Management
and
Performance

Defining the
Manager's Job

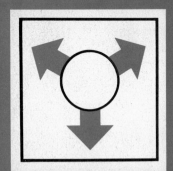

Planning

Organizing

Leading

Control

Change

Andrew D. Szilagyi, Jr.

University of Houston

Management and Performance

Scott, Foresman and Company
Glenview, Illinois
Dallas, TX   Oakland, NJ   Palo Alto, CA   Tucker, GA   London, England

Library of Congress Cataloging in Publication Data

SZILAGYI, ANDREW D

    Management and performance.

    Includes indexes.
    1. Management. 2. Organizational effectiveness.
I. Title.
HD31.S94   658   80-24344
ISBN 0-673-16101-3

10 9 8 7 6 5 4 3 2

0-673-16101-3

Book design: Mike Yazzolino

2 3 4 5 6-RRC-86 85 84 83 82 81

This book is dedicated to my children,
Darin, Dana, and Drew.

Contents

v

**Part II Developing the Framework for Performance—
       Planning 91**

Part IV Directing Performance—Leading *401*

Part V Evaluating Performance—Control 549

Preface

The factors contributing to the success or failure of an organization are seemingly limitless. The external environment can offer significant opportunities, or it can be quite hostile; governmental activities can facilitate or constrain an organization's operation; raw materials can be inexpensive or scarce and costly; or other organizations may provide society with better products and services.

No one factor is more important to organizational effectiveness than the performance of managers. Managers influence everything the organization does, from analyzing the environment to planning and controlling the work of employees. The link between the activities of managers and the level of effectiveness of the organization is the theme and title of this book—*Management and Performance*.

Focus of the Book

As a look at any management professor's bookshelf will attest, there are many ways of presenting management in a first course. Some texts take a behavioral or situational approach, others believe that a quantitative orientation is necessary in these computer times, while still others focus on the different schools of management thought. While each of these approaches has merit, your author believes that there is no one best way to manage or to present the topic of management. Rather than build on any one approach, the focus of this book is on what the manager actually does—in other words, *the manager's job*. By learning what managers do, future managers will be able to develop an approach that works best for them.

The manager's job orientation is presented throughout this book in a fourfold manner:

1. First, managers perform similar *functions* in their work. They plan what needs to be done and organize work flows, communication, and people. In addition, they lead employees toward goal accomplishment and attempt to control efficiently the resources of the organization.

2. In performing these functions, managers act out certain *roles*. They are superiors to groups of employees, they are themselves subordinates to other superiors, information flows through them from sources internal and external to the organization, they represent the organization to other organizations, and they make decisions that influence how well the firm achieves its goals.

3. Success as a manager is highly dependent on whether the individuals acquire important *managerial skills*. These include how well they know their work, proper relationships with other employees, the degree to

which they can see how the different components of the organization fit together, and the ability to pinpoint opportunities and problem areas.

4. Finally, the name of the game as a manager is *performance*. It is important for managers to understand that performance cannot be simply stated in dollars and cents. It is many-sided and includes such factors as cost control, sales revenue, adherence to laws, satisfied and productive employees, and good corporate citizenship.

The presentation of the manager's job is in six parts. Part I defines the manager's job, with special emphasis on the field of management and the important foundations of management thought. Part II (Planning) discusses how managers develop the framework for performance, highlighting the impact of the environment, goals, planning, and decision-making. In Part III (Organizing), establishing order, function, and design is the main subject In Part IV (Leading), the way managers direct performance is discussed, focusing on motivation, leadership, and group behavior. Part V (Control) presents the important process of evaluating and controlling performance. Finally, Part VI (Change) discusses trends and issues that are important to adaptive management, managerial careers, and organizational change.

Unique Features

In addition to a strong manager's job orientation, how does this book differ from other management texts? There are at least five distinguishing components:

Realism. It is important to present real life situations that managers face daily. This has been accomplished by making extensive use of current managment periodicals, such as *Business Week* and *Fortune,* for examples and special *The Practice of Management* and *The Manager's Job* sections in each chapter. Most of these illustrations are as current as possible— in fact, some have been added up to the printing deadline.

Involvement. The best way to get students involved is to have them actually experience management. While this cannot be accomplished solely in a textbook, a good way to achieve involvement is by introducing situations faced by managers through the use of cases and experiential exercises. These cases and exercises are found in every chapter.

International perspective. Management is not something only practiced in the fifty states. And today, as more and more organizations become multinational, future managers must be prepared to manage effectively in foreign cultures where customs and resources demand various management approaches. This has been recognized by integrating an international perspective throughout the book.

Organizational focus. Management is crucial to the success of *all* types of organizations, not just profit-making enterprises. We have included many illustrations of management concepts from health care, governmental, and service sector viewpoints. In addition, the growing importance of operations management and production are covered in Chapter 18.

Keys to success. There are certain guidelines and operating philosophies that have been generated from the experiences of managers that will immeasurably assist the young management recruit. These guidelines, which we call Keys to Success, are included in each chapter.

Acknowledgments

As in any task as large as writing a textbook, I am indebted to a number of colleagues who improved this book in many different ways. I am especially grateful to the following individuals who took valuable time to offer comments and reviews:

PETER J. FROST
University of British Columbia

DAVID A. GRAY
University of Texas, Arlington

RICKY W. GRIFFIN
University of Missouri, Columbia

LAWRENCE R. JAUCH
Southern Illinois University

MARVIN KARLINS
University of South Florida

WILLIAM R. LaFOLLETTE
Ball State University

HARRY N. MILLS
East Texas State University

WILLIAM L. MOORE
California State University, Hayward

W. ALAN RANDOLPH
University of South Carolina

CELESTE M. SICHENZE
Northern Virginia Community College

MARY S. THIBODEAUX
North Texas State University

The students at the University of Houston are also recognized for enduring the classroom testing of many of the book's concepts, cases, and exercises.

Special thanks go to a group of individuals whose time, commitment and support of my work were extensive. First, appreciation is given to Lyman W. Porter and Joseph W. McGuire, University of California, Irvine, who contributed significantly throughout the writing and review stages in their role as consulting editors to Goodyear Publishing Company. Second, I would like to single out present and former students of mine—Dennis Duchon (University of Houston), Ricky Griffin (University of Missouri, Columbia), Dave Hunt (Miami University), and Bruce Johnson (Marquette University)—whose suggestions and comments on all chapters were highly valued. Since each of them endured my comments and criticisms during their years at the University of Houston, I believe they really enjoyed this role reversal. The typing responsibilities were in the capable hands of Joann Olivares and Cheryl Willis, who are due a special thanks for meeting my sometimes unreasonable deadlines. Roger Holloway and Hal Humphrey of Goodyear Publishing are also singled out for their continued support and contributions to the manuscript. It is not often that an author can say he or she has had the opportunity to work with true professionals. I believe I am justified in making such a statement. Finally, I would like to acknowledge A. Benton Cocanougher, dean of the College of Business Administration, University of Houston, for his continued support of my efforts over the last seven years.

Of course, the individuals who suffered the most were my wife, Sandy, and my children, Darin, Dana, and Drew. The need to meet deadlines many times took precedence over recreational activities, and "vacation" was a word seldom used during the last two years. To my family, I can only express my love and appreciation, for without their support, *Management and Performance* would only be an idea.

ANDREW D. SZILAGYI, JR.

I

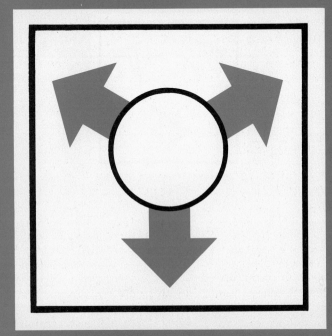

Defining the Manager's Job

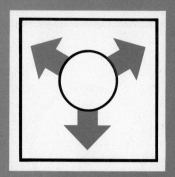

1

The Field of Management

CHAPTER OUTLINE

The Practice of Management

The Field of Management
    The Process of Management
    The Manager's Job
    Is Management Art or Science?

The Need for Managers
    The Forces Affecting Managerial Performance
    Managing in the International Realm

The Plan of This Book
    Managerial Topics
    Bringing Management to Life

Summary for the Manager

A Case for Analysis: William "Pat" Patterson of United Air Lines

KEY POINTS IN THIS CHAPTER

1. Management involves resources, tasks, and goals effectively integrated.

2. Management is a process involving planning, organizing, leading, and controlling.

3. The manager's job is best described as one that consists of functions, skills, and roles.

4. Management draws from art and science. It is more accurately depicted as a field of study and practice that is situationally based.

5. The challenges to managers originate from internal and external sources.

6. The forecasted shortage of managers will place an increased emphasis on managerial selection, education, and training.

7. Success in the future for managers may depend heavily on the ability to understand the importance of international organizations and on the ability to manage in different countries and cultures.

THE PRACTICE OF MANAGEMENT

Walt Disney

To people around the globe, Walt Disney was known for his creative genius and his contributions to the world of entertainment. Yet, in none of the separate arts that made his company famous—drawing, painting, photography, writing, music, acting, and architecture—did he himself excel. What Walt Disney did do well was inspire, stimulate, restrain, plan, and coordinate hundreds of talents brighter than his own into producing at levels of quality that could not have been accomplished without him. In essence, he was an excellent manager.

Born into a working-class family in the Midwest, Disney quickly exhibited skills for hard work, perseverance, and use of new technologies in work. To his credit, he built an organization around these same skills and principles so effectively that the company continued to prosper after his death in 1974.

Each success forced him toward more difficult goals. Mickey Mouse was succeeded by the Silly Symphonies, which broke new technical ground in the coordination of sound and color. In 1938, he gambled with the first feature-length cartoon, *Snow White and the Seven Dwarfs*. He then produced *Fantasia,* which blended color, shape, and motion with classical music. In the fifties the studio produced an ambitious program of cartoons (*Cinderella, Peter Pan*) and live-action movies (*20,000 Leagues Under the Sea*).

With the introduction of television, most people in the movie industry trembled. Disney did not. He set out to master the new entertainment medium with his *True-Life Adventure* features and, eventually, the highly successful *Disney's Wonderful World of Color* weekly series. His movie ventures did not stop during this time, as the success of the Davy Crockett epics attests. When he turned his attention to the design of Disneyland, he achieved effects of structural coordination that amazed even the most skilled city planners.

Out of the public's eye, Disney established a well-run organization that could produce his entertainment products. He set up different departments to concentrate on ventures for the various markets (e.g., T.V., movies). In this way, he kept his pulse on the needs of the viewing public. He also maintained a separate technical and idea development unit to ensure that the creative skills that made his organization so successful were not impeded. His skills at management even made an impact in the financial area when he established formal financial controls systems.

Disney's biggest contribution, however, was instilling in his people ideals of hard work, creativity, teamwork, and attention to detail. This style of management cascaded through the organization and into every job. Overall, Walt Disney made a profound impact not only on twentieth-century culture, but also on management in the creative industries.

Suggested from Max Ways, "The Business Hall of Fame," Fortune (January 1976): 121.

1

Throughout our lives, from adolescence through adulthood, each of us has been a participant in various types of organizations. We can be members of church choirs, little league teams, a fraternity or sorority, a branch of the armed services, or a business or institution from which we receive income and establish careers. Some of these organizations, such as a neighborhood baseball team, are informally organized and may exist for only a short time. Others, such as a large corporation, are organized more formally and function for long periods. Most organizations, however, have a number of important characteristics in common.

Three common characteristics are more important to organizations: (1) resources; (2) tasks; and (3) goals, or desired results. An organization's set of *resources* are its financial, physical, and human components and how they are allocated and used. The *task* characteristic concerns the specific job assigned to each organization member. Finally, a *goal* is that specific end result or objective that an organization desires to achieve. It is the most important characteristic because without a goal, an organization has no real reason to exist.

Consider, for example, a major league baseball team such as the Chicago Cubs. It consists of players and equipment and performs on a field (resources). Players are assigned particular positions (tasks) and attempt to perform at a level that will win as many games as possible (goal). On the other hand, a hospital involves employees, equipment, buildings, and finances (resources), functioning through individual specialists such as physicians, nurses, and therapists (tasks), whose objective is to improve the health of the patients (goal). The job of integrating resources and tasks for goal attainment is a key function of *management*. While the responsibilities of managers vary greatly—from choir director and baseball manager to corporation president—we can say that without some form of management, many organizations would eventually cease.

This text has two major objectives: (1) to focus on the manager's job by examining how managerial performance at every level affects the performance of individual workers, departments, and entire organizations; and (2) to present concepts and techniques for improving managerial performance. These objectives are independent of the type of organization under study. All organizations strive to accomplish goals, be they oil companies (return on investment, profit margin), hospitals (patient health, cost control), police departments (crime prevention), or a local chamber of commerce (drawing new industry to the area).

THE FIELD OF MANAGEMENT

A careful examination of the writings of management scholars and practitioners reveals a number of definitions of management. While there are some differences in these definitions, there is a core of factors that have most frequently been used to define management. For our purposes, we will define *management* as:

> The process of integrating resources and tasks toward the achievement of stated organizational goals.

Management is concerned with resources, tasks, and goals. More importantly, however, management involves a *process;* in other words, a systematic and organized way of doing things![1] All managers, regardless of their particular organizational affiliations, engage in a systematic, interrelated set of activities in order to achieve some desired objective. Understanding this process is the key to successful management. A schematic describing the managers' job as a process is shown in exhibit 1–1.

The Process of Management

In exhibit 1–1, we have identified the major managerial activities that will serve as the foundation for our discussion. First, managers must focus on *deciding what to do*. This involves establishing the framework for performance, or *planning* the work to be done. At this stage, for example, the product manager of household detergents at Procter & Gamble would be concerned with such external factors as consumer attitudes toward household products, personal disposable income levels, recent innovations in product development, and the source and strength of the competition. Integrating the influences of the external environment with the resources and goals of the organization (e.g., market share, profit margin) will lead to the achievement of these goals. Second, managers must *decide how to*

EXHIBIT 1–1   A Simplified Description of the Manager's Job

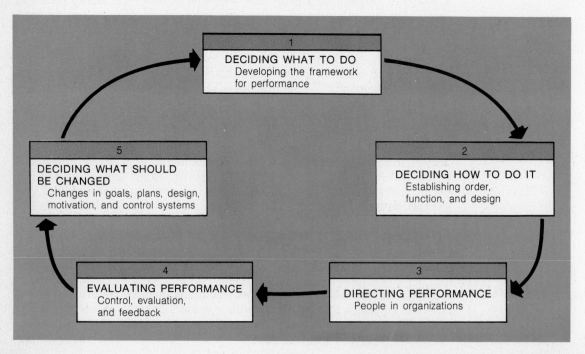

do it; in other words, *organizing* to establish order and function and to design their unit to achieve the stated goals. At this stage, the product manager would focus on selecting people to make up the team; training them to do their respective jobs; establishing authority, responsibility, and accountability relationships; and acquiring and allocating the necessary financial and physical resources.

Third, a concern for *directing performance* becomes dominant. In essence, the focus is on *leading* employees in the most effective manner possible. At this stage, the hospital administrator, for example, would concentrate on improving worker motivation and cooperation between groups, and on examining his or her own leadership style as it relates to goal achievement. Fourth, managers become involved in *evaluating performance*. This is the *control* function, which, for the hospital administrator, involves evaluating individual and group performance, examining financial indicators of effectiveness and efficiency, and investigating any problems that may have developed in communication, resource allocation, and interpersonal relationships.

Finally, attention is given to *what needs to be changed*. This emphasis on adaptability concerns evaluating all previous activities—plans, goals, employee selection and training, motivation, group behavior, and control systems—in order to determine what factors or activities may or may not need *change* so that goals are achieved.

It should be pointed out that the four activities of planning, organizing, leading, and controlling—what we will term the management *functions*—are unique activities. The change component, however, generally occurs *within* each of the four management functions and thus is not considered as a separate activity. Given the rapidly changing environment of management, we will highlight its importance throughout the book and in the last two chapters.

The Manager's Job

As we will discuss in the next chapter, describing the manager's job in a process framework involves an analysis of managerial *functions, skills,* and *roles*. For example, in planning for the addition of a new hospital wing with 100 beds, the hospital administrator must understand the process of planning (functions), be adept at the techniques and methods of planning (skills), and act as a spokesperson to the hospital board of directors and various financial lending organizations concerning the details of the hospital expansion (roles). This combination of functions, skills, and roles provides a better description of the manager's job, and it will serve as the framework for the remainder of the book.

Is Management Art or Science?

The best response to this question is that management is both an art and a science.[2] If we define *art* as a personal aptitude or skill, then management clearly has certain artistic components. To manage effectively, individuals must have not only the necessary abilities to lead but also a set of critical skills acquired through time, experience, and practice.[3] On the other hand, management involves certain aspects that have a strong scientific orientation to them. To perform at high levels in a variety of sit-

"To my mind, the secret of executive performance is the ability to delegate authority. For instance, nothing ever reaches this desk."

Drawing by Whitney Darrow,
© 1969 The New Yorker Magazine, Inc.

uations, managers must be able to draw on the sciences—particularly economics, psychology, sociology, political science, mathematics, and anthropology—for assistance and guidance.

For our purposes, it might be more appropriate to present management as being a *field of knowledge* that is heavily *applications and practitioner* oriented and is *situationally* based. This presentation recognizes the necessity of systematically studying why and how people work together to accomplish specific goals. In other words, management is more accurately defined as a field than as a science because its foundations are built with components of several sciences rather than with self-contained theories and laws.

Similar to the physician, lawyer, or engineer, the manager is a practitioner. As the physician draws on the basic sciences of chemistry, biology, and physiology, the manager draws on the sciences of mathematics, psychology, and sociology to solve practical problems. Like the physician or lawyer, the manager frequently is confronted with problems that cannot be answered by science. These problems cannot wait for science to catch up, but must be solved in a short period of time.

This *situational* nature of management concerns two important facts about managing.[4] First, not all problems faced by managers can be solved with an equation or theory. For example, solving the problem of low motivation for two subordinates may require additional training for one and assigning more challenging tasks for the other. Each situation is different and will require an equally different corrective strategy by the manager. Second, no matter how often we hear about the "behavioral sciences," "management science," and "scientific management," in planning activities, leading people, and controlling performance, it is very important to be able to draw on intuition, subjective beliefs, or just pure common sense.

For example, Delta Airlines, unlike many of its competitors during the late 1960s and early 1970s, resisted the stampede to replace their fleet of first generation jets with the new, more expensive jumbo jets.

Their decision on aircraft needs was based on a combination of analysis and common sense. Delta's detailed analysis indicated that most of their routes were relatively short (less than 500 miles on an average), making the larger jets uneconomical. Intuition and common sense told them that their main aircraft—the Boeing 727—was far from being obsolete. They felt that the plane was well built and ideally suited for short- to medium-distance routes. More than anything, however, Delta's management believed that the plane was adaptable to changes that could make a good plane a better one, such as improved engines, navigation equipment, and cabin design. Along with Braniff and Continental Airlines, Delta convinced Boeing not to give up on the 727.

Delta eventually ordered only enough jumbo jets to cover some of their longer routes. In addition, they were able to purchase a new series of 727s with such modifications as more fuel-efficient engines. As a result, they not only have a modern, new fleet of efficient planes, but they are not overly burdened by a large debt as are their competitors who purchased many jumbo jets.[5]

One area in which the common-sense manager has had some success has been in figuring out the fickle American appetite. Confronted in 1960 with what his lawyer called a bad deal—$2.7 million for the McDonald's name—Ray Kroc says: "I closed my office door, cussed up and down, threw things out the window, called my lawyer back, and said, 'Take it!' I felt in my funny bone it was a sure thing."[6] Kroc's feelings proved correct, as systemwide income from the McDonald's fast food chain are approaching $5 billion.

Some individuals state that "knowledge (science) without skill (art) is useless" and "skill (art) without knowledge (science) means stagnation"; we may add that "managing without common sense is often wrong." The key to management success is the ability to tie together knowledge, skill, and common sense into a workable framework.

THE NEED FOR MANAGERS

We have all frequently heard the comment that most large corporations are impersonal, self-perpetuating, machinelike entities where the efforts of individuals are neither valued nor felt.

Granted, some organizations are large and ponderous. They are, however, made up of people like you who make decisions and chart the future direction of the organization. Managers make such companies and institutions as Exxon, IBM, the Mayo Clinic, and Stanford University successful. Managers also contribute to corporate disasters and embarrassments. Firestone Tire and Rubber's 500 radial, Lockheed's political kickbacks, and Penn-Central's bankruptcy are classic examples of the impact of management on the total organization. We hope that by studying the field of management future managers will contribute to the continued success of many organizations and apply various management tools and techniques to bring errant institutions under control.

The Forces Affecting Managerial Performance

In some respects, the need for managers in the 1980s and beyond will be greater than at any time during this century. To illustrate this point, consider the following random list of article titles taken from such publications as *Fortune, Business Week, Forbes,* and *The Wall Street Journal:*

"American Motors' Plan for Survival"

"Space Will Be the Next Big Construction Site"

"When We'll Start Running Out of Oil"

"It Takes Long-Range Planning to Lick Inflation"

"The Lack of Management Talent in the 1980s"

"Those Worrisome Technology Exports"

"How SOHIO Bet Its Life in Alaska"

"China's Bureaucracy—You Think You Have It Bad"

"The EEOC's Bold Foray into Job Evaluations"

"Allied Chemical's $20 Million Ordeal with Kepone"

"The Growing Schism Between Management and Labor"

"Doing Business in the Middle East"

To some respected scholars and practicing managers, articles such as these highlight the coming crisis in management during the remainder of this century. There are three specific issues that are most frequently discussed. First, many organizations are becoming increasingly more *internally complex.* Many of the traditional ways of running an organization are giving way to such methods as free-form designs, flexi-time, dual authority systems, computerized information systems, self-governing teams, behavior modification programs, along with the growing use of management and technical specialists. As one would expect, the greater the internal complexity, the greater and more varied the demands on management.

Second, the *external environment* of most organizations is also becoming increasingly *complex* and *dynamic.* Organizations must monitor constantly not only the competitive market environment but the political, social, and technological environments as well. Consider the following examples: (1) One of IBM's major competitors in the business typewriter market is a division of Exxon, an energy company; (2) the majority of sales revenue from Gillette's shaving goods comes from products that were introduced since 1972; (3) Volkswagen is now assembling its cars in the United States, a competitive factor no auto manufacturer would have considered even ten years ago; (4) administrative paper work associated with governmental rules and requirements costs organizations as much money as they contribute to employee pension plans; and (5) the impact of OPEC is felt in the daily lives of every American.

Finally, the complexities of the internal and external environments will challenge *management talent.* The cold, hard fact is that due to population and demographics, there will be an extreme shortage of experienced managers to train young future managers who climb onto the organization's career ladder during the 1980s.[7] As a result, management is faced with three important and crucial problems: (1) how to design jobs so that the young manager can gain valuable experience without the constant supervision of an experienced manager; (2) how to identify and train "high risers" so that they can perform effectively in top management positions early; and (3) what to do in the late 1980s and early 1990s when these young managers have gained experience and fight for the small number of top management jobs.

Some people view this situation as a challenge to management rather than a crisis. It is a challenge to both the student and teacher of management to develop and participate in an educational system where the necessary skills are taught and acquired to meet the demands of organizations in the future. The burdens are many, but so are the rewards.

Managing in the International Realm

One of the greatest needs for managers will be in the international sphere, including both profit and not-for-profit organizations. Managers in the U. S. must recognize that their profession should not have a limited geographic perspective. The need for managers in the international realm means that managers should understand international and cross-cultural differences, as well as understand how to manage on foreign soils.

Managers should no longer believe that the impact of what they do and help produce is limited to their immediate environment. On the contrary, the products and services produced in this country and products and services produced in other countries, must be considered within an international arena of influence. American managers help produce computers that are sold overseas, for example, and we also import oil, automobiles, and other goods from other countries. Knowledge of this integration of management among many countries is now an important factor in the manager's job.

Operating in other countries is also now a crucial feature of the manager's job. Many students reading this book will one day live and work in foreign countries. There are important differences in managing in foreign cultures (and in some countries, managers have developed procedures and approaches that rival ours in effectiveness). For example, in Japan, managers must consult with lower-level workers before a major decision is made. Some German workers actually sit on the organization's board of directors. Volvo and Saab automobiles in Sweden are manufactured with a modified assembly-line process, in which the emphasis on teamwork and job design has turned boring jobs into those that offer a high level of challenge. In some countries, laws and cultural or religious beliefs can constrain the manager's ability to manage.

International management is one of the most important topics facing managers today and in the future. For this reason, we will discuss the influence and impact of the international perspective throughout this book.

THE PLAN OF THIS BOOK

The focus of this book is the *manager's job*—what managers do, how they do it, what elements determine effective performance, and what is learned while doing the job. From a format point of view, we will attempt to integrate managerial *functions, skills,* and *roles* into a framework for analyzing the manager's job. This framework will be established in chapter 2.

Managerial Topics

The book is divided into six major sections. Part I provides the basic foundation for analyzing the manager's job and a discussion of the historical origins of the field of management. Part II will focus on "Developing the Framework for Performance." We will look at the impact of the internal and external environment on the organization and the manager's job. Of prime importance will be an analysis of the dimensions of the environment, how goals are set, the development of organizational strategies and plans, and the basic foundations of managerial decision making.

Part III will emphasize the activities involved in "Establishing Order, Function, and Design." The topics include designing an effective organizational structure, developing a competent workforce, and establishing communication networks. Part IV focuses on the human element of management, or "Directing Performance." The elements of employee motivation, group behavior, and leadership will be stressed.

In Part V, the focus will be on the process of "Evaluating Performance." We will present the foundations for evaluation and control and will discuss controlling behavioral and other organizational resources. The topics include employee performance evaluation and reward systems, management information systems, and budgetary and production approaches to control. Finally, Part VI will highlight the need for adaptability by both the organization and the manager. Throughout this book, we will continually stress that the topics and concepts presented are related to all forms of organizations, not just businesses.

Bringing Management to Life

In this book, the *application* nature of the material presented is emphasized. In each chapter, a number of components dealing with applications are used. First, each chapter begins with a section entitled, "The Practice of Management," comprised of adapted discussions from recent journals such as *Business Week, Fortune, Forbes, Wall Street Journal,* and other practitioner-oriented publications to illustrate the chapter's content. Second, at the end of the text presentation in each chapter, we encapsulate the material under the heading, "Summary for the Manager." This is more than a summary section; it contains certain suggestions and thoughts for future applications of the material.

Third, after most major topic presentations, we offer certain "Keys to Success." These suggestions have been gathered from the experiences of many managers in applying the presented material. Fourth, each chapter has a set of discussion questions that focuses on the main points in the chapter. Fifth, a short case study to illustrate the important concepts is presented. The cases are real-life situations that highlight both the complexities and challenge of the manager's job. Sixth, because involvement in the education process is so important, an "Experiential Exercise" is included at the end of many chapters. The exercises simulate the learning of critical skills, roles, and functions required of a manager. Finally, most chapters contain an insert entitled, "The Manager's Job." This is a discussion by a manager concerning how he or she has applied the topic being presented.

Students, however, should not think that a management text will teach them all that they need to know to be successful managers. On the contrary, this book—and every other management text—can focus only on a portion of the process of acquiring managerial skills. As we discuss in the next chapter, one must combine education with other factors in order to become a successful manager.

SUMMARY FOR THE MANAGER

1. Management involves the integration of resources, tasks, and goals.

2. Management is a process that concerns deciding what to do (planning), deciding how to do it (organizing), directing performance (leading), and evaluating performance (controlling). Involved in each of these managerial functions is the element of change.

3. A true picture of the manager's job is one that emphasizes managerial functions, needed skills, and the roles that must be performed.

4. Management contains elements of art and sci-ence. It is more accurately a field of study and practice that adapts to the situation.

5. Present and future managers must, among other things, recognize that most organizations are becoming more internally complex. This greater complexity will place increasing and different demands on managers.

6. The dynamic and complex nature of the external environment will create new and more difficult challenges for the manager.

7. Increasingly, it is necessary for managers to understand the importance of international activities and how to manage in these foreign envioronments.

QUESTIONS FOR REVIEW AND DISCUSSION

1. What is *your* definition of management? How is it different from the one presented in this book?
2. Why is management discussed as a process?
3. What are the important elements of the manager's job?
4. Why is it stated that management draws from both art and science?
5. What are some internal and external factors that may affect the manager's job?
6. Why is consideration of the international nature of management so important in the manager's job?

NOTES

1. J. F. Mee, *Management Thought in a Dynamic Economy* (New York: New York University Press, 1963).

2. L. Gulick, "Management Is a Science," *Academy of Management Journal* (March 1965). 7–13.

3. P. F. Drucker, *The Practice of Management* (New York: Harper & Row, 1954).

4. J. W. Lorsch, "Making Behavioral Science More Use-ful," *Harvard Business Review* (March–April 1979). 171–81.

5. "Flying High at Delta Airlines," *Duns' Review* (December 1977). 60–61.

6. R. Rowan, "Those Business Hunches Are More Than Blind Faith," *Fortune* (April 23, 1979). 114.

7. "An Uneven Flow of Management Talent," *Business Week* (February 20, 1978).

A CASE FOR ANALYSIS

William "Pat" Patterson of United Air Lines

One day in 1927, a young assistant cashier at Wells Fargo Bank in San Francisco, William Patterson, was managing the bank while his superiors were at lunch. He was approached by Vern Gorst, an independent pilot, for a loan to buy a new airplane to be used to fly mail to the East Coast. After listening with fascination to Gorst, Patterson gave him $5,000, the first loan Patterson had ever made on his own.

The bank's president, who saw no future in aviation, was shocked at the loan transaction. He told Patterson to stay close to those flying-machine men until the money was paid back. Patterson stuck so close that he became Gorst's unpaid financial advisor. The loan was repaid, but Pat Patterson was hooked. Four years later he moved to Chicago as general manager of a new company—United Air Lines. In 1934, he became president, and thirty-two years later he retired from the company, which he had built into the largest airline in the free world.

Patterson's three-plus decades as head of United Air Lines were characterized by an emphasis on innovation, management style, tight organization, and control. In innovation, he saw that the future for airlines lay in passenger traffic, not mail. He understood, however, that passengers would not fly unless flying was safer.

In rapid succession, his newly created engineering department perfected the first air-to-ground radio and the wing de-icer. Patterson, who was not a pilot, later proved the safety of the first workable instrument landing system to his own satisfaction by sitting in the co-pilot's seat during twenty-two blind landings. Stewardesses were another Patterson innovation. At first they were registered nurses in white smocks, but soon he realized that this hint of possible disaster conveyed the wrong meaning. He switched to pretty young women in pleasant outfits.

Patterson was a complex personality who could be reclusive one day and very aggressive the next, especially if the topic was the expansion of United's route structure. To his employees, he was a friendly and highly visible leader. He was always walking around the Chicago headquarters, bumming cigarettes and calling vast numbers of workers by their first names. In managerial decision-making activities, he preferred to lead by example rather than tell people how to do their jobs.

Beyond his open, friendly nature Patterson believed in tight control over United's activities. He not only developed an organizational structure that was quickly copied by other companies in the industry, but the main elements of his financial control system exist today. Even other companies felt the effects of his style. For example, he rejected the 707 because Boeing wouldn't make some modifications to the plane's instrument panel. This shock led Boeing to its present policy of close consultation with its customers in the design of new aircraft.

Patterson wasn't always successful at United. His biggest mistake was in not grooming a successor. This "leadership vacuum" created many problems until Patterson's long-time friend Edward Carlson took over as chairman of the board.

Suggested from: Donald D. Holt, "The Business Hall of Fame," Fortune (April 21, 1980): 106.

Questions for Discussion

1. What were the important elements of Patterson's approach to management?
2. Did he consider management to be an art or a science or both?
3. Do you think Patterson would be successful today as manager of a major airline?

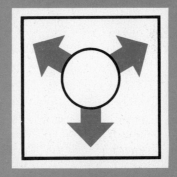

2

The Manager's Job

CHAPTER OUTLINE

The Practice of Management

Types of Managers
    Levels of Management
    Line and Staff Managers

What Managers Do: The Process of Management
    Developing the Framework for Performance: Planning
    Establishing Order, Function, and Design: Organizing
    Directing Employee Performance: Leading
    Evaluating Performance: Controlling
    The Adaptive Organization

Where Managers Spend Their Time

Managerial Skills
    Managerial Skills and Management Levels
    How Managerial Skills Are Acquired

Managerial Roles
    Interpersonal Roles
    Informational Roles
    Decisional Roles

An Emphasis on Performance

Managerial Ethics
    Definition of Managerial Ethics
    Categories of Unethical Behavior
    Sources of Ethical and Unethical Behavior
    Ethics and the Manager's Job: Keys to Success

The Manager's Job: An Integrative View

Summary for the Manager

A Case for Analysis—Standard Brands, Inc.: Executive Replacement

Experiential Exercise—Defining the Manager's Job

KEY POINTS IN THIS CHAPTER

1. The manager's job concerns the integration of functions, skills, and roles to achieve performance goals.

2. Three types of managers exist—executive, middle level, and first line.

3. Four managerial functions are identified: planning, organizing, leading, and controlling.

4. The important skills that should be acquired by managers are technical, human, conceptual, and diagnostic.

5. Applying managerial skills in the different functions requires behavior in at least three roles: interpersonal, informational, and decisional.

6. In defining managerial performance, one must be concerned with the standards of performance, level of analysis, time frame, and measurement components.

7. Managerial ethics or codes of conduct play an important part in how managers perform their jobs.

8. Managing cannot be reduced to a simple checklist of activities; it requires a high degree of flexibility in adapting to many complex situations.

THE PRACTICE OF MANAGEMENT

Harry Cunningham of K-Mart

Technological advance has played such a large part in the rise of twentieth century business that there's a tendency to assume the presence of an invention behind every important business innovation. Harry Cunningham's achievement in the ancient field of retailing is a reminder that business is still a matter of knowing what employees can do and how customers will react. The man who, by an innovation called K-Mart, revitalized the stagnant S.S. Kresge Co. did it without test tubes or patents.

Cunningham had not set out to be a retailer. He studied journalism during two years at Miami University, Ohio, then got a job on a newspaper in Harrisburg, not far from his birthplace, Home Camp, Pennsylvania. He met a Kresge executive and saw more chance of advancement there. Starting at the bottom as a stock boy in a Lynchburg, Virginia store, he worked seventy, eighty, ninety hours a week. Promotions came fast. In 1957 he was given the title of "general vice president" with no specified duties and no staff. He seemed to be in line for the top job, but the incumbent, who didn't want a crown prince around the Detroit headquarters, suggested that he travel. Cunningham had noticed that many corporate executives competed so intently for the chief executive office that they didn't know what to do with it when they got it. He set out to find what the company needed; after two years of travel he had visited all except fourteen of Kresge's 725 stores.

Sebastian S. Kresge's successors had preserved the sound management he built before his retirement in 1925. (Kresge died in 1966 at ninety-nine.) But the chain's customers had been moving to the suburbs, stranding central-city stores. Though sales inched up year by year, profits inched down. Cunningham, searching for new directions, studied the discount stores that were booming, especially in New England. Here was, he soon concluded, an idea that Kresge, with its strong national organization, could carry further than the discounters. He did not trumpet this conclusion in a company that looked down on discounters. "If I had announced before being elected president my intention to take Kresge into discounting, I'm quite sure I would not have been elected president."

He wanted a broad management consensus to understand why and how Kresge should make a major shift. An executive group carried out an elaborate study of discounting and, before the first K-Mart opened in 1962, management's confidence in the idea was such that it had made an $80 million commitment for thirty-three K-Marts. The new stores carried fast-moving lines of nationally advertised goods, relying on high turnover to keep prices down.

Kresge's sales volume had been $483 million in 1962, less than half that of the Woolworth chain. In a few years Kresge overtook Woolworth, which moved slowly into discounting with Woolco stores. In 1979 Kresge, its name changed to K-Mart Corporation, had sales approaching $10 billion. Profits rose from $9 million in 1962 to around $300 million in 1979. No large retailer in the last fifteen years had a comparable record of growth.

Cunningham, who retired as chairman in 1972, is a director of several big companies, including K-Mart. In his two years of roving exile from headquarters, he did more than generate a bright marketing idea; he discovered that his organization had capabilities for change that nobody else had seen.

Source: Max Ways, "The Hall of Fame for Business Leadership," Fortune (January 30, 1978): 94.

When the seemingly simple question, "What do managers do?" is asked, the variety of responses is surprising. Some attempts at defining the manager's job include the use of such words as *leader, motivator, coordinator, professional,* or *organizer;* some simply say, "they manage." In reality, these are all true, which provides some indication of the breadth, scope, and complexity of the manager's job.

In this chapter, we will attempt to answer the question, "What do managers do?" in a way that will capture the realities of this important position in organizations. Four major points will be covered. First, we will describe the different *types* of managers that can be found in all organizations. Second, we will discuss a three-part definition of the manager's job. The emphasis will be on: (1) managerial *functions,* (2) managerial *skills,* and (3) managerial *roles.* Third, we will focus on an important criterion of the manager's job: *performance.* Finally, we will discuss a crucial but frequently misunderstood part of the manager's job—*managerial ethics*—and how it affects managerial performance.

TYPES OF MANAGERS

As you are aware, there are many different types of managers in organizations with varying tasks and responsibilities. In this section, we broadly classify managers into two categories: (1) level and (2) line and staff managers.

Levels of Management

In order to illustrate the different levels of managers, exhibit 2–1 depicts the organizational chart of a medium-sized chemical company, and exhibit 2–2 isolates the manufacturing function of the company.

In exhibit 2–2, three levels of management are shown. These levels are usually called executive, middle, and first-line management.[1]

Executive Managers. Sometimes termed "top management," this small group of individuals makes up the highest level of management. Managers who hold these positions are responsible for interacting with representatives of the external environment (e.g., financial institutions, governmental and political figures, important suppliers and customers) and establishing organizational goals, plans, strategies, and broad operating policies and guidelines. While there is a great variety across different organizations, typical titles include president, chief executive officer (CEO, or COO for chief operating officer), executive vice president, senior vice president, and vice president.

Middle-Level Managers. A number of management levels are included within this category, such as the positions of general manager,

EXHIBIT 2–1   A Typical Organizational Chart

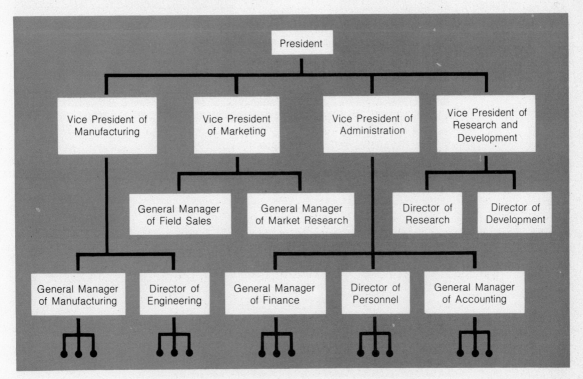

plant manager, and operations superintendent shown in exhibit 2–2. The responsibilities of these managers include translating executive orders into operation, implementing plans, and directly supervising lower level managers. This is probably one of the most important management levels because it is a prime training ground for future executives, and it is at the center of the organization's activities.

First-Line Managers.   Characterized by such titles as sales manager, clerical supervisor, and lab supervisor, these managers are responsible for directing first-line, nonsupervisory employees. Additional duties include evaluations of day-to-day performance indicators such as volume produced, quality control, inventory, and preventive maintenance. It is the level at which the majority of management graduates will be within the first three to five years of full-time employment.

Line and Staff Managers

A second way of describing types of managers is to distinguish between *line* and *staff* responsibilities. A line manager's responsibilities and activities have a *direct impact* on the main product line or service of the organization. In the company depicted in exhibit 2–1, the marketing and sales managers are considered line managers. A plant manager would also be a line manager.

EXHIBIT 2–2
Levels of
Management in a
Manufacturing
Company

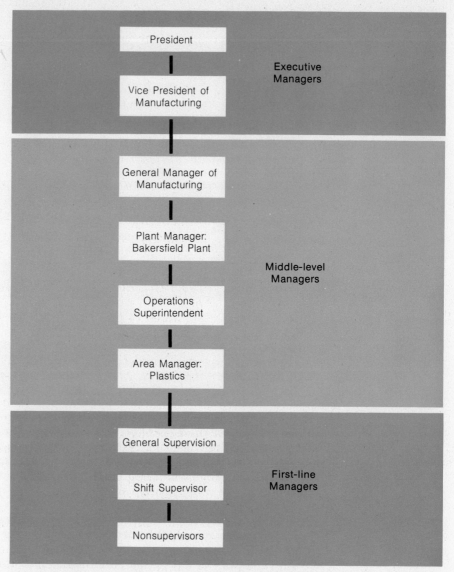

A staff manager's responsibilities and duties *support* the activities of line managers. Examples are managers of personnel, finance, research and development, and accounting. The personnel manager of a chemical plant, for example, would be responsible for the human resources of the facility, including: (1) identification of plant staffing needs; (2) selection, placement, and training of newly hired employees; (3) company compliance with federal guidelines on safety, antidiscrimination, and pay policies; (4) development and implementation of a performance evaluation system; and (5) maintenance of the plant's compensation, employee benefit, and employee relations functions. We will discuss the differences and similarities between line and staff managers in later chapters.

WHAT MANAGERS DO: THE PROCESS OF MANAGEMENT

In chapter 1, we presented four management process activities: the functions of planning, organizing, leading, and controlling. We now present these management functions in greater detail. Exhibit 2–3 is a representation of this process.

Developing the Framework for Performance: Planning

Planning is probably one of the most important functions because it sets the pattern for the other activities to follow. Planning activities usually encompass four elements:

1. Evaluating environmental forces and organizational resources.
2. Establishing a set of organizational goals.
3. Developing strategies and plans to achieve the stated goals.
4. Formulating a decision-making process.

While these elements are not all-inclusive, they do capture the essence of the planning phase.

To illustrate the planning functions, consider a large petroleum corporation during the early 1970s. The oil embargo and the influence of OPEC countries had drawn attention to the corporation's vulnerability to environmental forces. The majority of the company's crude-oil supplies were controlled by the foreign governments, and top management believed that the long-term impact of uncertain raw materials would be detrimental to the organization's survival (evaluating environmental forces). An evaluation of the strengths of the corporation concluded that the organization: (1) was really an energy company with untapped resources in coal reserves; and (2) the refining division had developed skills that could be easily transferred from the manufacture of oil products to industrial chemicals (evaluating organizational resources).

Therefore, top management strongly believed that the future stability of the company rested on the expansion of activities related to the manufacture (mining) and distribution of coal and industrial chemicals. A corporate goal was established: by the year 1990, at least 50 percent of the company's revenues will come from coal and chemical products (establishing corporate goals). Formal five- and ten-year plans were developed to meet the stated goal. Included in the plans were allocation of resources (financial, human, and physical), statements of responsibility for all levels of management regarding implementation, and a timetable of expected events (developing plans and the formulation of a decision-making process).

Establishing Order, Function, and Design: Organizing

As shown in exhibit 2–3, once management has established goals and developed plans to achieve these goals, emphasis is placed on designing and developing an organization that can successfully implement the stated plans. It is important to recognize that various goals will require dif-

EXHIBIT 2–3   The Process of Management

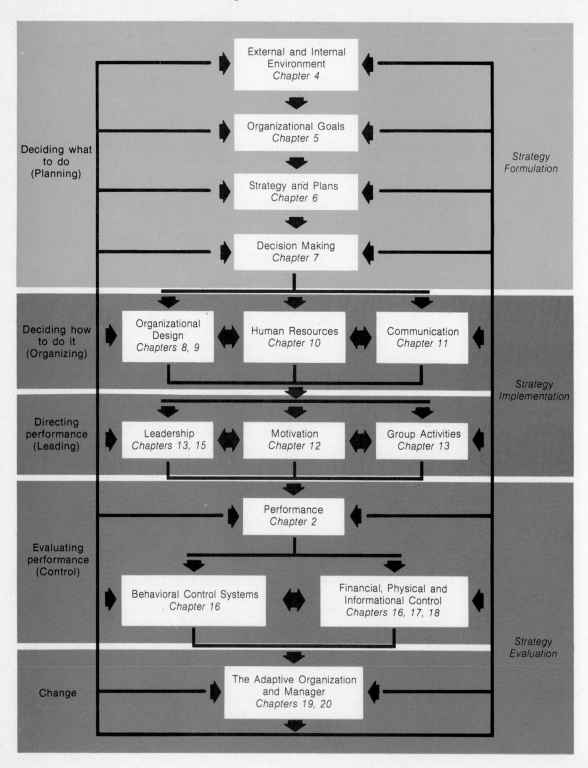

ferent kinds of organizations. For example, in the oil company, the type of organization developed in the petroleum division may not be effective in the coal or chemical divisions.

Three elements are essential to organizing:

1. Developing the structure of the organization.
2. Acquiring and training human resources.
3. Establishing communication patterns and networks.

As an example, assume that you are the administrator of a soon-to-be-opened medical diagnostic clinic in Seattle. The clinic will employ physicians, nurses, technicians, and a maintenance staff and function primarily as an outpatient clinic specializing in comprehensive physical examinations. Although it will serve the general public, the clinic will rely on contracts to perform physicals on the employees of local firms and institutions.

Once the planning phase has been completed, your concern switches to internal organization. First, elements of the clinic's structure are formulated. Policies and procedures for authority relationships, reporting patterns, the chain of command, departmentalization, and various administrative responsibilities are established (designing the structure of the organization). Second, steps are taken to hire a competent work force. Where required, programs are established for training new employees in skills necessary to their jobs (acquiring and training human resources). Finally, formal communication and information networks are formulated, emphasizing horizontal and vertical communication, the types of information that are to be communicated, the manner in which communication is to flow, and reduction of the barriers to effective communication (establishing communication networks).

Directing Employee Performance: Leading

After the organization's goals and plans have been formulated and the issues of structure and staffing have been resolved, the next step is directing the human resources toward attaining the stated goals. The essential function of *leading, directing,* or *motivating* is getting the organization's employees to perform in ways that will assist in achieving the defined goals.

Four components make up the leading function:

1. Motivating employees.
2. Influencing employees to perform.
3. Forming effective groups.
4. Improving job performance.

As can be seen, the focus of the leading function is on the individual employee as well as on the interrelationships between employees in groups.

Returning to the example, the clinic administrator's attention will be directed toward establishing conditions that will result in high employee motivation, such as providing a performance-based pay and promotion program and jobs that are designed to offer challenge, variety, and development. For newly appointed managers, emphasis is next placed on acquiring knowledge in the most effective leadership styles and reinforcing behaviors that will hopefully influence employees to high performance (influencing employees). Third, attention is given to how groups will be formed; i.e., to which composition and structural characteristics of the groups can yield high levels of performance (forming effective groups). Finally, the manager ties motivation, leadership styles, and group formation together with methods to improve the unit's performance (improving job performance).

Evaluating Performance: Controlling

The major objective of the control function is ensuring that the organization is in fact moving toward achieving the formulated goals. Three basic components constitute the control function:

1. Elements of a control system.
2. Evaluating and rewarding employee performance.
3. Controlling financial, information, and physical resources.

An effective control function allows the manager to know whether the organization's performance is on target or if corrective actions are required to meet performance standards.

To accomplish this, the overall organizational goal is translated into performance standards (control system elements) by establishing individual goals and a formal performance evaluation system to rate the extent to which the goals have been accomplished. Depending on their performance, employees are given rewards such as pay increases and promotions. If performance is consistently below standard, a decision to terminate employment may have to be made (evaluating and rewarding employee performance). Next, a formalized (usually computer based) reporting system is developed. Frequently called a management information system (MIS), it is used to collect data and report organizational performance in such terms as financial indicators, adherence to scheduled deadlines, and the degree of utilization of the organization's resources. Attention is given to the important nonbehavioral aspects of organizational performance, such as cost analysis, budgeting, production, inventory, quality control, etc. (controlling resources).

The Adaptive Organization

One of the most important factors that managers need to fully understand is that organizations are rarely static creations. More often than not, there are major changes in the internal or external environment that force the organization to change.

For example, any of the following situations would cause a radical change in the functions of management in our oil company illustration:

1. One or more of the Mideast oil-producing countries is overthrown, and a communist government takes over.
2. Workers at the newly opened chemical plant join a militant union and go out on three wildcat strikes over a nine-month period.
3. Congress passes a law requiring divestiture of assets (i.e., oil companies

can no longer control the flow of gasoline from the ground to the service station pump).

Similarly, what reaction would the clinic's management have in any of the following situations?

1. A national health insurance law is enacted.
2. Insurance companies refuse to cover medical malpractice suits.
3. Federal and state governments pass laws that limit hospital cost increases.

Reading daily newspapers will reveal that these situations are not unrealistic. They can occur!

These examples suggest that managers must not only be able to adapt to changing conditions but, whenever possible, must develop methods to forecast changes and their impact. It is also important to recognize that adaptation and change involves how the organization is managed as well as the skills, duties, and career development of the manager.

The Strategic Activities of the Manager's Job

Exhibit 2–3 also indicates that the functions involved in the process of management can be broken down into three broad *strategic activities:* (1) strategy formulation; (2) implementation; and (3) evaluation. *Strategy formulation* is planning to achieve organizational goals, stated in a way that defines what business the organization is in or is to be in, and the kind of organization it is or is to be. Of concern are answers to the questions of what the organization *might do,* in terms of environmental opportunities; what it *can do,* relating to present and future organizational resources; what it *wants to do,* reflecting the aspirations of top management; what it *ought to do,* bringing ethical and societal issues to the forefront; and integrating these decisions into a statement of what it *should do.*[2] *Implementation* and *evaluation* deal with mobilizing organizational resources to accomplish its goals. Since ineffective implementation and evaluation can make sound plans thoroughly unsuccessful, managers must give increasingly more attention to these important activities.

Consider the case of Scripto, a familiar name in writing instruments. The company had planned to be the world's foremost producer of pens and pencils. In implementing this plan, Scripto initially ignored the market for cheap, disposable ballpoint pens (18–25 cents), preferring instead to concentrate its efforts in the market for higher priced writing instruments. This error allowed Bic Pen the opening they needed to introduce a line of less expensive pens and felt-tip instruments. As a result, Bic has overtaken Scripto in sales and market share and far exceeds Scripto in almost all the important financial measures of performance.

The Realities of the Process of Management

From a functional orientation, management is a systematic way of getting things done in organizations. However, managerial functions and activities cannot simply be relegated to a checklist of things to do, how to do them, and when they should be done. On the contrary, the process of management should be viewed as the basic framework for performance, not a universal, all-encompassing theory or set of procedures. Reality must be faced on at least three points.

First, the functional approach to management should not be viewed as a rigid, step-by-step system. In other words, it is erroneous to think that on Monday, managers plan; on Tuesday, they restructure the department; on Wednesday, they motivate; and so on. Managers do all these things *every day* that they work. Planning may follow goal setting, but motivation, leadership, communication, and control are daily occurrences. For example, the project manager who is responsible for the construction of a warehouse may systematically go from planning through to control on one project before it has been completed. However, if this manager is overseeing the construction of three warehouses at the same time, all management functions will definitely be part of each day. This overlapping of management functions indicates the need for a flexible approach to the manager's job.

Second, individual levels of proficiency in each managerial function differ. That is, one manager may feel most skilled in planning, another's strength may be in motivating subordinates, and a third may feel most comfortable with the quantitative aspects of the control function. This does not mean that the corporate planner does only planning, the construction supervisor only supervises, or the manager of internal audit only works with figures. Managers must be skilled in all the management functions to be effective in their work. As will be pointed out in the next section, managers at different levels in the organization allocate proportionately different amounts of time to planning, organizing, leading, and control. However, although the individual may be most proficient in one managerial function, the need to develop skills in the other functions cannot be overlooked.

Finally, we must all recognize that there is no "one best way" to manage an organization. The process of management should be viewed as a basic framework, not as answers or solutions to organizational problems. Each situation faced by managers may require a slightly different application of the framework. This *situational* approach to management has been termed the *contingency* approach, and it is directed toward developing managerial actions that are most appropriate for the specific situation and the people involved.[3] By considering and weighing the important variables in a situation, the manager can take the most appropriate actions needed to achieve organizational goals. In other words, managers must be able to *recognize, diagnose,* and *adapt* to the situation in order to be most effective.

The situational or contingency approach to management is conceptually appealing, but extremely difficult to follow. It is definitely not an "it all depends" philosophical position. After performing a careful analysis of a particular situation and thoroughly reviewing the variables, a manager must be satisfied that the actions taken are the most appropriate.

Established situational or contingency approaches will be covered throughout this book. Knowledge and application of these approaches immediately notifies the manager that pat answers to organizational problems do not exist. If they did, all we would need to do is list them and refer to them at the appropriate time. Predicting performance is certainly much more elusive than this. Simple answers for complex situations just do not exist, and this is why the field of management is so challenging.

WHERE MANAGERS SPEND THEIR TIME

Our discussion to this point has focused primarily on the types of managers and what functions they perform. While most managers are concerned with each function, the time devoted to each varies by management level in the organization.

Exhibit 2–4 is a suggested profile of the amount of time that the three levels of management—executive, middle, and first line—devote to the main functions. Some interesting differences evolve from an analysis of this exhibit.[4] Executive management spends the most time on issues of planning and change. This is in line with the duties and responsibilities of chief executives, which concern overall policy and *strategy formulation*. The main function of a chief executive, such as in Sears, J.C. Penney, and Montgomery Ward, is to chart out, plan and direct the company's progress, along with keeping a sharp eye out for possible important changes. For example, top management in these three merchandising firms would be concerned with such issues as overall pricing strategies and the location of new stores, and they would frequently analyze changes in consumer preferences, mobility, and disposable income.

At the middle manager level, the time allocation switches to an emphasis on organizing and leading. This is what we call *strategy implementation*. In other words, these managers are primarily responsible for putting into action the plans and strategies of the executive management team. For example, store managers at Sears would devote most

EXHIBIT 2–4 Distribution of a Manager's Time

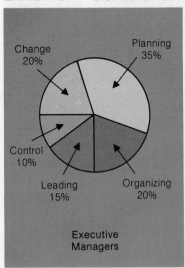
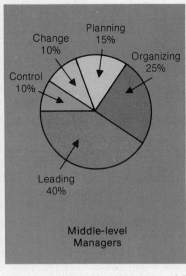
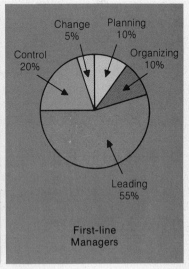

Suggested by: H. Mintzberg, The Nature of Managerial Work *(New York: Harper & Row, 1975).*

of their time to organizing their stores and directing subordinate department managers in implementing the company's new product and pricing policies.

Finally, an emphasis on leading and controlling performance are prime duties that first-line managers use to allocate their time. In essence, the focus is on *implementation* and *evaluation* of the organization's plans to achieve the stated goals. In our Sears example, the department manager of women's fashion goods is responsible for seeing to it that the new product line and pricing policies are carried out, as well as for evaluating the consumer's response to the new policies (e.g., sales revenue, inventory, etc.). The data on this evaluation are communicated through organizational channels to top management, which then considers if any change is needed in these policies.

As this simplified merchandise example illustrates, the level in the organization has a strong impact on where managers spend their time. Although most executive managers spend the majority of their time on long-range issues, they probably have gained a wealth of experience when they were "down on the firing line" during the early part of their careers. As individuals progress through the levels of management, the time they spend on the management functions allows them to learn and acquire the skills needed to be a high performer.

MANAGERIAL SKILLS

Our approach to management suggests that the manager's job can be studied from at least three perspectives. In the preceding section, we discussed the *management function* approach. The second approach deals with the needed *managerial skills*.

Most successful managers have acquired a certain set of skills during their working lives that has had a strong impact on their levels of achievement. Four specific managerial skills are needed by all managers: (1) technical; (2) human; (3) conceptual; and (4) diagnostic skills.[5] A summary of these skills is shown in exhibit 2–5.

Technical Skills.   The ability to use tools, techniques, procedures, or approaches in a specialized manner is referred to as a technical skill. Examples would be the civil engineer, heart surgeon, accountant, or patent attorney. In a sense, people with technical skills are recognized as experts at what they do. For the manager, the nature of technical skills is twofold. First, the manager should have developed some expertise in the work being done. The project manager in a research and development (R&D) laboratory normally has made some scientific contribution to the particular field. Second, there are skills involved in managing the work being done. To successfully run an R&D group, the project manager would need to know how to plan scientific studies, how to organize the group, how to evaluate scientific performance, and so on.

Human Skills.   The second skill needed relates to the ability to select, motivate, work with, and lead employees, either individually or in groups. To be effective, the R&D project manager needs to know the qualifications

EXHIBIT 2–5 Managerial Skills

SKILL	DESCRIPTION	EXAMPLE
Technical	The use of tools, techniques, and procedures in a specialized manner.	1. Pathologist analyzing a blood sample. 2. An engineer designing a bridge.
Human	Interpersonal relationships dealing with selecting, motivating, and leading other employees.	1. An accounting manager supervising a group of audit accountants. 2. A manufacturing manager resolving conflict between an inventory supervisor and a loading supervisor.
Conceptual	The ability to see the total organizational picture by integrating and coordinating a large number of activities.	1. An analysis by the executive vice president of the potential effects of a merger with another firm. 2. Examining the total impact of a proposed labor contract in the firm by the personnel vice president.
Diagnostic	The ability to quickly get at the true cause of a certain situation through a maze of data, observations, and facts.	1. Analyzing the causes of employee turnover. 2. Anticipating changes in consumer buying habits by a marketing manager.

of other scientists in order to select members of the team properly, as well as have a knowledge of what motivates these scientists, how to structure communication and information flow networks, and the degree of direction they should be given to get the work done.

Conceptual Skills.   This third managerial skill relates to the ability to integrate and coordinate the organization's activities. In a sense, it concerns the ability to see the "total picture," how the different parts of the organization fit together and depend on each other, and how a change in one part of the organization can cause a change in another part. The director of the R&D lab must be able to see how the most theoretical of research activities (those dealing with new discoveries and innovations) fit with applied research efforts (specific projects designed to solve a particular consumer problem) into the overall purpose of a research and development function. And he or she must be able to link the work of different groups together when the greatest impact of their efforts comes from their joint effort. For example, until recently most chemical plants used an expensive, time-consuming procedure to test air pollution levels around their facilities. Upon observing this procedure, a sharp-eyed R&D manager recalled a much simpler test, which had been developed in a research effort on a different problem, that could easily be adapted for this use. Using this simplified, faster method has resulted in a savings of thousands of dollars.

Diagnostic Skills. Diagnostic skills include the ability to determine, by analysis and examination, the nature and circumstances of a particular condition. In other words, it is not only the ability to specify *why* something occurred, but also the ability to develop certain speculations in a *what if* situation. Individuals who have developed diagnostic skills have the ability to cut through unimportant aspects and quickly get to the heart of the problem. For example, a problem being faced by all managers is the issue of employee turnover. High turnover usually means increased costs associated with hiring, placement, training, and the intangible costs related to not having the right people around to do the work. After a number of unsuccessful attempts to reduce the turnover of clerical personnel in an insurance claims department (i.e., changing the office layout, replacing supervisors, and so on), the department manager used a questionnaire survey and a series of employee interviews to find out about the concerns of the employees. Both the survey and interview data confirmed that the main problems concerning departmental employees were issues of low pay raises and a lack of proper job training. A revised compensation system coupled with an increased emphasis on employee training resulted in a 40 percent drop in turnover in one year. Diagnostic skills are probably the most difficult skills to develop because they require the proper blend of analytic ability with common sense and intelligence to be effective.

Managerial Skills and Management Levels

The four managerial skills essential to performance also vary in importance according to level in the organization. As shown in exhibit 2–6, technical skills increase in importance as one goes down the organizational structure. A head nurse in a pediatric ward, for example, is likely to have greater technical skills with patients than the director of nursing, because these skills are needed to deal with everyday activities and problems. Similarly, because first-line managers spend most of their time on leading matters (see exhibit 2–4), we would expect that human skills are most important at the lower levels. This does not mean that top management should not be concerned with human skills; on the contrary, human skills are very important to executive management. However, executives are required to do more than lead subordinates.

Conceptual and diagnostic skills are most important at the higher levels of management because executives are responsible for broad-based, long-term decisions that have a significant impact on the survival and performance of the total organization. These skills have some importance at the lower levels of management, but they are usually related to specific problems for specific situations.

How Managerial Skills Are Acquired

Managerial skills, besides having differing importance to various levels of management, differ also in the ease or difficulty with which they can be acquired. Technical skills appear to be the easiest to acquire because they can be taught through educational and training activities. Human

EXHIBIT 2–6 Skills Needed for Effectiveness at Different Management Levels

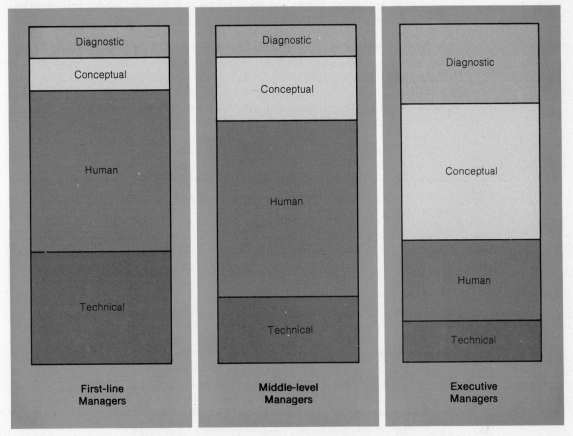

First-line Managers | Middle-level Managers | Executive Managers

skills, on the other hand, are much more difficult to acquire because interpersonal relations involve consideration of the differences in attitudes, emotions, and cultural characteristics of peers, subordinates, and superiors. These characteristics vary with different employees, and their impact on performance is hard to predict. The entire field of organizational behavior has developed in response to the problem of describing and predicting the behavior of people in organizations.

Finally, conceptual and diagnostic skills are the most difficult to acquire, mainly because they involve time and a certain level of intellectual ability. In addition, conceptual and diagnostic skills development depends, to a certain extent, on the degree to which technical skills and human skills have been acquired and mastered. In essence, conceptual and diagnostic skills are *mature* skills that require a capacity to learn and a level of experience in observing and practicing acceptable behaviors.

There are at least three mechanisms that facilitate the acquisition of managerial skills. These include: (1) education; (2) experience; and (3), a mentor relationship with a higher level manager.

Education as a method to develop managerial skills involves the participation in undergraduate, graduate, and continuing education programs. The fast growth in M.B.A. degrees and executive development programs across the country are examples of the importance being placed on education as a skill developer. Some individuals, however, argue that management courses neglect to teach people what they must do to become effective managers. Livingston maintains that what is stressed in business schools is analytical ability—an emphasis on problem solving and decision making.[6] What is missing, he states, are the crucial elements of problem finding and opportunity finding. Analytical skills are important, but a manager's success will ultimately depend on his or her ability to anticipate problems and opportunities long before they arise. In our terminology, educational programs are effective in developing technical skills; other mechanisms are required to develop human, conceptual, and diagnostic skills.

COMMENTS ON THE PRACTICE OF MANAGEMENT
(See p. 17.)

The brief summary of Harry Cunningham's career at K-Mart (formerly S. S. Kresge) provides an illustration of the importance of developing managerial skills. First, many of his skills were acquired through experiences in a variety of jobs. His two years of traveling to the company's individual stores was important because it probably had a major impact on developing knowledge of the retail business. Second, Cunningham's diagnostic skills were most important in the decision to enter the discount field. Finally, the way he handled entry into the discount area involved an important human skill. Rather than announce his intention to take Kresge into discounting, he formed an executive group to carry out a detailed study of the issue. In the end, the group not only came to the same conclusion as Cunningham, but because of their involvement in the study, they became committed to the discounting strategy.

"*Experience* is the best teacher" is an old saying that contains much truth for managerial success. Experience in management generally refers to three facets. First, experience is the *exposure* to a variety of situations, problems, and demands. For example, a project manager in a large engineering design and construction company may have held positions in design, contract administration, and construction before advancing to this important post. Exposure is "learning the ropes" by being an integral part of various organizational activities. Second, gaining experience involves *time*, which is necessary to allow enough exposure to various managerial situations. Finally, experience is a level of *maturity*, which is a philosophical attitude or belief about the individual at work. It is the ability to resist panic in crisis situations and replace it with rational and analytical reasoning; the ability to look beyond trivial matters to the cause of the problem; and a crucial managerial quality that comes from exposure to a variety of situations over a length of time. This chapter's introductory section on Harry Cunningham of K-Mart Corporation is a good example.

Consider the case of John James, the president of Dresser Industries, a diversified organization specializing in the manufacture of high-technology products for the energy industry:

> If I were to give an ambitious, young person advice about getting ahead today, I'd tell them first of all, that they must undergo a continual learning process. Someone, for example, who starts out in finance should be willing to cross-train or learn all they can about, say, engineering, manufacturing or marketing, and so on. In other words, don't let yourself get stuck in some specialized niche. . . . You can never stop learning or growing, you have to keep improving your ability to listen—to be open to other people's ideas—you must be able to take criticism. You can't be a know-it-all. As the old saying goes, if you can't take the heat, stay out of the kitchen![7]

Mentor relationships, a recent topic presented in the management literature, is a longstanding activity in management practice. In simple terms, it is a situation where a young manager learns a set of managerial skills from observing, working with, and relating to a more seasoned manager. Mentorship can be a formal activity, such as programs at Hughes Aircraft or the Jewell Company where each aspiring manager has a higher level executive as an organizational sponsor, or an informal activity, such as a developing friendship between a young and older manager. A recent survey of top management in a variety of companies revealed that: (1) over two-thirds of the surveyed executives had developed a mentor relationship with an older executive during the first fifteen years of their careers; (2) those with mentors were more likely to follow a career path, had learned more about the business they were in, and were more satisfied with their work and careers; and (3) executives who have had a mentor in turn sponsor more proteges than executives who have not had a mentor.[8]

What is gained from a mentor relationship? For the protege, it not only is an opportunity to learn the business from an experienced manager (technical skills), but it also affords a learning experience on how to relate to people (human skills) and how to approach various problems faced by the organization (conceptual and diagnostic skills). More than this, however, it is an opportunity for the protege to acquire some career *direction,* and it is a mechanism to develop a personal *philosophy* of *management* and the invaluable quality of *self-confidence* in managerial ability.

For example, consider the case of Susan Swan, a vice president at Morgan Guaranty Trust. At the ripe old age of 30, she is responsible for managing the $1 billion pension fund for this fifth largest of U.S. banks:

> "I have earned the success I now enjoy. However, I have not forgotten that I received a little help along the way—a mentor," Susan notes. "A mentor is someone who smooths the edges, who helps you along the road to success. If you attract someone to play that role, you have to demonstrate that you're worth it. I earned my stripes when I became a vice president."[9]

Mentoring is not solely an American phenomenon. Joachim Zahn, head of Daimler-Benz (maker of Mercedes-Benz automobiles) credits Dr. Fritz Brinckmann, a noted German accountant and industrialist, for being a mentor, or *Meister,* when he worked for Brinckmann's accounting firm early in his career. Brinckmann not only supported Zahn and gave him invaluable advice, but he introduced Zahn to the top influential people in German industry. These acquaintances proved to be significant in Zahn's later career with the auto maker. For the mentor, working with a protege provides a feeling of intrinsic satisfaction—a sense of pride and accomplishment in developing a capable manager who will carry the company's banner into the future.

The important conclusion to be drawn from this discussion is that acquiring the skills necessary to be a successful manager is a complex activity. It is more than just reading a book, listening to lectures, or on-the-job experience. The successful manager has acquired technical, human, conceptual, and diagnostic skills through a continual education process, extensive exposure to a variety of organizational conditions, and hopefully a relationship with an individual who acts as a mentor. The end product is a manager who has the necessary skills, maturity, and confidence to perform at high levels.

MANAGERIAL ROLES

To this point in our discussion, we have drawn attention to two important aspects that define the manager's job: (1) to manage involves a systematic way of doing things consisting of a set of managerial *functions*—planning, organizing, leading, and controlling; and (2) successful achievement as a manager is dependent on acquiring a set of crucial management *skills*—technical, human, conceptual, and diagnostic. The last perspective necessary in discussing the manager's job is the set of behaviors, or roles, that are required.

The concept of a *role* is drawn from the behavioral sciences and is defined as an organized set of observable behaviors that are attributed to a specific office or position. As applied to the manager's job, a role would be viewed as the *capacity* in which the manager acts. For example, a manager may act as a leader of subordinates, a spokesperson of the organization, a source of information, or one who makes decisions. In a simple way, we may say that managers "wear many hats" while performing their jobs.

In a detailed study of managerial activities, Mintzberg identified a series of roles relating to *interpersonal, informational,* and *decisional* activities.[10] The individual roles are shown in exhibit 2–7. Mintzberg argued that all managers have formal authority and status given to them by the organization. Authority and status give rise to interpersonal relations with subordinates, peers, and superiors, who in turn provide managers with information to make decisions.

In the discussion of the different managerial roles, consider the position of a regional sales manager of a medium-size electronics company. The sales manager supervises eight sales representatives and three office workers in the Detroit office, which is responsible for the sales and service of the company's products in the states of Ohio, Indiana, and Michigan. A summary of the managerial roles is shown in exhibit 2–8.

Interpersonal Roles

Three interpersonal roles characterize managerial activities. First is the *figurehead,* which for the sales manager involves ceremonial work, such

EXHIBIT 2–7
Managerial Roles

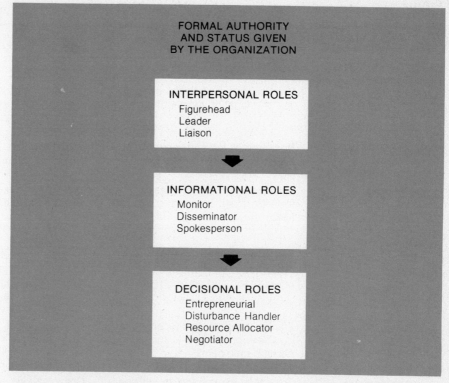

FORMAL AUTHORITY
AND STATUS GIVEN
BY THE ORGANIZATION

INTERPERSONAL ROLES
Figurehead
Leader
Liaison

INFORMATIONAL ROLES
Monitor
Disseminator
Spokesperson

DECISIONAL ROLES
Entrepreneurial
Disturbance Handler
Resource Allocator
Negotiator

Source: H. Mintzberg, "The Manager's Job: Folklore or Fact," Harvard Business Review
(July–August 1975): 55.

as receiving visitors, and hierarchical duties, such as requesting a subordinate to follow up on a specific job. Second, the sales manager in a
leader role hires, trains, and motivates field and office personnel. Third,
the *liaison* role consists of interactions with other managers external to
the organization. For example, in establishing a sales contract with a
customer, the sales manager is acting as a liaison for or representative
of the organization.

Informational Roles

In performing the interpersonal roles, the manager is involved in a number of interactions that give rise to information flow. The result is that
many managers emerge as focal points for information exchange in organizations. Three individual informational roles are prominent. First,
as a *monitor,* the sales manager is a receiver and collector of information,
and thus often becomes well informed on various organizational activities. This role involves such activities as gathering information on
changes in consumer attitudes toward the product, learning of competitors' plans, and the future marketing plans of their company. The *disseminator* role involves transmitting information to peers, subordinates, and
superiors *within* the organization. Finally, as a *spokesperson,* the sales
manager transmits information to individuals *outside* the organization
by such means as a meeting with a customer on an upcoming product

EXHIBIT 2–8   Description and Examples of Managerial Roles

ROLE	DESCRIPTION	EXAMPLES
Interpersonal Roles		
Figurehead	Symbolic head; performs routine duties of a legal or social nature.	Greeting visitors; signing legal documents (university president signing diplomas); usually at executive manager level.
Leader	Responsible for motivation of subordinates and for staffing and training.	Most activities involving subordinates: formal authority position.
Liaison	Maintains network of outside contacts to obtain favors and information.	"Keeping in touch" with the external community through phone calls, meetings, etc.
Informational Roles		
Monitor	Seeks and receives information to obtain thorough understanding of organization and environment.	Reading periodicals and reports, conversations, and other activities related to changes in consumer activities, competitors' plans, etc.; "keeping one's ear to the ground."
Disseminator	Transmits information received from outsiders or insiders to other organization members.	Formal reports, memos, or phone calls to other company managers regarding activities in the business or local community.
Spokesperson	Transmits information to outsiders on organization plans, policies, actions.	Conversations with suppliers, customers, speeches to local groups.
Decisional Roles		
Entrepreneur	Initiates and supervises design of organizational improvement projects as opportunities arise.	Realigning subordinates' jobs and responsibilities; new product or promotional ideas.
Disturbance handler	Responsible for corrective action when organization faces unexpected crises.	Resolving employee conflicts; adjusting to strikes at suppliers; reacting to a bankrupt customer.
Resource allocator	Responsible for allocation of human, monetary, and material resources.	Scheduling time for projects; awarding bonuses and pay raises.
Negotiator	Responsible for representing the organization in bargaining and negotiations.	Negotiating shipping rates and schedules with transportation companies; labor-management contracts.

Adapted from H. Mintzberg, *The Nature of Managerial Work* (New York: Harper & Row, 1973).

price change, a telephone call to a trucking company to discuss problems of product delivery time, or a speech to a local chamber of commerce on the company's plans to build a new shipping and receiving warehouse in their community.

Decisional Roles

Managers' unique access to information and their interpersonal relationships put them at a central place in the organization where important decisions are made. Four specific decisional roles can be usually adopted. First, the *entrepreneurial* role involves some change or improvement initiated by the manager. For example, the sales manager may realign the responsibilities of the sales representatives such that they specialize in certain products, rather than handling all products for a set of customers. This decision may be based on the recognition that the product line of the company has grown too complex for each sales representative to become an expert. Specialization may permit better service to customers. Second, as a *disturbance handler,* the manager takes charge when the organization is put in a difficult position. Responses to a bankrupt customer, to conflicts between sales representatives, or to a strike by trucking companies that affects delivery of the product are examples. In the *resource allocator* role, the manager decides how the resources of the organization are to be divided. In this role, the sales manager decides how much money to spend on training and supplies, how much time to spend structuring the work of subordinates, and whether or not to bid on a contract with a new customer. Finally, as a *negotiator,* the manager enters into negotiations with internal or external parties on behalf of the organization. For the sales manager, this would involve such situations as negotiating shipping schedules with customers, establishing a lease on office space, and coming to an agreement with transportation companies on the shipping rates.

Mintzberg's work has not only highlighted the various functions of management, but it also calls attention to the dynamic environment in which managers frequently operate. The systematic and rational functions of planning, organizing, leading, and controlling that serve as the foundation of what managers do in their jobs are usually interrupted by the realities of organizational life. Managers must constantly adapt to changes, react to crises, and be able to wear a variety of hats to do their jobs properly.

AN EMPHASIS ON PERFORMANCE

Our definition of *management* says, in effect, that the major objective of a manager is to achieve organizational goals; in other words, there is a strong emphasis on performance. Typically, managerial performance has been discussed in terms of *efficiency* and *effectiveness*. As the noted management scholar, Peter Drucker, has stated, efficiency means "doing things right," and effectiveness means "doing the right things."[11]

Efficiency is a concept based on the physical and engineering sciences and concerns the relationship between "inputs" and "outputs." For example, the efficiency of an automobile engine is based on the energy

BEETLE BAILEY

value of the fuel that is necessary to generate a given level of power output. In organizations, the inputs are the human, physical, and financial resources available to the manager. Efficient managers achieve high levels of output (goal accomplishment) with a given base of inputs. When managers are able to minimize the cost of the resources that are used to attain goals, they are functioning efficiently. In discussing sports, we are speaking of efficiency when we say that "this team went further than we could ever imagine, given the talent the manager has to work with." Casey Stengel and the 1969 New York Mets baseball team and the U.S. hockey team in the 1980 Winter Olympics are classic examples.

Effectiveness is the degree to which the goals of an organization have been met. In essence, effective managers have selected the correct approaches and therefore have achieved their goals. For example, Procter and Gamble, Texas Instruments, and Federated Department Stores have consistently outperformed other organizations within their industries on such measures as return on investments, sales margin, growth in earnings, and so on.

It is often stated that a manager must be both effective and efficient. While few people would disagree with this statement, it is both too broad and ambiguous for our purposes. A more concise framework is needed.

A Framework for Performance

The term *performance* will be used as a somewhat global concept that represents the outcomes or results of organizational activities. Effectiveness and efficiency will be viewed as subcomponents of performance.[12]

As an aid in our presentation of the manager's job, we provide a framework for performance that managers should carefully consider in attempting to achieve organizational goals:

1. Performance is not a single standard, but consists of *multiple criteria*.
2. The *level of analysis* of performance ranges from the individual employee to the user of the organization's products and services, and society in general.
3. The *focus* of performance can concern maintenance, improvement, and developmental goals.

EXHIBIT 2–9   A Framework for Managerial Performance

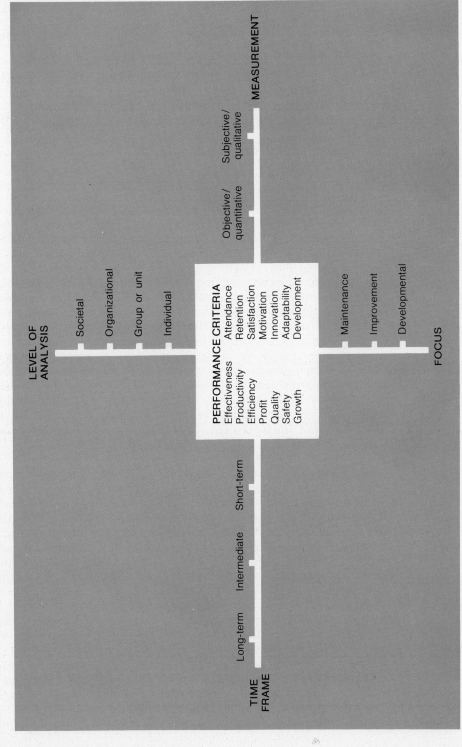

4. The *time frame* for performance, from short term to long term, must be established.
5. How performance will be *measured,* ranging from quantitative/objective to qualitative/subjective measures, should be considered.

Performance Criteria.   As shown in exhibit 2–9, the concept of performance involves many different standards. This part of the performance framework suggests that managers must judge performance with multiple criteria. For example, a dean of a university business school could identify teaching, research publications, and community service as performance criteria to evaluate faculty.

Level of Analysis.   This factor concerns whether performance criteria apply to the individual, group, department, or society. For example, the manager of an audit group in an accounting firm could be interested in the morale of individual employees, the productivity of the group, and the client's satisfaction with the group's activities, and would apply different criteria in evaluating each.

Performance Focus.   A frequently overlooked aspect concerns the focus or kind of performance that is desired. Three distinctions can be made: (1) *maintenance,* or performance designed to maintain a specific level of activity; (2) *improvement* performance activities, usually described in terms of an action verb such as increase/decrease or add/reduce, which implies some change is desired; and (3) *developmental* performance activities, which are related to growth, learning, or advancement issues. For example, the quality control manager in a steel pipe manufacturing company could be interested in maintaining daily product inspection rates at 50 percent of production (maintenance), reducing quality rejects by 25 percent (improvement), and training subordinates in the use of laser technology in quality control (developmental).

Time Frame.   When goals are to be achieved relates to the time frame component of our performance framework. Putting performance activities in some time frame (scheduling) stresses the need to consider goal attainment in short-term, intermediate, and long-term perspectives. The manager of a data processing department, for example, may want to immediately reduce, from three days to one day, the turnaround time on financial reports, to decrease employee turnover in the department by 40 percent within one year, and have a new computer installed in four to five years.

Performance Measurement.   Finally, the manager needs to be concerned with how performance will be measured. Performance measurement usually involves the use of objective/quantifiable and/or subjective/qualitative data. Objective measurement concerns data to which some hard number can be assigned as a value, such as sales dollars, percentage reduction in costs, or the number of days allotted for project completion. Subjective measurement, on the other hand, usually involves obtaining an opinion or evaluation through perceptual means. Job satisfaction measurement, questionnaires, or supervisory evaluations of subordinate performance are examples.

In summary, organizational performance is a complex dimension that is more than "doing things right" or "doing the right things." It is the responsibility of the manager to consider carefully who or what is performing, what performance is to be measured, how performance is to be measured, and when it is to be measured. An added concern relates to the ethical consideration of a manager's performance. This is the subject of the next section.

MANAGERIAL ETHICS

As an executive of a large U.S. based corporation, what would you do if . . .

1. In the process of negotiating a multi-million dollar contract with a foreign nation, a key governmental official asks you for a $250,000 personal consulting "fee." In return, he promises to give your organization special assistance in obtaining the contract from his country. You are aware that not only are such "fees" common practice, but that if it is not paid, the contract would certainly be awarded to one of your major competitors. Would you pay the consulting "fee"?

2. During a luncheon meeting, a representative of a major competitor for one of your key product lines suggests that the two companies come to an "informal agreement" on the prices that will be set on the competing products. You know that the recent price competition between you has all but eliminated the profitability on the products. The new suggested price would bring profits back to acceptable levels. Should you agree on the new price?

3. You have the opportunity to hire a major research scientist from a major competitor. This scientist was involved in the development of a new product that, when introduced to the market later this year, will adversely affect the market share and profitability of your product. By hiring the scientist, you can reduce your reaction time to the new product by two years. Should you hire the scientist?

4. In preparing a bi-annual report to the Environmental Protection Agency (EPA) you come across data that show that one of your agricultural products manufacturing plants had been discharging high quantities of a toxic pesticide into the local river. You investigate and find out that the cause of the discharging was due to a piece of malfunctioning equipment. The plant manager decided not to repair the equipment because it would have meant a six to eight day shutdown of the plant during the busiest season of the year. You are aware that reporting the data will result in a stiff fine from the EPA and in an increase in community opposition to the plant, which is already quite high. What should be in the report?

The above situations are all true and represent an important factor in the manager's job—namely, the *ethical* considerations that govern a manager's behavior. In this age of instant information from the media, concerns over the environment, and questions of the role of organizations in our society, the concept of managerial ethics gains significant importance. As is becoming clearer every day, corporate integrity and sound professional ethics are *essential* conditions for managerial effectiveness and even for survival of the organization.

Definition of Managerial Ethics

Ethics is derived from the Greek word *ethos,* which refers to a person's fundamental orientation toward life. Initially the word meant a dwelling place, but for Aristotle, it came to mean an inner dwelling place, or what we call *internal character.* Carrying this further, the Latin translation of ethos is *mos, moris,* from which we get our word *moral.* In Latin, the emphasis shifts from internal character to actions—external behavior, acts, habits, and customs.[13] For our purposes, managerial ethics will refer to internal *and* external standards or codes of conduct used not only to govern the behavior of individuals or groups, but also to determine what is right or wrong, good or evil.

From a managerial point of view, the distinction between illegal and unethical should be made. *Illegal* behavior are acts that violate a law, or laws, in a particular area or society. *Unethical* behavior, on the other hand, are acts that are contrary to the moral standards or codes of conduct established by society. The difference between the two is important to note. While laws that govern legal behaviors are finite and relatively stable, ethical concepts may change over time or between cultures. As the first example indicates, political bribes or payoffs may be acceptable in one culture but not in another. The manager is thus faced with acknowledging (or developing) a complex set of ethical codes.

Categories of Unethical Behavior

Defining unethical behavior can be an elusive activity due to cultural changes. There are, however, certain practices or categories of behaviors that can raise questions of ethics. Some of the most publicized practices are as follows:

1. *Political gifts.* Corporate gifts to politicians or their committees are prohibited by U.S. law.[14]
2. *Political bribes.* Political gifts are usually indirect contributions, a bribe or payoff is a direct payment that assumes preferential treatment. Some payoffs are illegal under the Foreign Corrupt Practices Act.[15]
3. *General business practices.* A global category that can include such practices as Olin selling weapons from its Winchester division to South Africa.[16]
4. *Improper reporting procedures.* Refers to internal practices that provide an inaccurate appraisal of the organization's position. Includes, for example, Fruehaufs Trailers' improper reporting of excise taxes.[17]
5. *Employee privacy.* Subjecting employees to probing interviews, psychological testing, investigative reports, or lie detectors, which can be considered as "loyalty" tests or help in creating "blacklists."[18]

EXHIBIT 2–10   Examples of Questionable Managerial Ethics

ORGANIZATION	DESCRIPTION
Ashland Oil, Inc.	Paid more than $300,000 to foreign officials, including $150,000 to President Albert Bernard Bonogo of Gabon to retain mineral and refining rights.
Braniff Airlines	Admitted to the C.A.B. that it had given 21,600 free tickets worth $750,000 to travel agents to promote the company. It also admitted to illegally contributing $40,000 to the Nixon campaign.
Exxon Corporation	Paid $740,000 to government officials and others in three countries. Admits its Italian subsidiary made $27 million in secret but legal contributions to seven Italian political parties.
Fruehauf Trailer	Company top two executives found guilty of conspiring to defraud the government of excise taxes.
Lockheed Aircraft Corporation	Gave $202 million in commissions, payoffs, and bribes to foreign agents and government officials in the Netherlands, Italy, Japan, Turkey, and other countries. Admits that $22 million of this sum went for outright bribes.
Merck & Company, Inc.	Gave $3 million, largely in commission-type payments, to employees of 36 foreign governments between 1968 and 1978.
Northrop Corporation	SEC charged that it paid $30 million in commissions and bribes to government officials and agents in Holland, Iran, France, West Germany, Saudi Arabia, Brazil, Malaysia, and Taiwan.
Olin Corporation	Illegally shipped $1.2 million worth of arms and ammunition to South Africa. Company salesman had lied about the destination of the goods to the U.S. government.
Southwestern Bell	Lost a $1 million suit for illegally tapping the telephone of a Bell manager.
United Brands Company	Paid a $1.25 million bribe to Honduran officials for a reduction in the banana export tax. Admits paying $750,000 to European officials. Investigators say the payment was made to head off proposed Italian restrictions on banana imports.

Some of the more notable examples of reportedly unethical behavior are shown in exhibit 2–10.

Sources of Ethical and Unethical Behavior

Where do standards of ethical conduct originate; what is the role of society, government, and industry; and why do we have occurrences of unethical behavior? The answers to these questions are just as elusive as attempting to explain cultural differences between nations. A discussion of four factors may assist in our understanding of these issues: (1) societal attitudes and beliefs; (2) competitive pressures; (3) the legal environment; and (4) industry codes of conduct.

Societal Attitudes.   Exhibit 2–11 presents the results of a survey of over 1,200 managers in a variety of organizations that dealt with the topic of ethical standards.[19] An examination of the factors influencing

EXHIBIT 2–11   Factors Influencing Ethical Standards

FACTORS CAUSING HIGHER STANDARDS	PERCENTAGE OF RESPONDENTS LISTING FACTOR	FACTORS CAUSING LOWER STANDARDS	PERCENTAGE OF RESPONDENTS LISTING FACTOR
Public disclosure; publicity; media coverage; better communication	31%	*Society's standards are lower;* social decay; more permissive society; materialism and hedonism have grown; loss of church and home influence; less quality, more quantity desires	34%
Increased public concern; public awareness, consciousness, and scrutiny; better-informed public; societal pressures	20	*Competition;* pace of life; stress to succeed; current economic conditions; costs of doing business; more business competing for less	13
Government regulation, legislation, and intervention; federal courts	10	*Political corruption;* loss of confidence in government; Watergate; politics; political ethics and climate	9
Education of business managers; increase in manager professionalism and education	9	*People more aware of unethical acts;* constant media coverage; TV; communications create atmosphere for crime	9
New social expectations for the role business is to play in society; young adults' attitudes	5	*Greed;* desire for gain; worship the dollar as measure of success; selfishness of the individual; lack of personal integrity and moral fiber	8
Business' greater sense of social responsibility and greater awareness of the implications of its acts; business responsiveness; corporate policy changes; top management emphasis on ethical action	5	*Pressure for profit* from within the organization from superiors or from stockholders; corporate influences on managers; corporate policies	7
Other	20	*Other*	21

Note: Some respondents listed more than one factor. There were 353 factors in all listed as causing higher standards and 411 in all listed as causing lower ones. Categories may not add up to 100 percent because of rounding errors.

Source: Steven N. Brenner and Earl A. Molander, "Is the Ethic of Business Changing?" *Harvard Business Review* (January–February 1977). 57–71. Copyright 1977 by the President and Fellows of Harvard College; all rights reserved.

ethical standards and causing lower standards suggests that there may be at least three contributing factors. First, there may be the perceived decline in certain of society's norms and attitudes, such as a greater emphasis on permissiveness, the decline in the influence of church and family, and the orientation toward quantity as opposed to quality. Second, as already noted, society is increasingly concerned with unethical behavior, with the emphasis on public disclosure and media information. This increased awareness and consciousness may assist in creating, or at least enforcing, existing ethical standards.

Finally, there is the important influence of groups on our behavior. As some well-known writers have stated, as a society we are becoming less independent as individuals and more oriented to be members of groups. For example, in the same survey described in exhibit 2–11, the respondents were asked what were some of the factors that can influence unethical decisions. The responses are as follows:

Factors Influencing Unethical Behavior   *Rank*

Ranking scale of 1 (most influential) to 6 (least influential)

Behavior of superiors	2.15
Formal policy or lack thereof	3.27
Industry ethical climate	3.34
Behavior of one's peers in the company	3.37
Society's moral climate	4.22
One's personal financial needs	4.46

As this survey indicates, the influence of group members, from superiors to peers, can have a significant influence on ethical behavior.

As we will discuss in chapter 14, groups (such as committees, task forces, and interest groups) establish norms that can have a significant impact on individual behavior. This social ethic can vary from group to group, and from organization to organization, resulting in conflict and confusion concerning which standard should be followed.

Competitive Pressures.   Our economic system is built on two fundamental concepts: *effort* (the Protestant work ethic)[20] and *competition.* The essence of these beliefs is that working hard and outperforming others in achieving certain goals will be rewarded with high levels of success. In recent years, however, we have seen an increase in a "winning at all costs" philosophy, which leads to other behaviors, possibly unethical, being substituted for hard work and competition. We see examples all around us frequently, such as the increase in cheating on exams, falsifying documents, or making questionable advertising claims. In many organizations in which the managers' pay increases and promotional opportunities are based on their past performances in contributing to the organization's profits, various ways have been devised to inflate their profit pictures.

For example, at a truck assembly plant of one of the "Big Three" U.S. automobile companies, managers were given a production goal each week that assumed that everything would go perfectly. The problem was that on an assembly line, nothing ever does. There are frequent conveyor breakdowns, or high absenteeism, or something else. As a result, production goals were being missed with regularity, and higher level managers were putting pressure on the plant to do something about it.

In response, plant management installed a secret control box in a supervisor's office that overrode the control panel governing the speed of the assembly line. With the secret box, managers were able to speed up the line and increase production. The use of the secret box, however, violated the labor contract with the United Auto Workers' Union. The workers eventually discovered the secret device and later were awarded $1 million in back pay from the courts. The ill feelings between management and labor still pervade the plant today. Plant management, when questioned on the matter, claimed that higher level executives had to know about the device, but never asked any questions. So while they knew they were doing something ethically wrong, plant management figured that it must have been okay in the eyes of the company.[21]

The Legal Environment.   The legal and legislative environment, contrary to some beliefs, is confusing and full of loopholes when it comes to determining what is or what isn't legally acceptable behavior. Legal interpretations and entanglements often make it difficult for managers to know exactly what course to take or what decision to make.

For example, consider the previously mentioned Foreign Corrupt Practices Act of 1977. The law specifically outlaws "foreign gifts or bribes to any foreign official, political candidate, or party paid by domestic concerns—defined as U.S. corporations, partnerships, or individual representatives of same—for purposes of inducing them to influence their government to assist the giver in obtaining or retaining business." Violation of the act will cost the individual five years in jail and a $1 million corporate fine.

Sounds simple, right? Wrong. Two significant loopholes exist within the act that may put the manager in a difficult position.[22] For example, the act exempts "facilitating payments made solely to expedite nondiscretionary official actions." Translated into street language, this means that "grease, dash, or squeeze" payments are not illegal. In this most important area, the act *excludes* from the definition of *foreign official* (to whom it is a crime to pay bribes and gifts) any foreign employee whose duties are essentially ministerial or clerical. This leads to the startling conclusion that bribes in any amount, for any purpose, are apparently permissible under the anti-bribery law if they are paid to clerical or ministerial employees. There is no guarantee, however, that the clerk will not pass on the bribe to the boss.

Second, the law also excludes foreign extortion from its coverage. The Senate Report on the law refers to an example of a "payment to an official to keep an oil rig from being dynamited" as being exempted. The loophole here is whether the extortion exemption is limited to threatened physical or property damage or extends to economic damage as well. What if a foreign minister or cabinet official states, "pay me $100,000 or I'll put you out of business in this country"? Is this asking for a bribe or demanding a permissible extortion payment? When faced with this situation, many managers have been going to the Justice Department to report the demand before any payment is made.

These are a few of the many ambiguities in the manager's legal environment. Since most courts have not ruled on all the implications, the manager is put into a situation where common sense and good personal ethics must be called upon.

Industry Code of Ethics.   An industry code of ethics is an internally enforced code of conduct that serves as a guide to all members of the profession or industry. Examples of codes of conduct are most noticeable in the medical, legal, and accounting professions. There are, however, few if any professional codes of conduct that serve as guidelines for business or other organizational leaders. There is also some question about whether such an ethical code can be developed.

Arguments for a code of ethical conduct include:

1. It will improve the confidence of customers, suppliers, and others in the quality of goods and services that they expect.
2. The complexities of organizational activities demand some standards of behavior be set and followed.
3. In the long run, adherence to a set of standard ethical codes will increase the quality of management talent that reaches the highest levels of organizations.

Arguments against a code of ethical conduct:

1. Codes of conduct will result in a severe restriction of the manager's freedom to act; a code that is too strict can actually restrict some modes of ethical behavior.
2. The environment of any organization is too dynamic for any specific code of conduct. A code that is too strict can limit behavior, and a loosely written code may contain meaningless generalities that can be interpreted in an infinite number of ways to suit the particular situation.
3. Enforcement of codes of conduct would be an almost impossible task.

Some form of ethical conduct code is needed. However, until the problems of overly restrictive behaviors, deceptive statements, and enforcement procedures can be overcome, a universally accepted code will be difficult to establish and enforce.

Ethics and the Manager's Job: Keys to Success

This discussion may leave the manager or future manager with a feeling of helplessness when it comes to defining what is right and wrong in managerial practice. One can easily develop the attitude that virtue does not always triumph or that ethical practices are not necessarily the most profitable. However, managers who are convinced that ethical behavior is necessary can do many things to promote this view. For example, consider the following thoughts:

1. **Take the lead by setting a good example.**

   If many managers feel pressure from superiors to perform (which may lead to unethical behavior), then top management that adopts a strong ethical mode of behavior can have the same effect. By this action, managers can cultivate the professional nature of employees.

2. **Are there any internal systems that can promote unethical behavior?**

   For example, reward systems that promote the achievement of organizational goals at any cost should be examined carefully. If unethical behavior by employees is rewarded by the organization, others will follow. Unethical behavior should be punished severely to eliminate its reoccurrence.

3. **Broaden organizational communication both internally and externally.**

   Many high-level executives from such organizations as Union Carbide, Du Pont, G.M., and IBM have taken the lead in attempting to communicate to employees and external constituencies the nature of organizational activities.[23] The idea is to explain to employees and to the public how and why business operates, how decisions are made, the difficulties in institutionalizing a social point of view, and what roles organizations play in the socioeconomic life of a nation. For such efforts at communication to be successful, managers must be as open, candid, and forthright as possible in their dialogue.[24] Remember a key principle: secrecy can breed distrust and contempt.

4. **In the short term, unethical behavior may prove successful; in the long run it will not succeed.**

    Ethics should be evaluated in terms of long-range consequences for the individual and the organization. Not only does short-term unethical behavior lead to a poor reputation, but continued unethical practices can only result in stiff governmental regulations.

    In an environment that is becoming increasingly dynamic and complex, managers must recognize the importance of ethical behavior in both their short-term and long-term activities.

THE MANAGER'S JOB: AN INTEGRATIVE VIEW

In this chapter, we provided a contemporary definition and description of the manager's job. Our view of the manager's job focuses on four elements: (1) functions; (2) skills; (3) roles; and (4) performance. A summary illustration of this presentation is shown in exhibit 2–12.

EXHIBIT 2–12
The Manager's Job

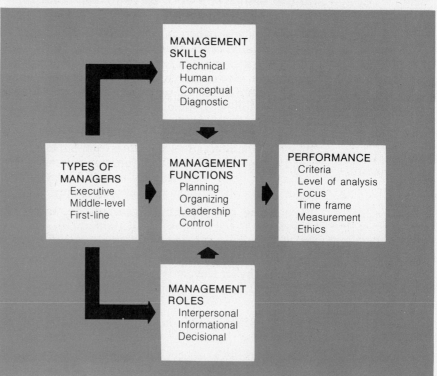

MANAGEMENT SKILLS
Technical
Human
Conceptual
Diagnostic

TYPES OF MANAGERS
Executive
Middle-level
First-line

MANAGEMENT FUNCTIONS
Planning
Organizing
Leadership
Control

PERFORMANCE
Criteria
Level of analysis
Focus
Time frame
Measurement
Ethics

MANAGEMENT ROLES
Interpersonal
Informational
Decisional

This exhibit highlights certain important characteristics of the manager's job that will serve as the foundation for the remainder of this book. First, the major focus of activity for the manager is on *performance*. This is the ultimate test of the manager's job. Second, at the core of the manager's job are the *functions* of planning, organizing, leading, and controlling. They serve as the basic framework for managerial activities. Third, the manner in which the individual performs the managerial functions is dependent both on the extent to which the necessary *skills* have been acquired and applied and in what *behavioral role* the manager is performing. Finally, there is the recognition that managerial behavior differs by the particular *level* in the organization. Executive, middle, and first-line managers differ in the time they devote to specific functions, the nature of the skills they require, and the role in which they perform.

SUMMARY FOR THE MANAGER

1. Our definition of *management*—the process of integrating resources and tasks toward the achievement of stated organizational goals—clearly suggests that management is results, or *performance,* oriented. For the manager, this performance approach requires a knowledge base and proficiency in the managerial functions, skills, and important roles.

2. A way of classifying managers is by their level in the organization. Such terms as *executive manager, middle-level manager,* and *first-line manager* have been used to distinguish between different types of managers.

3. Four managerial functions were identified: planning, organizing, leading, and controlling. It is important to note that these functions should not be considered a rigid, checklist approach to management. On the contrary, most managers probably perform these functions daily, allotting different amounts of time to each depending on the level in the organization that the managers occupy.

4. Effectiveness as a manager requires that the individual develop a set of skills that can be applied to most managerial situations. The four identified skills—technical, human, conceptual, and diagnostic—vary in importance by levels in the organization. The manager (or future manager) must realize early that these skills cannot be acquired solely from textbooks. Beyond education, the two most important mechanisms for acquiring these skills are experience and developing a mentor relationship with a senior manager.

5. In addition to functions and skills, the third important aspect of the manager's job is the set of roles that must be performed. The three broad role categories—interpersonal, informational, and decisional—not only cut across the main managerial functions, but require the development and use of the important types of managerial skills. This orientation to the managerial functions, skills, and roles serves as our foundation for defining the manager's job.

6. Performance in the manager's job is complex and requires more than a discussion of the differences between the terms *effectiveness* and *efficiency*. In particular, to define *managerial performance*, at least five different aspects should be considered: multiple criteria; level of analysis; focus; time; and measurement characteristics. It is the responsibility of each manager to define the important performance criteria, who or what is performing, how performance is to be measured, and when performance is to be measured.

7. There is no one best way to manage; there are no hard rules, laws, or equations. The key to managerial success is the ability of the individual to analyze and understand each situation and to perform the necessary functions, skills, and roles that can lead to effectiveness.

8. Ethics will continue to play an important part in the manager's job. Although ethics help in determining what the manager *ought to do,* cultural differences between countries and the lack of a general code of managerial ethics may put added pressures on the manager, resulting in different behaviors.

QUESTIONS FOR REVIEW AND DISCUSSION

1. Why would some people call management an art, and others call it a science?
2. Why do we suggest that management cannot be reduced to a simple checklist approach?
3. Describe the differences between a first-line manager and a middle-level manager in terms of functions, skills required, and roles.
4. What is the function of a mentor in an organization?
5. What are the major differences between interpersonal and decisional roles?
6. How may an individual acquire human skills? Diagnostic skills?
7. Do you favor the development of a code of managerial ethics? Why?
8. Using exhibit 2–11, discuss managerial performance for a postmaster of a suburban post office, a head nurse in a hospital, and a manager of a group of accountants specializing in auditing.

NOTES

1. R. Steward, *Managers and Their Jobs* (London: Macmillan & Co., 1967).

2. C. R. Christensen, K. R. Andrews, and J. L. Bower, *Business Policy* (Homewood, Ill.: Richard D. Irwin, 1978).

3. F. E. Kast and J. E. Rosenzweig, *Organization and Management* (New York: McGraw-Hill, 1974).

4. T. A. Mahoney, T. H. Jerdee, and S. J. Carroll, "The Job(s) of Management," *Industrial Relations* (February 1965): 97–110.

5. R. L. Katz, "Skills of an Effective Administrator," *Harvard Business Review* (September–October 1974): 90–102.

6. J. S. Livingston, "Myths of the Well-Educated Manager," *Harvard Business Review* (January–February 1971): 79–89.

7. W. G. Smith, "John James: Don't Get Stuck in Some Specialized Niche," *Texas Business* (December 1979): 36.

8. See A. Zaleznik, "Managers and Leaders; Are They Different?" *Harvard Business Review* (May–June 1977): 67–68; E. Collins and P. Scott, "Everyone Who Makes It Has a Mentor," *Harvard Business Review* (July–August 1978): 89–101; and G. R. Roche, "Much Ado About Mentors," *Harvard Business Review* (January–February 1979): 14–31.

9. K. White, "The Woman Executive," *Sky* (August 1979): 51.

10. H. Mintzberg, *The Nature of Managerial Work* (New York: Harper & Row, 1973).

11. P. F. Drucker, *Managing for Results* (New York: Harper & Row, 1964), p. 5.

12. P. S. Goodman, J. M. Pennings, and Associates, *New Perspectives on Organizational Effectiveness* (San Francisco: Jossey-Bass, 1977).

13. W. J. Byron, S.J., "The Meaning of Ethics in Business," *Business Horizons* (November 1977): 32.

14. See T. Griffith, "Payoff Is Not Acceptable Practice," *Fortune* (August 1975). 122–25; and W. Robertson, "The Directors Woke Up Too Late at Gulf," *Fortune* (June 1976): 120–25.

15. J. S. Estey and D. W. Marston, "Pitfalls (and Loopholes) in the Foreign Bribery Law," *Fortune* (October 9, 1978): 182–88.

16. H. D. Menzies, "The One-Two Punch That Shook Olin," *Fortune* (June 5, 1978): 120–22.

17. W. Kiechel, "The Crime at the Top in Fruehauf Corp.," *Fortune* (January 29, 1979): 32–35.

18. A. F. Westin, "The Problem of Employee Privacy Still Troubles Management," *Fortune* (June 4, 1979): 120–26.

19. S. N. Brenner and E. A. Molander, "Is the Ethics of Business Changing?" *Harvard Business Review* (January–February 1977): 57–71.

20. J. D. Long, "The Protestant Ethic Reexamined," *Business Horizons* (February 1972): 75–82.

21. G. Getschow, "Overdriven Execs: Some Middle Managers Cut Corners to Achieve High Corporate Goals," *Wall Street Journal,* 8 November 1979, p. 1.

22. Estey and Marston, p. 184.

23. H. D. Menzies, "Union Carbide Raises Its Voice," *Fortune* (September 25, 1978): 86–90.

24. J. F. Steinger, "The Business Response to Public Mistrust," *Business Horizons* (April 1977): 74–81.

ADDITIONAL REFERENCES

Barnard, C. I. *The Functions of the Executive.* Cambridge, Mass.: Harvard University Press, 1938.

Bowman, J. S. "Managerial Ethics in Business and Government." *Business Horizons,* October 1976, pp. 48–64.

Caroll, A. "Managerial Ethics: A Post-Watergate View." *Business Horizons,* April 1975, pp. 75–80.

Child, J. "What Determines Organizational Performance?" *Organizational Dynamics,* Spring 1975, pp. 2–18.

Drucker, P. F. *Management: Tasks, Responsibilities, and Practices.* New York: Harper & Row, 1974.

Ghorpade, J. *Assessment of Organizational Effectiveness.* Santa Monica, Calif.: Goodyear Publishing, 1971.

Koontz, H. *Toward a Unified Theory of Management.* New York: McGraw-Hill, 1964.

McAdams, T., and Miljus, R. C. "Growing Criminal Liability of Executives." *Harvard Business Review,* March–April 1977, pp. 36–58.

McGregor, D. M. *The Professional Manager.* New York: McGraw-Hill, 1967.

Owens, J. "Business Ethics: Age-Old Ideal, Now Real." *Business Horizons,* February 1978, pp. 26–36.

Price, J. *Organizational Effectiveness.* Homewood, Ill.: Richard D. Irwin, Dorsey Press, 1968.

Sayles, L. R. *Managerial Behavior.* New York: McGraw-Hill, 1964.

Steers, R. "Problems in the Measurement of Organizational Effectiveness." *Administrative Science Quarterly,* December 1975, pp. 546–58.

Wortman, M. S., and Sperling, S. *Defining the Manager's Job.* New York: Amacom, 1975.

A CASE FOR ANALYSIS

Executive Replacement: Standard Brands, Inc.

Reuben Gutoff's sudden fall from the presidency of Standard Brands, Inc., marks the end of more than a year of tension within the company—a period of conflict apparently brought on by his management practices and personality.

Gutoff came to the diversified food company in 1976 as the ideal staff executive—a strategic planner who developed much of the finely honed system at General Electric Co. and a firm believer in centralized management and strong controls emanating from headquarters. His managerial sophistication was to play a large part in transforming Standard Brands from a rather stodgy company, relying heavily on its food ingredients business, to an aggressive marketer of branded consumer items. Cast in that role, Gutoff rose quickly, receiving two promotions in fifteen months to become president in May 1977.

He did not fare as well as an operating officer. "Gutoff ran into trouble right from the start," says a former senior executive who recently left the company. "As soon as he became president and assumed line responsibility, the animosity began."

Yet the frictions that eventually led to Gutoff's departure from active management were present even before that. In late 1976, when it was clear that Gutoff was soon to take the president's job, a number of top officers met with Chairman F. Ross Johnson to lodge their complaints. This "palace revolt," as one former executive put it, was reportedly squelched by assurances from Johnson that any differences between Gutoff and the other officers could be ironed out. But, notes a second former executive who departed within the past six months, "Those problems were obviously never worked out."

Part of the trouble, as those reporting to Gutoff saw it, was that he wanted to make too many operating decisions himself, even in areas where he had little experience. "It was over-centralization all right," explains an alumnus of Standard Brands, "but mostly in the sense that Gutoff wanted his hands in everything. And he interfered in operating matters in an imperious fashion."

Gutoff's style aggravated the frictions created by substantive differences, according to others. "His main problem was his rigidity," claims a former officer. "He's very bright, and he's also very opinionated. Often he did not leave room for any sort of team involvement." Still other observers question how effective the vaunted planning tools Gutoff introduced at Standard Brands have been. One former executive complains: "Things were bogged down by the perceived need to plan. You don't have the same luxury of time in the consumer food business as Gutoff did at GE."

But even his detractors concede that Gutoff, 51, is a brilliant individual whose expertise in solving conceptual, organizational, and systemic problems is impressive. Gutoff's supporters also note that he had many years of operating experience at GE, even if it did not seem to help much at Standard Brands. And his step down—Gutoff will stay on as an executive associate to the chairman, working on new ventures— might have been largely because the job of repositioning the company was about complete, say present Standard Brands executives. "Reuben Gutoff has done what he came here to do," says one vice president. "His time is over now."

Though Gutoff may have accomplished much, his departure from the presidency was not exactly his idea. "He didn't really have a choice," says one director, noting that the board voted in favor of the change. The man taking over as Standard Brands' new president, O. Lester Applegate, could hardly be more different, in both experience and manner, from Gutoff. Applegate, 61, left the company in 1976 following a rift with then-Chairman Henry Weigl. Applegate, who originally joined Standard Brands in 1942, returned to the company in mid-1977.

Assessing the old president and the new one, a former executive who knows them explains: "Applegate is an outgoing, gregarious guy, with the sort of operating experience that the old hands there respect. Gutoff is another animal altogether— the sophisticated, abrasive staff man." Adds a Standard Brands vice president: "Applegate is the more qualified of the two to be president, I think Gutoff would admit that, though perhaps grudgingly."

Suggested from Business Week, *October 16, 1978.*

Questions for Discussion

1. Discuss Mr. Gutoff's activities in terms of managerial functions, skills, and roles. What functions, skills, and roles were required of the job?
2. Identify the performance criteria for Mr. Gutoff's job. Did they change over time?
3. What factors led to Mr. Gutoff's replacement? How do you think Mr. Applegate will perform as Mr. Gutoff's replacement? Discuss your reasons.

EXPERIENTIAL EXERCISE

Defining the Manager's Job

Purpose

1. To examine the key components of a manager's job.
2. To gain an understanding of the variety of demands on a manager.

Required Understanding

The functional, skills, and role perspectives of a manager's job.

How to Set Up the Exercise

Set up groups of four to eight students for the forty-five minute exercise. The groups should be separated from each other and students asked to converse only with members of their own group.

Instructions for the Exercise

You are to consider the job of a divisional sales manager in a large suburban branch store of a major national retail organization. This manager's area of responsibility includes women's fashions, teen sportswear, children's clothing, and women's accessory goods. Each of these four areas is headed by a department manager who reports directly to the divisional manager. The branch store employees, approximately 600 people, recorded sales last year exceeding $5 million. Of this, the divisional manager was responsible for 185 employees and sales of $2 million. The divisional manager reports directly to the assistant store manager.

Exhibit 2–13 presents a list of activities in which the divisional sales manager has engaged during the last year. Individually and as a group, you are to rank in order these ten activities in terms of the amount of time that the divisional manager has devoted to these activities.

1. *Individually,* each of the group members should rank in order the ten activities on the basis of the amount of time devoted to each activity, from one (1), the activity that demanded the most time by the divisional manager, to ten (10), the activity that demanded the least time (*no* ties, please). Mark your responses on exhibit 2–13.

2. *As a group,* repeat the instructions presented in step 1 above.

3. The group rankings should be displayed and a spokesperson from each group should present and discuss the group decision with the class.

EXHIBIT 2–13
Allocation of Time
for a Divisional
Sales Manager

MANAGERIAL ACTIVITY	RANKING	
	INDIVIDUAL	GROUP
1. Evaluating employee training programs		
2. Conducting employee performance evaluations		
3. Training new department managers		
4. Evaluating sales and cost data		
5. Planning future personnel needs		
6. Defining limits of authority for department managers		
7. Developing department and employee performance goals		
8. Discussing sales and cost performance with the assistant store manager		
9. Planning for sales and introduction of new fashions		
10. Identifying promotional ladders for employees		

3

Foundations of Management
Thought and Practice

CHAPTER OUTLINE

KEY POINTS IN THIS CHAPTER

1. The study of management consists of at least three different schools: classical, behavioral, and management science. The contingency approach is emerging as an alternate viewpoint.

2. The classical school of management involves two separate branches: the scientific management branch, which introduced the scientific method to management; and the administrative theory branch, which stressed the managerial functions of planning, organizing, and controlling.

3. The behavioral school focused on the need for managers to consider the psychological reactions of employees to work. It served as the foundation of the contemporary field of organizational behavior.

4. The management science school was oriented toward a quantitative analysis of managerial problems through mathematical models and use of the computer.

5. A contingency view stresses the need for managers to adapt their managerial activities to the external and internal environmental components of the organization.

6. Contributions to management thought originated not only from scholars and scientists but also from practicing managers.

7. The schools of management differ in their orientation to the functions, skills, and roles that define the manager's job.

8. Although management has a rich and significant history, a single, universally accepted approach to effective management does not yet exist.

THE PRACTICE OF MANAGEMENT

William Cooper Procter (1862–1934): Procter and Gamble

The essence of business is how people relate to people: producers to consumers, management to labor. Whoever improves these relations exercises business leadership. In 1883 when Cooper Procter, fresh out of Princeton, went to work for Procter & Gamble, the firm was already forty-six years old and had been successful under the direction of his grandfather and father. Cooper Procter, however, changed his silver spoon into a golden reputation as a pioneer in more equitable treatment of the work force.

With Procters running the office and Gambles in charge of production, the firm had taken an early lead over numerous other Cincinnati soapmakers partly because of a strict policy of giving honest weight and consistent quality to customers. Cooper Procter soon found a new dimension in which to deploy this tradition. Starting at the bottom, he picked up a keen sympathy with the workers' sense of economic insecurity and with feelings that today would be called "alienation." He was a junior executive when he persuaded his elders in 1885 to shorten the work week to five and a half days and in 1887 to establish what seems to have been the first profit-sharing plan in a sizable U.S. company.

Profit sharing, Cooper argued, made sense on business as well as on humanitarian grounds. The company then had a 50 percent labor turnover and had been plagued by small but costly strikes. "The root of existing trouble," said young Procter, "lies in the fact that the employee takes no interest in his work and has no consideration of his employer's property or welfare." Profit sharing did not change that attitude overnight, but strikes and turnover diminished. In 1894, Procter & Gamble had only six terminations from a staff of more than 600. Later, when profit sharing had been tied to a stock-ownership plan, the company could point to small fortunes amassed by longtime employees.

In 1923 Procter put through his boldest stroke of labor relations: the company guaranteed most employees forty-eight weeks of work in every year. To do that Procter had to restructure its merchandising by selling directly to retailers. Sales increased as, once again, concern for the workers turned out to be also good for profits. When in 1930 Procter stepped down after twenty-three years as head of the company, sales had risen from the 1907 level of about $20 million to over $200 million.

Suggested from Max Ways, "The Hall of Fame for Business Leadership," Fortune *(January 1976): 120.*

The field of management, as we know it today, has a history of development that cuts across many centuries. Since people first grouped together, they have tried to organize their activities in order to achieve some mode of effectiveness and efficiency. While many of these activities have come to us through the ages, there is yet no single, unified theory of management that can be applied successfully to all situations.

Managers have at their disposal many ways of looking at the activities, authority, responsibilities, and behavior of people in organizations. Each of these ways may be more useful for some problems than for others. For example, the manner in which Texaco approaches the energy exploration problem is different from the way General Motors looks at the energy consumption of its cars. Similarly, the manner in which a head nurse solves a motivation problem among subordinates is different from the way a merchandising vice president approaches the issue of managerial turnover. Because there is no universal theory of management, managers must be able to integrate theory with insight and common sense to solve a problem.

Analyzing and understanding the development of management thought should be viewed as much more than a history lesson. It is interesting to find out "whence we came"; much can be learned about management today and tomorrow by investigating how historical counterparts approached their problems.

The foundations of management thought will be presented here in three parts. First, we will provide an overview of the three major schools of management—classical, behavioral, and management science. An emerging view of management—the contingency approach—will also be discussed. Second, we will provide a more detailed theoretical discussion on each approach. Because the discussion in the second part will concentrate on the contribution of management scholars, the last section will focus on the contributions of practitioners to the foundations of management thought.

SCHOOLS OF MANAGEMENT THOUGHT

The literature on management includes a variety both of topics and writers. Early contributors were management practitioners who wrote about their experiences and attempted to generalize to some basic principles. Later many of the contributions came from writers who could be classified as more scientific and scholarly in their orientation. The professional affiliations of these later contributors were primarily in the fields or disciplines of engineering, psychology, political science, mathematics, economics, and philosophy. These writers attempted to build the emerging field of management on a foundation of the known sciences.

As a result of these two perspectives—the practitioner and the scholar—numerous classification schemes have been presented as schools of management thought; some count as few as three approaches, and others as many as seven.[1] In order to present the essence of the management movement, we have chosen to discuss three schools.

The *classical school* of management evolved in the early part of this century and to some extent is accepted and practiced by many managers even today. Over time, two separate branches of the classical school have developed: the emphasis on the *management of jobs* (scientific management); and the emphasis on *management of organizations* (administrative theory).

The first to develop was the *management of the job* branch. At the most basic level the writers and practitioners in this area were engineers and scientists who were concerned with issues of *efficiency* (i.e., getting the most performance out of a certain amount of resources). The concern for improvement in efficiency led to the development of many methods related to machine design, plant layout, tools, work methods, and material flow.

With the emergence of large, complex organizations, managers became more concerned with managing the larger organizations than with improving the efficiency of individual jobs. The literature in this era sought to describe management in terms of the functions performed by the manager, with particular emphasis on coordinating the resources of the organization (e.g., people, tasks, finances, and equipment) toward achieving stated goals. Although many variations or descriptions of managerial functions have been presented, the three major functions most frequently mentioned are *planning, organizing,* and *controlling.*

The *behavioral school* of management offered a somewhat different perspective. Whereas the classical school gave attention to the efficiency of job activities, the behavioral school of management sought to understand the psychological and sociological processes—attitudes, motivation, group structure—that affected employee performance. In simple terms, the classical approach focused on the *jobs of workers,* and the behavioral school focused on the *workers in these jobs.*

The *management science* school emphasized the quantitative aspects of the manager's job. Evolving out of World War II research on the application of quantitative methods to military and logistical problems, this approach features highly sophisticated use of mathematics and statistics. Because of the technical nature of the approach, management science is more closely aligned with the classical approach, particularly in quantitative applications to planning and control problems. The popularity of the management science approach owes a great deal to the development of the computer because it can generate previously impossible solutions to complex problems.

Although not recognized as a separate school, a contemporary view of management called the *contingency* or *situational* school is emerging. In its most basic formulation, the contingency approach is concerned with the relationship between an organization and its environment, both *internal* and *external*. This approach is more *eclectic* than the other three schools. That is, it borrows the managerial functions (planning, organizing, and controlling) from the classical approach, the cooperation and humanism of the behaviorists, and the competitive strategies of the management science approach. In other words, it does not teach "one best way" to manage, preferring to emphasize flexibility, adaptability, and survival as its goals.

In the next sections of this chapter, we will discuss the schools of management in more detail. The short but dynamic existence of formal management thought has seen the emergence of many concepts and contributors. As an introduction to the remainder of this chapter, a brief summary of these contributions and contributors is presented in exhibit 3–1.

EXHIBIT 3–1   Summary of Concepts and Contributors to Management Thought

	SELECTED CONTRIBUTIONS	SELECTED CONTRIBUTORS	ENVIRONMENT
Classical School	Scientific management Control systems Time & motion studies Management functions Administrative theory	Gantt (1908) Taylor (1911) Gilbreth (1911) Church (1914) Fayol (1916) Mooney & Reiley (1931) Davis (1935) Urwick (1943)	Expanding size of organizations Market growth for goods & services World War I Depression Post-Industrial Revolution Decline of owner/manager Rise of professional manager
Behavioral School	Participation Motivation applications Professional managers Hawthorne studies M.B.O.	Roethlisberger (1939) Mayo (1945) Barnard (1938) Drucker (1954) McGregor (1960)	World War II Unionization Need for trained managers Federal regulations Worker unrest
Management Science School	Operations research Simulation Game theory Decision theory Mathematical models	Churchman (1957) March & Simon (1958) Forrester (1961) Raiffa (1968)	Growth in corporation size Conglomerates Cold War Recession Military/Industrial complex
Contingency View	Dynamic environment Organic-mechanistic Technology Matrix designs Social responsibility Organizational change Information systems	Burns & Stalker (1961) Woodward (1965) Thompson (1967) Lawrence & Lorsch (1967)	Expanding economy Space race High technology products Vietnam War Civil rights International trade increase Social discontent Growth of skilled professions

Possibly one of the most important features of exhibit 3–1 is the "Environment" column. As we discussed in chapter 2, one of the crucial factors in becoming a successful manager is the ability to learn and apply the needed managerial skills.[2] We suggest that the skills needed for effective managerial performance are, to some extent, dependent on the state of the environment at any given time. In other words, the environment makes demands on the organization and the manager, and successful adaptation to the environment will facilitate attaining high performance levels.

For example, during the time of the development of the classical school, the environment helped create a need for managers who were proficient in "technical" skills. What was required for success was the ability to change businesses effectively from the informal owner/manager-operated establishment to the more formal organization needed in the post-Industrial Revolution society. Use of engineering practices coupled with the effective utilization of planning, organizing, and controlling techniques provided the means to achieve levels of success. Toward the middle of this century, the changing work force and population characteristics demanded that more attention be given to the individual worker's needs and growth. This required the ability to learn and use behavioral or human skills.

Finally, in the second half of this century, the environment of most organizations became much more complex and changeable. The competitive market became more dynamic, technological innovations increased at a rapid pace, the economy was subject to fluctuations, governmental influence increased, foreign markets and competitors grew in importance, and the like. The complexity of the environment required equally complex conceptual and diagnostic skills.

SEEDS OF MANAGEMENT THOUGHT

We often refer to the development of formal management thought as having its origins in the early part of the twentieth century with the formulation of the classical school. Many of the ideas that formed the foundations of formal management thought, however, originated much earlier than this century.[3] Some of the most prominent contributions include the following:

Sumerian Priests.   The Sumerian civilization, which dates back to about 3000 B.C., put priests in charge of the formal tax system. Recognizing a need for better control of that society's resources, one of the first reporting or auditing procedures was developed by the priests. Their contribution to control and accounting systems is felt even today.

The Egyptians.   The obvious contribution by Egyptians to management thought was the construction of the pyramids. The planning and organization of resources, both physical and human, is impressive even by today's standards.

Chinese Civil Service.   Among the wondrous tales brought from the Far East in the late sixteenth century were accounts of government rationally administered by an elite corps of scholars/decision makers.[4] Chosen through competitive examination, these Chinese civil servants were the ablest and most learned members of their society. Later it was determined that the Chinese imperial bureaucracy was subject to extensive manipulation and corruption by clerical subordinates and lesser employees. Higher officials, although required to demonstrate competence in classical scholarship, were lacking in practical administrative knowledge and were unable to deal with everyday problems.

Karl von Clausewitz.   In his book, *The Principles of War,* von Clause-witz dicussed the management of war.[5] His basic principles are used even today: (1) decentralize command; (2) use entire force with all energy; (3) concentrate power at the enemy's weakest point; (4) never waste time; and (5) follow up success with utmost energy.

The Industrial Revolution.   The development of the steam engine and other mechanized equipment helped establish the foundation of modern society and organizations. The result, the Industrial Revolution, involved both economic and social changes. It brought about the mechanization of production, caused a major shift in emphasis from the craftsman to large-scale manufacturing, and finally facilitated the development of the professional manager. What emerged was a society that encouraged business and profit and an increased need for more capably trained and skilled individuals to serve as managers.

CLASSICAL SCHOOL OF MANAGEMENT

The Industrial Revolution gave rise to the need for a more sophisticated approach to administration. The development of new manufacturing tech-nologies concentrated great quantities of raw materials and large num-bers of workers in the emerging factories. Since it was apparent that it would be difficult to coordinate all resources into a smoothly running process, people began to pay more attention to the problems of manage-ment.

Our presentation of the classical approach will cover the two per-spectives mentioned earlier: (1) the *management of jobs,* founded on the literature of "scientific management," focusing on the jobs of individual workers; and (2) the *management of organizations,* its foundations in the literature on "administrative theory," focusing on the total organization.

Scientific Management

Scientific management arose during the first decades of this century out of a need to improve manufacturing productivity through more efficient utilization of physical and human resources. Factories at that time were experiencing problems in formulating proper work procedures, establish-ing the boundaries of jobs, and coordinating the flow of raw materials. A breakthrough occurred when certain members of the engineering profes-sion became interested in the process of work flow. One engineer in par-ticular, Frederick Taylor (1856–1915), became known as the father of scientific management.[6]

Taylor's Scientific Management.   Taylor's ideas about management of jobs grew out of his years of experience in three companies: Midvale Steel; Simonds Rolling Machine; and Bethlehem Steel. His basic approach was to observe the separate functions and the motions that each worker performed in his job. After careful analysis of his observations, he would redesign the job in a more efficient manner, or the "one best way."

Taylor's approach to management was influenced by his basic phi-losophy of work. First, he believed that prosperity for the employer and the employee could be achieved only through *maximizing* productivity. Productivity improvements, however, could come only from developing more *efficient* jobs. Second, there was too much "soldiering" among factory workers. The term *soldiering* came from his observations of military personnel. Today we would call this "goofing off." Third, the continued growth of industry could come only from a complete revolution in the *mental attitudes* of employers and employees toward work. In other words, the future economic well-being of the worker would come from more efficient work methods and habits. Finally, the heart of scientific management is in the *cooperation* between management and the worker. Through cooperative effort of all concerned, the betterment of society would result.

In his work at Midvale Steel, Taylor began his studies with an analysis of the job of a lathe operator. He was concerned with a number of factors. For example, there were no work standards that specified daily work output for the operator, nor was there a relationship between output and the wage system. He was particularly concerned that there was no standard for a "fair day's work for a fair day's pay." He also blamed management's practice of making decisions based on hunch and "rules of thumb" as the primary contributors to the large amount of waste that was present.

In his studies of lathe operators, pig iron handlers, and shovelers, Taylor developed a process of fact gathering and objective analysis that focused *exactly* on what the worker did to perform his task. He identified each element of the worker's job and measured every factor that was adaptable to measurement. From these studies, a set of "scientific management" principles evolved.[7] Some of the more important principles are as follows:

1. *Develop a science for each element of a worker's job that replaces rules of thumb.* Use the scientific method rather than intuition and experience to determine the activities engaged in by workers. Ensure that each motion and movement is the most efficient possible. For example, his analysis of the process of loading pig iron onto a flatcar resulted in a 400 percent increase in the tonnage loaded per worker.

2. *Job specialization should be a part of each job.* Taylor believed that each worker should be a *specialist* in what he did because this would ensure that each worker knew his job well. This specialization also included management, which he termed "functional foremanship." Taylor's foremanship concept held that each employee should be supervised by several foremen, each with distinct responsibilities. One foreman would be responsible for machine speeds, another for repair, still another would serve as an inspector, a disciplinarian, a cost and time foreman, and the like.

3. *Ensure the proper selection, training, and development of workers.* Taylor believed that it was important to properly identify the person for the right job. Proper selection of people with the appropriate abilities, coupled with specific training, would facilitate good perfomance. Taylor suggested that tests be used to determine whether or not a person had the necessary attributes for a particular job. For example, he developed a speed and reaction test for quality control inspectors.

4. *Planning and scheduling of the work were essential.* Everything in the organization had to be done by plan, from yearly plans for the total organization to daily plans for the individual worker. Planning and sched-

uling activities involved getting the people and the materials at the right place, right time, and in the proper condition to be used.

5. *Standards with respect to methods and time for each task should be established.* Using observational methods, the worker's movements along with the time needed to complete a particular movement were studied. The redesigned job involved highly efficient motions with specific times required for each step in a task. This was the forerunner of contemporary time and motion studies.

6. *Wage incentives should be an integral part of each job.* Taylor instituted a program whereby workers were paid for what they did, which meant different wage rates for different jobs. In addition, workers were paid a bonus if they did better than the standard time established for the task.

As an illustration of Taylor's scientific management, consider his shoveling experiments. Through his analysis of the job, Taylor determined that the optimum size shovel for handling materials carried about twelve and a half pounds of material. This meant that small shovels should be used for heavy materials, such as sand, and larger shovels should be used for lighter materials, such as cinders. Combining shovel size with worker training and incentive wages enabled Taylor to increase the productivity of the workers from sixteen to fifty-nine tons shoveled per day. This productivity increase per worker decreased the number of shovelers needed per day from 500 to 140.

This and other applications of Taylor's work led to significant increases in productivity and higher wages for workers. Later, however, workers and unions became increasingly uncomfortable with scientific management approaches. Workers feared that working harder or faster would exhaust the available work and would bring about layoffs of personnel as did the shoveling experiment. Thus, as Taylor's ideas spread and were accepted by management, resistance was growing among front-line workers to scientific management because it quite possibly would mean the loss of their jobs.[8] In a sense, scientific management appreciation gave rise to interest in human needs and behavior.

In the final analysis, Taylor made a lasting contribution to making jobs and the management of these jobs more efficient and productive. His observational methods of analysis led not only to the development of time and motion study but also stimulated others to continue the formulation of management thought.

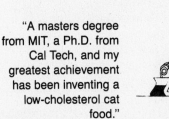

"A masters degree from MIT, a Ph.D. from Cal Tech, and my greatest achievement has been inventing a low-cholesterol cat food."

Cartoon by Randy J. Glasbergen

Other Contributors to Scientific Management.   Further development of scientific management principles continued to expand as Taylor's ideas gained acceptance by managers. Three of the more prominent contributions were made by the Gilbreths, Gantt, and Emerson with their studies in work simplification, scheduling and control, and principles of efficiency.

Frank B. and Lillian M. Gilbreth (1869–1924 and 1878–1972, respectively) worked as a husband and wife team to produce significant contributions in motion study and *work simplification.*[9] During his early work experience as an apprentice bricklayer, Frank Gilbreth recognized that his work could be improved greatly through studies of fatigue and motion. His analysis of the job convinced him that many of the body movements could be combined or eliminated so that the bricklaying procedure could be simplified and production increased. Craftsmen who adopted Gilbreth's methods were able to increase their productivity by 200 percent.

Gilbreth's contributions were based on the principle that motion and fatigue were highly related, and that every motion that was eliminated would reduce fatigue. With the use of motion picture cameras, the Gilbreths found the most efficient and economical motions for each task, thus upgrading production and reducing fatigue. This improved worker morale not only because of its obvious physical benefits, but it also showed management's concern for the welfare of the worker.

EXHIBIT 3–2 An Example of a Gantt Chart*

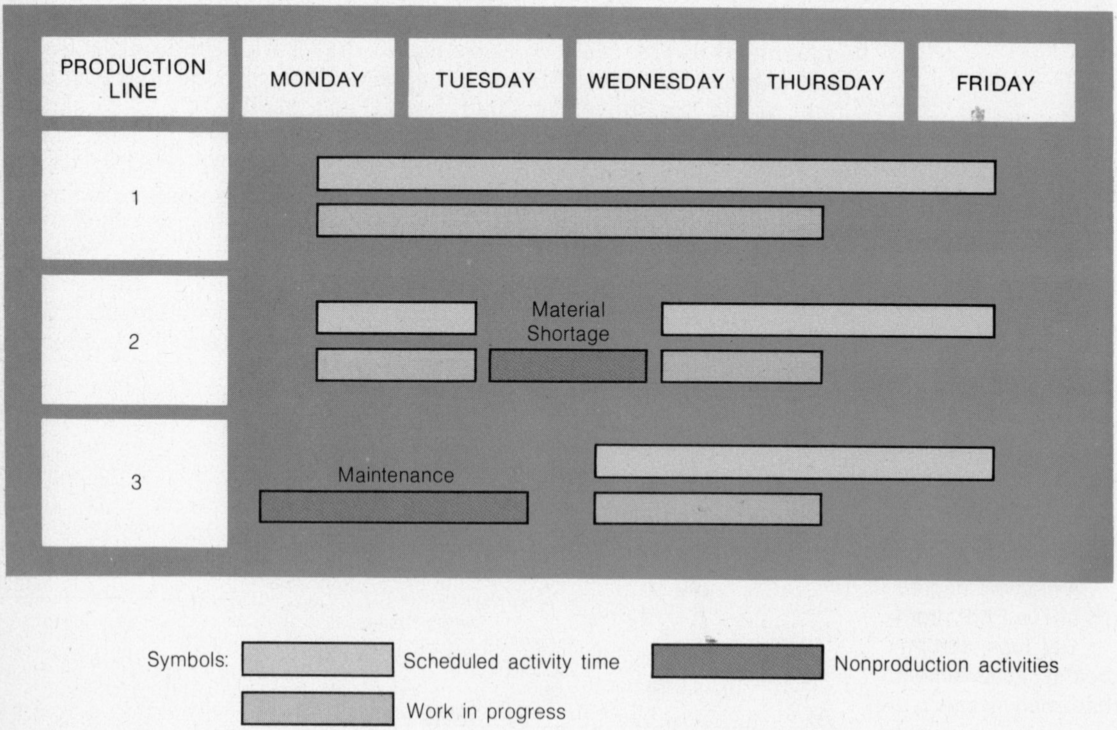

PRODUCTION LINE	MONDAY	TUESDAY	WEDNESDAY	THURSDAY	FRIDAY
1					
2		Material Shortage			
3	Maintenance				

Symbols: ▭ Scheduled activity time   ▬ Nonproduction activities

▭ Work in progress

*Chart reviewed at 11:00 a.m., Thursday.

An important, but little-known factor in their work was the three-position promotion plan for workers. According to the plan, the three positions included the worker doing his present job, training his successor, and learning new skills for movement to the next highest job. This was a significant morale factor because workers could look ahead to development and avoid dead-end jobs.

Contributions toward *work scheduling and control* were made by Harry L. Gantt (1861–1919), who was an associate of Taylor at Midvale and Bethlehem Steel.[10] Gantt's most famous contribution was the Gantt chart, a system of control and scheduling still in use today. A typical chart (shown in exhibit 3–2) depicted the relationship between the work planned and completed on one axis and the time elapsed on the other axis.

His contributions, however, go beyond just the Gantt chart. For example, he developed a task bonus system different from Taylor's in that it provided fair remuneration regardless of output. Unlike Taylor's system, which was a pure incentive system, Gantt set a standard wage for each job, but work over and above the standard was rewarded with a bonus. He also recognized the importance workers placed on job security and proper training procedures. Above all, Gantt believed that improved efficiency in organizations resulted from the work methods of the manager, not solely the worker.

The *principles of efficiency* were further developed by Harrington Emerson in 1913 with his book, *The Twelve Principles of Efficiency*.[11] His basic principles of efficient use of organizational resources are summarized as follows: (1) use of clearly defined jobs with the use of objective and fact-based analysis; (2) the need for standard operations, conditions of work, and schedules; (3) the fair use of discipline; (4) the need for accurate records and job-related instructions; (5) the necessity of integrating all jobs into a whole; and (6) rewards for workers for performing jobs in an efficient manner.

In some of his additional work as one of the first management consultants, Emerson presented two concepts that today can be found in most organizations. First, he believed that the most efficient organizational design was one with strict distinctions between line and staff functions; that is, certain individuals were responsible for the production and marketing of the organization's goods and services, and others acted in a support or advisory position to the line managers. For example, a line manager would be a manufacturing superintendent, and a staff manager would be the personnel manager. Second, Emerson strongly advocated the use of clear statements of goals and objectives for the total organization. In some respects, these two concepts identified Emerson with those who later contributed to management thought along the lines of the management of the total organization, or administrative theory.

Administrative Theory

Scientific management, with its emphasis on efficient production, was quite limited in scope. While efficiency of production certainly was of great importance, of equal or greater concern were issues related to the *management of the total organization*. Organizations and the manage-

EXHIBIT 3–3   Fayol's Business Activities

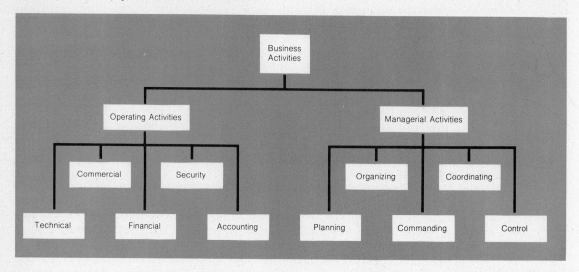

ment of organizations had become much more complex than could be handled by scientific management principles.

From this situation emerged a body of ideas that is known as *administrative theory*. As we will see, many individual contributors have been identified within this approach. They all had in common their concern with the development of the basic *functions* of management. We will briefly discuss the contributions of Fayol, Urwick, and Davis.

Henri Fayol (1841–1925): Principles and Functions of Management.   Similar to many of the management contributors of the time, Henri Fayol was an engineer with extensive business experience. Working as the managing director of a large coal-mining organization in France provided Fayol with his particular perspective on the management process. His book, *Administratim Industrielle et Generale* (later translated as *General and Industrial Management*), had a major impact on the emerging field of management.[12]

Fayol's contributions to management thought were fourfold. First, as shown in exhibit 3–3, he made the distinction between *operating* and *managerial* activities of an organization. This was a subtle but important influence in elevating the importance of managerial activities.

Second, Fayol elaborated on the managerial activities by being one of the first to clearly identify specific *management functions*. His five major functions included the following:

1. *Planning*. The activity that attempts to forecast future actions and directions of the firm. It is used to develop operating procedures and assists in the decision-making process.

2. *Organizing*. This management function is concerned with establishing the organization's structure of authority, responsibility, and tasks.

3. *Commanding*. Closely related to our earlier discussion on the function of leading, this activity is concerned with the *direction* of subordinates.

EXHIBIT 3–4   Fayol's Principles of Management

1. *Division of labor.*   Specialization of labor results in increased productivity through the reduction of job elements required of each worker. Specialization of labor permits large-scale production at minimum cost.

2. *Authority.*   Fayol defined *authority* as the "right to give orders and the power to exact obedience." He distinguished between the official authority that derives from holding a given position and the informal authority that derives from the officeholder's own personality, experience, moral worth, and other personal characteristics that enable him to influence the efforts of subordinates.

3. *Discipline.*   The basis of discipline is obedience to rules and procedures reached between parties in the firm. He believed that clear statements of agreements are necessary and that the state of discipline of any group of people depends on the worthiness of its leaders.

4. *Unity of command.*   Fayol believed that an employee should receive orders from only one superior. Recognition and observance of this principle would eliminate conflict and breakdown in authority and discipline.

5. *Unity of direction.*   Each group of activities with the same goal should be managed under one head and one plan.

6. *Subordination of individual interest to the common goal.*   This principle states that the whole is greater than the sum of its parts, and that the overall objectives that the organization seeks to achieve take precedence over the objectives of individuals.

7. *Remuneration.*   The compensation of all employees for services rendered should be based on a systematic attempt to reward good performance.

8. *Centralization.*   Centralization is the degree to which the importance of subordinates' roles is reduced. He stated that managers should retain final responsibility but should give subordinates enough authority to do the task successfully.

9. *Scalar chain.*   The hierarchy from top to bottom through which all communications flow. This chain implements the unity-of-command principle and provides for the orderly flow of information.

10. *Order.*   Fayol applied the principle of order to the material and human resources of the firm. This principle states that materials and people should be in the right place at the right time.

11. *Equity.*   Fayol defined equity as the use of established rules tempered by a sense of kindliness and justice. Employees respond to equitable treatment by carrying out their tasks with a sense of loyalty.

12. *Stability of personnel.*   Fayol noted that successful firms usually had a stable group of managers. As a general principle, top management should implement practices that encourage the long-term commitment of employees, particularly of managers, to the organization.

13. *Initiative.*   Employees should be given the freedom to develop and implement a plan of action.

14. *Esprit de corps.*   Fayol defined *esprit de corps* as unity of effort through harmony of interests. The most effective means for achieving esprit de corps is through unity of command and through oral rather than written communication.

Also included within this activity were concepts related to communications, managerial behavior, and reward and punishment activities.

4. *Coordinating*. This function concerns all activities and efforts needed to bind the organization together in order to achieve a common goal.

5. *Controlling*. This function was concerned with the evaluation of organizational activities as they related to stated goals and plans.

While some have criticized Fayol's management functions as lacking in priorities and clarity, they comprised one of the first such statements. As a result, he has been duly recognized for his contribution.

Third, Fayol proposed fourteen *principles of management* that should guide the thinking of managers in resolving concrete problems. These principles are shown in exhibit 3–4. It is likely that many of these principles were practiced by managers during his time. It was Fayol,

EXHIBIT 3–5   Various Descriptions of Management Functions

CONTRIBUTOR	PLANNING	ORGANIZING	CONTROL	OTHERS
Dale	X	X	X	Staffing, innovation
Davis	X	X	X	
Drucker	Set objectives	X	Evaluation	Motivation
Fayol	X	X	X	Commanding, coordination
Koontz, O'Donnell	X	X	X	Direction, staffing
McFarland	X	X	X	
Mee	X	X	X	Motivation, innovation
Newman	X	X	X	Resource assembling, direction
Terry	X	X	X	Coordination, direction
Urwick	X	X	X	Forecasting, coordination, command
American Management Association	X	X	Execution	
Air Force	X	X	X	Commanding, coordination
Chrysler	X	X	Appraisal	Guiding
Firestone	X	X	Evaluation	Direction
General Electric	X	X	Measuring	Integration
Texaco	X	X	X	Motivation, innovation

X indicates function included

however, who first presented these principles in a coherent form, making it possible for all managers to learn from them. While some scholars have criticized Fayol's principles because they lack specificity, Fayol stated that these principles would not relieve management from the responsibility for determining "the appropriate balance" of behaviors.

Fayol was also a leader in recognizing the need for managers to acquire and learn certain abilities and skills. He noted that skills and abilities varied not only by the manager's level in the organization (types of managers as we discussed in chapter 2), but also by the size of the organization. Fayol also strongly urged that managerial training be introduced into schools, rather than the on-the-job experience method for learning. He was one of the early promoters of formal managerial training activities in schools and of organizational "in-house" training programs. He felt that such training would go far beyond the manager's job to affect family, church, military, and political activities of the manager.

Fayol's contributions to management thought were both large and significant. More than anything else, he established the foundation for further work in managerial functions.

Other Contributors to Administrative Theory.   Many other individuals contributed to the administrative theory branch of the classical approach by building on the management functions first presented by Fayol. Some of these contributors are shown in exhibit 3–5.

Lyndall Urwick's book, *The Elements of Administration,* was a landmark contribution to management thought for two reasons.[13] First, he attempted to blend scientific management and administrative theory into a more comprehensive package. The book provided scholars and practitioners of management with a broad understanding of the management of the total organization. Its level of discussion ranged from the job level to the organizational level but was specific enough to provide insights into how principles of the managerial functions could be generalized.

Second, like Fayol, Urwick noted that the management process consisted of three functions: planning, organizing, and controlling. He added further insight by stating that the three functions were guided by the subfunctions of forecasting, coordination, and command. More importantly, he expanded on the controlling function to include three subfunctions: staffing, selecting, and placing. Urwick's expansion of the control function not only founded the personnel function in organizations, but it served as the forerunner of the behavioral approach.

Ralph C. Davis, in *The Principles of Business Organization and Operation,* provided a significant synthesis of the basic factors involved in organization and the operation of a business.[14] Similar to Urwick's concept, he founded his approach on the functions of planning, organizing, and an expanded control activity. His discussion of the concept and classification of business objectives was a unique contribution. Davis identified *primary* and *secondary* objectives of a business. Primary objectives were called *service* objectives of the firm, including social objectives and personal objectives of individuals and groups. The secondary objectives related to the economy and effectiveness of operations. In a sense, Davis was ahead of his time in identifying social objectives and survival above profitability as prime objectives of an organization (see chapter 5).

Summary of the Classical School of Management

Exhibit 3–6 provides a brief overview of the contributions of the classical approach to management thought. At least three aspects should be noted concerning this management approach. First, the focus on managerial activities has moved from a concern for the management of jobs to management of the total organization. This is an important evolutionary process. Second, the expansion of management thought within this approach strongly suggests the need for different *skills* in order to achieve high levels of managerial performance. The need for technical skills is foremost in the scientific management approach. In the administrative theory approach, the management of the organization requires a growing awareness of human skills and conceptual skills. Finally, the *roles* that managers perform is distinctly different in Taylor's scientific management than it is in Fayol's approach. Taylor's manager is very much an occupant of interpersonal *roles,* particularly the figurehead and leader roles. Fayol's manager, however, must be proficient in operating in all three major role categories: interpersonal, informational, and decisional. Overall, the discussion of the classical approach to management provides an excellent stage for the reader to evaluate the importance of the three key factors in a manager's job: functions, skills, and roles.

BEHAVIORAL SCHOOL OF MANAGEMENT

The practice of management, as suggested by the contributors to the classical approach, was built on the thoughts and experiences of engineers and professional managers. It was proposed that with efficiently designed jobs, the right kind of incentives, and the proper use of managerial func-

EXHIBIT 3–6 Summary of the Classical School

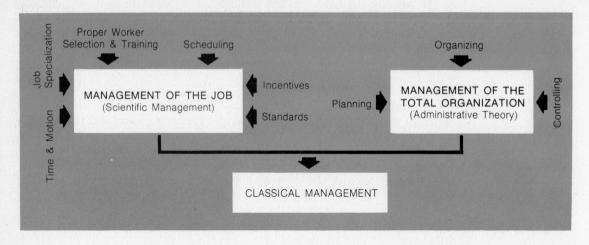

tions, productivity would increase. It is not surprising that this formal, impersonal approach to management would meet with some resistance from the workers themselves.

This resistance, along with other challenges to the classical approach, gave rise to the development of the *behavioral school of management.* Two branches contributed to the behavioral school: the human relations movement, and the development of organizational behavior. These approaches were concerned with a better understanding of how psychological processes interacted with the activities and jobs in the organization. Whereas the classical approach focused on the *jobs of workers,* the behavioral approach was concerned with the *people in these jobs.* Several individuals made significant contributions to this approach.

The Human Relations Movement: Elton Mayo

A group of Harvard researchers, headed by Elton Mayo (along with his associates, including Fritz J. Roethlisberger), conducted a landmark study of human behavior in the Hawthorne plant (Cicero, Illinois) of Western Electric from 1927 to 1932. Since then, this research has been known as the *Hawthorne studies.*[15]

Mayo and his associates were called in by Western Electric after an experiment carried out by the company engineers between 1924 and 1927 with work-area illumination or lighting produced confusing results. The engineers, true to the scientific management tradition of seeking answers to industrial problems through research, studied two groups of workers to determine the effects, if any, of different levels of lighting on worker performance. In one group (test group) the level of illumination was changed, while the other (referred to as the control group) experienced no change in illumination.

In their initial tests, the engineers found that productivity improved in the test group when the lighting conditions increased. But what concerned the engineers was that productivity also increased in the test group when illumination was decreased! To add to this confusion, the control group's productivity kept increasing even though this group experienced no changes in work-area illumination. Mayo's subsequent entry into the illumination experiment formally ushered in the behavioral approach to management.

Mayo conducted a series of experiments over the next few years to further investigate the Western Electric situation. The research was conducted in four distinct phases:

1. Experiments to determine the effects on worker productivity of changes in illumination.
2. Experiments to determine the effects on worker productivity of other work-related factors. These factors included salary increases, introducing varying lengths of rest periods and coffee breaks, shortened workdays and workweeks, and other changes in working conditions (the relay assembly room experiments).
3. An extensive employee interview program to determine worker attitudes.
4. An analysis of the various social factors at work (the bank wiring observation room experiment).

As in the original experiments, productivity increased in both the test and control groups in the new tests. After a thorough analysis of the total results, Mayo and his associates concluded that what caused the productivity changes was a series of *psychological reactions* by the participating workers. Briefly stated, it appeared that because the test and control groups had been singled out for special attention, they had developed a sense of group pride that motivated them to increase performance levels. The change in supervisory styles from a directive to a more sympathetic style further reinforced their levels of performance.

The Harvard researchers suggested that the way people were treated had an important impact on performance. In other words, the workers in the tests were not reacting to changes in illumination but to the experiment itself and to their involvement in it. They acted in a way that they thought the experimenters wanted and because they were the center of attention. Since that time, this phenomenon is known as the *Hawthorne Effect*.

Mayo further concluded that the social environment of work, particularly the effect of the informal work group, had a great influence on productivity. From this conclusion the researchers suggested that management must recognize the importance of the worker's needs for recognition and social satisfaction. Management should make an effort to turn the informal group into a positive, productive force by providing workers with a new sense of dignity and well-being. Mayo termed this the concept of the *social man:* individuals are motivated by social needs and good on-the-job relationships and respond better to work-group pressure than to management control activities. What was needed was a totally new approach to the human in the workplace—a view that people are motivated to work not solely by economic means, but by complex needs.

The Hawthorne studies had a significant impact on management thought. The teachings and practices of the classical school were being seriously questioned, especially the "dehumanizing" nature of scientific management. As a result of this and other studies, both practitioners and scholars began to take a second look at the importance of human resources in organizations. Training programs were begun to teach supervisors to better understand how people and groups behave in work situations. Improved selection and placement activities evolved along with further work on incentive systems. In the workplace, the worker, rather than the job, became the focal point for managerial activities. The impact on scholarly research is felt even today with the behavioral science emphasis in management theory.

Other Contributors to the Human Relations Movement

The contributors who followed the Hawthorne studies were as numerous as those who built on Fayol's work. Many of these contributions will be discussed in detail in our chapters on motivation, leadership, and group behavior. Two contributors, however, deserve specific mention: Chester Barnard and Douglas McGregor.

Chester Barnard.   As president of New Jersey Bell, Chester I. Barnard (1886–1961) combined his work experience and extensive readings in sociology and philosophy into an analysis of the executive's job in an organization. The result, his book *The Functions of the Executive,* is one of management's few classic texts.[16]

According to Barnard, people form organizations in order to achieve goals they could not achieve working alone. This "cooperative effort" is the basis of his definition that, "An organization is a system of consciously coordinated activities or forces of two or more persons." His major point was that an organization can operate efficiently and survive only when both the organization's goals and the goals and needs of the individuals working for it are kept in balance. This formed his basic elements of organizations: (1) a system of cooperation; (2) common purpose; and (3) an emphasis on efficiency and effectiveness.

Barnard also stimulated interest in the fields of motivation, decision making, communications, and the importance of objectives. For example, he proposed that worker cooperation and motivation were related to the balance between *inducements* and *contributions*. Inducements were the sum total of financial and nonfinancial rewards available to employees in exchange for their efforts (i.e., contributions). The nature of the communications system provided employees with the necessary information to evaluate the balance between inducements and contributions. Finally, he set forth an approach that was later called the *acceptance theory of authority*. This theory stated that employees will determine whether an order is legitimate and whether they will accept it or not. In other words, employees will accept an executive order only if required behavior on their part is consistent with their view of the goals of the organization and their own personal interests.

Douglas McGregor: Theory X and Theory Y.   One of the main contributors to the behavioral science movement was Douglas McGregor.[17] In his major work, *The Human Side of Enterprise,* McGregor advanced two beliefs about human behavior that could be held and practiced by

EXHIBIT 3–7 Theory X and Theory Y Assumptions

THEORY X	THEORY Y
1. The average human being has an inherent dislike of work and will avoid it if possible.	1. The expenditure of physical and mental effort in work is as natural as play or rest.
2. Because of this human characteristic of dislike of work, most people must be coerced, controlled, directed, threatened with punishment to get them to put forth adequate effort toward the achievement of organizational objectives.	2. External control and the threat of punishment are not the only means for bringing about effort toward organizational objectives. People will exercise effort toward organizational objectives to which they are committed.
3. The average human being prefers to be directed, wishes to avoid responsibility, has relatively little ambition, wants security above all.	3. Commitment to objectives is a function of the rewards associated with their achievement.
	4. The average human being learns, under proper conditions, not only to accept but to seek responsibility.
	5. The capacity to exercise a relatively high degree of imagination, ingenuity, and creativity in the solution of organizational problems is widely, not narrowly, distributed in the population.
	6. Under the conditions of modern industrial life, the intellectual potentialities of the average human being are only partially utilized.

managers: Theory X and Theory Y. These beliefs are summarized in exhibit 3–7.

Theory X represented the traditional approach to management as suggested by adherence to Taylor's scientific management principles. From the Hawthorne studies and other behavioral research efforts, many practicing managers recognized the need to adopt a totally different set of assumptions about people at work. The acceptance of the Theory Y approach, with its tenets of participation and a concern for employee morale, encouraged managers to begin practicing their profession in a radically different manner. Theory Y encouraged the following: (1) delegating authority for many decisions to lower level workers; (2) making an effort to make worker jobs less routine and boring; (3) increasing the level of responsibility in each worker's job; (4) improving the free flow of information and communications within the organization; and (5) recognizing that people are motivated by a complex set of psychological needs, not just money.

In a sense, the contribution made by McGregor may be more significant than that made by Mayo. Whereas Mayo's work was a data-based research study in one organization, McGregor's work represented a major philosophical change for managers. Though some have criticized the approach because it lacks specific details on "how" to manage, it suggested that a major reorientation in managerial thinking was necessary.

From Human Relations to Organizational Behavior

Mayo, McGregor, and others pioneered the movement toward a better understanding of people at work in organizations. Later researchers, who were more rigorously trained in the social sciences (such as psychology, sociology, political science, and anthropology), began investigating the human resources issue in management with more sophisticated research techniques. The work of these later researchers helped to found the field called "organizational behavior."[18]

As shown in exhibit 3–8, the field of organizational behavior is identified by five distinguishing characteristics: (1) a foundation built on the scientific method; (2) an interdisciplinary orientation taken from the social sciences; (3) a level of analysis that includes a focus on the individual, groups, and the organization; (4) a contingency orientation, suggesting that there is no universally accepted theory or approach to the study of people in organizations; and (5) an important concern for applications. The contributions of researchers in organizational behavior are shown most notably by the tremendous expansion of the literature on such topics as motivation, leadership, group and intergroup behavior, and the design of work. We will discuss each of these topics in later chapters in this book.

Summary of the Behavioral School of Management

The human relations movement and the growth of the contemporary field of organizational behavior made significant contributions to our understanding of people at work, people in groups, and people in organizations. Through courses in higher education and continuing education programs, in-house training classes, published articles, and on-the-job experiences, the behavioral school of management has motivated managers to become more aware and sophisticated in dealing with subordinates.

COMMENTS ON THE PRACTICE OF MANAGEMENT
(See p. 56.)

William Procter was one of the earliest proponents of the behavioral school of management. His philosophy concerning the equitable treatment of the work force was as many as forty years ahead of its time. By recognizing that workers have many complex needs that require some level of satisfaction, Procter contributed significantly to the success of his firm. Through the use of such mechanisms as profit sharing, challenging jobs, and guaranteed jobs, Procter gained the commitment of his people to the improved performance of Procter and Gamble.

There are certain important points of information that should be recognized by the reader before total adoption of the behavioral approach is contemplated. First, the potential contribution of the behavioral approach has not been fully realized due to the reluctance and resistance of many managers in accepting behavioral principles. As we noted in chapter 2, managers acquire certain attitudes and skills through many mechanisms (e.g., education, experience, mentor relationships). Once these attitudes have developed, it is difficult to change them. In other words, managers with many years of experience will not readily admit

EXHIBIT 3–8
The Key
Characteristics of
the Field of
Organizational
Behavior

CHARACTERISTICS	DESCRIPTION
Scientific Method Foundation	Armchair speculation and common sense are not completely disregarded in the field of organizational behavior; the use of the scientific method takes precedence in attempting to predict and explain behavior and performance.
Interdisciplinary Foundation	Organizational behavior has borrowed concepts, theories, models, and the orientation of the behavioral sciences in understanding behavior and performance.
Analysis Level	Organizational behavior as a field is concerned with the in-depth analysis of individuals, groups, and formal organizations. Each level is of equal importance and needs to be scientifically studied.
Contingency Orientation	The organizational behavior field has no universally applicable set of prescriptions for managers. Instead, the contingency theme, which encourages the development of action plans that are based on the situation and the people involved, is considered the most relevant.
Concern for Application	Organizational behavior knowledge is suited for the practicing manager in an organization. Consequently, theories, research and models need to be eventually communicated in language that is understood by the manager faced with individual, group, and organizational problems.

that they cannot handle people or that their ways are now outdated. This situation, hopefully, will change as more and more of our future managers are trained in behavioral principles.

Second, behavioral scientists are equally to blame for the unrealized potential of the behavioral approach. Too often, behavioral scientists communicate their findings in academic journals that are neither appealing nor accessible to the applied practitioner. When these researchers attempt to write for the practitioner audience, many times they use language that the manager cannot understand. This acts to further inhibit transfer and acceptance of their ideas. Third, because the study of human behavior in organizations is both relatively new and complex, behavioral scientists often differ in their recommendations on a particular problem, making it difficult for managers to decide whose advice to follow.

Finally, as we noted in chapter 2, the behavioral approach is strongly oriented to human skills. As we noted, although human skills are important, effectiveness as a manager requires proficiency in many skills.

THE MANAGEMENT SCIENCE SCHOOL

Shortly after World War II, a new approach to management emerged that attempted to solve people and work problems in organizations using a more sophisticated, mathematically based scientific approach. This is called the *management science school.*

Foundations of the Management Science School

During World War II, a significant research program was begun to investigate the applicability of quantitative methods to military and logistical problems. Some of the projects included methods of increasing bombing accuracy, development of search procedures to locate enemy submarines, and the transportation of supplies and equipment to needed locations. Most of the research projects were conducted with the use of interdisciplinary teams, culled from such fields as engineering, mathematics, statistics, economics, psychology, and political science. After the war many individuals recognized that there was great potential for the newly developed methods in the industrial world.

The application of management science principles followed a two-step sequence. Initially, since many of the new methods were oriented toward the manufacturing function, applications in *production management* quickly emerged. Use of management science principles provided significant benefits when applied to such problems as the flow of raw materials, quality control, inventory control, and new manufacturing processes. Later, both management science scholars and practitioners recognized that the principles being applied to the manufacturing function could be applied to other organizational functions. (See chapter 18.) This change to a much broader focus created the second stage of development in the management science approach called the *operations management focus*. Management science principles were now being applied to problems such as personnel scheduling, business planning models, simulated decision-making activities, and so on.

The management science approach differs from the classical and behavioral schools of thought in a number of important ways. The distinguishing characteristics include the following:[19]

1. *Managerial decision making.* Management science differs from scientific management primarily in focus. Scientific management is concerned with production tasks and the efficiency of workers and machines. Management science stresses that efficiency comes from proper planning and making the right decisions. In other words, improper decisions can be implemented in an efficient manner. Management science principles and techniques provide the format to make proper decisions.

2. *Mathematical models.* A model is a simplified representation of a real situation. In management science, a mathematical model attempts to reduce a managerial decision to a mathematical form so that the decision-making process can be simulated and evaluated *before* the actual decision is made. For example, a manager may be concerned with the relationship between production rates and inventory requirements for customer orders. By reducing such variables as production rates, inventory storage space, available manpower, and the frequency and quantity in customer orders into a mathematical model, the manager can test different values of each variable until an acceptable solution is found.

3. *Computer applications.* More than any one factor, the use of the computer has been the driving force in the emergence of the management science approach.[20] With its speed, the computer can handle in minutes extremely complex problems with an immense volume of data and calculate nu-

merous variations on the solution that would take a team of experts many months using manual calculations.

4. *Evaluation criteria.* Because the main focus of the management science approach is on proper decision making, models were evaluated against a set of effectiveness criteria. Examples include cost savings, revenue, return on investment, improved scheduling and the meeting of deadlines.

As management science and operations management began making inroads into many organizational applications, the term *operations research* became accepted as representing the various models and techniques that were being used. This term was applied to identify the desire to use scientific analysis in the solution of managerial problems in all types of organizations.

In exhibit 3–9, we have summarized some of the main operations research techniques. The seven techniques identified—break-even analysis, linear programming, queuing (waiting in line) theory, network models, simulation, probability analysis, and regression analysis—are by no means all-inclusive of the techniques that are being applied today. They are provided to give the reader an overview of current uses.

EXHIBIT 3–9   Examples of Operations Research Techniques

TECHNIQUE	DESCRIPTION	EXAMPLE
Break-Even Analysis	Determining the particular point of operations at which total revenue equals total cost and profit is zero.	With the use of price, quantity, and cost data, finding the level of sales that will result in a profit for the firm.
Linear Programming	A model that determines the best way to allocate limited resources to reach an optimum solution.	With a given number of warehouses, customers, and shipping costs, determining the routes that will minimize transportation costs.
Queuing Theory	Investigating the relationship between waiting time (of people, materials, or equipment) and the cost of additional facilities.	Deciding whether to add new bank tellers given the number of customers waiting in line.
Network Models	Planning the activities of a project so that it can be completed on schedule.	Constructing a new plant.
Simulation	Simulating a process with the use of a mathematical model and the computer.	Aircraft trainers that simulate landings and takeoffs.
Probability Analysis	Attempting to predict the decisions of people using probabilities.	Deciding whether or not to expand a retail store size with probabilities associated with an increase, decrease, or no change in area population size.
Regression Analysis	Attempting to predict the effects on one variable with changes in other variables.	Predicting the effects on sales with changes in price and advertising.

Summary of the Management Science School

With its emphasis on decision-making, models, and the computer, the management science school has become an integral part of the problem-solving framework in many organizations. Management science techniques are used in many settings, not just in manufacturing.

The management science school has made a significant impact on the practice of management; however, it still does not have a high level of acceptance by many managers. First, using our managerial *skills* theme, management science techniques have helped in the acquisition of technical and conceptual skills (and maybe, to a certain extent, some diagnostic skills). However, management science has not yet reached the state where it can effectively deal with the human skills issue. Most applications have been found in planning and control activities; its contributions have been only modest in such areas as organizing, motivating, staffing and leadership. Second, from a managerial *role* framework, the management science school leans heavily toward decisional roles at the expense of interpersonal and informational roles. Thus, its contributions to date have only covered a portion of the manager's job.

Finally, there is a growing resistance to management science schools on the basis that "experts" are trained to the teeth in the *techniques,* but not in the *practice* of management.[21] In other words, some practitioners and scholars point out that mathematical models are no substitute for native shrewdness, sound common sense, and abundant energy. In their zeal to solve more and more so-called complex problems, management scientists develop models that are far from the realities of the management situation. This bridge between theory and practice must be overcome before management science can continue to make contributions to management thought.

THE CONTINGENCY VIEW OF MANAGEMENT

The contingency view of management emerged from the real-life experience of managers, researchers, and consultants. More often than not, these individuals found that the methods, techniques, and prescriptions suggested by the three management schools—classical, behavioral, and management science—did not consistently work in every situation. Why, for example, would strict adherence to the managerial functions of the classical approach result in high performance in one situation, but not another? Why would workers in one group respond well to a Theory Y approach, while those in another did not? Why would a mathematical planning model perform effectively for one product, but less effectively for another product in the same organization? In response to these and other questions, a contingency view began to emerge.

The contingency view suggests that the effectiveness of various managerial practices, styles, techniques, and functions will vary according to the *particular* circumstances of the situation.[22] This approach also recognizes that the state of management thought has not advanced to the point at which definitive prescriptions for the best way to manage in every situation are available. In fact, there are some who believe that because of the complexities of the environment, organizations, and humans in these organizations, we may never reach a point where we will have answers or approaches for solving most problems. For this reason, the contingency approach is not recognized as a formal management school.

Components of the Contingency View

As shown in exhibit 3–10, we believe that the contingency approach can be best understood by analyzing the determinants of contingency thought and the managerial questions that arise from adopting this view of management. It is only through gaining knowledge about the facts surrounding various situations that we can improve our effectiveness as managers.

It is suggested that the main determinants of the contingency view are related to the external and internal environments of the organization. The *external environment* concerns the state of the economic, social, political, and technological areas and their impact on or relationship with the organization. For example, consider the following illustrations: (1) Mideast oil problems have significantly changed the thinking of many energy company executives about the future of crude oil as a fuel; (2) the development of miniature electronic components has totally reoriented the business machine industry; (3) federal laws and enforcement policies on equal opportunity and safety have caused the personnel function in most organizations to be elevated in importance; and (4) national concerns over the environment have forced automobile manufacturers to radically change their new cars to be more fuel efficient.

The *internal environment* is more commonly referred to as the state of the organization with respect to the various constraints and resources that are available. At least three components are used to describe the internal environment:

1. **Technology constraints.**

Technology refers to the type and nature of the processes used to produce the organization's goods or services. For example, the technology used to manufacture plastics is different from the technology of banking. Two constraints, or limiting factors, are most important. First, how *flexible* is the technology to changes in external environmental demands? In the manufacture of steel, large capital investments in machinery and equipment are necessary to produce the product. As such, steel companies cannot change their processes around very quickly to meet new consumer demands. The impact of the Japanese steel industry on U.S. companies, with its new equipment and technology, is well documented. On the other hand, the retailing industry, with its emphasis on human resources rather than on physical plant and equipment (i.e., it is labor intensive), can adapt readily to changes in consumer demands and taste. In other words, every industry is constrained by its technology, some more than others.

Second, the type of technology that is used in an organization determines the nature of the *interdependence* between different units. Interdependence concerns the degree to which one individual, group, or organization is dependent on another for materials or services to perform the task. For example, workers on an automobile assembly line are highly dependent on one another. The tire mounters cannot do their job until the brakes have been installed; the bumpers cannot be installed until the car has been painted, and so on. The key factor with technology is that

EXHIBIT 3–10 Summary of Contingency Management

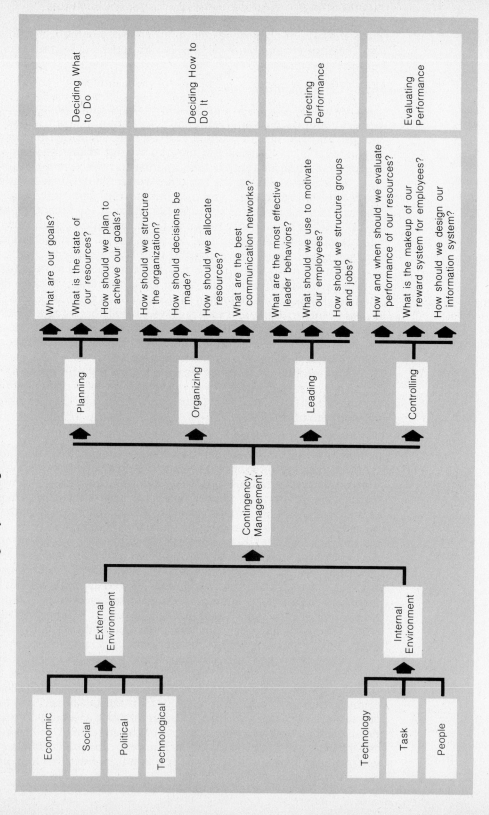

the greater the level of dependence, the greater the need for *coordination* and, hence, managerial attention and decisions.[23]

2. **Task constraints.**

The nature of the tasks performed by individual workers is also a contingency factor. Employees who work on *routine* tasks perform their work in a repetitive fashion. Such jobs require a more precise set of instructions, training, directing, and control than do jobs that are nonroutine and *complex*. For example, newspaper press operators perform their jobs according to a set of procedures and guidelines that dictates their responsibilities, quantity and quality requirements, and scheduling. On the other hand, the manager of product planning for a company such as General Foods or Procter and Gamble follows only a minimum of procedures because the job contains many uncertainties with respect to consumer acceptance, production requirements, and product specifications. The important contingency aspect is that the task will dictate how a manager will act in various situations. A manager supervising a group of workers in routine jobs will be heavily concerned with the control functions because much of the subordinates' job is described by rules, policies, and procedures. The manager of a group of subordinates who perform complex tasks will be less concerned with the control aspects than with the planning and change aspects.

3. **Individual or people constraints.**

This third contingency factor relates to the types of individuals employed in the organization and their levels of competence. First, the manager must be concerned with the dominant psychological needs of the work force. Do workers seek high wages and job security, or are the needs for advancement, learning, and personal development more important? The Chevrolet Lordstown plant taught a valuable lesson in the mismatch between the workers and their jobs. It was not until after many strikes that management of this assembly line plant recognized that many of the employee-relations problems could be traced to the fact that the workers—who were more highly educated than employees at other plants—were reacting negatively to both the boring nature of the assembly line jobs and the lack of any opportunity for advancement.

Second, the abilities, skills, and levels of competence of the organization's work force must be carefully analyzed before any major decisions affecting the survival of the firm are made. In essence, the question is how good is the managerial and nonmanagerial work force? In the 1950s and 1960s, American Motors' decision to compete head-on with Ford and G.M. resulted in failure because they did not have the necessary personnel to compete effectively. In other words, they went in over their heads!

As shown in exhibit 3–10, the focus of a contingency orientation to management is a series of questions (or problems) that must be faced by managers. These questions stress the recognition of two points. First, the questions cannot be answered with the adoption of one specific management approach—there just is no "one best way" to handle all possible contingencies and constraints. Second, these questions should make the reader keenly aware of the need to consider the importance of functions, skills, and roles in performing the manager's job. These three characteristics of the manager's job must be integrated in order to attain high levels of achievement.

Summary of the Contingency View

The contingency view approaches management from a totally different perspective than do the formal schools of management. Rather than apply a universal technique to each situation, it suggests that different situations will require different approaches.

The contingency view supports the use of classical, behavioral, or management science ideas in various situations, depending on the state of the external and internal environments. The basic managerial functions of planning, organizing, and control are the important elements of any management approach. They must, however, be adapted to the situation. Planning is always important, but it is only as effective as the quality and quantity of information that is used. Organizations must set goals, but these goals must recognize the capabilities and resources of the firm. One must emphasize structural design, but what type of design should be chosen? Concern for people in the workplace is without question an important consideration. Yet, managers must recognize that a Theory X approach may be more effective in a particular situation than use of Theory Y would be. Finally, operations research techniques can be of tremendous value only when we have some confidence in the quality of the assumptions and of the input data. No matter how complex and sophisticated our mathematical model, unreliable input information will result in an unreliable solution.

More than any approach to management, the contingency view provides a clear representation of the realities of the manager's job. There is a constant emphasis on managerial functions, skills, and roles. It recognizes the importance of the management functions of planning, organizing, and control as a key to effective performance. It focuses attention on acquiring proficiency in all four of the major managerial skills—technical, human, conceptual, and diagnostic. With its emphasis on investigation, observation, and analysis of various managerial problems and the possible courses of action, it highlights the conceptual and diagnostic skills, a focus that was lacking in the other approaches. Finally, the contingency view recognizes that the manager is more than just a leader of subordinates or a decision maker or an information handler. In reality, the manager is all three.

The contingency view is not without its critics and thus should not be portrayed or accepted as the best or only way to manage. There is criticism that stressing the "it all depends" stance of the contingency view adds more *confusion* than *order* to the practice of management. By accepting contingency approaches, the practitioner is swamped with more "what ifs" and "what happens when" ideas than it is humanly possible to comprehend, and is then thrown into a difficult managerial position and allowed to sink or swim without the use of tested and proven prescriptions, techniques, or methods. Still others point out that the contingency view is without a theoretical foundation, thus making it near impossible to research, gain valuable information, or develop a knowledge base. Whether management is an art, a science, or a field of study and practice, certain elements should serve as a foundation for continued growth and development.[24]

These criticisms, and those directed at the other management schools, certainly have some validity and should, therefore, be carefully considered by the manager. Our approach to management is neither based, nor limited, by adherence to a particular popular school. It is our view that a manager's job revolves around certain basic but broad *functions,* that require different *skills,* and performs a variety of *roles.* The ultimate test is *performance,* no matter what approach is used.

SUMMARY OF THE SCHOOLS OF MANAGEMENT THOUGHT

In this chapter, we have attempted to provide an overview of approaches to management thought. A summary of our presentation is shown in exhibit 3–11. This exhibit has been developed around our belief that a manager's job is best described in terms of *functions, skills,* and *roles.* There are at least three points of importance for the manager to consider.

First, the description of the managerial *functions* has grown significantly from the classical school to the contingency orientation. We have seen how the functions performed by the manager have developed from a concern for efficiency and the basic ideas about planning, organizing, and control to an emphasis on human factors and mathematical models, and finally to a recognition that what the manager does is determined to a great extent by the state of the environment, both internal and external to the organization.

Second, the different schools of management each stress the importance of acquiring certain managerial *skills.* The differences involve not only priority but also complexity. Scientific management and the human relations views each stress the importance of a primary skill—technical for the former, human skills for the latter. On the other hand, the organizational behavior branch of the behavioral school and the contingency view each stress the need to acquire proficiency in multiple skills.

Finally, the scope of managerial activities is represented by the different *roles* that the management schools emphasize. The classical approach looks at the manager's roles as being primarily interpersonal in nature, but the behavioral school and contingency view present the manager's job in much greater scope.

The differences in functions, skills, and roles are an important distinguishing characteristic of the four management schools. More than any one factor, however, this summary exhibit should remind the manager of the importance of the growth of management as a profession—one that is not only becoming more and more complex, but one that can afford a highly rewarding career as well.

CONTRIBUTIONS BY PRACTICING MANAGERS

Throughout the twentieth century, many contributions to the development of management have been made by practicing managers. Taylor, Fayol, and Barnard, for example, all held managerial positions when they presented their views and approaches to management. Being an applied field of study, we should expect significant contributions from practicing professionals. We have singled out four additional practicing managers

EXHIBIT 3–11   Summary of Management Schools

	BASIC FUNCTIONS	SKILLS REQUIRED	ROLES STRESSED
Classical			
1. Scientific Management	1. Developing more efficient jobs through job specialization, planning, motion and time standards.	Technical	Interpersonal
2. Administrative Theory	2. Planning, organizing, and controlling.	Technical Human Conceptual	Interpersonal Informational
Behavioral			
1. Human Relations	1. Emphasis on the person's psychological reactions to a job.	Human	Interpersonal
2. Organizational Behavior	2. Exploring the effects on employee behavior of the job, supervisory relations, group structure, and organizational practices.	Human Conceptual Diagnostic	Interpersonal Informational Decisional
Management Science	Developing mathematical models to assist managerial decision making.	Technical Conceptual Diagnostic	Informational Decisional
Contingency	There is no one "best way" to manage. Managerial activities and behavior are determined by the state of the situation.	Technical Human Conceptual Diagnostic	Interpersonal Informational Decisional

for discussion. Charles P. McCormick, James F. Lincoln, Pierre Du Pont, and Alfred P. Sloan have been chosen because each made a unique contribution to management thought.

Charles P. McCormick: Employee Participation in Management

Employee participation in management became an important concept for the McCormick Company, a food products company, during the 1930s. Developed by the company's president, Charles P. McCormick, the plan stressed how employees in the headquarters, factory, and sales force could share both the responsibilities and opportunities of company management. "Multiple management," as it became known, was the forerunner of many of today's participative management approaches.[25]

McCormick's first venture into participative management was the junior board of directors. The junior board consisted of seventeen promising young employees who were given free access to many company records, including detailed financial data. They were instructed to review various parts of the business and make recommendations that would supplement (or oppose) the judgments of the senior members of the main board of directors. The junior board was highly successful and made a number of suggestions that helped the company through the Great Depression. The concept was expanded later in the development of two other boards: (1) the factory board, which included supervisors and non-supervisory workers; and (2) the sales board, made up of various members of the sales and distribution staff.

McCormick's participative management plan involved a number of important points:

1. *Involvement.* It permitted workers and lower level managers to get involved in the company's major decision making.
2. *Communications.* Both vertical and horizontal communications networks were opened up in the company.
3. *Management development.* The various boards could be used to identify and evaluate the special talents of employees and attempted to put them in more challenging jobs.
4. *Sponsorship.* Each board member was sponsored by a higher level executive (see the discussion of "mentors" in chapter 2). This helped the lower level employee become socialized more quickly in the organization and became an invaluable means of gaining experience.
5. *Evaluation.* With the use of a senior board and a junior board, the company benefitted from having a variety of sources of ideas and points of evaluation on new and existing programs.

McCormick's vision of future management was also early for its time. He noted that the primary purpose of management was to build people. It should place the human factor above profit, knowing that if its human organization is constructed of the right kind of material, the profit will take care of itself.

James F. Lincoln: Incentive Management

At Lincoln Electric, a Cleveland based firm, James F. Lincoln became known for his approach to individual motivation through the use of incentives and profit sharing.[26] During the late 1930s Lincoln was concerned that pride in one's work, self-reliance, and other time-tested virtues were being replaced by a greater dependence on someone else—principally the government. He felt that it was time to return to the days when individual ambition was dominant. In other words, people were not primarily motivated by money, nor by security, but by recognition of their skills and performance.

Lincoln's incentive plan sought to develop all employees to their highest abilities and then reward them with a "bonus" based on their contribution to the firm's profits. This bonus, which many times exceeded the individuals' annual wage, was given over and above regular compensation, which was already comparable to area wages. At Lincoln Electric, there were no work stoppages or strikes, turnover for all types of employees was almost nonexistent (there was, and still is, a waiting list for new jobs), worker productivity was five times as great as for other manufacturing companies, and profits were rising along with bonuses. The incentive plan at Lincoln is still as successful as ever today, and is being copied by many other small- to medium-size organizations.

Beyond Lincoln's contribution to motivation by incentives, the basic philosophy of management is both interesting and adaptable even by today's standards. Some of his more important points are as follows:

1. Occasionally give workers jobs over their heads; challenge brings out the best in most people.
2. Personal advancement is based solely on the individual's performance and contribution to the firm.
3. Stress teamwork; every worker must feel responsible to a team.
4. You are a leader, not a boss.

Lincoln's emphasis on motivation, teamwork, and leadership were to serve as foundation elements of many contemporary organizational programs in the management of human resources.

Pierre Du Pont: The Coming Age of Modern Top Management

When Pierre Du Pont took over as chief executive of the family firm, E.I. Du Pont de Nemours, the company was already a century old. He knew Taylor; in fact, he hired him as a consultant on a number of occasions. However, Du Pont was more concerned with higher level management problems. While Taylor worked on problems at the job and factory level, it was with Du Pont that modern top management thought and practice came into being.

During Du Pont's early tenure, most industrial companies were one-man shows, such as Carnegie, Ford, and so on. Du Pont revolutionized the executive office, setting up the procedures for forecasting, long-range planning, budgeting and allocating resources that are taken for granted today. He created functional departments for manufacturing, sales, purchasing, finance, and transportation. On top of the functional arrangement, Du Pont set up a tightly centralized general office for the total company. The company's governing body was the *executive committee,* composed of the president and the heads of the major functional departments. To enable the executive committee to make resource allocation decisions, Du Pont set up a system to provide it with information about departmental expenditures, including data on expenses, rates of return, and proposed spending plans.[27] The executive committee also coordinated the flow of materials through the company, attempting to control inventory, the physical movement of goods at all stages, and the fluctuating demands of working capital. While some students of management consider John D. Rockefeller the founder of top management thinking, the committee system he established at Standard Oil was scrapped almost entirely in favor of the Du Pont system.

The Du Pont system, however, was not without its problems. When the company diversified into paints, dyes, chemicals, and fibers, the complexities created by massive diversification coupled with a severe economic recession brought about big losses. As a result, the company separated top management from day-to-day decisions about resource allocation. This move was the beginning of management decentralization, to which Du Pont also contributed.

Alfred P. Sloan: Management Decentralization

Du Pont's organizational expertise carried over to an emerging firm in the 1920s, General Motors. In order to save the young company from financial failure, the Du Pont family invested millions of dollars along with many of its management ideas. Influenced by the emerging decentralized structure at Du Pont, G.M.'s new president, Alfred P. Sloan, formalized the system of decentralized operations and centralized control and review.[28] Essentially, the system enabled top management to control the various parts of the company in a more efficient and rational manner. Each division, or department, was considered as an *individual operating company,* with its own functional departments (e.g., manufacturing, sales, and purchasing). But each division would have to operate according to a set of guidelines—from personnel to finance—established by top management. Under the system, the divisions were required to develop detailed data on costs, sales, purchases, and profits so that top management could then authorize production levels. While the divisions made day-to-day decisions, it was ultimately top management that made the major policy decisions on how resources would be deployed and the direction of the company.

The idea of decentralized product divisions enabled each division to react much more quickly to the ever-changing environment. In the late 1920s, G.M. recognized the changing trends in consumer tastes for automobiles. Consumers no longer wanted the bland looking but reliable car. What they were beginning to express was a desire for variety of products based on style, not just low cost and engineering. By 1927, G.M. was offering a full line of cars that covered a wide price and style range. The decentralized structure not only permitted G.M. to react to the market faster but also enabled them to pass Ford in size and sales—a lead they have not relinquished even today. Sloan's decentralization idea, later revised as "profit-center" management, is still a dominant force today.

SUMMARY FOR THE MANAGER

1. Each of the management schools of thought developed during different parts of this century. The important point of this evolution is that the particular management school was appropriate for the environment at that time: management thought adapted to the conditions of the organization's environment. Because of this, the schools of management differed in their emphasis on the functions, skills, and roles of the manager's job.

2. The classical school of management consisted of two branches. The scientific management approach stressed the use of the scientific method toward developing a better understanding of the management of jobs. This orientation resulted in emphasizing control aspects, technical skills, and interpersonal roles of the manager's job. The administrative theory branch, with its focus on the management of the total organization, first noted the importance of the managerial functions of planning, organizing, and controlling. This branch also expanded the view of the manager's job in terms of the needed skills and the required roles to be performed.

3. Employee reactions to certain features of the classical school, coupled with changes in the environment of many organizations, created a need to refine the manager's job. This need resulted in the development of the behavioral school of management. Managerial functions, skills, and roles were changed to give greater emphasis to the importance of managing an organization's human resources.

4. Two major events gave momentum to the development of the management science school. First, World War II created a need for more sophisticated methods of handling and solving complex managerial problems. Second, the advent of the computer enabled managers to solve these problems with great speed and accuracy. These two factors resulted in redefining the manager's job to stress the technical and conceptual skills applied to informational and decisional roles.

5. The complex and dynamic environment of the 1960s and 1970s clearly revealed that there was no universal approach to management that could be applied to every situation. The contingency view of management emphasized adaptation to the organization's external and internal enviornment. The manager's job became equally complex and dynamic. The focus of managerial activities was on all functions (planning, organizing, leading, controlling, and change), skills (technical, human, conceptual, and diagnostic), and roles (interpersonal, informational, and decisional). To be successful, the manager was required to carefully analyze each particular situation and apply the needed functions, skills, and roles.

6. Over the history of management thought, major contributions came from both scholars and practitioners of management, stressing the need for management scholars and practitioners to interact frequently to exchange ideas and thoughts.

QUESTIONS FOR REVIEW AND DISCUSSION

1. Why is the study of the history of management thought of interest to today's managers?
2. Why were the two branches of the classical school termed the management of jobs and the management of the total organization?
3. What were Taylor's major contributions to management?
4. In what ways are Fayol's principles of management different from those proposed by the contingency approach?
5. What were the key factors in the development of the behavioral school of management?
6. What is the "Hawthorne Effect"?
7. What factors or events facilitated the development of the management science school?
8. What are some of the issues or problems with the management science school?
9. What major skills and roles are stressed by the contingency school of management?
10. Why have the contributors to management thought come from the academic and practitioner orientation?

NOTES

1. H. Koontz and C. O'Donnell, *Management: A Systems and Contingency Analysis of Managerial Functions* (New York: McGraw-Hill, 1976).

2. J. D. Thompson, *Organizations in Action* (New York: McGraw-Hill, 1967), p. 147.

3. D. A. Wren, *The Evolution of Management Thought* (Englewood Cliffs, N.J.: Prentice-Hall, 1968).

4. R. L. A. Sterba, "Clandestine Management in the Imperial Chinese Bureaucracy," *Academy of Management Review* (January 1978). 69–78.

5. K. von Clausewitz, *Principles of War* (Harrisburg, Pa.: Military Service Publishing, 1942).

6. F. W. Taylor, *Principles of Scientific Management* (New York: Harper and Brothers, 1911).

7. Ibid., pp. 36–37.

8. L. E. Davis and J. C. Taylor, eds., *Design of Jobs* (Santa Monica, Calif.: Goodyear Publishing, 1979).

9. F. B. Gilbreth, *Bricklaying System* (New York: Clark Publishing, 1909).

10. H. L. Gantt, *Work, Wages, and Profits* (New York: Engineering Magazine Co., 1911).

11. H. Emerson, *The Twelve Principles of Efficiency* (New York: Engineering Magazine, 1913).

12. H. Fayol, *General and Industrial Management,* trans. J. A. Conbrough (Geneva: International Management Institute, 1929).

13. L. Urwick, *The Elements of Administration* (London: Sir Isaac Pitman, 1943).

14. R. C. Davis, *The Principles of Business Organization and Operation* (Columbus: H. L. Hedrick, 1935).

15. F. J. Roethlisberger and W. J. Dickson, *Management and the Worker* (Boston: Harvard University Press, 1939).

16. C. I. Barnard, *The Functions of the Executive* (Boston: Harvard University Press, 1938).

17. D. McGregor, *The Human Side of Enterprise* (New York: McGraw-Hill, 1960).

18. L. L. Cummings, "Towards Organizational Behavior," *Academy of Management Review* (January 1978). 90–98.

19. H. M. Wagner, *Principle of Management Science* (Englewood Cliffs, N.J.: Prentice-Hall, 1976), p. 5.

20. J. W. Forrester, *Industrial Dynamics* (Cambridge, Mass.: M.I.T. Press, 1961).

21. T. Levitt, "A Heretical View of Management Science," *Fortune* (December 18, 1978). 50–52.

22. P. Lawrence and J. W. Lorsch, *Organization and Environment: Managing Differentiation and Integration*

(Homewood, Ill.: Richard D. Irwin, 1967).

23. Thompson, pp. 54–55.

24. See J. W. Lorsch, "Making Behavioral Science More Useful," *Harvard Business Review* (March–April 1979). 171–81.

25. C. P. McCormick, *Multiple Management* (New York: Harper and Brothers, 1938).

26. J. F. Lincoln, *Incentive Management* (Cleveland, Ohio: Lincoln Electric Company, 1951).

27. P. Smith, "The Masterminds of Management," *Dun's Review* (July 1976). 17–19.

28. A. P. Sloan, *My Years with General Motors* (Garden City, N.Y.: Doubleday, 1964).

ADDITIONAL REFERENCES

Argyris, C. *Integrating the Individual and the Organization.* New York: John Wiley and Sons, 1964.

Babbage, C. *On the Economy of Machinery and Manufacturers.* London: Charles Knight, 1832.

Burns, T., and Stalker, G. M. *The Management of Innovation.* London: Tavistock, 1961.

Church, A. H. *The Science and Practice of Management.* New York: Engineering Magazine Co., 1914.

Churchman, C. W.; Ackoff, R. L.; and Arnoff, E. L. *Introduction to Operations Research.* New York: Wiley, 1957.

Drucker, P. F. *The Practice of Management.* New York: Harper and Brothers, 1954.

Follet, M. P. *The New State.* Gloucester, Mass.: Peter Smith, 1918.

George, C. S. Jr. *The History of Management Thought.* Englewood Cliffs, N.J.: Prentice-Hall, 1968.

Gilbreth, F. B. *Motion Study.* New York: D. Van Nostrand, 1911.

March, J. G., and Simon, H. A. *Organizations.* New York: Wiley, 1958.

Mayo, E. *The Social Problems of an Industrial Civilization.* Cambridge, Mass.: Harvard University Press, 1945.

Mooney, J. D., and Reiley, A. C. *Onward Industry.* New York: Harper and Brothers, 1931.

Raiffa, H. *Games and Decisions.* New York: Wiley, 1957.

A CASE FOR ANALYSIS

Joyce C. Hall of Hallmark Cards

Among the more fascinating questions that can be asked about businesspeople are those concerning motive. What makes them tick? What drives them on? Anybody who looks for simple, universal answers will be misled. Motives differ from person to person, and each manager, as his or her career evolves, develops a changing mix of motivations, ranging from the primitive and obvious to subtle goals for which psychology has no clear definition. The point is illustrated by the career of Joyce C. Hall, who built Hallmark Cards, Inc., a privately owned $500 million company.

At nine years old Hall was selling perfume door to door in Norfolk, Nebraska, and by the time he was eighteen he had moved to Kansas City and opened his own postcard business. When asked recently what motivated him to work so hard back then, Hall has a clear answer: "a good appetite—a deep-set desire to eat three meals a day." At no time in the last fifty years or more has Joyce Hall had reason to worry about where the next meal was coming from. So why did he go on driving to expand his business? Why, at eighty-five, did he have "two weeks work" on his desk? Some people, extrapolating from Hall's boyhood motivations, might ascribe his later work to "greed." Their sort of moralism, widespread in this country today, contributes to public misunderstanding of business.

Almost everybody in Kansas City will testify that Joyce Hall is the reverse of greedy. In a business that many people would consider unglamorous, Joyce Hall found a lifetime of excitement in the pursuit of excellence or, as he calls it, "quality." Hall says he learned about quality from a Kansas City grocer whose grocery stores sold nothing but the best. People were glad to shop in them even if they had to pay a little more for quality.

Hall's first important innovations, which helped Hallmark rise from a small regional business to national leadership, was a display case built around 1930. Up to then cards had been kept under store counters, usually in a mess. If a customer wanted a birthday card, the clerk fished around until he found one that would do. Hall, working with an architect, designed an open case where cards were displayed in slots. The retailer replenished the slot from a box in a drawer below. This case led to a second innovation, a method of inventory control. At the bottom of each storage box Hallmark put a reorder card for the retailer to mail. He did not necessarily get back cards of the same design. The system kept track of which designs were selling well, so a reorder card for a slowly selling design might touch off a shipment of a different design in the same category. This inventory system is now computerized, and the Hallmark warehousing operations are a marvel of modern management.

The life of a card design averages nine months. To replace about fourteen thousand designs a year, Hallmark employs more than 300 artists. Until a few years before his retirement at seventy-five, no new design went into production without his "O.K.J.C." He could tell with amazing accuracy which designs would sell and which would not. To illustrate what he meant by quality, he dug out a recent "To My Husband on Valentine's Day" with a copper-colored border. "The copper is wrong," he said. "If it had been gold, it would have sold 20 percent more." How does he know? "The vapor of past experience."

Until about twenty-five years ago Hallmark broke up artists' jobs into repetitive tasks. As designs became more numerous and more sophisticated, the artists' work was reintegrated; now a single artist does the whole design. Joyce Hall sent his artists to New York and to Europe to absorb new ideas for cards by looking in art galleries, clothing-store windows, and theaters.

In the 1930s Joyce Hall thought the company was ready for national advertising. He approached a number of agencies where he was told to forget the idea because a brand name could not be established in greeting cards. He proved that prophecy wildly wrong. In the early 1950s his "Hallmark Hall of Fame" was first turned down by the television networks because of a strict rule that time would be sold only in thirteen-week blocks. Finally, NBC agreed to let him buy time when he wanted it—an exception that led to the TV "spectaculars" and then to the "specials" sponsored by other companies.

He was much involved in the conception of Crown Center, an eighty-seven-acre area in Kansas City that is regarded as one of the best ongoing U.S. urban redevelopments. Joyce Hall's son, Donald, who now runs the company, grew up—literally—in the business. In the days when sales meetings were held in the Hall farmhouse, Donald, a toddler, was allowed to attend.

Joyce Hall drives himself to the office every day in a 1963 Buick. It costs a lot to keep the old car in tip-top condition, but Hall doesn't mind. That model's transmission has the quality he likes.

Suggested from Max Ways, "The Business Hall of Fame," Fortune (January 1977): 123.

Questions for Discussion

1. What was Hall's philosophy of management? Did he adhere to any of the schools of management thought?
2. Discuss Hall's performance as a manager in terms of functions, skills, and roles.
3. What effect, if any, did the external environment have on Hall's success as a manager?

II

Developing the Framework for Performance
-Planning-

4

The External and Internal Environment of Organizations

CHAPTER OUTLINE

KEY POINTS IN THIS CHAPTER

1. An analysis of an organization's external and internal environment in one of the most important parts of a manager's job.

2. The main external environmental components—economic, political, social, and technological—vary in importance to different organizations.

3. The external environment determines the opportunities, threats, and constraints for the organization; in other words, what they *might do.*

4 The internal environment is defined in terms of organizational resources; financial, physical, human, and system and technological.

5. The special case of human resources includes the analysis of managerial values, an important determinant of managerial behavior.

6. The internal environment identifies certain strengths and weaknesses for the future organizational action; in other words, it defines what they *can do* and *want to do.*

7. Matching external environmental opportunities, threats, and constraints with internal resource strengths and weaknesses is a key managerial activity.

8. Forecasting concerns the prediction of future events of importance to the organization.

9. An organization's external and internal environmental analysis has a significant impact on the manager's job—functions, skills, and roles.

THE PRACTICE OF MANAGEMENT

External and Internal Environmental Problems: The U.S. Textile Industry

The external environment has not been kind to the U.S. textile industry; some of its current problems, however, have been brought on by significant internal problems. Fragmentation, over-capacity, increasing imports of foreign products, and cutthroat competition are bleeding the life out of the textile industry in the U.S. Even the ten largest textile companies managed only a small 3.3 percent average return on sales during 1978 versus 10.5 percent for industrial corporations as a whole. As a result, most textile companies have little capital to invest in sorely needed plant modernization. The early prospects for major changes appear to be slim due to tradition-bound management that has clung to outdated ways of doing business.

The problems faced by textile industry managers are many and serious. Imports of textiles and apparel have increased 7 to 10 percent annually while the domestic textile industry grows at only 2 to 3 percent yearly. Industry managers are particularly upset by the federal government's failure to break down nontariff barriers in counties that ship excessively into the U. S. but buy few American goods. Despite an agreement with over fifty countries to limit the growth of imports into this country to 6 percent annually, during 1978 imports grew by nearly 20 percent while exports by U. S. firms increased only 3 percent. Executives quickly point to Japan whose imports increased over 17 percent between 1977 and 1978.

Internally, many textile firms operate with outdated and inefficient plants. The industry is planning on spending about $22.5 billion during the 1980s for capital improvement, nearly triple the amount spent in the 1970s. However, little new capacity will be built. Much of the money will be devoted to modernization to change the industry from a labor-intensive to a more capital-intensive business. During this process, it is estimated that about one-third of the industry's nearly one-million person work force will be eliminated.

The work force is itself a major internal problem. Paternalistic personnel policies and an anti-union fever pervade the industry's management. The industry has long believed in averting worker layoffs as much as possible, resulting in many plants running at full capacity even though the market for the product has dried up.

A partial cause of this paternalistic practice of providing a steady paycheck to its workers is management's desire to keep unions out of the industry, now only 7 percent unionized. Things are changing rapidly, however. Not only are unions gaining a foothold in many firms, but textile firms are feeling the pinch of the growing industrialization of the South, the heart of textile manufacturing. When new industries move to the South, particularly rubber companies and breweries, they pay wages that are 50 or more percent higher than those paid by the textile firms. The result is high turnover textile companies.

Another worker-related problem concerns regulations on employee health and environmental protection. Recent decisions by the Occupational Safety and Health Administration (OSHA) and the Environmental Protection Agency (EPA) concerning the level of cotton dust in textile plants has significant implications for the industry. Cotton dust not only pollutes the environment but is a major cause of byssinosis in workers, or brown lung disease. Nearly 10 percent of the proposed new capital investment will be used to meet OSHA and EPA regulations.

What can the industry do to counter these developments beyond fighting for improved tariffs and increased capital expenditures? Some action is already being observed. First, there is a movement among the largest firms toward market expansion by increasing the number of products being manufactured, or diversifying into other businesses. Second, to retain top workers, textile mills have begun to modernize their plants and to pay workers more competitive salaries. Although these are large and costly jobs, they may have to be done because the survival of the industry is at stake.

Adapted from "More Gloom for U.S. Textiles," Business Week *(April 9, 1979): 66–69.*

4

In this first of four chapters dealing with the organizational planning function, we will be concerned with analyzing the important elements of an organization's external and internal environment. The material in this chapter and the following chapter on organizational goals have been termed the *premises* of the managerial planning process. This term reflects the fact that an environmental analysis and the establishment of organizational goals are the primary inputs into the actual planning phase. In other words, the environment and goals state "what it is" that the organization desires to achieve; the planning itself sets about detailing "how" it will be done.

In this chapter we will focus on the relationship between the environment and management with a four-step presentation. First, we will provide a more detailed discussion of the components and dimensions of an organization's *external environment.* Second, we will introduce the importance of the organization's *internal environment,* which will be defined in terms of the resources of the organization. Third, we will discuss the crucial managerial activity of *matching* the opportunities and demands of the external environment with the strengths and weaknesses of the organization's internal resources. Finally, we will turn to a brief analysis of the various forecasting techniques that are used to predict a future event. We will again stress the importance of managerial functions, skills, and roles in the process of effectively analyzing external and internal environmental factors.

THE EXTERNAL ENVIRONMENT OF ORGANIZATIONS

Organizations of every type are in constant interaction with the external environment. The important components of the environment that have a direct impact on the organization include suppliers, customers, competitors, government agencies, and the society in general. The interaction is both wide and varied, depending on the particular organization. For example, Eli Lilly, the pharmaceutical company, is concerned about raw material supplies from chemical companies, approval of new drugs from the Food and Drug Administration (FDA), the knowledge of its products by physicians, and the purchase decisions by pharmacists. On the other hand, the Newport News Shipbuilding Company requires orders for new ships by the Navy and private companies, metal plates from numerous firms, a good working relationship with the union representing the employees, and approval of its hiring and placement policies by the Equal Employment Opportunity Commission (EEOC). In order to cover this topic adequately, our discussion of the external environment will focus on two issues: (1) environmental components and (2) environmental dimensions.

Environmental Components—Domestic and International

Many external forces affect the daily operations of an organization. These forces, representing the external environment, are shown in exhibit 4–1. At least three conditions should be noted about the environment of an organization. First, while many groups in the environment interact with an organization, it is helpful to categorize them into four separate *components*.These correspond to the economic, political, and social, and technological components. Second, the individual environmental components will affect particular organizations in *different* ways. For example, the technological environment is of key importance to the computer industry but of lesser importance to furniture manufacturers. Third, at any one point in time, *changes* in certain environmental components will have a more significant effect on an organization than would changes in others. Changes in consumer demand for automobiles, for example, can result in revisions to production schedules and layoffs of workers in a rather short period of time. On the other hand, governmental imposed mile-per-gallon standards for cars will result in a somewhat more lengthy response by the same companies.

EXHIBIT 4–1   Environmental Components

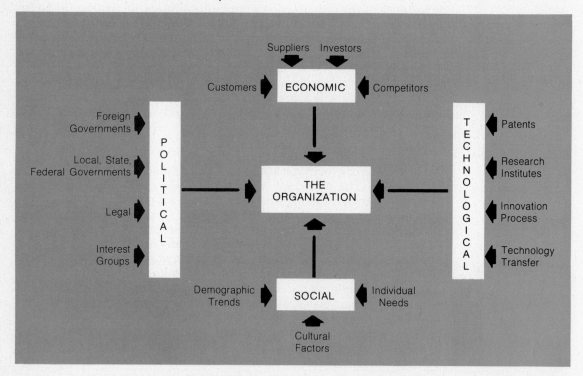

As an illustration, the four environmental components for a state-supported university and an energy company (e.g., Exxon, Gulf, Texaco, etc.) are presented in exhibit 4–2. This exhibit and the following discussion should serve to illustrate how the external environment interacts with and affects the functions of managers and organizations.

EXHIBIT 4–2   Environmental Components

	ENVIRONMENT	
Components	**State-Supported University**	**Energy Company**
Economic The state of the economy of different nations; relationships with customers, suppliers, and competitors.	Increasing education cost; declining enrollments; relationships with private foundations and other universities.	Increasing production costs; gas allocations; varying customer needs.
Political The general political climate of society; public image and attitudes toward product and services.	Funding levels from the state; tenure restrictions; faculty unionization.	Divestiture and regulation; oil embargo; nationalization by foreign counries; OPEC.
Social The general sociological and cultural changes in society.	Questions concerning the value of a college degree; continuing education programs; internal personnel policies.	Attitudes toward high gas prices, price fixing and kickbacks; concerns over pollution and destruction of natural resources; eliminating employment discrimination.
Technological The availability of resources and constraints facing organizations; the level of technology.	Availability of quality instructors; teaching innovations such as computers, video tape, etc.	Declining raw material sources (e.g., crude oil); availabiliy of alternative sources (e.g., solar, nuclear, coal, etc.).

Economic Environment.   Most organizations transform raw resources to produce goods and/or services for consumption in a competitive economy. Thus, the economic environment involves suppliers, customers, competitors, and investors.

1. *Suppliers.* Organizations must acquire raw materials, labor, equipment, and financial support from the environment in order to produce products and services. Physical, human, and financial resources are the critical raw material supplies for most organizations.

   In the case of *physical* raw materials, consider the environment of an electric utility company that uses coal to generate power. The purchasing agent for the utility is faced with a threefold supply responsibility: (1) obtain a steady supply of high-quality coal; (2) purchase the coal at minimum price; and (3) avoid becoming overly dependent on a single supplier. The usual procedure is to take bids from suppliers on price, quality, and amount and accept those from the one or two lowest bidders.

Organizations also need *human* resources to produce goods and services. In some cases the labor contract between management and a labor union provides the firm with a great portion of the needed human resources. In the absence of a union, the acquisition of human resources may depend on variations in labor market supply and demand. For example, during the late 1970s, there was a strong demand for computer systems specialists, petroleum exploration engineers, and certain skilled craftsmen in the building trades. We saw a similar strong demand for specialized scientists, engineers, and technicians during the space race era of the 1960s. To hire and retain these employees, the organization must provide competitive wages, working conditions, and employee benefits.

On the other hand, during the same period, an excess supply of applicants existed for certain teaching positions in elementary and secondary schools. Many qualified individuals competed for a few open positions. The organizations thus had the opportunity to choose the best candidates.

Financial resources can be provided to the organization from such investor sources as stocks, bonds, and from banks that give an organization a line of credit for daily operations. Like human resources, financial resources are subject to environmental supply and demand forces. An expanding economy coupled with a past record of good financial performance will enable the organization to sell equity and debt issues usually with a minimum of effort. On the other hand, a recession-prone economy and/or poor past financial performance will create a difficult situation for the organization in acquiring financial supprt.

2. *Customers and competitors*. We may look at the organization-customer-competitor relationship from at least two environmental viewpoints. First, using *economic* terms, we may classify such external relationships as being competitive, oligopolistic, or monopolistic. A *competitive* environment exists when there are a large number of buyers and sellers (producers) of goods and services. For example, restaurants in an urban area and clothing stores can be put into this classification. In such cases there is an emphasis placed on price, quality, product characteristics, and advertising claims. An organization may operate in an *oligopolistic* environment while there are few sellers or producers, but many buyers. The tire, automobile, and gasoline industries would be examples. In such environments price and product differentiation become quite important. Finally, a *monopolistic* environment may exist where there is only one seller, but many customers. Utility companies—telephone, electric, natural gas, and so on—would fall into this category.

The second way of looking at the organization-customer-competitor relationship is by considering the availability of *substitute* products and services. For example, with vacation traffic, airlines face competition not only from other airlines, but from AMTRAK, various bus lines, and auto rental agencies. A family looking for a residence may pick from a regular house, a patio home, or a condominium. In the not too distant future, our choices for fuel sources will include oil, gas, coal, solar, nuclear, and such exotic substitute sources as geothermal energy and the harnessing of ocean currents.

Political Environment.   Organizations of every type operate within and through various political systems. In a broad sense the interactions between the organization and the political environment is one of mutual influence. On one hand, organizations try to influence the political system in order to enhance their opportunities and chances of survival. The most visible of these are the extensive *lobbying* efforts by organizations at all levels of government. On the other hand, certain elements of the political system, such as regulatory agencies, attempt to influence the activities of organizations in order to promote environmental protection, avoid unfair competition, and so on.

1. *Sources of political influence.* The major sources of political influence originate from governmental bodies at the national, state, and local levels. With the emergence of such groups as OPEC, we have seen the governmental sphere of influence expand to include foreign governments as well.[1]

THE MANAGER'S JOB

Daniel Sharp of Xerox

Over the past decade, American corporation managers have been discovering one supposedly rich foreign market after another, only to have their hopes dashed or diminished by unexpected political changes or upheavals. Because of this situation, these managers are gradually acknowledging that they need both new skills and fresh insights to thrive overseas.

Analyzing the foreign political environment is one of the main responsibilities of Mr. Daniel Sharp, Director of International Relations for Xerox. Rather than hire political analysts to diagnose the international environment, Mr. Sharp relies primarily on a well-placed group of foreigners. Two years ago, Xerox's Latin American managing directors were made formally responsible for both anticipating and planning how to deal with local political risks. Now their annual raises partly depend on their political savvy. Sharp insists on quarterly reports from the local managers to keep U.S. executives informed about forseeable moves that may affect their business in each country.

Xerox consults outside authorities on some major issues, but Sharp says that "our best sources" are the local managers. As he explains: "They are better educated and informed about their environments than anyone here at staff headquarters. Often they went to school with those who run the government and other important institutions in their countries."

Adapted from L. Kraar, "The Multinationals Get Smarter About Political Risks," Fortune *(March 24, 1980): 92.*

An organization's political environment also extends beyond governmental bodies to the whole complex set of groups and individuals possessing power to influence the activities of organizations. These *interest groups* include in their membership trade associations, consumer protection groups, and unions. Many interest groups have exerted a great deal of pressure and influence on organizations, particularly in recent times. The Ralph Nader organization on automobile safety, the Sierra Club on land and wildlife conservation, and the A.F.L.-C.I.O. on worker interests are just three of many examples. Others are the National Organization of Manufacturing and local chambers of commerce.

2. *Activities of political sources.* The interaction between organizations and the federal government has become more involved and extensive during the last thirty years. Sometimes a part of the federal government such as the defense department acts as a consumer of goods and services. In most cases, however, the interaction concerns the relationship between an organization and a growing number of regulatory agencies. These agencies not only establish certain rules and procedures under which organizations must operate, but they then act to police the industry to ensure that those rules are obeyed.

These regulatory agencies may focus on a specific industry or some specific organizational activities.[2] For example, the Civil Aeronautics Board (CAB) and the Federal Aviation Agency (FAA) oversee airlines and aircraft, the Securities and Exchange Commission (SEC) oversees the securities industry, the FDA regulates drugs, and the Federal Communications Commission (FCC) regulates telecommunications organizations.

Other agencies have a broader focus. The EPA looks after environmental affairs, OSHA is concerned with the safety and health of workers, and the EEOC attempts to eliminate work-related discrimination. Organizations are also concerned with the acts of Congress. Recent legislation will have an impact on merger possibilities, tax laws, and foreign trade activities.

In addition to these federal activities, managers are faced with numerous points of interaction with state and local governments. These can include state and local corporate income taxes, zoning laws, governmental services (fire and police), and so on.

Interest groups also become involved in organizational influence activities. Consumer boycotts of goods and services, independent trucker slowdowns due to lower speed limits and rising diesel prices, demonstrations against nuclear power, and class action suits against utility companies because of high rates are just a few examples that we read in daily headlines.

The effects of these political sources on the organization, particularly federal regulatory agencies, can be looked at from three perspectives. First, there are certain *gains* for the organization in being influenced by these forces. Most people would agree, for example, that workers have benefited from certain actions of OSHA, the society in general is better off because of the scrutiny given to new drugs by the FDA, and the air we breathe and the water we drink have improved because of decisions by the EPA.

While there are certain gains, there are heavy *costs* to the organization in adhering to federal guidelines. These costs can take the form of added research and development on a new product, "opportunity costs" associated with delaying the introduction of a new product that could result in a significant competitive advantage to the organization, and the ever-present costs related to completing the significant amount of paper work required by federal agencies.[3]

Finally, and most important to our discussion, elements of the political environment can act as *constraints* that limit a manager's freedom of action. In a sense, such activities add a degree of uncertainty to the manager's job that some believe may result in lower levels of efficiency and effectiveness. Whether the political environment is detrimental to the performance of many organizations is beyond the scope of this book; it is also not usually within the domain of responsibility for most managers. What is important is that the influence of the political environment exists now and probably will exist well into the future.

Social Environment. The social environment, involving informal guidelines associated with the customs, culture, and trends in population, can influence the manner in which most organizations and managers function. Such guidelines may vary by country and by region within a single country, and may be quite different when compared with the "home" country of the organization. Nevertheless, understanding the social environment is an extremely important element of the manager's job.

Our discussion will focus on three factors related to the social environment: (1) demographic or population trends; (2) individual needs; and (3) cultural differences. These factors are illustrated in exhibit 4–3.

EXHIBIT 4–3
Forces Shaping the Social Environment

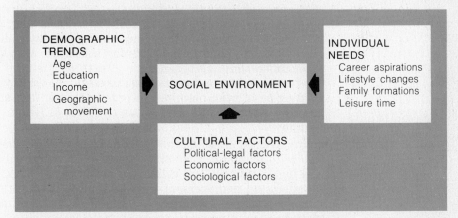

1. *Demographic trends.* The existence of significant shifts in demographic characteristics of the population will affect organizations in terms of the nature of the work force and the profile of the buying public, or customer. For example, many organizations are becoming more and more aware of the changing patterns and characteristics of the available management talent. Through a trend analysis it has been suggested that during the 1980s managers in the forty-five to sixty age bracket—traditionally the group of individuals with the most experience—will number only about 75 percent of the managers that will be needed.[4] Twenty-five year olds, on the other hand, will number 4.3 million in 1985—a 35 percent increase from 1970. The key question to which organizations must respond as a result of this trend is not only who will manage the organizaton, but who will be available to train and supervise the large number of young graduates just climbing onto the first rung of the management ladder. Certain changes in career planning and personnel acquisition and training may occur. (See chapters 19 and 20.)

    Changes in the behavioral profiles of customers are being felt even today. For example, the group of people known for years as constituting the "baby boom" are now themselves starting their own families and tend to be far more well off financially then other population sectors. Organizations are faced with the need to alter their marketing efforts to capture the buying power of this influential and affluent group. Changes in fashion, luxury goods, travel, and home furnishings represent this marketing effort. Even such fast food outlets as McDonald's are altering their menus to include breakfast and dinners to attract this population sector.

2. *Individual needs.* In some cases changes in demographic patterns will be felt by organizations as individuals begin to express the desire to satisfy different needs through the job. Two visible changes are currently being observed. One is the increased emphasis on the satisfaction of personal growth and career development needs.[5] Many employees want more than just money and security from a job—they see the job as a continuing learning and growth experience which may require frequent career moves.

A second trend that may be related to demographic patterns is one of changes in lifestyle. Individuals and families are more mobile, and many people wish to express certain creative needs through work or hobbies. To accomplish these and other activities, individuals need more leisure time than is presently being allocated. Many organizations and labor unions have recognized the growth of this need by adopting shortened workweeks or modified workweeks. A variety of options of this concept have been observed in organizations; for example, individuals must work forty hours, but can do so either in four days or four and one-half days.

3. *Cultural differences. Culture* has been defined in many different ways. Basically it relates to a society's economic, social, political, educational, and legal attitudes and beliefs. In recent years the study of culture and its effects on management have given rise to the study of comparative management. A significant amount of literature has been devoted to cross-cultural studies in an attempt to investigate the behavioral and performance characteristics of employees all over the globe.

Cultural factors can act to facilitate or constrain the performance of organizations. Among the cultural factors that should be considered by managers are the following:

Political-legal factors. Each country has its own laws that govern the practices of organizations. Many of these laws are quite similar to those in the home country of the organization. For example, operating in Canada can be similar to functioning in the United States. In other countries things may be quite different for the organization. In many cases the multinational corporation can expect such regulations as: (1) constraints on who can be hired by the firm; (2) tax laws that can take a significant part of earned profits; (3) laws that limit foreign operations and ownership in a country; (4) laws or tradition concerning the degree of participation of workers in policy decisions; and (5) regulations that require frequent discussions and approvals of day-to-day decisions by high-level governmental employees.[6] For example, multinational oil companies operating in Central and South America must hire a high percentage of native workers and managers. In addition, layoffs are not permitted, a governmental employee must be on site to observe daily activities, and products must be shipped in government-approved or owned tankers.

Economic factors. The competitive motive so dominant in the U.S. economy is frequently not found in other countries. For example, in selling or operating in communist countries, the only buyer may be the government. In addition, many countries prohibit a large percentage of profits earned within their boundaries to leave that country, and they require a certain percentage of profits to be reinvested in their countries. Labor also becomes a significant economic factor. Many times organizations cannot operate as efficiently as they wish due to restrictions or requirements on the number of workers that are to be employed. That is, a company may be forced to use less-efficient workers instead of a piece of machinery, to handle the work. Finally, many foreign countries require a part ownership of the local operation of the multinational company.[7] After a length of time, or when the makeup of the government changes, it is not uncommon to have the organization's holdings in a country "nationalized" by the foreign government.

Sociological factors. Behavioral patterns of workers in other cultures vary greatly. For example, in some cultures, the drive to work hard may be less than the drive for leisure time or other activities. This is particularly true in some underdeveloped countries. Even in some highly developed societies, such as Sweden, certain laws permit workers to make as much money in unemployment income as they would have had they worked during the same period. The leadership role of the manager, so well established in our own culture, is not so well accepted in others. In some cases, organizations have found it difficult to instill in foreign managers the need to accept responsibility and to use their authority over other workers. In Japan, the cultural philosophy of "lifelong employment" not only limits selection processes but how employees are rewarded.[8] Since the Japanese system is so heavily founded on the principle of seniority, the use of the merit system (i.e., rewards based on levels of individual performance) is restricted, limiting the motivational influence of management. Finally, managers must be aware that identification with certain groups can be a significant factor. Membership in certain groups— sex, age, caste, religion, or political associations—may reflect the degree to which the individual has access to economic resources, social relations, and hence, power. This affects not only whom the organization can hire, but with whom they must interact in order to perform as effectively as possible.

Cultural factors have become and will continue to be important considerations for managers operating in a foreign environment. However, despite these drawbacks in the social environment, managers should not lose sight of two factors. First, many international operations of U.S. based firms are highly profitable and in some cases, give the companies a higher level of return than its domestic operations do. These organizations *adapt* to the environment—in this case, the cultural environment. Second, some foreign companies have significant holdings in the U.S. For example, Volkswagen has an assembly plant here, Shell is a foreign-owned company, and the British Petroleum Company has a majority ownership share of Sohio, one of the largest contributors to the construction of the Alaskan oil pipeline.[9]

Technological environment.   From the point of view of management, developments in the technological environment are not only the fastest to unfold but can have the most far-reaching impact on the organization in extending or constraining its growth. For example, the introduction of microcomputer technology, resulting in the development of the pocket calculator, has proven to be a boon to the business-machine industry. It has, however, nearly eliminated the market for slide rules. In a similar vein, one can imagine the impact of the low-cost digital watch on the wristwatch industry.

Managers are generally concerned with two components of the technological environment: the process of innovation; and the process of technology transfer. The *process of innovation* refers to the efforts in the basic sciences to develop new technologies, processes, methods, and products.[10] In many organizations, this process is commonly called research and development (R&D). Examples, which are numerous, include laser technology and self-developing film used in cameras produced by Polaroid and Kodak. (See chapter 15.)

The *process of technology transfer* involves taking the new technology from the laboratory to the market, that is, the transfer of science to useful products and applications.[11] Technology transfer can occur both within and between industries. For example, we have seen the initial use of video-tape recorders by the television networks transferred into a commercial product that can be found in many homes today. Similarly, in less than twenty years, computer technology has progressed from large-scale units located only in the largest organizations to much smaller, efficient units that can be found in smaller organizations and even in some homes. Technologies can cross into other industries. Laser technology, for example, is used not only in medical surgery, but also to find flaws in metal products.

Factors in the technological environment have at least two important implications for managers. First is the knowledge that the primary impact of new technologies will be *increased product obsolescence* and *competition*. The risks, dramatized by rapid technological advances, can be offset by the identification of new opportunities for the organization to market its products and services. Second, there is the need for many organizations to develop sophisticated *monitoring and forecasting* methods and techniques. Managers must develop conceptual and diagnostic *skills* in order to monitor new technological developments, both within and outside their industry, in order for the organization to maintain a competitive position.

Environmental Dimensions

Our description of the individual components of an organization's environment—economic, political, social, and technological—serves as a mechanism to develop the *dimensions* of an organization's environment.

EXHIBIT 4–4   Environmental Dimensions

		DEGREE OF CHANGE	
		Stable	*Dynamic*
DEGREE OF COMPLEXITY	*Simple*	Stable, predictable environment Few products and services Limited number of customers, suppliers, and competitors Minimal need for sophisticated knowledge	Dynamic, unpredictable environment Few products and services Limited number of customers, suppliers, and competitors Minimal need for sophisticated knowledge
	Complex	Stable, predictable environment Many products and services Many customers, suppliers, and competitors High need for sophisticated knowledge	Dynamic, unpredictable environment Many products and services Many customers, suppliers, and competitors High need for sophisticated knowledge

UNCERTAINTY

As shown in exhibit 4–4, we have identified two key dimensions of the environment: degree of change; and degree of complexity.[12] These dimensions can be described as follows:

1. *Degree of change.* This dimension is the extent to which components of the environment are stable or in a dynamic state. It therefore describes whether a manager can predict future events, because a given environmental situation reoccurs frequently through time, or whether changes are so frequent that predictability of events is low. For example, a pottery manufacturer can expect to produce the same type of product year after year. On the other hand, a vice squad in a police department must treat each case differently with many unexpected findings and results.

A variety of factors can make an environment stable or dynamic, including unpredictable shifts in the economy, rapid change in customer preferences and demands, an unstable government, unnoticed changes in population characteristics, growth in the influence of interest groups, and a rapidly changing technology. The term *dynamic* does not refer to environmental factors that are "variable," such as the weather. For example, the demand for heating oil is strongest during the winter months, but this is known and can be forecast by the producer. Rather, a dynamic component is something that is not expected because it cannot be predicted from past patterns.

2. *Degree of complexity.* An organization's environment can range from simple to complex. Two factors contribute to the complexity of an organization's environment.[13] First, the number of units with which interaction is required—that is, the number of customers, suppliers, and competi-

tors—ranges from few in a simple environment to many in a complex environment. The manager of a dairy may interact with only a few owners of dairy herds and with fellow dairy owners. On the other hand, a flight director at N.A.S.A. may have to interact with a wide variety of individuals and contributing companies. Second, an environment becomes complex to the extent that it requires the organization to have a great deal of *sophisticated knowledge* about products, customers, and so on. In this respect, the dairy manager operates in a simple environment because processing milk from the farm to the grocery refrigerated case is relatively uncomplicated. The flight director at N.A.S.A., however, must be knowledgeable in all components of the operation, from propulsion and communications to life-support systems and reentry processes. To perform this role, the individual must acquire a complex set of knowledge, skills, and information. Hospitals, full-service banks, and computer manufacturers can also be considered as operating in complex environments.

Environmental quadrants.   A simplified way of studying the dimensions of an organization's environment is to divide each dimension in half, creating four quadrants as shown in exhibit 4–4. These four quadrants correspond to different environments faced by organizations.

Quadrant I corresponds to an environment that is stable and fairly predictable. Generally there are few products with a limited number of customers, suppliers, and competitors. Such an environment would describe that of a container company specializing in cardboard boxes. The environment has remained relatively unchanged over the years. In addition, the sources of raw materials, the number of competitors, and the major customers are few and easily identifiable.

Quadrant II is similar to the environment of quadrant I with respect to the degree of change, but the environment has become more complex. In other words, the number of customers, suppliers, and competitors and the sophistication of knowledge have increased. Examples include a home appliance manufacturer, such as Whirlpool or Maytag, large accounting firms, and a savings and loan company. In each case, not only is competition increased, but the variety of customers and the degree of knowledge associated with serving these customers is significantly greater than is the case for the cardboard box company.

Quadrant III organizations have a dynamic environment involving a limited number of customers, suppliers, and competitors. This is representative of the environment for a clothing manufacturer that sells its goods to retail outlets. The key to the dynamic nature of the environment is the rapidly changing styles of clothing, particularly men's and women's high-fashion goods.

Finally, *Quadrant IV* presents an environment that is both complex and dynamic. Not only is the environment highly unpredictable with respect to events and trends, but the number of customers, suppliers, and competitors and the degree of knowledge needed to compete is dramatically greater than in other quadrants. Organizations involved in electronics, computer software, and pocket calculators operate in this type of environment. Another example would be a public hospital that is faced with a rapidly changing and unpredictable environment, particularly with respect to new technological innovations (e.g., computer-based diagnostic equipment, microsurgery, and life-support systems) and the political climate (e.g., national health insurance, legislative control over costs). In addition, it must contend with an ever-expanding populace and with competition from the growing number of health maintenance organizations.

Environmental Uncertainty.   As exhibit 4–4 also shows, the two environmental dimensions may be combined to determine *environmental uncertainty*.[14] As the environment moves from stable-simple to dynamic-complex, the absence of concrete information about the environment and the lack of knowledge about the effects of specific organizational actions increases to such an extent that managerial decision making becomes a highly uncertain process. In our quadrant I example, decisions made by managers in container firms appear to be influenced by only a few factors and variables. Decisions can therefore be made with some *certainty* about the results. On the other hand, the hospital administrator in quadrant IV faces a quite uncertain state with respect to the attitudes, behavior, and actions of customers, suppliers, and competitors. The decisions are therefore made under conditions of *uncertainty*.

Summary

As shown in exhibit 4–5, an analysis of the environment is important to an organization because it provides a set of factors that are critical to managerial effectiveness. These include opportunities, threats, and constraints.

1. The environment identifies a set of *opportunities* for the organization to provide distinct goods or services. This is an important element. As we discussed in chapter 2, the management process begins with "deciding what to do"—in other words, recognizing opportunities for managerial action. The energy crisis of the 1970s and beyond has provided opportunities for organizations to develop other sources of fuel (e.g., solar, oil shale), to look into methods of energy efficiency (e.g., insulation of homes, more efficient electric motors), and so on.

2. At the same time, certain *threats* from the environment can become important. For example: (1) companies such as Singer are concerned that the demand for sewing machines will decline as more women take full-time jobs; (2) the gasoline situation has significantly influenced the recreational vehicle industry; and (3) a recession economy may cause the general public to cut back on charitable donations.

3. The environment provides certain *constraints* to managerial and organizational action. As we pointed out earlier in this chapter, the activities of organizations can be limited by governmental regulation, by cultural norms, by limited financial resources in the investment market, by limitations of existing technologies, and by many other external elements.

The combination of environmental opportunities, threats, and constraints establishes the foundation for future managerial action. In a basic sense, the environment dictates what the organization *might do* with respect to interactions with customers, suppliers, and competitors.[15]

EXHIBIT 4–5   Analysis of the External Environment: A Summary

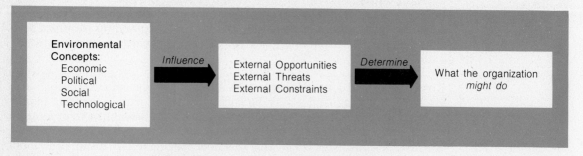

THE INTERNAL ENVIRONMENT OF ORGANIZATIONS

Environmental opportunities to produce and market goods and services provide a basis for organizational existence. In the automobile industry, for example, opportunities were recognized by General Motors for diesel powered cars, Porsche found a niche for itself in expensive sports cars, while Jeep (now a part of American Motors) has profited from market opportunities in off-the-road vehicles.

For an organization to capitalize on environmental opportunities, however, it must have the capacity and ability to accomplish, against many sources of opposition, what it sets out to do. This capacity and ability to achieve stated goals is related to the *resources* of the organization. In basic terms, environmental opportunities establish what an organization *might do;* the resources of an organization dictate what it *can do.*

Our discussion of the organization's internal environment will consist of three parts. First, we will identify the major resources of an organization. Second, the special case of managerial values, as they relate to organizational resources, will be discussed. Finally, the process of identifying resource strategies, weaknesses, and particular competencies will be discussed.

Organizational Resources

All organizations have at least four types of resources they can use to achieve their goals: financial; physical; human; and system and technological capabilities. These are shown in exhibit 4–6.

Financial Resources.   Financial resources are among the most important to all types of organizations, both profit making and not for profit alike. Three activities related to financial resources are important to managers:

1. *Acquisition of financial resources.* Managers are continually concerned with the *sources* of funds. Three major sources exist: (a) sale of equity on stock; (b) use of debt issues such as bonds; and (c) internal sources, particularly net income.
2. *Allocation of financial resources.* Commonly referred to as the *budgeting process,* allocating financial resources is providing funds to specific units

EXHIBIT 4–6
Organizational
Resources

RESOURCE	DESCRIPTION
Financial Resources	The acquisition, allocation, and control of money for financing plant construction, inventory, research and development, receivables, and working capital; involves, for example, cash flow, debt capacity, and new equity available.
Physical Resources	Includes: (1) efficient manufacturing plants and other facilities; (2) location of facilities with respect to markets, suppliers, or utilities; and (3) ownership or contractual access to needed raw materials.
Human Resources	The human resources include, but are not limited to, *specialized personnel* (engineers, scientists, and skilled labor) and skilled and experienced *management.*
System and Technological Resources	Expertise and particular competence in *process* elements (quality control systems, information systems, distribution systems, and the like) and *outputs* (patents, brand loyalty, and high-quality product)

or departments based on certain criteria. Frequently, most organizations find that the demand for funds is greater than the funds available. Generally speaking, organizations attempt to allocate financial resources where they can get the greatest return or where the survival of the unit is at stake. This poses a dilemma for many organizations. For example, should Ford Motor allocate funds to its highly successful European division in order to maintain high profit levels, or should funds be given to its less-successful domestic operations in order to regain a strong profit position? Should B. F. Goodrich continue to support its very profitable chemical and plastics division, or invest a majority of financial resources in the tire division, which has been less profitable in current times? Should the Mayo Clinic use its limited funds for expansion of the hospital, or for the purchase of the latest diagnostic equipment? Each example deals with the problem of allocating scarce financial resources to internal operations.

3. *Controlling financial resources.* Organizations must know how effectively financial resources are being *utilized.* Many financial tools can be used to assess an organization's short- and long-term financial resource performance, including ratio analysis, cash flow analysis, and computer-based financial models. In addition to these analyses, organizations have found it useful to calculate the amount of resources that it will have to reinvest in order to maintain or facilitate its current growth position. Some of the more important control procedures will be discussed in greater depth in chapter 17.

Physical Resources. Physical resources include the ownership and accessibility of physical plants and raw materials. At least three types of physical resources are important to managers:

1. *Physical plant.* This resource relates to the existence and level of *efficiency* of manufacturing plants, research and testing facilities, warehouses, office buildings, and other equipment. For example, the Japanese are known for their highly efficient steel plants, IBM for its research facilities, and Coors for its large brewery. As a physical plant, Walt Disney World in Florida is known for its efficiency as a people mover.

2. *Location of the physical plant.* Beyond the obvious benefits of efficiency and effectiveness, the *location* of the physical plant can be of great importance. The important features include closeness to customers and suppliers, accessibility to transportation, and availability of skilled labor. For example, the image of Sears as a retailer is enhanced by the neighborhood location of its major stores and catalogue outlets. The proximity of oil refineries to drilling and producing sites along the U.S. Gulf Coast is a benefit to various energy companies, and the center of financial activity in New York is a major reason why many corporate headquarters are located there.

3. *Raw material reserves.* Access to natural resources, by *ownership* or *contractual obligations,* can also be considered a physical resource. For example, Boise Cascade, which specializes in wood products, owns vast timberland reserves, and energy firms own coal and uranium deposits. Even the minor league system for the Los Angeles Dodgers and the New York Yankees can be considered physical resources. Raw material reserves can also be acquired through long-term contracts. For example, utility companies have contracts for oil, gas, and coal.

Similar to financial resources, the physical resources of an organization are important not only for continued operation but also for growth of the organization.

Human Resources. Stated simply, human resources make the other resources of an organization work. Two broad categories of human resources can be identified:

1. *Specialized personnel.* Most organizations contain individuals with unique or specialized knowledge in manufacturing, distribution, or scientific fields. Included would be scientists and engineers, sales representatives, computer systems analysts, production and quality control supervisors, and the like.

2. *Managerial personnel.* Certain organizations are known for their excellence in managerial activities. For example, General Motors has been known for its almost endless stream of capable chief executives, Delta and Northwest Airlines are recognized in their industry for the professional skill of their managers, and Procter and Gamble and Federated Department Stores have long been identified as sources of well-trained managerial talent in the food processing and retail industries, respectively.

In chapter 10, we will discuss human resources in more detail.

"I CAN REMEMBER WHEN ALL WE NEEDED WAS SOMEONE WHO COULD CARVE AND SOMEONE WHO COULD SEW."

© 1979 by Sidney Harris/Wall Street Journal

System and Technological Resources.   The previously discussed resource elements generally concern those factors that organizations have at their disposal to produce goods and services. Some organizations, however, have developed certain capabilities in the manner in which they produce goods and services. Two such resource elements are system and technological capabilities.

1. *System capabilities*. System capabilities are those *process* aspects that tend to support the main functions of the organization, such as quality control models, reward policies, and distribution systems. For example, Dow is known for its financial information systems, Lincoln Electric for its profit sharing, and Avon Products for its distribution system.

2. *Technological capabilities*. System capabilities concern certain process elements of an organization; technological capabilities deal more with the particular *output* of the firm. Examples include patents, customer brand loyalty, or a recognized high-quality product. Illustrations of technological capabilities include Polaroid's longstanding patent on its cameras, the fierce brand loyalty given to such beers as Coors and Strohs, and the recognition awarded to automobiles such as Mercedes-Benz, Rolls Royce, Maserati, and Aston-Martin.

Managerial Values: A Special Case of Human Resources

Values represent an individual's wants, preferences, and likes/dislikes of particular things, conditions, or situations. They also consist of opinions about what is right, fair, just, or desirable, as they relate to specific behaviors.[16]

An important factor for managers to recognize is that one cannot separate the external environment, organizational resources, and managerial values from each other. Managers do not look exclusively at what an organization *might do* (i.e., environmental opportunities) and *can do* (i.e., state of the organization's resources); they become heavily influenced by what they personally *want to do* (i.e., managerial value systems).[17] This is the key role played by managerial values.

Values affect managerial behavior in many ways. For example, managerial values:

1. Influence a manager's perception of various situations and problems.
2. Influence a manager's decisions and solutions to problems.
3. Influence the way a manager looks at other individuals and groups of individuals, thus affecting interpersonal relationships.
4. Influence the extent to which a manager will be affected by organizational pressures and stress.
5. Influence not only the perception of individual and organizational success but the entire definition of achievement.

Of course, value systems are not the sole property of managers. Other employees who are not managers have value systems that may or may not be similar to that of certain higher level superiors.

The topic of managerial values has received increased attention from behavioral scientists and practicing managers during recent years. The literature has focused on values, on various classifications of values, and on the value differences among people, professions, and cultures. One of the most useful schemes classifies managerial values into six value orientations:[18]

1. *Theoretical values.* A strong theoretical value orientation would classify a person as being primarily interested in the discovery of truth and the systematic ordering of knowledge. Such people are generally intelligent and show interests that are empirical, critical, and rational.
2. *Economic values.* One who adheres to economic values would be oriented toward practical and useful aspects of work. They are interested in the production and consumption of goods and the uses and creation of wealth. The typical stereotype of the American businessperson would fit well into this category.
3. *Aesthetic values.* Dominant interests in artistic features of an object, with an emphasis on form, symmetry, grace, and harmony would characterize someone with strong aesthetic values.
4. *Social values.* A person with dominant social values would place a primary value on the love of people and the warmth of human relations. They value people as ends, rather than means, and tend to be kind, sympathetic, and unselfish.
5. *Political values.* A dominant orientation toward power, influence, and recognition would characterize one who adheres strongly to political values. Competition plays an important role in their lives, in which power is the salient motive.

6. *Religious values.* People with an orientation toward unity and creation of satisfying relations with the environment have strong religious values.

There are at least two important points that this, and other, value classification schemes highlight. First, most values may be viewed as being culturally derived; that is, the various values are *learned* by a person through interactions with parents, teachers, friends, and other individuals. Second, managers can *order* or set priorities for these values differently. An example of this for ministers, purchasing managers, and research and development managers is shown in exhibit 4–7.

EXHIBIT 4–7
Ordering of Values
for Three
Occupations

MINISTERS	PURCHASING MANAGERS	RESEARCH AND DEVELOPMENT MANAGERS
Religious	Economic	Theoretical
Social	Theoretical	Political
Aesthetic	Political	Economic
Political	Religious	Aesthetic
Theoretical	Aesthetic	Religious
Economic	Social	Social

Adapted from R. Tagiuri, "Purchasing Executive: General Manager or Specialist?" *Journal of Purchasing* (August 1967): 16-21.

Evaluation of Organizational Resources

To complete our discussion, it is important for managers to conduct a resource *evaluation.* Two steps usually are involved in the process of evaluating internal resources: (1) developing a resource profile; and (2) determining resource strengths and weaknesses.

The basic objective of developing a resource profile is to provide a better idea about the state of the organization's resources. An effective way of doing this is to develop the profile along functional areas of the company. This is shown in exhibit 4–8.

An obvious benefit of developing a resource profile is that it provides the means for identifying where the organization is strong and where it is weak. Stated differently, the strengths of an organization determine not only what it can do, but *what it can do particularly well.* Specific weaknesses indicate what the organization cannot do, or *what it has difficulty doing.* For example, consider a small bank in a large urban area. The size of the bank offers both strengths and weaknesses. Because it is small, it can handle the needs of individual customers (e.g., savings accounts, home mortgages, checking accounts, and the like) quickly and efficiently. On the other hand, because of its size, it may experience difficulty in attempting to satisfy the needs of larger customers, such as corporate requirements for a credit line, investments, and expansion loans.

Two important managerial implications can be derived from identifying organizational strengths and weaknesses. First, weaknesses point out the *constraints* for managerial action—constraints that must be dealt

EXHIBIT 4–8 Resource Profile by Functional Area

	R & D ENGINEERING	MANUFACTURING	MARKETING	FINANCE	MANAGEMENT

Financial Resources	$ for basic research, new product development, product improvements, and process improvements	$ for plant
		$ for equipment
		$ for inventory
		$ for labor
			$ for sales and promotion
			$ for distribution
			$ for service
			$ for market research
				Credit rating
				Credit availability
				Leverage
				Price/earnings ratio
					$ for planning system
					$ for control system
					$ for management development

Physical Resources	Size, age, and location of R&D facilities Size, age, and location of development facilities	No., location, size, and age of plants Degree of automation Type of equipment	No., and location of sales offices, warehouses and service facilities	No. of major lenders Dispersion of stock ownership No. and types of computers	Location of corporate headquarters
Human Resources	Nos., types, and ages of key scientists and engineers Turnover of key personnel	Nos., types, and ages of key staff personnel and foreman Turnover of key personnel	Nos., types, and ages of key salesmen Marketing staff Turnover of key personnel	Nos., types, and ages of key financial and accounting personnel Turnover of key personnel	Nos., types, and age of key managers and corporate staff Turnover of key personnel Quality of corporate staff
Systems and Technological Resources	System to monitor technological developments No. patients No. new products % of sales from new products Relative product quality	Nature and sophistication of —Purchasing system —Product scheduling system —Quality control system Raw materials availability Trends in total constant $ Per-unit costs for: —Raw materials and purchased parts —Direct labor and equipment Productivity Capacity utilization Unionization	Nature and sophistication of: —Distribution —Service system —Pricing and credit staff —Market research staff Trends in total constant $ Per-unit costs for: —Sales and promotion —Distribution and service % retail outlet coverage Key account advantages Price competitiveness Breadth of product line Brand loyalty Service effectiveness	Type and sophistication of: —Cash management system —Corporate financial models —Accounting system	Sophistication of planning and control systems Delegation of authority Measurement of reward system Corporate image prestige Influence with regulatory and governmental agencies

Adapted from: C. W. Hofer and D. Schendel, *Strategy Formulation: Analytical Concepts* (St. Paul, Minn.: West, 1978), p. 149.

with to avoid failure. In other words, does the organization have sufficient financial, physical, human, system and technological resources to undertake an action? If not, a "red flag" should be waved.

More importantly, strengths identify specific areas of competence that the organization has. These are the organizational activities that can be done *extremely well,* such as the following:

1. Excellence in engineering.
2. Low-cost, high-efficiency manufacturing plants.
3. Well-established and effective distribution networks.
4. Efficiency in customer service.
5. Brand loyalty to the organization's products and services.
6. Effective advertising campaigns.
7. High inventory turnover.
8. Ability to influence legislation.
9. Ownership or control of low-cost or scarce raw materials.
10. Availability of capital for expansion.
11. Proven training and development programs.
12. High-quality products.
13. Capable managerial staff.
14. Location of physical facilities.
15. Low turnover of key personnel.
16. Corporate image.

This list is by no means all-inclusive of the potential competencies of various organizations. The importance to managers is that performing this type of analysis provides valuable information concerning the capabilities of the organization with respect to *what it can do and cannot do.*

MATCHING EXTERNAL AND INTERNAL ENVIRONMENT COMPONENTS

In this chapter, we have attempted to describe an important aspect of the manager's job: the crucial activity of *diagnosing* the elements of the organization's external and internal environment. Our discussion, summarized in exhibit 4–9, has focused on two major aspects:

1. An analysis of the *external environment* provides an understanding of the opportunities, threats, and constraints associated with the process of producing goods and services for society. In a simplistic manner, such an analysis provides managers with a definition of *what might be done* by the organization.
2. An *internal environmental* analysis, focusing primarily on the resources of the organization, identifies the strengths and weaknesses of the organization, and hence its specific constraints and competencies. In a sense, this determines what the organization *can do.* Additionally, the evaluation of the tangible resources of the organization—financial, physical, and so on—must be supplemented with a clear understanding of the intentions of management. This is what we have termed the values and ethics of managers (see chapter 2)—what they *want to do* and *ought to do.*

EXHIBIT 4–9   Matching External and Internal Environmental Components

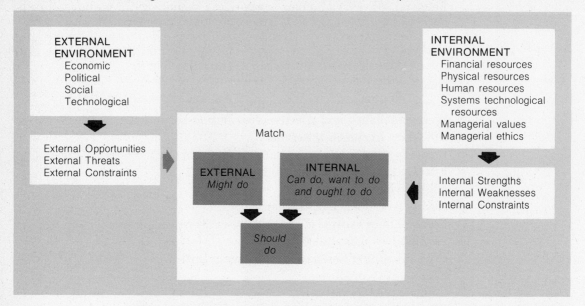

These analyses provide managers with information to make decisions that may affect the future of the organization, department, or unit. These decisions relate to the process of determining the proper *match* between the opportunities, threats, and constraints of the external environment with the strengths and weaknesses of the organization's resources; in other words, what the organization *should do.*

COMMENTS ON THE PRACTICE OF MANAGEMENT
(See p. 94.)

The textile industry is a classic case of the match—or mismatch—of the elements of the external and internal environment. Externally, companies in this important industry are faced with many serious threats, particularly foreign competition and the demand for skilled workers. Internally, outdated and inefficient plants coupled with a longstanding paternalistic view of employees have resulted in significant resource problems. To counter these threats and weaknesses, textile organizations must consider such activities as developing new products, diversifying out of the textile industry, renovating plants, improving employee working conditions and pay and benefit plans, and so on. Some managerial action is required because survival of the industry is at stake.

Deciding What Should be Done: Keys to Success

Developing a strong foundation on what might be done, what can be done, what ought to be done, and what management wants to be done leads to the inevitable decision of *what should be done.* Making decisions that will affect the activities of organizations, departments, or groups must be made with a clear understanding concerning the feasibility and capability of taking such actions.

To better understand the decision on "what should be done," let us examine a select set of examples. The examples will highlight some of the key success points associated with making such decisions.[19]

1. **Has the external environment been properly and accurately analyzed with respect to opportunities, threats, and constraints?**

   Ford Motor Company is known for both the best and the worst job of analyzing the external environment. The Mustang was a clear-cut success from the first day, while the Edsel proved to be a significant financial disaster. The main difference between the two models was that customer desires and transportation needs were accurately identified for the Mustang, but not for the Edsel. The Mustang was introduced when consumer desire for a small, sporty but economical car was growing. On the other hand, the Edsel was introduced into the large-car market, which was already overpopulated with Buicks, Oldsmobiles, Pontiacs, Chryslers, and to some extent, large Fords. Other examples of successful environmental analyses include the growth of discos, low-calorie beers, and discount department stores (e.g., K-Mart, Target, and the like).

2. **Is the decision consistent with organizational resources, both present and future?**

   The entry of IBM into the word-processing industry was consistent with its already established divisions. Word processing, basically a computerized information system, was a natural for IBM with its expertise in computers and electric typewriters. Kodak's decision to compete with Polaroid in the instant camera market was not only supported by their past experience and success in the still photo market, but also because they were a large firm with an enormous amount of resources (e.g., distribution network) to throw into the competition.

3. **How much risk is associated with the decision?**

   Competence in the aircraft-manufacturing industry involves a great deal of risk because of the huge outlays of money, fierce competition, and the limited number of customers. Even Boeing, the most successful of the firms, will invest money in the development of its new line of airplanes— the 757 and 767—that will equal more than *twice* its net worth.[20] Lockheed's turbo-prop Electra, McDonnell Douglas's DC-10, and the British-French Concorde are other examples of the great risk found in this industry.

   High risk is found even with the decisions made by such household names as Sears. The company, long known as the retailer to Middle America, recently attempted to change its marketing image.[21] In an attempt at market expansion, it decided to implement two new strategies: (1) enter into the high-fashion clothing market with higher-priced and quality garments to counter the growth of specialized retail stores; and (2) allow significant price reductions on many products in order to attract customers from the growing number of discount stores. The result of both these actions has been failure, forcing the management of Sears to totally reevaluate its decisions.

4. **What is the impact of the personal values and aspiration of key managers?**

As we have discussed, the values, preferences, and desires of managers play an important role in the direction of many organizations. For example, in the newspaper industry, *The New York Times* and *The Washington Post* generally reflect the attitudes and philosophies of the major owners. Also, some years ago, Pan American Airlines, under the executive direction of Juan Trippe, sought for some time to gain governmental approval as the "flag" airline of the United States, much the same as B.O.A.C., Air France, and KLM had achieved in their countries. This effort by Trippe not only failed, but the growth of foreign competition and the lack of acquisition of domestic routes has proved troublesome for Pan Am for many years.

As these limited examples illustrate, the match between environmental opportunities and resource capabilities is a most critical decision for managers. Although we have chosen to illustrate the decisions of top managers in well-known organizations, it should not be thought that such decisions are made by the executive management level only. The decision process of matching opportunities with capabilities occurs at *all levels* in the organization, from executives to first-line managers.

For example, consider the manager of a group of accountants in a large accounting firm who is responsible for auditing the accounts of an electronics company. From an *external* environmental standpoint, our manager is concerned with, among other things, new rules and guidelines established by professional and governmental bodies concerning the auditing process and the need by the client for an accurate and timely job. *Internally,* the manager is aware that not only is the audit group understaffed, but the majority of the subordinate accountants have less than one year's experience with the firm as auditors.

Similarly, consider the situation faced by the supervisor of a pathology laboratory in a large urban hospital. The hospital is in the planning stage for expanding from a 400- to 600-bed capacity. The supervisor recognizes that this expansion will affect the ability of the lab to handle the increase in patient tests. Since laboratory input into the expansion planning is desired, the supervisor must decide whether the increase in workload can be handled by increasing personnel strength in the lab, by the purchase of more automated equipment, or some combination of both. Just the same as the president of IBM, Sears, or Boeing, the auditing manager and the lab supervisor must be able to match these environmental demands with the capabilities of the available resources—human, physical, financial, and the like. In chapters 5 and 6 we will redefine "what should be done" as organizational *goals* and *strategy*.

Identification of factors in the organization's external and internal environment is a crucial activity in which managers must engage in order to improve their levels of effectiveness. Once these factors have been identified, the next step is to attempt to forecast events in the future.

FORECASTING

Forecasting concerns the process of predicting future conditions that will guide and affect the activities, behavior, and impact of organizational actions. As such, forecasts have an important role to play not only in the planning function but in the entire management process. Our discussion of forecasting will focus on two major elements: information inputs, and techniques of forecasting.

Information Inputs into Forecasting

Forecasting is frequently regarded as one of the main inputs into the organizational planning process. Forecasting, however, is only as good as the quality and validity of the information that is used to make predictions. Assessing information quality and validity is a difficult endeavor because it is usually only through experience or over time that we can judge these factors. Two major issues are related to information inputs into the forecasting process: the methods and sources of information.

Methods of Acquiring Forecasting Information.   Organizations and managers can acquire or collect information for forecasting purposes in at least three ways. First, there is *informal monitoring* by the manager. It is termed informal because the manager does not actively seek out information, but keeps his or her eyes and ears open to all inputs during the normal work schedule. For example, a purchasing agent for a hospital may listen carefully to various presentations by representatives of supply companies to detect if a price increase may occur in the near future for the products that the hospital purchases.

The second method is termed *formal scanning* because it involves a purposeful effort on the part of the organization to monitor the activities in the environment. Frequently, organizations set up a formal managerial position that has the responsibility for examining all media documents, speeches by politicians, and various reports from external sources (e.g., chamber of commerce) for important information.

Finally, there is the *formal search* method, which is a scanning process purposefully undertaken by the organization to obtain information for specific forecasting purposes. Such activities are usually performed by formal organizational units, such as market research or the fast growing environmental monitoring department.[22]

Sources of Forecasting Information.   A way of classifying the sources of information is by their origin: whether they are external or internal to the organization. *External sources* include suppliers, customers, professional acquaintances, and various media, such as trade publications, newspapers, magazines, and conferences. *Internal sources* can focus on contacts with superiors, peers, and subordinates through meetings, reports, and informal conversations.

In a study of managers in forecasting roles, it was found that managers show a great preference for personal sources, such as contacts with suppliers, customers, and colleagues, as opposed to impersonal sources, such as conferences and newspapers.[23] In other words, these managers rely heavily on face-to-face communications for the information they need. This strongly supports the need for managers to develop their informational roles and to sharpen their human skills, which are oriented toward interpersonal communications.

Forecasting Techniques

Managers can use a variety of techniques to forecast the possible occurrence of future events. Our discussion will focus on four broad categories of forecasting techniques: qualitative, time-series, causal models, and technological forecasting. It should be pointed out that this presentation of forecasting techniques is only a brief summary of those methods that are available. A more detailed discussion can be found in other sources.[24] An evaluation of the techniques is presented in exhibit 4–10.

Qualitative Techniques.   Qualitative techniques generally use informed experts when quantitative data are scarce or difficult to use. Three approaches are the most frequently used:

1. *Panel of executive opinion.* This method consists of combining and averaging top management's views concerning the event to be forecast. The organization generally brings together executives, sometimes at an offsite retreat, from areas such as sales, production, finance, purchasing, and staff positions. The advantages of this approach are that forecasts can be provided easily and quickly without elaborate statistics, and a range of management viewpoints can be considered.

2. *Delphi technique.* Delphi is another type of qualitative or judgmental technique that polls a panel of experts and gathers their opinions on specific topics. In the feedback gained through a succession of anonymous votes, a pattern of response to future events generally emerges.

3. *Historical analogy.* This technique is probably the most commonly used method of forecasting. It takes the form of past trends plotted on a graph or chart, providing a visual curve. It is based on the belief that future trends will develop in the same direction and at the same rate as past trends unless there is a clear indication of change.

Time-Series.   The general approach of time-series forecasts is to identify a pattern representing a combination of trend, seasonal, and cyclical factors based on historical data. That pattern is then smoothed to eliminate the effect of random fluctuations and extrapolated into the future to provide a forecast.

1. *Trend projection.* This technique fits a trend line to a mathematical equation and then projects it into the future by means of this equation. Data requirements vary with the techniques used, but several years of historical data are usually required.

2. *Moving average.* Each point of a moving average of a time-series is the arithmetic or weighted average of a number of points of the variable under study (e.g., sales). The number of data points is chosen so that the effects of seasonal variations or irregularities are eliminated.

3. *Exponential smoothing.* This technique is similar to the moving average, except that more recent data points are given more weight. The new forecast is equal to the old one plus some proportion of the past forecasting error.

EXHIBIT 4–10 Summary of Forecasting Techniques

TECHNIQUE	EXAMPLE APPLICATIONS	ACCURACY			TIME TO DEVELOP	TOTAL COST
		Short Term	Med. Term	Long Term		
Qualitative						
Exec. Opinion	New product development, sales, earnings	Fair	Fair	Poor	3 weeks	Mod. expensive
Delphi	Product and service development, technological breakthroughs	Good	Good	Good	3 months	Mod. expensive
Historical analogy	Sales, earnings	Poor	Fair	Fair	2 months	Inexpensive
Time-Series						
Trend projection	Sales, earnings, new product introduction	Very good	Good	Good	1 day	Inexpensive
Moving average	Sales, inventory control	Fair	Poor	Poor	1 day	Inexpensive
Exponential smoothing	Production and inventory control, sales, earnings	Good	Good	Poor	1 day	Inexpensive
Causal Models						
Regression analysis	Sales, earnings	Very good	Very good	Fair	1 month	Inexpensive
Econometric models	GNP, sales, economy shifts	Very good	Good	Good	3 months or more	Expensive
Economic indicators	Sales, inventory, purchases	Good	Fair	Poor	1 month	Inexpensive
Technological Forecasting						
Cross-impact	Impact of new developments	Good	Good	Fair	1 month	Inexpensive
Morphological analysis	New uses for product developments	Good	Good	Fair	1 month	Inexpensive
Substitution effect	Substitution of new product for old	Poor	Fair	Fair	3 months	Inexpensive

Adapted from J. C. Chambers, S. Mullick, and D. D. Smith, "How to Choose the Right Forecasting Technique," *Harvard Business Review* (July–August 1971); 55–64.

Causal Models.   When historical data are available and enough analysis has been performed to spell out *explicitly* the relationships between the factor to be forecast (sales) and other factors (price, advertising, and product availability), a causal model can be constructed. It expresses mathematically the relevant causal relationships and takes into account everything known of the dynamics of the variables under study.

1. *Regression analysis.* This method assumes that the variable to be forecast can be predicted on the basis of the value of one or more independent variables. For example, if auto sales were the variable to be forecast, they might be dependent on the economy, personal income, price, and time.

2. *Econometric models.* This approach uses a system of regression equations that take into account the interaction between various segments of the economy and/or organizational activities. While such models are useful in forecasting, their major use has been in attempting to answer the perennial "what if" questions. These also allow managers to investigate the impact of various changes in the environment and in major segments of the organization's services.

3. *Economic indicators.* Economic indicators are data that can forecast the future state of the economy, such as the dollar amounts of sales for raw materials. Each indicator may predict an event or change in the economy (leading indicator), coincide with the event (coincident indicator), or lag behind the event (lagging indicator).

Technological Forecasting.   Technological forecasting is a special forecasting approach that deals specifically with technological changes that can affect the organization.[25] The rapid pace of technological change has led many firms, hospitals, governments, and other organizations to recognize the importance of predicting future technological developments. Such technological developments as word processing, computerized calculators, lasers, and space technologies have drastically affected the operations of many organizations. While many techniques are incorporated into the classification (including the Delphi technique and trend projection), three are most widely used:

1. *Cross-impact analysis.* This technique attempts to identify and determine the significance of relationships and interactions between specific events.[26] A matrix displaying a two- or three-dimensional array of variables, factors, goals, and issues usually is developed. For example, the impact of solar heating is of interest to the housing industry as well as to energy companies and the management of many commercial buildings.

2. *Morphological analysis.* This technique consists of identifying the relevant dimensions of the object, listing all varieties and combinations of those dimensions, and finding practical applications for them.[27] For example, managers have successfully used this technique to find multiple uses for transistors, lasers, and microcircuitry.

3. *Substitution effect.* The substitution phenomenon is based on the belief that one product or technology that exhibits a relative improvement in

performance over the older product or technology will eventually be substituted for the factor with the lower performance. Mathematical formulations have been developed that indicate that such substitutions occur in a relatively patterned fashion for many technologies. Examples include jet engines over prop engines, microwave over conventional cooking, radial tires over bias-belted tires.

ENVIRONMENTAL ANALYSIS AND THE MANAGER'S JOB

Analyzing an organization's external and internal environment is a crucial activity because it sets the stage for the entire management process. It is also an activity in which the development and application of managerial skills and roles play an important part.

Each of the main managerial *skills* are involved with the environmental analysis process. Technical skills are required to perform such activities as forecasting. Interacting with people internal and external to the organization, particularly when gathering information for analysis, imvolves important human skills. Conceptual skills come to the forefront as the manager begins the process of matching external and internal environmental data. Finally, because the environmental process is investigative in nature, diagnostic skills may be the most important. In a sense, the development of these skills may be an important resource of the organization.

The environmental analysis process also involves each of the managerial *roles*. Maintaining liaison networks of outside contracts and generally keeping in touch with various situations—an interpersonal role—contributes to the overall effectiveness of the analysis process. The informational roles, especially the monitor role, are also an important part of this activity. Great emphasis must be placed on receiving information from the environment and transmitting it through the organization. The decisional roles are related not only to what needs to be done—the environmental role—but also to activities that are concerned with the evaluation and use of organizational resources—the resource allocator role.

SUMMARY FOR THE MANAGER

1. The process of analyzing the organization's external and internal environments is one of the most important activities performed by managers. It is important not only because such an analysis provides an evaluation of the state of the organization, but also because the resulting decision will have a long-term impact on the performance of the organization.

2. The external environment analysis highlights three crucial points for managers. First, it forces managers to view the external environment as consisting of economic, political, social, and technological components, each of which may have a different level of importance to and impact on the organization. Second, the external environment creates different degrees of uncertainty for the manager and the organization. Since high uncertainty is not desired by organizations, managers will attempt to control the uncertainty through various actions. Finally, the external environment provides opportunities, demands, and constraints for the organization—in essence, it draws attention to what the organization *might do.*

3. The internal environmental analysis focuses on the resources of the organization—financial, physical, human, and system and technological—which establish the competencies and constraints for future activities, or what the organization *can do.* Managerial values play an important part in the activities of an organization. These are the desires and preferences of management—what we have termed *what they want to do.*

4. From a managerial *function* viewpoint, an external and internal environment analysis provides necessary input into the *planning* function, which in turn guides the remainder of the managerial functions.

5. Together, the opportunities in the external environment and the main competencies of the internal resources play a major role in determining what the organization *should do.* The information and decisions that evolve from this environmental analysis stage serve as the important first step of the management process.

6. A variety of techniques are available to the manager to predict the occurrence of an event in the future, including qualitative, time-series, technological forecasting, and causal models. It is important for the manager to remember that forecasts, no matter how performed, are only as good as the quality and validity of the input information.

7. Performing an internal and external environmental analysis is not only for executive managers. The procedures apply to most levels of management, including first-line managers. At a minimum, all managers must get involved with evaluating the resources at their disposal in order to determine the particular competencies and constraints for future action.

8. Managerial skills and roles are important for the environmental analysis process. In a sense, the development of skills and performance in these roles may in turn become important resources of the organization.

QUESTIONS FOR REVIEW AND DISCUSSION

1. Why has it become more important for managers to analyze carefully the external environment before making major policy decisions?
2. What factors contribute to environmental uncertainty for an organization?
3. What are some important demographic trends that managers should recognize?
4. In what types of industries would changes in the technological environment be an important external component?
5. What are the important human resources of an organization?
6. How do managerial values affect organizational decisions?
7. Why have differences in managerial values systems been reported in cross-cultural studies?
8. Can you identify certain products whose image or acceptance is an important internal resource strength?
9. Why is it important to identify the internal competencies of an organization?
10. What role does forecasting play in the manager's job?

NOTES

1. L. Kraar, "The Multinationals Get Smarter About Political Risks," *Fortune* (March 24, 1980): 86–103.

2. T. Alexander, "Why Bureaucracy Keeps Growing," *Fortune* (May 7, 1979): 166.

3. See, "Red Tape Blues," *Newsweek* (August 30, 1976): 77.

4. "An Uneven Flow of Management Talent," *Business Week* (February 20, 1978): 87.

5. D. T. Hall, *Careers in Organizations* (Santa Monica, Calif.: Goodyear, 1976), p. 170.

6. R. Azzi, "The Saudis Go for Broke," *Fortune* (July 31, 1978): 110–19.

7. N. Foy and H. Gordon, "Worker Participation: Contrasts in Three Countries," *Harvard Business Review* (May–June 1966): 358–73.

8. "Japanese Managers Tell How Their System Works,"

Fortune (November 1977): 127–38.

9. A. L. Morner, "For Sohio, It Was Alaskan Oil—or Bust," *Fortune* (April 1977): 172–86.

10. V. J. Baldridge and R. Burnham, "Organizational Innovation: Individual, Organizational and Environmental Impacts," *Administrative Science Quarterly* (June 1975): 165–76.

11. J. M. Utterback, "Innovation in Industry and the Diffusion of Technology" *Science* (February 1974):620–26; and W. H. Gruber and D. G. Marquis, eds., *Factors in the Transfer of Technology* (Cambridge, Mass.: MIT Press, 1971).

12. H. Mintzberg, *The Structuring of Organizations* (Englewood Cliffs, N.J.: Prentice-Hall, 1979), p. 286.

13. H. E. Aldrich, *Organization & Environment* (Englewood Cliffs, N.J.: Prentice-Hall, 1979), p. 74.

14. R. Duncan, "Characteristics of Organizational Environments and Perceived Environmental Uncertainty," *Administrative Science Quarterly* (September 1972): 313–27.

15. K. Andrews, *The Concept of Corporate Strategy* (Homewood, Ill.: Dow Jones-Irwin, 1971), p. 37.

16. C. R. Christensen, K. R. Andrews, and J. L. Bower, *Business Policy,* 4th ed. (Homewood, Ill.: Richard D. Irwin, 1978), pp. 448–54.

17. M. Rokeach, *The Nature of Human Values* (New York: Free Press, 1973), p. 5.

18. G. Allport, P. Vernon, and G. Lindzey, *Study of Values* (Boston: Houghton Mifflin, 1960).

19. Andrews, p. 38.

20. L. Kraar, "Boeing Takes a Bold Plunge to Keep Flying High," *Fortune* (September 25, 1978): 42–53.

21. W. Robertson, "How Sears' Retailing Strategy Backfired," *Fortune* (May 8, 1978): 103–4.

22. P. Lorange and R. F. Vancil, "How to Design a Strategic Planning System," *Harvard Business Review* (September–October 1976): 75–81.

23. F. J. Aguilar, *Scanning the Business Environment* (New York: Macmillan, 1967).

24. S. C. Wheelwright and D. G. Clarke, "Corporate Forecasting: Promise and Reality," *Harvard Business Review* (November–December 1976): 52; and R. O'Connor, *Planning Under Uncertainty* (New York: Conference Board, 1978), pp. 2–3.

25. J. R. Bright, ed., *Technological Forecasting for Industry and Government* (Englewood Cliffs, N.J.: Prentice-Hall, 1968).

26. W. L. Swager, "Technological Forecasting in Planning," *Business Horizons* (February 1973): 37–44.

27. C. R. O'Neal, "New Approaches to Technological Forecasting: Morphological Analysis," *Business Horizons* (December 1970): 47–58.

ADDITIONAL REFERENCES

Aguiler, F. *Scanning the Business Environment.* New York: Macmillan, 1967.

Burns, T., and Stalker, G. M. *The Management of Innovation.* London: Tavistock, 1961.

Downey, H. K.; Hellriegel, D.; and Slocum, J. "Environmental Uncertainty: The Construct and Its Application," *Administrative Science Quarterly* (December 1975): 613–29.

Elbing, A. O. "On the Applicability of Environmental Models." In *Contemporary Management: Issues and Viewpoints,* edited by J. W. McGuire. Englewood Cliffs, N.J.: Prentice-Hall, 1974.

Lawrence, P. R., and Lorsch, J. W. *Organization and Environment.* Cambridge, Mass.: Harvard University Press, 1967.

Levinson, H. *Organizational Diagnosis.* Cambridge, Mass.: Harvard University Press, 1972.

Meyer, M. W. *Environments and Organizations.* San Francisco: Jossey-Bass, 1978.

Paine, F. T., and Naumes, W. *Organizational Strategy and Policy.* Philadelphia: Saunders, 1978.

Rokeach, M. *Beliefs, Attitudes, and Values.* San Francisco: Jossey-Bass, 1968.

Starbuck, W. "Organizations and Their Environments." In *Handbook of Organizational and Industrial Psychology,* edited by M. D. Dunnett. Chicago: Rand McNally, 1976.

Terryberry, S. "The Evolution of Organizational Environments." *Administrative Science Quarterly* (March 1968): 590–613.

A CASE FOR ANALYSIS

Howard Johnson Company: The Changing of America

The orange roof restaurant of Howard Johnson's has been a landmark for Americans for many years. The company, which once was very much in tune with this country's population, has fallen on hard times. Companies like McDonald's and Marriott have long since put Howard Johnson's in their shadow with their food and hotel operations, respectively. In addition, the company's recent poor financial performance has ignited takeover rumors due to its depressed stock price. How and why has Howard Johnson Company lost its position? Speculations abound from many sources.

Some analysts believe that competition in the food and hotel fields has increased dramatically. There are far more fast food restaurants and motel/hotel complexes located all around the country now than there ever were during the time of the company's late founder, Howard Johnson, Sr. Competitors in these fields have also been more successful in their decisions regarding the location of their facilities than Howard Johnson's has been.

Still others point to the significant change in the eating habits of U.S. citizens. There has been the explosion of fast food outlets, such as McDonald's, Burger King, and the like. In addition, in many young families, both husband and wife work, and working wives tend to be interested more in entertainment in the evening than in cooking a meal. The Howard Johnson's highway restaurants, oriented to mom, dad, and the kiddies, and with bland menus and decor, have been losing out to some of the "theme" restaurants, such as Victoria Station, with more elaborate menus.

During the 1974 oil crisis, the company reacted by stopping nearly all of its expansion plans. Highway travel was way down, resulting in low occupancy rates at many of the Howard Johnson's motels. It took until 1977 for the company finally to regain its momentum for expansion.

Internally, many problems appeared to surface. The company had long adhered to its founder's philosophy of avoiding the use of debt, preferring instead to be as liquid in cash as possible. Expansions were financed primarily through internal funds and equity issues. There also appeared to be some problems within the management ranks at Howard Johnson's. Many managers seemed to sense the changes going on in the United States before the current chief executive, Howard Johnson, Jr., reawakened. It was not until a group of managers confronted the chief executive with their concerns that the company began to move again.

The movement to retain its once-prominent position has been slow but noticeable. First, 103 Ground Round restaurants have recently opened. With a turn-of-the-century atmosphere, they sell nostalgia and nightly musical entertainment along with a varied menu. Revenues from these new outlets have averaged nearly twice that of the orange roof restaurants.

The orange roofs are themselves undergoing some renovations. The fast food counters have been replaced by a salad bar, tropical and airy new interiors, and more service. There is concern by management, however, that the company may lose a high percentage of the older clientele who have continued to patronize the traditional restaurants.

Howard Johnson's problems are far from solved. Energy problems continue to be present, and inflation is eating into the income of Americans. Takeover rumors may become fact in the future. The key question is, has Howard Johnson Company awakened too late?

Adapted from "To Be and What to Be—That is the Question," Forbes *(May 1, 1978): 25.*

Questions for Discussion

1. Perform an external environmental analysis on Howard Johnson Company.
2. Perform an internal resource analysis on the company.
3. Do you agree with the current activities of the company? What should they do next?

EXPERIENTIAL EXERCISE

Analyzing the External Environment

Purpose

1. To examine some of the important components of an organization's external environment.
2. To identify certain opportunities, demands, constraints, and the degree of uncertainty for select organizations.

Required Understanding

The student should have a basic understanding of the components of the external environment.

How to Set Up the Exercise

Set up groups of four to eight students for the forty-five minute exercise. The groups should be separated from each other and asked to converse only with members of their own group.

Instructions for the Exercise

Exhibit 4–11 presents eight example organizations for which the students should provide an analysis of the external environment. The instructor may substitute or add to the list.

1. *Individually,* each of the group members should take one of the example organizations and provide an examination of that organization's external environment. The analysis should include: (a) an identification of some key environmental components; (b) a suggestion as to the degree of environmental uncertainty being faced by the firm (see exhibit 4–4); and (c) a recognition of some of the important opportunities, constraints, and demands originating from the environment.
2. As a *group,* combine and discuss the analyses performed in the previous stage of this exercise. Refine the individual analyses as needed.
3. The group analysis should be presented to the total class.
4. As an *option* to shorten the exercise, each group should be given one or two of the example organizations to analyze. The analyses would then be combined by the total class.

EXHIBIT 4–11   External Environmental Analysis Exercise

ORGANIZATION	ENVIRONMENTAL COMPONENT ANALYSES	UNCERTAINTY (QUADRANT)	OPPORTUNITIES, DEMANDS, CONSTRAINTS
IBM	1. Economic: 2. Political: 3. Social: 4. Technological:		
McDonald's Corporation	1. Economic: 2. Political: 3. Social: 4. Technological:		
Boeing Aircraft	1. Economic: 2. Political: 3. Social: 4. Technological:		
Urban Hospital	1. Economic: 2. Political: 3. Social: 4. Technological:		
AMTRAK	1. Economic: 2. Political: 3. Social: 4. Technological:		
Dallas Cowboy Football Team (or others)	1. Economic: 2. Political: 3. Social: 4. Technological:		
Coor's Brewery	1. Economic: 2. Political: 3. Social: 4. Technological:		
Levi-Strauss Company	1. Economic: 2. Political: 3. Social: 4. Technological:		

5

Management and Goals

CHAPTER OUTLINE

KEY POINTS IN THIS CHAPTER

1. Goals generally are formed from an internal and external environmental analysis of the organization and serve as guiding factors for most managerial functions.

2. Certain criteria for good goals exist that apply to any of the different types of goal frameworks.

3. The major characteristics of goals include an emphasis on measurement, multiplicity, and order.

4. Concern is given to nonmarket (social) goals as well as market goals. Rapidly changing societal values dictate an increased managerial concern over social issues.

5. An organization's social behavior can take the form of social obligations, social responsibility, and social responsiveness from which the responses of tokenism, functional change, and structural change originate.

6. Activities in pollution control, affirmative action, consumerism, urban development, and philanthropy should be measured. This is the function of the social audit.

7. Achieving organizational and social goals can be hampered by certain internal problems and a lack of recognition of a number of constraining factors.

8. The successful achievement of organizational and social goals requires performance in specific managerial functions and roles and the acquisition of important managerial skills.

THE PRACTICE OF MANAGEMENT

Organizational Goals: Teledyne, Inc.

When interviewed, most corporation executives would probably state with respect to their organization's goals: "We're profit oriented, not product oriented." The fact is that few companies really are that way. Teledyne is a rare exception. "Forget products," says President George Roberts, "here's the key: We create an attitude toward having high margins (i.e., returns on both sales and assets). In our internal system, the company can grow rapidly and its managers can be rewarded richly for that growth if they produce high margins. If they have had low margins, it's hard to get capital from the organization. No one likes to have trouble getting new money for expansion."

Roberts is saying nothing exceptional. What is exceptional is the way Teledyne—a producer of a variety of products including offshore drilling units, auto parts, machine tools, electronic components, unmanned aircraft, and Water Pik home appliances—practices what it preaches. There are very few companies of any size, and certainly none of the billion dollar class, that are as tight with a capital dollar as Teledyne. Texas Instruments, a company of equal size and technological orientation, will spend more than three times as much for capital spending projects. Many companies normally spend more for capital projects than they take in as cash. Not so with Teledyne. This is the real secret to the company's ability to grow.

The key is goal discipline: no ego trips, only new investments that will pay off quickly in the form of enhanced cash flow. Says Roberts: "The only way you can make money in some businesses is by not entering them. Internally we hold up high profit margin companies as examples. Our margin on sales is now over 7 percent after taxes, versus a national average for manufacturing of 5.4 percent. Since we run a broad cross-section of business, it is clear the rest of American industry can improve, too.

"Take any big old giant company like U.S. Steel. If they really accounted for their business conservatively and line by line in detail as we do, they might conclude that they didn't have any margins at all. We make the point that the margin on every product, every project, is important."

The effect of these goals on restricting risk and insisting on a high return on sales and assets, Roberts says, is that he is able to stop preaching. "Now everyone understands that all new projects should return at least 20 percent on total assets. [their goal] . . . This is so ingrained that few lower-returning proposals are ever presented anymore."

As for Chairman Henry Singleton, he is a scientist and an intellectual, but he has an old-fashioned respect for cash. You cannot pay bills with bookkeeping profits. He knows that companies have gone broke after reporting big profits for years—Penn Central, for example, and W.T. Grant. He wants to see the color of some of that money in his companies' reports. Above all, he wants each unit in Teledyne to focus its activities on achieving a high return on sales and assets—returns that can be utilized for overall corporate purposes.

Abridged from R. J. Flaherty, "The Singular Henry Singleton," Forbes (July 9, 1979): 45–50.

5

How many times have we read in a newspaper or magazine, or listened to the radio or television and heard such statements from various organizations as, "We are planning to increase our market share from 12 percent to 15 percent this year," or, "A 20 percent improvement in sales revenue is what we're aiming for during this fiscal period," or, "This administration's objective is to reduce government spending in this city by 25 percent," or "Our goal is to make the Super Bowl this season." Many company annual reports contain more lengthy statements such as, "We are setting a goal of 18 percent return on invested capital and 12 percent growth in sales for the upcoming year. These overall corporate goals have been established to motivate our employees to be number one in our industry and to be able to attract capital from the investment community necessary to enhance our continued growth." Each of these statements concerns the important element known as organizational goals.[1]

As we will discuss in this chapter, goals serve an important function in the continuing existence of organizations. Realistically developed, stated, and implemented goals can be the guiding principle for increased effectiveness and continued growth. On the other hand, unrealistically developed and/or improperly implemented goals can lead to questions about the level of performance or even the survival of the organization.

In this chapter we will discuss the concept of organizational goals in two major parts. First, we will present a general framework of organizational goals. The focus will be on the definition and importance of goals, the criteria for good goals, the various types and characteristics of goals, and certain problems with goals and the manager's job. The second part of our discussion will focus on a special case of organizational goals—the issue of organizational social behavior. As managers or future managers we must be concerned with how our actions, and the actions of the organizations we represent, affect the society in which we live.

MANAGERS AND ORGANIZATIONAL GOALS

Definition of *Organizational Goals*

Organizational goals are desired states of affairs or preferred results that organizations attempt to realize and achieve.[2] An acceptance of this definition implies the existence of at least two factors concerning the relationship between goals and management. First, goals are influenced by the *aspiration* of the key managers in an organization. This was brought out in the last chapter. In other words, the aspirations of management help to form the concept of "what they should do," which itself is the result of an external ("what they might do") and internal ("what they can do" and "what they want to do") environmental analysis. For example, a goal of McDonald's to "double the number of fast-food restaurants located outside the U.S. by 1985" assumes that: (1) there are sufficient market opportunities in foreign countries; (2) the organization currently has or can easily obtain adequate resources to achieve the goal; and (3) such a goal is desired by the management of the company.

Second, goals reflect a desired *end result* of organizational actions— that which they wish to achieve. McDonald's may want to increase the number of outlets, Delta Airlines may wish to increase sales, the United Auto Workers (UAW) may want to have all their represented workers covered with adequate medical insurance, and General Foods may desire a larger share of the breakfast cereal market. As we will shortly point out, there are a variety of goals that organizations may want to achieve simultaneously.

At the outset, we should state that we consider goals, objectives, and purposes to be interchangeable. Some writers consider objectives as means for achieving goals, and others reverse the definition.[3] In this book, we will not differentiate between these concepts.

Importance of Organizational Goals

Goals are important to organizations for four reasons, as shown in exhibit 5–1. First, goals provide guidance to the direction of efforts of individuals and groups in an organization. For example, consider two automobile manufacturers, Volvo and Honda. Volvo has stressed the production of a low volume of high-quality and high-priced cars. Honda, on the other hand, is oriented toward a high volume of functional cars at a relatively low price. Even though each of these firms is in the business of providing transportation products, we should expect the two differing goals will guide or lead to different ways of producing and marketing cars.

Second, goals affect how the organization *plans* and *organizes* its activities. Consider two universities—a large, state-supported institution, and a smaller, but growth-oriented private university. The growth orientation (i.e., the goal) of the private institution may cause its planners

EXHIBIT 5–1   The Centrality of Goals to Management

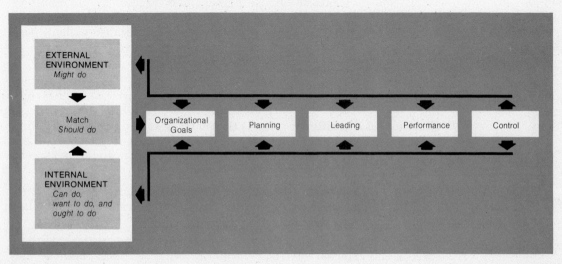

to be concerned with more external aspects—seeking outside funds from foundations and other agencies, drawing a wide variety of students to campus, and hiring quality professors. On the other hand, the large, public university may be more oriented toward internal factors in its planning activities, such as control over operating expenses, proper maintenance of the facilities, and support for existing programs.

Third, the use of goals provides the foundation to *motivate* individuals to perform at the highest levels of efficiency and effectiveness. Sometimes it may be better to be number two striving to be number one than it is to be number one. Many of us have been members of sports teams that are in second or third place, but see a chance to be in first place with the exertion of some additional effort. In a similar manner, we can investigate the competition in the auto rental industry over the past few years. Avis' well known "We try harder" statement has not only been successful as an advertising claim but has proved to be a strong internal motivator of employees. As we will note in later chapters, however, continued high motivation is a function of the level of rewards received by the individuals. If individuals receive rewards (praise, recognition, pay raises, advancement, or a sense of achievement and pride) that are equal with their levels of performance, they should continue to exert high levels of effort.

Finally, goals form the basis for *evaluating* and *controlling* the activities of the organization. Goals, plans, and motivated workers all work toward the achievement of some end result. Evaluation and control tell us how well we are doing in our attempts to reach these ends, and, if we are not on target, they provide certain guidelines for revising our efforts. Consider again the private university. The university's administration may have set a goal of collecting contributions from different groups of $10 million over a three-year fund-raising campaign. When only $2.5 million is collected the first year, an analysis of the contributors may reveal that donations from alumni are far short of what was expected. This may lead administrators to examine why this level of contribution has occurred and to develop mechanisms to correct the situation.

Goals permeate the entire management process by providing the foundations for planning, direction, motivation, and control. Managers must be continually involved in the goal process because without goals organizations could meander in any number of ineffective directions.

Criteria for Good Goals

There are certain criteria for oals that enable us to classify them as good or poor. Four criteria, shown in exhibit 5–2, are most important.

Clarity and Specificity.   Goals should be clear and specific concerning the desired outcomes. Clear and specific goals make it known to all employees where their efforts should take them; unclear and/or nonspecific goals create confusion and conflict among workers.

Timing.   A particular time or date of anticipated goal accomplishment is an important requirement. With a definite time frame, accurate plans can be developed.

Consistency.   Goals must be logically consistent, particularly with respect to the external environment and internal resources, because they

EXHIBIT 5–2
Criteria for
Organizational
Goals

CRITERIA	EXAMPLE OF POOR GOAL	EXAMPLE OF AN IMPROVED GOAL
Clarity and Specificity	Improve employee communications.	Hold monthly unit meetings to discuss issues and problems and initiate an employee newsletter within three months.
Timing	Improve production.	Increase production to 95% of capacity within two months.
Consistency	Eliminate air pollution from all plants.	Reduce particulate matter venting to the atmosphere by 90% within three years.
Difficulty and Achievability	Double sales.	Increase yearly sales revenue by at least 20%.

indicate whether the organization has taken the right path. For example, General Electric's purchase of a coal company was logically consistent not only because of its immense resource base, but because it already was a major manufacturer of power-generation equipment based on coal as a fuel.

Difficulty and Achievability. It is important for goals to be difficult enough to stimulate added effort by workers, but not so difficult that they create frustration. Easily attainable goals may not only be quickly forgotten by employees but may lead to complacency and neglect. For example, using its dominant position in denim pants, Levi-Strauss may set a difficult but achievable goal of being the number one manufacturer of men's and women's *sportswear*. American Motors' claim to outsell G.M. in auto sales revenue by 1985, however, may be farfetched and unachievable.

These criteria are important to managers in all types of organizations. They provide the direction and momentum that is needed for improved performance.

Types of Goals

As we suggested in chapter 2, there are many performance criteria or end results that organizations seek to achieve. Among the most frequently stated are the following:[4]

1. *Profitability*. Profitability is usually expressed in such terms as net income, earnings-per-share, return on investment, or other similar ratios. Not-for-profit or public-sector organizations are also concerned with this type of goal when we consider their desire to keep costs within specific budget levels.

2. *Productivity*. Productivity goals generally concern the levels of output per unit or worker across the organization. Examples include "units pro-

duced per day for each employee," "costs per unit of production," or "income generated per employee."

3. *Market*. Market goals can be described in a number of different ways. They can relate to a particular penetration of the market, such as "increase the market share for Product A to 20 percent," or an output orientaton, such as "sell one hundred thousand units of output this year in the health care industry." Many times, market goals relate to the coverage by a company's product line. An unsatisfactory coverage may prompt management to improve the product line by introducing new products for a variety of different uses.

4. *Resources*. Organizations may establish goals concerning changes in their resource base. Financial resource goals may include, "reduce the company's long-term debt by $30 million within three years," "decrease the collection period on accounts receivable to less than thirty days within six months," and so on. Physical resource goals could deal with increases in the number of plants or facilities, production capacity, storage capacity, or maintenance capabilities. Human esource goals may relate to decreases in absenteeism, turnover, and lost days due to accidents. They may also concern improvements in management-development programs, career-planning activities, and executive succession programs.

5. *Innovation*. For many organizations, continued growth (or survival) may depend on the development of new products, processes, or services. Example goals include, "development of a new manufacturing process that is more efficient than the existing process within five years," "developing a new automobile engine that will run on a variety of fuels and get 50 m.p.g. by 1990," or "increase our spending on R&D by 25 percent this year."

6. *Social responsibility*. Most organizations, and managers within these organizations, are becoming keenly aware of their role in society. Concerns over the quality of life, minority employment, pollution, and the deteriorating environment are becoming more important. We will devote the last part of this chapter to an in-depth discussion of this topic.

The manager should carefully note that the example goals above may, in many cases, apply equally to not-for-profit organizations as well as those with the profit motive. Hospitals, state and local governments, and social service agencies, for example, are concerned with cost control, output per employee, development and improvement of resources, implementation of innovative practices, and their relationship to society. Goals are applicable to any organization that seeks high performance levels.

Beyond the above classification scheme, there are other ways of describing the types of goals that can be found in all organizations. Three categories can be presented: (1) level of analysis; (2) focus; and (3) time.

Level of Analysis.   A classification scheme for goals may distinguish between official, operative, and operational goals.[5] *Official* goals represent the formal statement of purpose concerning the overall mission of the organization. This is usually a broad statement found in official organizational documents, such as annual reports. Examples include the public utility that "exists to serve the public," the university that is chartered to "disseminate knowledge," and the hospital that is designed to "improve the health of the patients." They are also typically vague and aspirational in nature (maximize profits or contribute to the welfare of society) with indefinite time horizons.

The real intentions of organizations are termed *operative* goals. That is, they reflect what an organization is *actually* trying to do. For example, an *officially* stated goal of a telephone company may be to serve customers in a particular geographical area in the most effective manner. *Operationally* this goal may be translated to "courteously handle all requests for information and to satisfy at least 97 percent of all requests for assistance."

Finally, *operational* goals are those that have agreed-upon criteria for evaluating the level of goal attainment. In other words, an operative goal is said to be operational to the extent that management can precisely state *how* and *when* the goal will be attained. For example, a farm equipment company may state an *official* goal as, "maximize profits through the sale of farm implements." From an *operative* view, the goal can be stated as, "attaining a level of 15 percent return on invested capital from the sale of the company's product line." Finally, as an *operational* goal, the statement can be made as, "improve return on invested capital to a level of 15 percent by December 1983 through the sale of the company's farm implement products."

As shown in exhibit 5–3, another way of viewing official, operative,

EXHIBIT 5–3 The Hierarchical Nature of Goals

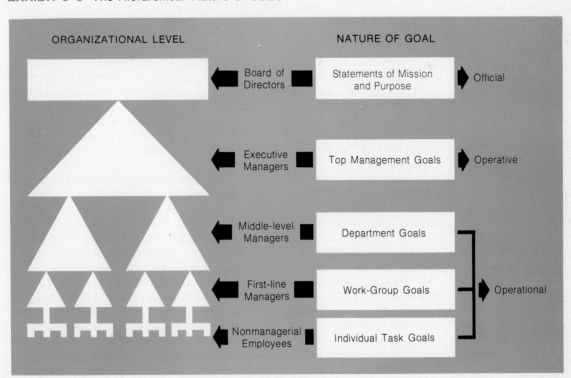

and operational goals is by the hierarchical level in the organization that they affect. Generally speaking, official and operative goals reflect the concerns of executive and middle level managers, respectively, and the lower managerial levels are concerned with operational goals.[6]

Focus.   Classifying goals by focus entails describing the *nature of the action* that will be taken. Three categories are most frequently used:

1. *Maintenance goals.* Maintenance goals imply that a specific level of activity or action is to be maintained over time. Examples include the desire to "operate at 95 percent of manufacturing capacity," and for an airline "to have at least 85 percent of its aircraft in service at one time."

2. *Improvement goals.* Goals that use an *action* verb to indicate a specific change is wanted seek improvement. "Increasing" market share, "decreasing" customer complaints, and "improving" return on invested capital are examples.

3. *Developmental goals.* Similar to improvement goals, developmental goals refer to a desire for some form of growth, expansion, learning, or advancement. Such goals could include increasing the number of new products introduced, establishing managerial training programs to improve managerial effectiveness, and so on.

Unlike the previous classification schemes, this approach is much simpler to understand and utilize by managers. The important characteristic, however, is the manner in which such goals direct the activities and actions of members of organizations.

Time Frame.   A dominant classification scheme for goals is based on the time period affected by the goals—either long-term or short-term goals.[7] *Long-term* goals refer to those goals that usually cover more than a one-year period of time. Examples may include such goals as, "doubling the number of beds in a hospital within four years," "capturing 30 percent of the market by 1983," or "obtaining a 10 percent growth in sales during the next five years." *Short-term* goals concern those that cover twelve months or less, even though their actual accomplishment may require more than one year. A "reduction in manufacturing costs by $2 million by the end of the year," or "completion of the construction of the warehouse before Christmas," are examples.

Two important aspects of long- and short-term goals should be pointed out. First, many times short-term goals are derived from long-term goals. In other words, a series of short-term goals may be under the umbrella of a long-term goal. For example, Colgate may desire an 8 percent market share for a new household detergent within three years of introduction. The first year, a 2 percent market share goal is set, 5 percent for the second year, and 8 percent for the third year.

Second, a high degree of flexibility and adjustment must be part of any long- or short-term goal. As we noted in the previous chapter, changes in the external environment can sometimes turn viable long-term goals into poor ones. These long-term goals must be based on the best possible forecasts available at the time and should not commit the organization to an unretractable position. Similarly, short-term goals should be sufficiently flexible as to not endanger the achievement of a long-term goal.

Characteristics of Goals

Like any other management concept, organizational goals have certain basic characteristics. As discussed below, goals should be measurable; many goals exist at the same time; and, because there are many goals, they are usually put in some kind of order.

Measurement. Goals of an organization, a department, or those of individual managers must be measurable. Unless there are criteria for effectiveness and methods of measuring the criteria, there can be no idea of when a goal has been achieved. As an executive acquaintance has stated, "If you can't count it, measure or describe it, why are you doing it?" Two types of measurement are most frequently presented:

1. *Quantitative measures* are those to which some "number" can be assigned. Examples include net income, return on investment, market share, units produced, turnover and absenteeism rate, and the like. These are also sometimes referred to as "objective" measures.

2. *Qualitative measures.* Managers frequently are faced with certain situations in which a quantitative figure cannot be assigned to a goal. In these cases one may be able to use qualitative or subjective measures to ascertain goal achievement. Surprisingly, many times qualitative measures are used to evaluate managerial performance. Although quantitative measures are easily adaptable to lower-level jobs (e.g., number of units produced or sold), measuring managerial performance or goal achievement is much more difficult. Many managers alleviate this problem somewhat by creating or attaching a number to the goal. For example, three most frequently mentioned managerial goals and their "qualitative" measures include: (a) "assessing the level of employee morale" through the use of survey questionnaires; (b) "developing future management talent" through participation in training programs or by the number of subordinates who have been promoted; and (c) "being a good corporate citizen" by the number of speeches to local organizations, reduction of customers' complaints, and so forth.

Multiplicity of Goals. Every organization and every manager has more than one goal that guides activities and actions. On an organizational level, the goals of a hospital may be related to patient health, control of costs, improvements in service, and reductions in turnover and absenteeism among personnel. On a departmental level, the marketing area in a consumer products company can consider unit sales, advertising effectiveness, market coverage, and number of new customers as possible goals. Exhibit 5–4 illustrates the multiplicity and hierarchical nature of goals for three levels and functions within an organization.

Ordering of Goals. Our previous discussion on the various types and characteristics of goals may suggest, even to the most casual reader, that goals in an organization entail a complex, complicated, and sometimes confusing process. In order to remove some of the problems associated with the goal concept, managers engage in a process of ordering goals. This ordering process involves three factors:

EXHIBIT 5–4   **The Multiplicity, Hierarchy, and Network Characteristics of Goals**

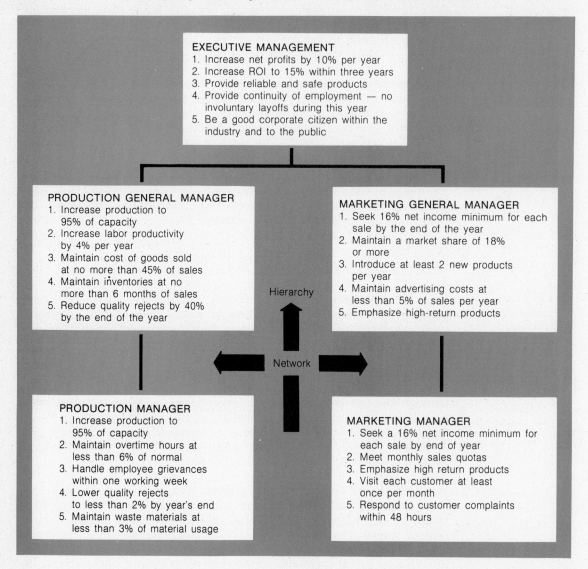

1. *Goal networks.* In our discussion of categorizing goals by the level of analysis in the previous section, we noted how a goal is transmitted *vertically* in an organization. In a similar manner, goals must be integrated horizontally in an organization, creating a network of goals. This is also shown in exhibit 5–4. If the goals of an organization are not interconnected and mutually supportive, managers may tend to pursue individual goals that can be detrimental to the overall organization. For example, consider two product managers in a marketing department of an electronics firm. The first may react to the global goal of "improving our market performance" by seeking out sales contracts that enhance

profit margins, while the second manager may work towards increasing sales revenue. These two behaviors may not be totally congruent with each other. As Sears and W.T. Grant painfully recognized, increased profit margins do not necessarily come with higher sales.[8]

2. *Goal priorities.* With the multiplicity of goals found *across* the entire organization, it becomes necessary for management to set *priorities* for goals. In general, goals are assigned an importance related to a primary or secondary rating. Primary goals are those that are of the highest importance to the organization. Secondary goals may be more oriented toward short-term considerations. For example, Teledyne has set margins as their primary goal.[9] All other goals—dealing with employee turnover, acquisitions, product development—are secondary but integrated with the primary goal. As an example of goal priorities, consider exhibit 5–5. The exhibit is a summary of a survey of 1,072 business-oriented managers at various organizational levels that was designed to gather information on what goals managers deemed *important* as well as *essential* to success of the organization.[10] The eight goals are divided into four categories: (1) overall efficiency; (2) growth and status; (3) employee concerns; and (4) social concerns. Two features of this survey data are interesting to note. First, there is a wide variation in the importance given to efficiency goals, suggesting that cost control and profit-oriented behaviors and values are still dominant among managers. Second, although 65 percent of the managers believed that employee welfare was of high importance, only 20 percent felt that it was essential to the success of the organization. This suggests the belief among the sample managers that managerial and behavioral theories are making an impact, but when it comes to a confrontation, profit goals win out over employee welfare goals.

EXHIBIT 5–5
The Importance
and Essentiality
of Goals

GOALS OF BUSINESS ORGANIZATIONS	% RATING HIGH IMPORTANCE	% RATING AS ESSENTIAL FOR SUCCESS
Overall Efficiency		
Cost efficiency	81%	71%
High productivity	80%	70%
Profit maximization	72%	71%
Growth and Status		
Organizational growth	60%	72%
Industrial leadership	58%	64%
Organizational stability	58%	54%
Employee Concerns		
Employee welfare	65%	20%
Social Concerns		
Social welfare	16%	8%

Source: G. W. England, "Organizational Goals and Expected Behavior of American Managers," *Academy of Management Journal* (June 1967): 108.

3. *Balancing goals.* In addition to setting priorities, managers find that they must trade off among goals so that an organizationally satisfactory set of goals emerges. Sales goals must be balanced with production goals; product development goals must be balanced with financial goals; short-term goals must be balanced with long-term goals, and so forth. Stressing one goal to the exclusion of all other goals may lead to suboptimum results, which may not be beneficial to the overall performance of the organization.

COMMENTS ON THE PRACTICE OF MANAGEMENT
(See p. 131.)

The Teledyne example in the Practice of Management section illustrates a number of important factors concerning organizational goals. First, their main goal is one that stresses profitability, a goal that clearly reflects the aspirations of top management. Second, this profitability goal is so internalized by other managers that it influences all planning, organizing, leading, and control functions. Third, it is a clear and consistent goal that is difficult but achievable. Finally, while other goals may exist, the profitability goal has been given top priority.

Keys to Success with Goals

As this discussion strongly suggests, goals are very pervasive factors for all types of organizations. They not only are the result of an external and internal environmental analysis, but they eventually form the basis for the important managerial functions of planning and control.

In operating with a goal-oriented framework, all organizations face problems that are not spelled out in theory. In many situations there are no set answers available to these problems for managers. Yet a knowledge of the following guidelines may be helpful to managers.

1. **Strive for goal acceptance and commitment by employees.**

Goals do not implement themselves. They need the support and cooperation of the entire organization. To reach high levels of achievement, it is necessary for employees both to accept and be committed to the goals.

The reasons for a lack of acceptance and commitment are many. Two are most prominent. First, *encouragement* may not be given by top management to the achievement of the goals, or they are simply ignored by key managers after their establishment. Without constant attention to integrating goal direction into activities, employees just "file away" the goals and little behavior has been changed. In other words, "if it's not important to them, why should it be important to me?"

Second, *acceptance* of certain goals may go against the values or better judgment of employees. They may feel that achievement of the goal is wrong ethically or managerially, thus they resist working toward its accomplishment. For example, it is not uncommon to see a number of hospital personnel quit their jobs when the hospital begins taking on abortion cases, or resistance is shown by potential workers to applying for positions in nuclear power plants. In each case, accepting the goals of these organizations would be counter to the individuals' value systems.

Beyond value issues, disagreement with changes in managerial decisions or policies can create a lack of goal acceptance. A number of key executives at Twentieth Century-Fox Studios, who were responsible for the highly successful films, "Star Wars" and "Alien," took jobs with other motion picture makers when Fox decided to use the large profits from these two films on projects *other* than producing pictures.[11] In addition, a frequent occurrence after the appointment of a new chief executive of an organization is the exodus of a number of high-level managers. These terminating managers may disagree with the choice of person, not only because they believe they should have had the job, but they may feel that they could not perform effectively with a new chief executive.

2. Emphasize communication and feedback.

The entire communications process involving goals is extremely important for goal success. Two parts of the communications process are of particular importance. First, many managers perceive a *lack of clarity* with respect to the newly set goals, either because the goals are stated in vague terms, or because the goals have not "filtered down" to all involved managers. The result is that some managers often make decisions that are inconsistent with the original intent of the goal. In a manner similar to a football lineman pass blocking instead of blocking for a run because he did not hear the signals from the quarterback, managers sometimes perform in ways that are inconsistent with expected activities.

Communication not only involves clarifying and stating clear goals, but it also involves *feedback* of results and the use of controls relative to these goals. Managers need to know through feedback of results whether goal-directed actions are on target, or if changes in the levels of goal achievement or effort levels are required. Charitable fund-raising campaigns are good examples of situations in which feedback of results may necessitate more effort being given in order to achieve a particular contribution goal.

3. Multiple goals should not conflict with one another.

It is not uncommon to find situations in which managers find that the achievement of one goal may come at the expense of another equally important goal. For example, a production supervisor who is given goals that include "maintaining a production rate of 95 percent of capacity" and "reduce production costs by 10 percent" quickly becomes aware that the two goals are in conflict. Maintaining the desired production rate can be achieved only by working employees overtime and increasing maintenance expenses. In other words, achieving the production rate goal will come at the expense of the cost goal. Needless to say, this can be a frustrating experience for many managers. This is a clear case in which priorities and goal balancing are necessary.

4. Rewards should be clearly related to goal achievement levels.

People join organizations because they seek the rewards (pay, advancement, status, recognition) for their levels of input. When rewards for goal achievement are unsatisfactory or not clearly related to the employees' performances, they may begin to exhibit little dedication or loyalty to the organization. They feel either that their contributions are meaningless or are not rewarded, thus causing them to direct their behaviors in other directions. We will give greater coverage to this subject in later chapters on motivation and rewards.

5. **Striving to reach a goal may create unproductive competition.**

There are times when the adoption of a goal results in managers pulling apart instead of pulling together. For example, in order to increase teller productivity, a savings and loan branch manager may institute an award/bonus program for those tellers each month who report the highest number of customer transactions and the lowest transaction errors and customer complaints. The result may be conflict and morale problems as tellers strive to better their own performance at the expense of the other tellers. Under a "profit center" approach (where a unit or department is rewarded on the basis of its contributions to profitability), it is a common occurrence to find managers in one profit center withholding information from another profit-center manager if the first believes that the information may benefit the second. Setting priorities and balancing goals, along with providing some flexibility in goal-directed behavior, are some of the ways of overcoming this problem.

6. **Personal survival should not be substituted for goal achievement.**

When the process of working toward the attainment of some goal may result in failure, many managers begin thinking about the personal consequences to their jobs and careers. Many instigate what we call "coping" behaviors or stress their innocence in all matters. The Firestone 500 radial tire debacle is a case in which many managers intimately involved do not accept any blame.[12] In cases such as these, efficiency, effectiveness, innovativeness, and imagination are relegated to secondary positions, replaced by personal survival motives.

The existence of goal problems does not suggest that punishment for any but improper, illogical, or illegal actions should be used. On the contrary, under normal circumstances, failures can be expected in many goal-directed activities. Sudden changes in the external environment or the organization's resource base may eliminate any chance that a particular goal can be fully achieved. This requires an adjustment process on the part of the organization and a recognition that some failures are good learning experiences that can benefit future decisions. Taking risks is an important part of a manager's job; eliminating risk may result in a stagnant, nongrowth attitude.

MANAGERS AND SOCIAL GOALS

Toward an Awareness of Social Goals

In the previous discussion of organizational goals, we noted how goals such as improving profit levels, increasing market share, and more efficient cost control were influenced by the external and internal environments of the organization (the "should do" component). These goals represent responses by the organization to *market* forces; the firm adapts by varying its product line, pricing strategies, promotion, and service to meet changing consumer needs, expectations, and organizational resource strengths.

In the process of working toward the achievement of market goals, there are many *nonmarket* goals and indirect consequences for society as a whole.[13] As we read and hear frequently from media sources, there have been increasing pressures from societal elements for organizations to minimize adverse nonmarket consequences and maximize the nonmarket benefits of its activities. While many business institutions can justifiably take credit for tremendous strides that have been made in improving living standards, they are frequently accused of being the cause of many environment-related and sociopolitical problems and for being relatively insensitive to the needs of society. There have been increasing pressures for organizations to take more active roles and assume greater responsibility for correcting the social ills that can occur. In other words, there is a growing awareness that market goals *and* nonmarket social goals should be part of an organization's goal set since each is an important part of what the organization "should do."

Dimensions of Organizational Social Behavior

While the concept of organizational social behavior has generated considerable discussion during recent years, it has been an elusive concept to define and classify. Frequently, such terms as *social awareness* or *social responsibility* have been used. For our purposes, we will define and classify *organizational social behavior* as a three-part concept.[14] This is shown in exhibit 5–6.

Social Obligations.   This first category concerns the typical activities of an organization directed in response to market forces and/or internal aspirations. According to this framework, an organization's social obligations are met by achieving its goals through its ability to compete for resources and conducting its operations within the legal constraints imposed by society (i.e., obeying the law). An example is an organization that maximizes profits by adherence to economic and legal criteria and constraints. This "normal" behavior by an organization has been criticized by many as being too narrowly defined in that economic and legal factors are insufficient for the long-term success and survival of most organizations. In other words, some believe that satisfaction of the profit motive does not totally insure the continued survival of the organization. More complex criteria and constraints are needed.

Social Responsibility.   This second category is much broader than the first in its definition and scope. Organizational social responsibility suggests that the organization should meet the prevailing social norms, values, and performance expectations of society (i.e., meeting social demands). At issue are not only the occasions when certain illegalities in organizations occur (see the discussion of managerial ethics in chapter 2), but also the increasing criticism that organizations have not done enough to meet such societal needs as minority employment, pollution control, education support, and the like.

Social Responsiveness.   Whereas the concept of social responsibility concerns current issues, social responsiveness is anticipatory in nature

EXHIBIT 5–6   Classification of Organizational Social Behavior

Dimensions of Behavior	Social Obligation	Social Responsibility	Social Responsiveness
Search for Legitimacy	Confines legitimacy to legal and economic criteria only; does not violate laws; equates profitable operations with fulfilling social expectations.	Accepts the reality of limited relevance of legal and market criteria of legitimacy in actual practice. Willing to consider and accept broader—extra-legal and extra-market—criteria for measuring corporate performance and social role.	Accepts its role as defined by the social system and therefore subject to change; recognizes importance of profitable operations but includes other criteria.
Social Accountability	Construes narrowly as limited to stockholders; jealously guards its prerogatives against outsiders.	Individual managers responsible not only for their own ethical standards but also for the collectivity of corporation. Construes narrowly for legal purposes, but broadened to include groups affected by its actions; management more outward looking.	Willing to account for its actions to other groups, even those not directly affected by its actions.
Operating Strategy	Exploitative and defensive adaptation. Maximum externalization of costs.	Reactive adaptation. Maintains current standards of physical and social environment. Compensates victims of pollution and other corporate-related activities even in the absence of clearly established legal grounds. Develops industrywide standards.	Proactive adaptation. Takes lead in developing and adapting new technology for environmental protectors. Evaluates side effects of corporate actions and eliminates them prior to the action being taken. Anticipates future social changes and develops internal structures to cope with them.
Response to Social Pressures	Maintains low public profile, but, if attacked, uses PR methods to upgrade its public image; denies any deficiencies; blames public dissatisfaction on ignorance or failure to understand corporate functions; discloses information only where legally required.	Accepts responsibility for solving current problems; will admit deficiencies in former practices and attempt to persuade public that its current practices meet social norms; attitude toward critics conciliatory; freer information disclosures.	Willingly discusses activities with outside groups; makes information freely available to public; accepts formal and informal inputs from outside groups in decision making. Is willing to be publicly evaluated for its various activities.
Reaction to Government Actions	Strongly resists any regulation of its activities except when it needs help to protect its market position; avoids contact; resists any demands for information beyond that legally required.	Preserves management discretion in corporate decisions but cooperates with government in research to improve industrywide standards; participates in political processes and encourages employees to do likewise.	Openly communicates with government; assists in enforcing existing laws and developing evaluations of business practices; objects publicly to governmental activities that it feels are detrimental to the public good.

Adapted from S. Prakash Sethi, "A Conceptual Framework for Environmental Analyses of Social Issues and Evaluation of Business Response Patterns," *Academy of Management Review* (January 1979): 67–68.

*"Granted the public has a right to know what's in a hot dog, but does
the public really want to know what's in a hot dog?"*

Drawing by Richter; © 1978 The New Yorker Magazine, Inc.

(i.e., anticipating and creating some demands). That is, the focus is not
only on how organizations should respond to current social forces and
pressures, but what their long-term position in society is to be. The organization in a socially responsive mode is expected to *anticipate* the
changes or the emergence of socially related problems that may be the
result of organizational activities.[15] The Alaskan pipeline is an example.
In an "idealistic" sense, those organizations involved in the project were
considered socially responsive when they considered in their planning
the long-term environmental, social, and economic impact of the pipeline
on the land and the people of the state.

Recent surveys have shown that few organizations went much beyond the social responsibility stage in their social activities.[16] These same
surveys found, however, that business activism will probably increase
significantly in the future.

Origins of Organizational Social Behavior

The concern over social issues by organizations has multiple origins. As
we will discuss, the origins are historical and come from experienced
problems.

Contrary to some beliefs, the concept of organizational social behavior—social obligations, responsibility, and responsiveness—is not a
revolutionary idea of the turbulent 1960s or 1970s. A close examination
of the writings on the history of management thought will reveal many
instances of concerns over social issues. Henry Gantt, R. C. Davis, and
Chester Barnard each challenged managers to be more active in the
affairs of the community.

Practicing managers also have made significant contributions to the
social behavior of organizations. For example, Sears, Roebuck instituted

the county farm agent concept during the early years of this century. Sears believed that before farm productivity could be improved by new farm technology, the farmer's knowledge needed improvement and some of the ignorance and isolation associated with agricultural work had to be removed. The county farm agent provided knowledge, information, and assistance that enabled farmers to produce more, to produce the right things, and to learn how to get more from their efforts on the land.[17]

Henry Ford I was best known for his radical manufacturing process, yet his social contribution of a guaranteed $5 a day wage to workers was even more radical. Even though the wage was almost triple that of the going standard, the company was convinced that the worker's sufferings were so great that highly visible changes would make an impact on other industries. In a similar fashion, during the Great Depression, IBM pioneered the concept of employment security by putting workers on salary instead of hourly wage. IBM's action was directed at a major social problem of that time—namely, the fear, insecurity, and loss of human dignity that resulted from the Depression. IBM turned a social malady into a business opportunity, and developed a human resource philosophy that pervades the organization even today. Sears, Ford, and IBM were socially responsive, an historical fact that even the severest critics of American business must accept.[18]

The past and current socially conscious practices of such organizations as Sears, Ford, and IBM unfortunately are not given the attention that is given to some of the less successful attempts at social behavior. The fact is that many more organizations are socially responsible than socially irresponsible. Because of the potential severity, however, the latter examples are the ones that gain our attention.

Some of the more publicized problems are as follows:

1.4 million *Ford* Pintos and Bobcats recalled due to exploding gas tanks.

1.45 million *Firestone* 500 radial tires recalled due to improper tread wear.

The *Amoco* Cadiz oil spill in France.

Mercury pollution in the Niagara River from an *Olin* plant.

1500 lawsuits filed against *Johns-Manville* by workers who have contracted asbestos-related diseases.

$20 million fines and settlements against *Allied Chemical* for discharging the toxic pesticide, Kepone, into the Chesapeake Bay.

Union Carbide's air and water polluting plants in West Virginia.

Three points should be noted by the reader with respect to this subject. First, some organizations have not been as socially conscious as they should have been. For example, there is some evidence that Firestone and Union Carbide knew of the existence of their respective problems *before* they became public. Second, as we will discuss shortly, many more organizations have made significant contributions to social issues, but have not received the notoriety that the less successful ones have received. Last, organizations, like individuals, *learn* from their mistakes. The bad experiences of these organizations have no doubt had an effect on other organizations in their social thinking.

Pros and Cons of Organizational Social Behavior

One might conclude from the discussion to this point that socially conscious behavior on the part of organizations is an accepted belief in the same category as motherhood, peanut butter, and the flag. Such may not be the case; there are as many equally strong arguments *against* social behavior as there are for it. The major pro and con arguments on the social behavior issue are shown in exhibit 5–7.

Two individual points of view may serve to highlight the major differences on this issue. The "against" view is best presented by the well-known economist Milton Friedman, who argues that the only responsibility of business is to *maximize profits* for its owners.[19] Friedman's argument assumes that managers are really agents of the owners and that diverting funds to social activities that do not contribute to profits may be illegal.

EXHIBIT 5–7   Arguments For and Against Social Responsibility

MAJOR ARGUMENTS FOR SOCIAL RESPONSIBILITY	MAJOR ARGUMENTS AGAINST SOCIAL RESPONSIBILITY
1. It is in the long-run self-interest of the firm to promote and improve the communities where it does business.	1. Violates profit maximization and is thus, illegal.
2. It improves the public image of the firm.	2. Cost of social responsibility too great and would increase prices too much.
3. It is necessary to avoid government regulation.	3. Business lacks social skills to solve societal problems.
4. Sociocultural norms require it.	4. It would dilute business's primary purposes.
5. Laws cannot be passed for all circumstances. Thus, business must assume responsibility to maintain an orderly, legal society.	5. It would weaken U.S. balance of payments because price of goods would have to go up to pay for social programs.
6. It is in the stockholder's best interest. It will improve the price of stock in the long run because the stock market will view the company as less risky and open to public attack and, therefore, award it a higher price to earning ratio.	6. Business already has too much power. Such involvement would make business too powerful.
7. Society should give business a chance to solve social problems that government has failed to solve.	7. Business lacks accountability to the public. Thus the public would have no control over its social involvement.
8. Business is considered by some groups to be the institution with the financial and human resources to solve social problems.	8. Such business involvement lacks broad public support.
9. Problems can become profitable if firms become involved.	9. Business plus government creates a monolith.
10. Prevention of problems is better than cures— so let business solve problems before they become too great.	10. Social responsibility cannot be measured.

Adapted from J. R. Mansen, "The Social Attitudes of Management," in *Contemporary Management,* ed. Joseph W. McGuire, (Englewood Cliffs, N.J.: Prentice-Hall, 1974), p. 616.

The "for" view has been well presented by Keith Davis and his *Iron Law of Responsibility*. The law states that in the long run, those who do not use power in the manner that society considers responsible will tend to lose it.[20] The argument is that since business is a major power in our society, it has an obligation and responsibility to attempt to solve problems of public concern. If business neglects this responsibility, then the only action that society can take is to withdraw some of the power that business enjoys and give it to institutions that may be better able to solve the problems. In other words, this would mean that in the majority of cases there would be increased government involvement in society's problems with no guarantee that government can do better, given its uneven and sometimes poor performance record in solving past public problems.

Organizational Responses to Social Issues

When organizations are confronted with issues of a social nature, they may adopt a number of different response patterns or behaviors. As shown in exhibit 5–8, there are three broad response categories that are most prevalent in organizations today: (1) tokenism; (2) functional change; and (3) structural change.

Tokenism.   Tokenism has been the most frequently used response mechanism by organizations for many years. It is the easiest, quickest, and least expensive way to respond to social issues. Examples include

EXHIBIT 5–8
Organizational
Responses to
Social Issues

RESPONSE CATEGORY	EXAMPLES	POSITIVE FEATURES	NEGATIVE FEATURES
Tokenism	1. Membership on community committees 2. Donation of funds 3. Donation of management talent	Inexpensive and adaptable	Usually is ineffective and inefficient in the long run
Functional Change	1. Ad hoc committees 2. Temporary task forces 3. Permanent committees	Provides support and expertise	Costly in terms of expanding duties; increasing potential for internal conflict
Structural Change	1. Vice president of consumer affairs 2. Environmental affairs department	Visible commitment; developing expertise; meaningful presentation	Costly expansion: value conflicts; makes decision making more complex

membership on local and state committees, donation of funds and executive talent to particular causes, and so forth. Token responses, however, are usually short term in nature and can be ineffectual and inefficient for the organization in the long run.

Functional Change. This next-highest level of response awareness generally involves a more complex reaction by the organization. The usual procedure is to establish a temporary or permanent committee whose members are responsible for handling specific tasks or for supplying information to management on social affairs. Examples include United Appeal campaigns, employment opportunity review boards, and the like. Such responses can not only be expensive in terms of staff and manpower costs but can create potential conflicts of interest when individuals are confronted with choices between their primary and secondary job duties.

Structural Change. Structural change is the most complex and costly response to social affairs. The typical mechanism is to create a new managerial position, such as vice president of consumer affairs, or a department, such as environmental and social affairs, each of which is formally incorporated into the structure of the organization. By adopting this mechanism, organizations are placing social issues on a relative par with other more traditional organizational concerns such as market share, profit growth, and management development. It can, however, further complicate an already complex decision-making process and bring about the potential for major conflicts between the new unit and the other functional areas.

There are three important points that this discussion suggests. First, such social responses by organizations generally can be placed in the social obligation and social responsibility and, at least partially, in the social responsiveness categories. In other words, these responses fall only within a portion of the potential social behavior pattern that we have discussed. Second, there is a varying level of cost, in terms of "real" and "opportunity" costs, to the organization. Tokenism may be the least costly, but it may leave the organization open to accusations of disinterest and insincerity. A major structural change requires more than just appointing a vice president of social affairs; it may involve a complete revision of the organization's thinking and decision making. Finally, whatever the response pattern chosen, the organization must carefully examine and diagnose its particular situation for information about its own unique problems and issues.

Social Issues and Projects

The social issues facing society in general, and business in particular, are complex and numerous. We have chosen five to discuss not only because of their importance but also because of their relationship with business organizations. As we will see, business organizations (along with not-for-profit organizations) have become involved in many of these issues already, some in a positive manner, some not so positive. The five include: pollution; affirmative action; consumerism; urban development; and philanthropic activities.

Pollution.   Perhaps no other issue has gained the level of attention and been the center of so much controversy as that of pollution and its impact upon the environment. Because most organizations use some form of natural resources as raw material inputs into their operations, they have been identified as one of the leading sources of the significant deterioration of a nation's land, air, and water resources. Five areas of possible pollution control have been most frequently identified and discussed:

1. Reduction of *air pollution* from automobile exhaust emissions, aircraft, and particle discharges from chemical, mining, metals, and other manufacturing firms.

2. Reduction of *water pollution* and the destruction of water life from the effluent discharges of a variety of industrial plants.

3. *Land conservation* and/or proper reclamation by lumber, mining, and petroleum firms along with limitations placed on sports activities (e.g., hunting, dune buggy and motorcycle racing in the deserts of California, snowmobiling in winter lands).

4. Reduction of *noise pollution* from industry and aircraft.

5. Reduction of *visual pollution* from the billboard industry.

As these issues impinge more and more upon the organization, there are at least three factors that the manager must recognize. First, the pollution issue will continue to take up considerable amounts of managerial time and energy. Not only will societal interest continue to grow, but the participation of federal, state, and local governmental agencies will increase. With its regulatory and financial power, the EPA will be able to exert a considerable amount of control over the creation and enforcement of air and water quality standards. In essence, concerns over pollution have or will become an integral part of the manager's *planning* and *control* activities.

Second, despite such highly publicized incidents as the Amoco Cadiz oil spill off the coast of France, Allied Chemical's problems with the pesticide Kepone, Hooker Chemical's Love Canal problems, the Pemex oil spill in Mexico, and the asbestos controversy at Johns-Manville, managers should resist taking a totally defensive position.[21] In many unfortunately unpublicized instances, organizations have taken the lead in trying to solve present and future pollution problems. A good example is the National Coal Policy Project, which is a group of leading conservationists and top executives from the coal-mining and coal-consuming industries that meet to try to devise environmentally safe ways to mine and use coal.[22]

Third, any plan by an organization to reduce or eliminate pollution—particularly air and water—must answer some key questions related to technology and cost. For example, some of the technical equipment required to totally eliminate most forms of air pollution is only on the drawing board and not commercially available. Such equipment may be years away from widespread use. As for cost, the amount of money necessary for total pollution elimination is staggering. Businesses are already spending nearly 25 percent of their capital improvement budgets on pollution control and worker safety. In other words, a cost-benefit or trade-off analysis that evaluates the economic and environmental effects must be considered carefully: At what point is the survival of the organization at stake? Our later discussion of the social audit will cover this point in more detail.

There is no doubt that organizations, particularly businesses, are concerned with the pollution issue. Solutions will be found, but it will take time, capital, and the cooperation and commitment of many individuals and groups.

Affirmative Action.   Perhaps no two documents have had a more significant impact on the management of human resources in organizations than the Fourteenth Amendment of the Constitution (1868) and the 1972 amendment of Title VII of the Civil Rights Act of 1964. The former promises "equal protection of the law to all persons born or naturalized in the United States," the latter "prohibits discrimination because of race, color, religion, sex, or natural origin in all employment practices including hiring, firing, promotion, compensation, job classification, and other terms, privileges, and conditions of employment." The result was not only the creation of the Equal Employment Opportunities Commission (EEOC), but an entirely revised way of thinking about people at work.

While we discuss this issue in greater depth in chapter 10, certain implications for organizational goals should be pointed out here. First, any discrimination in the work force will not be tolerated, and it is clearly illegal as well. Second, certain executive orders designed to supplement the previous acts require federal contractors (or any organization that receives federal monies) to file a written affirmative action program designed to eliminate any inequities that might exist as a result of past practices. In essence, organizations must supplement their goal set with goals that identify, for example, the percentages of minorities that will be hired or trained by certain future dates. Finally, much the same as McGregor's Theory X and Theory Y, the impact of equal employment opportunity and affirmative action has been to reorient significantly management's thinking about human resources. In many cases, concerns over the health and welfare of employees will take as much managerial time as that of capital expansion, mergers, or new product development.

Consumerism.   Our lives are touched daily in many ways by the products and services provided by numerous organizations. We have all at one time or another been disappointed by the performance of some product or service we have purchased. On a larger scale, these attitudes may represent a growing movement, termed *consumerism,* which reflects a judgment that organizations have not done their part in protecting the consuming public when it designs, promotes, sells, and guarantees its products and services.

In a recent survey of over three thousand managers in a variety of organizations, the following *business practices* were identified as causes of consumerism's growth.[23] In order of importance, they are:

1. Defective products.
2. Hazardous or unsafe products.
3. Defective repair work.
4. Misleading advertising.
5. Poor complaint-handling procedures by retailers.
6. Advertising that claims too much.
7. Deceptive packaging and labeling.
8. Poor complaint-handling procedures by manufacturers.
9. Failure to deliver merchandise that has been paid for.
10. Inadequate guarantees and warranties.

Important *economic factors* in consumerism's growth include concern over rising prices, deteriorating product quality, and the impersonal nature of the marketplace.

In response to the needs and desires of consumers, governmental intervention into the manufacture and marketing of products and services has been steadily increasing (an example of the Iron Law of Responsibility?). This governmental intervention has taken the form of various acts and creation of regulatory agencies with a variety of powers. Consumerism, consumer protection, more powerful regulatory agencies, and the like can all be of concern to the manager.

Urban Development. In many areas of the country, because of their location and resource potential, organizations have been called upon to give support (and in some cases, take the lead) in community efforts aimed at improving the quality of life within major population centers. This concern over urban development has resulted in a number of significant contributions by organizations.

Typical of some of the programs include the leadership by Ford Motor in the rebuilding of the downtown area of Detroit. In addition, Southern Pacific Company helped develop a program for eliminating substandard housing in Watts, and Kodak proposed the establishment of a fund and offered managerial consulting assistance for inner-city business ventures.

Organizations sometimes form a group to assist in urban problems. The Allegheny Housing Rehabilitation Corporation, composed of thirty-two large Pittsburgh area companies, was formed to rehabilitate deteriorating inner-city housing. After renovation, the homes are made available to low-income families.

Philanthropic Activities. For many years, organizations have been involved in philanthropic activities. Contributions to the arts, education, hospitals, and a variety of charities have averaged about $1 billion per year. Some of the contributions have been significant. For example: (1) by itself, IBM contributes over $20 million per year to charitable causes; (2) the railroads were instrumental in the formation and development of the Young Men's Christian Association (Y.M.C.A.); and (3) Texaco has sponsored the Metropolitan Opera radio broadcasts for over forty years.[24]

Some interesting questions develop when one considers philanthropy by private organizations. For example, why do organizations get involved in such activities? Is it to improve profits, is it done to be socially responsible, is it out of Christian charity of enlightened self-interest, or is it done as a tax write-off? The answer to all these questions is probably "yes," but it varies from organization to organization.

THE MANAGER'S JOB

Cornell Maier of Kaiser Aluminum and Chemical Corporation

Although many executives of large corporations are steering their firms increasingly toward social consciousness, Cornell Meier, chairman of Kaiser Aluminum and Chemical, does so with gusto. He goes out of his way to look for ways he and his firm can perform good community deeds. To Mr. Maier, corporate citizenship is a matter of conviction and remarkable personal interest. He feels that business has a clear social responsibility. Business is frequently critical of government involvement, but he believes that if business wants to criticize, it needs to become more involved itself.

To be sure, Kaiser does all the traditional things expected of a leading community employer. In its Oakland, California, headquarters area, for example, it hires disadvantaged workers, donates money to education, supports the local symphony and downtown renovation efforts, and offers financial and personnel backing to the United Way fund.

What sets Kaiser Aluminum and Maier apart, however, is their nontraditional activities. One of the newest is the unique "Summer on the Move" work-learn program developed last summer by Kaiser and the Oakland school district. Some 120 high school students attend morning classes, taught by University of California at Berkeley professors, and work in meaningful jobs in Oakland companies in the afternoon. In a related project, Kaiser has "adopted" Oakland High School, an aging inner-city school with a heavy enrollment of minority students. The company is buying needed facilities for the school and donating the time of its employees to work directly with the students.

In a different vein, Kaiser also has launched a program to educate wives of its male employees about the company and its role in society. Named Iris (after a Greek goddess, the "messenger of the rainbow"), the program is a pet project of bachelor Mr. Maier. He believes that businessmen have done the worst possible job in helping families understand what the free enterprise system is all about. "Some of the most vocal and aggressive critics are the sons and daughters of business managers," he says.

Mr. Maier attributes his crusading interest in social responsibility and free enterprise to his upbringing. Born to poor parents in South Dakota, he was reared by his mother who scratched out a living for her family as a grocery and department store clerk. Following a service stint in World War II, he graduated from UCLA and began his climb up the management ladder at Kaiser.

"I believe I'm one of the luckiest people on earth," he reflects. "I came from a very poor family, more so than most people. I was blessed with a mother who would rather starve than take aid. Also, I was fortunate in going to work for Henry Kaiser, the founder of the company. He was a great inspiration. He believed strongly in community service, and it rubbed off on me."

Suggested from S. Modic, "Maier," Industry Week *(October 29, 1979): 56–58.*

A number of points should be made. First, as an aggregate sum, $1 billion is a large figure, but it represents less than 1 percent of corporate pretax profits. In addition, the federal government has encouraged organizations to make charitable donations, as long as the sum does not exceed 5 percent of net income. The tax write-off argument, therefore, appears not to be very valid. Second, while many managers believe that charitable contributions are good for the organization (economically and in a social responsibility sense), the courts have stated that organizations need not show a direct benefit to profits by such contributions. In a stockholders suit against A.P. Smith Company, the New Jersey Supreme Court ruled that the company's contribution to a university was "essential to public welfare, and therefore, of necessity to corporate welfare." In other words, the court's decision implied that an "indirect benefit" was sufficient justification for such donations.

Organizations differ in the way they handle or manage philanthropic activities. Some make it a board of director's decision, others put it within the authority of an executive, and many others establish foundations for the sole purpose of being responsible for these activities. Whatever the reasons or ways of managing philanthropic activities, they will continue to be an important function in many organizations.

Social Audit

As the concern over the social behavior of organizations continues to grow, there has developed a need to find new methods to measure the performance of organizations in various social activities. The makeup of today's society almost insures that organizations will be held accountable for a much broader range of activities and results than ever before.

This broadened responsibility has led many organizations to develop specific assessment procedures that concern their involvement, support, and contributions to programs that deal with social issues. Several approaches under the heading of a *social audit* have been developed.[25] Four of the most used are the following:

1. *Inventory approach.* A descriptive method that lists the organization's social activities for a specific period of time. While it serves the purpose of informing various segments of society of the organization's activities, it provides little information or data on the extent of involvement or about the effectiveness of the various programs.

2. *Cost approach.* In addition to a list of activities and programs, an accounting of the amount spent, in terms of financial outlays, resources utilized, and so on is developed. Since only the "inputs" into social programs, not "results," are noted, such an approach gives no indication of the effectiveness of the activities.

3. *Program management approach.* Along with a list of programs and costs, this approach also requires a statement concerning whether the organization has met its goals with respect to each program. While this approach is more detailed than either of the previous two, it has been criticized because many of the stated goals can not be measured quantitatively.

4. *Cost-benefit analysis.* Incorporating the features of the other three ap-

proaches, the cost-benefit method attempts to quantify both the costs and values of each program. Such an analysis commonly follows an accounting procedure in which "assets" and "liabilities" are listed. As before, the problem of quantifying the benefits and then comparing them with actual costs remains an unresolved issue.

As the concept of organizational social behavior increases in importance, more and more organizations will attempt to develop methods for overcoming some of the problems of the current social audit approaches. The American Institute of Certified Public Accountants, the American Accounting Association, and the Securities and Exchange Commission have each offered procedures and guidelines for measuring the social performance of organizations.

ORGANIZATIONAL GOALS AND SOCIAL BEHAVIOR

In the second part of the chapter, we attempted to illustrate the importance of the organization's social behavior within the concept of goals. The relationship may be best summarized in exhibit 5–9. A number of points can be developed from an analysis of this exhibit. First, a thorough analysis of the subject must recognize that a three-way interaction involving the organization, society, and governmental elements exists. Second, each of the three main components in the exhibit have goals, not just the organization. Goal achievement must not only be measured by the number of interactions (organization-society, organization-government, and so on), but by whose point of view one takes.

EXHIBIT 5–9   Organizational, Societal, and Governmental Goal Interaction

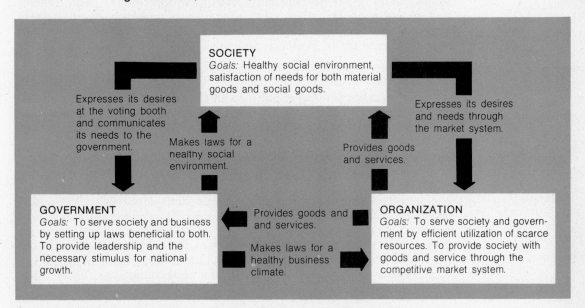

SOCIETY
Goals: Healthy social environment, satisfaction of needs for both material goods and social goods.

Expresses its desires at the voting booth and communicates its needs to the government.

Makes laws for a healthy social environment.

Provides goods and services.

Expresses its desires and needs through the market system.

GOVERNMENT
Goals: To serve society and business by setting up laws beneficial to both. To provide leadership and the necessary stimulus for national growth.

Provides goods and and services.

Makes laws for a healthy business climate.

ORGANIZATION
Goals: To serve society and government by efficient utilization of scarce resources. To provide society with goods and service through the competitive market system.

Adapted from C. W. Gross and H. L. Verma, "Marketing and Social Responsibility," Business Horizons (October 1977): 80.

Third, establishing social goals, as with setting market goals, implies that detailed policies, plans, and procedures must be developed, as well as information and feedback systems and a commitment to achieve the goals. In other words, a managerial system must be created that plans and controls an organization's social activities.

Keys to Success with Social Behavior

Managers are performance oriented. They attain their positions by proven success, or the potential for success, in achieving the goals of the organization. As such, the managers' first task and major responsibility is to the organization. The manager who through neglect causes the decline and erosion of an organization by becoming a public figure and taking the leadership in social problems at the expense of organizational goals is just as socially *irresponsible* as the manager who maximizes profits at the expense of society's good. The issue, therefore, concerns some keys to success with social behavior that managers must recognize.[26]

1. **Managers must not relegate economic performance to secondary status.**

Profit-making organizations survive and grow to the degree that revenues exceed costs; not-for-profit organizations continue to exist by providing services within certain cost constraints. An organization is not an employer of people, a contributor of goods and services, or a good neighbor in a community when it goes bankrupt and ceases to exist. This is not to say that a company that can no longer compete or one that produces unsafe or inferior goods should be allowed to continue to exist. Market forces should be the determining factor, as in the cases of Penn Central and W.T. Grant. Stated simply, whenever an organization disregards economic performance by assuming social responsibilities that it cannot support economically, it is asking for trouble.

2. **Solving social problems can be costly not only to organizations, but to society itself.**

As we have seen, solving social ills can take organizational profits that would normally go to further growth and development. However, most organizations will not sustain a continuing loss by seeking attainment of a nonmarket goal, but will transfer some of the responsibility to society. Two situations can be used as examples. First, the energy crisis could be partially eliminated through the development and use of synthetic fuels, coal, oil shale, and other alternative or substitute sources. However, no one organization or consortium of organizations can develop these new processes without governmental assistance. Governmental assistance, however, comes from funds provided by *taxpayers*. Second, solving social problems may result in the loss of jobs, or even a lower standard of living. Many manufacturing or chemical plants have been closed down for environmental reasons, resulting in layoffs or terminations. These "side effects" of solving social problems must be carefully considered by all.

3. **Organizations should lead from strength to solve problems.**

Organizations may actually be acting irresponsibly by taking on social tasks for which they lack the resources or required competence. There are resources inherent in all organizations that establish a certain degree of competence in specific activities (see chapter 4). Most organizations have managers who are proficient in certain managerial functions or who have acquired special skills that have some value. In areas beyond their specific competence or for which they are not responsible, the organization should limit their contributions. A business may donate the time of a number of skilled managers in order to help organize and control a charitable campaign such as United Appeal, American Cancer Society, and the like. Similarly, managers may give their own time to political candidates to assist in the management of their campaigns, or architects and engineers can contribute to urban renewal efforts. On the other hand, government has been less successful in attempting to make the post office a business-type organization or in effectively developing and managing training programs for the hard-core unemployed. These activities are beyond the competencies of governmental bodies, just as taking out an appendix is beyond a dentist's competence or organizing and operating a church is beyond the competence of a business such as Xerox or Bank of America.

4. **Social responsibility also implies social authority.**

As we will discuss in chapter 8, responsibility for certain actions also requires authority over these actions. For example, it was under Firestone's *authority* that 500 radial was developed, manufactured, and sold— they are, therefore, *responsible* for the product's malfunctions and impact. When the impact is the result of the exercise of an organization's authority, responsibility is also assumed. But what happens when an organization is asked to be socially responsible for a social ill or community problem for which it has no authority? If an organization is asked to take the lead in an urban renewal effort or a hard-core unemployed training program, does it have the authority to make decisions? Managers should consider carefully this authority-responsibility-impact relationship. By not recognizing this important relationship, managers are not only placing their organizations in a tenuous position, but they are throwing themselves (and their organizations) open to claims of "big brotherism" or "power grabbing" by certain elements in society.

Organizational and Social Goals: A Summary

As this chapter has attempted to present, the goals of an organization are important elements in the performance of the organization in addition to having significant implications for the manager's job. The major concepts discussed in this chapter are summarized in exhibit 5–10.

Goals and the Manager's Job

In what manner does the concept of social behavior by the organization affect the way its managers perform their jobs? In line with our format of defining the manager's job in terms of functions, skills, and roles, we can point out the following factors.

First, managerial skills are also important to the concept of social behavior by organizations.

EXHIBIT 5–10   Organizational and Social Goals: A Summary

GOAL CONCEPTS	DESCRIPTION
Organizational Goals	
1. Importance	Goals are guiding factors that affect the managerial functions of planning, organizing, leading, control, and change.
2. Criteria	Important criteria include: (1) clarity and specificity; (2) timing; (3) consistency; and (4) difficulty and achievability.
3. Types of goals	Goals can be classified by: (1) level of analysis; (2) focus; and (3) time frame.
4. Characteristics	Major characteristics include: (1) measurement; (2) multiplicity; and (3) ordering.
Social Goals	
1. Dimensions	Three dimensions identified: (1) social obligations; (2) social responsibility; and (3) social responsiveness.
2. Origins	History and experienced problems have contributed to the growth of social consciousness.
3. Arguments for and against	The main argument against social behavior is that any activity that does not contribute to profits for the organization's owners may be illegal. The "for" argument suggests that those who do not use power in the manner that society considers responsible will tend to lose it.
4. Responses	Tokenism, functional change, and structural change identified as organizational responses to social demands.
5. Issues and projects	Five major issues or projects discussed: (1) pollution; (2) affirmative action; (3) consumerism; (4) urban development; and (5) philanthropic activities.
6. Social audit	In an attempt to measure the social performance of organizations, four methods or procedures can be identified: (1) inventory approach; (2) cost approach; (3) program management; and (4) cost-benefit analysis.
7. Constraints	Organization's social behavior should consider the following limiting factors: (1) social behavior should not endanger the economic survival of the firm; (2) potential "side effects" should be identified and carefully considered; (3) the organization should evaluate its competencies before taking on social tasks; and (4) social responsibility also implies social authority.

1. *Technical skills.* Technical skills gain in importance when one considers the complexity of coordinating market and nonmarket goals and seeing them through to completion.

2. *Human skills.* Managers must develop human skills on an intragroup and intergroup basis. That is, they must be able to move the organization's human resources toward goal attainment but effectively deal with groups outside the organization (e.g., interest groups, community organizations, governmental agencies, and the like).

3. *Conceptual and diagnostic skills.* These higher level skills are closely related to our previous discussion on the realities of social behavior. Managers need to understand the competencies of the organization, where the organization fits in with social issues, and what the short- and long-term effects on society and the organization itself will be.

Finally, it is clear that all three managerial *roles* come into action when we consider the social behavior of the organization.

1. *Interpersonal roles.* As a figurehead, leader, and liaison, the manager performs important roles representing the organization to environmental units, keeping in touch with the external community, and motivating employees toward goal achievement.

2. *Informational roles.* Performing as a monitor, disseminator, and spokesperson, the manager is the key communications and information link with the external environment.

3. *Decisional roles.* Finally, as an entrepreneur, disturbance handler, resource allocator, and negotiator, the manager seeks out the environmental impact of the organization's products and services, attempts to resolve conflicts in setting and achieving goals, and determines the extent of the organization's involvement and commitment to social issues.

Managers in all types of organizations are finding out that their effectiveness as managers and the survival and effectiveness of their organizations depends to a large extent on its acceptance and relationship with societal elements. Thus, many managers have found it to be a requirement for performance to pay increased attention not only to market goals but to the equally important nonmarket, social goals as well.

SUMMARY FOR THE MANAGER

1. Some form of goal setting is necessary for proper performance by the organization and for the manager's job. Goals, the product of some environmental analysis (internal and external), serve as guiding principles for planning, organizing, leading, controlling, and change. Goals are among the major factors in the management process.

2. Managers must understand that goals can be viewed from a variety of frameworks. Of particular importance is the recognition that goals can be short term or long term; the focus can be some form of maintenance activity, improvement, or developmental action; and goals can vary through the different organizational levels, from corporate goals down to individual goals. In addition, no matter what type of organizational goal we are discussing, unless it is clearly stated and understood, is consistent with the organization's resources, and can be achieved without being overly difficult, it will result

in behavior and performance that is less than desirable.

3. Further recognition must be given to the fact that most managers attempt to achieve more than one goal during a particular period of time. This multiplicity places emphasis on how and when goals will be measured. In addition, it affects: (a) how they relate to the goals of other managers; (b) which goals are more important than others; and (c) the necessity for a "give and take" or balancing relationship with other goals.

4. Market, profit, and efficiency goals have been the main focus for managers for many years. Nonmarket or social goals have been increasing in importance as the organization's relationship with society and the environment gains attention. The result is increasing complexity in the manager's job. This situation also creates a dilemma for the manager. With rapidly changing societal values, is the manager's real responsibility to the organization, to the stockholders, to the larger community, or where? The answer is "all of the above," which requires the manager to set priorities and balance organizational goals.

5.   There are at least three frameworks for analyzing social behavior by an organization: (a) social obligations; (b) social responsibility; and (c) social responsiveness. Depending on the dominant framework, organizations will adopt a number of different response patterns when faced with increasing social pressures. Tokenism, functional change, and structural change are the three most used response patterns. Whatever response pattern is chosen, the manager must recognize that each differs in the cost, support, and commitment necessary from the organization, and the acceptance level by society of these responses can also vary greatly.

6.   The major issues on which some social goals can be developed are increasing at a rapid pace. Examples include: (a) pollution control; (b) affirmative action; (c) consumerism; (d) urban development; and (e) philanthropic activities. Each will require special knowledge and expertise by the manager.

7.   While it is difficult for the manager to be against anything that is for the "good of society," a careful analysis of constraints is needed before any commitment of organizational resources is contemplated. Above all, the manager must not relegate economic success to secondary importance for fear of jeopardizing the future survival of the organization. Also included in a constraints analysis is the identification of potential side effects of social actions, the limits of the organization's authority and the resources and competencies that can be allocated.

8.   Managerial functions, skills, and roles are all affected by the concept of organizational goals. Goals serve as the foundation for planning efforts and the establishment of a control function. The success that the manager obtains from interacting with environmental elements and internal units depends to a great extent on what skills are developed and what roles are enacted.

QUESTIONS FOR REVIEW AND DISCUSSION

1. Discuss the origins and importance of organizational goals.
2. What are the important criteria for organizational goals? Why are they critical for goal achievement?
3. In what jobs would qualitative goals be acceptable?
4. Why is it important for goals to be assigned priority ratings and balanced?
5. What skills and roles are emphasized in organizational goal formation?
6. Can you identify organizations that: (a) meet their social obligations; (b) are socially responsible; and (c) are socially responsive?
7. What are the advantages and disadvantages of the three response patterns to social pressure?
8. What social issues or projects are important in your community?
9. Can you suggest how social behavior by an organization can be better measured?
10. What is the relationship between organizational competencies and the level of their socially conscious behavior?

NOTES

1. See M. D. Richards, *Organizational Goal Structures* (St. Paul, Minn.: West, 1978), p. 1.

2. A. Etzioni, *Modern Organizations* (Englewood Cliffs, N.J.: Prentice-Hall, 1964), p. 6.

3. Richards, p. 5.

4. A. Raia, *Managing by Objectives* (Glenview, Ill.: Scott, Foresman, 1974), p. 38.

5. C. Perrow, "The Analysis of Goals in Complex Organizations," *American Sociological Review* (December 1961): p. 856.

6. Ibid., p. 857.

7. G. A. Steiner, "Comprehensive Managerial Planning," in Stephen J. Caroll et al., *The Management Process* (New York: Macmillan, 1977), pp.126–27.

8. See C. J. Loomis, "The Leaning Tower of Sears," *Fortune* (July 2, 1979): 78–85; and R. Loving, Jr., "W.T. Grant's Last Days as Seen from Store 1192," *Fortune* (April 1976): 108–14.

9. R. J. Flaherty, "The Singular Henry Singleton," *Forbes* (July 9, 1979): 48.

10. G. W. England, "Organizational Goals and Expected Behavior of American Managers," *Academy of Management Journal* (June 1967): 108.

11. L. Langway and M. Kasindorf, "Laddie, Come Home," *Newsweek* (July 9, 1979): 57–58.

12. A. M. Louis, "Lessons from the Firestone Fracas," *Fortune* (August 28, 1978): 44–48.

13. S. P. Sethi, "A Conceptual Framework for Environmental Analysis of Social Issues and Evaluation of Business Response Patterns," *Academy of Management Review* (January 1979): 64.

14. Ibid., pp. 65–66.

15. M. L. Lovdal, R. A. Bauer, and N. H. Treverton, "Public Responsibility Committees of the Board," *Harvard Business Review* (May–June 1977): 40–54.

16. See D. C. Aker and G. S. Day, "Corporate Responses to Consumerism Pressures," *Harvard Business Review* (November–December 1972): 114–24; and V. M. Buehler and Y. K. Shetty, "Managerial Response to Social Responsibility Challenge," *Academy of Management Journal* (March 1976): 67–78.

17. P. F. Drucker, *Management: Tasks, Responsibilities,* *Practices* (New York: Harper & Row, 1974), p. 338.

18. E. E. Jennings, "Make Way for the Business Moralist," *Nation's Business* (September 1966): 90.

19. M. Friedman, "Does Business Have a Social Responsibility?" *The Magazine of Bank Administration* (April 1971): 14.

20. K. Davis, "The Meaning and Scope of Social Responsibility," in *Contemporary Management,* ed. J. W. McGuire (Englewood Cliffs, N.J.: Prentice-Hall, 1974), p. 616.

21. See W. Kiechel III, "The Admiralty Case of the Century," *Fortune* (April 23, 1979): 78–89; M. H. Zim, "Allied Chemical's $20 Million Ordeal with Kepone," *Fortune* (September 11, 1978): 82–91; and S. Solomon, "The Asbestos Fallout at Johns-Manville," *Fortune* (May 7, 1979): 196–206.

22. T. Alexander, "A Promising Try at Environmental Detente for Coal," *Fortune* (February 13, 1978): 94–102.

23. S. A. Greyser and S. L. Diamond, "Business Adapting to Consumerism," *Harvard Business Review* (September–October 1974): 38–58.

24. N. K. Barnes, "Rethinking Corporate Charity," *Fortune* (October 1974): 169–82.

25. See R. A. Bauer and D. H. Fenn, Jr., *The Corporate Social Audit* (New York: Russell Sage Foundation, 1972); and D. Fetyko, "The Company Social Audit," *Management Accounting* (April 1975): 135–48.

26. Drucker, pp. 343–51.

ADDITIONAL REFERENCES

Abouzeid, K. M., and Weaver, C. N. "Social Responsibility in the Corporate Goal Hierarchy." *Business Horizons* (June 1979): 29–35.

Davis, K., "Five Propositions for Social Responsibility." *Business Horizons* (June 1975): 19–24.

Davis, K., and Blomstrom, R. L. *Business, Society, and Environment.* New York: McGraw-Hill, 1971.

Drucker, P. *The Practice of Management.* New York: Harper & Row, 1954.

Farmer, R., and Hogue, W. D., *Corporate Social Responsibility.* Chicago: SRA, 1973.

Fitch, H. G. "Achieving Corporate Social Responsibility." *Academy of Management Review* (January 1976): 38–46.

Granger, C. H., "How to Set Company Objectives." *Management Review* (July 1970): 2–8.

Greenwood, W. T., *Issues in Business and Society: Readings and Cases.* Boston: Houghton Mifflin, 1971.

Guzzardi, W., Jr. "The Mindless Pursuit of Safety." *Fortune* (April 9, 1979): 54–64.

Parker, I. R., and Eilbirt, H., "Social Responsibility: The Underlying Factors." *Business Horizons* (August 1975): 5–10.

Social Responsibilities of Business Corporations. New York: Committee for Economic Development, 1971.

Steiner, G. A., *Issues In Business and Society.* New York: Random House, 1972.

A CASE FOR ANALYSIS

The Beta Oil Company

Troy, Colorado, was a small town of slightly over thirty-five hundred people located at the base of the Rocky Mountains. Since it was founded in the late nineteenth century, the majority of its residents were employed in agricultural work. Much has happened to this town in the last ten years. It has gone from a sleepy little town, to a boom town, to a town in deep trouble.

Everyone knew that the town sat on top of one of the largest shale oil deposits in the world. However, as long as the technology to mine and produce crude oil from the shale rock cost more than normal drilling operations for crude, the town would not gain any economic value from the deposits. This was to change dramatically with the oil crises of the 1970s.

Early in 1970, Beta Oil Company, one of the nation's largest energy producers, announced plans for the construction of a pilot plant to produce crude oil from shale rock in Troy. The pilot plant would be built on a small scale in order to examine the feasibility of a new process that it had leased from a West German firm. When fully operational, the plan would only produce four thousand barrels of oil per day. If the process proved to be economically feasible in line with rising crude prices around the world, Beta had developed plans to expand the plant to produce seventy-five thousand barrels per day. Even though the plant was to be small initially, Beta planned to employ nearly five hundred people during the test plant stage at the facility. With their families, the total influx of new residents working for Beta would be about 1,800, increasing the size of Troy by over 50 percent.

Beta knew from past experience that such a venture would hit Troy like a big shock wave. In order to smooth out any problems and try to make the transition for the residents of Troy as easy as possible, the company established a unit of over thirty employees who were part of the Community Affairs Development Group. Attached to the Personnel Department, the main function of the group was to work with various community leaders and townspeople with regard to employment opportunities, pollution control, community development, and so on. The plant opened in 1971.

The impact of the Beta plant was felt almost immediately by the town. Homes and apartments were built for the transferred employees along with new schools and churches. The company built a new water purification plant for the town. To finance the construction of the new schools and sewer system, it was necessary for the town and district to be bonded: that is, capital improvement bonds were sold and were to be paid off on a yearly basis through a new taxing plan. In addition, the police and fire department were expanded to handle the town's growth. In total, slightly over $3 million dollars in bonds were sold.

For the next four years the town of Troy grew tremendously. Beyond the private and public facilities, the state began a program to double the number of miles of paved roads, new snow removal equipment was purchased for the winter months, and various state agencies established regional offices in Troy. The town also drew a significant number of new merchants and other businesses to serve the growth in population. A program was even started to expand and refurbish the small downtown area. By the summer of 1976, the population of Troy had grown to over eight thousand residents.

In the fall of 1976, however, things changed rapidly. Beta announced that it planned to shut down the pilot plant in early 1977. After four years of operation, the company concluded that even with rising crude prices, the present process was still not economically feasible. A skeleton work force of less than thirty employees would continue to maintain the plant, as the company left open the decision to restaff the plant, if and when a new process technology could be developed by the company's scientists or a new license could be obtained.

The impact on the people and businesses of Troy was immediate and disastrous. The town was faced with numerous problems including developing means of paying off the bonds, how to keep the new businesses in town, what to do about the sudden unemployment of teachers, city employees, and other workers, and the like. The high probability of a 25 percent increase in school and sales taxes was particularly distressing to the residents. Private groups would be hit particularly hard. Already committed were two new churches, a new department store, and land had been purchased for a new city park that would include little league facilities and a large swimming pool. One saving feature of the town's rapid growth was the building of a new ski resort five miles from the city limits. However, this was a seasonal business that could not counter the impact of the plant's closing.

The townspeople were extremely bitter and angry with Beta Oil. They felt that the company had lied to them about the plant and its future. They claimed that if they had known that the plant could possibly be closed within five years, the present expansion would never have been contemplated. In defense, Beta pointed to documents and communication that its Community Affairs Development Group had given to the town's leaders which clearly stated the potential temporary nature of the plant. They also pointed to the many facilities, especially the new water works, that the company had donated. Finally, they indicated that a new technology that they were developing in their laboratories in Houston showed great promise and that there was a good chance that the plant could be reopened within three years.

Questions for Discussion

1. Evaluate the social behavior of Beta in this case.
2. Could the company have handled matters any differently so that the current problems could have been alleviated?
3. Does Beta have any obligation to the town of Troy at the present time?
4. Evaluate the role of the leaders of the town in this case.

EXPERIENTIAL EXERCISE

Organizational Goals

Purpose

To study how goals influence managerial decision making.

Required Understanding

The reader should be familiar with the issues and concepts associated with organizational goals.

How to Set Up the Exercise

Set up groups of four to eight persons for the thirty- to forty-five minute exercise. The groups should be separated from each other and asked to converse only with their group members. Before joining the groups, each person is asked to complete the exercise alone, and then the groups should form and reach a consensus.

The Situation

Assume you are a member of the top management team of the Davis Industrial Gas Products Company, a large industrial gas supplier located in St. Louis, Missouri. The firm specializes in packaging and distribution of gas cylinders to industries within a two-hundred mile radius of St. Louis. The firm's main products are oxygen, hydrogen, helium, acetylene, and other gas mixtures used, for example, in hospitals (oxygen) and manufacturing firms (acetylene for metal cutting). The company purchases the various gases from chemical plants located nearby, processes the gases to improve the levels of purity, and then packages the product in different size cylinders. The firm's financial statement at the end of 1979 is shown in exhibit 5–11.

EXHIBIT 5–11
Income Statement
of Davis Industrial
Gas Products
Company

INCOME STATEMENT: 1979

A.

Revenue		$10,000,000
Expenses		
Raw materials	$5,600,000	
Salaries, wages, and benefits	2,850,000	
Depreciation	1,000,000	
Research and development	200,000	
Advertisement	50,000	
Training	40,000	
Public relations	60,000	
Interest expense	300,000	
Total Expenses		10,100,000
Net Loss		($ 100,000)

B. Net profit (loss) and revenues for four years

Year	Revenue	Net Profit (loss)
1978	$10,000,000	($100,000)
1977	9,500,000	380,000
1976	8,000,000	300,000
1975	7,800,000	($ 50,000)

Your top management team will meet shortly to discuss four problems or issues currently facing the company. Decisions on each of the four problems *must be made at this meeting.* The four problems, which are *occurring at the same time,* are:

Problem 1　The local civic club has frequently complained to your company and to the city council about the air pollution originating from your plant. Although this is not proven, the age of your equipment suggests a number of leaks could exist. Your legal advisors have told you that to prove air pollution exists and that Davis is the source would take a minimum of two to three years. Your options are to repair the possible pipe leaks, costing approximately $100,000 (option 1), or to do nothing (option 2).

Problem 2　Your company is pleased with the success in sales of oxygen cylinders to the area hospitals. Your management believes that there is good growth potential in selling other products to hospitals as well as in selling oxygen in smaller cylinders to doctors' offices and nursing homes. You would, however, face increased competition in each of these markets. The new equipment and increase in sales force will cost $300,000. The options are to spend the money (option 1) or to do nothing (option 2).

Problem 3   The relations with the union representing your hourly workers has been tense for years. The three-year union contract will expire in four months. In your initial bargaining, the union has made known its demands for a significant increase in wages and benefits. The cost over the three years of the new contract would be $250,000. Finished inventory at the time of the contract's expiration would last six to eight weeks. Your options are to settle with the union on terms similar to their demands (option 1) or to take a chance on a long and bitter strike (option 2).

Problem 4   Your company has experienced a 35 percent turnover in supervisory and management personnel during the past year. A recent consultant's report indicated that not only are salaries for managerial personnel below the area average, but the company is in need of extensive revisions in its training and development programs. Your options are to spend $100,000 on personnel selection, training, development, and salary upgrading (option 1) or to do nothing (option 2).

Instructions

1. *Individually,* group members should:

   a. Make decisions on each of the four problems discussed above. Remember: (1) decisions on these problems must be made now; (2) the problems are occurring simultaneously; and (3) you have only two options on each problem.

   b. *Rank in order* the underlying goals or objectives that were important in your overall decisions. Mark your responses on exhibit 5–12.

2. As a *group,* repeat the above decisions. Mark group choices, distribution of individual choices, and group ranks on exhibit 5–12.

EXHIBIT 5–12   Goals in Decision Making

Problems	Individual Decisions Option 1 Option 2 (circle your choice)		Distribution of Individual Decisions in Group Option 1 Option 2	Group Decision Option 1 Option 2 (circle group choice)	
1. Air pollution	1	2		1	2
2. Improved product line	1	2		1	2
3. Labor relations	1	2		1	2
4. Management development	1	2		1	2

B. Rank in Order the Underlying Goals in Individual and Group Decisions (1 = Most Important; 6 = Least Important)

Goal	Individual Rank	Group Rank
1. Company survival		
2. Improved competitive position		
3. Community image		
4. Stability		
5. Employee relations and development		
6. Internal cost control		

6

Strategy and Plans

CHAPTER OUTLINE

KEY POINTS IN THIS CHAPTER

1. Planning is a process that concerns the future impact of current decisions. It is a crucial managerial function that, when linked to control, strongly influences performance.

2. The premises of organizational planning include the analysis of the external and internal environment and the establishment of goals and strategy.

3. Strategy is different from planning. Strategy deals with the "what" of organizational activities, while planning concerns "how" goals and strategies will be achieved.

4. The types of strategies include stability, product and market development, vertical integration, merger, and retreat.

5. Types of plans, time frame, elements, repetitiveness, and focus are related to the dimensions of planning.

6. An important addition to the planning process is contingency planning, which focuses on the important "what if" events.

7. Scenarios, nominal group technique, and computer simulation models are some key aids in the planning process.

8. Managerial skills—especially human, conceptual, and diagnostic—and informational and decisional roles are all important factors of planning to the manager's job.

THE PRACTICE OF MANAGEMENT

Organizational Planning: Gulf Oil Corporation

In 1978, Gulf Oil Corporation received what might be called a nasty surprise from a competitor. Halfway toward its five-year goal of gaining and holding the number two position in the market for low-density polyethylene film (used in household food wrappings, sandwich and garbage bags), Gulf was jolted by Union Carbide's announcement that it had developed a new process to make low-density polyethylene at a cost 20 percent less than Gulf's conventional method. Gulf immediately cranked up its research and development effort, but unless the Pittsburgh oil and chemicals producer can come through quickly with a similar breakthrough, Gulf's long-range goals for its chemicals business are in jeopardy.

In seeking to attain the number two position in the low-density polyethylene film market, the chemicals division went about its planning: looking at its industry potential for growth, its competitors, its market position, and any inherent risks, as well as the funds needed to reach its goals. But Gulf's problems show that any plan is only as good as the assumptions and savvy underlying it. Gulf had forecast a projected growth in demand of 10 percent or more in each of the plan's five years. To meet such a demand, Gulf added into its plan the cost of a new plant to be built in 1979. In addition, a major assumption of the plan was that since technological breakthroughs in the manufacture of polyethylene were highly *unlikely,* research and development spending could be kept to a minimum. Not only did the Union Carbide announcement throw a rock into these assumptions, but market growth turned out to be only 8 percent annually, putting a big question mark on the decision to build the new plant.

The conception of Gulf's initial strategy for its chemicals business, the dovetailing of this into the overall organizational plan, and now the problems in those plans are typical of what organizations throughout the U.S. are facing these days. Questions of how to design plans and how to meet—or better still, anticipate—threats from competitors and a host of other outside factors have become the prime topic of concern in more and more organizations.

Divisional plans and corporate plans are two very different animals. A business plan usually covers a plan for a single product or group or related products, while a corporate plan seeks to unify all the product and service lines of an organization and point them toward an overall goal. Today most of the action is at the divisional level, where sophisticated tools and techniques permit analysis of such things as market growth, pricing, and the impact of governmental regulation and also permit the establishment of a plan that can sidestep threats from competitors, economic cycles, and social, political, and consumer changes in an erratic environment.

But, while divisional plans are becoming more sophisticated, corporate planning is still very fuzzy and ill-defined. A possible reason for this situation is that most top managers today have grown up in a tradition in which, as line managers, they were forced to play the cautious game. The people who have risen to power now are simply continuing what was for them a successful strategy—stability and minimum risk. The new style of planning, which requires line managers to be creative, flexible, and entrepreneurial, could end up breeding a new type of manager—one whose success is based on the entrepreneurial qualities that built today's most effective organizations.

Adapted from "The New Planning," Business Week *(December 18, 1978): 62–68.*

6

The function of planning affects our lives constantly, whether we are planning a vacation, a sales presentation to a customer, or our careers. In its simplest form, planning is the process of translating individual or organizational goals into ways to achieve the goals.

In an organization, planning is one of the most essential elements. While variations in the types of plans exist, it is important to note that *all* levels of management plan. From the head nurse in a hospital who plans the work schedule and assignment of tasks to floor nurses, to the corporation president who develops the five-year profitability plan for the organization, planning is an integral part of their jobs.

In this chapter, we will discuss the planning function in four parts. First, we will attempt to establish a fundamental understanding of planning, exploring some of the definitional elements, the importance of planning, and the significant distinction between planning and strategy. In the second part, we will develop and discuss a basic framework for planning, the important dimensions, and the key differences between the various types of planning activities. Third, three planning aids will be discussed. Finally, we will concentrate on the major issues of planning and how they affect the manager's job.

THE MEANING AND IMPORTANCE OF PLANNING

In more formal terms, we will define *organizational planning* as the set of policies, procedures, and methods used by managers to achieve their stated goals. Crucial to the understanding of this definition is a knowledge of what organizational planning is and is not.

Organizational planning is sometimes referred to as long-range planning, corporate planning, strategic planning, managerial planning, or some combination of these words. Although we will shortly attempt to distinguish between some of these terms, we should point out at least four ways of defining organizational planning:[1]

1. Organizational planning is a process.

Planning is a process that begins with an analysis of the external environment and internal resources, concerns the development of goals and strategies to achieve goals, and formulates detailed plans to make sure that the strategies are carried out. The discussion of planning began with the previous two chapters on the external and internal environment (chapter 4) and organizational goals (chapter 5). Whereas these two chapters identified *what* should be done, the remaining elements of the planning process deal with *when* it is to be done, *how* it is to be done, and *who* is going to do it.

2. Organizational planning is a philosophy of managing.

While planning has been identified in chapter 2 as a managerial function, there are many practicing managers and academicians who elevate planning to a special level of importance. To these people, planning is a way of life that has a great impact on managerial performance.

3. **Organizational planning deals with the future impact of current decisions.**

This means that planning tries to identify a series of cause-and-effect relationships that may result from a particular set of decisions. If the results of a planning effort are not to the liking of the managers, they can change the decision and develop alternative plans.

4. **Organizational planning is made up of a series of plans.**

It is in reality a series of different plans that differ by such characteristics as time frame, focus, and the level of management involved. Planning is more accurately viewed as an integrated structure of goals, strategies, policies, and functions of an organization.

As the previous discussion suggests, organizational planning has a wide domain of influence in organizations. Even with this wide domain, there are some aspects that are frequently confused with planning. Let us make clear what planning is not:

1. **Planning is not forecasting.**

As we discussed in chapter 4, forecasting concerns an attempt to predict the value of some particular variable (e.g., sales or personnel needs) based on current data, information, or trends. The variables of interest can be associated with either external or internal environmental components. In essence, forecasting is a pre-activity or *premise* of planning.

2. **Planning does not attempt to make future decisions.**

Quite the opposite, planning concerns the impact of *current* decisions on future events and the alternatives that are open to the manager.

3. **The end product of a planning effort is not inflexible doctrine.**

Rather than set in concrete, a plan must be an iterative, flexible activity that adjusts to changes in the external and internal environment. Planning attempts to invent the future for the manager; but when changes do occur during the period of the plan, certain alternatives can be chosen to get activities back on track. This is what we will refer to later as the *contingency* nature of planning.

4. **Planning is not done solely by executive managers.**

Planning is an integral part of every manager's job, from president to front-line supervisor. While differences in the nature and type of planning exist between managerial levels, the essential process of planning remains unchanged.

The Gulf Oil Corporation example in the *Practice of Management* section and the preceding discussion should provide some important insights into the reasons why managers emphasize planning. Planning is a crucial managerial function and one that involves everything a manager does. Without a plan, it would be difficult for managers to attempt to organize their areas of responsibilities, to try to staff the unit with needed employees, or to motivate these employees.

Beyond this general statement of importance, there are other factors that serve to highlight the planning function. First, planning enables the manager or organization to affect rather than accept the future—in other words, planning assists managers in *coping with change.* As discussed in chapter 4, the external environment of many organizations is becoming more and more dynamic and turbulent with each passing year. This includes all types of organizations from corporations to hospitals and universities. Many managers know that without good plans, they may be caught by surprise, which could have dire consequences.

Consider, for example, the impact on oil companies of the development of OPEC, the fall of the Shah of Iran, and the increased federal emphasis on other energy sources including synthetic fuels. Without plans developed for such situations, many of the organizations would have been forced into a reactive, crisis management mode. Or consider a university and the impact of changing population characteristics such as age distribution and education and skills needs. In absence of certain plans, universities in the future (or even today) could find themselves in an overstaffed and underfunded position with inadequate curricula.

Second, planning can improve the performance of the organization and its members. A number of studies have been reported that strongly indicate that organizations using formal planning activities significantly outperform those who do not plan, or who plan in an informal manner.[2] These studies have shown that not only does organizational performance improve when formal planning efforts are initiated, but the relationship holds up at all levels: organization, division, unit, group, and individual managers.[3] Consider the differences in performance between Ford and Chrysler, and G.E. and Westinghouse.[4] In each case, studies have shown that Ford's and G.E.'s growth and performance, in comparison with Chrysler and Westinghouse, was due in part to their meticulous planning.

Finally, planning and the important managerial function of *control* are strongly related. After goals and plans have been established, controls are necessary to ensure that resources are allocated properly and that individuals and groups perform to achieve the stated organizational goals. Planning states what is to be accomplished, and control systems are developed to evaluate how plans are progressing.

THE ORGANIZATIONAL PLANNING PROCESS

Exhibit 6–1 provides a framework for analyzing the total organizational planning process. As the exhibit shows, the planning process can be viewed as consisting of five distinct stages. Stage I involves what we will call the *premises* of the planning process. The premises, discussed in detail in chapters 4 and 5, concern how organizational goals are developed from an analysis of the external and internal environment. Stage II focuses on the key aspect of an organization's *strategy.* As we will shortly discuss, strategy involves the choice of particular actions to be taken.

Stage III is the heart of the planning process. In this stage, the important *plans, policies, procedures, budgets,* and *rules* are developed

EXHIBIT 6-1 Organizational Planning Process

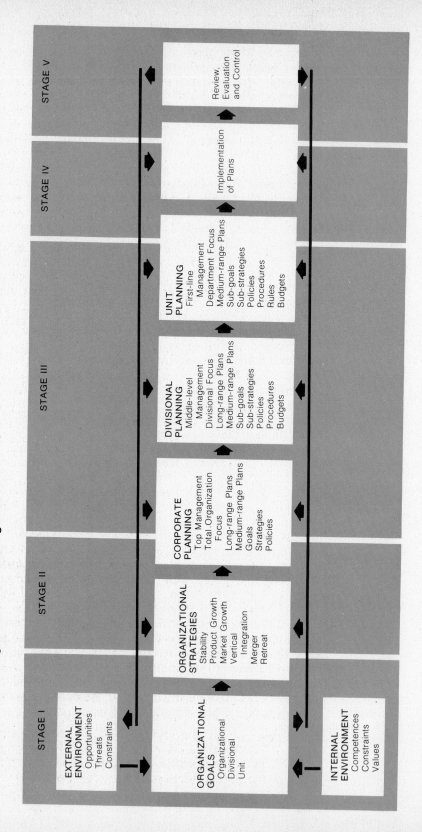

Suggested by G. A. Steiner, *Top Management Planning* (New York: Macmillan, 1969).

to put the organization's goals and strategies into action. Stage IV concerns the implementation activities of Stage III. This includes the establishment of the needed organizational design and control systems. Finally, Stage V deals with the *review, evaluation,* and *feedback* aspects of the implemented plans. Stages II and III will be discussed in detail in the next sections. The remaining stages will be covered in later chapters.

ORGANIZATIONAL STRATEGY

In their zeal to translate goals into action plans, managers sometimes fail to give sufficient attention to what comes between these two elements—namely, the concept of organizational *strategy*.[5] For our purposes, we will define *strategy* as a comprehensive and integrated framework that guides those choices that determine the nature and direction of the organization's activities toward goal achievement. This definition implies the existence of three important characteristics:

1. Strategy involves a *choice* of particular actions or activities.[6] Managers and organizations are faced with many choices during any time period. Examples include choices concerning an organization's products and services, the groups that will be served, and the allocation of resources.

2. Strategy is a function of *direction;* plans (Stage III) are a function of *how* this direction is put into action. Since strategy sets the direction, it must be formulated *before* plans are made.

3. If more than one strategy has been chosen by an organization, they must be *integrated* into a strategic framework, much the same as organizational goals are ordered (i.e., setting priorities, goal networks, and balancing as discussed in chapter 5). If choices are made without a framework, the manager abdicates the control over direction to whoever happens to be making decisions.

External and Internal Environmental Influences on Strategy

In chapter 4 we developed the concept that the organization's external environment, with its inherent opportunities, threats, and constraints, and internal environment, consisting of certain strengths and weaknesses, are major factors in determining the domain of management action—"what it should do." In essence, what the organization "should do" is translated into *goals* and *strategies,* the choice and direction components of the organizational planning process.

   We can integrate these concepts with the aid of exhibit 6–2, which is adapted from General Electric's "Stoplight Strategy" for planning.[7] The two dimensions of the presented "grid" represent an analysis of an organization's external and internal environments. The first dimension, *external opportunities* ("Industry Attractiveness" in G. E.'s framework) relates to certain market or service opportunities on which the organization can capitalize. It is determined by projections of a product's sales, profit, and return on investment along with such factors as volatility of market share, technology needs, competitive stance, and social needs. The result is a rating of high, medium, and low on the existence of external opportunities.

EXHIBIT 6–2
The Influence of
External
Opportunities and
Internal Strengths
on Strategy

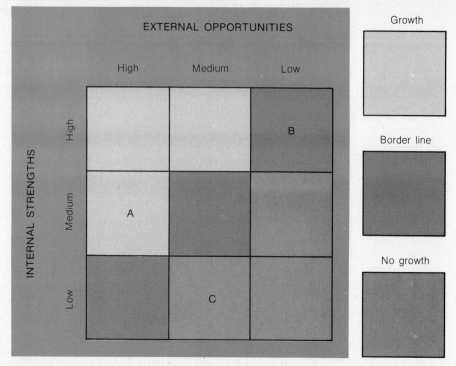

Adapted from "General Electric's 'Stoplight Strategy' for Planning," Business Week, *(April 28, 1975): 49.*

The *internal strengths* dimension represents the strengths and weaknesses the organization has developed over time. Consisting of an evaluation of the organization's internal resources, the dimension is also rated along a high, medium, and low continuum. The result is a nine-part grid that depicts three tentative strategies: (1) growth opportunities, (2) borderline opportunities, and (3) no-growth opportunities.

1. *Growth.* The three quadrants present a medium-to-high evaluation on both external opportunities and internal strengths. This evaluation suggests that there is a potential for expansion of goods and services in the chosen market. For example, consider the plans of Exxon, noted as "A" in exhibit 6–2. Seeking to diversify out of the turbulent energy field, Exxon invested in the electronics market (i.e., "QWIP" Systems) with the development of electric typewriters and other data-processing devices. In the grid, such a venture would be evaluated as being high in external opportunities because of the growth in that market. The internal strengths are shown as medium, representing not so much Exxon's lack of expertise in the electronics market, but its immense resource base.[8]

2. *Borderline.* This evaluation, which includes the diagonal cells of the grid, suggests that before the organization invests in the product, or continues in the market, a more detailed and cautious evaluation is needed. In other words, it is a "hold tight" strategy until more is known. An example is Bell & Howell's dilemma of whether or not to continue producing and

selling in the home movie equipment market.[9] Shown as "B" in exhibit 6–2, the company's strengths are evaluated as high because of its past performance and expertise developed over many years. The external opportunities are shown to be low. This is due to 25 percent decline in the demand for movie equipment since 1972 as more families turn to video games and other forms of home entertainment.

3. *No growth.* The three parts shown as a medium-to-low evaluation on each dimension suggest strategies that may involve a reduced investment, consolidation of resources, and a lack of growth opportunities. Consider, for example, the problems that have faced Gerber Products, Inc., the country's largest baby-food maker.[10] Shown as "C" in exhibit 6–2, the opportunities for investments into areas outside baby foods are evaluated as being medium, but the internal strengths are depicted as low. This evaluation represents Gerber's recent failures in entering the adult convenience food market and the marketing of life insurance policies to young parents. Gerber was faced with a decline in its primary market due to the decrease in birth rate during the 1970s. The market offered a medium level of opportunity, but the company lacked the necessary resource strengths to effectively compete in these areas.

It is important to note that this type of analysis is only preliminary. However, it does give the manager a good idea of what possible actions are available to the organization, and it provides time for a more careful evaluation.

Types of Strategies

At least six different strategies can be adopted by organizations to achieve their stated goals: (1) stability, (2) product development, (3) market development, (4) vertical integration, (5) merger, and (6) retreat.

Stability.   A strategy oriented toward stability is generally followed by an organization when it is satisfied with its present position. As long as the organization is doing well, managers may be reluctant to change. In most cases we may find successful strategies of stability when a firm is faced with a stable and simple external environment (see exhibit 4–4). A paper mill and certain utilities can be considered as organizations that have followed a stability strategy.

In addition to the external environment, another source of a strategy of stability (possibly the most influential) are the values, background, and orientation of the top management team. For example, consider the differences between two giants of the food industry, Campbell Soup and H.J. Heinz.[11] Most people consider the companies "look alikes," yet from a performance standpoint, they are quite different. From a growth perspective (e.g., sales, net income, and new products), Heinz is the hare, while Campbell is the tortoise. A look at the members of the top management team may provide some insights. Heinz is run by a group of managers who have a strong marketing background and orientation. On the other hand, among its top two dozen managers, Campbell doesn't list a single marketing person. Virtually all are production engineers. As we learned from the history of management thought (chapter 3), engineers are known for their concern over internal factors such as efficiency, production capacity, and manufacturing design. A dominant concern for external growth may not be a primary strategy of Campbell's; one of relative stability may fit well.

One of the major problems with a strategy of stability is that a certain degree of complacency can develop among managers. This can become a significant problem when the external environment of the organization undergoes rapid change. When this occurs, managers who have been conditioned to a stability strategy have a difficult time reacting to environmental changes.

Product Development.   Product growth strategies are followed by organizations when they wish to expand their product lines or services. As is the case for stability strategies, the external environment is an important influencing factor. When the environment of an organization becomes more dynamic, managers may find it necessary to move their organizations into new products or services to meet or better competition. Product growth strategies can originate from the values of the top management team, as with Heinz, or out of necessity when it is determined that the product service life is short or when obsolesence is fast becoming fact. Because of the dynamic nature of the environment, even the biggest computer company, IBM, must continually direct its strategic efforts toward expansion and improvement of its product line.[12] Such a strategy not only requires enormous resources and management commitment, but can cause other computer companies to rethink their strategies. Other examples of product growth include digital watches, and, in the distilled spirits industry, low-cal and dark beers and ready-mix drinks.

Market Development.   A market growth strategy can be adopted when the organization desires to expand the customers served by its products and services. Two types of market growth strategies can be identified. First, an organization can attempt to expand its market with the same products. For example, a university may adapt its normal curriculum to fit continuing education programs for the general public.

A second form of market growth—termed diversification—can come from new markets and new products. Being the largest airline in the free world was not a sufficient reason for United Airlines to sit back and be lulled into inactivity. It knew that competition among other airlines would continue to increase, particularly when deregulation occurred. Through a series of decisions, it acquired a number of hotels and a rental car agency. Not only had it diminished the impact of airline competition, but in the process it had become a diversified organization—it is now a *travel* company as opposed to being just an airline. The result was the formation of U.A.L., Inc.

Another method of diversification of markets is through internal development into areas that may be totally divorced from the previous line of competence. Not wanting to be totally dependent on the rubber and tire industry, B.F. Goodrich used its expertise in the manufacture of synthetic rubber to establish chemical and plastics divisions. Still known as a major tire company, it now not only derives less than 50 percent of its revenue from the sale of tires (the only major tire company to do so), but it is one of the largest manufacturers of basic plastic resins.

Vertical Integration.   Some organizations choose to redefine their direction through means that are less radical then diversification. A strategy known as *vertical integration* can be used by organizations who wish to stay close to their core area of competence. A good example is Goodyear Tire and Rubber. Unlike its competitor, B.F. Goodrich, Goodyear's management felt that their main business was in the manufacture and selling of tires. To strengthen their position, Goodyear chose to become more involved in the total process of tire manufacturing by expanding their control of the process from raw materials to consumption. In previous years, the company had purchased raw materials from other companies, converted them into tires, and sold the product to automobile companies and to the general public. After analyzing external and internal environmental elements, they made two major changes: (1) they chose to manufacture their own raw materials; and (2) they proceeded to build and open new expanded customer automobile and tire service centers in order to better serve the general public. With this *vertical integration,* Goodyear was able to control the process of tire manufacturing from the raw material stage to the hands of the final customer. As a total tire company, Goodyear adopted a strategy within their existing environment by emphasizing and using their strong resource base.

Merger.   A strategy that enables an organization to expand its products and/or markets by acquiring other organizations is known as a merger. Such a strategy fits well in an organization that wishes to expand through external means rather than wait for internal projects to generate growth.

For example, Tenneco began as an oil and gas company but saw opportunities in other areas that were not subject to the fluctuations and constraints of the energy industry. Using its financial resource base, it acquired a number of companies in vastly different businesses. In addition to oil and gas, it now manufactures and/or markets such products as tractors, containers, life insurance, chemicals, ships, and agricultural products. While the oil and gas divisions still contribute heavily to the company's revenues and profits, the addition of the other product lines through mergers have made it an even stronger organization.

Retreat.   As we have shown so far, organizations can adopt strategies that can involve some form of stability or growth in products and/or markets. There are times, however, when an organization finds that it must retreat, or retrench, from a previous position in order to survive or improve its performance.

Even the largest of companies find themselves in difficult situations with respect to the manufacturing and marketing of goods and services. Westinghouse and R.C.A. are good examples. Both are large firms with supposedly enormous resources and boundless opportunities. Yet each has recently made decisions that have redefined their services. In the case of Westinghouse, the household appliance division not only had a small percentage of the market, but it had been losing money for a number of years.[13] Something had to be done—either invest a large amount of resources to build the division to better compete with such firms as General Electric, or get out altogether. They chose the latter. In a similar situation, R.C.A., a large company overall, was only a small competitor in the computer manufacturing industry. Rather than invest resources to compete with IBM, R.C.A. chose not to continue in the computer market. Both of these examples illustrate a *retreat* strategy.

Classifying Organizational Strategies

The six strategies discussed can be classified into categories that represent differences in product and market orientation, shown in exhibit 6–3.

EXHIBIT 6–3
Classification of Strategies

PRODUCTS	MARKETS	
	Existing	*New*
Existing	**Strategies** Stability Vertical Integration Retreat	**Strategies** Market Development
New	**Strategies** Product Development	**Strategies** Diversification Merger

Existing Product–Existing Market.   In the first quadrant the strategies of stability, vertical integration, and retreat can be placed. Each deals with the same markets and products, but the choice and direction are quite dissimilar for the three.

New Product–Existing Market.   In the second quadrant, the strategy of product development can be placed. Beyond the IBM example, others may include the introduction of new household products by various firms, new style and model automobiles, fashion wear, appliances and the like.

Existing Product–New Market.   The third quadrant is clearly a market development strategy, such as the continuing education example. Another example is the Jeep Division of American Motors. The division was in a slow growth stage until management recognized that Jeep vehicles were ideal for off-the-road activities and the growing recreational market. AMC entered a new market with a relatively unchanged product.

New Products–New Markets.   In this fourth quadrant the strategies of diversification and merger can be categorized. Our United Airlines, Goodrich, and Tenneco examples illustrate this classification scheme.

DIMENSIONS OF ORGANIZATIONAL PLANNING

Although every manager is involved in the function of planning, many differences exist not only between managerial levels but across different organizations. Some of the most important differences can be seen by discussing the dimensions of organizational planning. These dimensions include: (1) type, (2) time frame, (3) elements, (4) repetitiveness, and (5) focus. (See exhibit 6–4.)

Types of Plans

As shown in exhibit 6–1 (Stage III), there are three types of plans that can be found in most organizations: corporate, divisional or business, and unit or functional plans. Exhibit 6–5 presents an example of the organizational planning process as it cycles through an organization.

EXHIBIT 6–4 Organizational Planning Dimensions

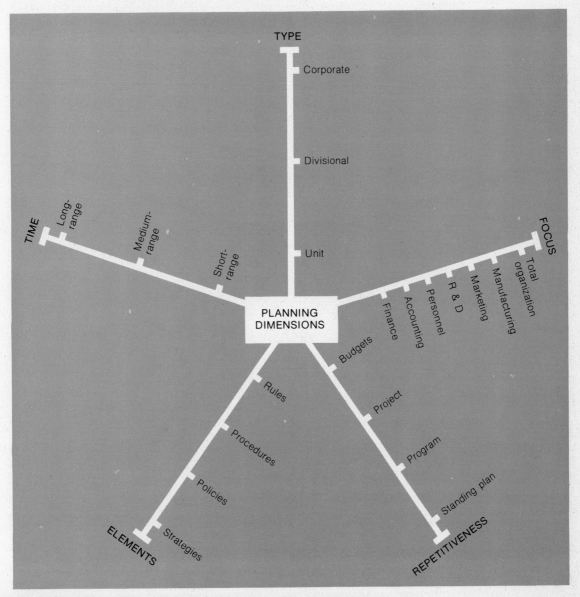

Suggested from G. A. Steiner, Top Management Planning *(New York: Macmillan, 1969), p.12.*

EXHIBIT 6–5 Organizational Planning Cycles

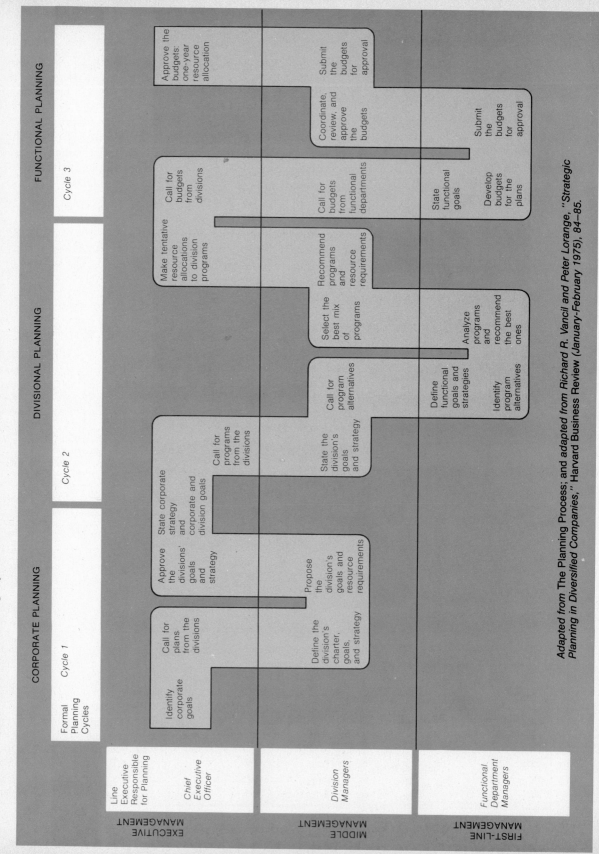

Adapted from *The Planning Process*; and adapted from Richard R. Vancil and Peter Lorange, "Strategic Planning in Diversified Companies," *Harvard Business Review (January–February 1975), 84–85.*

Corporate Planning.   Corporate planning efforts evolve from the decisions on organizational goals and strategies. In a sense, goals and strategy deal with the *what* of organizational planning, and corporate planning is the first step in activating the *how* of planning. This is why corporate planning is sometimes referred to as strategic planning.

Planning efforts at the corporate level are developed by the orga-

**THE
MANAGER'S
JOB**
Robert Burgin
of Leaseway
Transportation
Corporation

Leaseway Transportation Corporation of Cleveland is one of the most successful trucking firms in the United States. Sales are not only approaching $1 billion per year, but they have grown at a compound rate of 15 percent a year. In addition, the company holds lucrative contracts as the exclusive hauler of autos for General Motors and appliances for Sears and Whirlpool. One would think that the company would have the tendency to sit back and enjoy their success.

Not so, says Robert Burgin, president of Leaseway. He claims that their current success was achieved without vision of the future or any written strategy. Burgin notes, however, that the company has become dependent on the successes of its big customers, such as Sears and GM, and thus, is vulnerable to cycles in retailing and the auto industry. On top of this, it had no plan for growth.

"I took over a very successful company, but there will be a number of strategic decisions I'll have to make soon to move us into the 1980s," he says. "With sales estimated to be near $2 billion by 1985, it's critical how you manage that growth and decide what to do with that money. One of our plans is to balance our business."

Burgin is one of those managers who has replaced the company's general mission—trucking—with a more visionary target. He wants Leaseway to become the "best managed provider of physical distribution services and systems." This means he will consider moving Leaseway into air freight, barge shipping, and possibly Great Lakes shipping and leasing of railroad cars. His plans include acquiring other transportation companies outside trucking, developing the company's first advertising program, and changing the structure and executive compensation system. With respect to the latter, he wants to give more discretion in awarding bonuses to managers who take risks to achieve long-term gains as opposed to short-term profits.

"Strategic planning is something that has a big impact on a company beyond the individual business plans," he states. "How you intend to make use of your money is a strategic decision. The plans by which you actually spend it are business plans."

Adapted from "The New Planning," Business Week *(December 18, 1978): 64–65.*

nization's executive management and are generally, but not always, long term in nature. The most important aspect of corporate planning is that it is *original, energizing,* and *decisional* in its purpose. It is original in that it is the starting point of the formal planning process in an organization and, therefore, must cover the entire spectrum of organizational activities from production to final sale and accounting. It is energizing because it acts to stimulate and motivate employees to work toward successful achievement of the organization's goals. Finally, it is decisional in that it sets the foundation for all plans, policies, and procedures to follow.

Divisional or Business Planning.   Activities within a divisional planning framework concern the process of determining the scope of the division's actions that will satisfy the consumer's needs, of deciding on specific divisional subgoals within its defined area of responsibility, and establishing policies and budgets to attain these goals.

In some cases, divisional planning is referred to as *tactical* planning. Whereas corporate planning is concerned with the selection of broad plans to achieve the larger organization's goals, tactical planning redefines these goals as they apply to the divisional level and develops more specific plans for their achievement.

Functional or Unit Planning.   This lowest level of planning concerns the individual department's development of a set of feasible action plans to implement divisional plans. At this level, department managers or first-line supervisors focus on planning for day-to-day and month-to-month activities. There is concern for more short-range actions and adherence to planned schedules and budgets.

Time Frame

A second important dimension of organizational planning concerns the time frame or length of the planning horizon. Three planning horizons are usually identified: long-range, medium or intermediate range, and short-range plans.

Long-range plans are those plans that deal with decisions regarding the broad technological and competitive aspects of the organization and the allocation of resources over an *extended* period of time. Three aspects are crucial to long-range plans. First, it is necessary that goals and strategies be consistent with each other. Second, the long-range plans associated with the major functions of the organization must be specified. Finally, provisions must be made for periodic review and revisions.

A number of important factors should be pointed out with respect to long-range planning:

1. **The term *long-range* planning varies by organization.**

   Typically, most people consider five-, ten-, or fifteen-year intervals as long-range plans. However, this can vary significantly by industry. For example, a retail store may plan only three years in advance for clothing goods, but ten years when it concerns the construction of new stores. A lumber company, however, may plan as much as fifty years ahead when the planting and harvesting of trees is considered. Some industry differences are shown in exhibit 6–6.

2. **Specificity of plans decreases as the plan horizon increases.**

   Planning beyond a few years involves a great deal of uncertainty with respect to the occurrence of certain events. Rather than emphasize specific achievements, goals are usually stated in terms of acceptable ranges for extremely long periods.

2. **Long-range planning forces a dilemma on managers.**

   On one hand, organizations face a rapidly advancing technology, chang-

EXHIBIT 6–6   Time Span Covered by Long-range Plans

	TIME								
	3–5 Years		6–10 Years		Over 10 Years		Other		
Industry	No.	%	No.	%	No.	%	No.	%	Total
Food	22	84	3	11	0	0	1	4	26
Chemicals	40	87	5	10	0	0	1	2	46
Oil	10	58	5	29	1	6	1	6	17
Steel	7	63	2	18	0	0	2	18	11
Machinery	26	92	1	3	0	0	1	3	28
Electronics	34	91	1	10	0	0	2	5	37
Retail sales	25	89	3	10	0	0	0	0	28
Total	164	84	20	10	1	0	8	6	193

Source: L. W. Rue, "The How and Who of Long-range Planning," *Business Horizons* (December 1973): 29.

ing competitive and market conditions, increasingly active government, labor, and other interests that make forecasting the external environment extremely difficult. On the other hand, organizations must plan their activities over a long-run period and must commit resources *in spite of* future uncertainties. This need for a long-run commitment of resources in the face of an increasingly dynamic environment must be read by managers as the necessity for plans to be *flexible* in their approach.

4. **Long-range plans must be integrated together.**
   All long-range plans must be tied together and aligned with the stated goals and strategies of the organizations.

   Medium or *intermediate* planning generally focuses on a planning horizon between two and five years. These plans are usually more detailed than long-range plans when they concern the basic functions of an organization. For such functions as marketing and manufacturing, medium-range plans include appropriate budgets for selling, material purchases, labor, overhead, and administrative expenses.

   Short-range planning, like medium-range plans, is an extension of long-range plans. The planning horizon usually extends to about one year and includes more specific plans with respect to plant location, work methods, inventory plans and controls, employee training, and the like.

Planning Elements

A number of different elements make up the organizational planning process, some of which we have already discussed. The major difference between the elements is the degree of scope or breadth of involved activities.

Strategies, as we discussed earlier, concern choices of particular actions by the organization to achieve stated goals. As such, they have the broadest scope of any of the planning elements.

Policies, which are narrower in scope than strategies, are standing guidelines for organizational decision making. Policies not only flow from strategies, but set up boundaries around which decisions are made. In doing so, policies direct the behavior and actions of organizational members so that they are consistent with the stated goals. Examples of policies are shown in exhibit 6–7.

EXHIBIT 6–7
Example of
Organizational
Policies

Product Policies

1. Determining factory layout.
2. Maintaining movement of materials and work in process.
3. Production control and scheduling.
4. Machine utilization and inventory control.

Marketing Policies

1. Product—nature of product line, sizes, and quality of product or service.
2. Price—methods of pricing, trade, and quantity discounts.
3. Promotion—advertising, personal sales effort, and sales promotion.
4. Place—channels of distribution, types of outlets, and transportation methods.

Financial Policies

1. Established fixed and variable expense relationships.
2. Determining the degrees of risks involved and cost of capital in capitalizing potential earnings.
3. Utilizing financial ratios and control techniques in analyzing sources of funds.
4. Determining the methods used in valuing inventories in depreciating fixed assets.

Personal Policies

1. Developing job descriptions.
2. Recruiting and hiring employees.
3. Use of testing programs in establishing applicant capabilities.
4. Implementing training programs.
5. Developing fair compensation and fringe benefit programs.

Purchasing Policies

1. Deciding if established suppliers will be used exclusively, or if orders will be placed with any available vendor.
2. Determining how much should be bought on each order.
3. Determining the minimum inventory size of each item in computing the reorder point.
4. Utilizing purchase discounts.

Procedures are narrower guides to decision-making than are policies. Unlike policies, which many times involve the entire organization, procedures tend to be applied to departmental or interdepartmental activities. Examples include how customer orders are to be handled, hiring procedures, procedures for payments of supplies, and so on.

Rules are the narrowest of elements dealing with specific actions or approved behaviors. In general, rules usually guide the activities of individual members or of employees who hold a specific job classification. Wearing safety glasses in a plant, employment hours, and deadlines on particular activities are examples. As the most explicit of planning elements, rules do not serve as general suggestions for decision making, but as substitutes for them.

Repetitiveness

Plans can be characterized by the degree of repetitiveness with which they are used by the organization. Two distinctions are usually made:

standing plans and single-use plans.[14] *Standing plans* are those developed by the organizations to direct activities that will occur frequently over time. These include certain policies, methods, and standard operating procedures. Examples include the methods for computing overtime for employees in a manufacturing firm, the procedure for taking a chest X-ray in a hospital, and the policies in handling an overdrawn checking account by a bank.

Single-use plans deal with ill-structured, novel, or nonrepetitive problems to fit a specific situation and may become obsolete when the goal has been achieved. Three types of single-use plans can be found in organizations. First, *programs* are broad activities that include many different functions and interactions. Examples include the Space Shuttle Program, instituting a new motivation program based on profit-sharing, and a store expansion program for a retail organization.

Second, *projects* are single-use plans that are much narrower in scope and complexity than programs. In some cases, projects may be subsets of a larger program. For example, a project to review and revise maintenance procedures on DC-10s is part of the larger program to improve the safety of the airplane, or a portion of Chrysler's program to regain its declining market position is a project to purchase Volkswagen engines for installation in its line of small cars.

Finally, the third single-use plan is the *budget*. A budget is a plan for allocating certain resources to organizational activities. As we will point out in chapter 17, budgets also form a significant portion of the control process. Shown in exhibit 6–5, budgets are linked closely to the entire organizational planning process. In other words, establishing goals and strategies may be the most ill-defined parts of a plan, while budgets are the most precise.

Focus

As was shown in exhibit 6–4, the focus of organizational planning concerns the particular function of the organization that the plan affects. These functions include: marketing, production, personnel, finance, or the total organization.

A Summary

The individual planning elements are highly interdependent. Exhibit 6–8, for example, shows that corporate planning is usually long-range in nature, involves the highest levels of management, concerns broad strategies and policies, and can be directed at the entire organization. At the other extreme, the first-line managers usually operate with short-range plans that are functional or unit in nature; involve policies, procedures, and rules; and relate to the particular unit that is affected.

CONTINGENCY PLANNING

To this point in our discussion of organizational planning, we have taken what may be considered a "single-future" or "straight-line" approach— goals are set, and specific strategies, plans, policies, procedures, rules and budgets are developed to meet these goals. This straight-line approach is based on a series of expected events and certain assumptions regarding the internal and external environment. In such plans, however, provi-

EXHIBIT 6–8   Organizational Planning Dimensions: A Summary

ORGANIZATIONAL LEVEL	TYPE	TIME	FOCUS	ELEMENTS	REPETITIVENESS
Executive Management	Corporate planning	Long-range planning	Total organization	Corporate: Strategies Policies	Corporate: Standing plans Programs Projects Budgets
Middle-level Management	Divisional planning	Long-range planning Medium-range planning	Divisional or business	Divisional: Strategies Policies Procedures	Divisional: Standing plans Programs Projects Budgets
First-line Management	Unit planning	Short-range planning	Unit, function, or department	Unit: Policies Procedures Rules	Unit: Standing plans Programs Projects Budgets

sions are not made for unexpected events or situations that could occur and significantly alter the accuracy of the total planning process.

Taking into account unexpected events in the planning process is the focus of one of the fastest growing planning techniques—contingency planning. Basically, *contingency planning* is the preparation, *in advance,* of a course of action to meet a situation that is not expected, but that, if it occurs, will have a significant impact on the organization.[15] Similarly, it has been defined as a plan that can be put into effect when an unforeseen event actually occurs. For example, a divisional manager may develop an intermediate-range plan for the sale of a product line that is based on projection of the growth in the nation's economy. What happens to the manager's original plan when the economy begins taking a dip toward a recession not anticipated by the manager? Needless to say, not only has the original plan been significantly affected, but a totally new plan may be needed.

A number of benefits can be identified with the use of contingency planning. First, it helps avoid, or cushion, the effects of *surprise* in the planning process. The occurrence of unexpected events for an organization can be the cause of what we can term *crisis management*—the scrambling for answers and guidelines and the sometimes ineffective decisions that can result. Contingency planning usually permits more rational decisions because they are made in advance in a less critical fashion.

Second, involvement in contingency planning can sharpen managers' *skills*. It forces managers to anticipate problems and opportunities

CROCK

CROCK by Rechin, Parker and Wilder. © 1980 Field Enterprises, Inc. Courtesy of Field Newspaper Syndicate.

and prepare for them with different courses of action. Third, it requires managers to gain a better *understanding* of their environments. They are therefore not wedded to a particular plan, and they are able to get a "second look" at the environment. Finally, the result is an organizational planning product that emphasizes *speed* and *flexibility*—speed in foreseeing an event, and flexibility in reacting to it.

There are two main sources of contingencies: those that are within the planning process, and those that are outside the planning process.

1. Sources of contingencies *within* the planning process are similar to those that we discussed at length in chapters 4 and 5. These may include, for example: (1) changes in raw material sources or costs; (2) new product introductions by competitors; (3) mergers of firms that may upset the competitive balance; (4) labor problems; (5) stiffening of governmental regulations; and (6) increased influence of foreign governments. These factors are termed sources within the planning process because they are generally known to managers, at least so far as the range of their effects and probability of occurrence.

2. Sources of contingencies *outside* the planning process concern those events that may be considered unexpected or a surprise to the organizaion. Examples include: (1) natural disasters; (2) a takeover by another organization; (3) a major internal fraud uncovered in an audit; (4) product recalls; (5) a major legal suit brought by a governmental agency or competition; and (6) a death of an important high-level manager.

Contingencies outside the planning process can sometimes be built into a contingency plan. For example, an organization may limit or refrain from doing business in an area subject either to severe weather disruptions or political upheavals. In addition, many organizations have insured the lives of executives or provided for a sudden leadership vacuum through extensive management training and succession programs.

Contingency planning applies to the entire organizational planning process, including type of plan (corporate, divisional, and unit), planning horizon (long-range, intermediate-range and short-range), or particular focus (marketing, manufacturing, personnel, and so on). Unexpected events can occur anytime and anywhere.

The contingency planning process generally consists of three distinct steps: (1) identifying the contingent event; (2) establishing the point at which action should be taken (the action point); and (3) determining the

EXHIBIT 6–9   Example of a Contingency Planning Process

PLANNING STEPS	ACTIONS	DESCRIPTION		
STEP 1: Identify the Contingent Events				
What if . . . ?	List events that may occur in the future that are important.	Competitor develops new process.	Decline (20%) in market growth.	Substitute product
What is impact of event?	Evaluate impact of contingent event on corporate goals.	"B"— moderately severe	"C"—slightly severe	"A"—very severe
How probable is event?	Establish the likelihood of contingent event occurrence.	"I"—highly likely	"II"— somewhat likely	"III"—unlikely
STEP 2: Establish Action Points				
How known that event is about to happen?	List indicators and set action points that signal the impending occurrence of event.	Various media sources	Economic data	Various media sources
Who will alert us?	Assign responsibility for tracking indicators and issuing warnings.	Divisional Manager	Market research manager	Marketing manager
STEP 3: Develop Strategies and Plans				
What will we do when it occurs?	Determine the strategy that will neutralize (or capitalize) on the effects of the contingent event.	1. Develop new process; 2. Cut prices; 3. Get out of market.	1. Delay plant construction; 2. Maintain status quo.	1. Compete with new product; 2. Get out of market.
What effect will this have on the event?	Estimate the financial impact of the new strategies.	1. Will neutralize, if successful, in time; 2. Declining profit margin; 3. Significant reduction in revenue and profits.	1. Cost of construction plans; 2. Little impact.	1. Reduction in profit margin if price cutting occurs; 2. Significant reduction in revenue and profits.

nature of the response. The process is shown in exhibit 6–9. To help in the understanding of the process, the Gulf Oil example in the "Practice of Management" section will be developed further.

Identifying Contingent Events.   The process of identifying a contingent event is the most critical, but most difficult part of the contingency planning process. The problem is not so much in being able to identify events, but in identifying *too many!* Most managers have found it helpful to limit the identification of those "key risks," as they are called, to no more than a half-dozen events that can have a significant impact on the goals of the organization.[16]

How are these key risks identified? A number of methods have been employed by various organizations. The most popular is the formal planning process itself. These formal plans usually contain "assumptions" about the environmental situation such as economic data, market conditions, competitive behavior, and socio-political trends. In a contingency framework, managers are forced to *challenge* the validity and accuracy of these assumptions. This process forces managers to possibly rethink their assumptions.

A second method is the use of an informal or formal environmental monitoring and warning system. Data are constantly received from various internal and external sources and compiled for evaluation. Sources include media publications, meetings with customers, financial analysts'

COMMENTS ON THE PRACTICE OF MANAGEMENT
(See p. 170.)

The Gulf Oil Company example is an excellent illustration of the value of contingency planning to the overall planning process of an organization. Gulf's major assumptions on market growth and the absence of any technological breakthroughs in manufacturing became accepted as fact and served to guide future activities. Thus, it moved ahead to build a new plant and cut down on expensive research and development activity.

Could contingency planning have helped Gulf in this situation? Possibly, by causing the company to go slow on its plant construction and reduction of research and development. More than anything, an operative contingency plan could have made management more aware of warning signals of market decline and competitive activity sooner than normal. Stated differently, a contingency plan could have emphasized management's liaison and monitor roles in the process of seeking out and evaluating potentially valuable information from the external environment.

reports, and the "grapevine." A final method is the "nominal group" technique, which we will discuss later in this chapter.

In our example, Gulf has set a goal of being the number two (behind Union Carbide) producer of low-density polyethylene, which is used to make household food wrappings and large garbage bags. A contingency analysis may identify three important key risks: (1) development of a more cost-efficient manufacturing process by a competitor; (2) a significant decline (e.g., 20 percent) in the market growth; and (3) introduction of a substitute product not made of polyethylene.

Two other steps occur within this first phase. First, the identified key risks are evaluated on their severity to the organization should they occur. The usual procedure is to assign certain subjective characters or letters to represent the degree of severity. For example, "A"—very severe, "B"—moderately severe, and "C"—slightly severe.

The final step is to estimate the likelihood of the occurrence of the key risk. This is done either by actual probabilities or through a subjective evaluation system (e.g., "I"—highly likely, "II"—somewhat likely, and "III"—unlikely).

Establishing Action Points.   An action point is an event, or series of events, that signals the manager that one of the identified key risks is about to become reality. Three steps or activities are crucial to this stage:

1. *Gather information and track the contingent event.* This can be the function of an environmental monitoring system. For example, in the Gulf Oil situation, if market growth is expected to be around 10 percent, then economic data should be gathered frequently on the actual situation. With respect to the other key risks, constant monitoring of various sources should give the manager some idea as to what is occurring.

2. *Set the action point.* This is the point, quantitatively or qualitatively measured, that signals the manager that the contingency plan should be thrown into effect. For Gulf, if market growth is only 8 percent per year instead of the planned 10 percent, the action point would signal the manager that the original goals and plans are in doubt.

3. *Assign responsibility for enacting the action point.* Someone in the organization, possibly the manager in charge, should be given the responsibility to collect the data as well as to signal that the contingency plan should now be used.

In most organizations, the action point probably has already been established. That is, the process just described is nothing more than what a good *control* system would do. Since most control systems incorporate monthly and quarterly reports, the necessary data may already be available. The responsibility, however, for signaling the action point must still be determined.

Develop New Strategies and Plans.   Once the action point has been initiated, the process of determining the response—selecting new strategies and activities—involves the same sort of procedures that are employed in the development of the original plan. The main difference is that the new goals take on a two-level orientation. The first goal is to somehow neutralize the effects of the unexpected event as much as possible—in other words, the first actions are directed at reducing costs quickly. With this done, the second goal is to try to regain as much of the lost performance as possible. As in developing the basic strategies, the requirements of a contingency plan usually suggest that a variety of alternatives must be weighed and evaluated in order to find the most favorable outcome.

In our ongoing example, if a major competitor develops and puts into operation a new, more cost-efficient manufacturing process to produce polyethylene, the response by Gulf could be twofold. First, since the new process may enable the competitor to sell the product more cheaply, Gulf may decide to cut prices in order to protect its share of the market. By this action the company hopefully could temporarily neutralize the impact of the new process. Second, in order to regain some of the lost position, the company must decide whether they can internally develop a similar process or attempt to license the process from another organization. Of course, a possible strategy could be to get out of the polyethylene business if a new manufacturing process cannot be acquired internally or externally, or if the price-cutting actions result in an unprofitable product.

Keys to Success with Contingency Planning

Contingency planning in the organizational planning process has only been in use for a few years. Nevertheless, the number of organizations employing this technique has grown significantly. Their combined activities and experiences have pointed out a number of keys to success in the use of contingency planning.

1. **Contingency plans should be developed by the original planner.**
   Managers face a problem when it comes to the contingency plan. If they delegate the preparation of the plan to subordinates, the quality of the plan could be downgraded and not contain sufficient information for top management. On the other hand, if the managers also prepare the contingency plan, it may act to dilute the commitment to the original plan. Most organizations have found that well-prepared contingency plans are those that are drawn up by people with the greatest knowledge of the situation. If these people are the original planning managers, then they should also prepare the contingency plan.

2. **Contingency plans should be kept internally as well as externally secret.**
   While keeping regular plans from competitors is normal practice by organizations, contingency plans should probably be hidden from most employees as well. Should a plan that details a series of cost reductions—such as plant or office closings, layoffs, or the cancelling of certain project—became known to employees, it could lead to unnecessary speculations, conflict, or other demoralizing consequences.

3. **Contingency plans should include unexpected opportunities as well as unexpected crisis.**
   Too often, contingency plans are couched in terms of negative occurrences for the organization. Experience has shown, however, that there are many unexpected events that can be translated into positive consequences for the organization. The organization, therefore, should not be held to an original plan when it does not fully capitalize on opportunities. For example, if the growth rate in the use of polyethylene is actually found to be 12 percent instead of the planned 10 percent, plans should be ready to handle this contingency. Such a situation could be the driving force for the construction of a new plant, for example.

4. **Contingency planning should be integrated with normal planning activities.**
   While it is fairly common practice to prepare contingency plans that are not as detailed as regular plans, this should not be interpreted as justification for just "tacking on" contingency plans to regular organizational plans. On the contrary, contingency plans should be an integral part of the planning process from beginning to end.

5. **Contingency plans are frequently only as good as the organization's environmental monitoring and early warning systems.**
   This is an especially important consideration for organizations that operate in external environments that are dynamic and/or complex (see exhibit 4–5). Some organizations in this type of environment have ac-

tually set up formal functions to do nothing more than monitor the environment.

6. **Contingency plans should begin to be used as much in corporate planning as in divisional and unit planning efforts.**

Most uses to date of contingency planning have been in the more short-range, operational, or tactical planning in subunits of an organization, such as in divisions or profit centers. One of the problems with contingency planning at higher management levels is that so few people are involved, which may result in such plans being developed informally, or kept under extreme secrecy. Nevertheless, contingency plans apply to corporate plans and to the people who develop such plans.

The formal organizational planning movement began in the 1960s when organizations undertook to develop or refine basic planning systems. With the turbulent nature of the 1970s and 1980s, this movement will certainly continue to increase. Contingency planning is just one of many processes that will help organizations to be more flexible and adaptive to environmental changes, and it can be a significant aid in improving performance.

AIDS IN ORGANIZATIONAL PLANNING

As has been suggested throughout this book, the management of organizations has become a much more dynamic and complex activity over time. It has, therefore, become more difficult and more important for managers to make plans that are more effective and accurate. To assist managers in improving the quality of their planning, a variety of tools and techniques, some from the management science school, have been developed. In this section, we will provide a brief overview of three techniques that have been applied to the planning function: (1) scenarios; (2) nominal group technique; and (3) simulation models. These techniques are by no means all-inclusive of the planning techniques in use by organizations today. However, they are representative of the most popular and most frequently used methods.

Scenarios

In a formalistic sense, a scenario is a *hypothetical* sequence of events constructed to focus attention on causal processes and decision points.[17] In more practical terms, a scenario is a written description of a set of events *apt* to occur in the future that bears on organizational effectiveness. A scenario, then, is nothing more than a description of the organization's future activities based upon the occurrence of some event or events. It is a story describing a "what if" situation.

Similar to contingency planning, to which they are compared, scenarios have come into prominence only because of the dissatisfaction of managers over the utility of "single future" plans. Managers recognized quickly that single-future plans are not very valuable when there is a high probability of the occurrence of unexpected events. Scenarios are intended to raise awareness in managers and to prevent surprises. Alternate scenarios serve to broaden the outlook of managers to the external forces that shape the future of the organization and sensitize them to their vulnerabilities and to opportunities that lie within other possible futures.[18]

Developing Scenarios.   Three scenarios are considered the most practical to work with: (1) the "most probable" or most likely, on which the regular plan is developed; (2) a pessimistic or "worst case"; and (3) an optimistic or "best case" scenario. The "most likely" case usually carries a 50 to 70 percent probability; the worst and best cases each account for a 20 percent probability or less. While it might be perfectly valid to prepare more than three scenarios, it is doubtful that many managers would bother to prepare, read, or base their actions on so many cases.

The process of preparing a scenario can consist of the following steps:[19]

1. Identify and make explicit the organization's basic goals and strategies.
2. Determine how far into the future you wish to plan.
3. Develop a good understanding of the organization's points of leverage and vulnerability.
4. Determine factors that you think will definitely occur *and* may occur within the planning horizon.
5. Make a list of key variables that will have make-or-break consequences for your organization.
6. Assign reasonable values to each key variable.
7. Build three scenarios (most likely, worst case, and best case) from which the organization may operate.
8. Develop a strategy for each scenario that will most likely result in achieving the organization's goals.
9. Check the feasibility of each strategy in each scenario.
10. Select—or develop—an optimum response strategy and present it to management.

In most cases, the process of developing scenarios follows the same steps as would be followed in a regular planning exercise. The main difference is that at least three situations are evaluated, not just one. An example of two of many scenarios for a regional private brand gasoline marketer is shown in exhibit 6–10.

Subjects and Sources of Scenarios.   A number of areas of managerial concern can confront the scenario writer. Of immediate concern to the organization, and the easiest to develop, are those scenarios that relate to the organization's performance. Many organizations ask for scenarios based on upturns or downturns in sales, inventories, products, and so on. Other possible subjects for scenarios include economic (GNP, inflation, and interest rates), sociopolitical issues (energy problems), legislative and regulatory behavior (FTC, OSHA, and the like), climatology (for such agricultural based industries as tobacco and fruits), labor, and foreign nation activities.

A variety of individuals and groups can be responsible for preparing scenarios. Some, such as universities, institutes, and consultants, can be external to the organization. These external sources are primarily used when the organization lacks expertise on the issue. Internally, ad hoc committees, task forces, and formal planning groups prepare scenarios. Past experience has shown that internal groups that are interdisciplinary or interdepartmental produce the best scenarios because of the diversity of resources and experiences that are represented.

EXHIBIT 6–10   Two Possible Scenarios for a Small Gasoline Marketer: 1990

SCENARIO I	SCENARIO II
Assumptions: Inflation—10 to 20%; Gasoline Availability—No shortages; Price—Competitive; GNP—2 to 4% growth per year; Time Frame—1990.	Assumptions: Inflation—5 to 9%; Gasoline Availability—Tight; Price—Rising; GNP—Less than 2%; Time Frame—1990.
Advances in technology and design have made the automobile of the early 1990s safer, more reliable and efficient, and nearly service free. From the viewpoint of a gasoline retailer, however, the most significant change has been in fuel efficiency. Better gas mileage has offset the effects of increases in the number of cars on the road. Overall market demand has grown at an average of only 1.5 to 2.0%.	The gasoline-powered automobile is still the dominant mode of transportation. Even with the movement toward more gas efficient cars of the 1970s, gasoline remains in tight supply. National rationing was used twice in the last seven years. As a result of rising prices and tight supply, the number of retail outlets has declined slightly in the last three years.
Because of a low rate of market growth and a high cost of capital, the number of retail gasoline outlets has decreased only slightly since the late 1970s. Rapidly escalating costs and the service-free auto have been responsible for the demise of the full-service gasoline station. The high rate of inflation has made price-conscious consumers extremely receptive to the economies of the self-service stations. The price competition between the majors and independents is head on, so there is no pump-price spread.	One important trend has been the growth of the full-service outlet as hard-pressed consumers increasingly choose to repair rather than replace their automobiles. Marketers in a position to do so strive to retain brand loyalty through the service and repair portions of their operations. The economics of the full-service outlet benefit from the general availability of low-cost labor. The federal government, concerned with the survival of the small businesses in these difficult times, is especially watchful for anti-competitive practices by the large companies.

Adapted from R. E. Linneman and J. D. Kennell, "Shirt-Sleeve Approach to Long-Range Plans," *Harvard Business Review* (March–April 1977): 147.

Nominal Group Technique

The nominal group technique is a limited but extremely useful technique that has been used in conjunction with contingency planning and scenario development. It is a technique that is particularly useful for planning tasks or elements that require a high degree of innovation, idea generation, and creativity.[20] Examples include product development, future missions of the organization, and the development of new manufacturing and information processes.

Process.   The technique is usually applied to a group of knowledgeable people with different backgrounds and experiences whose pooled skills and judgments are needed to identify desirable goals and strategies. The typical steps followed in a nominal group exercise are as follows:

1. The manager brings together a group of about six to twelve individuals and outlines the problems to be discussed (e.g., what product lines should the organization be involved in within the next ten years).

2. Each member *separately,* without interaction with any other member, attempts to generate a number of ideas in writing.

3. At the end of a short period (e.g., fifteen to thirty minutes), each member verbally presents one idea to the assembled group. Each idea is recorded

on a blackboard or a large sheet of paper, and discussion is then limited only to clarifications of the presented idea.

4. The cycle is repeated until all developed ideas are presented and recorded.
5. Each idea is then openly discussed as to its merits and realism.
6. After sufficient discussion has taken place, the manager asks each member to evaluate—usually by ranking in order—the presented ideas by secret ballot. The group decision is the pooled or summed outcome of the members' evaluations. The manager can then accept or reject the results.

Evaluation of the Nominal Group Technique.   A number of organizations, including those in the industrial, service, and government sectors, have successfully used the nominal group technique for many years. Its most pronounced successes have been with issues or problems that are exploratory in nature, or where fresh ideas are needed.

The main benefit of the technique is that it attempts to minimize some of the inhibiting effects of group interaction, at least in the early discussions. In particular, the following benefits have been reported: (1) in the absence of personal criticism—since only the idea, not the person, is discussed—there is a greater sharing of ideas; (2) there is a greater concentration on the task as opposed to side issues; and (3) nominal groupings prohibit the dominance of the group by strong individual personalities since persuasion is not permitted, only open discussions.

Two concluding factors should be noted. First, on the positive side, individuals who participate in the exercise can develop a sense of "ownership" of the finalized idea. This can be translated into a high level of commitment should some of these ideas reach the formal planning stage. Second, on the negative side, since individual members put in a significant amount of time and effort into the exercise, the manager is put on the spot if he or she decides not to accept some of the group's ideas. In the future, the manager in charge may find some resistance by these members to further participation.

Simulation Planning Models

One of the fastest growing planning tools is computer simulation modeling, by which planners construct sophisticated models of an organization showing desired, reality-based characteristics. With the aid of the computer, managers can test certain hypotheses on a wide range of decisions at a much lower cost and with greater speed than ever before. From a definitional point of view, computer simulation in planning is a quantitative modeling technique developed to test alternative courses of action based on historical facts and managerial assumptions.[21]

Many different forms of planning models exist in organizations. Some models attempt to simulate a particular function, such as manufacturing, marketing, or finance. Others simulate the interaction and interrelationships of two or more functions for planning purposes. Still others, called corporate planning models, are capable of simulating almost the entire operation of an organization. The overall objective of these models is to assist in the development of long-, medium-, and short-range plans, A well-designed model is capable, at least in theory, of projecting the results (e.g., financial, sales, and manufacturing costs) of particular strategies over a number of years.

Process.   In preparing a simulation planning model, a number of steps are required. Among the most important are the following:

1. First, as shown in exhibit 6–11, a simulation model depicts a *logical* sequence of activities and functions. Of crucial importance are the interactions and interrelationships between the components, or submodels, of the larger model. For example, the marketing and manufacturing submodels must show the important relationships between these two functions. The marketing submodel must specifically describe how marketing demands affect production capabilities; production capacities and requirements (e.g., maintenance, downtime) must be shown to affect the total number of products available for sale.

2. The formulation of the model and the important interrelationships are based on the *assumptions* of managers. These aspects are usually translated into some form of mathematical equation that can be manipulated by the computer. The assumptions are based on historical data, managerial opinions, and certain forecasts of events, such as revenue growth, personnel and equipment costs, availability of raw materials, and so forth.

3. The model is tested on the computer to verify the validity of the assumptions and the input data. In other words, can the model predict today's results with today's data? Once this has been satisfactorily shown, the model is oriented more toward a forward-looking model by changing some of the input data and analyzing the results in an orderly fashion. Examples include changes in sales growth, impact of inflation and interest rates, manufacturing cost changes and price.

Many organizations, such as Ralston Purina, Digital Equipment, and R.J. Reynolds Industries, work with their models almost on a continual basis. For example, at Public Service Electric & Gas Co., the total corporate planning model is run on the average of once a day to test the impact on the New Jersey utilities costs, equipment use, and the financial effect of such events as an unexpectedly warm winter week on fuel purchases.[22]

Evaluation of Simulation Planning Models.   With the continuing knowledge and sophistication of computer usage, simulation models in planning activities will become one of the dominant techniques in our future. It not only can be used in long- and short-range planning studies, but special studies investigating the ever-present "what if" problems can be investigated with a high degree of accuracy.

A number of problems exist with simulation planning models that managers should evaluate carefully. As should be readily apparent, the performance of such models depends to a great extent on the model's construction and the assumptions that form the basis of the calculations. If the model is not a true representation of reality, the output will be equally unrealistic. Second, problems can arise if managers do not have a clear idea of the kind of information they want to get out of the computer. A common problem is to attempt to simulate too many variables, resulting in an unmanageable model. Finally, a simulation model has no perspective of some of the important qualitative aspects of organizational functioning. In other words, while it can help to find answers to certain questions, it cannot tell managers which questions to ask and what are the most important answers to get.

EXHIBIT 6-11   A Corporate Planning Model

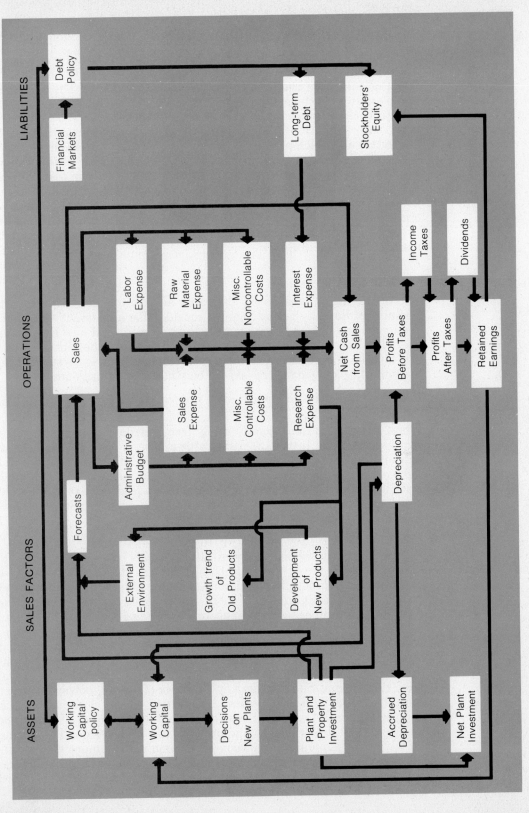

Adapted from James I. Morgan, Robert M. Lawless, and Eugene C. Yehle, "The Dow Chemical Corporate Financial Planning Model," in Albert N. Schrieber, ed., Corporate Simulation Models (Providence, R.I.: Institute of Management Science, 1970): 379.

PLANNING, PERFORMANCE, AND THE MANAGER'S JOB

This chapter has attempted to develop a basic framework for the understanding of the managerial function of planning. The effects of planning on an organization are both pervasive and far-reaching. The absence of any planning efforts, except in very isolated cases, usually will result in organizational performance that is lower than potential. On the other hand, the existence of planning and plans does not ensure that the organization will reach high levels of success. For every success in planning, such as G.E., we can point to a failure of planning, such as the General Foods acquisition of Burger Chef restaurants ($39 million loss), or Mattel's diversification attempt with Ringling Bros. Circus ($25 million loss).

These examples point out the "realities" of managerial planning in organizations. A discussion of these realities of planning will focus on two topics: (1) keys to success with planning; and (2) planning and the manager's job.

Keys to Success with Planning

One of the major reasons for the rapid adoption of the organizational planning philosophy is that there is considerable agreement among academicians and practitioners on what the concept is and how it should be used. The basic simplicity of the concept undoubtedly has contributed to this high level of agreement.[23] The experiences of managers suggest that the following keys to success should be studied by future managers.

1. **Planning is more than predicting the future by extrapolating from the present.**

When an organization projects solely from current activities, it acts to straitjacket the future. Starting with a base of current products and markets makes it difficult to obtain the new and eliminate the old in light of a changing environment. This does not mean that a strategy of stability is wrong for some organizations—indeed, it may be the only successful strategy. What it does mean is that planning is much more than an exercise in extrapolating trends.

2. **Planning should not degenerate into a game of achieving numbers.**

Planning usually translates organizational goals into terms that have a strong financial flavor (i.e., numbers). Through the processes of a goal hierarchy and corporate, divisional, and unit planning, these numbers cascade down the organization. As David Mahoney of Norton Simon, Inc., has said to his subordinate managers, "The way I make my numbers is for you guys to make your numbers. So make your numbers."[24] In and of itself, this situation is not bad because it develops commitment among organizational members and serves as the basis for evaluating managerial performance. The problem is that financial performance is invariably tied to *time*. Some of the key elements of a plan, however, are not controlled by a rigid time horizon. Innovation simply does not occur on an orderly month-to-month basis for product development. Neither does an acquisition follow a neat and orderly time progression. This creates an important managerial paradox—the same management that creates the plan ends up with the responsibility for accomplishing the financial goals of the plan *without control* over the events on which the plan is based. Stated differently, financial numbers should not be "force fit" to the goals-strategy-planning-performance sequence when they may not be realistic or applicable. Managers should be highly cautious of individuals who demand only to know "how much" and "by when" from a plan.

3. **Plans don't necessarily cope with change—managers do!**

Many managers feel that since a great deal of time is spent laying out an organizational plan, it must be so well thought out that it must be right and, therefore, a good mechanism for coping with change. This philosophy usually leads to the cry, "Why didn't you follow the plan?" when a manager deviates from the plan in a conscientious attempt to meet new problems. It results in the opposite effect than was designed for planning—rigidity instead of flexibility. It is rare, even with contingency planning, that a plan accurately assesses changes in the external environment. An organizational plan should serve as a guideline for action. Managers must be given the leeway to make judgments and to take risks, which are key ingredients in defining the manager's job.

4. **Developing a plan should not be an end in itself.**

In many cases, this situation is concerned with the human elements of the planning process. This usually involves two factors. First, there is an absence, or lack of communications between levels of management concerning organizational strategies and corporate plans. In light of this situation, managers developing divisional or unit plans are left in the open without guidelines concerning what to do. Second, there is the unrealistic assumption that people will be willing to cooperate with all facets of the plan. Most managers have pet ideas that they wish to see accomplished. A controller may want a tight budget and a market research director a new marketing image. When the corporate plan calls for the aggressive marketing of a new product line, all organizational members may not pull in the same direction. The key, then, is to stress communications and cooperation among and between managers.

5. **Many managers do not have an active enough role in developing plans.**

Organizational planning is essentially a line management function. A sure route to problems is to have all plans produced by staff planners and then issued to line managers for implementation. There is no real sense of "ownership" by line managers, which can result in less than enthusiastic support and commitment to the plan. Organizational planning is a people-interactive process, and the staff planner is only one player in a cast of characters. In other words, both the staff planner and line manager must serve as analysts, catalysts, and coordinators of plans.

6. **Goal-setting, strategy formulation, and developing plans should be separated.**

Managers must recognize that each of these important concepts are separate entities in and of themselves. Therefore, strategy comes after goals have been set, and plans are developed once a strategy (or strategies) have been selected. One must resist the temptation of diving into the "how we're going to get there" planning process without a clear understanding of "where we want to go"! Planning as a management tool can never reach its potentially high levels of effectiveness until this "chicken before the egg" syndrome is eliminated.

7. Stay flexible.

At least five components facilitate the flexibility of an organization's planning process. First, orient the plan's execution to events. As pointed out in the discussion on contingency planning, managers must be able to adapt plans to the events occurring in the internal and external environment. Second, commit organizational resources in a step-by-step process. For example, it might be better to build a smaller plant now that is easily adaptable to expansion than it would be to build a large plant, even though manufacturing managers rightly claim that the larger plant is more efficient. The five-year plan may call for a large plant, but a change in market growth may alter the assumption. Building a large plant now could lead only to overcapacity and an adverse impact on the balance sheet. Third, decide in advance on the criteria for abandoning a project. This relates to the "action point" of contingency plans. Fourth, make new five-year plans *every* year. Any organizational plan that is over twelve months old, given the rapidly changing environment of many organizations, is a dangerous document. At minimum, the plan should be carefully reviewed and revised as needed. Finally, set up a comprehensive monitoring system. The fundamental idea of a flexible forward planning system is one of regular review and evaluation. To achieve its maximum value, there is the requirement for accurate and timely information. All the reasons that a well-run organization needs information to manage existing operations are even more important when it comes to managing their future ventures with all the risks and uncertainties.

8. Analysis goes hand in hand with synthesis.

This final suggestion focuses on the erroneous assumption that good organizational planning is founded solely on analysis. Although we have stated a number of times the importance of analysis, the most valuable ingredient of good organizational planning is *synthesis*. Someone must creatively put together disparate items and come out with a plan that is practical and realistic. This point stresses the human skill element again in planning and the necessity of having the right people with the right skills performing planning activities.

Planning and the Manager's Job

Planning is one of the key factors that helps define the manager's job. All managers plan, whether it be planning a corporate acquisition or next year's budget in a neighborhood hardware store.

Planning and managerial *skills* are concepts that must be integrated together in order to achieve high levels of performance. Technical skills in planning relate not only to the ability to follow closely the steps required in developing a plan, but also concern the specific skills involved in acquiring the expertise to develop and manipulate some of the complex planning techniques and models. Since planning is highly people intensive, requiring the interaction and combined skills of many individuals, the human skill concept gains in importance. Conceptual skills relate to our previous point of synthesis as a key to planning effectiveness. Managers must be able to see and integrate the various components of a plan into a unified package. Finally, the emphasis on environmental monitoring and the assumptions about trends and events focus attention on the need to develop diagnostic skills.

Managers perform a number of different *roles* during the organizational planning process. In the interpersonal role they must act as a liaison, or contact person, with various elements of the environment. In addition, in the leader role, managers serve the important function of guiding or coordinating the plan from inception to evaluation. The informational roles are among the most important. Acting in a monitor, disseminator, and spokesperson role, the manager facilitates the information process from the acquisition of data about trends and competitive or consumer behavior to the collection of information about the performance of a plan. Finally, the decisional roles of entrepreneur and resource allocator directly affect the planning process. As an entrepreneur, the manager can be a source of ideas for improvements or planning projects; as the resource allocator, the manager is in the heart of planning, being involved in allocating human, financial, and physical resources according to the plan.

SUMMARY FOR THE MANAGER

1. Organizational planning has evolved into one of the most important managerial functions. It is a concept that begins with an analysis of the environment, the establishment of goals, strategies, and plans, and includes implementation and control procedures. Planning processes must be flexible, constantly monitor the environment, receive commitment from organizational members, and assist in adapting to changes.

2. While most people discuss planning in terms of the three key types of plans, it should be carefully noted that organizational planning also includes goals and strategies. These premises of the planning process set the stage for the development of actual plans.

3. Strategy precedes planning. It deals with the choice and "direction" that the organization desires to follow; planning concerns "how" these strategies will be attained. If more than one strategy is chosen by an organization, it must be totally integrated into a strategic framework, much the same as priorities have to be set for goals.

4. Six different types of strategies were presented: stability, product development, market development, vertical integration, merger, and retreat. Each strategy presents the organization with different choices of action that will influence its future.

5. Corporate planning, divisional planning, and unit planning were identified as the three main types of plans. They differ in terms of their emphasis, time

orientation, and level of management involved. The important point is that there are probably more similarities in the planning activities of managers than there are differences. The key factor is that managers are guided by goals, they must choose the direction that will best achieve the goals, plans must be developed to facilitate goal attainment, and proper control procedures should be developed to review and evaluate the process.

6. Policies, budgets, programs, and procedures are all important dimensions of organizational plans. Each applies to different levels of management and the particular purpose that is required of the plan.

7. Contingency planning has grown in popularity and importance because many planning efforts do not take into account the effects of a changing environment. This crucial "what if" question has led many organizations to include contingency planning as a major factor in the total planning process. The key features of a contingency plan involve identifying events that can occur during a planning period, their effect on the organization, how these events will be monitored, when the organization will take action on the occurrence of an event, and reformulating goals and plans.

8. Comensurate with the growth in planning's importance, the aids to planning have increased in recognition and use. Scenarios, nominal group technique, and simulation planning models are just a few of the many techniques that have been developed. The important aspect for managers to remember is that many of these techniques are only as good as the quality and validity of the input information. These aspects highlight not only the importance of a good monitoring and scanning program, but the necessity of maintaining flexibility in the planning process.

9. Effective planning efforts are those that allow the manager some flexibility in making decisions when faced with a new contingency, do not end with the development of a plan but continue to emphasize how the plan will be implemented and controlled, and involve many employees in the developmental process. By far the most inportant factor to planning success is the emphasis placed on synthesizing all goals, strategies, and plans. In their zeal to plan, some managers stress analysis to the exclusion of synthesis, resulting in an ambiguous document that few can follow.

10. In terms of the manager's job, the planning function stresses all the managerial skills, with particular emphasis on conceptual and diagnostic skills. The informational and decisional roles also are salient activities in the planning process.

QUESTIONS FOR REVIEW AND DISCUSSION

1. What is the difference between planning and forecasting?
2. Do all managers plan? Explain.
3. What is the relationship between planning and control?
4. Why is the concept of strategy so important to organizational planning?
5. Describe the basic types of strategy.
6. Is long-range planning done only by executive managers?
7. Compare divisional planning with unit planning in terms of their similarities and differences.
8. Why has contingency planning grown so popular among managers?
9. What are some of the advantages and disadvantages of scenarios in planning?
10. What managerial skills are important in the planning process?

NOTES

1. G. A. Steiner, *Comprehensive Managerial Planning* (Oxford, Ohio: Planning Executives Institute, 1972), p. 4.

2. See A. L. Comrey, W. High, and R. C. Wilson, "Factors Influencing Organizational Effectiveness: A Survey of Aircraft Workers," *Personnel Psychology"* (1955): 79–99; S. Thune and R. J. House, "Where Long-Range Planning Pays Off," *Business Horizons* (August 1970): 81–87; and D. R. Wood and R. L. La Forge, "The Impact of Comprehensive Planning on Financial Performance," *Academy of Management Journal* (September 1979): 516–526.

3. A. C. Filley and R. J. House, *Managerial Process and Organizational Behavior* (Glenview, Ill.: Scott, Foresman, 1969), p. 206.

4. See "The Opposites: G.E. Grows While Westinghouse Shrinks," *Business Week* (January 31, 1977); 60: and B. Tamarkin, "GM Gets Ready for the World Car," *Forbes* (April 2, 1979): 44–48.

5. F. T. Paine and W. Naumes, *Organizational Strategy and Policy*, 2nd ed., (Philadelphia: Saunders, 1978).

6. B. B. Tregoe and J. W. Zimmerman, "Strategic Thinking: Key to Corporate Survival," *Management Review* (February 1979): 9.

7. "General Electric's Stoplight Strategy for Planning," *Business Week* (April 28, 1975): 49.

8. "Exxon: Searching for Another Game that Equals Oil in Size," *Business Week* (July 16, 1979): 80–81.

9. "Bell & Howell: Moving to Abandon its Ailing Camera Business," *Business Week* (July 30, 1979): 88–89.

10. "Gerber: Selling More to the Same Mothers is Our Objective Now," *Business Week* (October 16, 1978): 192–95.

11. P. Gibson, "Win Some, Lose Some," *Forbes* (June 11, 1979): 101–2.

12. B. Uttal, "How the 4300 Fits I.B.M.'s New Strategy," *Fortune* (July 30, 1979): 58–64.

13. See E. Faltermayer, "Westinghouse Comes Back Home to Electricity," *Fortune* (August 1976): 147–56; and B. Uttal, "How Ed Griffiths Brought RCA Into Focus," *Fortune* (December 31, 1979) 48–57.

14. F. Kast and J. E. Rosenzweig, *Organization and Management*, 2nd ed., (New York: McGraw-Hill, 1974), p. 444.

15. R. O'Connor, *Planning Under Uncertainty* (New York: Conference Board, 1978), p. 13.

16. Ibid, p. 17.

17. H. Kahn and A. Wiener, *The Year 2000* (New York: Macmillan, 1967), p. 6.

18. O'Connor, p. 5.

19. R. E. Linneman and J. D. Kennell, "Shirt Sleeve Approach to Long-Range Plans," *Harvard Business Review* (March–April 1977): 141–50.

20. See A. Delbecq, A. Van de Ven, and A. Gustafson, *Group Techniques for Program Planning: A Guide to Nominal, Group, and Delphi Processes* (Glenview, Ill.: Scott, Foresman, 1975); and T. Green and P. Pietri, "Using Nominal Group to Improve Upward Communications," *MSU Business Topics* (1974): 40.

21. See Albert N. Schrieber, ed., *Corporate Simulation Models* (Providence, R.I.: Institute of Management Science, 1970; and J. S. Hammond III, "Do's and Don'ts of Computer Models for Planning," *Harvard Business Review* (March–April 1974): 110–23.

22. "The New Planning," *Business Week* (December 18, 1978): 66.

23. See A. Brown, "When the Planner Speaks, Does Management Really Listen," *Management Review* (November 1978): 59–61; F. W. Gluck, R. N. Foster, and J. L. Forbis, "Cure for Strategic Malnutrition," *Harvard Business Review* (November–December 1976): 154–65; R. N. Paul, N. B. Duncan, and J. W. Taylor, "The Reality Gap in Strategic Planning," *Harvard Business Review* (May–June 1978): 124–30; and E. C. Schleh, "Strategic Planning . . . No Sure Cure for Corporate Surprises," *Management Review* (March 1979): 54–57.

24. "The Way I Make My Numbers is for You Guys to Make Your Numbers," *Forbes* (February 15, 1972): 46–54.

ADDITIONAL REFERENCES

Ackoff, R. L. *A Concept of Corporate Planning.* New York: Wiley, 1970.

Anthony, R. *Planning and Control Systems: A Framework for Analysis.* Cambridge, Mass: Harvard University Press, 1966.

Bloom, P. N., and Kotler, P. "Strategies for High Market Share Companies," *Harvard Business Review* (November–December 1975): 63–72.

"Corporate Planning: Piercing the Fog," *Business Week* (April 28, 1975): 46–54.

Fahey, L. and King, W. R. "Environmental Scanning for Corporate Planning," *Business Horizons* (August 1977): 61–71.

Fulmer, R. M., and Rue, L. W. "The Practice and Profitability of Long-Range Planning," *Managerial Planning* (May–June 1974): 4–5.

Gerstner, L. V. "Can Strategic Planning Pay Off?" *Business Horizons* (December 1972): 5–16.

Koontz, H. "Making Strategic Planning Work," *Business Horizons* (April 1976): 37–47.

LeBreton, P., and Henning, D. A. *Planning Theory.* Englewood Cliffs, N.J.: Prentice-Hall, 1961.

Litschert, R. J. "Some Characteristics of Long-Range Planning: An Industry Study," *Academy of Management Journal* (September 1968): 315–28.

Mockler, R. J. *Business Planning and Policy Formation.* New York: Appleton-Century Crofts, 1972.

Schoeffler, S. "Impact of Strategic Planning on Profit Performance," *Harvard Business Review* (March–April 1974): 137–45.

A CASE FOR ANALYSIS

The Hoover Company

Many a consumer products company would covet Hoover Co.'s widely recognized brand name for vacuum cleaners, its 100,000-outlet marketing network, and its rock-solid balance sheet. Indeed, such assets attracted a suitor unwanted by management—Fuqua Industries, Inc., the Atlanta-based conglomerate. In 1979, Fuqua offered $22 a share, or double the stock's then-current price, in a bid to acquire the 42 percent of the company's shares held by Hoover family members as a base for a future tender for the remaining shares.

But if Hoover's assets are enticing, its performance decidedly is not. Despite a 29 percent increase in sales over the past five years to $692 million, Hoover's 1978 earnings of $24.6 million fell short of the peak 1973 level. By the accounts of insiders and outsiders, it appears that Fuqua has set its sights on putting the resources of a weakly managed company to better use by installing more aggressive managers.

Even some of Hoover's executives privately conceded that the company's conservative, slow-moving management has failed to capitalize further on the familiar red and white Hoover trademark, both in domestic markets and, more important, in markets overseas, where Hoover chalked up 70 percent of its sales in 1978. "I don't think they've been aggressive at all in utilizing their resources," says William M. Kreckmann, an investment officer at Philadelphia's Provident National Bank, which has held a large block of Hoover shares.

Management's cautious bent all but doomed the company's only major move to diversify. In the mid-1960s, Hoover introduced small appliances, such as toasters and blenders, but the new products fell victim to brutal competition. The company now seems reluctant to venture beyond its traditional floor-care products in the U.S. Eyeing sluggish demand for household vacuum cleaners, Hoover acquired Chemko Industries Inc., a $2.4 million per year maker of industrial carpet-cleaning equipment in May 1979.

Perhaps the boldest move in recent years has been the company's desperate effort to stave off Fuqua. In mid-May 1979, Herbert W. Hoover, Jr. (no relation to the former President), grandson of the company's founder and former chairman, announced that he planned to accept Fuqua's offer for his 1.1 million shares, or 8.2 percent of the outstanding stock. But Chairman Merle R. Rawson does not favor any linkup with Fuqua, a $1.6 billion per year concern with interests ranging from movie theaters to lawn mowers. "Fuqua Industries has been built over buying and selling companies," he says.

The Hoover board voted to exercise its right of first refusal on any sale of Herbert Hoover's shares, a byproduct of the settlement of a lawsuit launched by the former chairman following his ouster a dozen years ago. The company began looking for other merger partners, and it filed lawsuits claiming that Fuqua's moves violated federal securities laws and state anti-takeover statutes. In turn, Hoover family members owning half a million shares have sued to keep the company from buying the former chairman's stock, fearing the purchase might discourage Fuqua.

While Hoover has failed in diversifying into faster growing markets, it has at least attempted to bolster its position in vacuum cleaners in recent years. Earlier in the decade, plagued by intense competition from the number two maker, Eureka Co., and by a design flaw in one of its own models, Hoover lost several points of its roughly 30 percent domestic market share. But the company managed to regain the ground it lost with the introduction in 1978 of a more powerful line of cleaners, dubbed Concept One. Still, few observers believe the new models will stimulate much new growth in a mature market that has remained stagnant at just over 9 million units a year for three years. In 1969, Hoover stepped up its efforts to move into more glamorous consumer product lines by acquiring a manufacturer of small appliances, but its offerings were not competitive in price, and Hoover was either unable or unwilling to roll out the continuing stream of new gadgets that success in the small appliance field requires. The company sold off the operation in 1977.

Hoover is also taking a drubbing in Britain, its chief overseas market and one that supports a broader line of Hoover appliances. The company claims half the market for vacuum cleaners in Britain, but it has been hard hit by European overcapacity in the appliance business, and imports of Italian laundry equipment have cut its 40 percent share of Britain's market for clothes washers to 35 percent. Earnings of Hoover Ltd., in which Hoover Co. has a 55 percent interest, slid from $23.8 million in 1975 to $5.8 million in 1978. The company is responding by scaling back new product and plant expansion plans and by cutting its British work force. However, some of its British managers are reportedly upset that the popular Hoover brand is not reaching its full potential because of the limits corporate headquarters has put on planning and new product development. Such caution leads many observers to speculate that the new management that might result from an unfriendly tender by Fuqua is just what Hoover needs.

Questions for Discussion

1. Discuss Hoover's strategies since 1969.
2. Discuss Hoover's reaction to the takeover bid in terms of contingency planning.
3. What went wrong with Hoover in its attempts at diversification?
4. Discuss the comment that Hoover is weakly managed. Is it justified?

Adapted from "Hoover: How Stodgy Management Made it a Takeover Target," Business Week *(June 18, 1979): 149.*

EXPERIENTIAL EXERCISE

Organizational Planning: The Simpson Sporting Goods Company

Purpose

To study the steps in the organizational planning process.

Required Understanding

The student should be familiar with the elements of organizational planning.

How to Set Up the Exercise

Set up groups of four to eight persons for the thirty to forty five minute exercise. The groups should be separated from each other and asked to converse only with members of their group. Before joining their groups, each member is asked to complete the exercise alone and then to join the group and reach a consensus.

The Situation

The Simpson Sporting Goods Company is a medium-sized recreational product manufacturer with headquarters and the main manufacturing plant located in Kansas City, Missouri. Founded in 1948 by Mr. John Simpson, Sr., the company specializes in the manufacture and sales of sporting goods for use in tennis (rackets), baseball and softball (bats and gloves), and skiing (water and snow skis). The products are sold directly to retail stores across the country through a twenty-five person sales force. The company has attained an average growth in sales and net income of 14 percent over the last eight years; sales revenues at the end of 1979 were $8.7 million.

The current chairman of the board, Mr. John Simpson, Jr., has concluded that present and future economic and leisure time trends offer the company a unique and positive opportunity to expand its product line and significantly grow in sales and profitability. While the present product lines have proven to be quite successful, he believes that they are too narrow for the rapidly expanding recreational field.

To formalize his objective of future growth, Mr. Simpson made two important announcements during a meeting of the company's top managers. First, he set the following company goals he wishes the company to achieve within the next five years:

The company shall show a growth rate in sales and net income of a minimum of 20 percent annually.

The company shall introduce at least three new product lines in areas in which they currently do not manufacture or market.

Second, in order to manage the growth process better, he formed a new department of corporate planning, staffed by a director, four planners, and two clerical workers.

EXHIBIT 6–12   Topics for the Simpson Planning Group Meeting

	Individual Priority	Group Priority
1. Guidelines for the involvement of the various levels of the company's management in the planning process.		
2. Analysis for internal and external environmental contingency factors.		
3. Translate company goals into goals for each department or unit.		
4. Develop five-year economic forecast.		
5. Development of the total company manpower resource base to achieve the stated goals.		
6. Identifying market opportunities for the company's existing product being manufactured.		
7. Analysis of current retail strategies and development of new marketing strategies.		
8. Procedures for reviewing established and implemented plans.		
9. Identification of opportunities for manufacturing and marketing of new product lines.		
10. Development of capital budgets and profit and loss statements for the next five years.		
11. Establishing a timetable for the development, implementation, and evaluation of the plans.		
12. Analysis of the external environment influencing the demand for sporting goods.		
13. Analysis of the company's present resource base.		
14. Identification of the required level of physical facilities needed to achieve the stated goals.		

Instructions for the Exercise

In one of your first duties as Director of Corporate Planning, you have asked your planning staff to identify and develop a set of agenda items to be covered at the initial meeting of the planning unit. After a review of the individual lists, you have identified a set of items for discussion. These are shown in exhibit 6–12. A closer examination of the combined lists indicates, however, that the identified topics represent different stages of the planning process, thus necessitating a scheme for setting priorities. In response, you have developed the following classification or system for setting priorities:

I. Those topics that deal with the direction in which the company should head in the achievement of the stated goals. These topics concern the broad, corporate issues and the criteria for judging the quality of the final plan.

II. Those topics that come after consideration of the topics labeled "I." These topics should concern the more operational aspects of a plan.

III. Those topics that are related to the implementation of a plan, and which should be considered after those topics labeled "I" and "II."

1. *Individually*, each member should classify the topics in exhibit 6–12 as I, II, or III.

2. As a *group*, the same topics should be classified using the same scheme.

3. The group results should be displayed, and each group should justify its scheme.

Managerial
Decision Making

CHAPTER OUTLINE

KEY POINTS IN THIS CHAPTER

1. Decision making is a managerial activity that affects and involves all the management functions.

2. Decision making is a process that involves a sequence of rational steps.

3. Decisions vary by type (programmed and nonprogrammed) and conditions (certainty, risk, and uncertainty).

4. The manager's position in the organization, culture, individual characteristics, and certain organizational factors can act as constraints to decision making.

5. The manager's particular style can result in significant variations in the decision-making process.

6. The external environment can influence the way managers make decisions. This is especially noticeable in the evaluation of results stage.

7. The management science school has contributed to the solution of many complex managerial problems.

8. The decision-making process involves the development and use of all the managerial skills and roles.

THE PRACTICE OF MANAGEMENT

Managerial Decision Making: General Electric

General Electric, the largest diversified company in the world, has long been known for its strategic planning excellence, timely decision making, and the seemingly endless stream of competent managers. An example is Tom Vanderslice, Senior Vice President and head of G.E.'s power systems business.

The power systems business embraces the area that helped G.E. grow into the successful company that it is—manufacturing heavy equipment to generate and deliver electricity. With the demand for power growing more slowly now than before the 1973 and 1979 oil crises, the U.S. market for turbines and switchgear has not exactly been electrifying. Power systems also include the company's nuclear energy group, which was in financial trouble even before the Three Mile Island incident.

To this difficult task, Vanderslice brought skills acquired in a varied career with G.E. Like many managers, he has spent virtually his entire professional life inside the company, growing and learning new skills along the way. Holding a degree in chemistry and physics, he has gone from doing scientific research to managing scientific research, and then from managing scientific businesses to the general management of business. A meticulous decision maker, Vanderslice is more interested in figures than in words or their pronunciation. In conferences with his subordinates, he says, "I listen to the war stories, but then I go back to check the data." For some time, he has even kept a computer terminal at home so that he can summon up real-time financial results anytime he is not at his corporate office.

As an example of his approach to decision making, consider the problem he faced shortly after he took his current position in December 1977. Because four or five years can elapse between an order for heavy electrical equipment and delivery of the finished product, manufacturers can have trouble detecting long-term trends in their markets. Vanderslice found, for example, that his turbine group, representing about half the area's $3.5 billion in sales, still planned its production around a forecast of 7 percent annual growth in electrical usage in the U.S.—a figure that had not changed in a number of years.

Intuition told him that the figure was too high, but initially he lacked the data to back his conclusions. To verify his intuition, he kept after his managers repeatedly asking them to explain and justify the assumptions behind the 7 percent estimate. Finally, he hit upon the right question: "What about energy costs?" Experience had shown that consumers cut down their use of electricity during the mid-1970s as energy costs increased. To his surprise, using a hunch, he checked the electrical usage of G.E.'s own buildings during this time and found a significant reduction in the consumption of electricity. Such elasticity—energy costs versus demand for electricity—had not been factored into power systems' electrical usage forecasts to date.

After reworking the data, Vanderslice decided to lower the forecast to just over 4 percent. If it did nothing else, this change got the attention of G.E. managers who had been in the electrical equipment business for years. The major market impact of this decision was felt in the planning process. Carefully thought-out plans for virtually every product line in the power systems group had to be redrawn. Time has proven his approach to decision making to be correct.

Adapted from W. Kiechell, "Tom Vanderslice Scales the Heights at G.E.," Fortune *(July 30, 1979): 80–84.*

Decision making is an integral part of every manager's job. In fact many prefer to call managers "decision makers." Decisions involve everything from where to hold a meeting, to the level of resource commitment to a new product line, from who will be promoted (or hired) to fill a vacated managerial position, to the amount of money to be paid out in stock dividends this year.

The common theme running through these examples is that decision making involves some action or, in our terminology, deciding on a *choice* of particular actions. We will define *decision making* as a process involving information, choice of alternative actions, implementation, and evaluation that is directed to the achievement of certain stated goals.

Our discussion of decision making will be broken down into four parts. First, we will focus on the process of decision making, types of decisions, and the various factors influencing decision making. Second, the relationship between the decision-making process and the manager's style of decision making will be investigated. Third, we will introduce certain decision-making aids that have been contributed by the management science school. Finally, the relationship between decision making, performance, and the manager's job will be presented.

THE PROCESS OF DECISION MAKING

Decision making is a process that involves the following steps: (1) recognition and identification of the problem; (2) development and evaluation of alternatives; (3) choice among the alternatives; (4) implementation; and (5) evaluation of the results. The process is shown in exhibit 7–1. The exhibit suggests, first of all, that decision making is a logical *sequence* of activities. That is, before alternatives are evaluated, the problem must be defined, and so on. Second, decision making is an *iterative* activity. As shown by the feedback loop, decision making is a recurring activity, and managers can learn from past decisions.

Recognition and Identification of the Problem

This first step, that of recognizing and identifying the problem, is the *energizing* factor in the decision process. Important to this step are the questions, what is defined as a problem, and what are the sources for identifying the existence of problems?

Defining a Problem.   There are two sources of problems usually encountered by managers. First are *goals* set by the organization. While not exactly considered problems, goals are certainly energizing factors for decision making. Achieving such goals as "improving return on invested capital to 15 percent by 1985" or "reducing service cost by 25 percent this year" is the purpose to be served by the decision-making process.

The second source of decision-making problems is somewhat related to the first: that is, there is a *gap* between the desired level of goal achievement and the actual level. This may be as simple as an operator

EXHIBIT 7–1 Decision-Making Process

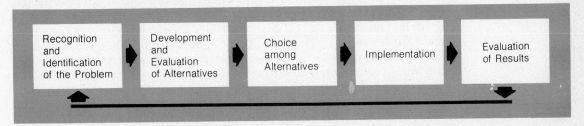

in a power-generating plant recognizing that the flow of coal into the equipment is below standard, or as significant as the "action point" in the discussion of contingency planning. In essence, signaling an action point (i.e., that a contingency has occurred) is a decision in itself.

Sources of Identifying Problems. The process of identifying problems, sometimes called "problem finding," is related to the particular information source available to the manager. These sources include:[1]

1. *Internal sources.* Managers can use comparative, or historical data, to examine a unit's performance in relationship with past performance to identify whether performance has increased, decreased, or remained the same. Another internal information source are data from organizational plans indicating that results do not meet the planned goals.

2. *External sources.* Customers, suppliers, actions by competitors and governmental agencies, either from written or verbal sources, act to initiate the decision process.

There are times when the identification and recognition of a problem is clear-cut, such as the case of the decision process involving goal achievement. There are other cases in which there is a lack of information to identify a problem, but the manager has a "hunch" that something has or will go wrong. These situations should not be passed off as pure folly because many hunches are founded on sound managerial experience.

Development and Evaluation of Alternatives

Once the problem (or problems) has been identified, the search for solutions can begin. This step is broken down into two separate factors: developing alternative solutions, and evaluating each alternative.

Developing Alternative Solutions. At this point, managers are concerned with gathering different ideas, thoughts, and resources to try to solve the problem. For example, Uniroyal faces the problems of high labor costs and inefficient equipment in its Akron, Ohio tire plant. Among the possible alternatives for solving these problems are: (1) remodel the plant; (2) close the Akron plant and build a new plant in a more favorable area; or (3) do nothing.

Evaluation of Alternatives. Each alternative, first of all, is considered for its *realism* and *feasibility*. This "weeding out" process eliminates those alternatives that are not practical or are too costly. For example, Uniroyal may eliminate the plant-remodeling alternative because it still would be faced with high labor costs.

Following the feasibility analysis, specific questions are asked concerning the degree to which the problem can be solved with the adoption of a particular alternative. The focus is one of *criteria*. As discussed in chapter 2, many different criteria can be used to evaluate an alternative, such as costs, potential profit contribution, maintaining a competitive position, and so on. For example, consider the decision on certain equipment for a new manufacturing plant. On one hand, the manufacturing manager may propose the purchase of a new packaging machine that has the latest technology and is the most cost efficient. It, however, will not be delivered for six months. The marketing manager, on the other hand, suggests that the company should instead purchase a more readily available packaging system, one that is less cost efficient but can be delivered and installed within eight weeks. This alternative, according to the marketing manager, would enable the organization to get the product into the market for sale earlier than any competitor, providing a significant competitive advantage. This example illustrates the issue of criteria (in this case, multiple criteria—costs savings versus time) in selecting alternatives.

Choice Among Alternatives

The final choice among a variety of alternatives depends on how well the alternatives serve the goals of the organization. Choice is an act of *judgment*. This judgment is made as to how well the outcomes or consequences of the alternative approximate the desired goals, or which alternative offers the most favorable combination of results. Some of these judgments made by managers are reasonably objective; others, however, are more subjective and are influenced by personal value systems of the managers.

COMMENTS ON THE PRACTICE OF MANAGEMENT
(See p. 211)

The example of Tom Vanderslice of General Electric illustrates a number of important points in making a choice among alternatives in the decision-making process. First, as Vanderslice did, a manager must always question the quality of the information that is being used to make a decision. Inaccurate information may lead to an erroneous decision. Second, if the quality of the information is suspect, go out and gather new information. Vanderslice's collection of data on energy costs and electricity usage in office buildings is an excellent example of this procedure. Finally, it is important for the reader to recognize that Vanderslice's approach to decision making may have been the result of his "varied" career with G.E. In essence, by working in a variety of jobs in different functions, he had apparently acquired the necessary managerial skills for success in his present position.

Choice is influenced by the *quality of the information* used in evaluating the selected alternatives. As we discussed in the last chapter, managers must be aware of this information quality/effective choice relationship. The choice of a particular course of action can also be altered if *new information* is received (such as in contingency planning), or if managers higher in the organization do not approve the decision. From experience, the most effective presentations of a decision to higher level executives are made by managers who thoroughly explain the problem, review the several actions that might be taken, offer a definite proposal, explain what results are expected, and why it is the most prudent action.

Implementation

Implementing a decision involves a number of important steps. As an illustration, consider the decision by an office equipment manufacturer to open a new sales office in a previously untapped territory. Initially the decision must be *communicated* to all involved employees. This is usually done through written communications and verbally to those who are most directly affected. Second, resources must be *organized* and *allocated* to the new office. This entails appointment of a sales manager and sales representatives, acquiring office space, and hiring the staff. Finally, *feedback* mechanisms are developed in order to check on the progress of the new office's sales performance. These topics will be covered in greater detail in Part III.

Evaluation of Results

Evaluating the results of decisions can be a time for cheer, a time for deep introspection, or a time to pick up the pieces. For every successful decision, such as the introduction of felt-tip pens or low-calorie beers, there is a less-successful one, such as the Edsel. In analyzing decision results, at least three questions should be asked by the manager.

First, to what degree have the goals been *achieved?* This is the most important to the organization. Miller Brewing's goal of obtaining the largest market share in low-calorie beer was achieved with its "Lite" product. On the other hand, Polaroid's goal of creating a large market for instant movie film with its Polavision unit ended up a significant failure.

Second, how *committed* are employees and customers or clients to the decision in the long run? This is crucial, for many times a decision is found to be successful in the short run, but a failure as time goes by. For example, in instituting a new employee performance evaluation system, a high level of commitment and participation is noted by all concerned. After the initial euphoria has worn off, some of the deficiencies of the new system become apparent, acting to reduce the commitment to the system.

Finally, what has been *learned* from implementing the decision—in other words, could we have done better making another decision? This is similar to second guessing a result that was successful but may have been better had some changes been made earlier. For example, in the case of McDonald's, some people have looked beyond the company's tremendous successes in fast food marketing and suggested that McDonald's missed out on higher profits by not diversifying its offerings into foods such as pizza and other specialty sandwiches. The important factor to be gained from this type of analysis is that the organization has learned from experience what has worked, and what may have worked better, so that the next time a similar decision is to be made, a different approach may be taken.

ORGANIZATIONAL FRAMEWORK FOR DECISION MAKING

Managers make decisions within a framework and under conditions usually dictated by the organization. In essence, the process of decision making can vary significantly depending on the situation that the manager faces. For our purposes, this framework is determined by the type of decision, conditions of decision making, and the focus of the decision.

Types of Decisions

Each of us has been in situations in which we have made decisions that were well defined and straightforward. We have also encountered other situations in which the decisions were quite ill-defined and not readily adaptable to a straightforward decision approach. In managerial terms, the former are defined as programmed decisions, while the latter are called nonprogrammed decisions.[2]

Programmed decisions are well-structured problems that are generally routine and repetitive in nature. Such decisions can be made using a systematic procedure, rule, or habit. For example, the decision to hire a new employee, the manner in which a patient is admitted into a hospital, and the way a product is checked for quality can be viewed as programmed decisions because they are quite similar each time they occur.

Nonprogrammed decisions are those that are ill-structured and unique in nature and for which standard routines cannot be developed. For example, negotiating a merger, introducing a new product line, or the selection of a new organization president are not well suited to structured rules or policies due to the relative infrequency of their occurrence.

Managers are faced with many nonprogrammed decisions in their work. This suggests that the ability or *skill* to make good nonprogrammed decisions can be a determining factor in the level of managerial effectiveness. Managers must rely heavily on their problem-solving ability, judgment, and common sense when they are faced with nonprogrammed decisions. To aid managers in this area, many organizations have developed training programs to teach their managers how to make nonprogrammed decisions in a logical manner.

Conditions of Decision Making

Managers make decisions so that certain goals can be achieved. Sometimes the achievement of these goals is assured when a particular decision is made. Unfortunately, most managerial decisions are made when the future is not so predictable. The difference between these decisions is the *amount of information* that managers have at their disposal and the *degree of confidence* managers have in the usefulness of the information in predicting the future. The information input into decision making determines the following conditions: certainty, risk, and uncertainty.[3] This is shown in exhibit 7–2.

Certainty.   When managers have sufficient information to make decisions so that the exact results are known in advance, they are making decisions under *certainty*. For example, a worker in a chemical plant may be responsible for monitoring the reaction between certain materials. The worker may view a dial that measures the reaction temperature and

EXHIBIT 7–2
Conditions of
Decision Making

| CERTAIN KNOWLEDGE AND INFORMATION | Certainty | Risk | Uncertainty | UNCERTAIN KNOWLEDGE AND INFORMATION |

see that the temperature is too low. Since a continued low temperature will result in an inferior product, the worker turns certain valves that act to raise the reaction temperature. This decision (in essence, a programmed decision) is made under conditions of certainty because the worker knows that raising the temperature will produce an acceptable product.

Risk.   Under conditions of *risk* the manager is faced with a situation in which the results are not totally known, but will probably fall within a certain range of outcomes. With the use of the word "probably," we are formally introducing the concept of probability to managerial decision making. *Probability* is defined as the percentage of times a specific outcome will occur over a large number of occurrences.

For example, consider the marketing manager of a firm that manufactures machine tools who decides to raise prices on a particular product line by 5 percent. The decision to raise prices is based on two assumptions: (1) the added revenue is needed to cover rising manufacturing costs; and (2) the price rise will hold because competitors will probably follow suit with their own price rises. From past experience the manager knows that competitors have matched price rises in 80 percent of recorded situations. However, there is a 10 percent chance that some competitors will not raise prices, and another 10 percent chance that other competitors will raise prices, but less than 5 percent. In other words, the marketing manager is operating under conditions of risk.

Uncertainty.   When managers have difficulty assigning probabilities to outcomes, either because there is a lack of information or an absence of knowledge concerning what outcomes can be expected, we say that the manager is operating under conditions of *uncertainty*.[4] In other words, there are too many variables or too many unknown facts (or both), and therefore the manager cannot predict the outcomes with any degree of confidence.

This situation is faced frequently by managers when new, innovative products or services are introduced. For example, such products as Chrysler's K car, microwave ovens, and videotape recorders for home use were introduced with much uncertainty.

Focus of the Decision

In the last chapter, we pointed out that there are different types of plans found at the three main managerial levels. In much the same manner, the focus of decisions is different at varying management levels. We shall identify these decisions as strategic, administrative, and operating decisions.[5]

1. *Strategic decisions.* These decisions are usually oriented toward establishing organizational goals, selecting strategies, and problems that con-

cern the relationship between the organization and its environment. They are fundamentally executive or top-management oriented.

2. *Administrative decisions.* Administrative decisions are directed toward developing divisional plans, structuring work flows, distribution channels, developing material sources, personnel training, acquisition of facilities, and the like. They are primarily middle-management oriented.

3. *Operating decisions.* Maximizing the performance of current operations is the major concern of operating decisions. For example, setting production schedules, determining inventory levels, and deciding on the relative expenditures in support of the functional areas of the organization are included in this category.

EXHIBIT 7–3
Decision Types, Conditions, and Focus

TYPE	CONDITIONS	FOCUS	EXAMPLES
Programmed	Certainty to Risk	Operating and Administrative	Hiring clerical personnel Quality control Hospital admissions
Nonprogrammed	Risk to Uncertainty	Administrative and Strategic	Negotiating a merger Introducing a new product Testing a new drug

The components of decision type, conditions, and management level can be integrated. That is, at the lower management levels (i.e., first-line managers), one can expect to be confronted with mostly operating decisions that lend themselves to programming and that contain a great deal of certainty. At the highest management level, however, decisions are more strategic in nature, are mostly nonprogrammed, and contain a high degree of uncertainty.

FACTORS INFLUENCING DECISION MAKING

It would be an error to assume that decision making is a straightforward, checklist approach that varies little over time. Decision making does vary because managers change and the situations they face also change. Organizational factors and culture appear to have a significant influence on managerial decision making.

Organizational Factors

Possibly nothing can facilitate or constrain decision making more than organizational factors. Typically, the manager has very little control over these factors and must learn to adjust to them. In essence, organizational factors establish the *boundaries* for managerial decision making. The manager's *level* or *position* is a contributing factor. The level or position in the organization influences the degree of freedom the manager has in making a decision. Some managers have flexibility and discretion in making a decision, while others must closely follow standard rules and procedures. This concerns the topic of organizational structure, which will be discussed in chapters 8 and 9.

Another organizational factor is the relative *importance* or *significance* of the decision to the organization. Decisions are not the same in terms of the impact they will have. For example, a decision to promote a manager is less important than one to close down a series of inefficient plants or offices.

The significance and importance of the decision is related to the amount of resources that are involved or can be affected. Promoting one person or laying off 400 people represent different levels of significance. The impact on the *financial stability* of the organization should also be considered. A decision to introduce a new product line that could affect the total survival of an organization is certainly more important than how the office space is designed. Finally, *time* is an important factor in and of itself. Time is related not only to how long it takes to make a decision, but to what is the long-term impact of the decision.

The third organizational factor concerns the different *groups* that have an influence on the manager. The influencing groups can include advisory committees, informal groups, and labor unions. Groups can many times act as constraining factors in managerial decision making. For example, with labor contracts, the manager is limited in ability to motivate, discipline, or assign work to subordinates. Contractual wage increases remove the powerful influence of merit increases, discipline in many cases is not permitted, and managers may have to assign specific workers to jobs not on the basis of skill, but seniority. In chapter 14, we will discuss the influences of groups in more detail.

Culture: International Factors

In earlier chapters, we discussed the importance of culture in the activities of organizations and managers. Nowhere is the cultural influence more pronounced than in decision making. Consider the difference between Western and Japanese managers.

For Westerners, the organizational decision-making process stresses individual responsibility and accountability. The Japanese, however, take a different approach by emphasizing *collective* or *consultative* decision making. This is primarily due to the fact that employees, managers and nonmanagers alike, spend more time in corporate activities than do their Western counterparts. They have tenure, are almost never fired, and job switching is quite rare.

Termed *hara gei* (where hara means "guts" and gei is translated as "art"), this collective decision making occurs in Japanese industrial and commercial organizations when an important strategic decision must be made that can affect many people both inside and outside the organization. The process is usually initiated by a series of memos and reports discussing the elements of the decision and the possible consequences. These memos and reports are then passed up and down the ranks in the organization and initialed by all recipients.

Whenever an individual wishes to express reservations about the decision, he will put his initials sideways on the circulating document. To express severe reservations, he may even sign it upside down. This will prepare his colleagues for a future memo that outlines his dissent, possibly discussing overlooked aspects that are deemed important.

To the Japanese, there are a number of advantages in the use of a collective form of decision making. Some of these advantages include the following:

1. **The thoroughness of the process insures that fewer aspects will be overlooked.**

    It is believed that satisfactory decisions are made when they are in accordance with the overall goals of the organization, are based on adequate information about the present and future, include all relevant factors, have been considered in the light of their long-term consequences, and so forth. It is the belief of the Japanese that when more people are involved in the decision process, each element in the process will be covered more thoroughly.

2. **Broad participation creates a sense of commitment by employees.**

    It has long been believed that people work harder to implement decisions when they understand and approve the decision. Several Western management techniques are also based on the principle of explaining goals and methods to those who are charged with implementation. For the Japanese, it is even more motivating to have employees participate in the process leading to the decision. The opportunity to study background memos and reports used to reach a decision is more informative than an ex post facto explanation or justification.

3. **The decision can be bolder and more radical in a collective decision system.**

    In Japan, the consultative decision process between workers and management has resulted in unanimous agreement on harsh but necessary courses of action. For example, the entire bicycle industry was abandoned and the workers were retrained for positions in new industries with greater potential, such as motorcycles, automobiles, and trucks. Through participation in decision making, it is easier for the workers to trade off short-term problems and disruptions against their long-term benefits.

While there are obvious benefits in the adoption of a collective system of managerial decision making, there are certain factors that make it difficult to implement in other systems. First, the collective system does not work well when decisions must be made quickly. Second, when secrecy is important, the collective system fails badly. A degree of participation can be used quite effectively in certain types of decisions, but on an overall basis the collective system seems to be culturally bound.

Recent research has shown that certain changes are occurring in the Japanese system of decision making.[6] In particular, one study has shown that there is a growing tendency for the Japanese to adopt a more Western style of decision making. It is a possibility that with time the consultative process may all but disappear.

DECISION-MAKING STYLES BY MANAGERS

Since decision making is influenced by a number of situational factors, one would expect that managers would exhibit different approaches or styles of decision making. One way of studying the differences in managerial decision-making styles is to examine the steps in the decision-making process. As we will discuss, managers can exhibit quite different styles within and across the individual decision-making steps.

Decision-Making Styles and Problem Identification

Although it is widely assumed that managers are concerned with the solutions to work-related problems, there is some evidence that some managers (and nonmanagers) *actively* go out of their way to find problems. In the same manner, we are all aware of some people who thrive in situations of high uncertainty, while others can be effective only in situations of calm certainty. This phenomenon relates to what has been called a manager's *problem-sensing style*.

Research in this area has shown that there are at least three types or styles that managers exhibit in problem-sensing situations:[7]

1. *Problem avoider.* A problem avoider is a person who expects order and predictability (i.e., certainty), and is motivated to maintain these conditions. Such individuals tend to block out or eliminate problems in advance either by ignoring information or by attempting to curb uncertainty with the use of detailed planning efforts.

2. *Problem solver.* This style reflects a manager who expects and strives to maintain a mix of certainty and uncertainty. Problem solvers do not tend to ignore problems, but attempt to solve them as they arise.

3. *Problem seeker.* A problem seeker is one who actively seeks out and thrives on uncertainty and the novelty that it provides. Managers who adopt this style usually will seek out problems to satisfy their needs for the challenge of uncertainty. They would be expected to be quite active in contingency planning efforts.

As we discussed in chapter 4, and will point out further in this chapter, the nature of the organization's environment plays an important role in determining where these styles are most effective. That is, an environment of relative stability may be conducive to a problem-solver style, and a complex and dynamic environment in which problems abound would fit well with a problem-seeker style of decision making.

Decision-Making Styles and Developing and Evaluating Alternatives

The process of developing and evaluating alternatives for decision making is based on *information*. Managers differ in their styles of gathering, interpreting, and evaluating information. Two distinct approaches can be identified: information processing, and information integration.

Information Processing. If we view decision making as a process through which managers organize the information they receive from the environment, we must be concerned with how these individuals think. The manner in which a manager thinks through the process of developing and evaluating alternatives is highly dependent on certain consistent modes of thought. These thought patterns develop through training and experience in much the same way as managerial skills develop.

As shown in exhibit 7–4, a manager's decision-making style in developing and evaluating alternatives can vary along two information processing dimensions: information gathering, and information evaluation.[8]

EXHIBIT 7–4
Information
Processing
Decision Styles

		INFORMATION EVALUATION	
		Systematic	Intuitive
INFORMATION GATHERING	Preceptive	Manufacturing manager Statistician	Marketing manager Psychologist
	Receptive	Accountant Physician	Architect Research chemist

Adapted from J. L. McKenney and P. G. W. Keen, "How Managers' Minds Work," Harvard Business Review (May–June 1979): 83.

Information gathering relates to the way managers organize the various sources of information they receive daily. In a sense, it involves a framework or standard by which some information is rejected while other information is summarized and categorized. Two specific managerial styles can be identified:

1. *Preceptive style.* A manager who adopts a preceptive style is one who emphasizes the process of "filtering" data or information. All incoming information is compared against some internal standards: the information that matches the standard is retained, and information that does not meet the standard is eliminated from further consideration. For example, consider a manufacturing manager who attends a meeting where the divisional vice president outlines the division's plans for the next five years. The manufacturing manager with a preceptive style would listen attentively to the vice president's comments concerning production aspects, but may filter out comments that are of little concern to his or her job, such as changes in the organization of the market research department.

2. *Receptive style.* The manager with a receptive style of information processing is attentive to *all* sources of information. Instead of trying to categorize information through filtering, emphasis is placed on looking at all the information for some meaning or new knowledge. Consider a doctor specializing in internal medicine who examines a variety of test results on a patient. In order to gain some understanding of the patient's condition, the doctor's receptive style would require that all test results are examined in total in order to pinpoint possible sources of illness.

Information evaluation is sometimes referred to as the process of problem solving. The different styles of information evaluation relate to the particular analysis sequence used by the manager. Two distinct styles can be described:

1. *Systematic style.* This style refers to managers who approach problems by structuring them in terms of some accepted method that if followed

will lead to a solution. An accountant auditing the books of an organization would use a systematic style of information evaluation.

2. *Intuitive style.* In contrast to the systematic style, a manager with an intuitive style would avoid being bound by a particular approach to a problem. The Practice of Management example concerning G.E. is a good illustration of an intuitive style. These managers prefer to look at the meaning of information from a trial-and-error framework and are much more willing to jump from one method to another. Consider the reaction of United Airlines in their attempt to regain lost airline business after their lengthy strike in 1979. In the past, airlines that come off a long period of inactivity would attempt to regain business through a slow process of winning back customers in a "business as usual" manner. Since competition in the air-travel business had significantly increased due to the deregulation, the management of United felt that a more dramatic and quick reaction was needed. This intuitive response, the half-fare coupon to passengers, not only regained lost business quickly, but sent reverberations throughout the airline industry.

THE MANAGER'S JOB
Robert P. Jensen of General Cable Corporation

Many managers believe that effective decision making is the result of the proper integration of detailed analysis and intuition. Consider the case of Robert P. Jensen, chairman of General Cable Corporation, who for three years was a tight end for the Baltimore Colts football team. Sensing the need for his company to diversify, he found himself faced with five major decisions that involved over $300 million.

"On each decision," says Jensen, "the mathematical analysis only got me to the point where my intuition had to take over"—as was the case with the $106 million cash purchase of Automation Industries. General Cable's strategic planning department had come up with a purchase price based on Automation's future sales. "It's not that the numbers weren't accurate," Jensen recalls, "but were the underlying assumptions correct?"

As an engineer not given to making hasty decisions, he calls "patience" crucial to the decision-making process. At the same time, he warns that the perfectionist who keeps waiting for new information never gets anything done. "Intuition is picking the right moment for making your move."

Adapted from R. Rowan, "Those Business Hunches are More Than Blind Faith," Fortune *(April 23, 1979): 111–12.*

Exhibit 7–4 also shows that the two information processing dimensions can be combined to describe particular managerial jobs. For example, statisticians can be described as those who utilize a preceptive and systematic style of information gathering and evaluation. They normally tend to filter out superfluous information and go about their decision making in a systematic manner. On the other hand, an architect is more receptive to a variety of information sources and depends on a certain mode of intuition in solving design problems.

Information Integration.   In what ways does the manager *combine* or *integrate* information from various sources in developing and evaluating alternatives? For example, consider the case of a manager making a decision to promote one employee from five candidates to a supervisory position. Suppose that the manager has four pieces of information on each candidate: tenure in the organization; individual performance data over the past two years; previous supervisory experience; and test scores measuring supervisory capability. In evaluating the five candidates (i.e., alternatives), in what manner should the information be combined or integrated? Exhibit 7–5 suggests that three approaches can be used.[9]

EXHIBIT 7–5
Information Integration Decision Styles

STYLE	DESCRIPTION	SUPERVISORY SELECTION EXAMPLE
Compensatory	High value on one criterion can offset low value on another criterion.	High test score on capability test offsets lack of supervisory experience.
Conjunctive	Minimally acceptable levels must be achieved on all criteria.	Must minimally have: (1) five years employment with the organization; (2) two years supervisory experience with any organization; (3) top 20 percent in performance; and (4) top 25 percent on scores of supervisory capability test.
Disjunctive	High value on any one of the criteria is acceptance.	Four years supervisory experience with the organization is sufficient to make decisions.

First, the manager could treat the information in a *compensatory* manner for each candidate. This approach is based on the assumption that a low score on one criterion can be *offset* or *compensated* by a high score on another criterion. One employee, for example, may have almost no previous supervisory experience, but scores high on the supervisory capability test. Because the high test score can offset the lack of experience, this candidate will be evaluated at the same level as a candidate who has an average amount of supervisory experience and who achieves an average score on the capability test.

A second approach, termed the *conjunctive* or multiple hurdles approach, can also be used by the evaluating manager. In this case, the manager establishes *minimally* acceptable levels that must be attained on *each* criterion. If candidates fall below the cutoff level on any one criterion, they can no longer be considered for promotion to supervisor. The manager, for example, may set the following minimum cutoff points: (1) five years with the organization; (2) two years of supervisory experience; (3) past performance that would place the candidate in the top 20 percent of fellow employees; and (4) test scores that place the candidate in the upper 25 percent of those who take the test. Note that in contrast to the compensatory model, under a conjunctive approach high scores on one criterion cannot offset a score below the minimum cutoff on some other criterion.

Finally, the manager might adopt an evaluation approach that is *disjunctive* in nature. Under this approach, the manager simply scans the information about a candidate looking only for some *outstanding characteristic*. If found, the candidate is promoted on the basis of this characteristic alone, and other pieces of information are ignored. In this case, the manager might determine that one of the candidates has had over four years experience as a supervisor in another organization and that this information alone warrants promoting the individual.[10]

Decision-Making Styles and Alternative Choice

When the problem or goals have been stated and the major alternatives have been identified and evaluated, the manager is faced with making the actual decision. The different decision-making styles that managers have been known to use at this stage can be classified under two approaches: classical decision approach, and behavioral decision approach.

Classical Decision Approach. To illustrate the classical approach to decision making, consider the problem facing the administrator of a private specialized hospital that deals with rehabilitation care for patients with spinal cord injuries and with nerve and muscle system disorders. Because of the relatively small size of the hospital (only 80 beds) and the growing patient load, a planning decision concerning the physical facilities must be made soon. The three strategies open to the administrator are: (1) maintain the present size; (2) remodel the existing facilities to increase the number of beds to 110; or (3) add a new patient ward to increase the number of beds from 80 to 150. The administrator wants to begin planning revisions to the hospital, if any are justified, as soon as possible. From a decision-making point of view, which alternative should be chosen? Two different approaches can be used: probabilistic, and non-probabilistic.[11]

The *probabilistic* approach, known as a Decision Tree, deals directly with the probabilities associated with various environmental events. The development of the decision tree for this example involves the following steps. The complete analysis is shown in exhibit 7–6.

1. *Identify the possible strategies.* The three strategies that have been chosen for analysis include no change, remodeling, and ward expansion.
2. *Identify the possible events that can affect the strategies.* Crucial to the analysis is the variation in patient load that could possibly occur. Three possible patient loads are identified: no change, 20 percent *decrease,* and a 20 percent *increase.*
3. *Estimate the probability of occurrence of each event.* On the basis of past experience and a recognition of current trends, the administrator estimates that there is a 50 percent probability that patient load will increase, a 30 percent probability that there will be no change in patient load, and

a 20 percent probability that the patient load will decrease.

4. *Calculate the expected payoff of each event and strategy.* The expected yearly payoff is calculated by multiplying the expected profit by the estimated probability of occurrence. Expected profits are the result of subtracting operating costs from expected revenue. For example, for decision tree branch "2" (maintain present size with no change in patient load), the expected payoff is ($2.2 million − $2.0 million × 0.3) $60,000. Similarly, for decision tree branch "6" (remodel with an increase in patient load), the expected payoff is ($2.7 million − $2.3 million × 0.5) $200,000.

5. *Choose the strategy that results in the highest expected payoff.* As shown in exhibit 7–6, the strategy to maintain the present size results in a $220,000 expected payoff, $230,000 for the remodeling strategy, and $330,000 for the ward expansion strategy. Therefore, the decision tree analysis indicates that the administrator should expand the hospital because it results in the highest expected profits, the original goal.

EXHIBIT 7–6   Decision Tree Analysis for Hospital Expansion

STRATEGY	PATIENT LOAD	REVENUE (Millions)		EXPENSE (Millions)		PROFITS (Millions)	PROBABILITY	EXPECTED PAYOFF	
Expand	Increase	9 [$3.0	−	2.4	=	$0.6]	× 0.5 =	$300,000	
	No Change	8 [$2.5	−	2.4	=	$0.1]	× 0.3 =	$ 30,000	$330,000
	Decrease	7 [$2.0	−	2.0	=	$0.0]	× 0.2 =	$ 0	
Remodel	Increase	6 [$2.7	−	2.3	=	$0.4]	× 0.5 =	$200,000	
	No Change	5 [$2.4	−	2.3	=	$0.1]	× 0.3 =	$ 30,000	$230,000
	Decrease	4 [$2.0	−	2.0	=	$0.0]	× 0.2 =	$ 0	
No Change	Increase	3 [$2.4	−	2.0	=	$0.4]	× 0.5 =	$200,000	
	No Change	2 [$2.2	−	2.0	=	$0.2]	× 0.3 =	$ 60,000	$300,000
	Decrease	1 [$2.0	−	1.8	=	$0.2]	× 0.2 =	$ 40,000	

Nonprobabilistic rules ignore the probabilities of the occurrence of various outcomes. In other words, decision makers act as if they had perfect information. Three different styles can evolve from this approach.

1. *Maximax Rule.* Some managers act *optimistically* about the occurrence of the events influencing a decision. By following this style, the manager will select the strategy under which it is possible to receive the most favorable or highest payoff. This is called a style that maximizes the maximum possible payoff, or *maximax*. As shown in table A of exhibit 7–7, the maximum payoff occurs when the hospital expands and patient load increases ($600,000). Using this style, the manager will decide to expand the hospital.

2. *Maximin Rule.* A *pessimistic* manager may make a decision believing that only the worst possible situation will occur. This is called the style that maximizes the minimum payoff, or *maximin*. Table A of exhibit 7–7

EXHIBIT 7–7
Classical
Decision Style to
Alternative Choice

TABLE A—MAXIMAX AND MAXIMIN RULES

Strategy	Patient Load Increase	No Change	Patient Load Decrease
Open new wing	$600,000[1]	$100,000	$0[2]
Remodel	$400,000	$100,000	$0[2]
No change	$400,000	$200,000	$200,000

1 = Maximax rule choice   2 = Maximin rule choice

TABLE B—MINIMAX RULE

Strategy	Patient Load Increase	No Change	Patient Load Decrease	Raw Total
Open new wing	$0	$100,000	$200,000	$300,000
Remodel	$200,000	$100,000	$200,000	$500,000
No change	$200,000	$0	$0	$200,000[1]

1 = Minimax rule choice

suggests that if the administrator adheres to a maximin rule, the choice will be to remodel or expand under a decrease in patient load condition because it maximizes the minimum payoff ($0).

3. *Minimax Rule.* If a manager chooses a particular strategy but the most favorable environmental event does not occur, a certain degree of *regret* develops. A decision-making style that takes regret into account is called minimizing the maximum regret, or *minimax.* For our purposes, we will define *regret* as the payoff for each strategy under every environmental event subtracted from the most favorable payoff that is possible with the occurrence of the particular event. The minimax analysis is shown in table B of exhibit 7–7. For example, if the hospital administrator decides to expand the hospital and patient load increases, the regret is $0 ($600,000 − $600,000). On the other hand, if the decision is to remodel and patient load increases, the regret would be $200,000 ($600,000 − $400,000). Taking all strategies into consideration, the manager adopting a minimax style would choose to do nothing because such a decision would be a "minimum of maximum regret" of $200,000.

The reader should carefully note that the various decision styles can yield vastly different results. Using maximax and maximin expected pay-off rules, the manager would decide to expand; a maximin rule would dictate remodeling as one of the decisions; and the minimax rule would result in a no-change decision.

BROOMHILDA

Reprinted by permission of the Chicago Tribune-New York News Syndicate, Inc.

Behavioral Decision Approach.   In contrast to the classical approach, the behavioral approach to decision making suggests that many managers often make decisions without knowing all the alternatives available to them and all the possible consequences. In other words, there is a *limit* to how logical or rational the decision can be. Under these circumstances, many researchers have implied that managers make decisions within what has been called *bounded rationality.*[12]

Adopting a bounded rationality approach implies the consideration of two factors. First, there is the quality of the information available to the manager—in other words, the state of certainty, risk, or uncertainty. Under conditions of uncertainty, managers many times have incomplete or highly speculative information on which to make a decision. This may result in a situation in which not all alternatives have been considered, or in which there are far too many complex variables and relationships for one person to effectively handle. Without placing some "boundaries" on this information, few decisions could ever be made.

Second, managers differ in their psychological approach to decision making. Some are problem avoiders, others are problem finders; one may adopt a systematic-preceptive approach, while another may prefer an intuitive-receptive approach; some may identify with a compensatory format, while others may focus on a conjunctive model. There is no one best way; therefore, managers choose the approach that they feel is the most effective under the particular circumstances. Later, we will offer some suggestions as to where these approaches may be more effective than others.

Under conditions of bounded rationality, managers make the most *logical* decisions they can, limited by the quality of the information and by their ability to handle and utilize the information. Rather than make the "maximum" or "optimum" decision as suggested by the classical approach, managers more realistically make a decision that will *adequately* serve their purposes. We call this making a *satisficing* decision.

As an example of satisficing behavior, consider the process of buying an automobile. Under the classical decision approach, in buying a car one would search out all models at all dealers within an area and bargain with the dealer representative until the best or "optimum" price or decision has been reached. If the person were to use a *satisficing* approach, a number of initial assumptions would be made to guide decision making. For example, one may want the decision to be limited to small, four-cylinder, two-door models that are manufactured by U.S. auto companies. Second, if the person lives in a large urban area, contacts may be limited to dealers in a particular part of the city. In bargaining with the dealer representative, the person may have established a range of desired prices. Whenever a price is quoted that is within this range, the person may accept it because it minimally satisfies (or satisfices) the criteria set.

Managers who act in a satisficing mode do not give up trying to make the best possible decisions. Rather, it simply means that they recognize that at some point it becomes too expensive, difficult, and complex, or there is too much of a "hassle" to try to acquire or analyze additional information.

Decision-Making Styles and Implementation

Managerial decision making is not a solitary process, whether it concerns the actual choice or the implementation activities. At times, it is appropriate for a manager to make and implement the decision alone. Other times, however, putting the decision into effect requires the involvement and participation—and hopefully the commitment—of others.[13] Recently, Vroom and his associates have developed and tested a model that focuses on the degree of *participation* between a manager and subordinates when making and implementing decisions.[14]

The model begins by making a distinction between two major types of decision problems: individual and group. Individual problems are those whose solutions affect only one of the manager's subordinates. Problems that affect several of the subordinates are defined as group problems. Research on the model has led to the identification of a number of different decision-making styles that can be followed to reach a solution. A model of these is presented in exhibit 7–8.

The letters A, C, G, and D represent decision processes that increasingly involve subordinate participation in the decision. "A" processes are very autocratic, not involving the subordinate at all. The Roman numerals denote variants of the same process. "C" processes are consultative; they involve the group in the actual decision process. "D" processes constitute delegation of the entire decision to individual subordinates or groups of subordinates. Thus, exhibit 7–8 contains five decision strategies each for individual and group problems that are commonly used by managers in actual situations.

The investigators have also asked under what conditions will each of these alternative decision processes result in a good solution? They have identified three basic criteria for evaluating the success of a decision: (1) the quality or rationality of the decision; (2) the acceptance or commitment on the part of the subordinates to execute decisions effectively; and (3) the amount of time required to make the decision.

These three criteria have been combined into a series of questions to be asked about the decision situation confronting the manager. Once

EXHIBIT 7–8 Decision-Making Implementation Styles

FOR INDIVIDUAL PROBLEMS	FOR GROUP PROBLEMS
AI You solve the problem or make the decision yourself, using information available to you at that time.	*AI* You solve the problem or make the decision yourself, using information available to you at that time.
AII You obtain any necessary information from the subordinate, then decide on the solution to the problem yourself. You may or may not tell the subordinate what the problem is in getting the information from him. The role played by your subordinate in making the decision is clearly one of providing specific information that you request, rather than generating or evaluating alternative solutions.	*AII* You obtain any necessary information from subordinates, then decide on the solution to the problem yourself. You may or may not tell subordinates what the problem is in getting the information from them. The role played by your subordinates in making the decision is clearly one of providing specific information that you request, rather than generating or evaluating solutions.
CI You share the problem with the relevant subordinate, getting ideas and suggestions. Then *you* make the decision. This decision may or may not reflect your subordinate's influence.	*CI* You share the problem with the relevant subordinates individually, getting their ideas and suggestions without bringing them together as a group. Then *you* make the decision. This decision may or may not reflect your subordinates' influence.
GI You share the problem with one of your subordinates and together you analyze the problem and arrive at a mutually satisfactory solution in an atmosphere or free and open exchange of information and ideas. You both contribute to the resolution of the problem with the relative contribution of each being dependent on knowledge rather than formal authority.	*CII* You share the problem with your subordinates in a group meeting. In this meeting, you obtain their ideas and suggestions. Then, *you* make the decision, which may or may not reflect your subordinates' influence.
DI You delegate the problem to one of your subordinates, providing him with any relevant information that you possess, but giving him responsibility for solving the problem by himself. Any solution that the person reaches will receive your support.	*GII* You share the problem with your subordinates as a group. Together, you generate and evaluate alternatives and attempt to reach agreement (consensus) on a solution. Your role is much like that of chairman, coordinating the discussion, keeping it focused on the problem, and making sure that the critical issues are discussed. You do not try to influence the group to adopt "your" solution and are willing to accept and implement any solution that has the support of the entire group.

these questions are answered, the model indicates the best decision process to use under the given circumstances. Vroom and his associates arranged these questions in sequential fashion and designed a decision tree, reproduced in exhibit 7–9 for managers to use in selecting an appropriate decision process.

The first step in using the model is to state and examine the problem. Questions A through H, arrayed in sequential fashion across the top of the decision tree, are a series of questions representing the criteria for

EXHIBIT 7–9 Decision Process Flow Chart for Both Individual and Group Problems

A. Is there a quality requirement such that one solution is likely to be more rational than another?
B. Do I have sufficient information to make a high quality decision?
C. Is the problem structured?
D. Is acceptance of decision by subordinates critical to effective implementation?
E. If I were to make the decision by myself, is it reasonably certain that it would be accepted by my subordinates?
F. Do subordinates share the organizational goals to be attained in solving this problem?
G. Is conflict among subordinates likely in preferred solutions? (This question is irrelevant to individual problems.)
H. Do subordinates have sufficient information to make a high quality decision?

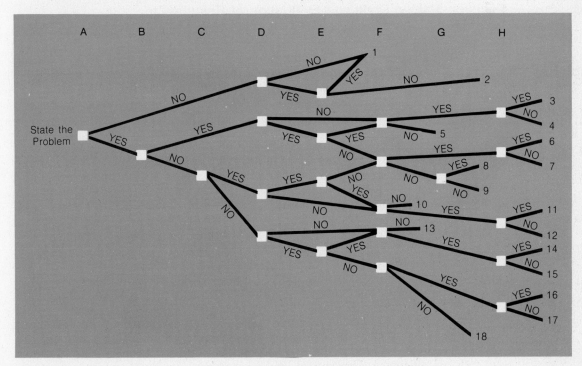

The recommended strategy for each problem type (1–18) for group (G) and individual (I) are as follows:

	Group	Individual		Group	Individual		Group	Individual
1	A1	A1	7	G11	G1	13	C11	C1
2	G11	D1	8	C11	C1	14	C11	D1
3	A1	A1	9	C1	C1	15	C11	C1
4	A1	A1	10	A11	A11	16	G11	D1
5	A1	A1	11	A11	D1	17	G11	G1
6	G11	D1	12	A11	A11	18	C11	C1

effective decisions. They can be answered with a "yes" or "no" response. The decision maker should work through the tree in sequential fashion until an acceptable decision process is indicated. For example, according to the tree, if decision process 1 is reached after analysis, AI is the best decision strategy for both group and individual problems. If the result is 2, GII is the best for group problems, and DI is the best for individual problems. The reader is urged to examine the decision tree and work through several hypothetical problems using it.

The Vroom model represents an important improvement over classical decision theory with rather immediate implications for decision making. They have identified major decision strategies that are commonly used in making decisions, and they have established criteria for evaluating the success of the various strategies under a variety of conditions. In addition, the Vroom approach is an applied model for managers to use in selecting decision strategies. It can improve the quality of decisions, acceptance of the decisions by subordinates, and minimize the time consumed in decision making.

Decision-Making Style and Evaluation of Results

Once the decision has been made and implemented, the manager becomes concerned with the performance of the decision—the evaluation stage. As we have suggested earlier in this chapter, the evaluation of decisions involves examination of criteria, the long-run commitment to the decision by employees and customers, what has been learned, and finally, how future decisions benefit from the organization's experience with this particular decision.

Similar to the other decision-making stages, managers can use different decision-making styles during the evaluation stage. One way of describing decision styles is to return to our discussion of the dimensions of the external environment in chapter 4. We stated that there are at least two dimensions, reproduced in exhibit 7–10, that can describe an organization's environment: degree of change, and degree of complexity. The resulting four-quadrant grid provides a framework or scheme with which to discuss decision-making styles at the evaluation stage.[15]

Computational.   In this first quadrant, decision-making evaluation is seen as being relatively mechanical and technical in nature. This is attributed to the external environment, which is both simple and stable, resulting in a low degree of environmental uncertainty. Decisions are made on problems for which there are well-established procedures that can be followed in a programmed format. Due to the environment, decisions are made with a high degree of certainty, and there is an emphasis on efficiency, cost control, and consistency.

As an illustration, consider a manager of loan processing in a small, rural savings and loan. Decision making is fairly routine and follows a definite sequence of steps. The evaluation of the decision is based on established interest rates and payback periods: in other words, it is computational.

Judgmental.   A judgmental decision evaluation style can be used when the environment is stable, but more complex when compared to the first

EXHIBIT 7–10 Decision Making Evaluation Style

		DEGREE OF CHANGE	
		Stable	Dynamic
DEGREE OF COMPLEXITY	Simple	Computational Type: Programmed Condition: Certainty Criteria: Efficiency Costs Consistency	Compromise Type: Nonprogrammed Condition: Risk to uncertainty Criteria: Reaction Flexibility Stability
	Complex	Judgemental Type: Programmed Condition: Certainty to risk Criteria: Efficiency Quantity/quality Variety	Adaptive Type: Nonprogrammed Condition: Uncertainty Criteria: Reaction time Innovation Growth

quadrant. Decisions are still somewhat programmed in nature, but due to the increased complexity of the environment, a degree of risk becomes more apparent. Efficiency is still a primary criterion for evaluation, but additional emphasis is also placed on quantity and quality as well as the variety of responses.

Consider the manager of the pension fund for a large industrial corporation. The manager's decisions are somewhat programmed in nature when they deal with the collection and distribution of funds to employees and retirees. However, in investing collected funds into market securities (stocks and bonds), a degree of risk is interjected. From an evaluation basis, the manager must be concerned with the quality and variety of the investments and the efficiency with which the total funds are handled.

Compromise. When the external environment becomes dynamic (but remains simple), a compromise decision evaluation style is dictated. Compromise is a situation in which there is a "give and take" relationship between interacting parties, where, for example, the achievement of one peformance criterion can come only at the expense of another. Decisions are generally nonprogrammed, and an increasing degree of uncertainty is present. Evaluation is made with such criteria as flexibility, stability, and reaction time.

An example can be the management negotiating team of a newspaper publishing company in discussions to achieve a new labor-management contract. The management team recognizes that, in order to reach an agreement with the labor team, a degree of compromise and bargaining over certain points will be necessary. For example, in order to achieve an agreement on productivity levels, a concession on cost-of-living advances or working hours may have to be made. This compromise type of style enables the management team to obtain a certain degree of stability in a dynamic environment.

Adaptive. In an external environment characterized by dynamic change and complex relationships, the manager is faced with many non-programmed decisions that are inherently high in uncertainty. Given this environment, an adaptive decision style for evaluation is usually adopted, stressing reaction time, innovation, and growth.

Consider the situation facing market development managers at Walt Disney Productions.[16] With the decrease in the company's primary market age group (five- to thirteen-year olds) and growing competition from other theme parks, the company's environment has shifted to one of complexity and dynamism. This increase in uncertainty and nonprogrammable decisions contributes to a need for decisions that stress innovation, growth, and reaction time. For example, Disney is contemplating building a large theme park similar to Walt Disney World in Japan. To attract an older audience, the development managers are considering building a ski resort in California, an adult "world's fair" type of exhibit in Florida, and even producing PG-rated films. Each of these decisions will be evaluated on the basis of their reaction time to environmental events, the inherent innovativeness, and the contribution to the organization's growth.

The key point in this discussion is that no one style or combination of styles is ideal. Each one works best in the right environment where there are differences in the types of decisions, conditions of uncertainty, and evaluation criteria.

Summary

As this discussion strongly suggests, the decision-making style of the manager can vary dramatically through the different stages of making a decision. The two most important influences, as summarized in exhibit 7–11, are the external environment and the individual characteristics of the manager. This not only implies that knowledge of the dynamics of the environment is important, but that managers must pay careful attention to their own approaches to making decisions. More than anything, decision making is an activity that directly affects the development of managerial skills.

AIDS IN MANAGERIAL DECISION MAKING

In our discussion of the management science school in chapter 3, we pointed out how the development and use of mathematical models and the computer have revolutionized many parts of the manager's job. In a sense, the discussions of forecasting and planning aids have introduced the reader to some of the most important management science techniques and tools.

Classifying Management Science Models

There are at least three ways in which management science models can be classified in decision making.[17] This is shown in exhibit 7–12.

EXHIBIT 7–11
Summary:
Decision-Making
Styles

DECISION-MAKING STAGE	EXAMPLES OF PERSON-ENVIRONMENT INFLUENCES
Recognition and Problem Identification	Problem Sensing: Managers can be problem avoiders, problem solvers, or problem seekers.
Developing and Evaluating Alternatives	Information Processing: Managers differ in their ability to gather information (preceptive vs. receptive) and evaluate it (systematic vs. intuitive). Information Integration: Information may be integrated into a compensatory, conjunctive, or disjunctive format.
Choice of Alternative	Classical Approach: Decision choice can be based on nonprobabilistic rules (maximax, maximin, minimax) or probabilistic rules (maximize expected payoff). Behavioral Approach: Managers act in a bounded rationality manner by making satisficing decisions.
Implementaton	Decision Analysis: Managers can differ in the degree of participation that they give to subordinates in making decisions.
Evaluation of Results	Environmental Analysis: The dimensions of the external environment (degree of complexity and change) will assist in determining the style of evaluation (computational, judgmental, compromise, and adaptive).

First, models can be classified either as *descriptive* or *normative* in *purpose*. Similar to the discussion in chapter 3, descriptive models describe things *as they are*. They are used to define a situation more clearly, identify possible areas of change, and to study the impact and consequences of various decision strategies. They cannot, however, identify the best choice among all possible alternatives. A normative model, on the other hand, is used to identify the best available alternative on the basis of some decision criteria—in other words, things *as they should be*. They are sometimes referred to as optimizing models since their purpose is to identify the optimal solution under a given set of conditions.

Second, management science models can be *deterministic* or *probabilistic*. A variable that is deterministic is one that contains no element of chance—conditions of *certainty* in our framework. For example, the accounting model of assets equals liabilities plus capital (A = L + C) is deterministic because the variables are all known quantities, and the exact solution is stated by the above relationship.

EXHIBIT 7–12   Classification of Management Science Models in Decision Making

USE OF MODELS	PURPOSE		TYPES OF VARIABLES	
	Descriptive (As Things Are)	Normative (As Things Should Be)	Deterministic (Certainty)	Probabilistic (Uncertainty)
Inventory				
EOQ		×	×	
Inventory control models		×		×
Resource Allocation				
Linear programming		×	×	
Assignment		×	×	
Transportation		×	×	
Scheduling and Sequencing				
Queuing	×			×
Simulation	×			×
PERT		×	×	
Prediction				
Break even		×	×	
Regression		×	×	
Decision tree		×		×
Expected payoff		×		×
Monte Carlo simulation	×			×

Adapted from H. L. Lyon, J. M. Ivancevich, and J. H. Donnelly, *Management Science in Organizations* (Santa Monica, Calif.: Goodyear, 1976), p. 26.

When variables in a decision situation have an element of chance or *uncertainty* in them, the models for their analysis are termed *probabilistic*. Our decision tree example in the last section is an example of a probabilistic model.

The third way of classifying management science models in decision making is by their *use*. As shown in exhibit 7–12, there are at least four major areas of use:

1. *Inventory control*. Most organizations cannot exist without some form of inventory, either of raw materials or finished products. Inventories, however, create a dilemma for managers. On one hand, inventories must be kept on hand to insure the smooth flow of materials to production facilities and final product to the customer. On the other hand, maintaining inventories is costly, not only in terms of idle goods but also in the physical space necessary to hold them. The management science school has developed a number of decision-making techniques that have proven helpful to the manager in balancing product availability with cost considerations.

2. *Resource allocation.* A common problem for all types of managers is how to allocate the organization's resources effectively—people, space, finances, and equipment—to specific situations. Two problems are most prominent: where to allocate resources for their maximum potential; and how to allocate resources when there are not enough resources available to do all the jobs required by managers. Assignment, transportation, and linear programming methods have been used to assist managers in solving resource allocation problems.

3. *Scheduling and sequencing.* Scheduling and sequencing issues arise when a manager is concerned with designing facilities to meet a demand for services, or in deciding in what order the parts of a job or project are to be performed. Queuing models and network models have been used in solving those problems.

4. *Prediction.* Managers' jobs would be made significantly easier if they knew in advance the exact impact and result of their decisions. Under conditions of certainty, managers can approach such a situation. However, as we have pointed out throughout this book, managers are increasingly coming face to face with high degrees of uncertainty in their work. Management science tools have been developed to aid the manager in making predictions about the occurrence of future events or outcomes of their decisions. Regression analysis (chapter 4), decision trees, and simulation are some of the most popular techniques.

A discussion of these decision aids will be presented in chapter 18.

Issues with the Use of Decision-Making Aids

The examples we have given to illustrate different decision-making aids are both simple and straightforward. In most managerial situations, however, the problems are usually more complicated, requiring the use of more sophisticated techniques or more complex versions of the described methods.

The use of these more sophisticated methods has not received the high level of managerial support that one would expect. The more important reasons for this situation are noted below:[18]

1. *Limited time.* The process of developing a complex model, gathering data, and testing the model can be extremely time consuming. The model may prove to be quite accurate and valid, but this is little help when a decision must be made quickly.

2. *Inaccessibility of information.* Some data necessary to test decision models may be difficult to obtain or may be totally unavailable. This can add time and frustration to the decision-making process.

3. *Resistance to change.* The use of decision aids may be a relatively new development in many organizations. This can be a problem if managers have developed their own particular ways of making decisions, causing them to be unreceptive to novel ways of doing things. The fact that mathematical techniques seem so complex and mysterious to many managers makes it more difficult for them to accept these techniques.

4. *Oversimplification.* The problems addressed by decision aids are quite adaptable to mathematical formulations. The problems frequently confronting managers, however, are not easily quantifiable. These include

motivation problems, politics, and power struggles. The models then develop so-called optimum decisions, but prove to be useless because they have been oversimplified by leaving out some important variables.

DECISION MAKING, PERFORMANCE, AND THE MANAGER'S JOB

All managers are decision makers due to the fact that they are confronted every day with choices and situations that demand action. It is also an accepted fact that the effectiveness of managers is largely reflected in their performance or "track record" in making the "right decision."

Managers and future managers are many times lulled into an unrealistic belief that making the "right decision" is simply a matter of following a set of predetermined steps, from identifying the problem to evaluation. As our discussion of decision-making styles strongly suggests, there are a significant number of styles that a manager can adopt in decision making, none of which may be the best way.

Managers should also be cautioned that experience in making decisions does not ensure that future decisions will necessarily be easier or better. Decision making, unlike some other managerial activities, may not improve with repetition. The manager's environment is too dynamic to become attached to a particular way of handling all problems. Moreover, many decisions are not easy to make, and simply weighing the pros and cons involved is seldom enough to accurately decide the best course of action to take.

In this final section, we will attempt to integrate the skill and role factors of the manager's job, the decision-making process, with a series of "keys to success."[19] These success keys have been gathered from the author's research and experience, from the experiences of other managers, and from the growing body of research on decision making.

Keys to Success with Decision Making

Problem Identification

1. **Be problem oriented, not just solutions oriented.**

Most, if not all, managers must stay on their toes with respect to the emergence of potentially serious organizational problems. This entails the process of fine-tuning one's information sources, developing new information sources, and generally keeping one's ear to the ground. From the manager's job perspective, involved are key components of the *informational roles* and the development of *diagnostic skills*. The frequent cry by many managers is that they suffer from information "overload"; there is far too much information to handle and interpret. However, many have suggested that it is far better to have too much information than to have too little. It would be a wise strategy for new managers to try to position themselves in as many information and communication networks as possible. With this strategy, the manager can gain an awareness of the issues facing the organization. But far more importantly, the frequent activities involved in information processing will enable the manager to develop the necessary *diagnostic skills*.

A second point to be gained from this suggestion is that it has been too frequent an occurrence in many organizations that managers become so attached to a particular decision aid or method that they either try to fit all problems to this model, or they create problems in order to use the model. This is the case of the tail wagging the dog. As a *technical and diagnostic skill,* make sure you have identified the problem clearly before a choice of decision aid is made.

2. **Set decision-making goals.**

Somewhat related to the first point, a frequent error committed by managers in decision making is the tendency to jump over setting goals to the step of evaluating alternatives. This is a serious mistake because setting goals focuses management's attention on where they must get the information needed to accurately assess the implications of the problem. Without setting goals, the search for information will be costly and much less efficient than it could be.

3. **If you get stuck, ask for help.**

A useful technique that can increase a manager's decision-making effectiveness is to talk about the problem with someone else, especially when one reaches an impasse. Contrary to some opinions, such an approach does not identify the manager as incompetent. On the contrary, talking with someone openly about a problem not only forces the manager to think more precisely about the problem, but the other person may provide valuable new inputs into the potential decision. This is an important reality test that involves *human* and *conceptual skills* along with *interpersonal and information roles*.

Developing and Evaluating Alternatives

1. **Always check the accuracy of the information.**

Perhaps the most important aspect of this phase of decision making is the search for valid data, not merely opinions. People have a tendency to accept someone else's evaluation of a problem without spending time probing for the reasons for that opinion. There is nothing wrong with opinions, but they should be supportable. Even with the use of more objective or "hard" data, the manager should question its source and accuracy. As our Practice of Management example stresses, the manager should not only develop criteria for accuracy but should also seek operational support for the information. This point again emphasizes the nature of the manager's *informational roles* and how they interact to help form *technical skills*.

2. **Don't be afraid to develop innovative alternatives.**

Far too many times, managers fall into a rut when they develop alternatives for consideration based more on their potential level of acceptance by higher management than their ability to successfully solve a problem. Even if an innovative, or "off-the-wall" suggestion is rejected, the manager has gained an important *conceptual skill* from performing the *decisional role* that may be used at a later time.

3. **Carefully think through the implications and consequences of each alternative.**

In evaluating alternatives, many managers generally identify the main outcomes of a particular action and then move toward some action. Sometimes supposedly minor consequences or side effects of a decision are not given sufficient attention, which may lead to a poor decision. It would behoove the manager to think through *all* the implications of a potential decision before action is taken. This important *decisional role* helps in developing a manager's *diagnostic skills*.

Decision Choice

1. Don't be too hasty in making decisions.

The results-oriented manager understandably assumes that in most situations decisions must be made quickly in order to be effective. The problem with a total acceptance of this philosophy is that it develops a "make it now" decision pattern. This desire to make a quick decision pushes many managers into poor decisions that could be avoided if more time were spent identifying the problems, evaluating alternatives, and so on. We can point to many such quick decisions, such as the Bay of Pigs fiasco, when the evaluation of alternatives was given insufficient time. Another important tactic—classified as a *technical skill*—is to make a decision but *wait* a period of time before implementing it. This will allow more time for the manager to carefully think over the potential impact of the tentative decision. Behavioral scientists call this "cognitive dissonance" or post-decision awareness.[20] How many times have you made a purchase of an item such as a car or expensive clothing, returned home, and then begun thinking, "What have I done?" If the purchase is sufficiently large, a number of sleepless nights may be encountered. If time is available, use it!

2. Retain a high degree of flexibility in decision making.

Good decision makers do not persist in defining a problem one way if that approach is not leading anywhere. Instead, successful managers will jump from one approach to another until an acceptable solution is attained. Two suggestions can be made here. First, do not be a creature of habit. Keep your mind open for new ways to see and solve a problem. Second, solutions sometimes appear suddenly, so keep your mind open for new relationships or new combinations. The successful manager is one who is highly flexible in the *decisional role*. Flexibility leads to high performance and the development of important *technical* and *conceptual skills*.

3. There is nothing wrong with the use of common sense.

As we suggested in an earlier chapter, management is probably more an art than it is a science. As such, managers must give attention as much to common sense as they do to the other aspects of decision making. This is particularly applicable both to the use of decision aids and the development of *diagnostic skills*. Statements that claim that certain techniques "optimize," "maximize," or "minimize" should be viewed with caution.

Implementation

1. Gain commitment early for a decision.

Managers must not assume that a decision will be accepted by others in the organization without some preliminary work. If it is not a confidential matter, it would be wise to discuss your views with others, seek out their views, and try to pinpoint sources of support and possible resistance. Both *human skills* and *interpersonal* roles are involved.

2. Delegate decision implementation frequently, but wisely.

Delegation is an important *human skill* in achieving decision-making effectiveness. In an *interpersonal role,* a manager cannot know enough or control enough to do everything alone, so others must often be depended on to implement key parts of a decision. Delegation is one way to get people involved and committed to a decision. When employees are made to feel a part of a decision, they may naturally want to put out extra effort to ensure the effectiveness of the decision.

Evaluation of Results

1. Evaluation and follow-up is just as important as the other decision-making steps.

Many well thought out and implemented decisions fail because of a lack of follow-up by the manager. A lack of evaluation may signal to employees that a manager has lost interest in a problem or project or is no longer concerned about it. The attention, effort, and recognition that are by-products of following through are important parts of making decisions. There are important *technical* and *human skills* to be gained from involvement in these *decisional* and *informational roles*.

2. Be willing to modify the decision with time.

Evaluation also implies a willingness to modify a decision if such changes become necessary. This flexibility makes decision making easier since it removes some of the finality inherent in some decisions. This open-mindedness is another important human skill that future managers should try to develop.

3. Decisions need not always be a "yes" or "no" variety.

Earlier in this chapter we discussed an example of the decision to purchase a new piece of packaging equipment by an organization. The manufacturing manager wants to purchase a new, more cost-efficient machine that will be delivered in six months. The marketing manager, on the other hand, wants to purchase an older model that can be delivered in two months. Since both managers may be entrenched in their positions, a decision choosing one alternative over the other may be difficult. Instead of an ultimate solution, it might be worthwhile to consider an alternative that is initially agreeable to all that will automatically be reviewed or changed within a certain period of time. In our example, a possible alternative would be to lease the older equipment for six months or more until the new equipment becomes available. This flexibility encompasses *human* and *diagnostic* skills along with *interpersonal* and *decisional roles*.

Decision making is essentially a rational process, but there are limits to its rationality. It is not a mechanical checklist procedure that can be easily taught or learned. Unfortunately, too many managers are inclined to cut these processes short in order to make a quick decision. Time sometimes helps and sometimes hinders effective decisions. How managers handle these factors determines whether they make most decisions or whether decisions are made for them. Conscious decision making, as opposed to crisis responses, separates the effective from the less-effective managers.

SUMMARY FOR THE MANAGER

1. Decision making is one of the most important activities in which managers engage daily. There are some, in fact, who prefer the term *decision maker* to manager. Decision making pervades the entire management process, from planning to control. A manager's success as a decision maker, however, is made up of a combination of scientific analysis, experience, and common sense.

2. In making most decisions, managers follow a number of rational steps including problem identification, evaluation of alternatives, choice, implementation, and evaluation of results. Many of the problems managers face in making decisions result from not following these steps in a sequential manner. Managers take short cuts either because of time constraints or their own personal characteristics (procrastination). Whatever the reasons, the effectiveness of a decision is dependent on how well the individual process steps are followed.

3. Decisions vary by the type and the conditions of the problem. Many decisions faced by lower level managers are programmed in nature. The routineness and repetitiveness of these decisions make them amenable to set policies and procedures. Higher level managers many times face unprogrammed decisions, which are new, novel, or original and for which there is a scarcity of information. The amount of information also establishes the conditions of certainty, risk, and uncertainty. It is important for managers to recognize that the greater the uncertainty, the more time should be devoted (if available) to the decision process steps, particularly in the development and evaluation of alternatives.

4. Managers should be aware that certain internal and external factors in their job can act as constraining factors in decision making. Such factors as the manager's position in the organization and cultural influences may establish boundaries on what type of decisions they can make or how effective they can be.

5. While the decision-making process is sequential in nature, significant variations can develop in the manner each step is followed. Most of the variations can be attributed to the particular style that the manager utilizes. For example, managers can be problem avoiders, problem solvers, or problem finders in the problem identification stage; preceptive-receptive and systematic-intuitive in the way they process information in the evaluation of alternatives stage; optimizers or satisficers when it concerns decision choice; or participative-nonparticipative in the way decisions are implemented. These different styles create significant differences between managers who may be making the same decisions.

6. An important variation in decision-making styles is the influence of the external environment. The degree of complexity and degree of change, for example, establish four different ways of evaluating the results of decisions. These include computational, judgmental, compromise, and adaptive. The important factor for managers to consider is that the environment may dictate the particular style that may be effective for a given problem or situation.

7. A number of aids to decision making are available to managers. These aids, which originate primarily from the management science school, have had a significant impact on the effectiveness of a manager's decision. The manager should be aware, however, that these decision aids are not the final answer to making good decisions. Important issues such as resistance to change, time and cost constraints, and oversimplification may severely limit the applicability of many decision techniques.

9. The decision-making process involves many managerial skills and roles. Because decision making is an everyday activity, it is a primary area for the development of these skills.

QUESTIONS FOR REVIEW AND DISCUSSION

1. Distinguish between "problem solving" and "problem finding."
2. What is the difference between the terms *optimize* and *satisfice*?
3. Discuss the difference between normative and descriptive models.
4. Identify some jobs you are familiar with that: (a) involve mostly programmed decisions; and (b) involve many nonprogrammed decisions.
5. What important criteria should managers use in evaluating the effectiveness of their decision making?
6. Discuss the impact of the external environment on decision-making style.

7. Why has the issue of "resistance to change" become so important in the use of mathematical decision aids?
8. How are managerial diagnostic skills and the decision-making process related?
9. Why is it important for managers not to ignore their own intuition or hunches?
10. What is the relationship between decision making and the planning function?

NOTES

1. W. F. Pounds, "The Processing of Problem Finding," *Industrial Management Review* (Fall 1969): 1–19.

2. H. A. Simon, *The Shape of Automation* (New York: Harper & Row, 1965), p. 61.

3. See F. H. Knight, *Risk, Uncertainty, and Profit* (New York: Harper & Row, 1920); and S. A. Archer, "The Structure of Management Decision Theory," *Academy of Management Journal* (December 1964): 269–87.

4. C. A. Holloway, *Decision Making Under Uncertainty* (Englewood Cliffs, N.J.: Prentice-Hall, 1979).

5. H. I. Ansoff, *Corporate Strategy* (New York: McGraw-Hill, 1965).

6. W. M. Fox, "Japanese Management: Tradition Under Strain," *Business Horizons* (August 1977): 76–85; F. Kaufmann, "Decision Making—Eastern and Western Style," *Business Horizons* (December 1970): 81–86; and R. T. Pascale, "Communication and Decision Making Across Cultures: Japanese and American Comparisons," *Administrative Science Quarterly* (March 1978): 91–110.

7. M. J. Driver, "Individual Decision Making and Creativity," in *Organizational Behavior,* ed. Steven Kerr (Columbus, Ohio: Grid, 1979), p. 76.

8. J. L. McKenney and P. G. W. Keen, "How Managers' Minds Work," *Harvard Business Review* (May–June 1974): 79–90.

9. M. J. Wallace, Jr., and D. P. Schwab, "A Cross-Validated Comparison of Five Models Used to Predict Graduate Admission Committee Decisions," *Journal of Applied Psychology* (October 1976): 559–63.

10. R. M. Dawis and B. Corrigon, "Linear Models of Decision Making," *Psychological Bulletin* (1974): 95–106.

11. See R. D. Luce and H. Raiffa, *Games and Decisions* (New York: Wiley, 1957); D. W. Miller and M. K. Starr, *The Structure of Human Decisions* (Englewood Cliffs, N.J.: Prentice-Hall, 1967); and R. Schlaiffer, *Probability and Statistics for Business Decisions* (New York: McGraw-Hill, 1959), pp. 445–46.

12. J. G. March and H. A. Simon, *Organizations* (New York: Wiley, 1958).

13. J. M. Ivancevich, "An Analysis of Participation in Decision Making Among Project Engineers," *Academy of Management Journal* (June 1979): 253–69.

14. See V. H. Vroom, "A New Look at Managerial Decision Making," *Organizational Dynamics* (Spring 1973); and V. H. Vroom and A. Jago, "Decision Making as a Social Process: Normative and Descriptive Models of Leader Behavior," *Decision Sciences* (1974): 743–69.

15. J. D. Thompson, *Organizations in Action* (New York: McGraw-Hill, 1967), p. 134.

16. "Can Disney Still Grow on Its Founder's Dreams?" *Business Week* (July 31, 1978): 58–67.

17. H. L. Lyon, J. M. Ivancevich, and J. H. Donnelly, *Management Science in Organizations* (Santa Monica, Calif.: Goodyear, 1976), p. 23.

18. C. J. Grayson, "Management Science and Business Practice," *Harvard Business Review* (July–August 1973): 41–48.

19. N. C. Hill, *Increasing Managerial Effectiveness* (Reading, Mass.: Addison-Wesley, 1979).

20. L. Festinger, *A Theory of Cognitive Dissonance* (New York: Harper, 1957).

ADDITIONAL REFERENCES

Ebert, R. J., and Mitchell, T. R. *Organizational Decisions Processes.* New York: Crane, Russak & Company, 1975.

Elbing, A. *Behavioral Decisions in Organizations.* Glenview, Ill.: Scott, Foresman, 1978.

Goldberg, L. R. "Five Models of Clinical Judgment: An Empirical Comparison Between Linear and Nonlinear Representations of the Human Inference Process," *Organizational Behavior and Human Performance* (1971): 458–79.

Grey, R. J., and Gordon, G. G. "Risk Taking Managers: Who Gets the Top Jobs?" *Management Review* (November 1978): 8–13.

Harrison, E. F. *The Managerial Decision Making Process.* Boston: Houghton-Mifflin, 1975.

Janis, I. L., and Mann, L. *Decision Making.* New York: Free Press, 1977.

MacCrimmon, K. R., and Taylor, R. N. "Decision Making and Problem Solving," in *Handbook of Industrial and Organizational Psychology,* edited by M. D. Dunnette. Chicago: Rand McNally, 1976.

Rowan, R. "Those Business Hunches Are More Than Blind Faith," *Fortune* (April 23, 1979): 110–14.

Tversky, A., and Kahneman, D. "Judgment Under Uncertainty: Heuristics and Biases," *Science* (September 1974): 1124–31.

Wright, P. "The Harassed Decision Maker: Time Pressures, Distractions, and the Use of Evidence," *Journal of Applied Psychology* (1974): 555–61.

Roy Ash of Addressograph-Multigraph

Roy Ash is staking his managerial reputation and a substantial part of his personal fortune on an effort to turn around the troubled company that Wall Street analysts privately dubbed "Addressogrief-Multigrief." As both the chief executive and the largest individual stockholder, since 1977 he has been engaged in what he calls "a classic case of corporate decision making." The full recovery of Addressograph-Multigraph, he says, will take another four or five years, but the performance so far suggests that he probably won't come to grief.

Ash seems determined to recapture the luster he had in the 1960s as president of glamorous Litton Industries and one of the brightest stars on the U.S. business scene. In Washington, he created the idea of an Office of Management and Budget, a considerable accomplishment that was obscured in the general ruin of the Nixon Administration. Now Ash seems eager to prove that the managerial success of the glory days at Litton was not a fluke.

Rescuing a creaky maker of mechanical office equipment seems a very different kind of challenge from founding and running a high-technology conglomerate, but Ash believes that the right executive decisions can shape up any organization. "At a sufficiently high level of abstraction," he says, "all businesses are the same."

Ash's plans for testing that theory are summed up in the notes that he continually pencils on yellow legal pads. One of the most revealing of these notes says: "Develop a much greater attachment of everybody to the bottom line—more agony and ecstasy." As he sees it, the really important change in a company is a process of psychological transformation.

In trying to do that, Ash employs a decision technique he calls "immersion management." To reach the core of problems, he probes deeply into operations through relentless questioning, which one executive calls "excruciating." Ash batters down bureaucratic practices in the belief that they tend to become an end in themselves. He forbids long memos, which managers submit, he says, "to have the record show the right thing for a defense later." And to make managers fully aware of the impact of their decisions, he demands a penetrating financial analysis of everything the company does or considers doing.

Ash found plenty that seemed to need changing. A-M, in his words, was "slow in pace, conservative in attitude, and living in the past." Its once dominant line of "clanking machinery" for offset printing and addressing was being overwhelmed by quiet, more efficient electronic products of rivals that include Xerox, IBM, and Eastman Kodak. The previous management had floundered about, never coming up with a clear plan for the company's future.

Ash began his corporate revolution very quietly. The new chairman showed up in Cleveland without a single personal aide to become, he half-jokingly says, "the lion in the den, all alone." He told everyone to continue whatever they were doing and promised, "I'll catch up to you." This helped reassure A-M's management, which was still reeling from past reorganizations and personnel changes that had proved disastrous. "Lots of us," says one vice president, "were anxious about how we might fit into his plans."

Instead of immediately starting to revamp the company, Ash spent his first several months visiting its widely scattered operations and politely asking a lot of searching questions. That alone was a dramatic and generally welcomed change.

His predecessors had always summoned subordinates to the headquarters building, which had long lived up to its official name, the Tower. But Ash's aim was substantive as well as symbolic. He wanted to get a handle on all the operations and assess the key people who ran them.

As he learned about the company, Ash kept jotting down what he saw as the issues that had to be resolved. Those notes, still being revised, became what he calls "my brick pile" for redesigning A-M. They include some 200 items, ranging from problem products to organizational difficulties. Summing up his overall goal in his own form of mental shorthand, he wrote: "Rethink, redesign, rebuild, and re-earn." In the same spirit, he says that he wanted to make the company's executives "re-question everything."

Rather than announcing his ideas, Ash demonstrated them. He left his office door open, placed his own intercom calls to arrange meetings, and always questioned people in person, not in writing. By casually asking office secretaries to suggest ways to "debureaucratize" the company, he received some clues about which executives were heavily engaged in paper shuffling. Then he removed some of the company's copying machines "to stop breeding paperwork." Spotting a well-written complaint from an important customer in Minneapolis, Ash quickly flew off to visit him. As he now explains, "I wanted the word to get around our organization that I'm aware of what's going on."

Soon others began emulating him, even before they grasped his broader objectives. Above all, Ash wanted to "raise the excitement content" of A-M. And he wanted to make its managers personally accountable. "There's nothing like fear of failure," he says, "to motivate all of us."

Ash stirred both excitement and fear by his early discovery that no one in the corporation knew precisely which products were profitable. "I assumed that it was an innocent question," he recalls, "but the data didn't exist." Older hands at A-M had analyzed the profitability of broad product lines that include many different items, but Ash demanded that they break it down further—including the amount of salesman's time devoted to each product. Says one surviving manager: "Roy opened a lot of closets that we hadn't gotten into yet."

Finally, fifteen weeks after taking over, Ash gathered five of his key executives in St. Petersburg, Florida, and revealed his ideas for giving the company "a sense of direction." Working from his collection of notes, Ash told them, "I don't have nearly as many answers as you, but I am beginning to know some of the questions." He spent the working weekend reviewing and refining his list of problems, then assigned them to various subordinates with deadlines for action. Accustomed to Ash's style by then, the five had their own pads and pencils ready. In essence, Ash's plan is to extend the life of the company's mature products as long as possible while gradually acquiring new electronic office equipment to replace them. A-M steadily continues selling offset duplicators, and expects that its more than two hundred thousand operating machines will chug along for years—consuming supplies and requiring service. "This company," Ash says, "has a big flywheel that gives us the time and the cash throw-off to do other things." What is more, the corporation's ample hoard of cash, he says, "allows us to deal with this task deliberately, rather than frantically."

But within two weeks of the strategy session in Florida, Ash started shedding what he calls "millstone products"—either unprofitable or unpromising. "One of the things that I learned in Washington," Ash says, "is that a new guy doesn't have a proprietary interest in earlier decisions—or in impending mistakes."

As he began swinging the ax, a sense of alarm swept through the company, but Ash's management style eased the psychic pain. He guided the managers he had inherited into solving their own problems. "Rather than just pronouncing the outcome from on high," he explains, "you lead others through joint analysis to the same conclusion."

Ash concentrated on "structuring the problems"—posing the hard questions, which forced others to provide the answers that determined the fate of dubious products. Cancelling the model 9000 lithographic copier, which had been introduced with great fanfare, came as a major blow to sales managers, says Robert Hagy, the senior vice president for marketing. "But when all the facts and figures were in," he adds, "it was the obvious thing to do."

Ash soon found, he says, that "I'm not as cold-blooded as I should be." Last March he brought James Mellor from Litton to be the new president and chief operating officer, and to do the things "that I personally find distasteful." More than a hatchet man, Mellor, forty-seven, is an electrical engineer with eighteen years of experience in directing high-technology programs and a desire "to really put my stamp" on A-M. He shares Ash's penchant for letting decisions naturally emerge from the facts.

Armed with his own handwritten copy of Ash's list, Mellor quickly tackled the catalogue of unresolved issues. High on that list were questions about an important new product then under development: "Why work on Delta? What do we expect of it?"

Delta, an offset duplicating system that was supposed to be virtually automatic, had lingered in development for nearly five years and had already cost more than $10 million. Ultimately Mellor's sharp probing revealed that Delta managers had underestimated almost everything about it—development costs, production costs, the time required to complete it, and the position of competitors. Delta probably couldn't be introduced before 1979, and the analysis indicated that other companies practically had rival products on the shelf. At best, Delta would be a break-even program within five to seven years.

By the end of Mellor's final day-long session on Delta, no one was fighting for it. "With all the answers laid out," he says, "a person would have to be very dense to conclude that we should continue." But Mellor softened the blow by immediately declaring that the division's research money would go into making present products more salable as well as finding new ones.

Despite Ash's emphasis on cool, objective decision making, he is highly sensitive to the need for diplomacy with his board and stockholders. By initiating radical changes slowly and methodically, he won over even the wariest directors. As one says, "Roy had a reputation from Litton of being fast on the draw, but his prudent way of dealing with A-M's problems impressed everyone." For example, when Ash and Mellor decided to drop vice president Edwin Bruning, whose family owns nearly 3 percent of the corporation, Ash first went to Chicago to break the news gently to the family patriarch, Herbert Bruning.

Ash has not only attracted young executives from outside the country but has also persuaded the holdover managers to adopt his stern disciplines. Hagy, the marketing vice president, a twenty-two year veteran of A-M, notes that grueling monthly operational reviews force everyone to anticipate problems. "If there's a weak spot," he says, "Ash and Mellor will find it." But they delegate wide authority to the operating divisions, provided that they meet their profitability goals. As a rule Mellor homes in threateningly on any product that fails to provide at least a 20 percent return on investment.

By demanding more of all executives, Ash and Mellor have created an atmosphere of brisk precision. The new senior vice president for finance, James Combes, who held similar posts at NCR and Hertz, observes: "This company is less hung up with committee deliberations and is more action oriented than any I've known. And there's very little politicking."

Much of the turnaround campaign, Ash insists, hinges on "changing the self-perception" of A-M managers. By forcing closer analysis of the company's activities, Ash has laid bare a surprising source of strength that had been neglected.

Questions for Discussion

1. Discuss Roy Ash's style of decision making in terms of the five process steps.
2. Why has his style of decision making been successful so far?
3. Discuss the role of Mr. Mellor.
4. What interpersonal, informational, and decisional roles were performed by Mr. Ash?

Adapted from L. Kraar, "Roy Ash Is Having Fun at Addressogrief-Multigrief," Fortune *(February 27, 1978): 46–52.*

EXPERIENTIAL EXERCISE

The Templeton Manufacturing Company

Purpose

1. To study the elements of a manager's decision-making style.
2. To consider the important criteria that are used to make a decision.

Required Understanding

The reader should have a basic understanding of the process of managerial decision making and the various elements that constitute a decision-making style.

How to Set Up the Exercise

Set up groups of four to eight students for the thirty to forty-five minute exercise. The groups should be separated from each other and the students asked to converse only with the members of their own group.

Background Information

The Templeton Manufacturing Company is a medium-size company that specializes in the manufacture and assembly of mobile communications equipment. The company is located in Indianapolis, Indiana, and is not unionized.

A significant decrease in international sales of the company's main product line has forced management of Templeton to consider laying off one, two, or possibly three of the poorest performers on the transmitter assembly line. The layoff may be only temporary, but the company wants to be as fair as possible in its decision choice. The layoff decision will be made by the immediate line supervisor, with approvals from the personnel manager and the plant manager.

The eight employees on the transmitter line that is to be cut back to at most five workers are as follows:

Julie Budde: White; age twenty-four; single; high-school graduate; three years with the company.

Tom Bare: White, age forty-three; divorced; four children to support; high-school graduate; six years with the company.

Rich Gomez: Hispanic; age twenty-nine; married; two children; junior-college graduate; six years with the company.

Dick Jackson: Black; age thirty-eight; married; three children; high-school graduate; ten years with the company.

Jack Lustig: White, age thirty-one; single; high-school graduate; five years with the company.

Tina Pastore: White; age twenty-eight; married; no children; junior-college graduate; three years with the company.

Sam Morrison: White; age fifty-five; widower; three grown children; high-school graduate; three years with the company.

Ken Carlson: White; age forty-nine; married; two children; high-school graduate; seventeen years with the company.

The company has evaluated these transmitter line employees on a number of factors, including productivity data and supervisory evaluations. The performance information to be used in making the layoff decision is shown in exhibit 7–13. The information represents the average performance for each of the employees over the past twelve months.

Instructions for the Exercise

1. Each group member, alone, is to *rank* the eight employees from 1 (the first to be laid off) to 8 (the last to be laid off).

2. The group should then be convened and the same ranking decision should be made as a group. When this has been accomplished, the ranking for all groups should be displayed and a spokesperson for each group should explain how the rankings were reached.

EXHIBIT 7–13　Templeton Manufacturing Company Employee Performance Data

Employee	PRODUCTIVITY			SUPERVISORY EVALUATION			
	Average Weekly Output[1]	% of Defective Units[2]	% Absent[3]	Depend-ability[4]	Ability to Take Directions[4]	Coopera-tiveness[4]	Advancement Potential[5]
Julie Budde	21.2	9.8	9.2	Poor	Fair	Fair	Low
Tom Bare	20.9	5.3	6.2	Good	Good	Good	Moderate
Rich Gomez	20.9	3.8	6.0	Good	Fair	Good	Moderate
Dick Jackson	22.8	5.7	7.8	Fair	Fair	Fair	Moderate
Jack Lustig	19.2	5.2	4.9	Excellent	Excellent	Good	High
Tina Pastore	18.7	1.9	1.1	Excellent	Good	Excellent	High
Sam Morrison	23.7	7.4	3.5	Good	Good	Good	Moderate
Ken Carlson	21.3	5.1	13.0	Fair	Good	Good	Low

1. Higher score indicates more quantity performance.
2. Lower score indicates fewer defective units.
3. Lower score indicates less absenteeism.
4. Ratings are poor, fair, good, excellent.
5. Evaluation range is low, moderate, high.

III

Establishing Order, Function, and Design
– Organizing –

8

Dimensions
of Organizations

CHAPTER OUTLINE

KEY POINTS IN THIS CHAPTER

1. There are three key dimensions of organization: grouping, influence, and coordination dimensions.

2. The grouping dimension, which concerns the process of grouping jobs and departments, involves the concepts of job specialization, departmentalization, and line-staff relations.

3. Establishing authority within the newly formed units is the function of the influence dimension. Three sources of authority are identified: legitimate, acceptance theory, and the unity of command principle.

4. The chain of command, span of control, and the centralization/decentralization issue relate to how authority is implemented in organizations.

5. One of the most important authority implementation issues concerns the degree of decentralization that the organization adopts. This decision is dependent on such factors as culture, cost and risk of decisions, managerial philosophies, locus of expertise, and the availability of capable managers.

6. Coordination requirements in organizations are determined by the level of interdependence and the differences in time and goal orientation between interacting units.

7. Rules and procedures, hierarchial referral, planning, liaison persons, task forces, teams and integrating departments are identified as some of the mechanisms available to the manager to ensure coordinated effort.

8. The international division and the integrated structure are ways the organization's structure adapts to increased international activity. The success of decentralization attempts is highly dependent on cultural practices.

THE PRACTICE OF MANAGEMENT

Organizational Dimensions and Hitachi Ltd. of Japan

Most Americans, when asked about Japanese businesses, come up with familiar names like Sony, Nippon Steel, Mitsubishi, Toyota, and Honda. But ask managers at General Electric or IBM, and you get a different answer. A good many American managers acquainted with international business consider Hitachi the best managed company in Japan.

Mr. Hirokichi Yoshiyama, who heads this big, diverse, technically advanced company known as the G.E. of Japan, suggests that Hitachi's success can be traced to at least three factors: flexibility, decentralization, and management development. For a Japanese company, flexibility—the ability to adapt to drastically changing circumstances—is especially critical. Japan has had many shocks in recent years: the continual upward valuation of the yen, which has priced many Japanese goods out of world markets; the impact of OPEC on an economy that imports almost all its energy; rising labor costs at home that have eliminated many old markets. Hitachi knows how to roll with these punches. When the oil crisis hit in 1974 and Japan was rocked to its foundations, Hitachi managers, for example, willingly accepted pay cuts up to 15 percent. In addition, production workers hit the pavements to sell goods that had piled up in warehouses.

Within Hitachi's spartan headquarters in one of downtown Tokyo's oldest office buildings is found an impressive management structure that differs from the typical Japanese system in content as well as manner. Unlike many Japanese companies, each Hitachi factory is an individual profit center. The plants, not the sales divisions, are responsible for profits, which explains why the company puts less emphasis on sales and market share than other Japanese firms do. Each plant borrows capital from headquarters for operating needs and pays back interest, dividends, and quasi-taxes. This decentralized system not only puts a premium on conserving capital through inventory control and running plants at or near capacity, but it will work only when the plants and the staff functions—planning, accounting, finance, and personnel—perform in a cooperative manner. This they do with great success and pride.

In the management development area, the company prides itself on its extensive managerial training activities, much of it patterned after its U.S. counterparts. These activities, which stress the need for managers to acquire a variety of skills as opposed to being narrow specialists, has enabled Hitachi to move managers quickly across functions when the need arises.

Yoshiyama talks about Hitachi as a company with "nobushi spirit." The nobushi were freelance samurai who would often sit out a battle and then pick up the weapons left behind by their fleeing cousins. The meaning has changed over the years. *Nobushi* now refers to a person or group that marches to its own drummer. Those traditions explain much of Hitachi's present eminence. In its beginnings, Hitachi was a gutsy monument to Japanese pride; with the necessary changes and adaptations, it has remained so to this day. It is typical of Hitachi employees to say that the reason the company has been so successful in the face of many threats was that they followed Mr. Yoshiyama's advice: remain flexible and work cooperatively.

Adapted from N. Pearistine, "That Old Nobushi Spirit," Forbes (July 23, 1979): 42.

8

This discussion begins a series of four chapters that concern how organizations are ordered and designed—the *organizing* function. We will devote two chapters to the important subject of designing an effective structure for the organization. Once a structure has been developed, we will discuss the process of acquiring and training a work force to staff the organization. Finally, the crucial function of communication among employees within the organizational structure will be discussed.

In this first chapter the focus is on the foundation or basic *dimensions* of the organizing function. These basic dimensions concern the answers to the following *sequential* questions:

1. What should be the content of employee jobs and how should these jobs be grouped or clustered together? The answer to this question of *grouping* involves the concepts of job specialization, departmentalization, and line and staff positions.

2. How can patterns of *influence* be established within the groupings or units? Issues of authority, scalar chain of command, span of control and centralization/decentralization are related to this question.

3. What mechanisms are needed to insure the proper *coordination* between the different organizational units? A satisfactory response to this question requires a discussion of the determinants and mechanisms for coordination.

An in-depth discussion of each of these questions forms the main sections of this chapter. In the next chapter we will investigate an answer to a fourth question: What is the influence of the external environment and the organization's strategies and technology on its structure?

THE MEANING AND IMPORTANCE OF THE ORGANIZING FUNCTION

In the previous four chapters, our focus was on establishing the *framework for performance* in the manager's job. Setting goals, developing plans, and making decisions to achieve these stated goals, however, requires the *coordinated* effort of all individuals and groups within the organization. In other words, the previous chapters emphasized the *formulation* part of the manager's job; the next chapters deal with the process of *implementing* these formulated goals, strategies, and plans (see part IV of exhibit 6–1).

We will define the *organizing function* as the process of achieving a coordinated effort through the design of a structure of tasks, authority, people, and communication. This definition draws attention to at least three points:

1. The meaning of the word *design* implies that this is a rational and conscious *process* on the part of managers to develop the most effective interactions and interrelationships within the organization.

2. The *result* of the design effort is a structure or framework within the organization.

3. This structure includes grouping similar jobs, establishing authority relationships across and among different jobs, placing the most capable people in these jobs, and developing the most effective means of communications between jobs and jobholders.

An effectively structured organization, then, develops the framework for the organization to achieve its goals. It permits employees to know what their responsibilities are so that they can concentrate on the tasks at hand. Structure enhances the process of coordinating the activities of managers and subordinates so time and effort are put to the best use.

The remainder of this chapter focuses on the following structural dimensions: the grouping dimension—aggregating or clustering jobs and units; the influence dimension—establishing authority, command, and control; and the coordination dimension—developing coordination mechanisms. The relationships are shown in exhibit 8–1.

EXHIBIT 8–1 Dimensions Defining Organization Structure

THE GROUPING DIMENSION: CLUSTERING JOBS AND UNITS

One of the first and probably most important dimensions of an organization's structure is that of defining the content of jobs and then grouping these jobs into units. In formalistic terms this activity is a *grouping* function that has been called the division of labor.[1] We will discuss three aspects of the division of labor: (1) defining individual jobs, or job specialization; (2) the horizontal division of labor, or departmentalization; and (3) line-staff relationships.

Job Specialization

In order to accomplish the required work, managers generally divide the work into specialized tasks to be filled by employees. For example, the personnel department may have a training specialist, a wage and salary specialist, a college recruiting specialist, and a labor relations and contract negotiation specialist. On a different scale, a building contractor may employ carpenters, plumbers, electricians, and bricklayers. This specialization of tasks provides an identity for the job and those performing it. This indicator is often called the *job definition* because it establishes what the workers are to do, how they are to do it, and what the organization will give in return for the effort (e.g., wages).

The concepts of job scope and depth may be used to describe the extent or degree of job specialization.[2] *Job scope* refers to the number of movements that are involved in a job. Sometimes called *job variety,* the concept is related to the different things that a worker does within a certain cycle of work. *Job depth,* on the other hand, concerns the relative freedom the worker has in planning, organizing, and controlling the assigned duties. This relates to such factors as the degree of autonomy, responsibility, and the extent of decision-making freedom.

For example, consider two jobs within a manufacturing organization such as the Fisher Body Division of General Motors. The job of a stamping press operator can be considered to be quite narrow in scope and depth. The individual's job is to operate the press that stamps out car doors from a flat piece of sheet steel. The variety is limited in this job to positioning a sheet of steel from the conveyor belt in the press, initiating the stamping function by pressing a button, and moving the stamped piece onto the conveyor belt to the finishing operation. The cycle for this job is relatively short, something less than one minute per unit. The operator's responsibilities are also limited by well spelled out safety and operating rules and procedures.

On the other hand, consider the job of plant manager of this G.M. facility. This manager's job could be evaluated as being quite broad in scope and depth. There is considerable variety in what this manager does, involving responsibility for overall effectiveness of the production, maintenance, personnel, and accounting functions. From our view of the manager's job, the plant manager's position involves many aspects of planning, organizing, leading, controlling, and change. The manager operates relatively autonomously because that job contains a high degree of freedom in decision making.

As these two brief examples suggest, the degree of scope and depth of a job is also closely related to the individual's level in the organization. That is, as one advances from a nonsupervisory job to a higher level management position, the degree of scope and depth increases. While there may be differences across organizations for similar jobs (e.g., personnel manager in a hospital versus personnel manager in a research laboratory), the vertical level differences in job scope and depth within a single organization usually are quite apparent.

The degree of job specialization is highly dependent on the particular school of management thought adopted, as discussed in chapter 3. For example, a manager who believes in the principles of the classical school (scientific management) would approach the problem of defining an employee's job with an objective of improving efficiency. In defining the stamping press operator's job, the manager would be concerned with breaking the job down into its fundamental movements and then with attempting to make these movements as efficient as possible. One could expect that the result would be a job quite narrow in scope and depth.

The manager adopting an approach similar to that proposed by the behavioral school, however, would be concerned with the problems associated with overspecializing jobs, such as boredom, fatigue, and monotony. These problems can lead to adverse effects such as increased absenteeism, turnover, and poor workmanship. As we will discuss in chapter 12, the manager making job specialization decisions must be concerned not only with criteria associated with economic efficiency but with psychological criteria as well.[3]

Horizontal Division of Labor: Departmentalization

Once the manager has decided on the manner in which *individual* jobs will be defined, the next step is to determine how these jobs will be grouped into different units or departments. When this grouping is done horizontally in an organization, it is called *departmentalization*.

The basis for making departmentalization decisions is one of *focus,* either internal or external. An internal focus is called departmentalization by function; an external focus involves an orientation toward product, geographical dispersion, customer type, time, type of equipment, and so forth.

Internal Focus—Functional Departmentalization.   The functional approach is by far the most widely adopted form of departmentalization. An example of a functional arrangement in a manufacturing firm is shown in exhibit 8–2. (Note: When an organization's structure is shown in schematic form, it is sometimes referred to as an organization *chart*). It is termed an *internal* focus because it is designed on the basis of the operations or functions performed by employees. In exhibit 8–2, the functional arrangement is by manufacturing, marketing, research and development, finance, and personnel. We may also carry this approach to many other organizations. For example, a medical school can be arranged by such specialties as surgery, pediatrics, psychiatry, internal medicine, and the like.

The advantanges of the functional form are twofold. First, it can be highly cost efficient because the individual specialties are grouped together, which eliminates costly duplication of effort. Second, it makes management easier because managers have to be experts in only a narrow range of skills.

The major disadvantages of the functional structure are also twofold. First, as the organization becomes large and more complex, the functional arrangement can prove to be quite cumbersome. For example, a functional arrangement in a hospital may have a single department of nursing. However, within the department there may be included such specialties as trauma nurses (i.e., emergency rooms), heart attack specialists, cancer ward specialists, pediatric emergency nurses, nurses specializing in paraplegic/quadriplegic patients, and so forth. Second, closely aligned with the first point, the functional arrangement does not readily adapt to change. Obtaining quick decisions or actions on specific problems may require more time because such decisions have to be made by higher level

EXHIBIT 8–2 Functional and Product Departmentalization

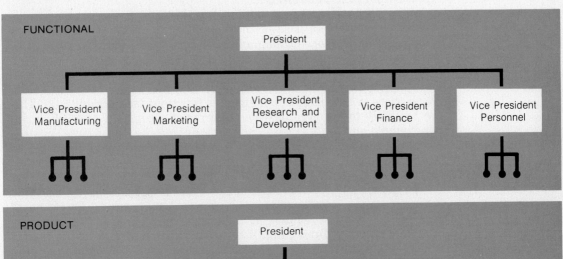

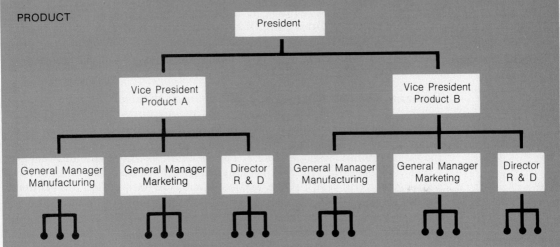

managers. In exhibit 8–2, if a problem of product quality arises with a customer, the marketing vice president must involve the manufacturing vice president and the president to solve it. This takes valuable time from the executives that might be better invested in such activities as environmental analyses and planning.

External Focus—Product Departmentalization. In a product arrangement, departments are grouped together on the basis of product or family of products and services marketed to customers. An example is also shown in exhibit 8–2. This type of arrangement is particularly applicable to those organizations that market a wide variety of products and services that require production technologies and/or marketing methods that differ markedly between products. For example, two of the main product lines for General Electric are consumer products (e.g., televisions) and electrical turbines. Another example could be General Foods, which produces and markets both breakfast cereals and dog food. There are too many *dissimilarities* between these product lines for them to be grouped together in a functional design.

The major advantages and disadvantages for the product arrangement are just the opposite of the functional form. That is, because it specifically is developed along external lines, the product form can be quite adaptable to change. It provides the mechanisms for the organization to react quickly to, for example, competitive changes or new customer needs. The main disadvantage is that there may be situations in which there is a duplication of effort or functions (see exhibit 8–2). This can be costly to the organization in terms of equipment and personnel. For example, in a product arrangement there may be two or more research and development labs, while in a functional arrangement there would be only one laboratory. This situation relates to the concept of "economies of scale."[4]

A variation of the product form is the *project* arrangement. This form groups jobs into departments by the particular project that is being performed. This is a popular arrangement used by large constructions companies such as Brown and Root, Fluor, and Bechtel. That is, project A may be an oil refinery in the Middle East, project B may be a large bridge in the state of Washington, and so forth. The other characteristics are similar to the product arrangement.

External Focus—Geographic Departmentalization.   As shown in exhibit 8–3, a geographic arrangement groups units on the basis of location. The exhibit represents a partial illustration of the geographic departmentalization used by Federated Department Stores and its regional merchandising operations. The rationale is that if the markets are widely dispersed in different regions, an improved response time to consumer needs will result if the particular units in each region are grouped together.

There are two additional factors or principles concerning departmentalization that should be pointed out. First, in most cases, the particular arrangement does not remain intact as one goes up or down managerial or organizational levels. This represents the principle of *alternation*. For example, as depicted in the product form of exhibit 8–2, the first organizational level after the president is arranged along a product departmentalization. The next level, however, is a functional arrangement, and so on. In another organization, the first level may be formed with a functional arrangement, and the next level would usually be a product departmentalization. The important point for managers to recognize about this situation is that departmentalization by different arrangements can and does occur at each level in the organization.

Second, exhibit 8–4 illustrates the concept of *mixed* departmentalization. There are times when an organization does not want to become a fully functional or product arranged firm. For example, the organization's top management may feel that a product arrangement will work effectively with groupings of manufacturing and marketing under the product structure. However, they may feel it necessary to keep planning, personnel, research and development, and finance in a functional form.

EXHIBIT 8–3 Geographical Departmentalization: Federated Department Stores

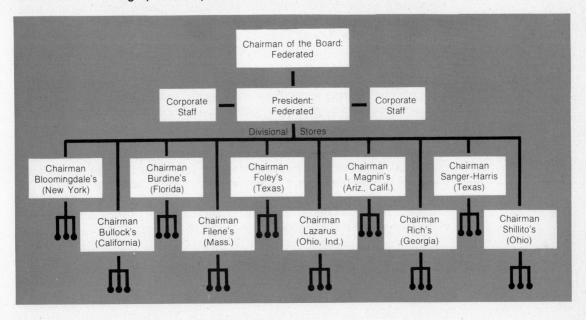

EXHIBIT 8–4 Mixed Departmentalization

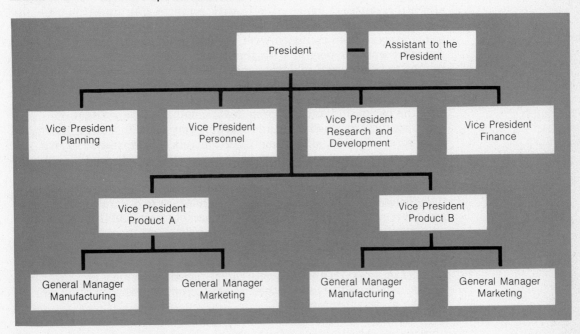

Using our cost and adaptive criteria, management may believe that adaptation or quick reaction time is needed in manufacturing and marketing. The remaining units (personnel, planning, and so on) may not need to be so adaptive and can be grouped in a functional form.

Line-Staff Relationships

As organizations increase in size and complexity, it is necessary to introduce personnel with specialized knowledge and skills. This creates the arrangement of line-staff relationships. Using exhibit 8–4 again as an example, *line* groupings are those units that are directly involved in producing the product or service. These are represented, for example, by the manufacturing and marketing departments. *Staff* groupings are those units that perform in *support* of the line functions but are not directly involved in manufacturing or marketing of the product or service. The personnel, finance, and research and development departments in the exhibit can be considered staff units.[5] Because of its importance, we will cover line-staff relationships in a number of later chapters.

THE INFLUENCE DIMENSION: ESTABLISHING AUTHORITY AND COMMAND

Once methods of departmentalization have been chosen and jobs have been grouped or clustered, mechanisms are needed to influence the behavior of employees within the departments. This influence dimension is referred to as *authority*. Before we discuss the sources of authority in organizations, the difference between authority, power, and responsibility should be pointed out.

For our purposes, *authority* is defined as the right to command and allocate resources.[6] Lines of authority serve to link and integrate the various organizational departments together in order to achieve stated goals. *Power,* often confused with authority, is defined as the ability to influence another person with the control of resources.[7] Power is thus related to the concept of dependence. Person A has power and can influence person B when A controls certain resources that are needed by B. For example, the manufacturing department of an organization has power over the packaging and shipping department because without manufactured products, no packaging and shipping can occur. In a sense, authority is a subset of power, since a manager controls certain resources (e.g., job assignments, wage increases, and so forth) that are desired by subordinates.

Finally, *responsibility* is accountability for the achievement of goals, the efficient use of resources, and the adherence to organizational plans, procedures, and rules. Once a manager accepts responsibility, it becomes an obligation to perform the assigned work.

Sources of Authority

At least three sources of authority can be identified in most organizations. These include legitimate authority, the acceptance theory of authority, and the unity of command.

Legitimate Authority.   Authority can be viewed as the right to influence other members of the organization. This is termed the *legitimate* source of authority.[8] Managers, because of their position in the organization, are given the right by the organization to influence others. A vice president has authority over his or her subordinate managers, and each of these managers has the right to influence subordinate employees.

Acceptance Theory of Authority.   One of the foundations of the authority concept was stated by Barnard in *The Functions of the Executive*.[9] He stated in 1938 that a person can and will accept a form of communication as authoritative only when four conditions exist: (1) the person can and does understand the communication; (2) at the time of the decision, the person believes it is not inconsistent with the purpose of the organization; (3) the person believes that the acceptance of the communication is compatible with personal interests; and (4) the person is able both mentally and physically to comply with it. These four conditions have been called the "acceptance theory of authority" because the right to command depends upon whether or not the subordinates obey. The manager can use punishment (or the threat of punishment) to assure acceptance. However, the subordinate may decide to endure the punishment or quit the organization rather than accept an effort at influence through authority.

Unity of Command.   The principle of unity of command originates from the classical school of management and concerns the relationship between managers and their subordinates.[10] Stated simply, the unity of command suggests that an employee should have *one and only one* immediate supervisor or manager. This principle is founded on two beliefs. First, it acts to further legitimatize the manager's authority by clarifying lines of authority. Second, it helps to eliminate the problems when an employee gets conflicting orders from two different managers. In this situation, the employee is put into an uncomfortable position—obeying one order will leave the other manager dissatisfied. When there are clear lines of authority, these problems are removed, thus permitting the employee to concentrate on the task at hand.

Implementation of Authority

Because authority is a key element in management, there are a number of ways that it has been implemented in organizations. Three specific implementation concepts will be discussed: (1) scalar chain of command; (2) span of control; and (3) the centralization-decentralization issue.

Scalar Chain of Command.   The scalar chain of command states that authority in the organization flows, one level at a time, through a series of managers ranging from the highest to the lowest managerial ranks.[11] It is commonly referred to as a *chain,* where each link is a single manager and the meshing of individual links in a vertical manner forms a chain. A chain of command for a manufacturing firm was shown earlier in exhibit 2–2.

The chain of command concept is founded on the unity of command principle. The latter is related to the interaction between superior and subordinates, and the chain of command takes this further by detailing how the principle works its way through the entire organization. The more clearly the lines of authority and responsibility flow from top management to every subordinate, the more likely there will be effective decision making and proper communication.

Span of Control.   The span of control is measured by the number of subordinates that report directly to a single supervisor or manager.[12]

Various mechanisms have been discussed to determine what is the optimum number of subordinates that should report to a single manager. One of the first versions of the span of control argument was presented by Sir Ian Hamilton during World War I.[13] He stated that a system with no more than six subordinates reporting to a superior would enable the superior to get his job done in an effective manner. Surprisingly, this number has held up for many years, even though the origins of Hamilton's number are quite unclear. In today's organizations, however, a manager's span of control can vary with a significant number of factors. Steadfastly adhering to the particular number may prove to be a much less effective strategy than a careful analysis of situational factors.

A. V. Graicunas later developed a mathematical representation of the span of control concept.[14] He pointed out that in selecting a workable span of control, managers should consider at least three factors: (1) the direct one-to-one relationships with the people they directly supervise; (2) the relationships the manager has with groups of two or more subordinates; and (3) cross-relationships between and among the individual subordinates.

From an anaysis of these three possible relationships, Graicunas developed the following formula to give the number of superior-subordinate relationships that may require managerial attention:

$$C = n(2^n/2 + n - 1)$$

where C designates the total potential contacts, and n is the number of subordinates reporting directly to the manager. According to the equation, the number of relationships increases geometrically as the number of subordinates increases arithmetically. For example, two subordinates require a total of 6 relationships; five subordinates require 100 relationships; and ten subordinates require 5,210 relationships.

Even without the use of this formulation, it was clear that the span of control of managers is directly related to the level of obtained effectiveness. It has been stated, "Harrassed supervisors and frustrated subordinates often mean that the supervisor has too broad a span of control." Conversely, harrassed subordinates and frustrated supervisors often are indicators of too narrow a span of control.[15]

Given this situation, what are the elements that the manager should consider in selecting managerial spans of control? There are at least three components:

1. *Types of control spans.* Two types of spans of control can be identified: executive and operative. *Executive* span of control includes middle and top management positions in the organization. Since these positions deal primarily with planning and policy-related matters, a narrow span of

control on the order of three to nine is usually adopted. *Operative* span of control is within the realm of first-line managers and some middle-level managers. The primary activities performed by these managers can many times be fairly routine, which requires less direct contact and interaction. In this case, the span of control can increase to as many as thirty. In essence, this argument suggests that span of control can and does vary by level in the organization—smaller for executives and larger for lower level managers.

2. *Situational factors.* Many internal situational factors can affect the decision on the span of control of managers. There are at least six factors for the manager to analyze: (a) The manager's ability and competence to supervise large numbers of people; (b) the relative similarity or dissimilarity of the work being performed; (c) the frequency and quality of employee interactions needed for effectiveness; (d) the incidence of new problems that are faced; (e) the need for supervision—the extent that rules, procedures, and other guidelines can direct the work of employees; (f) the physical dispersion of employees.[16]

3. *Tall versus flat structures.* The selection of a span of control will have a significant effect on the size and shape of the organization's structure. The words *tall* and *flat* have been used to describe an organization's shape; the number of employees can be used to measure its size.[17]

A simple example can be used to illustrate these concepts. Consider a personnel placement firm located in an urban area. The firm employs a total of forty-eight nonsupervisory counselors in conducting job search and placement activities. The question is, what structure is needed and how many supervisors and managers will be required? As shown in exhibit 8–5, at least three structures can be developed. Structure I uses two new managers (in addition to the owner/president), each with a span of control of twenty-four employees. Structure I is a flat structure with a narrow span of control for the president, but wide spans of control for the managers. Structure II adds a second level of management to I, and the resulting spans of control vary from two to six. Finally, structure III, a tall structure with narrow spans of control, adds a third new management level where the spans of control are two to four employees. The important factor to note about these three simple structures is that the size of the organization varies greatly—I uses a total of fifty-one employees (including the president); II uses sixty-one employees; and III uses seventy-one employees.

The proponents of both flat and tall structures point out certain advantages and disadvantages for each form. The flat structure is said to be more cost efficient and, by providing more variety of work, may result in high employee job satisfaction. On the negative side, it is not very adaptable to change and the large span of control may result in coordination problems. The tall structure can adopt to change better and there is better coordination, plus the narrow span of control facilitates the development of skills. The disadvantages include increased costs due to the added managerial levels and problems of employee dissatisfaction associated with performing routine, more specialized jobs.

EXHIBIT 8–5 Span of Control and Organizational Structure

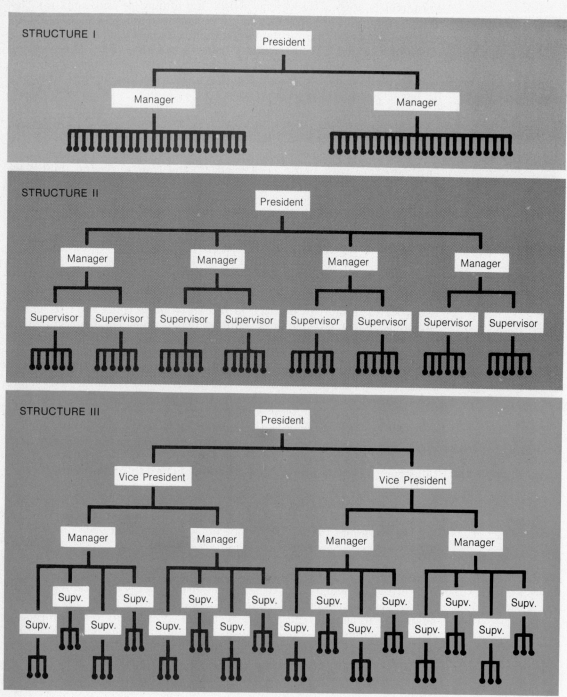

The many research studies that have been conducted over the years to study these factors, however, have been inconclusive, indicating that we cannot select the best span of control on the basis of some formula or set of rules. There are just too many variables involved in any organization that must be considered. For example, in the next chapter, we will suggest that the nature of the work being performed (what we will call *technology*) is an important factor. In a manufacturing firm, the routine and repetitive nature of the work may be appropriate for a tall structure. On the other hand, the innovative and creative work in a research and development laboratory may be best handled with a rather flat structure.

THE MANAGER'S JOB
Paul Elicker of SCM Corporation

In the decade since SCM Corporation acquired it, the company's Cleveland-based Glidden-Durkee division evolved into a big conglomerate in its own right. Its centralized approach to management, however, was getting in the way of successful operations. A capital expenditure proposed by a Glidden-Durkee plant manager, for example, would take seven months to wend its way through operating managers, be analyzed by the Glidden-Durkee financial staff, and then go to New York, where the SCM staff would do it all over again. The same lead time existed in budgeting and planning.

To solve this problem, Paul H. Elicker, President and Chief Executive Officer of SCM, decided to restructure Glidden-Durkee. His main move was to split Glidden-Durkee into four separate units: coatings and resins, with headquarters in Cleveland; food, also in Cleveland; chemical-metallurgical, based in Baltimore; and organic chemicals, with headquarters in Jacksonville, Florida. Decentralizing this way allowed for greater concentration of operations, and the promise of better performance.

In effect, Elicker recognized that the businesses that Glidden-Durkee was in were different and required specialists to run them. He noted that it was hard to mix a high-growth business, such as foods and chemicals, with low-growth operations, such as coatings and resins. Managing them requires a different approach. Coatings and resins growth will come primarily from expanding marketing and R&D efforts, and success in chemicals will come as a result of the skill with which capital investments are made.

So far, the restructuring has gone smoothly—no small feat considering the types of managerial jobs that were involved. One key reason for the smooth transition was that there was no loss of pay to any manager. Another factor is that a manager's chances of heading a division are greatly enhanced, since there are more divisions to go around. In addition, bonuses are now awarded based on the performance of the smaller division, where managers can have a more direct effect.

Adapted from "Streamlining the Management at SCM," Business Week (February 21, 1977).

Centralization/Decentralization.   The words *centralization/decentralization* have been discussed for many years, usually in a confusing fashion. For our purposes, we will present these concepts as the degree to which the *power to make decisions* is transferred to lower level managers. When all the power for decision-making is in the hands of a single, high-level executive, it is called a *centralized* structure. When the power to make decisions is dispersed among lower-level managers, it is called a *decentralized* structure.

Centralization/decentralization should not be viewed as two separate concepts, but opposite ends of a single continuum of *delegation*. At the decentralized end of the continuum, the phrase "You make the decision" would be representative; the phrase "I will make the decision" implies a centralization. In the middle of the continuum, the statement "Study this problem, but don't make a decision until you've checked with me first" would be appropriate.

There are two types of decentralization that can be identified in most organizations: vertical and horizontal. *Vertical decentralization* concerns the dispersal of power *down* the chain of command. This is the case of a higher-level manager delegating the power to a subordinate manager to make a decision. In some cases, this may be also called *vertical division of labor* (see the previous discussion on the grouping dimension).

Horizontal decentralization relates to line and staff relationships. When, as in the case of vertical decentralization, the authority and power to make a decision remains within a particular function, this is called *line* authority. When decision authority flows to managers outside the line structure to analysts, support specialists, and other experts, such a delegation is called decentralization to a *staff* authority. Staff authority is auxiliary and sometimes temporary in nature. For example, many organizations have created the position of "Assistant to ———", such as Assistant to the President, Assistant to the Senior Vice President, and so forth (see exhibit 8–4). In some cases, the line manager will instruct the "Assistant to" positionholder to attend a meeting and make inputs or decisions as if the line manager were present.

The use of centralization or decentralization has its value to the degree that it assists the organization in achieving its stated goals. The decision whether or not to decentralize is a complex process that involves a number of considerations. These include the following:[18]

1. *External environmental factors.* The impact of such environmental factors as governmental legislation; unions; federal, state, and local tax policies; and variations in the economic trends in different countries in which the organization operates are important influences on the decision whether to decentralize or not. As the environmental problems faced by an organization become more complex and dispersed, we would expect that some form of decentralization would be used. For example, many large multi-division/multi-product corporations face the prospect of negotiating labor contracts with ten, twenty, or more different labor unions. Rather than conduct the negotiation on a centralized basis with a headquarters unit, these organizations usually choose to delegate such decisions to the divisional level for resolution. This is also the way many organizations have decided to handle international operations. Rather than make decisions in the U.S., sometimes many thousands of miles away from the foreign operations, these organizations permit many of the day-to-day and long-term decisions to be made by the managers on site.

2. *Growth of the organization.* In managing a complex organization, it is nearly impossible to make all decisions in one location or in one head.

This is especially true for organizations that are in the midst of significant growth phases. Because situations, problems, and opportunities are developing at a rapid pace, it may be necessary for top management to delegate the decisions on these issues to lower levels in the organization. Unless this decentralization occurs, the organization may bypass a significant opportunity or be faced with a problem that has grown in size due to inattention. In some cases, organizations build decentralization into their strategies and plans to ensure proper attention.

3. *Cost and risk.* There is a reluctance on the part of many managers to delegate authority on a decision when the consequences may have a significant impact on the organization now or in the future. When the risks and costs are high, the tendency to centralize is strong. In the framework we developed in the last chapter, we can expect strategic decisions to be centralized; administrative and operating decisions would normally be decentralized.

4. *Management philosophies.* Some managers and organizations pride themselves on a policy, sometimes historical in nature, of making all the important decisions. Others point to a past practice of successful delegation to subordinate managers. This is nothing more than the adherence to a *habit* formed from past activities. As we all know, it is sometimes quite difficult to break a habit, whether it be smoking or centralizing all decisions.

5. *Locus of expertise.* There are many instances when managers do not have the necessary knowledge and understanding to make a decision. This *expertise* may reside at some lower level in the organization. For example, in selling consumer products in Europe, it may be a more effective policy to permit the marketing manager of Europe to make decisions rather than make them from the home office.

6. *Abilities of lower-level managers.* One of the basic assumptions of a policy of decentralization is that capable managers at lower levels are available to make effective decisions. However, too often there is a shortage of skilled and trained managers, forcing top management to centralize most decisions. This situation is somewhat circular in nature. That is, if decision-making authority is not decentralized because of lack of capable and skilled managers, how will these managers become skilled and capable unless they make important decisions? Also, if the organization is reluctant to decentralize some decisions, it will have a difficult time retaining young and ambitious managers who desire to get more involved in the decision-making process. When such people leave the organization, it makes the decision to decentralize that much harder. It is apparent that some form of decentralization should occur if the organization wishes to train and retain future managers. In fact, many organizations are using decentralization as a means of identifying future managers—those who perform successfully are moved quickly up the promotion ladder, and those who perform less successfully move much slower, if at all.[19]

There are certain factors that managers should be aware of that can alter the way decentralization is used in organizations. First, the decision to decentralize need not be permanent. Decentralization can occur over a period of time or for a particular set of decisions. Second, various levels of decentralization can occur within the same organization. For example, the marketing department may be highly decentralized so that regional sales managers are given the authority to change prices, propose bids on contracts, hire personnel, and select transportation methods for the delivery of product. The manufacturing department of the same organization, however, may be highly centralized so that most decisions, even on productivity rates, are made by top management.

Last, managers must recognize that subordinates may be reluctant to accept decentralization attempts by managers. This is especially true in organizations where decentralization has not been widely practiced. In these cases, managers must try to remove the barriers to decentralization attempts. Establishing goals, providing incentives, training subordinates in making decisions, and giving some direction and guidance are some of the mechanisms that the manager can use.

The decision to decentralize decision-making authority is obviously not as straightforward as the reader may have first thought, nor is it universally accepted in organizations. Such companies as General Electric, Sears, E. I. Du Pont, and General Motors have been successful with decentralized decision making. On the other hand, General Dynamics and International Harvester have used a more centralized approach and have met with equal success. Managers must closely diagnose their situations with respect to the previously discussed factors before deciding on the degree of centralization. Blind obedience to one approach or the other may lead to less than satisfactory levels of effectiveness.

THE COORDINATION DIMENSION

In our discussion of the grouping dimension of an organizational structure, we focused on the most effective means of grouping jobs and units. The influence dimension deals with establishing authority and command within units or departments. Finally, in our discussion of the coordination dimension, we will focus on developing mechanisms to *integrate* separate units and departments in order to achieve organizational goals. Without some form of coordination, individuals and larger units would go about their divided work activities and lose sight of their important roles and duties within an organization.

Determinants of Coordination Needs

There are many illustrations of the need for coordination in all types of organizations. Consider, for example, the emergency room in a hospital. In order to treat an automobile accident patient, the attending physician will need the assistance of members of the nursing staff as well as of the pathology lab personnel for blood analyses, X-ray technicians, and possibly other specialized physicians. In the same manner, the production control manager at a large chemical plant will need the help of manufacturing and sales personnel in order to schedule production rates and product grades that can satisfy both consumer demands for product and the needs of the manufacturing manager for steady and efficient production. These examples and others illustrate that coordination is both an important and complex managerial task in organizations.

Before discussing the mechanisms for coordination, it is necessary to identify the basic determinants and origins of coordination needs. For our purposes, three determinants will be discussed: (1) interdependence; (2) time orientation; and (3) goal orientation of interacting units.[20]

COMMENTS ON THE PRACTICE OF MANAGEMENT
(See p. 252)

The Hitachi example at the beginning of this chapter illustrates a number of important organizational dimensions. First, the need to be flexible during external and internal environmental changes implies that departmentalization practices should not be rigid, but adaptable to these changing conditions. Second, the form of decentralization, while unique to Japan, has served the company well. Note carefully that a key to success of this decentralization movement is the high level of mutual cooperation and coordination between line and staff units. Finally, authority and coordination dimensions are enhanced by managerial training and development programs. Managers are trained to work as a team no matter what function of the organization they are part of at the time.

Interdependence.   Interdependence between two or more departments is the degree to which the interactions between departments must be coordinated to attain a desired level of performance. Three types of interdependence are most frequently discussed: (1) pooled; (2) sequential; and (3) reciprocal.[21]

Pooled interdependence describes the relationship of departments that are relatively *independent* of each other but that provide a discrete contribution to the larger organization. The Chevrolet assembly plant in Oklahoma may be considered independent of the Cadillac assembly plant in Michigan on most manufacturing or coordination matters. They are, however, interdependent in a pooled fashion because each contributes to the overall performance of General Motors.

Sequential interdependence exists when some output of one group becomes the input to another group. For example, sequential interdependence exists between the departments of manufacturing and shipping in an organization. The outputs of the manufacturing department—finished products—are the major inputs for the shipping department.

Reciprocal interdependence exists when certain outputs of each department become inputs to these same departments. In other words, the departments are highly dependent on one another and thus require a significant degree of coordination. For example, consider the departments of operations and maintenance of a domestic airline company. These two departments are reciprocally interdependent because, on one hand, the outputs of the operations department—an aircraft needing repair—serve as an input to the maintenance department. On the other hand, the output of the maintenance department—a fully repaired aircraft—is an input to the operations department.

For successful performance, it is important for managers to understand that as one progresses from pooled to reciprocal, the three types of interdependence require greater interaction and hence greater coordination efforts. That is, when advancing from pooled to sequential and finally to reciprocal interdependence, there must be an increased awareness by everyone involved that the activities of one department are dependent on the actions and behavior of other departments. Effective performance is a direct result of how this interdependence is successfully coordinated. A summary of the interdependence concept is shown in exhibit 8–6.

EXHIBIT 8–6   Summary of Interdependence Types

TYPE	DEGREE OF DEPENDENCE	DESCRIPTION	EXAMPLE
Reciprocal	High	Certain outputs of each group become inputs for other groups, or to each other.	The interaction between operations and maintenance in a domestic airline company.
Sequential	Moderate	Outputs of one group become inputs of other groups.	Automobile assembly line activities.
Pooled	Low	Groups or units are relatively independent of each other, but contribute to the overall goals of the organization.	Separate manufacturing plants of a single organization that only infrequently interact.

Time Orientation.   Managers who spend a number of years in a particular type of job tend to become accustomed to organizing their work in a predictable fashion that helps them perform that job effectively. Many factors within the manager's job contribute to this situation, one of which is the *time orientation*.[22] For our purposes, we define *time orientation* as the length of time required to obtain information or results relating to the performance of a task. Manufacturing managers, for example, are usually concerned with problems and issues that can be solved quickly or within a short time. A production rate problem or an equipment malfunction requires the manager to seek a solution as quickly as possible. On the other hand, a research chemist may require months, or possibly years, to develop a new product or process.

The coordination issue posed by time orientation is important for units or departments that must get together to solve problems or perform other joint activities. For example, a serious problem has arisen in the quality of an important product of a plastics manufacturer. Because the problem is unlike any problem previously encountered by the company, the divisional vice president appoints a task force made up of representatives from manufacturing, marketing, production control, and research. Because of individual time orientations, the manufacturing representative may move for a "let's find a quick solution" approach while the research representative may opt for a more lengthy "let's investigate all the alternatives" route to solution. Given these divergent approaches, it may be difficult for the task force to reach a satisfactory solution.

Goal Orientation.   *Goal orientation* focuses on the particular set of goals that are of major concern to the manager.[23] To be effective, managers must focus their attention clearly on goals that are related to their work. For example, manufacturing managers are concerned with such goals as raw material costs, processing and inventory costs, production volume, and the quality of the product. The goals of marketing managers are oriented toward sales volume and revenue, market share, and customer satisfaction. Research scientists often concentrate on goals involving the development of scientific knowledge and translating this knowledge into potential market applications.

These examples point to three different goal orientations: (1) *techno-economic,* dealing with cost control and the implementation of manufacturing techniques (e.g., manufacturing and accounting departments); (2) *market* goals, concerning the response of the market to the organization's goods and services (e.g., marketing department); and (3) *science* goals, concerning contributions to scientific knowledge (e.g., research and engineering departments).

The different goal orientations provide a basis for establishing criteria for evaluating the performance of a particular unit or department. We would expect that the primary criteria of performance for manufacturing would focus on quantity, quality, and cost considerations (i.e., techno-economic), sales volume and market share for the marketing department (i.e., market goal), and the number of new products, new processes, and other contributions to scientific knowledge for research and engineering (i.e., science goal).

Two additional factors should be pointed out. First, as in the case of time orientation, the greater the difference in goal orientation, the greater the difficulty in achieving coordination between units or departments. This is due to the fact that different department orientations may force managers to act in dissimilar ways. When managers representing these units are asked to integrate their activities, they try to maintain their particular perspectives about work and how it should be done. To fully integrate the activities of widely different units requires a high degree of coordinated effort by management.

Second, as shown in exhibit 8–7, time and goal orientations are highly related to each other. That is, we would expect that manufacturing managers have a relatively short time orientation along with a techno-economic goal emphasis. On the other hand, the director of a research laboratory should have a much longer time orientation and goals that are more scientific in nature.

EXHIBIT 8–7 Differences in Time Orientation

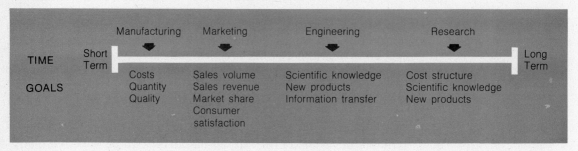

Coordination Mechanisms

There are a number of different methods or mechanisms available to managers to achieve high levels of required coordination. A total of seven methods will be discussed: rules and procedures, hierarchy, planning, liaison roles, task forces, teams, and integrating departments.

Two aspects should be noted about these coordination methods. First, advancing from the use of rules to integrating departments represents an increased level of difficulty and commitment of resources by the organization to achieve coordination. That is, the use of rules and procedures is the easiest coordination method, particularly appropriate for those situations that require low coordination. However, organizations will use integrating departments when coordination needs are great and when they are willing to commit significant organizational resources to achieve coordination.

Second, in moving from the use of rules and hierarchy to teams and integrating departments, a coordination method previously used will probably still be used along with other methods. That is, even though the organization may depend on task forces as the main coordination method, it is highly probable that rules, hierarchy, and planning will also be used.

Rules and Procedures.   The most basic or simplistic method for managing coordination is to specify in advance, through rules and procedures, the required activities and behavior of group members.[24] Interacting employees learn that when certain situations arise there is a particular set of actions that should be used. For example, the packaging and shipping department knows that when the manufacturing department changes the manufacturing process from producing the medium-grade product to the higher-grade product at 10:00 a.m. each day they must use a different packaging container and labeling process. Little, if any, interaction between the two groups is necessary because the procedures have spelled out in advance the required behaviors.

The principal benefit of rules and procedures is that they eliminate the need for extensive interaction and information flow between groups or units. Rules and procedures also provide a means of stability to the organization. Employees may come and go, but the procedures remain for future interactions.[25] Rules and procedures, however, are limited methods for managing coordination. They are most applicable when interacting activities can be anticipated in advance and when the responses or required behaviors can be developed.

Hierarchy.   When the use of rules and procedures proves inadequate for effective coordination, the use of the hierarchy, or common supervisor, becomes the primary managerial strategy. For example, when there are departmental problems between manufacturing and shipping, such as inadequate inventory to load a boxcar, the problem is brought to the attention of the manufacturing general manager by the supervisors of the two units.

The basic assumption for using the hierarchy or common supervisor as a coordination strategy is that higher level managers have the power and authority to make these decisions. However, as in the case of rules and procedures, this method has its limitations. Whenever interdependence and/or time and goal orientation differences become a problem, the manager's time may be totally taken up resolving these exceptions or problems of coordination. Less time can be devoted to more pressing issues, such as planning the construction of a new plant. Additional difficulties are encountered when problems between two separate units, such as shipping and sales, arise. The common supervisor may be the divisional vice president, who becomes the sole arbitrator of day-to-day problems, which is an ineffective way of using an executive's skills and time.

Planning.   As the problems between interacting departments develop beyond the control of rules, procedures, or hierarchy, organizations increasingly use planning activities to improve coordination. Planning activities involve setting targets and schedules that can lead to task accomplishment.[26]

For example, consider the construction of a new manufacturing plant. Various interdependent and interacting groups are involved in such aspects as erecting the frame of the building, installing the electrical and utility lines, installing the manufacturing equipment, and connecting all raw material and finished-product processing lines. Rather than having constant interaction between these groups, plans have been made so that each group or unit can perform its task over a specific period of time. Each group has a set of goals or targets for required hours of construction, delivery of construction materials, and completion dates.

Liaison or Internal Boundary-Spanning Roles.   When the number of interactions and volume of information between two or more units or groups grows, it may become necessary to establish a specialized role to handle these requirements. Such a role has been variously termed a *liaison,* or more formally, an internal boundary spanner.[27]

In the example shown in exhibit 8–8, a liaison or internal boundary-spanning role could be established between the applied research and market research functions. Individuals who operate in this role provide *lateral* communications and facilitate interaction between the two functions in a number of areas. One important area is the coordination of activity directed toward ascertaining the potential of a new product developed by the applied research unit. The effective interaction provided by the liaison role may enable the product to progress more quickly or may force research scientists to revise their work in light of a negative evaluation from the market research unit. In each case, decisions related to the new product may be made.

EXHIBIT 8–8
Liaison Role

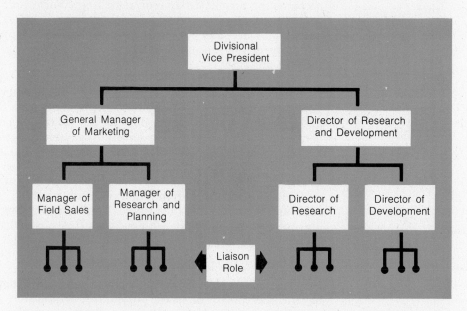

A number of negative consequences can develop when organizations use a liaison role strategy to manage coordination. First, performing in liaison roles may have negative effects for the individuals who hold these positions. A number of research studies have found incumbents of boundary-spanning roles to experience such dysfunctions as lower job satisfaction and higher stress.[28]

The basic explanation for these negative characteristics is that those in boundary-spanning roles must face conflicting performance expectations from the different groups with which they interact. In contrast, a person dealing only with the performance expectations from the group would face less conflicting and ambiguous expectations. Second, the effectiveness of interdepartmental relations is limited by the ability of the liaison person to handle the complexities and information flow between the interacting groups. In addition, as these aspects increase, more and more individuals begin functioning in liaison roles, which acts to remove them from performing their primary functions. When this situation arises, organizations seek other methods to manage coordination.

EXHIBIT 8–9 Product Development Task Force

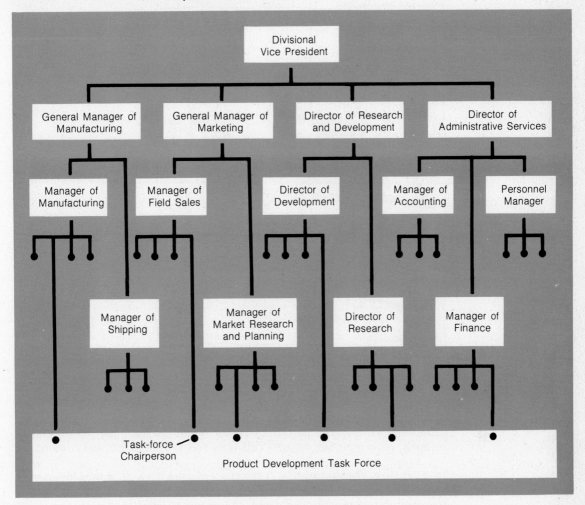

Task Forces. When the complexities of interaction increase, such as when there are more than two or three interacting departments, the coordinating or decision-making capacity of the liaison role becomes overloaded. One mechanism to overcome these problems is to establish a "temporary" task force (see exhibit 8–9) consisting of one or more representatives from each of the interacting units. Task forces exist only so long as the problem of interacting remains. When a solution is reached, each member returns to normal duties.[29]

Teams. Similar to task forces, teams are a collection of individual members used to manage coordination activities when there are more than two or three interacting units. The distinguishing aspect of the team concept is that the problem to be solved usually is long term in nature,

QUEENIE   By Phil Interlandi

"Why complain now? You should have asked what
'Special assistant to the President' meant before you
took the job."

requiring a relatively permanent formal assignment of the team. In addition, team members maintain a dual responsibility: one to their primary functional unit; the second to the team. When the team has accomplished its task, each member returns full-time to the functional assignment.

Integrating Departments.   As the complexities of interdependence, and time and goal orientations increase, the magnitude of coordination requirements may grow beyond the capacity of plans, task forces, or teams. In response to this situation, organizations may seek more permanent, formal, and authority-based mechanisms that represent the general manager's perspective. Such mechanisms are known as integrating departments.

In its basic form, an integrating department consists of a single person who carries a title such as product manager, project manager, brand manager, or group manager. These managers rarely supervise any of the actual work required in departmental interactions. They are, however, generally held responsible for the effective coordination of activities. Their decision-making authority is acquired through a direct reporting relationship to a higher management position; by increasing the managers' staffs with specialists from marketing, finance, and production; by giving the managers a major influence in the development and allocation of resources; or by allowing the managers to control a large budget. For example, with budgetary responsibility, the manager of the integrating department would have the authority to approve budget allocations in the engineering department in the product development process.

Summary.   A summary of the various mechanisms or strategies for managing coordination is shown in exhibit 8–10. This table indicates that as the complexities associated with coordination requirements increase, the organization focuses on two responses: (1) increase in the number of employees involved in managing coordination; and (2) move from informal to more formal managerial involvement. The effectiveness of achieving a high level of performance depends not only on the choice of a management strategy but also on the commitment that the organization gives to the improvement of coordination relations. The choice of such mechanisms as teams and integrating departments may require a significant departure from the organization's management philosophy.

EXHIBIT 8–10
Strategies for
Managing
Coordination

STRATEGY	DESCRIPTION
1. Rules and procedures	The required activities and behaviors between interacting groups are spelled out in advance. Employees learn that when certain situations arise, a particular behavior set should be used. Rules are a limited strategy; they cannot specify all behaviors in advance.
2. Hierarchy	When rules and procedures prove inadequate as a coordination strategy, the emphasis switches to the use of the hierarchy, or common superior. This is a limited strategy in that the higher level manager's time may be totally devoted to resolving intergroup plans.
3. Planning	Goals and targets are set for group interaction. The effectiveness of the strategy is limited by the complexities of interaction and how precisely future interaction patterns can be detailed in advance.
4. Liaison roles	A specialized, generally informational role is created to transmit vital information and coordinate activities. Certain dysfunctions, such as job stress, may affect the behavior of the liaison person.
5. Task forces	Selected members of interacting groups are brought together to form a task force. Task forces generally coordinate intergroup activities for a specific period of time, and thus are temporary in nature. They are also limited to an advisory role, leaving the final decision making to higher level managers.
6. Teams	Similar to task forces, teams are more permanent and may be given certain decision-making authority.
7. Integrating departments	These provide the most formal strategies for managing intergroup performance. The department manager generally reports to the highest management level and may be given great decision-making authority, consisting of a large staff and budgetary responsibility.

ORGANIZATIONAL DIMENSIONS IN THE INTERNATIONAL REALM

As an organization develops international operations, its structure must adapt to accommodate these foreign activities effectively. The structure that emerges will depend on many factors, including the scope, location, and type of international facilities; the goals and strategies of the organization; the impact of foreign operations on total organizational performance; and the degree of international management experience and competence. The relationship between strategy and structure is discussed in the next chapter.

An organization that begins operating in more than one national market normally recognizes that this new activity often leads to problems that require changes in its internal structure. The international organization must learn how to cope with geographically dispersed operations, personnel from many different cultures, diverse political and social environments, and a high rate of change in the economy. Many managers have found that an organizational structure designed for purely domestic purposes is ineffective for international operations. To illustrate the dimensions of organizations in international activities, we will briefly point out differences in the grouping and influence dimensions.

International Grouping: Evolution of Structure

The evolution of the grouping dimension, particularly departmentalization, can be viewed as a series of stages, with each stage a modification or adaptation of the structure of the previous stage. The rate of passing through the stages varies from organization to organization—some proceed cautiously one step at a time, while others move quickly through the stages. At least three stages have been identified: exporting, international division, and integrated structure.[30]

In order to enter international markets, many organizations *export* products. Organizationally, this can be done by assigning export responsibility to an independent trading company, by establishing an internal export department, or by the organization setting up its own sales, service, and warehousing facilities abroad. In this first stage, the structure of the organization remains essentially unchanged.

The second stage of evolution involves the establishment of an *international division* within the organization's structure. Exhibit 8–11 is a simplified structure for Bendix; similar arrangements can be found in IBM, General Motors, and Coca-Cola. An international division, which is usually headed by a vice president who reports directly to the president, normally results from four factors: (1) the level of commitment to international operations has reached an absolute size and importance to justify a separate unit; (2) the complexity of international operations requires the centralization of activities; (3) the organization has recognized the need for a group of specialists who are skilled in handling the special requirements of international activities; and (4) there is a need to improve the organization's ability to identify and evaluate external opportunities and threats through scanning the global horizon rather than simply responding to situations as they develop.[31]

During the 1960s, and well into the 1970s, the international division approach was the most common form of structure in large U.S. organizations with foreign interests. However, in many organizations, the international division structure became quite cumbersome and problem ridden. For instance, the international division normally does not have its own product development, engineering, research and development, and other staff units. The domestic divisions controlling these important activities were frequently reluctant to give priority to overseas needs because they were usually measured solely by their domestic performance. More importantly, it was the recognition by top management that, to function effectively, the control over strategic planning and policy decisions must shift from the decentralized international division to the headquarters unit, where a worldwide perspective could be used.

The third stage of structural evolution in the international realm is termed the *integrated structure*. Besides the need for a global strategic approach, managers became aware of the gains to be realized from coordinating functions and from motivating personnel to perform in accordance with the international interests of the organization.

EXHIBIT 8–11
International Structure for Bendix

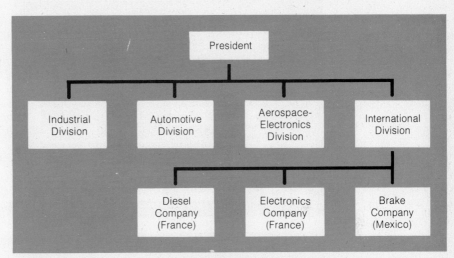

Source: Daniels/Ogram/Radebaugh, International Business, © 1979, 2nd ed., Addison-Wesley Publishing Company, Inc., Chapter 18, pp. 403, 404, figure 18.2, "Placement of International Activities Within the Organizational Structure." Reprinted with permission.

As shown in exhibit 8–12, at least three forms of grouping can be found in organizations adopting this structural approach: functional, geographic, and product. The functional structure (exhibit 8–12A) has the advantage of tight control over operations and uses only a relatively small group of executives to maintain line control over operations. On the other hand, the important functions of sales and production are separated, creating coordination problems. The geographic structure (exhibit 8–12B) is appropriate for organizations with a narrow range of products whose end use markets, technological base, and production methods tend to be similar. The major oil companies also prefer this structural form. The geographic structure permits the handling of market-to-market variations quite easily due to its decentralized approach. However, it requires a large number of internationally experienced managers to staff the regional operations and can prove to be quite inefficient when product lines become diverse.

EXHIBIT 8–12
Integrated
Structures in
International
Operations

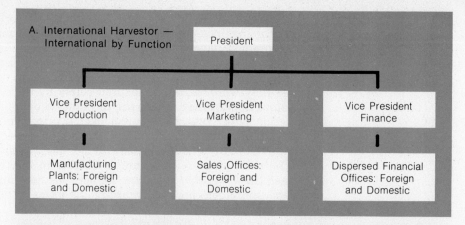

A. International Harvestor —
   International by Function

President

Vice President
Production

Vice President
Marketing

Vice President
Finance

Manufacturing
Plants: Foreign
and Domestic

Sales Offices:
Foreign and
Domestic

Dispersed Financial
Offices: Foreign
and Domestic

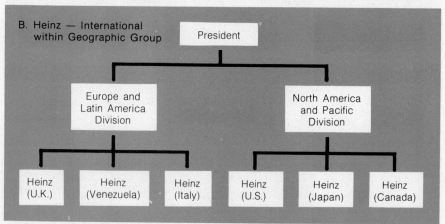

B. Heinz — International
   within Geographic Group

President

Europe and
Latin America
Division

North America
and Pacific
Division

Heinz
(U.K.)

Heinz
(Venezuela)

Heinz
(Italy)

Heinz
(U.S.)

Heinz
(Japan)

Heinz
(Canada)

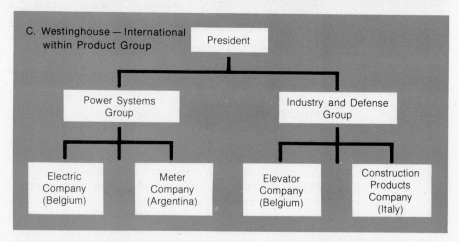

C. Westinghouse — International
   within Product Group

President

Power Systems
Group

Industry and Defense
Group

Electric
Company
(Belgium)

Meter
Company
(Argentina)

Elevator
Company
(Belgium)

Construction
Products
Company
(Italy)

Adapted from S. H. Robock, K. Simmonds, and J. Zwick, International Business and
Multinational Enterprises (Homewood, Ill.: Irwin, 1977), p. 436, © 1977 by Richard D. Irwin,
Inc.; and from Daniels/Ogram/Radebaugh, International Business, © 1979, 2nd ed.,
Addison-Wesley Publishing Company, Inc., Chapter 18, pp. 403, 404, figure 18.2,
"Placement of International Activities Within the Organizational Structure." Reprinted with
permission.

Finally, the product international structure (exhibit 8–12C) is best when an organization's product line is widely dispersed, when products go into a variety of end use markets, and when a high technological capability is required. Problems arise with this structure when managers are too narrowly trained in product responsibilities and when coordination is needed between the product divisions.

Some interesting variations are found when foreign organizations also attempt to go international. For example, many Japanese firms export through large trading companies that have grown to be quite powerful in international trade. In addition, some European organizations, because of their fast growth and diverse product lines, have bypassed the international division approach and have gone directly to the integrated structure from exporting.[32]

International Influence: Decentralization

As the international nature of management gains in importance, so does the concern by managers over the applicability of managerial concepts and the integration of these concepts with the dominant culture of the country. This is especially important for the centralization/decentralization issue.

Consider, for example, the differences among the U. S., Sweden, and Great Britain.[33] In the U. S., many decisions on decentralization are determined for the most part by the six factors previously discussed. In other words, it is a concept that is dictated by the needs of the particular situation. To the Swedes, decentralization of decision making, or participation, implies a classless cooperation between workers and management. This form of decision making is a basic and fundamental belief of the Swedish culture that is universally and passionately held. In other words, decentralization is an assumed concept in Sweden. On the other hand, the British look at decentralization as another arena for a class struggle. The British system is based on the adversary roles of bargaining for power, not in the cooperative roles of decentralization in decision making. The "them versus us" philosophy is as strong between levels in the organization as it is in education (elitist or democratic) or housing (public or private). In other words, decentralization occurs as a result of a group gaining power, rather than the problem at hand.

Though Sweden, Great Britain, and the U. S. differ significantly in their views and the degree of decentralization of decision making, these cultures are beginning to experience a growing demand from lower level managers and workers alike for more involvement in decisions. This is an important trend for managers to recognize. If managers understand these conditions and recognize the visible trends, they should be able to respond more effectively and decentralize appropriately.

ORGANIZATIONAL DIMENSIONS, PERFORMANCE, AND THE MANAGER'S JOB

The grouping, influence, and coordination dimensions of the organizing function are probably the most visible factors of the managerial process. These components help in determining the nature of jobs, how much authority and responsibility managers have, to whom they report and who reports to them, and what managers must do to obtain coordinated effort. Beyond these important dimensions, there are additional factors related to organizational structure that affect the manager's job.

Keys to Success with Organizational Dimensions

1. **Designing an organizational structure goes beyond developing an organization chart.**

   An organization chart, as shown in exhibits 8–2 to 8–4, is a schematic representation that shows only selected organizational dimensions such as departmentalization, span of control, and chain of command. Many managers, however, assume that the chart depicts all the necessary information related to the design of the organization's structure. This is false. Such important dimensions as decentralization, authority patterns, and coordination needs, and the exact nature of the manager's job cannot be displayed in such manner. The manager (or future manager) should not be lulled into acccepting the organization chart for more than it is.

2. **Organizational dimensions offer suggestions, not accepted laws or facts.**

   The discussions related to the grouping, influence, and coordination dimensions of organizational design do not offer the "one best way" to organize. Rather, they should be interpreted as suggestions to managers regarding what should be considered in the organizing function. For example, there is no such thing as the "optimum" span of control for a manager or the best way of coordinating the work of three departments in an organization. The manager must carefully diagnose the situation before choosing the appropriate degree of decentralization. Guidelines are available, but hard and fast laws and facts are not.

3. **An organization's structure should be adaptable to change, not rigid.**

   The key to success of an organization's structure is not only how effectively it organizes the work of the organization currently, but how it can adapt or be adapted to changing conditions. The organization's structure should not be assumed to be able to handle all situations that can occur. For example, situations can develop that may make the concept of decentralization less effective than one of centralization, or a wide span of control may not prove as effective as a much narrower span. The important key here is that the organization's structural dimensions are not set in concrete but must be flexible with changing conditions. An interesting fact for managers to consider is that most large organizations go through major structural changes every three to five years. This is because the conditions occurring at the time of initial development may have changed during the period.

4. **Don't automatically assume that what works in the U. S. will also work in the organization's foreign operations.**

   Many organizations have learned the hard way that certain U. S. concepts of organizing are not readily accepted in foreign countries. Cultural differences and other societal issues are important for the manager to consider in designing an organizational structure for a foreign operation. Differences exist in such aspects as the employees' readiness to accept authority, degree of decentralization, and acceptance of coordination mechanisms among foreign nationals and managers.

5. **The larger and more complex the organization, the more diversified its structure will be.**

As we have suggested throughout this discussion, a particular organizing concept may not be accepted through the entire organization. For example, marketing managers may have large spans of control, while manufacturing managers may have narrow spans of control. In applying the various organizational dimensions, managers must recognize that differences exist among the major functions which will necessitate equally different structural dimensions.

Organizational Dimensions and the Manager's Job

In our framework, organizing is a crucial managerial *function* in defining the manager's job. It is an important link between the planning process and the leading function. In our discussion of the planning process (see exhibit 6–1), organizing represents one of the elements of stage IV, the implementation of plans. In addition, the influence dimension (chain of command, span of control, and centralization/decentralization) establishes the foundations for managers to perform in their leadership position.

The development of managerial *skills* is also closely related to the organizing function. For example, the job specialization process is a significant factor in determining the nature and requirements of the jobs of individual employees—in other words, job specialization influences the development of technical skills. Employee reactions to the various organizing components demand that managers be cognizant of the quality of their human skills.

A manager's conceptual skills are tested throughout the entire organizing process. For example, in identifying the needs for departmentalization, the manager must be aware of what units or groups need to be placed together within a single authority structure. Similarly, the integrating activity, which is such an important part of conceptual skills, applies when coordination requirements are analyzed. Finally, a manager's diagnostic skills are important especially in recognizing when an organization's structure needs to be changed and what are the elements that may require the change.

The organizing function is one of the primary determinants of the manager's roles. Interpersonal roles, such as the figurehead and leader, are established by the chain of command, span of control, and the centralization concept (influence component). Informational roles and the liaison interpersonal role are created in part by the coordination dimension. Finally, a manager's decisional roles are developed by the interaction of the aggregation and influence dimensions.

SUMMARY FOR THE MANAGER

1. Analyzing the external and internal environments, establishing goals, and developing extensive organizational plans may turn out to be a futile exercise unless the manager gives a great deal of attention to the organizing function. In other words, goals and plans do not implement themselves—what is needed is some formal framework that permits the organization to use its resources effectively and efficiently. We call this framework the organization's structure.

2. Three basic dimensions make up the organization's structure: grouping; influence; and coordination. The important factor for managers to identify about organizational dimensions is that they represent a sequential process. That is, the first concern is with clustering or grouping jobs (grouping), followed by establishing authority and responsibility patterns within the newly formed units (influence), and finally by focusing on integrating the various units into a unified effort to achieve the organization's stated goals (coordination).

3. The grouping component consists of three aspects: job specialization; departmentalization; and line-staff relations. Job specialization, which involves grouping various jobs into units, can contribute significantly to effectiveness or be a big problem area. The key factor is the degree of specialization that is employed and the way workers react to this specialization. The manager must recognize that, on one hand, specialization provides the necessary mechanism for the development of skills and job expertise, and, on the other hand, too much specialization may create jobs that are quite routine, boring, and mundane, resulting in adverse employee reactions.

4. Departmentalization, the second grouping factor, involves grouping departments into such arrangements as functional, product, geographical, or mixed designs. The selection of one of these designs is based on a number of criteria; two of the most important are costs and adaptiveness. Whichever of these two criteria are salient will determine the choice of the particular design. Functional is best for control of costs; the product form is much more adaptive to changing conditions.

5. The influence component consists of assigning or recognizing authority, power, and responsibility relationships within the newly formed structure. The main concept, authority, has its origins in the legitimacy placed on the job by the organization, the degree of acceptance by subordinates, and the important unity of command factor. Authority is implemented in organizations with the use of the chain of command, span of control, and the principles of centralization/decentralization.

6. The centralization/decentralization decision is one of the most important that a manager will make because it involves giving important authority to certain subordinate managers to make decisions that only higher level managers have made previously. Such factors as the external environment, the size of the organization, the costs and risks, basic managerial philosophies, the locus of expertise, and the availability of competent managers all go into making a decentralization decision.

7. With the growing importance of international management, managers should be aware that various cultures around the world will adapt quite differently to decentralization attempts. That is, in some countries, such as Sweden, decentralization is a way of life, while in Great Britain attempts at decentralization may meet with great resistance.

8. Coordinating the units and departments of an organization is an extremely important but massive and costly managerial activity. The need for coordination is founded on three factors: the degree of interdependence and the differences in time and goal orientation between interacting units. As the degree of interdependence and the differences in time and goal orientation become more severe, the need for coordination also increases.

9. Depending on the degree of coordination that is needed, a number of mechanisms are available to managers. From the most basic mechanism, rules and procedures, to the most complex, integrating departments, these mechanisms vary in terms of the degree of managerial commitment that is required and the amount of organizational resources that must be used.

10. In terms of the manager's job, the organizing function acts as one of the major sources of development for the needed skills and roles performed by the manager. For example, the grouping factor has a significant impact on the nature and development of technical and human skills. The influence component relates strongly to developing conceptual skills, and the coordination component is a determinant of diagnostic skills. In a similar manner, the various interpersonal, informational, and decisional roles are affected by how the organization is structured.

QUESTIONS FOR REVIEW AND DISCUSSION

1. What is the purpose of the organizing function?
2. How are goals, planning and organizing related?
3. What are the sequential steps that are followed in developing an organizational structure?
4. What is the difference between organizational structure and an organizational chart?
5. What are some of the problems that a manager should look for if an organization's structure is not working effectively?
6. What is the difference between authority and responsibility?
7. What are the positive and negative features associated with performing in a liaison position?
8. What is the relationship between span of control and coordination?
9. Discuss the relationship between decentralization and the development of managerial skills.
10. Discuss the differences between functional and product departmentalization.

NOTES

1. H. Fayol, *General and Industrial Management,* trans. J. A. Conbrough (Geneva: International Management Institute, 1929); and L. Gulick and L. Urwick, *Papers on the Science of Administration* (New York: Institute of Public Administration, 1937).

2. J. L. Pierce and R. B. Dunham, "Task Design: A Literature Review," *Academy of Management Review* (October 1976): 83–97.

3. See D. McGregor, *The Human Side of Enterprise* (New York: McGraw-Hill 1960); A. Turner and P. Lawrence, *Industrial Jobs and the Worker* (Boston: Harvard University Press, 1965); and *Work in America: Report of a Special Task Force to the Secretary of H.E.W.* (Cambridge, Mass.: MIT Press, 1973).

4. R. T. Gill, *Economics,* 3rd ed. (Santa Monica, Calif.: Goodyear, 1978), pp. 111–18.

5. See G. G. Fisch, "Line-Staff is Obsolete," *Harvard Business Review* (September–October 1961): 67–79; and L. A. Allen, "The Line-Staff Relationship," *Management Record* (September 1955): 346–49.

6. H. A. Simon, *Administrative Behavior* (New York: Macmillan, 1961), pp. 133–34.

7. D. C. McClelland, *Power* (New York: Wiley, 1975).

8. J. R. P. French and B. Raven, "The Bases of Social Power," in *Studies in Social Power,* ed., Dorwin Cartwright, (Ann Arbor, Mich.: University of Michigan, 1959), pp. 150–67.

9. C. I. Barnard, *The Functions of the Executive* (Boston: Harvard University Press, 1938), pp. 165–66.

10. H. Stieglitz, "Optimizing the Span of Control," *Management Record* (September 1962): 25–29; and D. Van Fleet and A. G. Bedeian, "A History of the Span of Management," *Academy of Management Review* (July 1977): 356–72.

11. L. F. Urwick, *The Elements of Administration* (New York: Harper & Brothers, 1943), p. 46.

12. Fayol, p. 36.

13. Sir I. Hamilton, *The Soul and Body of an Army* (London: Arnold and Co., 1921), p. 229.

14. A. V. Graicunas, "Relationships in Organization," in *Papers on the Science of Administration,* ed. Gulick and Urwick, pp. 183–87.

15. Stieglitz, p. 28.

16. Ibid., p. 29.

17. R. Carzo, Jr., and J. N. Yanouzas, "Effects of Flat and Tall Organization Structure," *Administrative Science Quarterly* (June 1969): 178–91.

18. See E. Dale, *Organization* (New York: American Management Association, 1967).

19. W. D. Wooldredge, "Fast Track Programs for MBA's: Do They Really Work?" *Management Review* (April 1979): 8–12.

20. See A. D. Szilagyi and M. Wallace, *Organizational Behavior and Performance,* 2d ed. (Santa Monica, Calif.:

Goodyear, 1980), p. 237.

21. J. D. Thompson, *Organizations in Action* (New York: McGraw-Hill, 1967), pp. 54–55.

22. P. R. Lawrence and J. W. Lorsch, *Organization and Environment* (Homewood, Ill.: Irwin, 1967), pp. 34–39.

23. Ibid., p. 40.

24. J. G. March and H. A. Simon, *Organizations* (New York: Wiley, 1958), p. 44.

25. M. Weber, "The Theory of Social and Economic Organization," trans. A. M. Henderson and T. Parsons (New York: Oxford University Press, 1947).

26. J. W. Galbraith, *Designing Complex Organizations* (Reading, Mass.: Addison-Wesley, 1973), p. 12.

27. R. L. Kahn et al., *Organizational Stress: Studies in Role Conflict and Ambiguity* (New York: Wiley, 1964), p. 101.

28. R. T. Keller and W. E. Holland, "Boundary Spanning Activity and Research and Development Management," *IEEE Transactions on Engineering Management* (November 1975): 130–33.

29. Galbraith, p. 80.

30. S. H. Robock, K. Simmonds, and J. Zwick, *International Business and Multinational Enterprises* (Homewood, Ill.: Irwin, 1977), p. 428.

31. H. Schollhammer, "Organizational Structures of Multinational Corporations," *Academy of Management Journal* (September 1971): 345–65.

32. Robock, Simmonds, and Zwick, p. 426.

33. N. Foy and H. Gadon, "Worker Participation: Contrasts in Three Countries," *Harvard Business Review* (May–June 1976): 71–83.

ADDITIONAL REFERENCES

Etzioni, A. A. *Comparative Analysis of Complex Organizations.* Glencoe, Ill.: Free Press, 1961.

Filley, A. C., House, R. J.; and Kerr, S. *Managerial Process and Organizational Behavior.* 2nd ed. Glenview, Ill.: Scott, Foresman, 1976.

Frank, H. E. *Organizational Structuring.* New York: McGraw-Hill, 1971.

Galbraith, J. W. *Organization Design.* Reading, Mass.: Addison-Wesley, 1977.

Hall, R. H. *Organizations: Structure and Process.* Englewood Cliffs, N.J.: Prentice-Hall, 1977.

Kline, B. E., and Martin, N. H. "Freedom, Authority, and Decentralization." *Harvard Business Review* (May–June 1958): 69–75.

Litterer, J. A. *The Analysis of Organizations.* New York: Wiley, 1965.

Perrow, C. *Complex Organizations.* 2d ed. Glenview, Ill.: Scott, Foresman, 1979.

Walker, A. H., and Lorsch, J. W. "Organizational Choice: Product vs. Function." *Harvard Business Review* (November–December 1968): 129–38.

Widing, J. W. "Reorganizing Your World Business." *Harvard Business Review* (May–June 1973): 153–61.

A CASE FOR ANALYSIS

The Exeter Pharmaceutical Company.

The Exeter Pharmaceutical Company, headquartered in Switzerland, was one of the world's largest pharmaceutical organizations. The company had five major research laboratories that were located in Switzerland, the United States, France, Ireland, and Japan.

The lab in Switzerland, dating back to the early 1920s, was a general purpose facility that developed to further the knowledge that was gained from World War I. The U.S. facility was much smaller with specializations in penicillin chemistry. The largest facility was located in France where the massive scientific and technical effort in antibiotics was centralized. The Irish lab, created in 1954, specialized in agricultural and veterinary drugs. The decision to locate in Ireland was a result of the company taking advantage of the favorable Irish tax laws when locating a major new facility.

Since the techniques used in the lab were mostly new, there was a need for a large group of technical personnel.

During the late 1960s, the company attempted physically to centralize some of the labs in Switzerland. The Irish government resisted moving the facility to Switzerland (or France) because it did not want well-trained Irish scientists emigrating out of the country. In addition, many French scientists objected to the effort by the company to move them to the Swiss lab. The Swiss lab was located in an industrial area of Zurich; the French lab was situated in a rather scenic section on the fringe of Paris.

In terms of profitable new products, the Japanese lab was the fastest growing. Beginning as a small lab specializing in tropical diseases, the scientists at the facility began using their newly acquired technology in many other areas. Because of the tremendous physical separation between the headquarters unit and the Japanese lab, interactions and communications with other scientists were infrequent.

In 1978, the management of Exeter renewed their concern over the operations of the five laboratories. Growing competition coupled with rapidly increasing developmental costs made management aware that a change in the structure of the labs was needed. After a three month study, a special task force reported to the president of Exeter that there was a lack of coordination between the different facilities resulting in a massive and costly duplication of effort. In addition, not only was important and promising research not being done at all because each lab thought the other one was doing it, but no one in any of the five labs really knew where to go to find help, to get advice, or to talk over scientific matters of common interest.

In response to these pressures, the company president hired as director of research, Dr. Henry Malond, a Dutch-born, American-educated biochemist who had recently headed the main laboratory of a U.S. based pharmaceutical firm. Prior to Dr. Malond's appointment, Exeter had no full-time director of research. Instead, the director of the Swiss lab was expected to "coordinate" the research of the other labs along with the duties of the Zurich facility.

Dr. Malond, who would maintain offices in Switzerland, was charged by the company's president to *manage* Exeter's total research effort in any way he believed to be the most effective. As a visible means of authority, Dr. Malond was given control of the budgets of all the research labs.

Questions for Discussion

1. What organizational dimensions (i.e., grouping, influence, and coordination) are important for Dr. Malond to consider?
2. What are the structural alternatives open to consideration for Dr. Malond? What are the positive and negative features of each alternative?
3. What are the elements of coordination that should be considered by Dr. Malond?
4. What are the effects of a multi-cultural, multi-lingual, and multi-disciplinary situation?

9

Organizational Design

CHAPTER OUTLINE

KEY POINTS IN THIS CHAPTER

1. Three approaches have developed to study the organizational design process: classical; behavioral; and contingency.

2. The classical approach, most closely aligned with the bureaucratic model, offers the "one best way" to organize. It has been successful, however, only in specific environments.

3. The behavioral approach stresses participation, decentralization, and communications as its main components.

4. The contingency approach is based on the interaction of the environment, strategy, and technology as determinants of the most effective structure.

5. The studies of the environment have shown that stable environments are best for the mechanistic or functional structures, and dynamic environments are appropriate for the product-type structure.

6. The historical analysis of organizations has shown that organizations not only follow a similar strategic development process, but that structure follows strategy.

7. Technology is both a determinant and a constraining factor in the choice of a structure.

THE PRACTICE OF MANAGEMENT

Project Centers at General Motors

With giant corporations as with giant oil tankers, bigness confers advantages, but the ability to turn around easily is not one of them. Though General Motors does some things very well, one doesn't expect it to be nimble. In so huge an organization, decision-making processes are inherently complex, and sheer mass generates a great deal of inertia. The energy crisis, internal labor problems, and a slowly declining market share, however, forced G.M. into a mode that necessitated quick reaction. Though the company seemed ill prepared for change, it not only met the challenge but did so with success that surprised many observers of the auto industry.

While downsizing of its cars was the hallmark of this change, it was the organization behind the downsized "X" cars that created this achievement. Revolving around a project center concept, the new organizational design for engineering management was devised to coordinate the efforts of the five automobile divisions. A G.M. project center, made up of engineers lent by the divisions, has no exact counterpart elsewhere in the auto industry, much less other U.S. industries. The idea was used successfully by NASA for the space program before it found its way to the Delco Electronics Division, and then on to the entire company. Alfred Sloan himself would have appreciated the concept, for it is right in line with the coordinated decentralization approach to management.

G.M. adopted the project center idea in order to meet the special demands created by the sizing decision. Coordinating the development of a new body line among the various divisions is a complex undertaking even in normal times. To do what it wanted, the company would have to engineer its cars in a new way, using new design techniques and technologies, during a time when the margins for error would be especially tight.

The project center is not a permanent group. Every time a major new effort is planned—a body changeover, for example—a project center is formed. The X-body center also worked on its front wheel drive compacts. All project centers report to a board composed of the chief engineers of the auto divisions.

Project centers work on parts and engineering problems common to all divisions, such as frames, electrical systems, steering gear, and brakes. The project center augments, but does not replace, G.M.'s traditional "lead division" concept, in which one division is assigned primary responsibility for bringing some innovation into production.

The project center was probably G.M.'s single most important managerial tool in carrying out the bold decision to downsize. It has eliminated a great deal of redundant effort, and has speeded numerous new technologies into production. Its success, however, rests on the same delicate balance between the powers of persuasion and authority that underlies G.M.'s basic system of coordinated decentralization. Indeed, many of the company's engineers feel the project center innovation has helped enhance the division's individuality, by freeing some of them to work on divisional projects.

More fundamentally, G.M.'s entire approach to its business has changed. The company's downsizing plan and project center organizational structure were the first examples of a new strategic approach to the marketplace. It was shaped by a far better understanding of its external environment and the necessity to adapt the organization and its strategies to rapid change.

Adapted from C. G. Burck, "How G.M. Turned Itself Around," Fortune (January 16, 1978): 87–100.

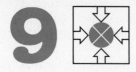

9

In the previous chapter, we began our discussion of the organizing function by identifying three major structural dimensions of organizations: grouping, influence, and the coordination dimensions. The focus was on the response to the questions of how to group jobs and units, how to establish authority within the units, and what mechanisms are available to ensure coordination between units.

In this chapter, our attention is directed to a discussion of the *process* of developing a structure for the organization—what is called *organizational design*. In other words, what are the important internal organizational and external environmental factors that will determine the level of job specialization, type of departmentalization, span of control, decentralization, and the choice of coordination mechanisms?

The chapter is divided into three major sections. First, we will review a number of studies that constitute the three main organizational design approaches: classical, behavioral, and contingency approaches. Second, we will attempt to integrate the three approaches into a discussion of the contemporary strategies for designing organizations. Finally, the relationship between organizational design, performance, and the manager's job will be presented.

CLASSICAL APPROACH TO ORGANIZATIONAL DESIGN

There have been a number of theoretical perspectives that have emerged over the years that can be classified as belonging to the classical approach. Among these, for example, is the work of Taylor and his scientific management.[1] However, the most dominant organizational design perspective in this approach is one that we hear the most about, but probably understand the least—*bureaucracy*.

Characteristics of an Ideal Bureaucracy

The bureaucratic approach to organizational design was conceptualized by a German sociologist, Max Weber, in the early part of this century.[2] Like Taylor, Weber believed that the key to the survival of an organization was through mechanisms that increased the *efficiency* of the organization's activities. The Weberian model can be considered a rigid approach, since it was proposed to be superior to any other form of organization structure. In other words Weber promotes the "one best way" to organize for all types of organizations.

The Weberian model is based on a number of important characteristics. Among these characteristics are the following:[3]

1. *Division of labor.* All tasks necessary to accomplish organizational goals must be divided into highly specialized jobs. A worker needs to master his or her trade, and this expertise can be more readily achieved by concentrating on a limited number of tasks. This is an example of the

important *grouping* dimension of organizational structure. What Weber proposed were jobs that were highly specialized. With high specialization, the worker can easily master the necessary activities and skills, becoming an expert in one area.

2. *Rules and procedures*. Each task is performed according to a "consistent system of abstract rules." This practice allows the manager to eliminate uncertainty due to individual differences in job performance. As discussed under the classification of the *coordination* dimension, the use of rules and procedures helps provide the order needed to achieve the organization's goals. Rules and procedures in a bureaucracy have sometimes been called "red tape," which is what may seem to be excessive use of forms, policies, systems, and so on.

3. *Authority*. Offices or positions must be organized into a hierarchial structure in which the scope of authority of managers over subordinates is well defined. This system, which we termed the *influence* dimension, insures that the organization is provided mechanisms to establish and hold some form of order.

4. *Impersonality*. Superiors must assume an impersonal attitude in dealing with each other and with subordinates. This psychological and social distance will enable the superior to make decisions without being influenced by prejudices and preferences. The thrust of this belief is that everyone in the organization, managers and nonmanagers alike, would be subject to the same rules and that all employees were to be evaluated on the basis of expertise and performance, not personality or emotional considerations.

5. *Careers*. Employment in a bureaucracy must be based on qualifications. In addition, promotion is to be decided on performance (i.e., merit). Because of this careful and firm system of employment and promotion, it is assumed that employment will involve a lifelong career and loyalty from workers. In other words, job security, incremental salaries, and retirement benefits were guaranteed so long as the employee was qualified and performed at acceptable levels. In government, this has evolved into the civil service system.

These characteristics of an "ideal" bureaucracy established a major organizational movement that even today is felt by many people. The idea that effectiveness as an organization could be achieved by an emphasis on efficiency, stability, and control is a very attractive concept to managers.

Issues with the Bureaucratic Model

Strict adherence to these characteristics was assumed by Weber to be the "one best way" to organize to achieve organizational goals. The benefits associated with implementing a structure that emphasized efficiency, stability, and control offered many organizations an opportunity to become more effective. As history has shown, the bureaucratic structure became the most widely adopted and successful form of structuring an organization that had yet been devised. Few alternatives, however, existed at that time.

As one may have suspected, some of the "ideal" characteristics of bureaucracy have undergone a transition over time and are now considered drawbacks. As shown in exhibit 9–1, a number of negative effects have developed from utilizing a bureaucratic approach in designing an organization's structure.[4] Some of these negative effects are as follows:

EXHIBIT 9–1
Characteristics,
Benefits, and
Problems of
Bureaucracy

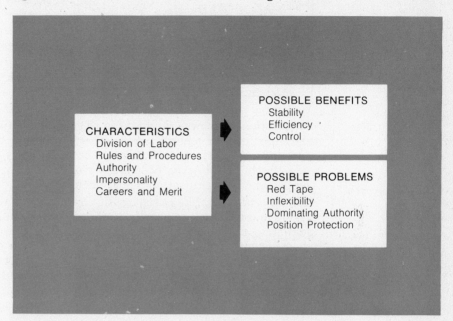

CHARACTERISTICS
Division of Labor
Rules and Procedures
Authority
Impersonality
Careers and Merit

POSSIBLE BENEFITS
Stability
Efficiency
Control

POSSIBLE PROBLEMS
Red Tape
Inflexibility
Dominating Authority
Position Protection

1. *Excessive red tape.* The use of formal rules and procedures was adopted in order to help remove the uncertainty in attempting to coordinate a variety of activities in an organization. In a bureaucracy, two negative effects can be seen with the use of rules. First, as we discussed in the last chapter, the use of rules and procedures is only a limited strategy in trying to achieve coordinated actions. Other strategies may be required, but bureaucracy's approach is to *add* more rules to try to cover all contingencies. This has resulted in the frequently heard cry of "too much red tape." Second, once established, it is very difficult in a bureaucracy to eliminate ineffectual rules or procedures. This results in more confusion, frustration, and a reduced level of motivation to perform.

2. *Inflexibility.* A careful examination of Weber's works reveals an almost total absence of the use of the word "environment." As we have stressed throughout this book, to be effective, managers and organizations must be flexible and adaptable to the changing environment. The mounting number of organizational experiences with a bureaucratic structure have shown that the "one best way" is not really best when faced with a rapidly changing external and internal environment.

3. *Dominance of authority.* The authority factor is one of the most powerful characteristics of the bureaucratic model. It is so strong and dominant that many managers are reluctant to give up some of this authority—for example, by decentralization—when the situation warrants. The end result is less effective decision making. Another form of the dominance of authority in a bureaucracy is an attempt by a manager to acquire as

much authority, power, and status as possible. This "empire building" takes the form of adding unneeded subordinates, acquiring excessive space (e.g., office space), requiring to be in on every important decision, and so forth. The objective of such motives is the preservation of authority and power, not organizational goal achievement.

4. *Position protection.* The bureaucratic characteristic that stresses lifelong careers and evaluations based on merit is one of those factors that is an ideal state but rarely found in actual practice. In some bureaucracies, advancement in jobs and salary is more a function of such variables as seniority and position than actual skill and performance. The idea of having the most competent people in the positions is not fully realized. Loyalty is obtained, but this loyalty is toward the protection of one's job and rank, not to the effectiveness of the organization.

Many of these negative effects have led to what some have called "bureaucratic blunders." For example:

A governor of a southern state a few years ago nominated to a state job a man who had been dead for two years.

One large drug company spends over $20 million a year filling out 27,000 government forms, thus adding nearly $1 to the price of each prescription.

The Food and Drug Administration took eleven years to decide how many peanuts should be required in peanut butter.

Former Secretary of HEW (now split into two cabinet positions, Health and Human Resources and Education), Joseph Califano, issued a 402-word job description for a chef to staff HEW's executive dining room and never once mentioned cooking skills.

Due to the foresight of the Board of Education of financially strapped New York City, at the current rate of consumption the city's schools have enough rubber softballs in warehouses to last students 23 years, enough magnets on hand for 32 years, and wooden beads sufficient to outfit kindergartens until the year 2626.[5]

Ideally, bureaucracy offered a number of features that were of great value to organizations in their formative stages. Many changes, however, have been made to the bureaucratic model that have significantly altered the purposes designed by Weber. Bureaucracy is not dead or unsuitable for use in the design of an organization's structure. As we will discuss later in this chapter, the bureaucratic model works well in situations where the emphasis on stable, routine tasks matches its stable external environment.

BEHAVIORAL APPROACH TO ORGANIZATIONAL DESIGN

The dissatisfaction with the classical design approaches led to the development of the behavioral approach to organizational design (see chapter 3). The Hawthorne research, and the more recent findings by researchers such as Rensis Likert, have offered significant modifications to the classical approach. These modifications are more scientifically based rather than derived from the personal experiences of the classicists. The work of Likert and Warren G. Bennis will be used to highlight the behavioral approach.

Likert's System 4

Likert's research led him to propose that effective organizations differ markedly from ineffective organizations along a number of important structural properties.[6] It is Likert's position that an effective organization is one that encourages managers to focus their attention on building effective work groups with challenging performance goals. In contrast, less effective organizations encourage managers to:

1. Introduce a high degree of job specialization.
2. Hire people with the skills and aptitudes to perform specialized job tasks.
3. Train these employees to do their jobs in the best and most efficient manner.
4. Closely supervise the performance of these jobs specialists.
5. Where feasible, use incentives in the form of individual or group piece rates.[7]

These five points are associated with the core features of the bureaucratic design. By examining organizations with such tendencies, Likert concluded that a more behaviorally or people-oriented design that encourages groups to work together is more effective. He describes this more effective, people-oriented organization in terms of eight dimensions and calls it a System 4 organization. The classical design is designated as System 1. Likert believes that System 1 organizations are ineffective because they cannot respond or cope with changes in their environments. Environmental changes naturally create pressures for change and to react to them, the organizational design needs to be more flexible. The System 4 and System 1 dimensions described by Likert are compared in exhibit 9–2.

The System 4 organization contains the features required to cope with changing environments, according to Likert. Communication flows freely, and this process is required to reach decisions, exercise control, and lend emphasis. Likert, like Weber with his ideal bureaucracy, assumes that there is a "one best way" organizational design. In Weber's case, it was the bureaucracy; in Likert's, it is System 4. It should be noted that it was not only the classicists who offered the "best way" but also behavioralists such as Likert.

EXHIBIT 9–2 Classical Design and System 4 Organization

CLASSICAL DESIGN ORGANIZATION	SYSTEM 4 ORGANIZATION
1. *Leadership process* includes no perceived confidence and trust. Subordinates do not feel free to discuss job problems with their superiors, who in turn do not solicit their ideas and opinions.	1. *Leadership process* includes perceived confidence and trust between superiors and subordinates in all matters. Subordinates feel free to discuss job problems with their superiors, who in turn solicit their ideas and opinions.
2. *Motivational process* taps only physical, security, and economic motives through the use of fear and sanctions. Unfavorable attitudes toward the organization prevail among employees.	2. *Motivational process* taps a full range of motives through participatory methods. Attitudes are favorable toward the organization and its goals.
3. *Communication process* is such that information flows downward and tends to be distorted, inaccurate, and viewed with suspicion by subordinates.	3. *Communication process* is such that information flows freely throughout the organization—upward, downward, and laterally. The information is accurate and undistorted.
4. *Interaction process* is closed and restricted; subordinates have little effect on departmental goals, methods, and activities.	4. *Interaction process* is open and extensive; both superiors and subordinates are able to affect departmental goals, methods, and activities.
5. *Decision process* occurs only at the top of the organization; it is relatively centralized.	5. *Decision process* occurs at all levels through group processes; it is relatively decentralized.
6. *Goal-setting process,* located at the top of the organization, discourages group participation.	6. *Goal-setting process* encourages group participation in setting high, realistic objectives.
7. *Control process* is centralized and emphasizes fixing of blame for mistakes.	7. *Control process* is dispersed throughout the organization and emphasizes self-control and problem solving.
8. *Performance goals* are low and passively sought by managers who make no commitment to developing the human resources of the organization.	8. *Performance goals* are high and actively sought by superiors, who recognize the necessity for making a full commitment to developing, through training, the human resources of the organization.

Source: Adapted from Rensis Likert, *The Human Organization* (New York: McGraw-Hill Book Co., 1967), pp. 197–211.

Bennis: A Behavioral Prescription

Bennis, like some of the classical organizational theorists, has forecast the demise of bureaucracy.[8] He assumes that bureaucracy will wither and become less prevalent in organizations because managers will be unable to manage the tension, frustration, and conflict between individual and organizational goals. In addition, bureaucracy will fade because of the scientific and technological revolution in industrialized nations. The revolutionary changes require adaptability to the environment, and bureaucracies have experienced difficulty doing this.

Based on experience, but no empirical foundation, Bennis outlines organizational life into the 1990s.

1. The environment will show rapid technological change with a large degree of instability or turbulence.
2. Because of their better education, people in jobs will want more involvement, participation, and autonomy in their work.
3. The tasks of organizations will be more technical, complicated, and nonprogrammed. There will be a need to group specialists together in a project design arrangement.
4. Organizational structures will be more temporary and adaptive. These adaptive organizational structures will gradually replace bureaucracy as described by the classicists.

As we have shown, the classical design approach sought to solve the problems of efficiency by emphasizing vertical, or top down, functional structure by relying on the hierarchical power of managers. Likert and Bennis, on the other hand, elevate the individual and groups to a status of prominence in design decisions. Both approaches, classical and behavioral, are "one best way" recommendations that do not consider enough of the complexities of organizational design. They are simplistic in that they are either/or choices. Organizational design decisions are anything but simple today. Consequently, it has been necessary to consider contingency design strategies.

CONTINGENCY APPROACH TO ORGANIZATIONAL DESIGN

The experiences of managers functioning in complex organizations have led to their seriously questioning the universal "one best way" proposals of the classical and behavioral approaches to organizational design. In most cases, they are rather simplistic in that they exclude many of the important variables that affect a manager's decision to structure the organization. In response, what has emerged in the literature and in practice is what is referred to as a *contingency* approach. It seems more reasonable to discuss approaches because no one model has been adopted as the final answer to design problems.

Definition and Importance of the Contingency Approach

Using the theories and research of classical and behavioral scholars enables one to offer a broad definition of the *contingency approach* to organizational design:

> A contingency approach attempts to understand the interrelationships within and among organizational units as well as between the organization and its environment. It emphasizes the complex nature of organizations and attempts to interpret and understand how they operate under varying conditions and in specific situations. The approach strives to aid managers by suggesting organizational design strategies which have the highest probability of succeeding in a specific situation. The success criteria revolve around the accomplishment of organizational goals.[9]

The contingency approach to organizational design appeals to practicing managers for a number of reasons. First, the contingency approach *supports no one particular design;* it encourages searching through the many variables that are important and selecting a design decision for the organization that is appropriate for a given period of time and in the existing environment.

Second, the contingency approach, although empirically based, incorporates personal opinions about the situation facing an organization. It encourages the use of different models, systems, scientific management, classical organization theory, bureaucracy and/or System 4, if they properly fit the situation. This openness and willingness to use what fits best is realistic if one considers the dynamic nature of organizations and their environments.

Finally, the contingency approach clearly points out that various departments of a single organization may require different organizational designs to accomplish goals. Thus, the same organization may have multiple designs as opposed to a strictly bureaucratic or System 4 structure. The exact designs used by an organization's departments are based on the situational mix of variables affecting their goal progress and achievement.

Contingency Factors in Organizational Design

As shown in exhibit 9–3, we have identified three major contingency factors that can influence the structure of an organization. Note that the central figure in the exhibit is a reproduction of exhibit 8–1. In other words, contingency factors will affect the grouping, influence, and coordination dimensions of an organization's structure.

The major contingency factors include the organization's external environment, strategies, and the internal technology used by the organization. In the following sections we will discuss the impact of these factors on organizational design.

EXHIBIT 9–3
Contingency
Factors in
Organizational
Design

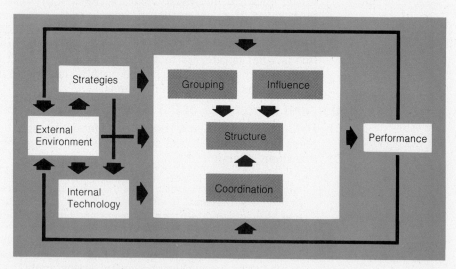

EXTERNAL ENVIRONMENT AND STRUCTURE

One of the most important influences on the development of an organizational structure is the external environment. As shown in exhibit 9–3, not only does the external environment directly affect structural dimensions, but there is an indirect impact through the environment's influence on the organization's strategies and technology.

The relationship between environment and structure has been the subject of a growing body of literature over the past four years. Among the most quoted and important are the studies of Burns and Stalker and Lawrence and Lorsch. These studies are briefly discussed below.

Burns and Stalker: Mechanistic and Organic Structures

Burns and Stalker examined approximately twenty industrial organizations in the United Kingdom.[10] They were interested in determining how the pattern of managerial activities in planning, organizing, and controlling was related to the external environment. Gathering their data by performing field interviews, it was their intent to analyze the responses and reach some useful conclusions about how the environment and organization interact.

Early in the course of their work, Burns and Stalker discovered that management processes were different in various industries and environments. They reached the conclusion that each firm in their study sample could be viewed as an information-processing network.

The Burns and Stalker study treated the predictability of environmental demands facing organizations. They rated environments on a five-interval scale, from "stable" to "least predictable." Each of the five environments was then discussed with regard to the different management processes.

They studied a rayon manufacturer, an engineering company, and an electronics firm. The rayon company operated in the most stable or predictable environment. Because of this stability, the organization was run on the basis of clearly defined roles, specialized tasks, limited information flowing downward, concentration of decision-making authority at the upper managerial levels, and a distinct scalar chain of command.

The engineering company operated in a rapidly changing commercial environment. The environmental fluctuations required frequent organizational design changes. Thus, the structure was more flexible or fluid. Tasks were not as clearly defined as in the rayon firm, and lines of authority and responsibility were not emphasized.

The organization operating in the least predictable environment was a newly created electronics development organization. Job tasks were not defined well; the specific task assignments were made on an individual basis between superiors, peers, and subordinates. This type of interactive and dynamic task decision making was the result of the organization's rapidly changing situation. The structural dimensions of this firm were matched with the unpredictability of the environment.

The perspective acquired from their analyses of over twenty companies resulted in the identification of two management systems: mechanistic and organic. The characteristics of mechanistic and organic organizations are presented in exhibit 9–4. A number of important points need to be emphasized. First, the structure in the organic organization is based on expertise in handling current problems. In this type of organization, there is a less rigid hierarchy, but there is a structure that

EXHIBIT 9–4 Differences Between Mechanistic and Organic Structure

MECHANISTIC	FACTOR	ORGANIC
Stable and changing	External Environment	Dynamic and unstable
Short range, efficiency oriented	Goals	Long range, development oriented
Programmed	Decision Making	Nonprogrammed
Formal structure	Structural Dimensions	Flexible structure
Emphasis on rules		Fewer rules
Centralized		Decentralized
Low job scope		High job scope
In a select group of executive managers (position power)	Locus of Authority	At whatever level skill or competence exists (skill power)
Directions and orders	Communications	Advice, counsel, and information
Vertical		Vertical and lateral
To the organizational system	Loyalty	To the project or group
Objective measures	Performance Criteria	Objective and subjective measures
Focus on results		Focus on activities and results
Short time span between actions and results		Longer time open between actions and results

is used to avoid confusion and chaos. Second, in the organic organization the individual's loyalty is developed around work unit membership. The group has a special value in satisfying needs of employees in the organic system. Finally, organic systems are associated with unstable environmental conditions. This type of system is more flexible and able to cope with and adjust to changes in technology and market situations. Rigidity of structure in the mechanistic organization hinders its ability to adapt to change. Thus, it is most appropriate to implement it in a more stable environment.

Lawrence and Lorsch: Differentiation and Integration

If the environment of an organization is complex and varied, it may be necessary to develop specialized subunits to deal with the parts of the environment. Lawrence and Lorsch conducted field studies to determine what kind of organizational design was best able to cope with various economic and market environments.[11]

They studied six firms in the plastics industry to sharpen their analytical procedures and theoretical propositions. After this phase of their study, they examined a *highly effective* organization and a *less effective* one in the plastics, food, and container industries. These three industries were included because they were assumed to be operating in environments that contained varying amounts of uncertainty (see exhibit 4–4). To assess environmental certainty, they asked executives in the organizations about clarity of market information, the rapidity of technological change in the industry, and the length of time required to determine product success in the marketplace.

In their research, Lawrence and Lorsch wanted to analyze the relationship between the environmental uncertainty facing an organization and its internal organizational design. They concentrated on three main subsystems—marketing, economic-technical, and scientific—and hypothesized that the structural arrangement of each subsystem or department would vary with the predictability of its own environment. They proposed that the greater the degree of environmental certainty, the more formalized or rigid (bureaucratic) would be the structure.

These contingency researchers also were concerned with what they called the differentiation and integration within the system. They assumed that by separating or grouping job tasks into departments, a need for coordination would develop. The unit members would become specialists in dealing with their tasks and would develop particular work styles. Thus, *differentiation* is defined as the state of segmentation of the organization's subsystems, each of which contains members who form attitudes and behavior and tend to become specialized experts (see time and goal orientation in chapter 8).

A potential consequence of differentiation is the problem of bringing these individuals together to accomplish organizational goals. Because the members of each subsystem develop different attitudes, interests, and goals, they often find it difficult to reach agreement. These built-in organizational conflicts illustrate the importance of integration. Lawrence and Lorsch define *integration* as the quality of the state of collaboration that exists among departments, which is required to achieve unity of effort (i.e., coordination mechanisms).

The researchers' questionnaire and interviews revealed that subsystems within each organization tended to develop a structure that was related to the certainty of their relevant environment. For example, a production subsystem tended to be faced with a relatively stable or certain environment. They had the most formal and structured design of the subsystems studied. On the other hand, research subsystems operated in a less predictable environment and had the least formal or rigid structure. Marketing operated in what Lawrence and Lorsch refer to as a moderately predictable environment and had a less formal structure when compared to production and research. Exhibit 9–5 illustrates the structural factors for high performing firms in these industries.

The Lawrence and Lorsch findings point out that successful firms in different industries achieve a high level of integration. The amount of managerial time and effort required to achieve successful integration seems to be dependent upon two factors: diversity and interdependence. The more diverse the tasks of the firm's main units, the more differentiated those units will be in an effective organization. Differentiation by creating and encouraging different viewpoints generates conflict. Thus, the greater the state of differentiation, the larger the potential conflict, and the more effort and time it takes the manager to resolve these conflicts to benefit the firm. Furthermore, the more interdependent the tasks

EXHIBIT 9–5   Dimensions of High Performing Organizations in Three Industries

	CONTAINERS	FOOD	PLASTICS
External Environment	Low uncertainty	Moderate uncertainty	High uncertainty
Key Interdependencies	Marketing–production	Marketing-research; research-production	Marketing-research; research-production; marketing-production
Degree of Differentiation	Low	Moderate	High
Key Unit to Goal Achievement	Production	Marketing	Integrating department
Major Problem	Scheduling; control	Consumer preferences	Innovation; change
How Conflict is Resolved	Confrontation	Confrontation	Confrontation
Type of Structure	Functional (mechanistic)	Functional/product (mechanistic/organic)	Product (organic)
Main Integrating Mechanisms	Rules; hierarchy	Plans, liaison person; task forces	Task forces; teams; integrating department

of the major subsystems, the more information processing is required for effective integration.

In our framework of investigating the determinants of organizational structure, one of the most important findings of Lawrence and Lorsch is the relationship between an organization's structure and its environment. As shown in exhibit 9–5, stable environments are best suited for a *functional* structure (mechanistic), with its emphasis on rules, procedures, and authority. On the other hand, the more dynamic the environment, the more suited will be a *product-type structure* (organic), where there is a focus on authority, decentralization, and coordination mechanisms.

STRATEGY AND STRUCTURE

Why do some growth-oriented, multi-industry organizations such as Texas Instruments and General Electric have internal organizational structures that are significantly different from such stable, single product or industry organizations as Alcoa? The response to this question has been the subject of the writings of many management scholars for a number of years.

It was not until the early 1960s that a concise answer to this question was presented in Alfred D. Chandler's book, *Strategy and Structure*.[12] Chandler studied over seventy of America's largest firms—Du Pont, General Motors, Sears, and Standard Oil, for example—in order to develop several principles about the relationship between an organization's strategy and its structure. First, he proposed that organization structure *follows* the growth strategy of the organization. Second, he also concluded that organizations do not change their structures until they are provoked or forced to by a state of inefficiency.[13]

Structure Follows Strategy

Chandler's best-known contribution was his statement that the structure of an organization follows from its growth strategy. In other words, as an organization changes its growth strategy—in order to use its resources most effectively in the face of changing external environmental conditions—the new strategy creates new internal structural problems. These internal problems, such as ineffective departmentalization, lack of proper authority over projects, or an absence of coordination, can be solved only by changing the structure of the organization. If a structural rearrangement does not occur, then the strategy will be less than effective (see the practice of management section on General Motors).

Chandler's historical studies identified four different growth strategies that were followed in his example firms. In stage I, Volume Expansion, many organizations began as single offices or plants. In most cases, only a single function was performed, such as manufacturing, sales, wholesaling, or warehousing.

Stage II, Geographic Expansion, is a growth strategy that created multiple field offices or plants in the same function or industry, but in different locations. Coordination, standardization, and specialization problems arose almost immediately. To counter these problems, a new structure was adopted that established the *functional* department. This was a problem faced early in the development of the railroads. Later, this same problem was faced by the financial industry with the development of branch banking and the retail industry with the geographic expansion of department stores.

Stage III, Vertical Integration, involved the organization staying within the same industry, but expanding its functions. Retail stores initially specialized in clothing, but expanded to include the sale of appliances, furniture, yard products, and so on. The new strutural problems that developed included issues of interdependence and the coordination of product flow and others. The resulting structural arrangement we now know as a *functional* structure (see exhibit 8–2).

Stage IV, Product Diversification, involved the process of organizations moving into new industries with new products and services in order to employ existing resources as the primary markets began to decline. Structural problems of this new strategy concerned the appraisal and evaluation of new products, allocation of resources, and issues of departmentalization and coordination. The new structural arrangement created a division of labor that was based on time horizon and product/service class—what we have called the *product structure* (see exhibit 8–2).

General Motors, Du Pont, Sears, and Standard Oil were some of the first multi-divisional firms that Chandler studied. In each case, the firms followed the four-stage pattern from volume expansion to product diversification by altering their structures from the simple unit structure to the more complex product structure.

Not all organizations in Chandler's study went fully through the four-stage pattern. For example, metal-processing firms in the copper and aluminum industries did not diversify into the product diversification stage (stage IV). Instead, they grew only in one industry, supplied the same customers, and employed strategies that were consistent with the stage, namely vertical integration. In other words, in each case structure followed strategy—General Motors adopted a product diversification strategy and implemented a product-type structure, while Alcoa was successful by staying within a vertical integration strategy and using a functional structure. Those firms that remained and grew within a single industry retained the centralized functional structure; those that diversified adopted the multi-divisional, product structure. The strategy-structure linkage held true.

Initiating Change

Chandler's historical studies pointed to a second important finding. He found that the process of changing strategy and structure was usually a painful one, especially during the early stages.[14] He found that the individual who started the organization—the *entrepreneur*—became entrenched and protective of the organization. As a result, entrepreneurs were resistant to change. On the other hand, the next generation of managers—the *professional organizers/managers*—had acquired different skills and knowledge bases that were more adaptable to the latter growth stages (i.e., vertical integration and product diversification).

The entrepreneur wanted a "business as usual" approach; the professional organizer/manager, skilled in analysis and diagnosis, saw the necessity for change in order to survive and grow. It was only when economic inefficiency and mounting internal problems surfaced that the entrepreneur gave up control to the professional organizer/manager and the new structure was developed and implemented. Thus, the differences between the entrepreneur and the professional organizer/manager created a delay in the formulation of new strategies, and the implementation of a new organizational structure occurred only after a forced and sometimes painful situation. The historical analyses of such entrepreneurs as Henry Ford I and Andrew Carnegie generally support Chandler's position.

Current Views on Strategy and Structure: International Development

Vertical integration, product development, and market development were some of the strategies available to organizations as presented in chapter 6. In the last chapter, we discussed the evolution of structure in the international realm. By integrating the material in these two chapters, we can develop a framework like the one shown in exhibit 9–6. The exhibit illustrates the most popular structural approaches used by organizations during their growth phases. It is not an all-inclusive view, since the retreat strategy is not shown. When such a strategy is adopted, the organization usually reverts back to a former structure.

One of the most important aspects of exhibit 9–6 is that international development can result in a functional or product structure. This confirms the statement made in the last chapter that organizations with a narrow product line prefer to maintain a functional type structure when they go international, while a wide range of products may necessitate an international product structure.

TECHNOLOGY AND STRUCTURE

Few concepts in the study of organizations are so important, yet so ill-defined or understood as organizational technology. In recent studies, the concept of technology has been viewed in terms of the extent of task

EXHIBIT 9–6
Current View of
Structure Follows
Strategy

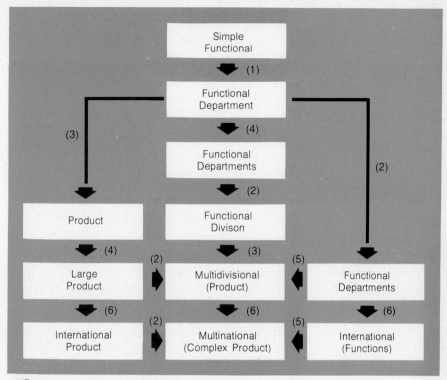

KEY:
Strategy   (1) Volume Expansion
            (2) Vertical Integration
            (3) Product Development
            (4) Market Development
            (5) Diversification
            (6) International Expansion

Adapted from: J. R. Galbraith and D. A. Nathanson, *Strategy Implementation: The Role of Structure and Process* (St. Paul, Minn.: West, 1978), p. 115.

interdependence (see chapter 8), degree of equipment automation, uniformity or complexity of materials used, and the degree of routineness of the task.[15]

There seems, however, to be some convergence on certain important points concerning the technology concept. First, there seems to be some agreement that technology concerns either the mechanical or intellectual processes by which an organization transforms raw materials into final goods or services. In other words, technology refers to a *transformation* process by which mechanical and intellectual efforts are used to change inputs into products.

Second, the diversity of opinions on a technology definition may relate to the level of analysis on which the concept is viewed. Some individuals may study technology as an organizationwide concept, such as an assembly line process in auto manufacturing. On the other hand, others may view technology at the individual level, relating to the concepts of job depth and scope (see chapter 8).

Finally, there seems to be some agreement that technology is a concept that is influenced by the environment *and* influences the structure of the organization (see exhibit 9–3). As one example of the former, consider pocket calculators in the office machine industry. Only a few years ago business calculators were bulky, slow, expensive, and generally a business as opposed to a personal possession. With the development of microcomputer circuitry, coupled with a growing consumer demand (technological and economic environment in chapter 4), office machine companies were forced to develop new manufacturing technologies to produce the new, inexpensive pocket calculators. An example of technology influencing structure is the steel industry. The process for manufacturing steel is well defined, standardized, and expensive (i.e., capital intensive). Since this process technology is fairly rigid, effective control and maintenance functions must be provided by the structure of the organization. In other words, structure adapts to technology.

COMMENTS ON THE PRACTICE OF MANAGEMENT
(See p. 290)

The project center concept at General Motors is a good example of the contingency approach to organizational design. First, it is a classic illustration of the relationship between environment, strategy, and structure. The energy crisis and changing market conditions (environment) resulted in a decision to downsize its cars (strategy), which created a need for more effective internal operations (structure). Second, from an organizational dimension viewpoint, the temporary "grouping" by project centers cut horizontally across the vertical automobile divisions, "influence" was given to the project board, and "coordination" of activities became the major key to success. The project center concept was temporary—a more formal and permanent approach using these same concepts will be discussed later as matrix design. Finally, the type of structure adopted by G.M. is one that can apply to other organizations—note that the idea came from NASA, a government agency.

Types of Technology

If we are adequately to study the relationship between technology, structure, and performance, a scheme for categorizing or classifying different technology types is needed. One of the best-known approaches to technology classification was presented by Thompson.[16] This classification scheme, based on the manner in which units are organized for task accomplishment, involves three types of technologies: (1) mediating; (2) long-linked; and (3) intensive. A summary of these technology types is shown in exhibit 9–7.

A *mediating technology* is characterized by linking of otherwise independent units of an organization (pooled interdependence in chapter 8) through the use of standard operating procedures. A simple example would be a commercial bank, characterized by low interdependency between the different functions (e.g., savings, investments, loans). Effectiveness is obtained through rules, procedures, and other control mechanisms. Such a technology is moderately adaptable or flexible to changing demands.

EXHIBIT 9–7   Technology Types

Technology Type	Illustration	CHARACTERISTICS			
		Interdependence	Basis of Coordination	Flexibility	Communication Demands
Mediating	*Bank*	Low (pooled)	Rules, standard procedures and supervisory control	Medium	Low
Long-Linked	*Auto Assembly Line*	Medium (sequential)	Planning and supervisory control	Low	Medium
Intensive	*Hospital*	High (reciprocal)	Cooperation and mutual adjustment	High	High

Long-linked technology stresses sequential interdependency between different units. Characterized by an automobile assembly line, this type of technology attains effectiveness through planning and supervisor control, coupled with a moderate emphasis on communication. Because of the rigid sequential nature of interdependence (along with the usual high cost of equipment and materials), this type of technology is not very flexible or adaptable to changing demands.

Finally, an *intensive technology* involves a variety of techniques drawn upon to transform an object from one state to another. The key point is that the choice of techniques is influenced by feedback from the object itself; that is, how the object responds to the application of the different techniques. The best example is that of a hospital. The object being transformed is the patient and the patient's health; the techniques are the various specialties of the hospital (e.g., surgery, pediatrics, X-ray, nursing, physical therapy). The manner in which the patient responds to one of the specialties (e.g., knee surgery) dictates the level of application of other specialties (e.g., physical therapy). As shown in exhibit 9–7, this type of technology is characterized by a great deal of interdependence between units, coupled with a need for good cooperation and high levels of flexibility and communications.

There have been a number of studies that have investigated the technology-structure relationships. One of the most important and most cited is the work of Woodward.

Woodward: Technology

The studies of Joan Woodward and her associates involved a sample of 100 firms that employed at least 100 people, in South Essex, England. Through reviewing company records, interviews, and observation, they developed a profile of specific dimensions for each organization in the sample.[17]

The analysis of the profiles resulted in a number of disconcerting discoveries. First, the researchers found that the organizational data did not relate, as they had hypothesized, to the size of the organization or to its general industry affiliation. For example, job specialization did not seem to be more intense in larger companies than in smaller ones. Second, the twenty organizations that were classified as effective had little in common with regard to organizational properties. This was also the case among the twenty least effective organizations. These two findings implied that the classical design principles (bureaucracy) were not significantly related to organizational effectiveness. Approximately one-half of the successful organizations utilized an organic management system, which, of course, is contrary to the prescriptions of Weber.

In seeking answers to the issues they discovered, the Woodward team found that by classifying firms on the basis of technology a better interpretation of the data emerged. The Woodward system of classification seems to interpret technology as "who does what with whom, when, where, and how often."[18] The three categories of technology were:

1. Unit and small batch (custom clothing, furniture, and electronics).
2. Large batch and mass production (automobiles and industrial equipment manufacturers).
3. Long-run process production (oil refinery and chemical plant).

This three-category system and the subgroups comprising it provided Woodward's team with a rough scale of *predictability of results* and the *degree of control* over the production process. In unit and small-batch manufacturing, each unit of production is made to order for a customer, and operations performed on each unit are nonrepetitive. Mass-produced products, such as automobiles, are usually more or less standardized, and the production steps are predictable. In our earlier framework, the unit and small-batch group could be considered an *intensive* technology, large batch and mass production a *long-linked* technology, and process production similar to *mediating* technology.

The results of classifying organizations on the basis of technology among effective firms in the sample are summarized in exhibit 9–8. The number of managerial levels varied among the three technological categories, with process production firms having the longest chain of command. Similarly, the chief executive's span of control varied with technology, with managers in process manufacturing having the widest span. The first-level supervisors' span of control also varied with type of technology, but in this case the relationship was curvilinear. Unit, small-batch, and process first-level supervisors tended to have smaller spans of control; those in mass-production facilities had the highest. Furthermore, the more advanced technologies utilized proportionately more administrative and staff personnel.

Woodward's research team also found that there were differences in operational procedures in the different technology categories. At what she calls the "top and bottom of the technical scale" (i.e., unit and process firms), there was a tendency for fewer rules, controls, definitions of job tasks, and more flexibility in interpersonal relations and delegation of authority compared to the middle-range mass-production firms. Furthermore, organizations in the technological category that deviated from

EXHIBIT 9–8   Summary of Woodward's Research Findings for Effective Organizations

	TECHNOLOGIES		
Levels of Organization and Characteristics	**Unit and Small-Batch Production**	**Large-Batch and Mass Production**	**Process Production**
Lower levels	Informally organized	Organized by formal structural arrangements	Organized by task and technological specifications; wide spans of control
Upper levels	Informally organized; no clear distinction between line and staff	Organized hierarchically with clear line and staff distinction	Informally organized; no line-staff distinction
Overall characteristics	Few levels; broad span of control; no clear hierarchy; low ratio of administrators to operating employees	Clear job specialization; clear chain of command	Many hierarchical levels
Keys to success	Sense and adapt to market changes	Efficient production of a standardized product	Product development and new scientific knowledge
Focus	External	Internal	External
Most effective structure	Organic (product)	Mechanistic (functional)	Organic (product or project)

this general pattern were most often less effective. The most effective mass-production firms were those that emphasized job specialization, tight controls, rigid chain-of-command adherence, and that in general followed classical design principles. A mass-production firm that was more flexible or organic tended to be less effective. On the other hand, organic and flexible process production firms were more effective than more rigid and bureaucratically inclined process firms.

Woodward aptly summarized the thrust of her contingency-oriented research by using the Burns and Stalker concepts: "Successful firms inside the large-batch production range tended to have mechanistic management systems. On the other hand, successful firms outside the range tended to have organic systems."[19]

What are the implications for managers from the research of Woodward? These implications may be best understood by examining the basic organizational functions and the keys to success (see exhibit 9–8). The unit and small-batch organization, such as a manufacturer of furniture, functions by taking customer specifications, developing the product, and manufacturing it. The keys to success depend on the organization's ability to sense and adapt to environmental change through the product development function. Since the focus is *external,* a product or organic structure would seem to be more appropriate.

On the other hand, the mass-production technology depends on producing a standardized product or service—automobiles, food, appliances—for an existing market. The keys to success concern the degree to which the product can be produced through routine methods as efficiently and economically as possible. The focus is *internal*, which supports scientific management, bureaucracy, and the adoption of a functional or mechanistic structure.

Finally, organizations that use a process technology also depend on product development as the focal point. The key to success is the ability to discover a new product, or a new use for a product—such as a new chemical compound, a new fabric for use in radial tires, or a new additive in detergents—through scientific research and development. New production facilities or the use of existing facilities also work into the scheme. Since the focus is *external*—adapting to changing scientific knowledge—a product or organic structure is most appropriate.

Current Technology-Structure Views

Since the publication of Woodward's study, a number of other research efforts have been conducted to verify, refute, or further develop her findings. Besides noting that organizational size (i.e., number of employees) can influence structure, one of the most important findings was that an organization can consist of a variety of technologies, and hence, a variety of structural forms.[20] For example, a production department using a long-linked technology may effectively operate with a function structure, while the marketing department or research and development function may successfully adopt a product structure. This confirms the growing preference among organizations to use a "mixed" structure (see exhibit 8–4).

CONTEMPORARY ORGANIZATIONAL DESIGN

Throughout this two-chapter sequence on organizational design and structure, we have made the point that there is no "one best way" to structure every organization. There are too many factors—including differences in strategies, environment, and technology—that vary from organization to organization that can influence the effectiveness of an organizational structure. A recognition of these factors establishes the foundation of the contingency approach to organizational design.

A Contemporary Organizational Design Framework

If there is a dominant and unifying concept that characterizes the contemporary approach to organizational design, it would be the focus on the impact of the *external environment*. As we have shown, the environment not only directly influences an organization's design alternatives, but it also has an indirect influence through the choice and implementation of the organization's strategies.

There also is an indirect influence of the environment on organizational design through the technology. In essence, technology acts more as a *constraint* to an organization. Operating a bank usually requires the adoption of a mediating technology; manufacturing automobiles almost automatically assumes a long-linked or assembly-line technology. The degree to which the technology matches the requirements of the environment will be reflected in the effectiveness of the organization's structure. That is, a long-linked technology is usually heavily capital intensive (i.e., requires large amounts of expensive equipment and processing mechanisms), and thus is not very adaptable to change. If an organization with a long-linked technology, such as a radio manufacturer, is placed in a relatively stable environment, the technology and environment are closely matched.

On the other hand, if the long-linked technology is confronted with a dynamic and complex environment, such as manufacturing business calculators, the need for adaptation to the environment cannot be satisfied with the stable technology. In this situation, the organization is faced with a need for an "organic" structure, but an internal technology that is primarily effective with a "mechanistic" structure. This organization must, therefore, depend on such complex and costly coordinative mechanisms as task forces and integrating departments to ensure some

EXHIBIT 9–9 Contemporary Organizational Design

ENVIRONMENT			DESIGN CHARACTERISTICS					
Degree of Change	Degree of Complexity	Example Strategies	Example Dominant Technology	Job Specialization	Decentralization	Span of Control	Coordination Needs	Structure
Stable	I Simple	Maintain existing competence; stability; vertical integration	Mass production or long-linked; high capital investment; programmed decisions	High	Low	Narrow	*Low* Use of rules, procedures and hierarchy	Mechanistic or functional structure (exhibit 8–2)
	II Complex	Expand competences; market development; vertical integration	Mass production or long-linked; high capital investment	Moderate	Low to Moderate	Wide	*Moderate* Use of rules, hierarchy planning, and task forces	Functional or product structure (exhibit 8–2)
Dynamic	III Simple	Expand and improve competences; product development or diversification	Continuous/process or unit/batch; mediating technology	High	High	Narrow	*High* Use of rules through integrating department	Organic or product structure (exhibit 8–2)
	IV Complex	Adapt to rapid change; seek new competences; product development; market development; merger	Unit/batch; continuous/process; mediating or reciprocal	Low	High	Wide	*High* Use of rules through integrating departments	Product or matrix structure (exhibits 8–2 and 9–10)

level of acceptable performance.

Some of the ideas expressed in this discussion are expanded in exhibit 9–9. The framework is based on exhibit 4–4, which identified two major dimensions of the external environment: *degree of change* (stable/dynamic) and *degree of complexity* (simple/complex). The four quadrants establish the elements that link organizational structure to effectiveness.

In *quadrant I,* the external environment for an organization is characterized by a relative lack of rapid change (stable) and a minimum number of interactions with external entities (simple). An example could be a city government or a paper products company. Such organizations usually adopt a stable strategy and use a mass-production form of technology. The necessary organizational design characteristics that will lead to high performance are high job specialization, centralization of authority, narrow span of control, and low coordination needs. The recommended structure would be a mechanistic or *functional* design. Since the environment is not rapidly changing, the keys to success for this type of organization reside in the control of *costs,* which is the strength of a functional structure. The astute reader should have recognized that under these conditions, a bureaucratic form of organization would probably work well. In other words, bureaucracy can be considered as an element of the contingency approach, being most effective in this particular environment.

In *quadrant II,* the external environment remains fairly stable, but the degree of complexity increases because of an expansion in the number of external interactions (e.g., customers, suppliers, and competitors). Manufacturers of home appliances—washing machines, dryers, and refrigerators—are an example of organizations that sell a variety of products across different markets (direct to customers or to commercial establishments and national retail stores under a brand name), all of which exhibit a fairly stable demand. Strategies usually involve improved or expanded competencies and market development (see chapter 6), and the dominant technology is one of mass production. Internally, there is a moderate degree of job specialization and centralization, wide spans of control, and moderate coordination needs. A *functional* structure, using task forces, or *product* structure would be a recommended design form.

A dynamically changing, but simple environment characterizes organizations in *quadrant III.* Specialty producers, such as clothing manufacturers, are an example. Such organizations generally specialize in only a few products that are made to order (or fashion) in a rapidly changing environment. A strategy of product development coupled with a unit/batch or continuous technology is usually found. The key design characteristics involve high job specialization and decentralization, narrow spans of control, and high coordination needs. In this case, a *product* (or organic) structure would probably be most effective.

Finally, in *quadrant IV* organizations are faced with a highly complex and rapidly changing environment. Energy companies, engineering firms, electronics manufacturers, and some multinational firms fall within this quadrant. Organizational strategies usually emphasize adaptation to change, diversification, and mergers coupled with a unit/batch or process technology. Job specialization is low, a wide span of control exists, and decentralization and coordination needs are high. A complex *product* structure is preferred by many organizations. Another structure that is gaining in popularity is the matrix structure.

The Matrix Design

The term *matrix* has been used to describe organizations that include a number of projects, programs, or task forces.[21] Decentralization was and still is a typical response to growth in organizational size, markets, and competition. Decentralization is feasible because it is possible to break the organization up into fairly autonomous units. However, rapid changes in technology, the environment, and preferences of the work force have posed problems for decentralized organizational design. These changes have made it necessary for organizations to have large numbers of specialists to handle research and development, market research, and human resources development. Thus, the increased interest in the matrix or program management approach is a consequence of problems inherent in the decentralization of decision-making authority.

When a matrix design is formulated, the easiest description is that of a product structure *superimposed* on a functional structure. As an example, consider exhibit 9–10, which depicts the structure of an engineering firm that specializes in the construction of large projects, such as bridges, oil refineries, and dams. The vertical components of the matrix structure reflect the typical functional departments of manufacturing, marketing, contracts, and so on. Since each project requires a different orientation with different needs, the product structure is placed on the functional structure—the horizontal components of exhibit 9–10. The result is that the *control* advantages of a functional structure and the *adaptive* advantages of a product structure are obtained in one design.

For effective functioning, a matrix design requires recognition of certain important factors. First, the *classical scalar chain of command* principle (i.e., each subordinate has only one supervisor) is thrown out. In our example, a construction engineer reports to both the functional construction vice president and the project manager (point *A* on exhibit 9–10). Second, the key managers in this design must agree on a balance or *sharing of power* over resources. Decisions over financial, physical, and human resources must be made *jointly* and with a knowledge that power will be shifting between the two units over time. Third, since conflict inevitably will occur, there must be an open and frequent use of *confrontation* as a resolution mechanism. Conflict over financial resources, for example, will create severe problems unless confronted and solved early.

There are both positive and negative features associated with the matrix design. For example, consider the construction engineer again in exhibit 9–10. This engineer reports to the functional manager on general construction matters and to the project manager on specific project concerns. The question is: How is this engineer's time to be divided? Is it 60/40 to the project—or is it 80/20, or 50/50? Not only will this situation create a state of tension and stress for the engineer if not resolved, but there is the key issue of who evaluates the engineer's performance—is it the functional manager, the project manager, or some combination of both, and what method of evaluation is to be used?

EXHIBIT 9–10   Matrix Structure for an Engineering and Construction Organization

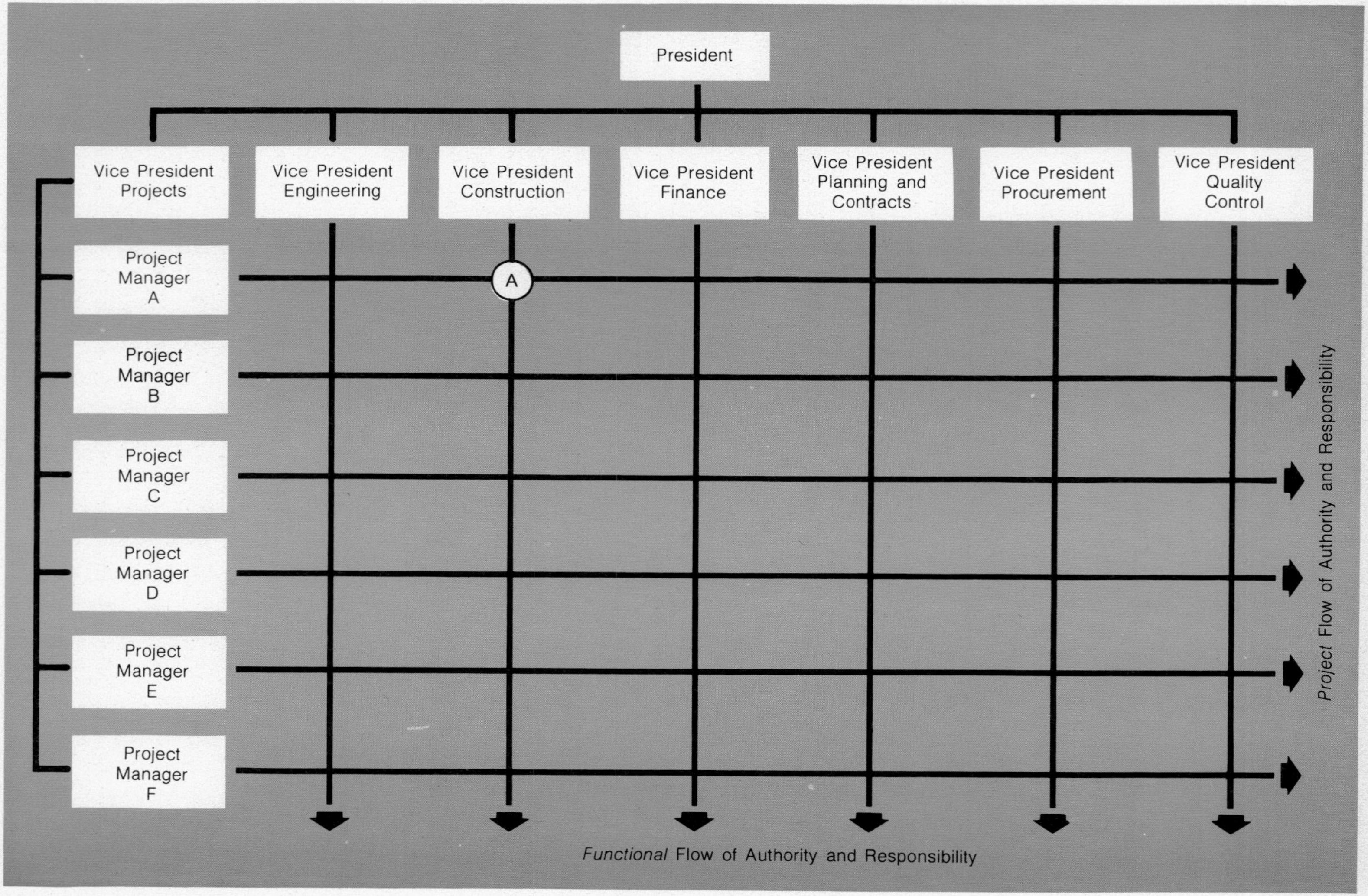

President

Vice President Projects

Vice President Engineering

Vice President Construction

Vice President Finance

Vice President Planning and Contracts

Vice President Procurement

Vice President Quality Control

Project Manager A

Project Manager B

Project Manager C

Project Manager D

Project Manager E

Project Manager F

A

Project Flow of Authority and Responsibility

Functional Flow of Authority and Responsibility

Naturally, these are questions that are answered differently by various organizations. Generally speaking, organizations tend to stay away from hard time allocations (e.g., 70/30) in favor of a flexible time schedule.

**THE
MANAGER'S
JOB**
Anthony E.
Cascino of
International
Minerals and
Chemicals

In the mid-1970s, Tony Cascino, vice chairman of International Minerals and Chemicals Corporation (IM&C), faced a crisis that threatened to break down the company's problem-solving and decision-making processes. The company, a major producer of fertilizers, animal products, energy, and such chemicals as phosphates, potash, and nitrogen, was operating with an organizational structure that did not fit with its growing and dynamic environment.

The company's structure had evolved from a simple functional design to one that was a complex array of project management and decentralization. Cascino recognized, however, that internal complexities and external environmental turbulence can increase to such a degree that a more effective structure has to be devised. To IM&C and Cascino, the answer was a matrix structure.

After six years with matrix management, Cascino learned a number of important lessons from which other managers may benefit. Some of the most important include:

—In the early stages of implementation, the structure should not only be put in place in manageable degrees, but minimal concern should be given to rules, titles, and authority. Experience is the best guide to establishing procedures.

—Success rests more on the behavior of people than on structure—the internal operations, therefore, must stress cooperation, not power plays.

—Avoid the condition of "two bosses": the preference was to refer to the "peer group," which minimized authority challenges.

—Keep top management informed, but don't let them get too involved in day-to-day activities; whenever this occurred, otherwise good working sessions deteriorated into a series of unproductive meetings and presentations.

—The compensation package for managers must be structured to accommodate both vertical (functional) and horizontal (product) obligations.

—Top management must, in spirit, philosophy, and practice, promote and support the matrix approach.

Matrix structure has helped IM&C improve operations, productivity, profitability, and overall working relationships. Its major contribution has been in the development of managers—experience with the matrix approach has improved managerial skills and performance.

Adapted from A. E. Cascino, "How One Company Adapted Matrix Management in a Crisis," Management Review *(November 1979): 57–61.*

Such a scheme, however, requires frequent monitoring and audit. Performance evaluations are generally conducted by the functional manager with major input from the product manager, though this can vary in different organizations.

Despite the relative youth of the matrix design, companies such as Honeywell, Texas Instruments, and General Electric have used it for some time. When General Electric decided to quit the computer business,

Honeywell acquired the pieces. It set up twenty managerial task forces, made up of approximately 200 people from both its own staff and General Electric's, to integrate manufacturing, marketing, engineering, field sciences, personnel, software, and the inventory of actual product lines. Honeywell's top executive claims that this design approach resulted in a smooth and effective merger of two large organizations.

Before the matrix design is even considered as effective as bureaucracy or System 4 in various settings, it needs to be more thoroughly studied. It is different and appealing for some situations, but determining the right situations is necessary and important.

ORGANIZATIONAL DESIGN, PERFORMANCE, AND THE MANAGER'S JOB

With today's increasingly turbulent environment, coupled with the growing size and complexity of all types of organizations, the topic of how to structure an organization for goal achievement has been given significant attention by managers and scholars alike. The topic of organizational design is important to performance and the manager's job.

Keys to Success with Organizational Design

As this chapter has suggested, there are an enormous number of factors that a manager must consider when designing an organization's structure. Aligning and integrating all these factors is a task that can be fraught with problems, resulting in less than satisfactory levels of performance. In exhibit 9–9, we have attempted to provide at least some order to the difficult task of picking the right structure. The experiences of managers in the organizational design process may also help to shed further light on this situation.

1. **Structuring (or restructuring) an organization is a complex and involved process.**

The manager or future manager should not underestimate the time, commitment of resources, and the extent of involvement that is required when restructuring of an organization is contemplated. A major reorganization will require a change in the grouping, influence, and coordination dimensions, which is a significant undertaking. Many organizations have learned the hard way with adopting a matrix design, for example, that many unforeseen side effects add up to major problems. Still, in order to maintain or improve performance levels, most large organizations go through the restructuring process every few years.

2. **Most organizations consist of many different technologies, not just one.**

The reader should not be misled by the simplicity of the technology concept. In reality, organizations are made up of many technologies, not just a single one. If the technology-structure argument is valid, this helps to explain why certain parts of an organization are functionally structured, while others are similar to a product/project structure (see the discussion of mixed designs in chapter 8). For example, the vice president of manufacturing may adopt a functional structure because manufacturing, in reality, does not frequently interact with the external environment. Thus, the stability and emphasis on control are strong features in this structure. On the other hand, the vice president of marketing and marketing department subordinates may interact frequently with a dynamic environment. Because of this, a product structure may be found in this area.

3. **The matrix design is not the final answer to structuring problems.** Although we discussed matrix designs at the end of this chapter, this should not be interpreted as the "ultimate" or "final" answer to structuring organizations. On the contrary, it is one of only many structures that have evolved from the development and knowledge base of the organizational design concept. The matrix design is suited only for those organizations with unique external environmental problems and even those organizations that have adopted the design will attest to some of the major problems that it creates. The essence of this argument, and that of the entire chapter, is that a manager must choose a design that best fits the situation.

4. **Managers must be as flexible as the design of the organization.** The fact that organizations must adapt to the environment is a major point of this chapter. Let us not overlook the fact that managers must also adapt to the organization's changing structure. For example, changing from a functional structure to a product structure will entail major revisions in a manager's authority and responsibility patterns (see the Ray-O-Vac case in chapter 8). Managers must be able to adapt to these changes in order to achieve high performance levels.

Organizational Design and the Manager's Job

The organizing function has a direct and significant impact on the manager's job. Point 4 above is only one of many direct relationships that exist with the daily functions of a manager's job.

From a managerial *skill* perspective, conceptual and diagnostic skills are probably the most important. In other words, the manager must be able accurately to diagnose the needs of the organization in relationship to a structure. This includes a knowledge of the environment, the importance of the chosen organizational strategies, and the impact, or constraining effect, of the dominant technology. In addition, the manager must conceptually be able to integrate the structuring needs of the organization into an effective package. In adopting a matrix design, the manager must recognize the potential problems associated with a dual authority system, the problems of power sharing, and so on.

Organizational design also relates to *managerial roles*. The structure of the organization will establish or change the manager's interpersonal roles, particularly authority and responsibility relationships. Informational roles will also be altered, especially when a change from a functional to a product structure occurs. Whom the manager communicates with and what networks are established will all be affected. Finally, in decisional roles, the manager's power to allocate resources, handle disturbances, and negotiate with other managers will be influenced.

SUMMARY FOR THE MANAGER

1. Organizational design is viewed as the managerial process that concerns the development of a structure for the organization. In essence, it focuses on the investigation, analysis, and decisions that establish the grouping, influence, and coordination dimensions of organizations. The process is organizational design; the result is the organization's structure. Three approaches to organizational design are most frequently discussed: classical; behavioral; and contingency.

2. The classical approach to organizational design usually relates to a discussion of the bureaucratic model as developed by Weber. In its ideal state, the bureaucratic approach offers the manager—with the emphasis on rules, authority, impersonality, and lifelong career development—a means to stress stability and control. In many situations, however, bureaucracy has come under severe criticism because of problems associated with red tape, inflexibility, dominance of authority, and the protection of position. It is important for the manager to recognize that the bureaucratic approach is quite effective for organizations operating in a relatively stable and unchanging environment where there is strong need for control. It is, however, not the "one best way" to organize for all organizations as its founder and supporters claim.

3. The behavioral approach to organizational design, like the classical approach, proposed the one best way to organize. The emphasis of this approach, particularly by Likert, was on the behavioral and humanistic issues of people working in an organization. Likert's approach emphasized participation, decentralization, and frequent communications as the means to overcome the problems associated with a bureaucratic form of governance. It, too, found success in some organizations, but not all.

4. The contingency approach has been offered by many as the most appropriate way of organizing. It presents no one best way, but is more a diagnostic approach that stresses the interaction of the external environment, the organization's strategies, and the internal technology as determining factors of structure.

5. The work of Burns and Stalker and Lawrence and Lorsch drew attention to the importance of considering the environment in the organizational design process. For managers, the lesson to be learned is that as the environment becomes more dynamic and complex, the structure of the organization should be made more decentralized and flexible. In our framework, a dynamic and complex environment is most appropriate for the product type of structure.

6. Chandler's major contribution is the finding that "structure follows strategy;" in other words, structure is determined, in part, by the chosen strategies of the organization.

7. Technology was viewed as another contingency factor in organizational design. It has, however, been viewed more as a constraining factor than a pure determinant. That is, the technology of a bank, hospital, or assembly plant, for example, is a given item, as it is in any company when it chooses to produce a particular good or service. The question for organizational design specialists is how flexible is this technology to the needs that are imposed on the organization by the environment? A heavily capital and equipment intensive organization may not have the flexibility of an organization that is more labor intensive, especially in a dynamic environment. To counteract this constraining problem of the environment, many organizations have made use of temporary task forces or permanent project managers to ensure flexibility.

8. The matrix design, which is simply a product structure superimposed on a functional structure, is fast becoming the most popular form of organizational structure. It is certainly not the final answer, particularly with the many problems that have arisen with organizations that have adopted this design. It is quite appropriate for organizations that operate in dynamic and complex environments but that need both the cost control *and* flexibility offered by the functional and product structures respectively.

QUESTIONS FOR REVIEW AND DISCUSSION

1. What is the difference between organizational design and organizational structure?
2. What are the major proposals or elements of the bureaucratic model? Why has the model failed to be the "one best way" to organize?
3. How do bureaucracy and Likert's System 4 differ?
4. Why does the contingency approach to organizational design not subscribe to a "one best way" system?
5. How are the external environment, strategy, and structure related?
6. Does Chandler's analysis pertain only to large organizations?
7. Why is the concept of technology important to the study of organizational design?
8. What are some of the advantages and disadvantages associated with the matrix structure?
9. How are managerial skills and organizational design related?

NOTES

1. F. W. Taylor, *Principles of Scientific Management* (New York: Harper & Brothers, 1911).

2. M. Weber, *The Theory of Social and Economic Organization,* trans. A. M. Henderson and T. Parsons (New York: Oxford University Press, 1947), p. 330.

3. C. Perrow, *Complex Organizations,* 2nd. ed. (Glenview, Ill.: Scott, Foresman, 1979), pp.4–6.

4. See B. Reimann, "On the Dimensions of Bureaucratic Structure: An Empirical Reappraisal," *Administrative Science Quarterly* (1973): 462–76; and T. Parsons, *Structure and Progress in Modern Societies* (New York: Free Press, 1960).

5. R. Levy, "Tales From the Bureaucratic Woods," *Dun's Review* (March 1978): 94–96.

6. R. Likert, *New Patterns of Management* (New York: McGraw-Hill, 1961).

7. R. Likert, *The Human Organization* (New York: McGraw-Hill, 1967), p.6.

8. W. G. Bennis, *Changing Organizations* (New York: McGraw-Hill, 1966).

9. F. S. Kast and J. E. Rosenzweig, *Contingency Views of Organization and Management* (Chicago: Science Research Associates, 1973), p. 313.

10. T. Burns and G. M. Stalker, *The Management of Innovation* (London: Tavistock, 1961).

11. P. R. Lawrence and J. W. Lorsch, *Organizations and Environment* (Homewood, Ill.: Irwin, 1969).

12. A. D. Chandler, *Strategy and Structure* (Cambridge, Mass.: MIT Press, 1962).

13. J. R. Galbraith and D. A. Nathanson, *Strategy Implementation: The Role of Structure and Process* (St. Paul, Minn.: West, 1978), pp. 12–16.

14. Ibid.

15. J. D. Ford and J. W. Slocum, "Size, Technology, Environment and the Structure of Organizations," *Academy of Management Review* (October 1977): 561–75.

16. J. D. Thompson, *Organizations in Action* (New York: McGraw-Hill, 1967), pp.15–18.

17. J. Woodward, *Industrial Organization: Theory and Practice* (London: Oxford University Press, 1965).

18. E. D. Chapple and L. R. Sayles, *The Measures of Management* (New York: Macmillan, 1961); and C. Perrow, "A Framework for the Comparative Analysis of Organizations," *American Sociological Review* (1967): 194–208.

19. Woodward, p. 71.

20. See J. Child and R. Mansfield, "Technology, Size and Organization Structure," *Sociology* (1972): 369–93; D. J. Hickson, D. S. Pugh, and D. C. Pheysey, "Operations Technology and Organization Structure: An Empirical Reappraisal," *Administrative Science Quarterly* (1969): 378–97; C. Perrow, *Organizational Analysis: A Sociological View* (Belmont, Calif.: Wadsworth, 1970); and A. H. Van De Ven and A. L. Delbecq, "A Task Contingent Model of Work Unit Structure," *Administrative Science Quarterly* (1974): 183–97.

21. S. M. Davis and P. R. Lawrence, *Matrix* (Reading, Mass.: Addison-Wesley, 1977).

ADDITIONAL REFERENCES

Galbraith, J. R., *Designing Complex Organizations.* Reading, Mass.: Addison-Wesley, 1973.

Gillespie, D. F., and Mileti, D. S. "Technology and the Study of Organizations: An Overview and Appraisal," *Academy of Management Review* (January 1977): 7–16.

Hall, R. H. *Organizations: Structure and Process.* 2nd. ed., Englewood Cliffs, N.J.: Prentice-Hall, 1977.

Harvey, E. "Technology and the Structure of Organizations," *American Sociological Review* (1968): 249–58.

Hrebiniak, L., *Complex Organizations,* St. Paul, Minn.: West, 1978.

Jackson, J. H., and Morgan, C. P. *Organizational Theory.* Englewood Cliffs, N.J.: Prentice-Hall, 1978.

Jelinek, M. "Technology, Organizations, and Contingency." *Academy of Management Review* (January 1977): 17–26.

Keller, R. T., Slocum, J. W., and Susman, G. I. "Uncertainty and Type of Management System in Continuous Process Organizations." *Academy of Management Journal* (1974): 56–68.

Lorsch, J. W. "Organizational Design: A Situational Perspective." *Organizational Dynamics* (Autumn 1977): 2–14.

Miles, R. E., and Snow, C. C. *Organizational Strategy, Structure, and Process.* New York: McGraw-Hill, 1978.

A CASE FOR ANALYSIS

The Mueller Engineering Company

The Mueller Engineering Company is a medium-size engineering design and construction company located in Muncie, Indiana. The company, founded by its president, Mr. Henry Mueller, in 1972, specializes in the design and construction of small manufacturing and processing plants. Since the company was founded, sales have increased steadily at approximately 20 percent per year. In 1978 the company recorded sales of $9 million and after-tax profits of $950,000. The vast majority of the company's projects have been located in a five-state area including Indiana, Kentucky, Ohio, Michigan, and Illinois. An increasing number of construction projects, however, were being contracted each year in the states of Georgia, Tennessee, and Arkansas.

Initially, president Mueller had four department managers reporting directly to him: (1) manager of engineering design; (2) manager of construction; (3) manager of contract sales; and (4) manager of administrative services. This arrangement proved to be successful during the early years of Mueller's growth when only one or two construction projects were in process. During the last two years, however, an average of four to six projects were in various stages of completion at any one time.

With the increasing business, Mr. Mueller was concerned that the departmental arrangement was not adequate for handling the numerous coordination problems that had developed. Of particular concern were problems that had arisen with current projects related to increased costs and the inability to meet schedule deadlines.

In order to overcome these problems, early in 1979 Mueller created the project manager position and promoted three of the company's best engineers—Bob James, Kent Tucker, and Martha Simmons—into these positions. The project managers, who reported directly to Mueller, were given full responsibility for coordinating one or two projects from the design stage through construction. To accomplish their job, the project managers would have to depend upon the expertise, resources, and cooperation of the other four departments. Only a secretary and a planning and cost analyst were under direct supervision of each of the project managers. The new organizational arrangement is shown in exhibit 9–11.

EXHIBIT 9–11
H. C. Mueller
Engineering
Company:
Organizational
Structure

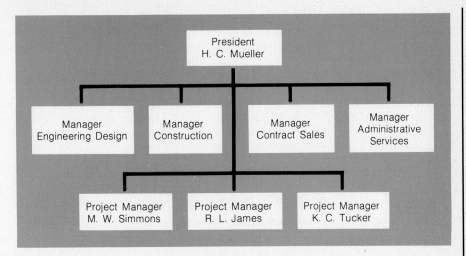

After the project manager arrangement had been in effect for approximately one year, Mueller had the following conversation with project manager Kent Tucker.

MUELLER   *Kent, I called you in today to get your informal evaluation of the way the project manager concept has worked out for you. As you know, I created your position in the belief that our growing number of projects could be better coordinated. I must say, however, that I really haven't seen any major improvement in our ability to meet time or cost schedules.*

TUCKER   *Let me say that I really enjoy my job. It's exciting, and I truly like the autonomy I have and the opportunity to work with all areas of the company and with a variety of customers. On the other hand, I feel totally frustrated and powerless in trying to get the projects done.*

MUELLER   *What do you mean, Kent?*

TUCKER   *Well, it basically boils down to a job that's all "responsibility" but no "authority." We're supposed to coordinate our different projects from beginning to end, but we don't have the power or authority over resources to get the job done.*

MUELLER   *I don't understand. You report directly to me—isn't that authority enough?*

TUCKER   *Not really, Henry. I can come to you with big problems, but for everyday work I have to depend on the design and construction departments for assistance. Getting help out of them is like pulling teeth. I have to "beg, borrow, and steal" just to keep a project moving forward. This is the major reason why Bob James quit two months ago. He plainly got frustrated with the lack of cooperation from the other departments.*

MUELLER   *When I set up this new arrangement, I thought I made it clear to everyone that the project managers were the key people in our organization. I hoped that the total organization would cooperate and support you people.*

TUCKER   *There's cooperation, but only to a point. The problem is that over time, the different department managers have developed particular routines and* *procedures for doing their work. When we come in with requests that are different from what has been done before—like asking for more design engineers to be put on a project than we have done before—all we get is the big "put off" or comments like, "We just don't operate that way in this department." It's just frustrating!*

A few days later, Mr. Mueller called Fred Carter, manager of construction, into his office for a conference on a number of matters. Toward the end of the meeting, Mr. Mueller brought up the issue of project management. The following are excerpts from that conversation:

MUELLER   *Fred, I'm getting a little worried that the projects we have going are not being as well coordinated as I wanted them. What's the problem? Is it with the function management or the project management?*

CARTER   *I was wondering when you'd get around to questioning something we have been fighting for months. The problem is with the project managers. Before, they were good engineers, but as project managers, they cause more trouble than they're worth.*

MUELLER   *Come on, Fred, explain yourself.*

CARTER   *Well, if you want to get down to brass tacks, the project managers seem to be more concerned with how much authority and power they have over a project than in actually getting the job done. Just because they have the title "manager" doesn't mean that they can overstep their authority by sticking their noses in my, or others', areas.*

MUELLER   *For example?*

CARTER   *For example, they are continually running into my office demanding more people on this job, quicker turnaround on that job, special consideration given to certain customers, and so on. They think that they run the organization, and consider the other functional managers as their subordinates and pawns. We've developed a good design and construction company without their help. If I went along with all their demands, they would have all the decision-making power and employees reporting to them, which would leave me and the other department managers out of a job. They are supposed to coordinate projects, not constantly give orders that disrupt a well-running organization that has been run on well-established plans and procedures.*

Questions for Discussion

1. Evaluate the project manager concept as an organizational design change.
2. What are some of the causes of the problems as presented by Messrs. Tucker and Carter?
3. What should Mr. Mueller do to remedy the situation?

10

Human Resources
in Organizations

CHAPTER OUTLINE

KEY POINTS IN THIS CHAPTER

1. A variety of external and internal environmental events have significantly increased the importance of human resources to managers.

2. The human resource process consists of human resource planning, recruitment, selection, orientation, training and development, performance evaluation, rewards, and separations.

3. The human resource planning activity involves the analysis of current and future trends as they relate to the organization's resource base.

4. Recruitment concerns the process of securing people and insuring that they remain in the organization.

5. Selection involves identifying the most capable people to fill a position. For managerial selection, the concept of assessment centers has grown in importance.

6. Orientation relates to the process of induction and socialization.

7. Training and development activities are used to develop managers and management skills.

8. Current issues in human resources include women in management and staffing international operations.

THE PRACTICE OF MANAGEMENT

Procter and Gamble

Consider the following statement: "We don't believe in mothering our managers. We grow our own managers by giving them responsibility very quickly, which sometimes means putting them in jobs they aren't quite ready for." If you think an organization adopting such a philosophy is asking for trouble, think again—it is the basic management development philosophy of Procter and Gamble, a company with an uninterrupted profit growth that is impressive by any industry's standards.

P&G starts the process by finding the right people through an extremely intensive selection process, followed by continuing on-the-job training, and tied neatly together with a substantial compensation system. The details of the compensation system are a guarded secret, but it is known to consist of competitive salaries, bonuses, and a significant profit-sharing program. A manager's profit share is invested in P&G stock, which is a powerful incentive to work hard—that is, the better the company performs, the better the manager will do.

The essence of the P&G system is to put new managers through their paces—a process that draws talent out early. At P&G new managers go to work, not to school. Except for a limited amount of formal training for those in technical areas, such as research and development, formal classroom training is not the P&G way. Instead, they give them something to do.

That "something" is responsibility for a piece of business and, if the manager does well, quick promotions into other jobs. Some of these jobs may require skills and abilities that the manager may not be fully equipped to handle. Yet the risks are much less than one might imagine. For one thing, the new manager, who is labeled a "development person," is backed up by a superior who is always close by (i.e., a mentor). By strictly limiting the number of people reporting to any one individual, the bond between superior and subordinate managers can grow tight. In addition, there is P&G's policy to promote from within, and managers are expected to train their successors. From day one, managers get the message that the best way to advance is for the person under them to be so good that they push the manager out of a job.

Just as important, the P&G system of management development gives managers a built-in loyalty and sense of respect for company traditions. Confidence is built because managers have been able to handle jobs that may have originally seemed over their heads. Each successive assignment, which at first seems a crisis, reinforces the manager's level of confidence.

If consistency is the keyword of P&G's management development, it pays off in corporate stability. While its executive ranks are not totally immune to raiding by other companies, turnover is surprisingly low. Many managers spend their entire careers at P&G. One advantage of this outcome is that employees know if there is a change in the management the basic conduct of the business will be the same. Employees know that managers who get new positions have been in the company for a period of time, which means they accept what is successful for the company and won't try any unnecessary major changes.

Adapted from "P&G: We Grow Our Own Managers," Dun's Review *(December 1975): 48–51.*

10

To this point in our discussion of management and the manager's job, we have analyzed the organization's external and internal environment, presented the process of establishing goals, plans, and decision-making elements, and discussed the activities involved in developing the structure within which goal-achieving functions are performed. The next important step is to place people in the established jobs and structure.

One of the most important resources of an organization are its people. Employees supply the talent, skills, and creativity and exert the effort and leadership that contribute to the organization's performance. Managers in all types of organizations are taking a greater interest in the management of human resources and are supporting many practical changes in longstanding and traditional human resource activities.[1] This interest is prompted by such factors as increased activities by governmental bodies (e.g., equal employment opportunity and affirmative action), rising labor costs, and questions concerning the supply of competent and skilled managers and employees (e.g., labor force trends and turnover rates).[2]

The topic of human resources in organizations will be presented in four parts. First, we will discuss the human resource process—sometimes called the *staffing* function.[3] Second, five important elements of the human resource process—human resource planning, recruitment, selection, orientation, and training and development—will be singled out for discussion. Third, two contemporary issues in human resources—women in management and staffing in the international realm—will be highlighted. Finally, we will present the relationship between human resources, performance, and the manager's job.

THE HUMAN RESOURCE PROCESS

The human resource process, like many other organizational activities, is a dynamic system. Changes in the external environment (e.g., competitive pressures, consumer needs, technological advances, and demographic characteristics), organizational goals and strategies, and other internal factors add up to a need for a flexible human resource system. In our discussion, the human resource process consists of two major components: (1) the premises of the process; and (2) the actual steps in the process.

Premises of the Human Resource Process

The premises of the human resource process involve those factors that come *before* the development of the human resource plan. This is shown in exhibit 10–1. For instance, as presented in chapter 5, *organizational goals* describe the state of affairs or desired results that the organization attempts to achieve. From a human resource point of view, this involves

EXHIBIT 10–1
Premises of the
Human Resource
Process

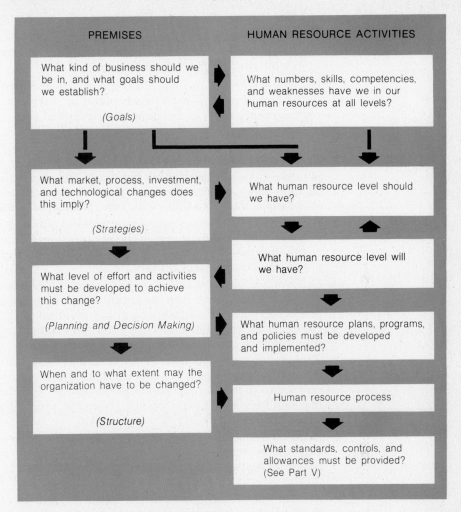

PREMISES

What kind of business should we be in, and what goals should we establish?

(Goals)

What market, process, investment, and technological changes does this imply?

(Strategies)

What level of effort and activities must be developed to achieve this change?

(Planning and Decision Making)

When and to what extent may the organization have to be changed?

(Structure)

HUMAN RESOURCE ACTIVITIES

What numbers, skills, competencies, and weaknesses have we in our human resources at all levels?

What human resource level should we have?

What human resource level will we have?

What human resource plans, programs, and policies must be developed and implemented?

Human resource process

What standards, controls, and allowances must be provided?
(See Part V)

not only developing knowledge of the numbers, skills, competencies, and weaknesses of the current work force but also what changes are needed in a future work force in order to achieve the stated goals. In the same manner, *organizational strategies* provide direction to the organization. The knowledge of where the organization wants to go reinforces the need to develop and acquire a skilled and competent work force.

As we have seen in chapters 6 and 7, the process of translating goals and strategies into specific activities concerns *planning and decision making*. Organizational plans must be developed that contain subplans for the development of an effective work force. Finally, establishing the framework within which performance will occur—the grouping, influence, and coordination components of the organization's *structure*—follows from the stated goals, strategies, and plans. From a human resource view, this involves the development of a comprehensive staffing plan.

Elements of the Human Resource Process

The human resource process can be viewed as consisting of a series of steps that are performed continuously by all managers. The steps, shown in exhibit 10–2, include the following:

1. *Human resource planning.* Meeting current and future human resource needs begins with a plan. Such planning involves an analysis of the organization's goals and strategies, the needed skills, abilities, positions, and competencies coupled with a knowledge of trends in employment laws and in personnel availability.

2. *Recruitment.* Once human resource needs have been identified, an effort is made to locate acceptable candidates. This may include such methods as newspaper and professional journal ads, college recruiting, recommendations from existing employees, placement firms, and so forth.

3. *Selection.* The selection process involves evaluating various candidates and selecting those that match the organization's requirements. Methods of evaluation include application forms, interviewing, testings, reference checks, and assessment centers.

4. *Orientation.* This important step involves the process of integrating the newly hired employee into the organization. Included are the more formal activities, such as acquainting the individual with the organization's rules and policies, along with the informal activities of "socializing" them into the work group.

5. *Training and development.* Training and development concern the activities that are directed toward improving the employee's capability to contribute to one organization's performance. Training involves improving employee skills; development concerns preparing the employee for additional responsibility or advancement.

6. *Performance evaluation.* This step involves the process of evaluating the employee's performance in relationship to certain standards or goals. Essential features of this step are: (a) the feedback to the employee; and (b) the direction needed to continue or improve performance.

7. *Reward system.* To maintain an effective work force, the organization must be able to reward good performance or punish poor performance. This is the function of the reward system. Included within this step are aspects related to compensation, promotion, career development, transfers, and demotions.

8. *Separations.* Because the human resource process in an organization is dynamic, there will be a constant inflow and outflow of people. Of concern to managers are such actions as voluntary turnover, retirements, layoffs, and discharges.

The discussion in this chapter concerns the process steps through training and development. The last three steps—performance evaluation, reward system, and separations—will be the focus of chapter 16.

HUMAN RESOURCE PLANNING

A few years ago, a large farm equipment manufacturer was in the process of building a plant in one of the Southern states. Financial planning had been conducted and the actual construction of the plant had begun. One

EXHIBIT 10–2
The Human
Resource Process

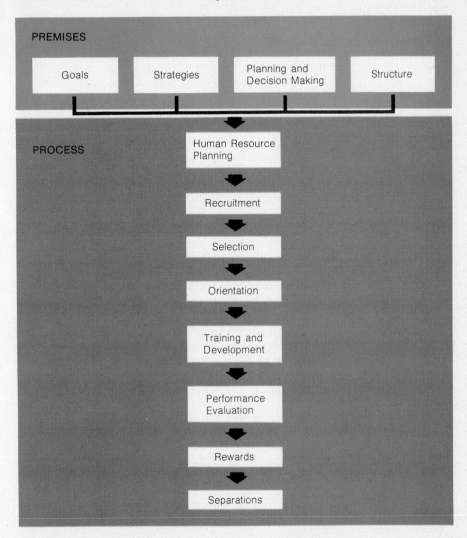

PREMISES

| Goals | Strategies | Planning and Decision Making | Structure |

PROCESS

Human Resource Planning

Recruitment

Selection

Orientation

Training and Development

Performance Evaluation

Rewards

Separations

element was missing—no one had given much thought to the issue of staffing the new plant. When the issue finally did come up, the new plant manager in charge indicated that when the plant was finished, then they would start worrying about hiring employees to staff the plant.

To the human resource planner, such a statement is not only a frequent occurrence, but is sure to bring on premature greying of the hair! Fortunately, most managers have come to the realization that acquiring and allocating human resources is not a process that can be turned on and off like a light bulb. The process takes time, effort, and a commitment by management—lack of attention to the process will result in many problems, such as higher costs and lower performance.

The human resource planning function involves at least four different factors, including: (1) the organization's goals and strategies; (2) the recognition of important labor force trends; (3) the current human resource audit and replacement analysis; and (4) the legal environment.

Organizational Goals and Strategies

The organization's stated goals and strategies identify what the future human resource needs are for the organization. In other words, how many people will be needed (an increase or decrease) to staff the organization in the near and distant future, and what skills and abilities will they require?

For example, vertical integration, market development, product development, and diversification (see chapter 6) strategies may require the organization to increase its number of employees and necessitate the development of new skills. Consider the situation faced by AT&T.[4] Long protected as a monopoly, the Bell System is now faced with increased competition in the sale of communication equipment and service from other companies. Since these products and services do not fall under the monopolistic umbrella, AT&T altered its strategies in an attempt to meet the new competition. The main effort is being directed at the marketing group, which must acquire skills in *selling,* not just servicing equipment—no small task, given the past practices they have learned and used.

A strategy of stability will probably mean that the organization will attempt to reach a status quo, being concerned with replacements for terminated workers. A retreat strategy, on the other hand, may require some major work force reductions. For example, the decisions by General Electric no longer to compete in the computer business, Westinghouse's divesting of its home appliance divisions, and the closing of plants by Chrysler all involve a shrinkage in the number of employees in the organization.

Labor Force Trends

In human resource planning, managers must be aware of certain trends in the distribution of the labor force. For example, consider the data shown in exhibit 10–3, which represents the actual and projected numbers in the national labor force by sex and age. At least two important points should be noted from the exhibit.[5] First, the decrease in the 20–24 year old group represents the well-known decline in birth rate that the U. S. has been experiencing. To management, this may signal a potential shortage of managerial talent during the latter part of this century. The knowledge of this situation may force organizations to rethink some of their expansion plans, or to revise their selection and training processes in order to provide for early identification and development of future managers.

Second, the increases in the 35–54 year old groups represent the "baby boom" population. By the end of this century, organizations will be faced with a large group of people who will be entering retirement. Thus, an effort may be needed to revise and reemphasize the organization's retirement programs. Coupled with the first point, many organizations will be faced with the problem of retiring a large group of experienced managers, but having an insufficient number of younger managers to replace these retired executives. The time to plan for this situation is now, not in 1990.

The process of forecasting human resource needs has evolved into

EXHIBIT 10–3 Labor Force Data (Actual and Projected) by Age and Sex

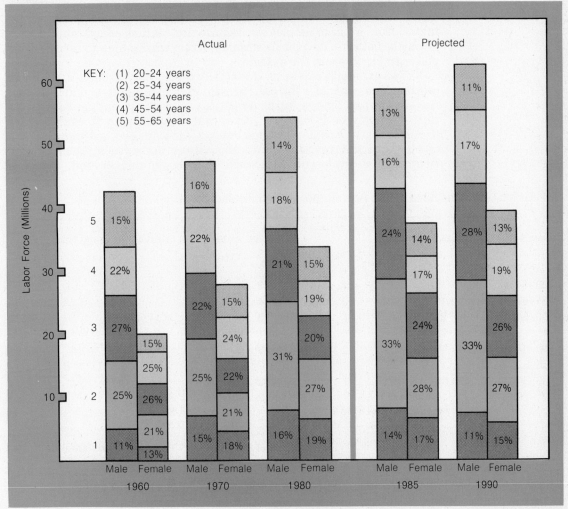

Source: *Current Population Reports,* Series P-25, no. 493; and W. Guzzardi, Jr., "Demography's Good News for the Eighties," *Fortune* (November 5, 1979): 96.

a major activity by managers in all types of organizations. The techniques available to managers to forecast are much the same as those we discussed in chapter 4 for environmental forecasting. The most frequently used techniques include judgmental (Delphi, trend extrapolation), quantitative (linear programming), and computer simulations. As human resource problems continue to grow in importance and complexity, the use of sophisticated forecasting techniques will increase commensurately.

Human Resource Assessment

At the same time, or shortly after the analysis of human resource trends, the emphasis switches to an examination of the organization's present personnel. This is called the human resource assessment or audit. The objective of the assessment is to evaluate current strengths and weaknesses of personnel and to match this evaluation against future requirements. Most organizations emphasize locating the needed skills and potential from *existing* employees because, for reasons of cost and morale, it may be better to develop and promote from within than to recruit, hire, place, and train from the outside.

Two examples can be used to clarify the human resource assessment process. First, consider the data presented in exhibit 10–4, which depicts the distribution by age, turnover rates, and replacement ratios (i.e., the ratio of employees at one age bracket that are waiting to fill each opening that occurs at the next-oldest age bracket) for managers in three divisions of a hypothetical company.[6] Such an analysis, known as a *resource audit*, would reveal any problems associated with age distribution. Turnover

EXHIBIT 10–4   Resource Audit: Age, Turnover, and Replacement

AGES	AGE DISTRIBUTION				TURNOVER RATES			REPLACEMENT RATIOS		
	A	B	C	TOTAL	A	B	C	A	B	C
60–64	7	6	7	20	4%	3%	3%	0	0	0
55–59	14	10	22	46	0	4	2	6	7	2
50–54	22	21	20	63	0	3	5	30	20	34
45–49	73	22	30	125	0	1	6	25	21	16
40–44	47	15	18	80	12	3	2	50	13	17
35–39	38	7	8	53	4	2	4	13	5	8
30–34	45	14	12	71	3	2	5	16	14	7
25–29	44	15	20	79	0	2	3	22	8	6
20–24	20	4	10	34	2	3	2	4	5	3
	310	114	147	571	3	8	6	31	18	22
					(Divisional Averages)			(Divisional Averages)		

Adapted from W. E. Bright, "How One Company Manages Its Human Resources," *Harvard Business Review* (January–February 1976): 85.

rates can be too high, indicating excessive replacement costs, or too low, indicating insufficient weeding out. In addition, high replacement ratios indicate that some blocking of lower level personnel is occurring; low ratios indicate that a shortage of capable managerial replacements exists.

If you were a manager in division A, you might be concerned with the following analysis from exhibit 10–4:

1. Of your 310 managers, there are 73 that are in the 45–49 year age bracket, which is not only disproportionate with the other age groups, but is the worst of the three divisions. Questions regarding the morale of the lower age group may develop. It is possible that some of these younger managers may move to other firms where there is more advancement potential. Or, these same managers may lose some of their effectiveness while waiting for slow-coming promotions.

2. The turnover rates for your division are the lowest of all the divisions and are one-half that of the organization as a whole. This is good from

the view of reducing turnover costs, but it may also be a signal that you may not be weeding out poor performers or there may be blocking of younger managers for promotions (note the turnover rate for the 40–44 year old group).

3. The analysis of replacement ratios supports the previous results. Your division has the highest replacement ratios, indicating that many more younger employees are waiting for promotion and advancement than the other divisions.

In summary, while on the surface your division may appear to be in good shape, a serious problem may be on the horizon concerning younger employees and their career development. A number of solutions can be considered, including more frequent promotions, use of special assignments, and so on. The most important factor, however, is that you have *diagnosed* the problem before it becomes critical. This, as we have stressed throughout this book, is an extremely important managerial skill.

A second form of human resource assessment is known as the *management replacement analysis*. As shown in exhibit 10–5, the replacement analysis for division A consists of three steps: (1) developing the organization chart; (2) evaluating the current performance of the existing managers; and (3) evaluating the promotion potential of the managers. The results are twofold. First, an evaluation of each department is given, providing higher level management with an assessment of human resource strengths and weaknesses. Second, the analysis provides the first step in the development of a *managerial succession plan,* identifying those managers that are likely candidates for future promotion.

In a simplistic manner, the analyses provided in exhibits 10–4 and 10–5 are very valuable to the manager. Not only have certain problems been uncovered, but the future needs and potential of the managerial staff have also been identified. These data, plus an analysis of labor force trends, provide the foundation for the human resource plan for the manager.

The Legal Environment of Human Resources

One of the most important developments in the human resource planning process has been the evolution and growth of the legal environment. Based primarily on civil rights legislation, the legal environment has made a significant impact on human resource activities for all types of organizations.

A number of the most important laws affecting the human resource process are shown in exhibit 10–6. By far the most dominant are those legislative acts that prohibit discrimination in the workplace on the basis of age, race, and sex. These laws have also served as the foundation for affirmative action programs, which require organizations to have a positive plan to reduce and/or eliminate internal imbalances or inequities among affected groups. Failure to do so can result in fines, loss of government contracts, or other actions.

AT&T, for example, agreed to pay over $15 million in back wages to women and other minority groups whose pay was "arbitrarily" low because of discriminatory practices. In addition, AT&T's affirmative action plan required that the number of women and blacks in lower level management positions be increased by over 80 percent and 40 percent, respectively. The plan also called for a 150 percent increase in the number

EXHIBIT 10–5 Management Replacement Analysis

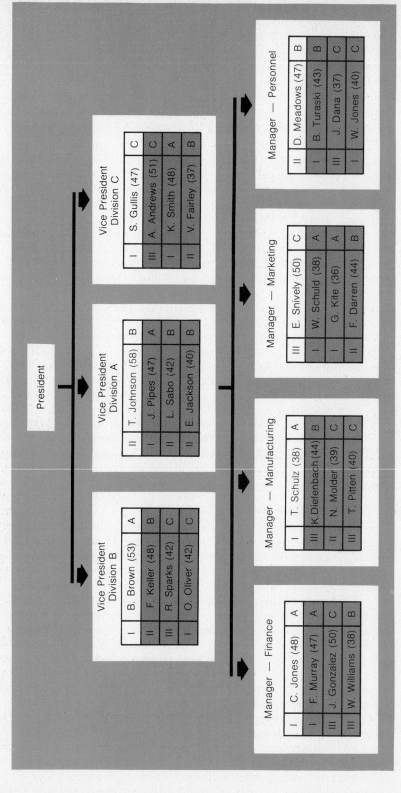

President

**Vice President
Division B**

I	B. Brown (53)	A
II	F. Keller (48)	B
III	R. Sparks (42)	C
I	O. Oliver (42)	C

**Vice President
Division A**

II	T. Johnson (58)	B
I	J. Pipes (47)	A
II	L. Sabo (42)	B
II	E. Jackson (40)	B

**Vice President
Division C**

I	S. Gullis (47)	C
III	A. Andrews (51)	C
I	K. Smith (48)	A
II	V. Fairley (37)	B

Manager — Finance

I	C. Jones (48)	A
I	F. Murray (47)	A
III	J. Gonzalez (50)	C
III	W. Williams (38)	B

Manager — Manufacturing

I	T. Schulz (38)	A
III	K. Diefenbach (44)	B
II	N. Molder (39)	C
III	T. Pitten (40)	C

Manager — Marketing

III	E. Snively (50)	C
I	W. Schuld (38)	A
I	G. Kite (36)	A
II	F. Darren (44)	B

Manager — Personnel

II	D. Meadows (47)	B
I	B. Turaski (43)	B
III	J. Dana (37)	C
I	W. Jones (40)	C

KEY

Present Performance
I   Excellent
II Satisfactory
III Needs Improvement

Advancement Potential
A Ready Now
B Needs More Experience
C Not Ready

EXHIBIT 10–6 Major Federal Laws Related to Human Resources

FEDERAL LAW	DESCRIPTION
1. U.S. Constitution: 1st, 5th, and 14th Amendments.	Prohibits deprivation of employment rights without due process of law—federal, state, and local governments.
2. Civil Rights Act of 1866 and 1870	Prohibits race discrimination in hiring, placement, and continuation of employment for private employers, unions, and employment agencies.
3. Title VI, 1964 Civil Rights Act	Prohibits discrimination based on race, color, or national origin—employers receiving federal financial assistance.
4. Title VII, 1964 Civil Rights Act	Prohibits discrimination based on race, color, religion, sex, or national origin—private employers; federal, state, and local governments; unions; employment agencies.
5. Executive Orders 11246 and 11375 (1965)	Prohibits discrimination based on race, color, religion, sex, or national origin (affirmative action)—federal contractors and subcontractors.
6. Title I, 1968 Civil Rights Act	Prohibits interference with a person's exercise of rights with respect to race, religion, color, or national origin.
7. National Labor Relations Act	Prohibits unfair representation by unions that discriminates on the basis of race, color, religion, sex, or national origin.
8. Equal Pay Act of 1963	Prohibits sex differences in pay for equal work—private employers.
9. Age Discrimination in Employment Act of 1967 and 1975	Prohibits age discrimination against those between the ages of 40 and 65 years—all employers.
10. Rehabilitation Act of 1973	Prohibits discrimination based on physical or mental handicap (affirmative action).
11. Vietnam Era Veterans Readjustment Act of 1974	Prohibits discrimination against disabled veterans and Vietnam era veterans (affirmative action).
12. Occupational Safety and Health Act (OSHA—1970)	Established mandatory safety and health standards in organizations.
13. Revised Guidelines on Employee Selection (1976)	Established specific rules on employment selection practices.
14. Mandatory Retirement Act	Employee cannot be forced to retire before age 70.
15. Privacy Act of 1974	Employees have legal right to examine letters of reference concerning them unless they waive the right.

of men in clerical positions and a nearly 120 percent increase in the number of women in craft and skilled jobs. The result is that women now climb telephone poles to repair circuits and men answer requests for long distance assistance.

The effect of affirmative action policies has been significant on organizations. Recent research has shown that the existence of such policies, supported by top management, has been effective in counteracting racial and sex biases in selection and promotion decisions.[7]

Due to the significance and complexity of human resource legislative acts, managers at all levels must become cognizant of their employment policies and behavior. Support and commitment to the laws must come from all managers, from the chief executive to the lowest levels.

RECRUITMENT

Recruiting concerns the set of activities that an organization uses to attract job candidates who have the abilities and skills needed to assist the organization in the achievement of its goals. For our purposes, recruitment will be concerned with the dual problem of *securing* people the organization needs and *insuring* that these people will remain.[8]

Recruiting to Secure People

In recruiting future employees, most organizations divide their recruiting into at least two types. First, for lower level positions, the organization employs a process we will call *general* recruiting. This is a continual process that is directed at filling positions that frequently open up in most organizations. Examples include various clerical personnel, janitorial staff, and other nonskilled or semiskilled workers. Second, to fill particular positions, an organization may opt for a *specific* recruiting orientation. This is most appropriate for positions in management, professional employees such as engineers and nurses, and certain skilled workers such as machinists and other equipment operators.

College recruiting can fall into each category. For example, most of the tire and rubber companies and financial institutions hire a number of college graduates for their management training programs. In this general classification, the new recruits enter the training program for a period of up to two years, after which they join a particular department where there is a match between the needs of the unit and the skills of the individual. Some recruiting of MBA graduates can be specific in nature, particularly if the graduate is being hired for an identified position, such as financial analyst or cost accountant.

Two issues are important in this recruiting category: job analysis and the sources of recruitment.

Job Analysis.   Before the organization can recruit personnel, it must know what type of position is open. This is the purpose of job analysis. *Job analysis* consists of a statement that depicts the following: (1) a description that identifies the title, duties, and responsibilities for that position; and (2) an acknowledgement of the desired background, experience, and personal characteristics an individual must have in order to perform effectively in the position. For example, an open position for an auditing manager in an accounting firm may state: "Position requires a BS or MS in accounting, CPA, minimum five years experience, some as a supervisor; motivated with well-established interpersonal and analytical skills."

Recruitment Sources.   Two broad sources of recruitment can be used by organizations. First, there are *internal* sources within the organization. These may include job posting systems, friends of present employees, or the replacement analysis. Many organizations have found it a beneficial practice to recruit or promote existing employees to open positions. At least two advantages can accrue to organizations from promoting from within: (1) it significantly reduces the sometimes excessive recruiting and placement costs; and (2) it promotes improved morale and loyalty among employees because they believe their performance will be rewarded with a promotion if it is consistently high.

External sources are also frequently used by organizations. The external sources include walk-ins, agencies or placement/search firms, newspaper and journal ads, school and college recruiting, unions, military services, and professional associations. External sources offer mixed advantages and disadvantages to the organization. On the positive side, the vast variety of sources will almost ensure that the organization will be able to find an adequate number of candidates. On the negative side, external sources such as college recruiting can be quite costly. Most organizations must interview between twenty to thirty candidates before one is hired. Newspaper and journal ads can also be expensive, as is using a placement firm for more specialized or high-level managerial positions.

The growing body of research that has investigated the relationship between recruiting source and rates of turnover have yielded surprisingly consistent results.[9] These studies indicate that internal sources, particularly employee referrals, were consistently good sources of personnel who remained in the organization for a significant length of time. Employment agencies, on the other hand, were poor sources of long-term employees. That is, employees hired through employment agencies left the organization sooner than did employees who were hired from internal organizational sources.

Realistic Recruiting

Recruiting philosophies and policies in many organizations are too often based on the objective of filling the immediate job opening, as opposed to the more long-term objective of finding a person who will be both productive and will stay in the job. The first is called the *flypaper* approach to recruiting: if the organization is able to attract people, they will get stuck and stay.[10] The latter approach is the *realistic* method, which emphasizes telling the prospective employee what to expect in the job in order to avoid establishing unrealistic expectations that may lead to later dissatisfaction.

The realistic recruiting approach stresses, through a variety of mechanisms, what the prospective employee will actually find on the job. This can be done with the use of interviews, booklets, films, and/or videotapes and other forms of communication.

A number of studies have been conducted to investigate the effects of the realistic recruiting approach.[11] Among the groups were included telephone operators, insurance sales representatives, and assembly-line workers in an electronics plant. In each study, the results were nearly the same: (1) newly hired employees given realistic job previews had greater job survival rates than those hired by traditional methods; (2) greater job satisfaction levels were reported by realistic job preview employees; and (3) contrary to the belief of many people, the use of realistic job previews did not reduce the flow of highly capable applicants.

In summary, the traditional approach to recruiting (i.e., flypaper approach) may result in the short-term benefit of hiring capable people, but can create long-term problems with respect to dissatisfaction and turnover. The realistic approach, on the other hand, has resulted in lower turnover rates with no decrease in the number of people applying for jobs.

SELECTION

The basis of the selection process is *matching*. On one hand, the organization decides whether the candidate's qualifications match the needs of the job; on the other hand, the candidate decides whether or not the job in the organization matches personal goals and needs.

Ideally, both the organization and the candidate enter the selection process on an equal basis. In reality, however, many factors, particularly the nature of the external environment, create a state of inequality. For example, if the labor market is "tight"—known as a buyer's market, because there are more candidates than jobs—the organization may have the opportunity to choose from a number of qualified people. If the labor market is "open"—known as a seller's market, because there are more jobs than qualified candidates—the candidate may be able to choose from a number of job opportunities. In the late 1970s the labor market for elementary school teachers was quite tight, while an open market was apparent for nurses, secretaries, and certain accountants. For engineers, the labor market has varied from tight to open frequently over the past fifteen years.

The Selection Process

Exhibit 10–7 presents an example of the selection process for an organization. While there are many variations in the degree of formality that organizations adopt, the detailed steps are usually followed.

Step 1. The first step involves the establishment of the *criteria* for selection by the organization. As in the job analysis procedure, the criteria usually consist of information related to formal education, experience, physical characteristics, and other specific skills.

Step 2. This step includes the *initial screening interview* and the completion of an application form. The objectives of this step are as follows: (1) get basic information; (2) determine the level of interest of the candidates; and (3) determine whether or not the selection process should continue.

Step 3. The *formal interview* is part of almost all selection procedures, and probably one of the most important steps. It is important for two major reasons. First, it provides a great variety and volume of information about the candidate (for the organization) and the organization (for the candidate). Second, the candidate generally meets face to face with many organizational members, which is invaluable in determining the degree of fit or match with organization's needs.

There are three general types of interviews that are most frequently used: structured, semistructured, and unstructured. In the *structured* interview, the interviewer prepares a list of questions in advance and does not deviate from the list. If the responses are to be made in a forced-choice manner (i.e., yes or no), a great deal of information can be gathered from a structured interview because it eliminates idle chatter. The *semistructured* interview consists of a limited set of questions that are asked of the candidate. This procedure allows not only for collection of needed

**EXHIBIT 10–7
The Selection
Process**

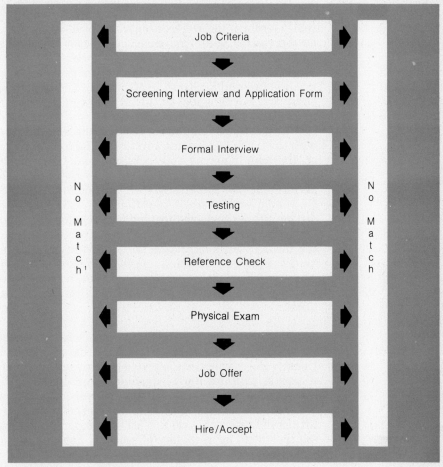

Job Criteria

Screening Interview and Application Form

Formal Interview

Testing

Reference Check

Physical Exam

Job Offer

Hire/Accept

No Match[1]

No Match

[1]Organization or Candidate Decision

data, but the extra time permits the interviewer or interviewee to delve deeper on a number of points. Finally, in the *unstructured* interview little preparation other than a set of example topics is made. The overriding advantage of this type of interview is that it allows a great deal of freedom to the interviewer to adapt to the situation and cover areas of interest to the candidate.

While the organization wishes to gain as much information as possible from the candidate. there are limitations that have been imposed as a result of antidiscrimination laws. Many questions that appear to be harmless can be construed as discriminatory in selection decisions. The important criterion is that unless a question relates directly to the job, or to specific needs, such as future insurance needs, it normally cannot be asked.

Step 4.   *Employment testing* involves a number of different procedures, each attempting to estimate the candidate's ability to perform effectively on the job. Two general categories of tests are usually employed by organizations. First, in *performance tests* or simulations, candidates actually perform the work or a portion of it. Examples include typing tests for secretaries, speed and accuracy tests for computer keypunch operators, and a standardized driving exam for forklift drivers. The second category concerns *pencil-and-paper tests* that are designed to measure the general intelligence and aptitude levels of the candidate. Also in the second category are *psychological tests* that are oriented toward measuring certain personality and temperament traits.

In the use of employment tests, the manager needs to be concerned with three characteristics. First, does the test relate to *actual performance* on the job? If not, it may possibly lead to a charge of discrimination. Second, is the test *valid*? That is, does the test measure a component of performance, or something else? For example, a speed and accuracy test for computer keypunch operators is quite valid for measuring or predicting future performance, but a psychological test supposedly measuring "achievement motive" may not only not be measuring this factor, but the factor itself may not be an important determinant of future performance. Finally, is the test *reliable*? The key criterion is whether the test gives approximately the same score each time it is taken over a short period of time, assuming that nothing important has occurred between tests.

Step 5.   Background and *reference checks* are one of the most valuable, but equally controversial, aspects of the employment selection process. Usually the candidate is asked to provide letters of reference or the names of people who are knowledgeable about his or her background. If the reference person is sufficiently knowledgeable and is truthful, then valuable information is obtained. However, many times this does not occur. Either the references do not know the person well enough or they hide the true facts for a variety of reasons. For this reason, reference checks have been criticized for their lack of reliability.

Cooper, if I had wanted someone who squealed every time I told him to come in on Sunday, I would have hired Porky Pig!

Weber for FORTUNE Magazine

**THE
MANAGER'S
JOB**
Phillip J.
Raymond of
Massachusetts
Mutual Life
Insurance Co.

A problem that has faced insurance companies for many years is the retention of insurance agents. According to industry statistics, an unimpressive 13 percent of agents stick it out for even four years. Massachusetts Mutual Life Insurance Company, however, believes that they have found a way to beat the odds by emphasizing a selection process to identify agents with more potential staying power.

The selection system, according to Phillip J. Raymond, who administers the company's program, is made up of two components. First, the crux of the new selection system is assigning weights or points to certain aspects of the candidate's personal data and then making a decision on the basis of total points. Of the five main areas, age, aptitude, and college background are given a 1 to 5 point rating, while orientation toward selling and the candidate's longevity and performance on former jobs are rated along a 1 to 10 point continuum.

Candidates who pass this first screening are then moved into the second stage of the selection process, consisting of interviews in the region and at headquarters. Each piece of information is again examined carefully resulting in a hire or no-hire decision.

The selection system, particularly the point system, may seem arbitrary, but the company has spent years fine tuning it. Its overall four-year rate of agent retention is 27 percent, more than double the industry average. More of the company's agents have passed the chartered life underwriter test than any in the industry. In addition, the company has more agents who have sold $1 million-plus policies than any other firm.

Mr. Raymond indicates that the success of the system is somewhat clouded because some claim it presses against the edge of privacy and anti-discrimination laws. The company has tried to stay within legal guidelines on hiring, and as a result, questions on sex and race were eliminated along with the requirement for a photo of the candidate. The age data are of continuing concern and may have to be changed.

Adapted from "Spotting a Winner in Insurance," Business Week (February 12, 1979): 122–23.

Another problem closely related to the above issues is that created by the Privacy Act of 1974. Under this law, persons have a legal right to examine letters of reference concerning them *unless* they waive the right to do so. Because of this, many people are reluctant to provide negative information for fear of being sued by the candidate. Besides attempting to have candidates waive their right to view the letters, many organizations have tried two techniques to obtain the valuable information from references. First, they may decide to telephone the reference and ask for a verbal recommendation. This helps somewhat to eliminate the problem of having the data down on paper. Second, the organization may contact people *other* than those identified by the candidate. This provides wider coverage to the needed information.

Step 6.   Some organizations require future employees to take a *physical examination*. The reasons are threefold: (1) to eliminate insurance claims for injuries or illnesses contracted outside the workplace or before the individual was hired; (2) to prevent the hiring of people with communicable diseases; and (3) to verify that the candidate can actually do the required work. The most important is probably the third—organizations must carefully state and prove that certain specific physical requirements are needed for acceptable on-the-job performance. For many years, certain handicapped persons were excluded from any jobs because of some non-performance-related physical requirements. In the same manner, women were not permitted to apply for jobs in city fire departments for physical reasons. With time—and the influence of anti-discrimination laws—such practices are slowly being eliminated.

Step 7.   The job offer generally concludes the first cycle of the selection process. A person who has successfully passed the key criteria of the process is offered employment. As we pointed out in the recruiting discussion, many offers are turned down before an acceptance is received. This means that the selection process is a *continual activity* that is time consuming, costly, but necessary.

Management Selection

Because managers are the focal point of an organization's activities, the selection decision for them is one of the most important made in the organization. The selection process we have just discussed is generally followed, except for some important modifications.

First, whether the manager is promoted from within or is recruited from the outside, the organization must recognize that the requirements for managerial positions differ from lower-level jobs, and that differences exist across the organizational functions (i.e., marketing, accounting, production). In other words, there should be a clear understanding concerning the skills and roles that are required of the manager (see chapter 2).

Second, in managerial selection, there is far more emphasis placed on *behavior* than on employment test *scores*. The reason is fairly clear: the manager's job has yet to be successfully reduced to a set of finite characteristics or traits that can be measured by simple paper-and-pencil tests. By the word *behavior* it is assumed that we are referring to the manager's past performance on the job.

Last, a recognition of these two points results in the increased importance of the employment interview. The interview process usually involves a number of interviews with the management team of the organization, sometimes one on one, other times in a group; formally in an office or informally during lunch or dinner; frequently in a semistructured format, or other times, quite unstructured. The goal of the interviews is to assess and evaluate the candidate's capabilities and potential match to the job.

Interviewing is a highly subjective process that is susceptible to a great deal of error. Nevertheless, most organizations believe that over a number of interviews, the candidate's true profile will be revealed. A good example to review is the case on Standard Brands at the end of chapter 2 in which there was a major problem with the managerial behavior of the new executive and the prevailing philosophies and behaviors in the organization.

As the reader may have realized, the process of managerial selection is less than scientifically rigorous and is highly dependent on subjective evaluations. Unfortunately, at this time in the emergence of the management profession, this may be the best most organizations can hope for. This situation, however, may be a blessing in disguise. If one can reduce the manager's job to a simple list of individual characteristics, scores on certain paper-and-pencil tests and psychological profiles, and other evaluation mechanisms, then much of the freedom, individuality, and creativity may be lost. As we have stressed throughout this book, the manager's job not only consists of functions, skills, and roles, but a significant portion of the success that is obtained is due to hunches, common sense, and innate judgements that are not easily reduced to quantitative measurement.

Managerial Assessment Centers

An approach to the selection of managers that has steadily gained in popularity is the *assessment center*. Beginning with the selection of intelligence officers during the Second World War, followed by the pioneering work of AT&T, the assessment center approach offers the organization a valuable tool for the selection of managers.[12]

In brief, assessment centers attempt to predict the behavior of individuals in management situations from their performance in a series of simulated exercises. Assessment centers usually involve the participation of candidates for one to three days in a number of exercises, interviews, and testing. A brief description of the most frequently used assessment center methods are shown in exhibit 10–8.

The following procedure is an example of how an assessment center works:

1. Management decides on the types or categories of jobs that are to be used in the exercises. They can be specific jobs that are to open up in the future or a series of managerial positions for which there is a high frequency of personnel movement.

2. A set of raters is chosen by management. The rating team can consist of skilled and competent managers from the organization; however, the usual procedure is to have a mix of internal management personnel and external experts, such as management professors, psychologists, sociologists, and consultants.

3. The management staff and assessment raters spend considerable time defining the job (or jobs) to be assessed and the criteria for performance. This can vary significantly from job to job and from organization to organization. Since the criteria for performance will be evaluated through the observation of behavior in simulated settings, it is crucial that there be a clear understanding of the definition of the particular criteria. For example, the job for which the candidates are being assessed is a middle-management position in the production scheduling and control division. The following skills were deemed important:

Organization and planning: Effective in planning and organizing one's own work and that of the group as well.

EXHIBIT 10–8   Typical Management Assessment Center Methods

METHOD	DESCRIPTION	EXAMPLE TRAITS ANALYZED
Management game or simulation	Participants perform in a simulated setting, sometimes with a computer simulation, make necessary decisions and analyze the results.	Organizing ability, financial aptitude, decision making, efficiency under stress, adaptability, and leadership capacity.
Leaderless group discussions	Participants in a group with no formally appointed leader are asked to solve a business problem.	Aggressiveness, persuasiveness, verbal skills, flexibility, and self-confidence.
In-basket exercise	A mail in-basket for an ill executive is given to the participant to analyze, to set priorities and to take action on.	Organizing ability, decision making under stress, conceptual skills, ability to delegate, and concern for others.
Role playing	Participants are asked to take the roles of hypothetical employees, as in a performance evaluation interview.	Insight, empathy to others, human and technical skills, and sensitivity to others.
Psychological testing	A series of pencil-and-paper instruments are completed by the participants.	Reasoning, interests, aptitudes, communications tendencies, leadership and group styles, motivation profile, and the like.
Case Analysis	Participants are given a case to analyze individually and present to a group of evaluators.	Verbal ability, diagnostic skills, conceptual skills, technical skills, and so on.
In-depth interviews	Participants are interviewed by raters—usually after some of the above exercises have been completed—regarding a variety of personal interests, skills, and aptitudes.	Verbal ability, self-confidence, managerial skills, commitment to career, and so on.

Recognition and integration: Effective in understanding the details of complex problems as well as integrating the details into a comprehensive plan.

Decision making: Ability to reach logical and rational decisions with the available data and be able to defend one's decisions when challenged.

Group leadership: Effective both in structuring group activities toward goal achievement and being aware of the feelings and needs of others.

Oral communication: Effective in communicating through such verbal skills as eye contact, grammar, vocabulary, voice and tone emphasis, and hand movements.[13]

In the actual assessment center activities, the raters look for behaviors by the candidates that represent various levels of effectiveness on these criteria.

4. The selection of the candidates to participate in the assessment center occurs next. Two methods are usually used to identify candidates: nomination by a superior or self-nomination.

5. The actual assessment activities occur with the candidates performing in group activities (role playing or leaderless group discussion, and in individual sessions (in-basket exercise, case analysis, or in-depth interviews).

6. Finally, a short time later (usually less than two weeks), the candidates are given feedback on their assessment center performance. In both written and verbal form, the individuals are counseled concerning their managerial potential, strengths and weaknesses in managerial skills, and areas that need to be developed further.

Since their introduction, assessment centers have been adopted by many organizations including IBM, Sears, Sohio, Caterpillar Tractor, and a number of health care organizations. Recent research studies and surveys have reported that the most frequently used assessment techniques are the in-basket exercise, management games, and leaderless group discussion.[14]

While the emerging studies indicate the superiority of assessment centers over other management selection methods, a number of problems exist that managers must consider.[15] First, an assessment center is costly—a three day assessment center not only ties up the time of candidates but the raters as well. Multiply this by the number of sessions per year, and you have a large resource commitment by the organization. Second, raters must be chosen carefully, with an emphasis on their experience, knowledge, and judgment. Finally, there must be a clear understanding that high ratings in the assessment center do not by themselves assure promotion, though they can speed it up. Low ratings are not a blemish on one's record, either. Studies have shown that the number of low-rated managers who quit the organization was not any different than the high-rated managers who also terminated with the organization.[16]

If the organization can tolerate the high cost, one can expect the use of assessment centers to spread across most industries. The advantages over existing procedures for managerial selection are too strong to ignore. Assessment centers are also now being used in such activities as minority employment and in college recruiting.

ORIENTATION

The process of *orientation,* which is defined as the activities involved in introducing the individual to the organization, provides the foundation for the new employee to begin to function confortably and effectively on the new job. In organizations, the orientation process serves multiple purposes. Among the most important are:

1. Clarifying the job and developing realistic expectations about what is expected of the individual.

2. Reducing the amount of stress and anxiety a new employee experiences.

3. Reducing start-up costs.

4. Properly done, strengthening the relationship between the new employee and superiors and peers.

Two different types of orientation usually occur in most organizations. The first is called *induction,* which is the initial phase in which the new employee learns what to do, where to go for help, and what are the important rules, policies, and procedures, and so forth. The second, termed *socialization,* is a longer-term process in which the new member learns the value system norms, and the required behavior patterns of the organization and group.

Induction

The induction phase of orientation involves an interaction between the new employee, the direct supervisor, and formal orientation programs. In these activities, the new employee usually learns the following:

1. The history of the organization.
2. A description of the organization's products and services.
3. The structure, authority, and responsibility relationships in the organization.
4. Rules, regulations, and policies regarding such things as safety, lunch hours, and methods of formal communication.
5. Personnel policies including compensation, benefits, and other employee services.
6. Meeting other employees as soon as possible after arrival.

In most organizations, the immediate supervisor of the new employee is required to complete a form that lists the items of orientation to be covered and when and who presents the material to the employee.

There is a growing body of research that suggests that the orientation process and the employee's early job experiences with the organization have a significant effect on the long-term career commitment to the organization. The crucial factor is one of expectations. That is, the individual has certain expectations of the organization, and the organization also has expectations of the new employee.[17] When these expectations match, a workable climate between the individual and the organization has been established; when the expectations do not match, a state of dissatisfaction can develop, creating tension, stress, and pressure that can possibly result in termination.

Socialization

A newly hired sales representative for an electronics firm, calling on a customer, encounters a quality problem with a recent shipment of the firm's electronic components. To show concern over the quality problem, the sales rep places a long distance call directly to the plant where the defective product was manufactured to notify them of the difficulty. Returning to the sales office two days later, the sales rep is confronted by the sales manager who states that the next time a similar problem is encountered with a customer, the sales rep should not contact the plant manager, but should call the sales office and report the problem to the sales manager.

This example is an illustration of the socialization process in organizations. Commonly referred to as "learning the ropes," socialization involves the various activities directed toward communicating to the new member what is and what is not acceptable behavior to the organization. By communicating to the new member in this manner, the organization hopes to build commitment and loyalty that can lead to future effectiveness.

Socialization Process.   The socialization process generally involves two stages: unlearning and relearning.[18] *Unlearning* consists of a series of events that serve the function of undoing old work values so that the new employee will be prepared to learn new values. Two mechanisms are most frequently used by organizations. First, as in the example, there is some form of direct communication with the new employee regarding a specific behavior. The first time such unacceptable behavior occurs, the communication usually is in a positive form, suggesting that lack of knowledge was the major cause of the behavior. With each occurrence, however, the form of communication becomes more coercive (i.e., more like punishment).

The second mechanism involves the allocation of time. That is, the new member is given a variety of assignments or problems to solve that require a great deal of time to complete. This is a common procedure that is used by educational institutions in the first weeks of the semester for new students and by fraternal organizations on campuses with new pledges or associate members. The overall objective is to take up so much of the time of the new employee with new learning episodes that old work habits and values do not have a chance to be used.

After a period of time of intensive unlearning, the *relearning* process begins. Among the mechanisms that are used are:

1. Observations of organizational members going about their work. This can be done by following a manager around during the day or through the mentoring process as discussed in chapter 2.

2. Frequent use of rewards and punishment. Just as the sales rep example illustrates, higher level managers make it a point frequently to point out satisfactory and less than satisfactory activities.

3. Extensive training programs that are more relevant to the job.

4. Frequent counseling sessions with superiors.

The length of time that is devoted to the socialization process can vary significantly with the type of job. With low-level positions (e.g., janitor, and machine operators), it can take only a few days. With managerial positions, due to the inherent complexity, socialization may take weeks or months.

Successes and Failures with Socialization.   The success of the organizational socialization process is dependent on at least two factors. First, the level of initial motivation by the new member is important—in other words, how much does the individual want to be accepted as a member of the organization? In the case of certain fraternal organizations, the "hazing" process is used to test the candidate's motivation.

Second, there are certain factors that the organization can use to hold the new member "captive" until the socialization process has made an impact.[19] For example, new employees are almost immediately asked to participate in stock option programs, medical insurance plans, and other benefits. Other mechanisms include the extensive process of locating housing, or the simple statement by a superior that it will "take many months to learn the business." Rather than leave in the middle of the learning process, the individual remains, thus permitting the socializing process to continue.

The acceptance or rejection of organizational socialization attempts is basically one of individual choice. An important point to remember is this: As a member of an organization, the individual can work to *change* certain beliefs that were deemed unacceptable when he or she went through the socialization process. The norms and values of an organization represent the attitudes and beliefs of the people who make up its fabric, and thus, make up a dynamic process. The process of change may take a great length of time, but the result may be an improved organization, and hence, higher performance.

TRAINING AND DEVELOPMENT

In today's complex and dynamic environment, it is no longer necessary to debate whether training and development activities are luxuries in which only the largest of organizations can indulge only in prosperous times. Most organizations—large and small—have come to the realization that the development of an effective work force is no more a luxury than having a sales department or an accounting function. It is an accepted fact that training and development are necessary for the spirit, survival, and performance of an organization—they must develop those who will manage the organization in the years to come.

The training and development function in an organization involves a multi-faceted purpose and definition. *Training* is an activity that is primarily directed at improving an employee's current job performance. It generally involves the acquisition of technical skills, and some human skills, by nonmanagerial and managerial personnel. Learning to operate a computer terminal, how to write a business report, or the right way to conduct a performance evaluation are examples.

Development, on the other hand, involves two equally important components.[20] First, there is *management development,* which is concerned with the question, "What kind of managers and professionals will the organization need tomorrow in order to achieve its goals in a changing environment?" Management development is oriented to issues of the age and skills of the managerial staff and what is needed in the future. It is also concerned with the structure of the organization and the types of managers that are required to operate in this structure. The focus of management development is *outside* or *external*—it is heavily oriented toward responding to the strategic questions of what business and service activity are we in, and what should it be in the future.

The focus of *manager development* is internal—on the manager. The objective is to improve the skills and advancement potential of individuals so that they may better contribute to the organization and to society in the future.

In this chapter, our focus will be on management development and training activities. In chapter 20, we will provide a more detailed discussion of the process of manager development.

Training and Development Process

Exhibit 10–9 depicts an example of the training and development process that occurs in many organizations. There are a number of important steps in this process:

1. The first step is to conduct a "training and development needs analysis." As shown in exhibit 10–9, a needs analysis has a threefold focus: *organizational analysis* (analyzing the needs of the total organization now and in the future); *operational analysis* (analyzing the needs of a specific group of jobs); and *individual analysis* (analyzing the needs of the specific employee).[21]

2. Once the needs have been identified, the specific goals and criteria for the training and development activities must be set. This includes establishing both the short-term and long-term objectives of the programs, and the criteria on which the programs will be evaluated.

3. Training and development methods are selected that emphasize both on-the-job and off-the-job programs.

4. Program evaluation provides an important assessment of the training and development process. Evaluation occurs during three stages: (a) during training and development; (b) at the end of the training and development experience; and (c) after a length of time back on the job.

Because of its particular importance to organizations, the topic of training and development sources and techniques will be discussed separately.

Training and Development Sources

There are a number of sources of training and development programs that are available to the organization.[22] Programs that are conducted *within* the organization (internal) usually involve on-the-job or off-the-job activities. On-the-job activities consist of programs that are designed for the individual to learn during work. Examples include apprenticeship programs and internships. Off-the-job activities are more oriented to separate classroom-type instructions by the training and development staff.

EXHIBIT 10–9   Training and Development Process

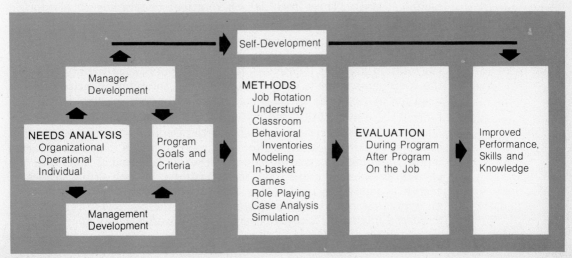

Training and development programs can also be conducted *outside* the organization (external). Such activities generally involve sending the individual to an association-sponsored program, such as the American Management Associations; or through one of the many university-sponsored programs. These external activities usually cover topics in more depth or completely new topics that the organizational staff are unable to cover.

A continuing debate in many organizations is the comparative value and effectiveness of internal and external programs. Internally sponsored training and development programs are generally less expensive and require less of the individual's time than external programs. On the other hand, external programs typically present concepts and topics from experts in a field, which is a plus in the acquisition of knowledge. In addition, a frequently overlooked factor is that learning of new skills and approaches may occur more effectively when the individual is removed from the day-to-day activities and demands of the job. This allows for a greater concentration on the concepts being presented. There is also the positive feature of meeting and interacting with managers from other organizations. The interchange of ideas and approaches to problems among program participants is itself a very valuable learning experience.

There is no pat answer to which is best, internal or external programs. Managers should diagnose the particular needs of the organization and the individual before choosing between the different techniques. Cost and learning value must be carefully weighed.

Training and Development Techniques

With the growing importance of training and development activities, there has been a commensurate growth in the number of techniques that have been used. The various techniques range from basic classroom instruction to complex simulation gaming and experiential learning. To simplify the presentation of the vast number of techniques, we will discuss them as they relate to the specific managerial skills that they are intended to influence. A summary is shown in exhibit 10–10.

Technical Skills.   Three techniques are most frequently used to impart technical skills. These include: job rotation; understudy or mentoring relationships; and classroom instruction.

1. *Job rotation.* With job rotation, the individual employee works on a series of jobs in the organization or in a specific unit. The primary benefits of job rotation are that it provides for learning of a wide variety of tasks, the individual is made aware of the critical interdependencies and the need for cooperation, and it enables the individual to develop a better view of the entire unit or organization.

2. *Understudy or apprenticeship.* Like job rotation, this technique is highly oriented to on-the-job activities. The understudy is asked to observe, follow, and emulate an experienced worker for a period of time until the particular technical skills have been mastered. In such skilled trades as carpentry, electrical installation, and others, the approach is known as an *apprenticeship.* At the managerial level, the *mentoring* relationship discussed in chapter 2 could be considered an understudy approach.

EXHIBIT 10–10   Training and Development and Managerial Skills

SKILLS	CRITERIA	Job Rotation	Under-study	Class-room	Behavioral Inventories	Modeling	In-Basket	Games	Role Playing	Cases
Technical	Improved Performance	X				X		X		
	Skills Development	X	X			X	X	X		
	Knowledge	X	X	X	X	X				
Human	Improved Performance	X				X		X	X	
	Skills Development	X	X	X	X	X		X	X	
	Knowledge	X	X	X	X	X		X		
Conceptual	Improved Performance	X						X		X
	Skills Development	X	X	X	X	X	X	X		X
	Knowledge	X	X	X	X	X	X		X	X
Diagnostic	Improved Performance	X	X			X	X			X
	Skills Development	X	X			X	X	X		X
	Knowledge	X	X	X		X	X		X	X

Adapted from T. J. Von Der Embse, "Choosing a Management Development Model," *Personnel Journal* (October 1978).

3. *Classroom instruction.* Similar to that of formal instruction in educational institutions, many organizations use lectures and seminars to conduct training activities.

Human Skills.   The importance of human skills to managers and management makes them quite popular for inclusion in most training and development programs. Yet their complexity and acquisition problems make them equally difficult to present. Many techniques, including role playing (as discussed in the section on assessment centers) have been created for purposes of developing human skills. Among the most used are behavioral inventories and behavioral modeling.

1. *Behavioral inventories.* A number of pencil-and-paper instruments have been developed that provide an evaluation or description of certain behaviors exhibited by the manager. Examples include descriptions of the manager's leadership style, communications patterns, and orientation toward working in groups.

2. *Behavior modeling.* Behavior modeling is a technique that uses a combination of role playing and video-tape feedback to present a new concept or skill.[23] For example, to introduce a new approach to college interviewing, the participants review a series of films or video tapes that depict acceptable and unacceptable interviewing techniques. To ensure the realism of the tapes, employees in the organization are used as actors in

the role-playing episodes. The participants are then asked to do the role playing of the new interviewing techniques after which the tapes are evaluated and repeated.

Conceptual and Diagnostic Skills.   The development of conceptual and diagnostic skills is more difficult to accomplish through training and development programs. As we implied in chapter 2, these skills are primarily developed through time and experience. There are certain techniques, however, that can facilitate the recognition and development of these two important skills.

In-basket exercise, simulation gaming, and leaderless group discussions, as used in assessment centers, have been used in the development of conceptual and diagnostic skills. One of the most popular techniques is that of the comprehensive *case analysis*. Either through internal programs or more frequently through externally sponsored management development programs (or graduate school courses), the participant is forced to: (1) identify the main problems and their causes; (2) develop a set of alternative actions to resolve the problem or problems; and (3) choose the most appropriate solution. The ensuing group discussions not only force the participant to justify a position, but may help promote tolerance of others' viewpoints in solving complex organizational problems, which itself is a valuable human skill.

Characteristics of Successful Management Development Programs

Organizations such as Xerox, Citibank, General Motors, AT&T, Kaiser Aluminum, IBM, Caterpillar, and Raytheon have been known for their successes in developing effective managers. It may be helpful to note what similarities and differences exist in the way these programs are conducted. A recent analysis of some of the best-managed companies in the United States revealed some interesting findings regarding management development practices.[24] The study revealed that there is no best way, or universal approach followed by these companies. AT&T, for example, depends heavily on the assessment center approach to identify managers with potential and then involves them in a long series of formal training activities along with frequent job rotations. IBM emphasizes formal training programs that can last from one to four weeks in duration. Lower-level managers participate primarily in in-house programs, and higher-level executives may be sent to university programs or other external associations. Raytheon almost totally depends on in-house training programs.

Second, without exception, the studied companies believe that the vast majority of actual management development occurs *on the job,* through handling of progressively more responsible assignments and problems under fire. On-the-job experience, coaching by superiors (mentoring), and job rotation were identified as the most important development means.

Third, formal training in management skills required at different organizational levels is used to prepare for and enhance on-the-job development. Specific job assignments are made to utilize the new skills after development occurs.

Fourth, the content of formal management training varies by organizational level. At the supervisory level, the emphasis is on handling organizational policies and procedures, communication, personnel practices, and motivation of subordinates. At the middle-management level, performance evaluation, effective leadership styles, group dynamics, time management, and counseling of subordinates are stressed. Finally, at the executive level, the focus is on effective decision making, dealing with the external environment, and the development of strategies and policies.

Fifth, the larger the organization, the greater the probability that they will have their own training operations physically separated from the headquarters. Thus, internal programs are preferred over external programs. This allows the organization to tailor the training programs more closely to on-the-job development activities.

Finally, it was unanimously believed that the development of subordinates is a primary responsibility of all managers. Their ability to develop capable people is a significant element in their own development and advancement.

COMMENTS ON THE PRACTICE OF MANAGEMENT
(See p. 325)

The brief discussion of Procter and Gamble's approach to management development at the beginning of this chapter illustrates how one company has reached a high level of success in this important area. First, it should be noted that the process begins with an intensive selection program, particularly on college campuses. While not stated in the introductory section, P&G consistently attempts to hire a steady group of potential managers no matter what the state of the economy. In time of recession, when some companies decrease their emphasis on college recruiting, P&G continues at its same level of effort. Consistency in recruiting ensures some consistency in management.

Second, the company places almost all its emphasis in management development on the mentoring process and on-the-job training. The latter approach is stressed quite heavily. Although some managers may believe that classroom training is necessary, P&G feels that the only way to learn is to get in there and do it. Much like cream rising to the surface, managers with the skills and abilities to tackle successfully challenging jobs are identified early and moved on to other assignments. Last, the compensation system is important. However, we will delay our discussion on this topic until chapter 16.

CURRENT ISSUES IN HUMAN RESOURCE MANAGEMENT

The human resource process, not unlike the other facets of the managerial functions, is being faced with many complex and difficult issues today. We have selected two of these issues for a brief discussion: women in management and international staffing.

Women in Management

During the past decade, women have made significant inroads into this nation's work force. Today, four out of ten workers in the U. S. are women. Among the professions, they account for about 12 percent of doctors, up from 6 percent in 1950, and close to 15 percent of the nation's lawyers, up from only 4 percent in 1950. Even more dramatic has been the increase in the managerial ranks, where nearly 15 percent hold management jobs, which is more than double the rate of twenty years ago.[25]

A number of reasons have been given for the increase of women in managerial positions.[26] First, there has been significant *governmental pressure* in enforcing equal opportunity for women through various legislative acts, including Title VII of the Civil Rights Act and the Equal Pay Act of 1963.

Second, there have been dramatic shifts in *social trends* in this and other countries. Women are more highly educated than ever before— nearly one-half of business school graduates today are women. The rising cost of living has also influenced the entry of wives into the managerial labor market to supplement the inflation-crushed income of their husbands. Many times it is the salary of the woman that provides the family with the larger home, car, and vacations that would be impossible on one income.

There is also the increased need by women for self-satisfaction and fulfillment in their careers. Because of their education, skills, and training, they no longer are satisfied with a clerical job when higher positions are available. So, no matter what management's view may be concerning the "woman's place," the fact is that women are working and must be considered as a valuable resource that needs to be effectively managed, motivated, utilized, and rewarded.

Many organizations are also concerned over their *public image*. Because women represent 51 percent of the population, product-based organizations are now seriously considering the implications on their market activities of their internal discrimination. Because women are the prime buyers of this nation's goods and services, they are taking a hard look at the policies of the companies that produce the products. For example, a recent General Mills training program consisting of sixty-five people, sixty-four of them white males, was the target of a formal charge filed by the National Organization for Women (NOW) and the Urban League. Not only was the publicity damaging, but both groups threatened to launch a nationwide boycott against the company's Betty Crocker products, Wheaties, Cheerios, and Gold Medal flour.[27]

Finally, and probably most important in the long run, is the issue of *human resource availability*. Many managers are coming to the recognition that industry's biggest problem in the coming years will be a shortage of capable people at all levels of management. Therefore, organizations can no longer ignore one-half the population when they are looking for creative executive talent. It has long been obvious that organizations are not utilizing the capabilities of women, having kept them in jobs in which their aptitudes, skills, intelligence, and education are not fully utilized. From a resource point of view, the female work force constitutes an important reservoir of talent that is increasingly needed by all organizations to remain competitive and successful.

The road to total acceptance of women in management, however, has been and will continue to be faced with many barriers. The lack of acceptance by male managers will continue to plague many organizations. There is also the problem of the influence of culture. Almost from the time they walk, men are thrown into competitive team activities that hone skills in interpersonal relationships, power behavior, and cooperative-competitive activities. Women have not been subjected to such cultural influences, which has an adverse effect on their organizational performance, particularly in leading others and in committee-type activities. To counter these influences, many organizations, such as the State of California, have embarked on large-scale training and development programs to educate and train managers—both male and female—in helping them to be better managers.[28]

Human Resources in the International Realm

One of the most significant changes in management during the last twenty years has been the development of the multinational corporation. This development has been the natural result of the evolution and growth of organizations in taking advantage of prevailing market opportunities and demands. The importance of an international awareness is vividly illustrated by the fact that companies such as Gillette and Ford Motor derive a large percentage of their sales and profits from overseas operations.

Stages of Human Resource Development. From an industrial organizational viewpoint, the international human resource development and usage process generally goes through four stages.[29] These stages include:

1. *Stage One—Transfer.* This first stage involves the transfer of an executive or executives from the home country to fill key positions in a foreign operation. In many cases, the vast majority of the jobs are held by U. S. personnel, and only a minimum of jobs are held by foreign nationals. Such decisions are normally not made out of prejudice toward foreign employees but a concern that there is a lack of needed expertise to handle the work.

2. *Stage Two—Mixed resources.* In this second stage, sometimes due to pressures from the foreign government (or because foreign nationals have been suitably trained for the work), most foreign operation jobs are held by local personnel. The exception is that the top management team is still from the home country of the firm. The organization wishes to be a good neighbor to the country by employing some of its citizens, but is reluctant to relinquish total control of operations.

3. *Stage Three—Unitary resources.* At this stage in the evolution process, the entire operation is staffed by foreign nationals, including the top management positions. Such a situation may be forced on the organization, as in Japan and Zambia where it is expected that the top management positions are to be filled by executives from that country. In other situations, the organization's operations may have matured to the point at which foreign nationals at all levels have been trained to handle all jobs effectively.

4. *Stage Four—Interchange.* In this final stage, there is the recognition that a manager's skill and competence rather than his or her passport should be the basis of advancement, privileges, and rewards. In other words, there is not only the opportunity for U. S. managers to obtain international assignments, but foreign managers within the organization are given assignments at the home office. There are few organizations that

have fully passed through this stage, but in time many will because the forces behind this movement are quite strong. The main force is the search for excellence and performance—choose the manager best for the job without consideration of nationality.

One of the most successful international staffing efforts is the one conducted by American Standard, Inc., a large New York based manufacturer of plumbing supplies, transportation equipment, and mining machinery. In order to instill a more global orientation, the company began tapping foreign managers to run its key U. S. operations, along with sending U. S. nationals overseas. Nearly one-third of all vice presidential positions at corporate headquarters have been filled by foreign-born personnel.[30]

Besides differences in managerial style, American Standard's biggest problem was in getting qualified foreign managers to come to the U. S. The company found out that many foreign managers resisted the potentially career-boosting move because their cultural roots were deep in their countries. American Standard overcame this problem with the use of a careful selection program. Interestingly, they found that the most successful moves were by foreign managers who were educated in U. S. universities.

Issues in International Human Resource Development.   The development of the human resource function on an international basis has been one of the most troublesome problems faced by many organizations. The reluctance on the part of many organizations to go from stage one to stage two and/or stage three in the development process has been a major stumbling block to effectiveness. The salient problem, however, has been the insistence on the part of organizations to impose U. S. management methods and techniques on foreign operations without certain modifications that are important to the particular culture. As we discussed in earlier chapters, for example, assigning authority and responsibility to a manager, so accepted in our culture, is not so readily accepted in others. Similar problems related to differences in cultural norms regarding employee terminations or the acceptance of high levels of foreign national absenteeism have also been difficult for managers to adjust to in the short run.

In addition to these points, there are other important issues that organizations face in performing in the international sphere. A recent survey of executives of U. S. based multinational corporations identified the major problem in their foreign operations as being the lack of qualified personnel in the particular country.[31] In order to have as many foreign nationals in their operations as possible, many organizations are investing millions of dollars in developing extensive training programs to teach the nationals the important skills and knowledge needed for high performance.

Finally, there are the problems associated with transferring a U. S. based manager to a foreign operation. Beyond learning the language, a major issue is adapting to the customs of the country. This is a particular problem for managers who wish to take their spouses and families with them on a job assignment in the Middle East, where the role of women is quite different than it is in the U. S. Other family adjustment problems can occur concerning education for the children or simple housing needs. To counter some of these problems, many organizations ask managers *and* their families to participate in orientation and training programs before the transfer so that their "socialization" process goes smoothly.

A 1976 amendment to the U. S. Tax Code can have significant implications for the manager contemplating an overseas assignment. Prior to 1977 U. S. citizens employed in foreign countries could exclude up to $25,000 of income from U. S. taxes and reduce their U. S. tax bill further by deducting all foreign income tax payments. Beginning in 1977, only $15,000 of income can be excluded, and foreign taxes may not be deducted from U. S. taxes. Further, if an organization reimburses a manager for housing or schooling costs, that payment must be considered as an income item. Needless to say, these tax law changes have had a significant impact on the decision of managers to take an overseas assignment.

These issues are not insolvable, but they must be adjusted to in order to deal with the demands of an international organization. As more and more organizations engage in international trade in goods and services, the process of managing human resource activities in an intercultural environment will be of increasing importance.

HUMAN RESOURCES, PERFORMANCE, AND THE MANAGER'S JOB

Today, as in the past, most organizations view policies toward human resources in a defensive manner. Management frequently does not know exactly what it wants done with respect to personnel, but it knows quite well what it doesn't want—namely, costly and recurring problems. During the 1980s most organizations will be confronted with a significant challenge in adjusting to rapidly changing circumstances in an environment likely to be more hostile than in recent years.

Keys to Success with Human Resources in Organizations

In this chapter, we have attempted to point out the key factors related to the human resource elements of human resource planning, recruitment, selection, orientation, and training and development. There are certain additional points that need to be mentioned that concern how human resources relate to the manager's job and some of the important trends that managers should recognize.

1. **The human resource process involves all managers, not just the personnel department.**

   The responsibility for the acquisition and allocation of human resources in an organization is part of *every* manager's job. It is an activity that cannot be effectively delegated in toto to someone else with the expectation of consistent success. Ineffectiveness can result just as easily from the improper placement of a manager as from the purchase of an inefficient piece of equipment or improper financial accounting.

2. **Managers in the 1980s will face many complex human resource issues.**

   The future impact of human resources on the organization will be both dynamic and complex. Human resource planning will become more sophisticated; recruiting processes will be made more realistic and hence more costly; selection activities, particularly for managers, will involve a complex set of methods and approaches; more emphasis will be given to the socialization process; and training and development activities will be given increased importance. Along with these basic factors, such components as women in management, the impact of federal and state employment and discrimination laws, flexible work schedules, employee rights, and the problem of international human resources will gain the attention of managers in all types of organizations.

3. **Improved employee productivity will be a salient concern for managers in the future.**

The effects of spiraling inflation and prices will force managers to be more aware of the productivity levels of subordinates. Managers must try to get more productivity from the same number or fewer employees. To do this, greater emphasis will be placed on proper selection, placement in jobs, and reward systems.

4. **The manager's job—particularly skills and roles—is strongly related to the elements of the human resource process.**

Managers must recognize that the human resource process, especially training and development activities, is the primary source for the acquisition of managerial skills. Various training and development activities affect the effectiveness by which the individual acquires technical, human, conceptual, and diagnostic skills. In addition, the emphasis on on-the-job activities and job rotation relates to the important acquisition of knowledge about what roles the manager is to perform.

5. **An important criterion in evaluating the performance of managers is their success in developing capable employees.**

We often look at the performance of a manager in such narrow terms as making decisions on time, signing a large contract for the sale of goods to a customer, or maintaining or exceeding the production capacity of a plant. While these are certainly important performance criteria, they are somewhat short term in nature. The long-term performance, survival, and success of any organization is related to the degree to which it can continue to provide a stream of skilled and competent managers and nonmanagers who are able to handle the changing and dynamic role of management. Thus, it is important that every manager pay particular attention to identifying and developing the managers of the future. In effect, this may be the most important impact that a manager may have on the organization.

SUMMARY FOR THE MANAGER

1. The acquisition, training, and allocation of human resources in organizations is one of the most important functions of management. No longer can management assume the existence of an unlimited employee pool that can be easily trained to accomplish the organization's goals. Issues of equal employment opportunity, the need for improved productivity, and the development of the managers of the future all highlight the need for a revised view of the human resource function. The effectiveness of the human resource function is the job of every manager, not just the personnel department.

2. The human resource process—consisting of resource planning, recruitment, placement, selection, orientation, training and development, performance

evaluation, reward system, and terminations—begins with an analysis and knowledge of its premises. These premises involve much of the material covered up to now in this book—goals, strategies, decision making, and organizational design. These components serve as the starting point for the human resource process.

3. Human resource planning involves the analysis of at least the following points: what does the organization want to do (i.e., goals and strategies); what are the significant labor forces and legal trends that can impinge on this organization; and, what is our present state of evaluation with respect to our human resources? By responding to these issues, managers can have a good start in identifying the organization's human resource needs now and in the future. Of particular concern for managers at this stage is the growing body of laws regulating the human resource process. Beginning with the Civil Rights Act, managers are continually being faced with issues regarding the legalities of the organization's human resource activities.

4. Recruiting involves the twofold process of securing people and insuring that they stay in the organization. Beyond the growing variety of recruiting sources, the issue of realistic recruiting is of particular concern to the manager. Unless a true picture of the organization is given, the possibility of increased turnover may develop.

5. Selection is a process that concerns establishing criteria for the job, interviews, testing, reference checks, and the like. The selection of managers requires a special emphasis by the organization because of the key role that managers play in the survival of the organization. Particular emphasis is placed on the individual's potential, past performance, and the evaluation of extensive interviews. Management assessment centers have been given increased attention during the past few years.

6. Orienting the new employee to the organization must go beyond the simple induction activities. The process of socialization—learning the ropes—is an activity that is undergoing a significant revision in many of today's organizations. The effectiveness of the unlearning and relearning phases of socialization can have a tremendous impact on the employee's subsequent performance.

7. The training and development stage of the human resource process is one of the most important. It is at this stage that the key managerial skills and roles are learned. Organizations use a wide variety of methods and techniques to train and develop their managers and nonmanagerial employees; by far the most used and successful relate to job rotation and on-the-job training. The important function of mentoring also can be used to impart new skills to the manager.

8. Many human resource issues face today's manager. Among them are the growing importance of women in management and staffing the international operation. These and others will continue to make the human resource aspect of the manager's job much more complex.

QUESTIONS FOR REVIEW AND DISCUSSION

1. Why is the concern over human resources the responsibility of every manager?
2. What are the premises of the human resource process?
3. Distinguish between a resource audit and management replacement analysis?
4. Why do many organizations resist the use of realistic recruiting?
5. What are some of the positive and negative features of managerial assessment centers?
6. Why are interviews so important in management selection?
7. What is meant by the term *organizational socialization*?
8. What is the difference between manager development and management development?
9. Can conceptual and diagnostic skills be acquired in training and development programs?
10. What are the forces behind the women in management movement?

NOTES

1. J. W. Walker, "Human Resource Planning: Managerial Concerns and Practices," *Business Horizons* (June 1976): 55.

2. A. D. Szilagyi, "Keeping Employee Turnover Under Control," *Personnel* (November–December 1979): 14–28.

3. H. Koontz and C. O'Donnell, *Management,* 6th ed. (New York: McGraw-Hill, 1976), p. 449.

4. B. Uttal, "Selling Is No Longer Mickey Mouse at AT&T," *Fortune* (July 17, 1978): 98–104.

5. W. Guzzardi, Jr., "Demography's Good News for the Eighties," *Fortune* (November 5, 1979): 92–106.

6. W. E. Bright, "How One Company Manages Its Human Resources," *Harvard Business Review* (January–February 1976): 81–93.

7. B. Rosen and M. F. Mericle, "Influence of Strong Versus Weak Fair Employment Policies and Applicant's Sex on Selection Decisions and Salary Recommendations in a Management Simulation," *Journal of Applied Psychology* (August 1979): 435–39.

8. B. Schneider, *Staffing Organizations* (Santa Monica, Calif.: Goodyear, 1976), p. 99.

9. P. J. Decker and E. T. Cornelius, "A Note on Recruiting Sources and Job Survival Rates," *Journal of Applied Psychology* (August 1979): 463–64.

10. Schneider, pp. 99–100.

11. J. P. Wanous, "Tell It Like It Is at Realistic Job Previews," *Personnel* (July–August 1975).

12. R. B. Finkle, "Managerial Assessment Centers," in *Handbook of Industrial and Organizational Psychology,* ed. M. D. Dunnette (Chicago: Rand McNally, 1976), pp. 861–88.

13. C. L. Jaffe and F. D. Frank, *Interviews Conducted At Assessment Centers* (Dubuque, Iowa: Kendall/Hunt, 1976), p. 93.

14. J. M. Bender, "What Is Typical of Assessment Centers?" *Personnel* (July–August 1973): 51.

15. W. C. Byham, "Assessment Centers for Spotting Future Managers," *Harvard Business Review* (July–August 1970): 158.

16. See J. R. Hinrichs, "An Eight-Year Follow-up of a Management Assessment Center," *Journal of Applied Psychology* (December 1978): 595–601; and J. O. Mitchel,

"Assessment Center Validity: A Longitudinal Study," *Journal of Applied Psychology* (October 1975): 578–84.

17. L. W. Porter, E. E. Lawler, III, and J. R. Hackman, *Behavior in Organizations* (New York: McGraw-Hill, 1975), pp. 173–76.

18. D. C. Feldman, "A Practical Program for Employee Socialization," *Organizational Dynamics* (Autumn 1976): 64–80.

19. J. Van Maamen, "People Processing: Strategies of Organizational Socialization," *Organizational Dynamics* (Summer 1978): 19–36.

20. P. F. Drucker, *Management: Tasks, Responsibilities, and Practices* (New York: Harper & Row, 1974), p. 425.

21. M. L. Moore and P. Dutton, "Training Needs Analysis: Review and Critique," *Academy of Management Review* (July 1978): 532–45.

22. H. H. Hand, "The Mystery of Executive Education," *Business Horizons* (June 1971): 35–38.

23. See A. I. Kraut, "Behavior Modeling Symposium," *Personnel Psychology* (1976): 325–69; and "Imitating Models: A New Management Tool," *Business Week* (May 8, 1978): 119.

24. L. Digman, "How Well Managed Organizations Develop Their Executives," *Organizational Dynamics* (Autumn 1978): 71.

25. A. L. Malabre, Jr., "Women at Work: As Their Ranks Swell, Women Holding Jobs Reshape U. S. Society," *Wall Street Journal* (August 28, 1978): 1.

26. M. B. Boyle, "Equal Opportunity for Women Is Smart Business," *Harvard Business Review* (May–June 1973): 85–95.

27. Ibid., p. 87.

28. K. Anundsen, "Keys to Developing Managerial Women," *Management Review* (February 1979): 55–58.

29. H. V. Perlmutter and D. A. Heenan, "How Multinational Should Your Top Managers Be?" *Harvard Business Review* (November–December 1974): 121–32.

30. "American Standard's Executive Melting Pot," *Business Week* (July 2, 1979): 92–93.

31. U. E. Weichmann and L. G. Pringle, "Problems that Plague Multinational Marketers," *Harvard Business Review* (July–August 1979): 120.

ADDITIONAL REFERENCES

Anderson, H. J. *Primer of Equal Employment Opportunity.* Washington, D.C.; Bureau of National Affairs, 1978.

Bass, B. M., and Vaughn, J. A. *Training in Industry: The Management of Learning.* Belmont, Calif.: Brooks/Cole, 1966.

Blue, J., and Haynes, U. "Preparation for the Overseas Assignment." *Business Horizons* (June 1977): 61–67.

Bowen, C. P. "Let's Put Realism into Management Development." *Harvard Business Review* (July–August 1973): 80–87.

Bray, D. W.; Campbell, R. J.; and Grant, D. L. *Formative Years in Business: A Long-Term AT&T Study of Managerial Lives.* New York: Wiley, 1974.

Dunnette, M. D. *Personnel Selection and Placement.* Belmont, Calif.: Brooks/Cole, 1966.

Foulkes, F. K., and Morgan, H. M. "Organizing and Staffing the Personnel Function." *Harvard Business Review* (May–June 1977): 142–54.

Gabarro, J. "Socialization at the Top—How CEOs and Subordinates Evolve Interpersonal Contracts." *Organizational Dynamics* (Winter 1979): 3–23.

Mills, T. "Human Resources—Why the New Concern?" *Harvard Business Review* (March–April 1975): 120–34.

Orth, C. D., and Jacobs, F. "Women in Management: Pattern for Change." *Harvard Business Review* (July–August 1971): 139–47.

Reha, R. "Preparing Women for Management Roles." *Business Horizons* (April 1979): 68–71.

Reynolds, C. "Managing Human Resources on a Global Scale." *Business Horizons* (December 1976): 51–56.

Ritti, R. R., and Funkhouser, G. R. *The Ropes to Skip and the Ropes to Know.* Columbus, Ohio: Grid, 1977.

Wright, O. "Summary of Research on the Selection Interview Since 1964." *Personnel Psychology* (Winter 1969): 391–403.

Zeira, Y. "Sequential Evaluation of Management Development." *Business Horizons* (April 1974): 87–93.

A CASE FOR ANALYSIS

The State Organization

Beth Irving, director of training for one of the largest state governments in the U. S., faced a perplexing problem. She needed to start a development program for women in management that: (1) satisfied equal employment opportunity demands; (2) met the organization's own needs for supervisory and management talent; and (3) did not create male backlash. She faced many problems, not the least of which was working for a bureaucracy burdened by red tape and the long-term effects of a culture that had excluded women from management positions.

Irving's first priority, when she began thinking about a women-in-management program, was to build a support system in which women could help each other grow and learn to work effectively in teams and committees. As a number of management theories on management women point out, teamwork is something most men learn at an early age through competitive team sports, which young women do not. As a result, men in organizations tend to adapt easily, while some women have difficulties.

The State was no exception. While they had an excellent record of hiring women—over twenty thousand had been hired—few women were in top management. Developing them into managers was a constant challenge. What was needed was a network for women, similar to a mentoring process; a group that would span a number of functional areas. Such a network would take a long time to develop; the immediate concern was some form of training program for the State's high management potential women.

Working with a group of consultants and an advisory board composed of senior-level women within the state organization, the training program established a foundation. First, certain basic guidelines were set up, including: (1) the program should be free of animosity toward men (eliminating the win-lose situation); (2) the management skills to be learned would be oriented to jobs at any organizational level; and (3) there would be an emphasis on on-the-job activities.

Second, the program would require a serious commitment by both the participants and the State because it involves at least 150 hours of each individual's personal time plus 120 hours of the organization's time (some of the program would be conducted on weekends; the rest would be held during working hours). In addition, not only would the participants attend a two-day (weekday) workshop every quarter, but they would be responsible for carrying out assignments in self-organized teams on their own time during the year.

Finally, selection to the program would be based on recommendations by division heads, followed by screening interviews by the headquarters personnel unit. The first program utilized selection by the headquarters personnel unit that resulted in approximately forty-five women from across the state being chosen. In summary, it was hoped that the year-long program of a comprehensive series of workshops and assignments, combining education in the operations of the organization with the development of management skills, would result in personal growth and a better knowledge of on-the-job issues.

The first of the quarterly workshops, held at a conference center in a state park along the coast, was a disaster. Almost from the beginning of the first day's program it was apparent that the participants were uneasy about their attendance at the meeting. Soon after the introductions and a statement about the objectives of the program, questions from the participants began. Some wanted to know about the selection procedure for participation in the program, others objected to the large amount of personal time that was needed, while still others complained that they lacked the support of their immediate supervisors for such a large undertaking. Rather than spend the entire day answering questions, it was decided to proceed with the program for that day, which involved breaking the participants into small groups to discuss a case that would be discussed at the beginning of the next day's meeting.

Before the second day's program could begin, the leaders were confronted with a group of angry participants. They felt that the program was a waste of time. They had spent the night analyzing the content of the program and came to the conclusion that many of the topics and skills to be learned were already aspects that the participants had acquired from their work. They concluded that they were not only jeopardizing their jobs by participating in the program, but some claimed that they had been brought to the training site under false pretenses and that the state already owed them promotions. A lengthy discussion ensued, but to no avail. The participants voted unanimously to terminate the program and return to their respective offices.

That afternoon, while driving back to her home, Irving tried to pick up the pieces. She knew that the basic idea of the program was solid, but something had gone wrong in the way it had been planned and implemented. She was determined that the program should continue in the future, but with some significant modifications. The modifications, however, would require much more thinking and analysis.

Questions for Discussion

1. What went wrong at the first training program?
2. Is the idea of such a training and development program sound?
3. What modifications should be made to future programs?

EXPERIENTIAL EXERCISE

The Application Form

Purpose

To distinguish between the lawful and unlawful items that can be asked on an application form for employment.

Required Understanding

The student should have a basic understanding of laws related to employment.

How to Set Up the Exercise

Set up groups of four to eight students for the thirty to forty-five minute exercise. The groups should be separated from each other and group members asked to converse only with members of their own group.

Instructions for the Exercise

You are the Director of Human Resources for the Fire Department for a large Midwestern city. From recent conversations with the city's legal department and with some of your counterparts in other cities, it has come to your attention that certain items on your application for employment form contain potentially discriminatory items that are illegal.

On examining your department's employment application form, you notice that the form asks for a total of eighteen questions to be answered by the candidate. These questions are noted in exhibit 10–11. The form is used for candidates wishing to become fire fighters.

1. *Individually,* review the eighteen questions and decide (lawful or unlawful) whether the question can be discriminatory in nature (i.e., on the basis of sex, race, age, and so on). Mark your responses on exhibit 10–11.

2. *As a group,* repeat the instructions discussed in step one.

3. The group decisions should be displayed for discussion.

EXHIBIT 10–11   The City Fire Department Employment Application Questions (for Fireman)

| | INDIVIDUAL | | GROUP | |
QUESTION	Lawful	Unlawful	Lawful	Unlawful
1. Name				
2. Age				
3. Sex				
4. Marital status				
5. No. of children				

6. Physical data:
  a. Height
  b. Weight				

7. Military status				

8. Housing:
  a. Do you own, rent a
    home or apartment?				

9. Religion				
10. Birthplace				
11. Citizenship				
12. Education				
13. Relatives in city				
14. Outside activities				
15. Past work history				
16. Criminal record				
17. References				
18. Recent photograph				

11

Communication

CHAPTER OUTLINE

KEY POINTS IN THIS CHAPTER

1. Of all the management activities, none takes up as much time as that of communication. Managers communicate to influence others, to express feelings, for information exchange, and to control.

2. Interpersonal communication generally involves the interaction between two people. Such communication can be one way or two way in nature.

3. Three main types of communication are found in organizations: verbal, written, and nonverbal.

4. A manager's interpersonal communication style concerns the degree of emphasis given to dimensions of exposure (giving information) and feedback (receiving information).

5. Perceptual errors, language, filtering, and information overload are among the many problems that act as barriers to effective interpersonal communication.

6. Organizational communication—communication between two or more members—occurs within networks that vary according to speed, accuracy, centrality, and member satisfaction.

7. Organizational communication flows vertically (up and down) and laterally in organizations.

8. Important differences exist among verbal, written, and nonverbal communication in the international realm.

9. Communication relates closely to the manager's informational roles of monitor, disseminator, and spokesperson.

THE PRACTICE OF MANAGEMENT

Communication: Learning How to Communicate to the Public

In today's complex and dynamic environment, an organization's success in the public's eye depends heavily on its ability to respond quickly and effectively to public concerns and opinion. Unfortunately, managers are not good communicators, particularly when it involves communicating to elements external to the organization.

Robert J. Wood, a communication consultant, relates the following incident to illustrate this point:

The chief executive of a major company called me last winter and said, "I've spent 32 years of my life working to get this job, and now my staff wants me to learn show biz!" He had been invited to appear on the program of a well-known TV reporter, and his colleagues felt their boss needed professional advice before tangling on national television with a man famous for putting his guests on the spot. To decline to appear on the program, in view of certain delicate developments within his company that had recently been made public, would have been unwise.

The executive was reluctant and resentful of this supposed criticism of his managerial skills. But reluctance vanished when we played back the videotape of the simulated interview with which we started his session. Our staff members spent a week studying his company, familiarizing themselves with public statements of every officer, and poring over congressional records in which the company had been involved. One of the group took the role of the host and threw the book at our guest, firing one difficult question after another. When the videotape was played back there was a long moment of silence. Then he said, "Let's get to work. I need help."

It began with each member analyzing his performance. First time around they criticized it for content. He had contradicted a previously published statement of one of his senior officers. He had hedged on two other questions. It would have been better to say, "I don't know that answer, but I'll be glad to send it to you." In answering another question he had taken almost three minutes to get to the heart of the matter. Start with your major point. Say, "Our company believes in doing such and such because . . . ." Then tell them why.

Next they criticized his style. He looked more at the camera than at the interviewer. He fingered the knot of his tie too often. He didn't use the interviewer's name in answering the questions. He should have said, "I'm glad you asked that question, Pete. It gives me a chance to tell you about . . . ."

I don't remember how many simulated interviews took place during the two-day cram session, but the progress was visible, vertical, and exciting to watch. It got so that he began to criticize himself: The TV screen is a great teacher. Before he left he also saw quite a few videotapes of the interviewer in action. This was designed to acquaint him with the interviewer's style and to refresh him on the kind of hostile questioning he was likely to encounter.

This manager spent two days that he later described as among "the hardest working days of my life." But on the day of the interview, he acquitted himself well. He had the facts at his fingertips, made his points clearly, quickly, and concisely. He sounded confident and looked at ease.

Adapted from R. J. Wood, "Communication: Top Executive Priority," Management Review *(May 1979): 49–51.*

11

Dan Rather and Gary Paul Gates, in their book *The Palace Guard,* describe an episode in their account of Richard Nixon's presidential administration:

> The president was working alone, very late at night in a hotel room while on a trip. He opened the door, beckoned to a waiting aide and ordered, "Get me coffee." The aide immediately responded to the request. Most of the activities of the hotel including the kitchen were not operating at such a late hour. Hotel personnel had to be called in and a fresh pot of coffee brewed. All this took time and the president kept asking about coffee while waiting. Finally, a tray was made up with a carafe of coffee, cream, sugar and some sweet rolls and was rushed to the president's suite. It was only at this point that the aide learned that the president did not want coffee to drink, but rather wanted to talk to an assistant whose name was Coffee.[1]

As this example illustrates, communication is an important activity in all types of organizations, yet it is also the activity that can create problems even for a president.

In this last chapter in part III, the focus will be on the various mechanisms that people use to communicate within the organization's structure. The first of five main sections of the chapter will discuss the importance of communication to the organization. This will be followed by two major sections on the types of communication that are found in organizations: interpersonal communication, dealing with the information exchange between two people (e.g., manager and subordinate); and organizational communication, concerning the network of information exchange between people and groups of people internal and external to the organization. The fourth section will be devoted to an analysis of communication in the international realm. The emphasis will be on communication difficulties across cultures. Finally, we will attempt to integrate the various themes of this chapter into a discussion of communications, performance, and the manager's informational roles. In part V, we will reintroduce the subject of communication with the presentation of the relationship between managerial control and management information systems (MIS).

THE PURPOSES OF COMMUNICATION

In one way or another, managers spend the vast majority of their time communicating, whether presenting a long-range strategic plan or directing a subordinate to do a particular task. If communication is hampered, the entire organization suffers; when it is accurate, thorough, and timely, the organization can move effectively toward goal achievement.

There are at least four major purposes served by communication that make it central to management.[2] The first major purpose is to *influence* the performance of organizational members—to motivate, direct, instruct, and evaluate. Second, communication networks are made up of people, and much of what people communicate has emotional content. Communication, formal and informal, is a primary means used by people to clarify and express their *feelings*. Third, communication is a vital activity that serves as an *information input* or *exchange* to many of the managerial functions. As we have already seen, information is important in setting goals, planning, and decision making. Finally, communication and organizational structure are closely related. Organization charts, for example, represent *formal channels* of communication in organizations.

INTERPERSONAL COMMUNICATION

Over the years, many studies have examined how managers spend their time (see chapter 2). Concerning communication, these studies have generally found that managers: (1) spend between 50 and 80 percent of their time at work communicating with other individuals; and (2) not only prefer face-to-face communications, but spend most of their time in this type of communication.[3]

This form of communication is referred to as *interpersonal* communication because it concerns the one-on-one information exchange between two organizational members. In our discussion of interpersonal communications, four topics are of importance: (1) the process of interpersonal communication; (2) types of communication; (3) interpersonal communication styles; and (4) barriers to effective communication.

Interpersonal Communication Process

In its most basic form, interpersonal communication involves a sender, a message, and a receiver.[4] However, as the model shown in exhibit 11–1 illustrates, we need to be more specific about these terms.

First, the *sender* is the source, or initiator of the communication. In initiating interpersonal communication, there are two important factors about the sender that must be considered: sender intent and sender expression. Concerning *intent,* the sender is a person with ideas, intentions, information, and a purpose for communicating. In other words, the sender has something with a meaning to communicate to another person. Consider again the example in the last chapter of socialization where the sales representative improperly or incorrectly contacted the plant manager of the facility that produced the defective goods. The sales rep's supervisor, the sales manager, wishes to communicate (intention) to the rep that such behavior is not acceptable and that future instances like this should come through the sales manager (meaning).

The *expression* of the intent by the sender, sometimes termed *encoding,* involves translating the sender's intent or ideas into a systematic set of symbols or gestures. The symbols, gestures, or words chosen must be such that the receiver understands what is being communicated.

Second, the sender's intent and expression are communicated by means of a message sent through a channel. The *message* is the physical form into which the sender encodes or expresses the information. This may take the form of speech, written words, or gestures. In the example of the sales rep, the sales manager may choose to use a verbal message,

EXHIBIT 11–1   An Interpersonal Communication Model

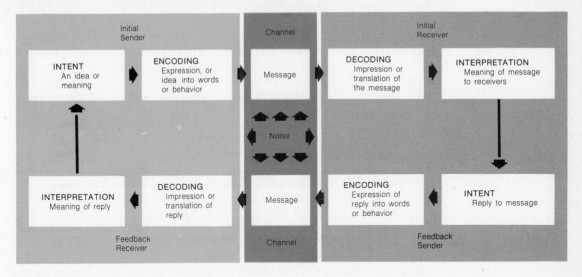

such as a formal conversation on a face-to-face basis. Physical gestures are also frequently used. For example, most children learn at an early age the meaning of "yes" and "no" from the nodding or shaking of the parent's head. In organized sports, the raising of one hand by an umpire in baseball may indicate a strike or that the runner is out trying to steal; in football raising both hands by a referee indicates a touchdown.

The *channel* is the carrier of the message, and is many times inseparable from the message. In organizations, the channel or medium of information exchange can take the form of such components as face-to-face communication, telephone calls, meetings, written memos, computer outputs, or other writtten reports.

Third, the receiver of the sender's message must sense and interpret the meaning of the communication. This involves two factors. First, there is the translation or *impression* of the message, or what is heard or sensed by the receiver. Second, the *interpretation* or *decoding* factor involves the process of translating the message into meaning for the receiver. Receivers interpret the message in light of their own past experiences and various personal frames of reference. The important aspect is that for effective communication, the meaning of the message sent by the sender must be interpreted in the same manner by the receiver.

For example, the sales manager in our illustration could verbally indicate to the sales rep that direct contact with manufacturing personnel is not acceptable. The sales rep, on the other hand, may interpret the message in at least three ways: (1) don't repeat that behavior; (2) you can repeat that behavior only in serious situations; or (3) the sales manager has done his duty by telling you the rules, now go about your business and contact the plant manager when you feel it is necessary. From the view of the sales manager, any behavior or message interpretation other than the first is unacceptable.

Communication Noise and Feedback.   As exhibit 11–1 also shows, there are two other aspects that are of importance to the interpersonal communication process. First, in the framework of interpersonal communication, *noise* is any factor that disturbs or distorts the message. The sender may send a confusing memo, the sender may speak too softly or indirectly to the receiver, the receiver may not be paying attention, or there are other sounds or sensations in the environment. An example could be the manager who attempts to conduct a conversation with another manager while simultaneously responding to various telephone calls.

Second, there is the *feedback* from the receiver to the sender, this time with the roles reversed. Because the receiver now becomes the sender, feedback goes through the same steps as the original communication with the same encoding and decoding problems. Feedback can take the form of verbal expression, a simple nod of the head, or questions directed at clarifying the original communication.

In organizations, three types of feedback are usually found: informational, corrective, and reinforcing.[5] *Informational* feedback is not evaluative; that is, it does not stress whether something is right or wrong. It is merely information that one person gives another that may be of value to the work of the first. Examples include giving a credit manager information on the account of a specific customer, sales revenue and market share information given a sales manager by a staff specialist, or laboratory results sent by a lab technologist to a physician concerning a patient.

The second type of feedback is called *corrective* feedback. This type of feedback is evaluative and instructional because it deals with the need of the receiver to correct something in the sender's message. Examples include correcting an assumption about a project design specification by an engineer, or resolving a problem with an accounting report that contains an improper procedure as presented to the accounting manager.

John Wooden, who led his UCLA basketball teams to ten national championships in twelve years, was the master of corrective feedback. Observations of his behavior in practice sessions showed that 75 percent of his contacts with players were instructional in nature.[6] He used instructions simultaneously to point out a mistake *and* indicate the correct way of performing. An interesting part of Wooden's behavior that may be of value to managers is that the use of corrective feedback always centered on the task, not on the personality of the player as an individual.

The third type of feedback is termed *reinforcing* feedback. That is, when a particular message has been sent clearly and/or correctly, there is a positive acknowledgement by the receiver. For example, a personnel manager may state to a subordinate, "well done," with respect to a recently submitted comprehensive human resource audit for the organization. We will discuss the reinforcement approach in more detail in the next chapter on motivation.

One-Way and Two-Way Communication. The existence or absence of feedback gives rise to the concepts of one-way and two-way communication. In *one-way* communication, such as statements of organizational rules and policies, the sender communicates without expecting or asking for feedback from the receiver or receivers. *Two-way* communication occurs when the receiver is permitted to or actually does provide information in return. A manager giving a project to a subordinate and receiving clarifying questions in return concerning deadlines and other guidelines is an example.

Over the years, a number of research studies have been conducted to investigate the various features of one-way and two-way communication.[7] In general, the results have shown the following:

1. One-way communication takes less time than does two-way.

2. Two-way communication is more accurate, since it allows both parties to refine their messages.

3. While receivers feel more secure about their interpretation of communication in the two-way manner, senders sometimes feel threatened when the receiver questions the sender's lack of clarity or mistakes.

4. One-way communication, although less accurate, appears to be more orderly than two-way communication in certain situations.

What implications are there for managers from this research? The answer deals with the criteria of time and accuracy. If communications must be made fast, and accuracy is not a problem or is easy to achieve, then one-way communication is preferred. Consider a divisional manager presenting changes in the organization's compensation plan to a large group of employees in an auditorium. Because of time considerations, executives cannot speak to each employee individually; therefore, a large meeting is appropriate. It also is much more organized, which is important in getting the point across.

When the accuracy of the communication is important, then two-way communication is required. Such cases as evaluating an employee's performance and assigning a complex task are examples. The feedback from the receiver provides the sender with a better understanding of the way the message was interpreted by the receiver.

Types of Communication

As shown in exhibit 11–2, there are a number of methods available to the manager for sending messages in an organization. These consist of verbal, written, and nonverbal types. The choice of the particular communication type is dependent on a number of factors, which are discussed below.

Verbal Communication. By far the most prevalent form of communication in organizations is that of verbal information exchange. Usually taking the form of face-to-face conversations or telephone calls, verbal communication can be both accurate and timely. On the other hand, unless one of the participants tapes the conversation, there is no record of the exchange, which leaves open questions of clarity and the chance

EXHIBIT 11–2   Types of Communication

TYPE	DESCRIPTION
Verbal	
1. Personal	Face to face or telephone conversation
2. Group	Face to face in a meeting
3. Impersonal	Public address system, closed circuit or video-tape television
Written	
1. Personal	Letters, memos, reports
2. Organizational (impersonal)	Newsletters, posters, announcements, policies, rules, computer outputs, and other organizational publications
Nonverbal	
1. Body language	Hand signals, body and eye movements, facial expressions, pitch and tone of voice
2. Physical or symbolic	Signs, horns, sirens, "beeping" paging devices, office size, desk, carpet, number of secretaries, number of windows, badges, clothing, and so on.

that certain aspects of the communication may be forgotten in a lengthy conversation.

In recognition of the importance of verbal communication, two major innovations are being adopted by many organizations. First, there has been the growth in the use of telecommunication equipment. Examples include picture-phones and video-tape cassettes. One of the most intriguing forms of interpersonal communication is known as *télématique* or *compunications*.[8] This is the merging of telephone, computers, and television into a single system that allows for transmission of data *and* interaction between persons through cables, macrowaves, or satellites. Thus, the total communication message can be packaged and organized into a much faster and accurate channel. These methods provide both verbal and face-to-face communication between interacting parties even when they are physically separated.

Second, there is the increased attention being given to the physical layouts of the workplace, particularly the design of the office. Managers are coming to the recognition that verbal communication among organizational members is facilitated when the ability to interact with members is improved. For example, consider the designs of two hypothetical offices shown in exhibit 11–3: the first represents the "typical" office design with floor-to-ceiling walls and solid doors; the second is the newer "open plan" design using partitions and no doors. The exhibit shows that the two offices are similar when it comes to physical density (i.e., the straight line distance between members), but are quite different when it relates to social density (i.e., the needed walking distance for members to interact physically). Recent studies have shown that the open plan design improves communication and performance between organizational members when there is a need for frequent verbal (face-to-face) communication.[9]

EXHIBIT 11–3
**Physical Density
and Social
Density in Offices**

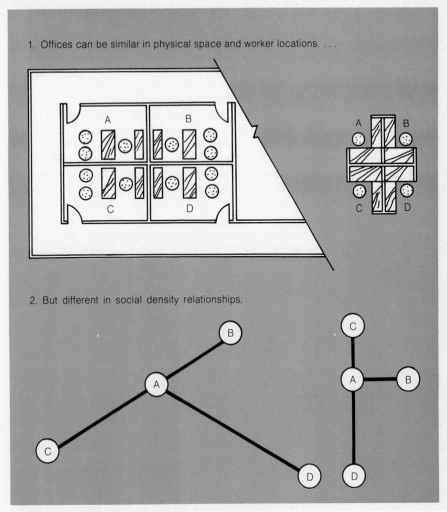

Source: A. D. Szilagyi, W. E. Holland, and C. Oliver, "Keys to Success with Open Plan
Offices," Management Review (August 1979): 26–41.

Written Communication.   Written communication within organizations can take many forms, including memos, reports, procedure manuals,
and other organizational publications. They are preferred by managers
who wish a record of their interactions, or for such items as technical
reports, which would be impossible to communicate verbally. Written
communication also forces the sender to use clear and concise thinking
to present the message.

On the negative side, since written communication (such as memos)
is essentially one-way, there is no opportunity for the receiver to question
or comment on the message, at least not initially. A second problem, one
that we alluded to in our discussion of bureaucracy, is that the overre-
liance on written communication may create a state of "red tape" confusion. Having a record of everything may put a severe burden even on

the most effective of organizations. Finally, having a record of an interaction may backfire on the participants. One such case discussed in the
last chapter is the letter of reference. Sometimes, certain confidential
letters are obtained by various media sources and made public, revealing
some less than ethical behaviors performed by organizational members
(see chapter 4).

Organizations differ in their emphasis on the use of written communications. Some managers prefer verbal communications and shy
away from the use of a written memo as if it were a plague (see National
Can case at the end of this chapter); other managers prefer to put everything in writing. For example, a part of Procter and Gamble's management development program (see practice of management section in chapter 10) is the emphasis given to written reports:

> The manager . . . first has to learn how to write the P&G memo, a one-page
> report considered essential to analytical thinking. The idea, of course, is
> that if a manager can put his thoughts down on paper in a concise and
> orderly fashion, they are, in fact, rational and orderly thoughts. Conversely,
> if his recommendations or analysis contain illogical elements, they are
> immediately apparent. Memos by the typical trainee . . . are scrutinized
> with the same kind of care that a writer's story is blue-penciled by an editor.
> Why all the fuss? At P&G, memos are not only central to the commu-
> nication system, they are a basic decision-making tool. P&G's conversative
> management approach rests on written analyses that must go through a
> series of endorsements up the line. . . . As one top company executive says,
> "We don't go in for any of this 'Let's get together and rap' nonsense. A brief
> written presentation that winnows out fact from opinion is the basis for
> decision-making around here."[10]

For maximum effectiveness, most managers will use a combination of
verbal and written communication to exchange information. After a conversation, one may hear the phrase, "Fine—why don't you confirm our
agreement in a memo." In this way, the positive features of one-way and
two-way communication can be obtained.

Possibly the most significant advance in written communication has
been the introduction of *xerography,* or photocopying equipment. Because
of this technological advance, various forms of written communication
(memos, reports, and other documents) can be given wider distribution
and hopefully communicate a better understanding and knowledge. Another advance having an impact on management is the *facsimile* system.
With this system, written documents can be sent electronically to a receiver by telephone lines or satellites much faster than by postal systems.

Nonverbal Communication.   When we transmit a message without
the use of the spoken or written word, we are using nonverbal communication. Such communication can take two forms: physical and body.
Physical or symbolic nonverbal communication involves the various symbols with which we come in contact each day. Examples include traffic
lights, stop signs, no-smoking signs, and sirens. Sometimes organizations
use nonverbal communication to imply status of an individual. The size
of an office, thickness of the office's carpet, a private elevator, and the
like are used by many organizations.

The second form of nonverbal communication involves expressions by a person's *body*. As in the practice of management section, voice tones, facial expressions, eye movements, and other gestures are frequently used by managers, either consciously or unconsciously. People can show their tension by crossing their arms and/or legs and clenching their fists. Boredom can be shown by yawning or slouching down in a seat.

Interpersonal Communication Styles

As we have all experienced, people differ in their style of communicating with others. Consider the following example dealing with the communication styles of two U. S. presidents:

> Soon after President Eisenhower took office, I asked one company's vice president of governmental affairs to comment on the different communication styles of President Eisenhower and President Truman. She told me that President Eisenhower depended almost completely on all news going through regular channels, with each key man giving him a briefing on what was happening. As a result, he had to see very few people.
>
> President Truman, on the other hand, saw practically everyone. People came and went constantly, until it was almost like having Andrew Jackson back in the White House. To the casual observer, President Truman was the most disorganized person in the world. But through his methods, he was able to personally determine the things that were important. He really *knew* what was going on.[11]

In the organizational world, some managers find comfort in following formal communication channels; others prefer an open-door policy. Both may be successful in their own particular situations.

In an attempt to assess a manager's interpersonal communication style, a pencil-and-paper instrument known as the "Johari Window" has received widespread use in many organizational training programs.[12] The instrument, named after the first names of the developers (Drs. Joseph Luft and Harry Ingram), attempts to measure a person's tendency to facilitate or hinder the flow of interpersonal communication.

The model, shown in exhibit 11–4, consists of two dimensions: exposure and feedback. *Exposure* involves the open and candid expression of one's feelings, knowledge, and information in a conscious attempt to communicate with others. The greater the exposure—the more one communicates—the more information is known by others. The second dimension, *feedback,* entails the active requests by the manager to learn or know about information held by others. The more information that is provided, the greater the feedback, and the more the manager knows. The combination of exposure and feedback is an example of the two-way communication process. Information is sent to others by the manager (exposure) and received by the manager from others (feedback).

Various combinations of exposure and feedback can create, as shown in exhibit 11–4, four different regions or cells of interpersonal communication: arena; blindspot; hidden; and unknown. The *arena* represents the amount of information known by both the manager and others. The larger the arena, the more effective the communication process between two or more persons. The second cell, the *blindspot,* concerns information

EXHIBIT 11–4
The Johari
Window

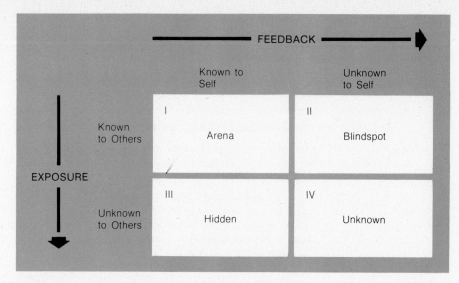

Adapted from J. Hall, "Communication Revisited," *California Management Review* (Spring 1973): 30–48.

that is known to others, but not known to the manager. It represents the information that others are withholding from the manager, or information that is not perceived or heard by the manager for reasons such as excessive noise in communications channels.

The *hidden* cell, like the blindspot, can contribute to decreased communication effectiveness because it concerns the amount of information that is known by the manager but not communicated to others. In some cases, it is a protective strategy by the manager, out of fear or desire for power, or because the managers feel others know that they know. Finally, the *unknown* relates to information that is unknown by the manager and others. In a sense, it represents unconscious or repressed feelings, hidden skills, and creative tendencies.

Because managers vary in their use of exposure and feedback, different interpersonal communication styles result. As shown in exhibit 11–5, at least four different styles can develop. *Type A* style reflects a minimal use of both exposure and feedback. A manager adopting this impersonal approach to interpersonal communication would tend to exhibit withdrawal from interactions, substituting a preference for rules and procedures that limit interpersonal communication. To others, this manager would seem to be aloof, rigid, and uncommunicative. *Type B,* on the other hand, is a style characterized by an aversion to exposure, but a desire for feedback. The typical manager using this interpersonal style would continually seek information from others, but would provide little in return. An aversion to the use of exposure can be interpreted as a sign of basic mistrust of others, which can lead to feelings of anxiety and hostility on the part of subordinates. With time, the manager using this style would be treated as a superficial person. As a result, effectiveness suffers.

The *type C* style reflects an overuse of exposure with a neglect of feedback. Managers adopting this style may feel very confident of the value of their own opinions and a mistrust of the opinions of others. Such managers are sometimes referred to as autocratic because they prefer to

EXHIBIT 11–5 Interpersonal Communication Styles

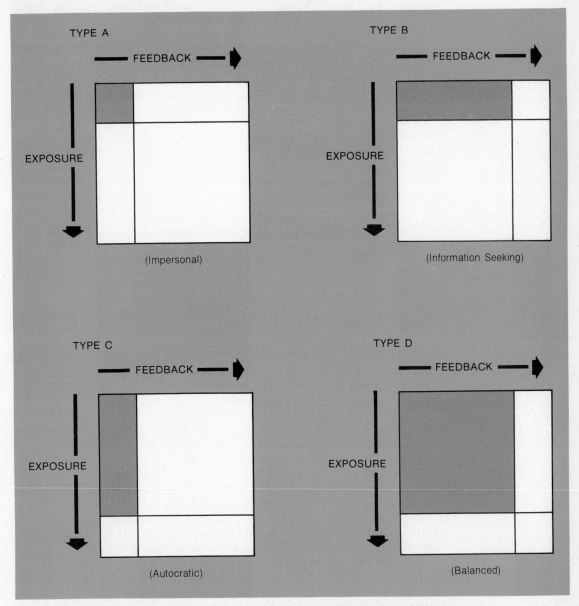

Source: J. Hall, "Communication Revisited," *California Management Review* (Spring 1973): 30–48.

tell people what to do, but wish to hear nothing in return that might be critical of their decisions. Since the manager using this style has little use for the contributions of others, people begin to develop feelings of hostility, insecurity, and resentment toward the manager.

The final interpersonal style, *type D,* reflects a balanced use of both exposure and feedback. Openness and a sensitivity to others' needs to participate in interpersonal communication are the major features of this style. The arena is the dominant cell of the model, and effectiveness may be expected to result.

If one believes that improved communication through exposure and feedback will result in higher levels of performance, then the Johari Window has a value to managers. Three major questions remain that should be examined by all managers wishing to adopt the model's framework. First, what will happen when a type D manager interacts frequently with other employees who are not the same type? Will the type D manager become the frustrated participant? Second, how are interpersonal communication styles acquired and developed in managers? One might speculate that similar to a manager's style of decision making, one's interpersonal communication style also is acquired through a complex process of culture, work experience, and personality traits over time. Finally, there is the question whether a manager's style of communicating is rigid, or can change and be flexible with the situation. This leaves open the potential influence of training and development programs to assist managers in their communication processes with others.

Barriers to Effective Interpersonal Communication

In the famous movie, "Cool Hand Luke," the chain gang boss stands over a beaten prisoner (played by Paul Newman) and states, "What we have here is a failure to communicate." While most managers would not be expected to find themselves in such a physical predicament, it is highly likely that in many of their interactions with others, they would feel justified in uttering the same words!

Communication problems in organizations are frequent occurrences and can have many complex sources. To illustrate this phenomenon, four major types of barriers to effective interpersonal communication have been chosen for discussion. These include perceptual errors, filtering, language, and information overload.

Perceptual Errors.   Perception involves the process of the stimulation of a person's senses. We see, hear, touch, and taste various factors in our daily lives that not only cause us to interpret what we have sensed (e.g., seeing a stop sign ahead while driving a car) but serve as significant learning situations (e.g., a child touching a hot stove for the first time).

Perception, and more specifically perceptual errors, play an important part in contributing to communication problems. Two perceptual errors are most prominent: stereotyping, and halo effect.[13] In *stereotyping,* managers seek to *simplify* their perceptual process by categorizing people into specific classes where there is a similarity of traits and characteristics. For example, a male manager may receive a memo from a woman manager describing a potential safety hazard in one of the organization's facilities. Because this manager "stereotypes" all women as being "too emotional and nonanalytical," he may disregard the warning in the memo even though it may have made legitimate points. Similarly, a manager of an engineering design group may ignore a recommendation by a young engineer on improving a design procedure because the manager has stereotyped young engineers as "lacking in creative ideas."

The second perceptual error, *halo effect,* concerns the biasing of an evaluation because of a single trait or incident. For example, a college recruiter for an organization may be on campus interviewing prospective employees. A particular candidate may have an excellent academic rec-

HAGAR THE HORRIBLE

ord, but may come to the interview wearing jogging shoes. This single appearance trait may cause the interviewer to rate the candidate quite low. Similarly, a manager may lose interest in a speech given by an executive because the speaker does not look people in the eye while talking, stands too far from the microphone, or uses slang words excessively.

Eliminating perceptual errors from the interpersonal communication process may be a difficult proposition because many of the errors have developed over time and may be culturally influenced. Some stereotypes, particularly those that are discriminatory, are clearly illegal, as in the case of refusing to hire a person on the basis of race. Halo effects, especially those related to the interviewing process, can be corrected through training programs. Even some stereotype errors can be changed through proper training. Others, however, may be changed only with the passage of time, or with the replacement of the individual.

Filtering.   Filtering is a phenomenon in communications when the sender purposely modifies the message to highlight the strong or weak points. For example, a manager may report to an executive committee that the "present high turnover rate of employees in the department is only a passing situation that will correct itself with time." The manager has filtered out some important facts that point to significant internal problems that are at least helping to cause the turnover problem.

Correcting problems of communication filtering can occur if the manager attempts to create an environment among employees in which subordinates feel free to pass on all information without fear of coercion or punishment. We will discuss this point further in chapter 12.

Language.   Language factors have at least a twofold impact on communication barriers in interpersonal communications. First, from the study of semantics, we know that: (1) words mean different things to different people; (2) words vary in degree of abstraction; and (3) the use of particular words reflects not only the personality of the individual but also the culture of the society. With respect to the first point, consider a manager's statement to a subordinate that, "It's important that we have your part of the report finished by the fifteenth of the month. Try to get it in on time, if you can." To the subordinate, these two sentences do not make sense. The first stresses the importance of the completion of the report; the second takes a weaker stand. How would you react to such a communication? In communicating one must be cognizant of the clarity of the message and how the receiver will react.

Concerning the second point, consider the plight of a plumber who wants to know whether to use hydrochloric acid to clean stopped-up drains. A reply such as, "The efficacy of hydrochloric acid is indisputable, but chlorine residue is incompatible with metallic permanance," leaves much to be desired and does not tell the plumber much. A better reply would have been, "Don't use hydrochloric acid—it eats the heck out of the pipes."[14] For the manager, the need to keep communication straightforward and simple is a worthwhile rule to follow.

Information Overload.   One of the major problems that all managers face is the fact that they are frequently deluged with all types of incoming communications. Phone calls, memos, written reports, computer outputs, or people just dropping in to the office create a state where it is beyond the capacity of the most successful manager to handle it all efficiently and effectively. Many people attribute this situation at least partially to the computer, photocopying machines, and the growth of telecommunication.

Many successful managers alleviate this problem by setting priorities. They divide the communications into different categories on the basis of when and what action must be taken. Another method to help reduce information overload is to delegate some of the communication to subordinates to handle. This assumes that subordinates are capable and skilled in this activity. A third strategy is to insist that all communication be direct and without excessive frills. This is why most business reports emphasize the use of a beginning abstract section, a short but direct narrative section, and an extensive, but optional appendix section. Remember a key managerial credo: a manager's time is most valuable—success will come when this time is used most efficiently.

Keys to Success with Interpersonal Communication

To counter many of the barriers to effective communication, successful managers have developed certain communication skills and practices. Some of the most important are noted below:

1. **Practice communicating.**

The old adage that "practice makes perfect" may have some validity to the interpersonal communication process. The only way to improve these skills is through frequent use. One can participate in training programs, observe and evaluate the practices of others, or join such clubs as Toastmasters. Many organizations permit managers to use video-tape equipment to practice a speech ahead of time, for example, and then play it back for an evaluation (see the practice of management section).

2. **Encourage feedback from others.**

Whether in verbal or written form, feedback can be one of the most valuable communication activities. For example, the transmission of a complex message between managers may need to be repeated or questions may need to be asked to ensure that an understanding has been reached. The best approach is to assume that we are relatively weak communicators: therefore, certain checks must be introduced to facilitate understanding.

3. **Develop good listening skills.**

Among the aspects that a manager can employ to develop good listening skills are: (a) stop talking—refrain from rushing others into a response; (b) set aside sufficient time without interruptions—nothing is more devastating to effective communication, for example, than attempting to communicate verbally to another while being interrupted by answering the telephone; (c) seem genuinely interested in the message—showing interest will help to open some people up; and (d) at the end of the message, restate it to confirm the message's content.

4. **Understand the situation from the other's point of view.**

Sometimes referred to as "empathy," it is important to understand the receiver or sender's situation in the communication process. For example, the purchasing agent of a large savings and loan association may not share the viewpoint of a branch manager concerning the importance of ordering a rush shipment of printed return business envelopes for the branch. To the purchasing agent, this request is only one of many that must be processed during the workday or week. To the branch manager, without business envelopes the entire process of mailing out monthly statements and the return of mortgage payments would be held up. To the purchasing agent, the request may receive low priority; to the branch manager, the request should be given high priority. If the purchasing agent were to empathize with the branch manager, the interpersonal relationship between the two might improve significantly.

COMMENTS ON THE PRACTICE OF MANAGEMENT
(See p. 366)

The Practice of Management section provides an enlightening illustration of the problems of interpersonal communication. First, it shows that no matter what we individually believe about our own communication abilities, others may view them differently. Since it is these others with whom we wish to communicate, their evaluations and opinions should be carefully analyzed. Second, actually seeing oneself in a communication episode can be a tremendous learning experience. The method described in the section can be termed "behavior modeling" (see chapter 10). Finally, the phrase "practice makes perfect" is one that every manager should consider thoroughly. Practice can ensure that we are actually getting our point across to the other person. Being a good communicator takes work and effort.

5. **Try to keep emotions out of communication.**

When the situation creates conditions in which people are either upset or highly emotional, the message of a communication may be lost in the tension and stress of the situation. In such cases, it might be a wise move to defer any form of communication until calm has reappeared.

6. Choose the right channel.

Many times, the importance of a message is lost because the information was transmitted through the wrong channel. Simple and clear messages can be communicated best by verbal means, such as a direction or order. More complicated messages may be best sent by a memo or report. The key point, however, is that the greater the importance, the more channels should be used. Back up verbal communication with a memo, or follow up on a report with some form of verbal communication. The manager runs the risk of information overload by using more than one channel; however, the accurate transmission of the message may take precedence.

ORGANIZATIONAL COMMUNICATION

Communication between individuals is of obvious importance; the flow of data and information through the various channels and networks within an organization is of equal importance. In our discussion of organizational communication, we will focus on general communication networks, vertical and horizontal (lateral) communication, and communication from the organization to elements of the environment.

Communication Networks

There are a variety of networks that an organization can develop to channel communication. Some networks can be very rigid. For example, a number of years ago telephone operators were prohibited from talking with anyone other than their supervisors while on duty. On the other hand, some networks can be much more loosely designed so that communications between people is encouraged. A director of a research and development laboratory may encourage the organization's scientists to frequently interact in the hope that the pooling of knowledge may help in solving a complex research problem.

Communication networks have been the subject of many research studies. The emphasis has been on comparing the advantages and disadvantages of various networks in handling the communication process in organizations. Using five people in a two-way communication pattern, four of the most popular networks, termed the chain, wheel, circle, and all channel are shown in exhibit 11–6.[15] In terms of their application to organizations, the chain can be viewed as representative of the typical chain of command, from executive management to the lowest management levels; the wheel is closely aligned with the communication from a single manager to four subordinates; the circle can be looked at as the communication that flows between members of a task force; and the all channel is similar to the informal communication network in organizations (i.e., grapevine).

As exhibit 11–6 indicates, the four networks offer managers different advantages and disadvantages. The chain is a moderately decentralized network with moderate communication speed, predictability of leadership, and a high degree of accuracy. For participants in this network, however, the satisfaction level is moderate because of its formalistic nature and the low degree of participation. For simple communication tasks, the centralized wheel network is both accurate and fast and lead-

EXHIBIT 11–6 Organizational Communication in Networks

EVALUATION CRITERIA	Chain	Wheel or Star	Circle	All Channel
		TYPE OF NETWORK		
Centrality	Moderate	High	Low	Very low
Speed	Moderate	1. Fast (simple tasks) 2. Slow (complex tasks)	Slow	Fast
Accuracy	High	1. High (simple tasks) 2. Low (complex tasks)	Low	Moderate
Predictability of leadership	Moderate	Very High	Low	Very low
Average group satisfaction	Moderate	Low	High	Very high
Example	Chain of Command	Supervisor to four subordinates	Task force	Informal Communication (Grapevine)

ership predictability is very high, but satisfaction is low for the participants for essentially the same reason as with the chain. On the other hand, for more complex tasks, the speed of communication is reduced along with the level of accuracy. The reason is that with more complex tasks, the central person in the network may become overloaded with communication and feedback, which may have an adverse effect on accomplishing the task.

The circle is slow with a low degree of accuracy and leadership predictability. The participants, however, report high degrees of satisfaction because of their involvement in the communication process. In a task force, where the need for speed is not crucial, accuracy can be improved with constant interactions of members. The high satisfaction level of participants will help in keeping the members' attention directed on the task at hand.

Finally, the all-channel network is very decentralized. The speed of communication is fast; accuracy is moderate, with a very low level of leadership predictability. For the same reasons as the circle, the satisfaction level of participants is very high.

What implications are there for managers from this information? Clearly, if the task being performed is simple and employee morale is not an issue, then a centralized network is preferred, particularly a wheel arrangement. If the task is complex, a decentralized network, either a chain or a circle, is recommended. If speed and accuracy in accomplishing a complex task are important, then clearly the chain is best.

Vertical Communication

Vertical communication is information that flows through the chain of command of an organization. In general, two categories of vertical communication are used: downward and upward communication.[16]

Downward Communication. This system of communication involves the transmission of information from higher levels of management to lower levels in the organization. The goal-setting and planning processes are examples of downward communication. Another example of downward communication is the process of informing employees of changes in the fringe benefit program of the organization. With the rapid change and complexity of today's organizations, it is important that close ties between the organization and its employees be maintained. This means that downward communication must be current, effective as well as personal.

As shown in exhibit 11–7, the identified types of downward communication vary in terms of their effectiveness ranking in communicating the message to the employee. It appears that those mechanisms that are both personal and direct (small group meetings, company publications, and supervisory meetings) are the most effective. Those mechanisms that are both indirect and impersonal (bulletin boards and posters) are the least effective.

EXHIBIT 11–7
Effectiveness Ranking of Downward and Upward Communication Types

DOWNWARD COMMUNICATIONS	UPWARD COMMUNICATIONS
1. Small group meeting	1. Informal discussions
2. Direct organizational publications	2. Meetings with supervisors
3. Supervisory meetings	3. Attitude surveys
4. Mass meetings	4. Grievance procedures
5. Letters to employees' homes	5. Counseling
6. Bulletin boards	6. Exit interviews
7. Pay envelope inserts	7. Union representatives
8. Public address system	8. Formal meetings
9. Posters	9. Suggestion boxes
10. Annual reports, manuals, media advertising	10. Employee newsletters

Adapted from "Upward and Downward Communication Channels," *Small Business Report* (October 1979): 12–14; and *Employee Communications, Bureau of National Affairs & Personnel Policies Forum Survey No. 110* (July 1975): 5–9.

This information can have significant implications for the organization. In particular, most of the information that is transmitted to employees is through such impersonal and indirect means as employee manuals. Concern over whether or not information presented in this manner can be understood has grown in recent years. When used, many organizations are making such impersonal mechanisms more readable for the employee. To improve this form of communication, many other organizations are moving in the direction of utilizing the small group meeting where the communication is direct and mechanisms for two-way communication are available.

Upward Communication.   Communication from management to employees in a great number of organizations is heavily downward in nature. When this happens, the positive benefits of two-way communication are lost. Upward communication is that form of communication that originates at the lower levels in the organization and flows to the higher levels.[17] An effective upward communication system not only can help management evaluate the performance of the downward communication system, but it enables management to learn of some of the problems that the employees are facing.

THE MANAGER'S JOB
Gerald H. Trautman of Greyhound Corporation

It was in 1978 that Gerald H. Trautman, chairman of Greyhound Corporation, suddenly realized that he had been neglecting the company's original business—its bus line. Communication played a big part in his reawakening.

First, he came across an internal memo, written by an angry employee who had just completed an unpleasant cross-country bus trip; it set forth a host of customer service problems, including filthy conditions and poor security at terminals. After reading some of the increasingly numerous letters of complaint from passengers and maintenance reports, he knew he had a big problem on his hands.

Second, to confirm this written communication, Trautman hired his own team of fifteen investigators—all ex-military officers—and sent them on an undercover mission to gather more details. Armed with a checklist covering everything from driver courtesy to baggage handling, they fanned out across the country. They brought back reports of air conditioning out of order, poor morale, and buses out of service.

Finally, the icing on the cake was provided by the president of the 14,000 member Amalgamated Council of Greyhound Local Unions. The union leader invited Trautman to an unprecedented private meeting in the union's offices. There, for two hours, the union leader spelled out grievances that included inadequate staffing at terminals and buses that were in terrible shape.

Armed with this information, Trautman began to make changes. Besides making significant changes in the company's route structure (i.e., to eliminate the attempt to compete with the airlines on long-haul routes), he stressed improved communication by decentralizing decision making to the local level and instituted frequent meetings with company employees to discuss mutual problems. These and other improvements Trautman has made—coupled, of course, with increased use of public transportation because of rising gasoline prices—have clearly contributed to the Greyhound's upturn in passenger traffic.

Adapted from J. Quirt, "How Greyhound Made a U-Turn," Fortune (March 24, 1980): 139–40.

In general, four major types of information are involved with upward communication: (1) the level of performance and achievement of employees; (2) identification of any unresolved problems and issues faced by employees; (3) ideas and suggestions for improvement in the organization; and (4) how employees generally feel about their jobs, fellow employees, and the organization. In a sense, such information is valuable to management because it provides a needed evaluation of the organization as viewed by its important human resources.

Exhibit 11–7 also shows some of the many types of upward communication that can be found in most organizations, along with a ranking of their relative effectiveness as evaluated by a sample of organizations. In much the same manner as downward communication, the most effective means are those that have direct and personal characteristics (informal discussions and meetings with supervisors). The least effective are those communication means that are both indirect and impersonal.

Issues With Vertical Communication.   Vertical communication is the most formal and probably the most important type of communication found in organizations. It is also the type of communication that can present the most problems for a manager. First, because downward and upward communication must flow through different layers of management, it is highly subject to distortion, condensing, modification, or blockage. As we pointed out in our discussion of barriers to interpersonal communication, issues of perceptual errors, filtering, language, and/or information overload can occur at any management level. The key concept to remember is that the more people there are in a network, the greater the chance that problems in vertical communication will occur.

Second, since vertical communication involves differing levels of management, one must be concerned with the effects of status and power. Research has shown that the more dissimilar people are who communicate, the less vertical communication is aided. For example, a general manager communicating to a vice president usually does so in a formalistic manner. Because of this situation, the true feelings and attitudes of the general manager may be hidden from the communication.

Finally, vertical communication networks are enhanced when there is a high level of trust and respect among the various participants. Without such factors, subordinates will usually not communicate information that may be interpreted as weaknesses in their ability, skills, or performance. Likewise, subordinates are likely to screen out problems and complaints when they feel strongly that there is a possibility that the higher level manager will use this information to punish them in some way.

Lateral Communication

Vertical communication systems in organizations generally follow the chain of command. As we pointed out in chapters 8 and 9, in today's increasingly large and complex organizations, communication *across* the chains of command has become quite important to organizational performance. This type of communication is referred to as *lateral* communication.[18]

The need for lateral communication is created primarily because of problems with the organization's structure. First, there is the issue of *time*. Frequently, information must be transmitted across organizational functions for decision-making purposes, such as a customer complaint on product quality that is received by a sales representative, but must work its way to the production unit manager (see exhibit 11–8). Under normal circumstances, this information would be transmitted along the chain of command of the marketing function, across to the manufacturing function, and then down the manufacturing chain of command to the responsible manager (note: this is also an example of a chain network as shown in exhibit 11–6). When time is critical, as in solving a serious customer problem, this form of communication can be less than satisfactory.

The second need for lateral communication, closely aligned with the first, concerns the need for *coordination* between different units in an organization. In a hospital, for example, before the nursing staff can administer medication to a patient, the lab test results must be communicated to the right people. In a university, there must be close coordination between the registrar's office and the director of facilities during the registration process, particularly in making sure that there are adequate classrooms available for classes.

EXHIBIT 11–8   Vertical and Lateral Communication Example (Customer Quality Complaint)

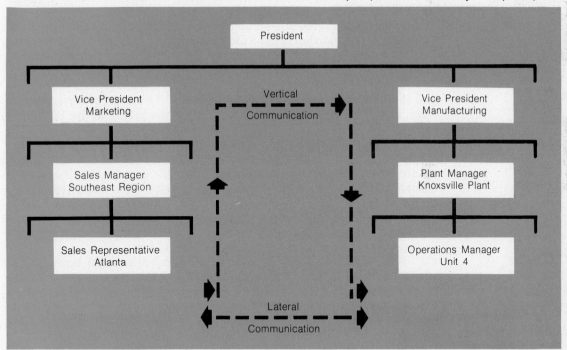

Because of the need for lateral communication, many organizations have adopted a number of facilitating mechanisms. The most frequently used mechanism, especially when time is important, is *direct contact* and communication across functional boundaries. In the hospital example, lab personnel may be given the go ahead to phone in the results of tests on patients to the physician or the nursing staff. As discussed in chapter

8, another frequently used mechanism for channeling lateral communication between different units is *liaisons roles*. For example, a project coordinator at NASA during the space program was responsible for making sure that there was adequate and accurate communication between private contractors and the particular NASA unit. Finally, some organizations facilitate the flow of lateral communication between a number of units with the formation of *task forces*. Instead of fighting the problem of communicating information vertically and across many functional divisions, representatives from the involved units are formed into a task force.

These examples are certainly not all-inclusive of the mechanisms used by organizations for facilitating lateral communication. The key point for managers to recognize, however, is that the structure of the organization, with all its formalistic components, may act to impede important communication. The need for lateral communication is not a failure of management, only a justified recognition that most organizational structures cannot effectively adapt to the growth, complexity, and dynamism of today's organizations.

External Communication

To this point in the discussion of organization communication, our focus has been on the *internal* communication process. A factor that is growing in importance is the way that the organization communicates with elements of its external environment.

The need for external communication by organizations to the general public is one that has arisen because of a number of serious situations. Consider, for example, the reaction by the public to the 100 to 200 percent increases in profits by the oil companies in 1978 and 1979. Irrespective of the validity or justification of these profits by the oil companies, it is hard for the general public to accept them when they personally are fighting high inflation. Or, consider the nuclear power industry and its desire to increase the construction of nuclear power plants after the Three Mile Island problem in Pennsylvania. Additional examples include significantly higher rates by auto and health insurance companies, increases in utility rates by gas, electric, and telephone companies, or rapidly increasing health care expenses.

From a communication viewpoint, organizations are beginning to adopt a number of new strategies to communicate to the general public. A frequently used mechanism by organizations, the *speakers' bureau,* is a volunteer group of employees who devote a portion of their time to discussing various important issues with community organizations. For example, a plant manager of a manufacturing facility may speak to a local civic club on the topic of the plant's plans to reduce air and water pollution, hiring the hard-core unemployed, or possible plant expansion.

In addition, many organizations are reemphasizing the use and power of the press in communicating to the public. This usually involves more frequent *news releases* on organizational activities, interviews with managers and employees, and so on. The use of this strategy, however, runs the risk of being misquoted or misunderstood by the media representative, which may end up doing more harm than good.

More frequently, the voices presenting the view of organizations are the various *professional associations* in which individuals and organizations are members. Examples such as the National Association of Manufacturers, the American Medical Association, and the Off-Shore Technology Association serve as communicators to the general public.

Finally, one of the main mechanisms for transmitting information to the public is the growing number of business councils. The most prominent are the Conference Board and the Business Roundtable. The latter is a group of nearly 200 chief executives who analyze issues, take positions, and argue them at the White House, on Capitol Hill, with regulatory agencies, or state or local bodies.[19] Their strategy is relatively simple: after being passive to the charges from many consumer and environmental groups, they suggest that organizations begin presenting their viewpoint in a more forceful and positive manner.

As the external environment becomes more dynamic and turbulent, organizations will be increasingly faced with having to state their cases to the public on a variety of issues. Managers can no longer take an "avoidance" view, hoping that the problem will blow away with the next breeze. The issues of our times will need open and straightforward information and communication if they are to be solved.

Keys to Success in Organizational Communication

Organizational communication, much like interpersonal communication, depends on senders, receivers, and the clarity of the messages to achieve effectiveness. Unlike interpersonal communication, however, organizational communication involves many people operating in networks. Thus, the problems we identified earlier (i.e., filtering, language, and so on) are multipled manyfold in organizational communication networks.

Achieving effectiveness in organizational communication may seem like an insurmountable task given the variety of people, jobs, environments, and goals that are involved. While communication has been, is now, and probably will be a major problem for managers in all types of organizations, there are certain suggestions for improvement that have been identified through the experiences of many managers. Some of these suggestions, or keys to success, in organizational communication are noted below.

1. **The structure of the organization should be adaptable, not a barrier to communication.**

If the organization is large and complex, with confusing lines of authority, overlapping functions, improper policies and procedures, and inadequate coordination mechanisms, it will tend to make communication difficult and sometimes haphazard. To counter these problems, managers must be willing to adapt or revise the structure to permit better communication between units. This can involve the use of different networks, liaison roles, task forces, direct contact, and the like.

2. **Learn how to regulate information flow.**

This involves the process of monitoring and regulating the massive flow of information and communication methods to ensure optimum results.

With today's emphasis on telecommunication, photocopying, and computer outputs, information overload is more a fact of life than a myth. Two practices can help managers overcome this situation. First is the practice of delegation of information and communication to subordinates to handle. The second is known as the *exception* principle, which states that only significant deviations from plans, policies, and procedures should be brought to the attention of higher level managers.

3. **Develop a good climate for communication.**

The research of communication specialists and the experiences of managers have shown that communication flows more freely and is more accurate and timely when there is mutual confidence and trust among the communicating personnel. Managers who develop this sense of trust among subordinates will find that communication is more effective because they have fostered high source credibility among subordinates. Key activities include the use of informal meetings, an open-door policy, absence of fear of reprisal for communicating a message, and the lowering of perceived status differences between people.

4. **Remove intergroup hostility.**

When two or more groups are in conflict, it hinders the communication between the groups. Examples are numerous: line versus staff; sales versus manufacturing; and management versus labor. This form of rivalry and conflict serves only to distort and block effective communication. While we will discuss the topic of conflict in Chapter 15 in more detail, it is important for managers to recognize at this point the need for such activities as confrontation between parties, settlement through negotiations, use of a third party as an arbitrator, and smoothing over differences to ensure good communication.

5. **Use of grapevine.**

The grapevine is probably the main informal communication channel that exists in all types of organizations. Grapevines exist in organizations for at least two reasons.[20] First, because of certain deficiencies, the formal vertical and lateral communication networks are bypassed, enabling employees to receive and send information more quickly and accurately. For example, in many organizations the news of an upcoming promotion of a manager may be known to most employees long before the formal announcement is made. Second, due to the great emphasis placed on verbal communication, there is always time for idle chatter (or gossip) between interacting employees. Frequently, this idle chatter communicates a message of greater value than the formal message. The important aspect for managers to understand is that not only is the grapevine an inevitable factor in the organization's communication system, but frequently it can be an effective means of transmitting information. The grapevine can also have damaging consequences. The fact is that there is a distinction between a grapevine and a rumor mill; the latter contains more inaccurate information than the former. One way to minimize some of the undesirable effects of informal communication networks is to improve other forms of communication. If relevant and accurate information and data exist in normal communication channels on important issues, then damaging rumors are less likely to develop or be transmitted.

COMMUNICATION IN THE INTERNATIONAL REALM

Communication across cultures and different languages has presented many perplexing and sometimes embarrassing problems for organizations.[21] For example, consider the following illustrations:

Coca-Cola's management was disturbed over the decline in sales of their soft drink in some Asian markets. The reason was that consumers were confused over the company's advertising claims—the "Coke Adds Life" theme had been translated as "Coke Brings You Back From the Dead."

Colgate Palmolive had to change the name of their toothpaste in French-speaking countries—the name "Cue" is a pornographic word in French.

Exxon's "Put a Tiger in Your Tank" ad was offensive to people in Thailand.

In Germany, General Motors' "Body by Fisher" translates to "Corpse by Fisher."

In some South American countries, the name "matador" has criminal implications. For American Motors, this presented problems because one of its main car lines had this name.

In marketing a new tire cord in Germany, Goodyear demonstrated its strength by showing how the cord could break a steel chain. The German government intervened and stopped the advertising claim—it seems that it is illegal to imply another product is inferior in Germany.

Before managers can use communication to the fullest, they must understand some of the problems imposed by international differences. Among the most important differences are consideration of language, especially in verbal and written communication, nonverbal communication, issues of etiquette, and formal versus informal communication.

Language difficulties can have a significant impact on verbal and written communications between managers and organizations. These differences surface not only in translations, but also in the actual meaning of words and phrases. For example: (1) in Spanish, the word *empleados* refers to white-collar workers and *obreros* relates to laborers—this differentiation reflects important class differences that must be recognized by the manager;[22] (2) in Japan, the word for yes—*hai*—does not indicate agreement, only that the other person has understood what has been said; and (3) the terms *corn, maize,* and *graduate studies* in the United Kingdom translate into *wheat, corn,* and *undergraduate studies* in American English.

What can the manager do to lessen these problems of language? At least three approaches can be used. First, the manager can attempt to learn the local language. With concentrated effort, a person can acquire a casual speaking knowledge of another language within six to twelve months. A casual knowledge may not be enough given the complexities of many languages. Second, employing a good interpreter appears to be a preferred approach by many organizations when there is a lack of well-versed or bilingual managers. Finally, English is rapidly becoming the international language of business, thus overcoming some of the language problems. Among non-U.S. organizations, such firms as Siemans and Hoechst (German), Philips (Dutch), Hoffman-LaRoche (Swiss) and Volvo (Swedish) have adopted English as their official tongue.[23]

These approaches should not imply that there is no advantage for an international manager to learn languages other than English. Nor does it imply that all transactions can be conducted in English. A working knowledge of the language spoken where one is operating may help in adapting to the foreign country as well as gaining acceptance by persons there. However, unless fully fluent in the language of the country, managers should not attempt serious negotiations in it or expect the foreigners to do so in English. Good translators are essential in these circumstances. Perhaps of greater importance than the ability to use a language is an awareness of the importance of language in the decision-making process. The capacity and structure of a language to a significant degree determines the nature of a person's thought and emotion and hence of behavior. In other words, for a manager to understand how foreign managers think and make decisions, they must have established clear communication channels.[24]

Managers should also be aware of nonverbal communication differences. For example, color conjures up meanings to us based on experience within our own cultures. Black in most Western countries historically has been associated with death, yet in parts of the Far East and in Latin America, white and purple mean the same thing, respectively. In some countries, particularly in Latin and South America, businesspersons prefer to stand quite close to another manager while they are communicating. Not knowing this approach, the U.S. manager continues to back up. At the end, both parties may have developed an unexplained distrust of each other. In addition, cues concerning a person's relative position may be particularly difficult to grasp. A U. S. manager may underestimate the importance of a foreign counterpart because he or she has no large private office with a wooden desk and carpeting. Similarly, the foreigner may feel the same because the U. S. manager opens garage doors or mixes drinks without benefit of a servant.

Even etiquette can influence communication between managers in the international realm. For example, if a U. S. manager in the Far East fails to bring small but thoughtful gifts to the Far Eastern counterpart, that official may not only consider it a breach of etiquette, but also feel that the U. S. manager places little interest or emphasis on the meeting. At the same time, if not invited into private homes, the U. S. manager may develop the same wrong opinion of the Far Eastern associate, not realizing that such invitations are not customary.[25]

Taken together, many organizations have found that for the best results, communication in the international realm should be conducted on a formal basis. This means the frequent use of an interpreter and a great reliance on written reports, both between headquarters and a foreign operation and between two organizations.

COMMUNICATION, PERFORMANCE, AND THE MANAGER'S JOB

Managers spend a large portion of their time in the communication process. This communication can take place internally or externally to the organization, formally or informally, and through vertical and lateral communication channels. As the focal point, or nerve center of the organization's activities, it is crucial to performance that managers understand their communication roles.

Performance and the Manager's Informational Roles

In chapter 2, and throughout this book, we have stressed the importance of the manager's informational roles—monitor, disseminator, and spokesperson. By performing in these roles, the manager becomes an active receiver and communicator of information. As shown in exhibit 11–9, these informational roles are linked with certain interpersonal and decisional roles as well. Let us look at how the manager can perform more effectively in these roles.[26]

The MonitorRole. Managers as monitors are continually seeking, and being bombarded with, information that enables them to understand and make sense about what is happening in the organization and its environment. The manager seeks information to identify or detect changes, to locate problems and opportunities, to build knowledge about the internal and external environment, and to know when information must be transmitted and decisions are to be made.

In the monitor role, the manager receives or seeks out information from at least two sources: internal and external to the organization. Consider the job of product manager for a large household products company such as General Mills. From an *internal* information source perspective, the product manager performing this monitor role would be cognizant of information on the progress of operations related to the product line from such sources as operating reports, committee reports, and general observations. Of interest would be such information as the present capacity of the manufacturing plant, sales by region of the country, and the progress being made on a new product.

EXHIBIT 11–9 Managerial Roles in Communication

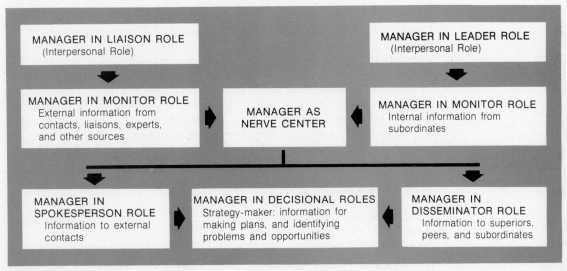

Adapted from H. Mintzberg, *The Nature of Managerial Work* (New York: Harper & Row, 1973), p. 72.

Externally, the product manager seeks and receives information concerning customers, competitors, suppliers, as well as information on market changes, political moves, and developments in new technologies. As a result, to learn about important trends the product manager may attend conferences, pay attention to letters from customers, read many trade publications, and listen to any information that may come through the formal and informal channels.

Successful performance in a monitor role involves a number of factors. Some of the most important include the following:

1. **Develop your own information system.**

This includes not only being aware of all sources of information that concern one's job, but in building important *liaison* contacts (see exhibit 11–9) with key people internal and external to the organization. A brief conversation with a sales representative or a customer may provide as much valuable information as a year-long market research study.

2. **Train subordinates to be equally aware of important information.**

A manager's subordinates are an important part of the information system. Properly trained, they can make valuable contributions to the understanding of the manager's situation.

3. **Develop good listening and reading habits.**

Important information can be lost unless the manager operates with a set of clear senses. This includes learning how to listen carefully when another person is trying to communicate. In addition, since much of the communication received by a manager is in written form, effective reading practices and habits are of great value. Three types of reading are most important: (1) inspectional reading, or skimming to identify key points; (2) analytical reading, or in-depth analysis of the important points found through inspectional reading; and (3) comparative reading, which is the process of examining a number of messages simultaneously in order to determine or detect trends, relationships, and so on.[27]

The Disseminator Role. As a disseminator, the manager acts as the main channel sending external information into the organization and transmitting internal information from one subordinate to another. Two general types of information are usually communicated. First, there is *factual* information, such as the product manager passing on information to executives about the introduction of a new product by the competitor. Second, information can have a *value* orientation, where some preference or judgment is assigned. An example would be the statement by the product manager of the need to develop a comparable product to meet the competitor's challenge.

Similar to the monitor role, certain keys to success have been noted by experienced managers:

1. **Whether factual of value oriented, make sure your information is accurate.**

When a supposedly important piece of information comes to the attention of a manager, there is a tendency to communicate it upward and/or downward without much thought given to its validity. Before communicating any information, take time to check it out with other sources. There is nothing more damaging to a manager than to be known as one who "cries wolf" too often.

2. **Choose communication methods and channels carefully.**

Try to disseminate information when there is less interference or fewer barriers to communication. This means learning the *timing* of communication (usually when you have the receiver's attention) and the most appropriate method and channel to fit the situation.

3. **Follow up your communication.**

This can be done by asking questions, using verbal communications after written communication, encouraging the receiver to express reactions, or the use of informal contracts. The key factor is to ensure that every important communication has a provision for feedback for optimal understanding.

The Spokesperson Role.   The disseminator role is primarily concerned with communication within an organization; in the spokesperson role, the manager is concerned with transmitting information to elements of the organization's environment. Because of their positions, managers have the authority and right to speak on behalf of the organization. As the focal point, or nerve center, managers have the information to perform this role effectively.

Certain keys to success in the spokesperson role are discussed below.

1. **Make sure the information communicated to the environment is accurate.**

For much the same reasons as given for the disseminator role, the accuracy of the information that is communicated will ensure the continued respect receivers have of your position.

2. **Share information with liaison sources.**

A manager's personal information system is not a one-way system; it entails two-way communication. To ensure the continued sending of information from other sources, it is a wise practice also to feed them information that they consider to be valuable. In this manner, the liaison network is strengthened. Consider the example of the product manager again. This manager may have developed a good liaison contact with a representative in the purchasing department of a customer. In the recent past, this customer liaison person may have informally indicated to the product manager that the organization may be interested in a higher grade of the product than is now being purchased. The product manager disseminates this information to key people within his or her organization such that when the customer requests becomes formal, the product manager's organization is ready with a proper strategic response. In a reciprocal manner, the product manager may informally tell the purchasing representative that his or her company is thinking about changing the size of the package for the product or is contemplating using other transportation means. Through this reciprocation, this important communication network remains open and viable.

3. Become recognized as an expert source of information.

A manager's ability to be influential in a spokesperson role is highly dependent on whether or not the receivers consider the manager to be an expert in what he or she is talking about. This means that the manager must demonstrate current, up-to-the-minute knowledge of the organization and its environment. Just the same as "crying wolf" too often will hurt one's performance in a monitor role, being taken by surprise often with new information in a spokesperson role will be detrimental to the manager's overall performance.

The Link to Decisional Roles.   As shown in exhibit 11–9, the final component in analyzing the manager's information roles in the organization's communication system is to recognize the important link with the decisional roles, or strategy-formulating activities (see chapter 6). The relationship is a logical link: the manager has the authority to make decisions (through interpersonal roles) and the necessary information (through informational roles) to make decisions effectively regarding strategy and policies.

In the case of the product manager, through performance in the monitoring role an entirely new use for one of the products has been identified. An example could be slightly changing the quality or grade of a household soap and marketing it as an industrial detergent. Since the product manager has the information and the authority to make the decision, plans are developed to enter the industrial market.

SUMMARY FOR THE MANAGER

1. Of all the activities and functions that are performed by a manager, none takes up more time than communication. Communication in organizations is conducted for a variety of reasons, including attempting to influence others, expressing feelings, exchanging information, and controlling. The way managers communicate has a significant effect on their overall levels of performance.

2. The interpersonal communication process involves a sender, a message sent through a channel, and a receiver. The process can be one way or two way in nature. While one-way takes less time, it is less accurate than two-way communication. An important part of two-way communication is the feedback given to the sender. Whether informational, corrective, or reinforcing, feedback is extremely important given the growing complexity and dynamism of today's organizations.

3. Three main types of communication are found in most organizations: verbal, written, and nonver-

bal. It is important for managers to recognize that in trying to communicate a message, it is a wise strategy to use more than one form of communication. Examples include following up a conversation with a phone call or asking for comments on a memo or report during a face-to-face interaction.

4. One of the most popular ways of presenting a manager's interpersonal communication style is the Johari Window. The major dimensions of the model, exposure and feedback, relate to how the manager provides *and* receives information from others. The key point is that one should not stress one dimension over another: effectiveness is a function of the maximum use of both exposure and feedback.

5. Interpersonal communication does not occur without problems or barriers. Four of the main barriers include perceptual errors, language, filtering, and information overload. Overcoming these errors involves a combination of training, experience, guidance, and practice.

6. Organizational communication—that form of communication that may involve more than two people—is conducted through communication networks. The four networks that were discussed—chain, wheel, circle, and all channel—differ in many characteristics, including centrality, speed, accuracy, and member satisfaction. For highest performance, the manager should carefully analyze the situation and choose the network that will work best. In formal superior-subordinate interactions, the chain and wheel are appropriate; for committees or task forces, the choice should be the circle or all channel.

7. Communication in organizations flows both vertically and laterally. The most effective vertical communication methods (upward and downward) are those methods that are both direct and personal. Lateral communication needs generally develop because of the need for speed and the deficiencies of the structure of the organization. Direct contact, liaisons, and task forces are used effectively by many organizations to speed communication throughout various units.

8. Communication in the international realm presents a number of problems to the manager. Among these are the problems of language (should the manager learn the local language or use a skilled interpreter), nonverbal communication, and etiquette. Because of these problems, formal communication is stressed heavily.

9. Communication relates directly to the manager's roles. Information is gathered from the performance in the liaison role (external information) and the leader role (interpersonal role). It is processed through the monitor, disseminator, and spokesperson roles, and then put to use through performance in the decisional roles. Effectiveness in these managerial roles involves developing one's own information system, learning how to read effectively, making sure the information is accurate, following up on communication, and being recognized as an expert in the material that is communicated.

QUESTIONS FOR REVIEW AND DISCUSSION

1. Why are organizational structure and communication closely related?
2. What are some examples of noise in the communication process?
3. Why is filtering a significant barrier to interpersonal communication?
4. Why are vertical communication methods emphasizing a direct and personal approach rated the most effective?
5. Give an example of the three main forms of feedback. Why is feedback important to the communication process?
6. What key characteristics should a manager consider when choosing a communication network?
7. Identify some of the reasons that many managers and organizations are increasing their emphasis on external communication to the general public.
8. How can the organizational grapevine be used effectively by a manager?
9. Identify some of the reasons for the need for lateral communication.
10. Discuss the importance of the manager's monitor role in organizational communication.

NOTES

1. D. Rather and G. P. Gates, *The Palace Guard* (New York: Harper & Row, 1974), p.109.

2. W. G. Scott and T. R. Mitchell, *Organizational Theory: A Structural and Behavioral Analysis* (Homewood, Ill.: Ir-win, 1976), p.193.

3. H. Mintzberg, *The Nature of Managerial Work* (New York: Harper & Row, 1973), p. 39.

4. See W. V. Haney, *Communication and Organizational*

Behavior, 3rd ed. (Homewood, Ill.: Irwin, 1973); and J. Wofford, E. A. Gerlof, and R. C. Cummins, *Organizational Communication* (New York: McGraw-Hill, 1977).

5. R. Kreitner, "People Are Systems, Too: Filling the Feedback Vacuum," *Business Horizons* (November 1977): 54–58.

6. R. G. Tharp and R. Gallimore, "Basketball's John Wooden: What Coach Can Teach a Teacher," *Psychology Today* (January 1976): 74–78.

7. See D. M. Herold and M. M. Greller, "Feedback: The Definition of the Constrict," *Academy of Management Journal* (March 1977): 142–47; and H. J. Leavitt and R. A. H. Mueller, "Some Effects of Feedback on Communications," *Human Relations* (November 1951): 401–10.

8. D. Bell, "Communications Technology—For Better or for Worse," *Harvard Business Review* (May–June 1979): 20–42.

9. A. D. Szilagyi and W. E. Holland, "Social Density: Relationships with Functional Interaction and Perceptions of Job Characteristics, Role Stress, and Work Satisfaction," *Journal of Applied Psychology* (February 1980): 28–33.

10. "P&G: We Grow Our Own Managers," *Dun's Review* (December 1975): 48.

11. H. O. Golightly, "The What, What Not, and How of Internal Communication," *Business Horizons* (December 1973): 49.

12. J. Hall, "Communication Revisited," *California Management Review* (Spring 1973): 30–48.

13. S. S. Zalkind and T. W. Costello, "Perception: Some Recent Research and Implications for Administration," *Administrative Science Quarterly* (September 1962): 218–35.

14. S. Chase, *Power of Words* (New York: Harcourt, Brace, 1953), p. 259.

15. See H. J. Leavitt, "Some Effects of Certain Communication Patterns on Group Performance," *Journal of Abnormal and Social Psychology* (January 1951): 38–50; and M. E. Shaw, "Communication Networks," in *Advances in Experimental Social Psychology,* ed. Leonard Berkowitz (New York: Academic Press, 1964), pp. 111–47.

16. B. Harriman, "Up and Down the Communications Ladder," *Harvard Business Review* (September–October 1974): 143–51.

17. W. H. Read, "Upward Communication in Industrial Hierarchies," *Human Relations* (February 1962): 3–15.

18. R. L. Simpson, "Vertical and Horizontal Communication in Formal Organizations," *Administrative Science Quarterly* (September 1959): 188–96.

19. W. Guzzardi, Jr., "Business is Learning How to Win in Washington," *Fortune* (March 27, 1978): 52–58.

20. K. Davis, "Grapevine Communication Among Lower and Middle Level Managers," *Personnel Journal* (April 1969).

21. D. A. Ricks, M. Y. C. Fu, and J. S. Arpas, *International Business Blunders* (Columbus, Ohio: Grid, 1974).

22. J. D. Daniels, E. W. Ogram, Jr., and L. H. Radebaugh, *International Business* (Reading, Mass.: Addison-Wesley, 1979), p. 78.

23. Ibid., p. 512.

24. R. D. Robinson, *International Business Management* (Hinsdale, Ill.: Dryden, 1973), p. 267.

25. Daniels, Ogram, and Radebaugh, p. 79.

26. Mintzberg, pp. 65–77.

27. M. Adler and C. Van Doren, *How to Read a Book* (New York: Simon & Schuster, 1972).

ADDITIONAL REFERENCES

Allen, R. K. *Organizational Management Through Communication.* New York: Harper & Row, 1977.

Argyris, C. "Double Loop Learning in Organizations," *Harvard Business Review,* (September–October 1977): 115–25.

Daft, R. L., and Wiginton, J. C., "Language and Organization," *Academy of Management Review* (April 1979): 179–92.

Ellis, D. S., *Management and Administrative Communication.* New York: Macmillan, 1978.

"Game Playing to Help Managers Communicate," *Business Week* (April 9, 1979): 76–78.

Greenbaum, H. H. "The Audit of Organizational Communication," *Academy of Management Journal* (March 1974): 139–154.

McMaster, J. B. "Getting the Word to the Top," *Management Review* (February 1979): 62–65.

Nadler, D. A. *Feedback and Organization Development: Using Data Based Methods.* Reading, Mass.: Addison-Wesley, 1977.

Nadler, D. A.; Mirvis, P. H.; and Cammann, C. "The Ongoing Feedback System." *Organizational Dynamics.* (Spring 1976): 63–80.

Roberts, K. H., and O'Reilly, C. A. "Organizations as Communication Structures: An Empirical Approach." *Human Communication Research* (Summer 1978): 287–94.

Rockney, E. H. *Communicating in Organizations.* Cambridge, Mass.: Winthrop, 1977.

Tubbs, S. L., and Widery, R. N. "When Productivity Lags, Check at the Top: Are Key Managers Really Communicating?" *Management Review* (November 1978): 20–25.

A CASE FOR ANALYSIS

National Can Corporation

Before Frank W. Considine arrived at National Can, the firm had succeeded largely on the strength of its skillful, old-fashioned salesmanship. The company was adept at patiently cultivating close relationships with customers and in providing extra help and service. National still has important customers who have remained faithful because of special efforts made on their behalf decades ago.

Even as National grew into a billion-dollar company, Considine deliberately preserved a lean and informal style of management. One of National's most valuable assets today is a small-company spirit rare among corporations of its size. Sales have doubled since 1973 (excluding the food and pet-food divisions), but with Considine keeping iron control over executive staffing, the number of salaried employees has remained virtually unchanged.

This strategy, however, leads a lean, if not austere corporate life. The company's four-year-old headquarters building, which stands alone out near O'Hare airport, is a plain tower of the sort that generally houses a swarm of small-time sales offices and one-person law firms. Most of National's vice presidents work out of spare, white-painted cubicles; senior vice presidents get offices that are not much larger, though most are at least corner rooms. There are no company planes—Considine purposely located near the airport to take advantage of what he calls "our corporate jet fleet, the largest in the world: American, United, T.W.A. . . . ." Everybody, including Considine, flies coach unless the flight is long or a customer is going too.

Informality is crucial to National's operating style. Because of the lean managerial staff, no one ever has trouble knowing whom to call when a problem arises. The only expensive-looking things in those executive offices are multibuttoned phone consoles, backed up with a system of WATS and tie lines, through which practically any National executive can reach practically any other. Written memos play a small part in National's communication flow.

Considine's own operating style sets the tone. He is very much a hands-on manager, with a relish bordering on obsession for involving himself in operations. He has a keen eye for detail and a memory for names, faces, numbers and minutiae that endlessly amazes his executives. Considine takes the phone in hand dozens of times a week to call down the executive line. One day recently, for example, the president of Jos. Schlitz Brewing Co. asked Considine for help on a problem involving printing on cans. Considine wanted to waste no time in putting the right man to work; he called directly to a plant where he knew he could find a suitable technician.

It could be argued, of course, that a chief executive should not spend a great deal of his time on such matters. But attention to details is an essential part of Considine's management style and a reflection of his philosophy. Good managers, Considine thinks, must be highly involved with their work and with their fellow managers. For a leader, he believes that involvement consists of asking the right detailed question at the right time. The results of doing that lie not just in getting the question answered, but in setting a pattern of managerial involvement.

Considine's style of close involvement works both ways. His executives feel free to call him directly, without going through channels, if they have problems too pressing to wait on someone above them who may not be available. They are free to call anyone else, up or down the chain of command, without observing hierarchical priorities. At National, customers get their problems attended to quickly, and manufacturing lines do not sit idle awaiting the appropriate executive's decision on a production problem. The freedom of communication in all directions undoubtedly contributes to National's prowess as an efficient maker and marketer of cans.

Considine has take original and unconventional measures to improve the flow of communications. Typical of his whole approach to management is a major structural reorganization he sponsored a number of years ago. He had hired a new head of operations, a shrewd and down-to-earth veteran of twenty-three years in plant management at Continental Can. Considine had observed that engineers and plant operations men, although linked by a common corporate interest, were not good at communicating with each other. It was almost as if they spoke different languages.

With Considine's backing, managers got together to work out a program for integrating the two staffs, with the goal of achieving smoother and more efficient plant operations. It took two years to bring the project off, but since 1974, National's engineering department has reported to manufacturing. The integration works at all levels, from senior management to factory floor. Executives can visit a plant and talk about either engineering or manufacturing.

A notable aspect of Considine's character as a manager is an unusual degree of concern for the people who work under him. He believes that a corporation doesn't have to hurt people to be successful. He is perpetually interested in the well-being of his employees' families. Not many billion-dollar corporations have ever held anything quite like the open-house fiestas, complete with refreshments and circuses, that took place at two National Can plants. Considine's purpose was to make it possible for spouses and children to see firsthand the workplaces that were such an important part of employee's lives. The open-house program was a smashing success, and Considine plans more such events for the future.

Considine's hands-on, highly personal operating style has clearly served National well to date, but there are questions about how well it will continue to do so. National's officers and directors are unanimous in saying that Considine is overly involved, given the size of the company today. Moreover, there is no chief operating officer to share the burdens.

Even if National seems not to have suffered from Considine's overinvolvement, he himself has: a little over a year ago, he was hospitalized for three weeks after a small heart attack. Since then he has taken his directors' advice to bring in help.

Pulling back is not likely to be easy for Considine. Past experience has convinced him that someone needs to be on the lookout for problems. For instance, he recently caught a major underbilling that just slipped by everyone else. Spotting even a major underbilling, however, is not part of the chief executive's job in a large corporation.

Adapted from C. G. Burck, "How Frank Considine Runs a Billion-Dollar Company," Fortune (July 3, 1978): 74–77.

Questions for Discussion

1. Describe and evaluate Frank Considine's communication style and its effects on the company and other employees.
2. How would you describe the company's communication networks?
3. Using exhibit 11–9, what managerial roles does Mr. Considine perform?
4. Can Mr. Considine continue to use his communication style? Can others?
5. What is the relationship between communication and organizational structure in this case?

IV

Directing
Performance
– Leading –

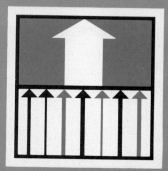

12

Motivation

CHAPTER OUTLINE

KEY POINTS IN THIS CHAPTER

1. Motivation is a process that has been examined through two major approaches: content theories (arousal factors) and process theories (arousal and direction factors).

2. Maslow's need hierarchy, a content theory, concerns motivation from the desire to satisfy needs.

3. Herzberg's two-factor theory, also a content theory, focuses on the nature of the job as the key motivator.

4. Expectancy theory is a process approach concerned with how individuals choose motivated behaviors that lead to valued rewards.

5. The second process theory, reinforcement theory, emphasizes learning motivated behaviors from the rewards received for performance.

6. Job design is applied managerial approach to motivation that stresses the use of intrinsic rewards.

7. Behavior modification, founded on reinforcement theory, emphasizes the use of extrinsic rewards to motivate subordinates.

8. Through assigning work, identifying subordinate needs, guiding work, and evaluating and rewarding performance, the manager is a key factor in the motivation process.

THE PRACTICE OF MANAGEMENT

Two Views of Motivation

George Sampson is a lucky man. The Hewlett-Packard factory in Palo Alto where he works is clean, pleasant, and quiet enough to permit Sampson to work on a challenging job, but also affords time to talk with other workers. Sampson, whose job is to assemble the company's complicated electrical-signal analyzers, takes a craftsman's pride in his work. "It's a cute little machine," he says of the device. He has even come up with a couple of tools and methods to make the assembling task more efficient. "They like you to come up with new ideas. When they have this policy, you think more and work harder."

Sampson is also pleased with the company's other policies, such as profit sharing, which he says makes you feel more a part of the company. Recently, the factory initiated a flexible schedule that allows employees to come to work any time between 6:30 and 8:30 a.m. and leave between 3:15 and 5:15 p.m. Sampson is usually at his work station by 6:30. "These hours give you a lot of freedom in the afternoon," he points out. When he goes home, Sampson does chores around the apartment building that his wife manages or spends time with his three sons.

      *   *   *

All too often, the career ambitions of a young man or woman are blocked by the realities of the labor market, and economic necessity forces a personal compromise. Sandy Jenkins is a case in point. Back home in Ames, Iowa, the twenty-three-year-old envisioned a career as an airline stewardess. Dreams of exciting jet travel and crowds of interesting people evaporated when her application was rejected. Now, as a secretary to three lawyers in one of St Louis's largest law firms, she finds that she is dead tired at day's end. In addition, she believes that her salary is too low to meet her needs. Some days she even feels like a machine, not a person.

A total of fifty-five secretaries work on her office floor. Each morning, she says, "we come in like a thundering herd of cattle." At work, Jenkins and the other secretaries are constantly supervised—by older secretaries who have many years of experience. Jenkins says that the supervisors react with impatience and show a high degree of displeasure toward younger workers who express dislike toward the many rules and procedures. As she tells it, the supervisors distribute debits and credits for tardiness or overtime, constantly look over the shoulders of the subordinates as they type, and warn them not to have a drink at lunch because it will make them sleepy and less productive. The system, she says, "just grinds you down."

Her father, a banker, is a driving, ambitious man. "He always told me that when you're working and making money, you're happy. But it's not as simple as that. To be happy, you have to feel that you're making some sort of contribution. And, believe me, that's very difficult when you have a supervisor standing over you every minute just waiting for you to make a mistake." Another thing that upsets Jenkins is not being told why she has to do certain things, and that when she does something right, no one says a kind word. Still, she plans to stay on her job for the near future. "After all," she says, "it's a job."

Suggested from Newsweek, *"The Job Blahs: Who Wants to Work?" (March 26, 1973): 81.*

12

With the topic of motivation, we begin a four-chapter sequence on the important managerial function of leading. Since the leading function is one that directly involves the relationship between the manager and subordinates, our discussion will cover the various facets of this relationship. The material will include an overview of the basic process of motivation, an analysis of the manager's activities as a leader, a discussion of how to understand and lead individuals in groups, and finally, a discussion on improving job performance.

This first chapter of part IV is concerned with how managers can motivate subordinates to perform. This chapter is presented before the formal discussion of leadership because it is important for the manager to understand the process of employee motivation before attempts at influence (i.e., leadership) are made. The chapter is divided into four major parts. First, a discussion of the study of motivation and its importance to management will be presented. Second, we will briefly cover some of the main approaches to motivation in organizations. Third, two important managerial motivation strategies—job design and behavior modification—will be discussed. Finally, we will end the chapter with a presentation of the relationship between motivation, performance, and the manager's job.

THE STUDY OF MOTIVATION

Managers in all types of organizations are continually faced with the fact that vast differences exist in the performances of individual employees. Some employees always perform at high levels, need little or no direction, and appear to enjoy what they are doing. Other employees perform only at marginal levels, require constant attention and direction, and are often absent. The reasons for these differences in performance are varied and complex, involving the nature of the job, the behavior of the manager, and the characteristics of the employee. At the core of each of these aspects is *motivation*.

Consider this statement from a recent General Electric publication:

When it comes to being highly productive on the job, to feeling a sense of success and achievement, to being a real contributor, what do you really believe about yourself and others? Does money count first—the desire to draw a bigger paycheck? Is it the competitive instinct—the urge to win over others? Is fear the principal factor or does motivation come from the promise of reward? Is it just ego—the desire for recognition, approval and status? Or is it the sheer enjoyment of being part of a busy, cooperative, professional team?

These are questions to which behavioral scientists have been addressing themselves for years. Yet, oddly enough, few of their findings and theories have been effectively applied by managers who have learned their managing skills from bosses or from managerial courses that have stressed

405

techniques, rather than a fundamental understanding of the manager's role in the human resource area.[1]

This illustrates that motivation has not only a complex meaning, but is applied in a variety of ways in organizations. The reasons for this variety will be discussed throughout this chapter.

Definition of Motivation

From years of research, behavioral scientists have developed slightly different viewpoints of motivation that emphasize different components. In general, the differing views about motivation have led to these conclusions:

1. The analysis of motivation should concentrate on factors that *arouse* or *energize* a person's activities. These factors include needs, motives, and drives.

2. Motivation is *process* oriented and concerns behavioral choice, direction, goals, and the rewards received for performing.[2]

Building upon these conclusions, we can provide a basic model of motivation that incorporates the concepts of needs, direction, and rewards. The model, shown in exhibit 12-1, presents motivation as a multistep process. First, the arousal of a *need* creates a state of tension (or disequilibrium) within the individual that he or she will try to reduce through behavior. Second, the individual will *search for and choose* particular behaviors or strategies to satisfy these needs. Third, *goal-directed behavior,* or actual performance occurs. An important individual characteristic, *ability,* intervenes between the choice of behavior and actual behavior. This is because individuals may not have the necessary background (e.g., skills, experience, or knowledge) to satisfy a need (as in the case of a person who wants to become president of a large organization before age twenty-five). Fourth, an *evaluation* of the individual's performance is conducted by the individual or by others. Performance directed at satisfying a need such as developing a sense of pride in one's work is usually evaluated by the individual. On the other hand, performance directed toward satisfying a financial need, for example, is generally evaluated by another person, such as a supervisor. Fifth, *rewards or punishment* are given, depending on the level of performance. Finally, the individual *assesses* the degree to which the chosen behavior has satisfied the original need. If this motivation cycle has satisfied the need, a state of equilibrium or *satisfaction* exists. If the need remains unsatisfied, the motivation cycle is repeated, with the possibility that a different choice of motivated behavior will result.

Consider, for example, a civil engineer recently assigned to the design and construction of a large bridge. Because the engineer has been with the company for a number of years, he recognizes a desire or need to be promoted to the position of project engineer (arousal of a need). A number of ways to satisfy this need are available, including continued excellent performance, obtaining an advanced degree, asking for the promotion outright, or moving to another company (search for behaviors). The engineer decides, after a discussion with higher-level management, to excel on this project as the strategy to satisfy the need (choice of behavior). Recognizing he has the necessary ability to excel in perfor-

EXHIBIT 12-1
A Basic Motivation Model

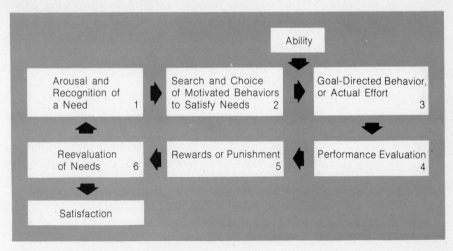

mance, the engineer works hard toward the successful completion of the project (ability and goal-directed behavior). After the project has been completed, the engineer's performance is evaluated by higher management (performance evaluation), resulting in a promotion to project manager (reward). Because the original need for promotion has been satisfied, our engineer is in a state of equilibrium (satisfaction) with respect to this particular need. Other needs may arise, such as a need for recognition, that will start the motivation cycle all over again.

Approaches to Motivation

Managerial approaches to motivation have existed for many decades. In previous chapters, the work of Taylor in scientific management and McGregor's theory X and theory Y represent contrasting views of how to motivate employees. These early approaches, however, lacked the specificity and concrete suggestions that are needed by managers in today's complex world. More comprehensive approaches were needed.

In the following sections, we will present four contemporary approaches to motivation. These approaches will be classified into two broad categories that correspond to our definition of motivation. Two approaches—Maslow's need hierarchy and Herzberg's two-factor theory—are classified as *content* approaches, since they concern those factors that energize or arouse motivated behavior. The approaches that deal with the direction of motivated behavior—Vroom's expectancy theory and Skinner's reinforcement theory—will be discussed as *process* approaches.

CONTENT THEORIES

Content theories of motivation focus on the question of what arouses, energizes, or starts behavior. The answer to this question involves the concept that needs drive people to behave in a particular manner. A need is considered to be an internal quality of the person. Hunger (the need for food), a steady job (the need for security), or career advancement (the need for promotion) are seen as needs that arouse people to choose specific acts or patterns of behavior. Two of the most popular content theories are Abraham H. Maslow's need hierarchy theory and Frederick Herzberg's two-factor theory.

Maslow's Need Hierarchy Theory

Maslow's need hierarchy suggests that people in organizations are motivated to perform by a desire to satisfy a set of internal needs (Step 1 in exhibit 12-1). Maslow's framework is based on three fundamental assumptions:[3]

1. People are beings who want and whose wants (needs) influence their behavior. Only *unsatisfied* needs can influence behavior: satisfied needs are not motivators.
2. A person's needs are arranged in an order of importance (hierarchy), from the most basic (food and shelter) to the complex (ego and achievement).
3. A person advances to the next level of the hierarchy (or from basic toward complex needs) only when the lower need is at least *minimally* satisfied. That is, the individual will be concerned with satisfying a need for safe working conditions before being motivated by a need for achievement from the successful accomplishment of a task.

From these assumptions, Maslow proposed five classifications of needs that represent the order of importance to the individual. These needs are (1) physiological; (2) safety and security; (3) social; (4) ego, status, and esteem; and (5) self-actualization. Exhibit 12-2 is a general representation of the need hierarchy.

Physiological needs are the primary or basic-level needs of people, such as food, shelter, and relief from and avoidance of pain. In the workplace, such needs concern base salary and working conditions.

When the primary, or physiological, needs have been minimally satisfied, the next higher level of needs, *safety and security needs,* assume importance as motivators. These are needs such as freedom from threat, protection against danger and accidents, and security of the job. In organizations, individuals view these needs in terms of safe working conditions, salary increases to meet inflation, job security, and an acceptable level of fringe benefits to provide for health, protection, and retirement.

Social needs become dominant when safety and security needs have been minimally satisfied. These needs concern such aspects as friendship, affiliation, and satisfying interactions with other people. In the workplace, these needs relate to the desire to interact frequently with other workers, good supervision, and acceptance by others.

The next level in the hierarchy, *ego, status, and esteem needs,* focuses on the need for self-respect from others for one's accomplishments, and a need to develop a feeling of self-confidence and prestige. Successful completion of a particular project, recognition by others of the person's skills, and the acquisition of organizational titles (e.g., manager, senior analyst, and director of nursing) are examples of these needs.

The highest need level in Maslow's framework, *self-actualization,* concerns the need to maximize the use of one's skills, abilities, and potential. People with dominant self-actualization needs could be characterized as individuals who seek work assignments that challenge their skills, permit them to learn and to use creative or innovative talents, and provide for advancement and personal growth.

To illustrate Maslow's approach, consider a newly graduated accounting student from a well-respected university in Indiana who takes a job as a staff accountant for a large accounting firm in California (see exhibit 12-3). The initial interview trip plus the follow-up visit to locate

EXHIBIT 12-2 Maslow's Need Hierarchy

GENERAL FACTORS	NEED LEVELS	ORGANIZATIONAL SPECIFIC FACTORS
1. Growth 2. Achievement 3. Advancement	Self-actualization	1. Challenging job 2. Creativity 3. Advancement in organization 4. Achievement in work
1. Recognition 2. Status 3. Self-esteem 4. Self-respect	Ego, Status, and Esteem	1. Job title 2. Merit pay increase 3. Peer/supervisory recognition 4. Work itself 5. Responsibility
1. Companionship 2. Affection 3. Friendship	Social	1. Quality of supervision 2. Compatible work group 3. Professional friendships
1. Safety 2. Security 3. Competence 4. Stability	Safety and Security	1. Safe working conditions 2. Fringe benefits 3. General salary increases 4. Job security
1. Air 2. Food 3. Shelter 4. Sex	Physiological	1. Heat and air conditioning 2. Base salary 3. Cafeteria 4. Working conditions

(Ascending Order — Basic to Complex)

housing remove his concerns about base salary and housing (physiological needs in exhibit 12-3a). Because the new accountant has a wife and a small child, he seeks out information about medical coverage, job stability, the tuition reimbursement program, and so on (safety and security needs in exhibit 12-3b). The collected information, coupled with a long discussion with his supervisor about job security, satisfy his concerns over these factors. The frequent interactions the accountant has with his supervisor, fellow workers, and clients prove to be most satisfying (social needs in exhibit 12-3c).

As time passes, the accountant concentrates more and more effort toward doing his job as effectively as he can. Within three years, he receives a promotion to the position of senior staff accountant (ego, status, and esteem needs in exhibit 12-3d). Subsequent years find the accountant in the newly created position of direction of administrative services, the external consulting arm of the accounting firm. Outside activities include active participation in civic, school board, and charitable affairs, plus a revitalized interest in building furniture in his garage workshop (self-actualization needs in exhibit 12-3e).

This example illustrates Maslow's basic concepts. That is, needs are: (1) motivational; (2) ordered in an importance, or basic-to-complex hi-

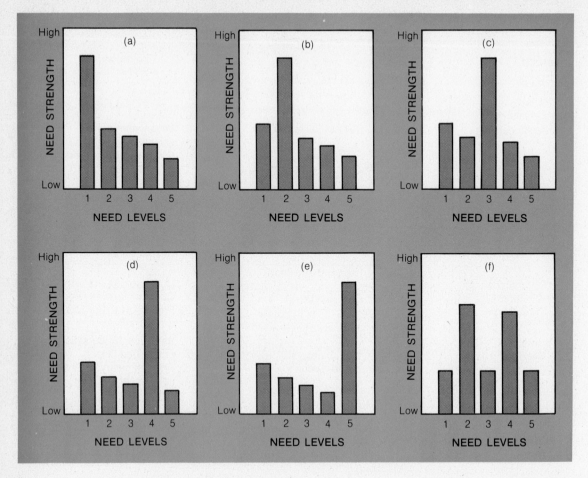

erarchy; and (3) ascending the hierarchy, based on the satisfaction of lower-level needs.

The Need Hierarchy in International Operations.   Since managers are becoming increasingly involved in international operations, knowledge of what motivates workers in other countries is beneficial. While our understanding of what motivates foreign workers is just emerging, what we know to date suggests that important differences exist.[4] For example, the analysis of needs for technical personnel in ten countries indicates that some employees are motivated by higher-order needs (e.g., in U. S. and United Kingdom), others are motivated by a combination of higher and lower-order needs (e.g., Japan), while still others have dominant lower-order needs that are highly motivational (e.g., Chile). Managers must recognize these differences when managing in these countries if high performance is to be achieved.

Issues and Implications of the Need Hierarchy Theory.   Since its development, the need hierarchy has stimulated a great number of research studies of organizations. Among the most interesting findings is the recognition that ego and self-actualization needs become most important as one climbs the management career ladder from first-line supervisor to higher-level executive.[5]

Even with these and other supportive findings, managers must be aware of the serious limitations of this theory. First, there is some question as to whether five need levels for individuals are found in all organizations. Some research has shown that the number of need levels can range from two to as many as seven.[6]

Second, managers must acknowledge that needs are not static, but are quite dynamic: in other words, one can go down the hierarchy as fast, or faster, than up. For example, managers in troubled organizations such as Chrysler, Lockheed, or Penn Central can go from being motivated by ego needs to security needs quite quickly after the announcement of impending manpower cutbacks.

Third, as shown in exhibit 12-3f, more than one need level can be operative at any one time, which is counter to the theory. Such a need profile was representative of your author shortly after graduating with a bachelor's degree in engineering. The high ego needs represent a desire to do well and the seeking of recognition for high performance. However, the equally high safety and security needs relate to the fact that your author had a young and growing family, plus his job involved production engineering in a chemical plant that manufactured highly toxic products. Such a need profile is inconsistent with the theory, but in fact, is found frequently.

Finally, the theory states that a satisfied need is not a motivator. Although in a general sense this may be true, it is also true that individual needs are never fully or permanently satisfied as a result of a single act or behavior. It is the nature of human needs that they must be continually and repeatedly fulfilled if the person is to perform effectively. If a number of needs are operating at one time—as is probably the case with the majority of people—this would seem to contradict the idea of need satisfaction occurring in a fixed hierarchial order.[7]

Herzberg's Two-Factor Theory

A second popular content theory of motivation was proposed by Herzberg. The theory, called the two-factor theory or the motivator-hygiene theory, has been widely received and applied by managers.[8] Herzberg accepted Maslow's concept of the importance of needs, but went further by suggesting that not all needs are motivational.

Herzberg's research led to the following conclusions:

First, there are *extrinsic* job conditions whose *absence* or inadequacy causes dissatisfaction among employees. However, if these conditions *are* adequate, it does not necessarily mean the employees are motivated. These extrinsic-contextual factors are the dissatisfiers, or *hygiene* factors. They include:

1. Job security
2. Salary

3. Working conditions
4. Status
5. Company policies
6. Quality of technical supervision
7. Quality of interpersonal relations among peers, supervisors, and subordinates
8. Fringe benefits

Second, *intrinsic* job factors exist whose *presence* helps to build levels of motivation that can result in good job performance. However, if these conditions are *not* present, it does not cause dissatisfaction. These conditions are intrinsic-content factors of the job and are called motivators, or *satisfiers*. These include:

1. Achievement
2. Recognition
3. Challenging work
4. Responsibility
5. Advancement
6. Personal growth, learning, and development

As shown in exhibit 12-4, Herzberg has reduced Maslow's five need levels to two distinct levels. The hygiene factors, or dissatisfiers, are similar to Maslow's lower-level needs (physiological, security, and social). They are essentially *preventative* factors that reduce dissatisfaction. In other words, hygiene factors, if absent in the job, lead to high levels of dissatisfaction; if present, they create "zero dissatisfaction" or neutrality.

EXHIBIT 12-4
Herzberg's
Motivator-Hygiene
Theory

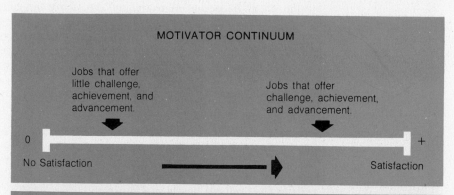

MOTIVATOR CONTINUUM

Jobs that offer little challenge, achievement, and advancement.

Jobs that offer challenge, achievement, and advancement.

0   +

No Satisfaction   Satisfaction

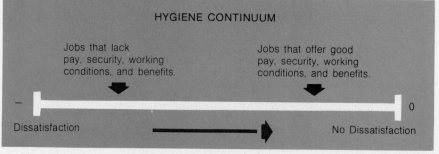

HYGIENE CONTINUUM

Jobs that lack pay, security, working conditions, and benefits.

Jobs that offer good pay, security, working conditions, and benefits.

−   0

Dissatisfaction   No Dissatisfaction

By themselves, hygiene factors do not motivate individuals to better performance.

The motivators, or satisfiers, are equivalent to Maslow's higher-level needs. These are the factors that motivate people to perform. According to Herzberg, the presence in a job of factors such as job challenge is motivational; when these factors are absent, the level of satisfaction is reduced to the zero point. Absence of these factors is, however, not dissatisfying.

Issues and Implications of the Two-Factor Theory. The implications of Herzberg's theory are significant. For example, consider assembly-line workers in the auto industry. For many years, these firms have experienced severe worker motivational problems, lower productivity, high turnover, absenteeism, grievances, and so on. In response to these many problems, the industry—usually with the blessing of the unions—instituted costly fringe-benefit programs, significant wage increases, and elaborate security and seniority programs. Yet, many of these problems remain.

According to Herzberg's framework, the problems remain because these firms try to motivate through hygiene factors, which he claims are nonmotivational. To motivate the workers, according to Herzberg, attention should be directed to the motivators—for example, changing jobs to remove the routineness, boredom, and lack of challenge. This point will be discussed further in this chapter.

The two-factor theory has received a great deal of notice and acceptance among managers in many types of organizations.[9] It has also been criticized by behavioral scientists on a number of points, including research methodology (i.e., short, written essays) and the research sample (i.e., engineers and accountants in Pittsburgh).

More importantly, the theory stresses the importance of *satisfaction*, rather than motivation. As shown in exhibit 12-1, satisfaction is more an outcome variable that occurs *after* actual motivated behavior has been exhibited. Finally, the two-factor theory fails to account for differences in individuals. Herzberg basically assumes that all employees will react similarly to motivational factors. A close examination of the people around each of us will reveal, however, that some people will indeed be motivated by a challenging job, achievement, and advancement, but on the other hand, there are many people who are highly motivated by money, security, and status symbols. In other words, trying to motivate employees through the content of the job is bound to result in only partial success.

Although the list of major criticisms is significant, the value or impact of the theory should not be underestimated. As in the case of the need hierarchy approach, Herzberg's theory has common-sense appeal to some managers. The serious student of management, however, should be cautious of approaches that have a subjective appeal and about which significant questions have been brought forth through scientific study.

Summary of Content Theories

The need hierarchy and two-factor theories have emphasized the basic motivational concepts of needs, satisfiers, and dissatisfiers. While each

"I FIND THIS WORK TRULY FULFILLING IN MANY WAYS — THERE'S THE EXERCISE, THE SENSE OF ACCOMPLISHMENT, AND, MOST IMPORTANT, THE OPPORTUNITY TO MAKE LOTS OF NOISE."

© 1975 by Sidney Harris/Wall Street Journal

has attempted to explain behavior from a slightly different perspective, neither of the two theories should be accepted as the only framework for understanding motivated behavior in organizations.

A manager should also be skeptical of theories such as these, which attempt to explain behavior solely from an analysis of arousal factors, because such factors provide only a minimal understanding of what actions the person will choose. Even so, people have needs, and various job factors result in differing degrees of satisfaction of these needs.

PROCESS THEORIES

The content theories, while identifying the key factors that arouse or energize motivated behavior, provide little understanding of why people *choose* a particular behavior to satisfy specific needs. This choice factor in motivation is the focus of two *process* theories: expectancy theory and reinforcement theory.

Expectancy Theory

In its basic form, expectancy theory concerns choice behavior that can lead to desired rewards. Specifically, the theory states that individuals will evaluate various strategies of behavior (e.g., working hard every day versus working hard three days out of five) and then choose that behavior that they believe will lead to those work-related outcomes or rewards that they value (e.g., pay increase, promotion, or recognition). If the individual worker believes that working hard every day will lead to a desired pay

EXHIBIT 12-5
Expectancy Theory of Motivation

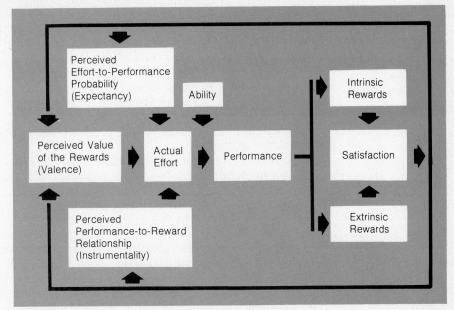

increase, expectancy theory would predict that this is the motivated behavior that he or she will choose.

Building on the work of other behavioral scientists, Victor H. Vroom presented expectancy theory in its most complete formulation.[10] As shown in exhibit 12-5, the theory involves three main variables—expectancy, instrumentality, and valence—that are derived from the relationship among effort, performance, and outcomes or rewards.

1. *Expectancy* is the perceived relationship between effort and performance. Similar to a probability, expectancy can range from 0 to +1.0. For example, if a financial analyst is given a project that he or she knows can be completed on time, the value for that expectancy would approach certainty, or +1.0. On the other hand, if completing the project on time (i.e., performance) would be difficult or near impossible given the available resources or skills, the value for this expectancy would approach zero.

2. *Instrumentality* is the perceived relationship between performance and outcomes or rewards and can vary in value from −1.0 to +1.0. For example, if high performance in an organization is always rewarded, then instrumentality will have a value approaching +1.0; if high performance usually yields no rewards, the value for instrumentality would be zero; finally, in the unlikely state that performing at a high level would result in a reprimand, instrumentality would have a negative value.

3. *Valence* is the strength of an employee's preference for a particular outcome or reward, which can be either intrinsic or extrinsic. Valence can either be given a positive or negative value by the person. In a work situation, we would expect such outcomes or rewards as pay increases, promotion, and recognition by superiors to have positive valences; such

outcomes as reprimands, job pressures, stress, and interpersonal conflicts may have negative valences. Theoretically, an outcome or reward has a valence because it is related to the *needs* of the individual; therefore, this variable provides a link to the content theories.

Consider, for example, a laboratory technician whose job is to analyze the results of an experiment for a research chemist. The technician is in a dilemma: it is Friday afternoon, only an hour before normal quitting time, and the analysis of the latest experiment results is incomplete. The technician knows that it will probably take at least two hours to complete the analysis.

At least two options are available to the technician. First, he could work to complete the analysis (i.e., performance). It would take a concentrated effort, possibly involving some extra time, but he knows that it can be done (i.e., expectancy). The technician also knows that his effort would not go unnoticed by the supervising chemist (i.e., instrumentality), since some form of valued praise or recognition would be given for the extra effort (i.e., valence). On the other hand, the technician could stop what he is doing at quitting time (i.e., performance). This behavior, which is easy (i.e., expectancy), would also not go unnoticed (i.e., instrumentality); however, this time the result would be an undesired reprimand (i.e., valence). The choice of behavior by the technician would probably be to work hard to complete the analysis, since this form of motivated behavior would lead to a valued reward (i.e., recognition).

The expectancy model in exhibit 12-5 identifies three additional factors.[11] First, as in the original motivation model (see exhibit 12-1), the relationship between actual effort and actual performance is moderated by the employee's ability. This is to recognize that unless the employee has necessary ability, no amount of effort will yield acceptable performance. Second, rewards for performance can be either or both intrinsic and extrinsic. In the case of the laboratory technician, an extrinsic reward would be recognition from the supervising chemist, while an intrinsic reward could be the feeling of accomplishment and pride associated with successfully completing an important task. Finally, the level of rewards leads to a state of satisfaction with work, which also acts as feedback into the main expectancy theory variables.

Issues and Implications of Expectancy Theory.   Expectancy theory, which stresses that people will be motivated to choose behaviors that result in valued rewards, has a number of implications for practicing managers. Among the most important points are as follows:

1. **Clearly identify what are good performance levels.**
   Before subordinates can be motivated to high performance, they need to know what is defined as good performance. Managers must identify what it is they want, when they want it, how it is to be done, and what rewards are available.

2. **Make sure that the employee can reach good performance levels.**
   Unless the organization has provided adequate training and resources and the individual exhibits the necessary skills and abilities, motivation levels may be low.

3. Determine what rewards are valued by the employee.

If motivated behavior is directed toward obtaining rewards, the manager needs to know what rewards are valued by the employee. The important aspect to recognize is that when it comes to rewards, people are different. Some employees value praise and recognition highly, others see their motivated behavior as leading to a good pay increase or an improvement in their chances for advancement.

Expectancy theory is not without significant criticisms.[12] The major issue concerns complexity: not only is it too difficult to fully research, but do people actually consider expectancies, instrumentalities, and valences every time they exert motivated behavior in an organization? Overall, however, the theory provides a valued addition to the study of employee motivation, if for no other reason than that it emphasizes that motivation involves *both* arousal and behavioral choice.

Reinforcement Theory

The second process theory of motivation, reinforcement theory, is an approach that emphasizes the application of rewards by the manager. Sometimes referred to as operant conditioning, reinforcement theory has its foundations in the work of B. F. Skinner.[13] Stated simply, reinforcement theory suggests that behavior (or motivation) is a function of its consequences (or rewards). In other words, if people are rewarded for performing at a high level, they should again perform at a high or higher level because of the knowledge of the rewards that will be received. If, for example, a market research analyst works hard to complete a comprehensive market study on time and is directly rewarded with recognition or a significant pay raise, the analyst will repeat that level of effort when a new project is given.

The reinforcement process can be illustrated as shown in exhibit 12-6. This process introduces formally a factor in motivation that is ex-

EXHIBIT 12-6
The
Reinforcement
Process

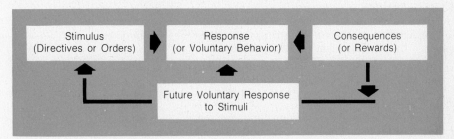

tremely important for all managers to consider. That is, much of the motivated behavior that is shown by people is *learned* behavior. Through experience, managers learn to be good managers or poor managers; in a similar manner, subordinates learn over time what is considered acceptable performance and what is not. This is the concept of learning.

The crucial element in this reinforcement process is the consequences or rewards for performance, because it is through the administration of rewards that the person learns acceptable or motivated behavior. Consider again the laboratory technician in the expectancy theory discussion. By choosing to work hard to complete the analysis (motivated behavior), the technician receives a valued reward. If a similar situation arose in the future, the technician would probably repeat that behavior because the reward would still be valued and desired. From a reinforcement point of view, the technician's improvement in performance would be a learned behavior that was the result of the proper use of the consequences of performance, or rewards.

Four fundamental principles are the foundation for reinforcement theory in motivation. These principles concern focus, types of reinforcement, schedules of reinforcement, and the nature of the reward.

Focus.   The focus of reinforcement theory is *objective, measurable* behavior (e.g., number of units produced, percentage of quality rejects, or adherence to budget and time schedules), as opposed to inner-person states (e.g., needs), which are difficult to measure or observe. This is one of the main distinguishing characteristics of reinforcement theory in comparison to the need hierarchy, two-factor, and expectancy theories. The latter approaches directly or indirectly involve the concept of human needs; reinforcement theory does not, emphasizing instead those behavioral components that can be easily observed and measured.

EXHIBIT 12-7   Types of Reinforcement

REINFORCEMENT TYPE	STIMULUS	RESPONSE	CONSEQUENCE OR REWARD
Positive Application increases the likelihood that a desired behavior will be repeated	Promotion will result from continued excellent performance →	Continued excellent performance	→ Promotion
Punishment Application decreases the likelihood that an undesired behavior will be repeated.	Tardiness will not be tolerated →	Tardiness	→ Reprimand
Avoidance Likelihood of desired behavior is increased by knowledge of consequence.	Reprimands will result from tardy behavior →	Punctuality	→ No reprimand
Extinction Removal of positive reinforcement to eliminate a now undesired behavior	1) Prizes awarded for attracting new savings account customers →	High effort directed toward attracting new customers →	Prizes
	2) Prizes for attracting new savings account customers halted. →	Reduction of effort to attract new customers →	No prizes

Types of Reinforcement. In reinforcement theory, there are four major types of reinforcement that can be used to motivate or modify a person's behavior in an organization: positive reinforcement, punishment, avoidance, and extinction (see exhibit 12-7).

1. *Positive reinforcement* is used to *increase* the likelihood that a behavior desired by the organization will be repeated by the employee.

2. *Punishment* is the use of negative consequences to *decrease* the likelihood that an undesired behavior by the individual will be repeated.

3. *Avoidance,* like positive reinforcement, is used by managers to strengthen the recurrence of a desired behavior. The employee avoids punishment by performing in the correct manner. The distinction between positive reinforcement and avoidance should be made carefully. With positive reinforcement, the employee performs to *gain* certain rewards; with avoidance, the employee performs in a manner to *avoid* undesired consequences.

4. *Extinction* is used like punishment to reduce or eliminate undesired behavior. In its simplest form, extinction involves the withholding of positive reinforcement for a previously acceptable behavior. With continued nonreinforcement, the behavior will disappear.

THE MANAGER'S JOB
James Parsons of Parsons Pine Products

Parsons Pine Products in Ashland, Oregon employs some 100 workers to cut lumber into specialty items—primarily louver slats for shutters, bifold doors and blinds, and wooden bases for rat traps. It is reportedly the U. S.'s biggest producer of these items. The company's owner, James Parsons, was concerned with ways of improving employee performance and attendance. His approach was to build a positive reinforcement plan with the use of four incentives: well pay, retro pay, safety pay, and profit sharing.

Well pay is an extra eight hours' wages for workers who are neither absent nor late for a full month.

Retro pay offers a bonus to workers based on any reductions in premiums received from the state's industrial accident fund. In operation, if accidents are reduced from one year to the next, the difference in insurance premiums is returned to the workers.

Safety pay equates to two hours' wages for remaining accident free for one month.

Profit sharing is a bonus whereby everything the firm earns over 4 percent after taxes is divided among the workers. Two-thirds of the bonus is paid in cash and the rest goes into the retirement fund.

The combination of the four incentives has resulted in an average 35 percent increase in the workers' take-home pay, a significant reduction in absenteeism and turnover, and a great jump in worker productivity.

The positive reinforcement plan has its drawbacks. The desire to increase one's income has resulted in many workers coming to work sick. These ill workers not only infect others, but the chance for accidents increases. Nevertheless, Parsons believes that his program is a success.

Suggested from "How to Earn Well Pay," Business Week *(June 12, 1978).*

The objective of each of the four reinforcement types is to modify the individual's motivated behavior to lead to goal achievement. Reinforcement will either increase the strength of desired behavior or decrease the strength of undesired behavior, depending on the goals of the organization.

Schedules of Reinforcement.   The degree of effectiveness of any reinforcement type is a function of time: the closer the reinforcement is given to the occurrence of the behavior, the greater impact it will have. Two broad classifications of reinforcement schedules have been identified and studied: continuous and intermittent. *Continuous* reinforcement is when each behavior is reinforced every time it is exhibited. Workers who assemble pocket calculators know that their behavior is correct when each unit passes a quality control check. Another example is a reprimand given after each tardiness.

When a manager recognizes that it would be impossible to reinforce each and every behavior, an *intermittent* schedule can be followed. With intermittent reinforcement, two distinctions are made. First, reinforcers can be given after a certain amount of time (an *interval* schedule) or after a certain number of acceptable behaviors (a *ratio* schedule). Second, reinforcers can be given in an unchanging format (a *fixed* schedule) or a constantly changing format (a *variable* schedule). As shown in exhibit 12-8, combination of these generates four reinforcement schedules: fixed interval (e.g., weekly paycheck), fixed ratio (e.g., sales commission), variable interval (e.g., promotion), and variable ratio (e.g., recognition).

A number of research studies have shown that the variable ratio schedule of reinforcement is the most powerful in sustaining motivated behavior in employees.[14] The reason is that reinforcement is tied to the behavior of the individual and is given closer in time to that particular behavior. This finding has significant implications for managers. Typically, organizations depend highly on such rewards as money and advancement to motivate employees; yet, the schedules associated with these rewards are not as effective as other schedules (see exhibit 12-8).

EXHIBIT 12-8   Intermittent Reinforcement Schedules

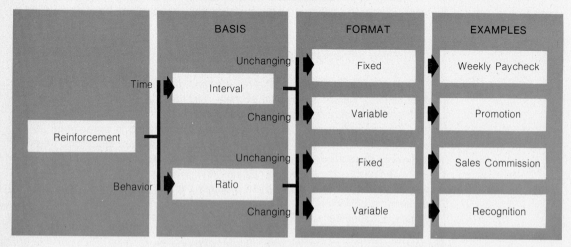

Nature of the Reward.   The nature of the reward, in terms of size and value to the person, can have a great effect on subsequent behavior. The key point for managers to recognize is that individuals differ in their

preferences for particular rewards. One subordinate may respond effectively to frequent praise and recognition. On the other hand, a subordinate desiring a promotion may not respond well to "pats on the back."

Issues and Implications of Reinforcement Theory.   A number of
implications for managers in motivating subordinates can be derived
from reinforcement theory.[15] The most important include the following:

1. **Tell subordinates what they can do to get reinforcement.**
   By setting performance goals or standards, the manager lets employees
   know what performance will lead to rewards. In this way, people can
   plan their work and behaviors.

2. **Administer rewards as close to the occurrence of the behavior as
   possible.**
   To ensure continued high motivated behavior, the appropriate reward
   must not only be clearly associated with the level of performance, but it
   must be given within a short time after the performance has occurred.
   This means that high performance should be highly rewarded as soon as
   possible, and low performance should not be rewarded, but punished as
   soon as possible. Unless this happens, motivation will suffer.

3. **Don't reward all individuals the same.**
   Rewards should be based on performance levels. Rewarding everyone the
   same way in effect reinforces poor or average performance and ignores
   high performance. The organization, or other external influences, may
   impose constraints on the manager with respect to this issue. As an
   illustration, consider the impact of the federal government when it imposes wage and price guidelines (or mandatory constraints), as was done
   in the late 1970s. The manager's ability to use pay as a reward becomes
   constrained. The manager cannot, for example, give high performers consistently large pay raises if such monetary increases surpass the established guidelines (e.g., 7 percent). This means that the manager must use
   other rewards to distinguish the high performer from the low performer.

4. **Failure to reward or punish can be reinforcing.**
   Managers can influence motivation not only by what they do, but by
   what they don't do. For example, failing to recognize a deserving employee
   may cause the person to perform less effectively the next time. Similarly,
   failing to punish poor performance will cause that performance to recur
   in the future. In other words, employees believe that since they weren't
   punished for what they did, they must have done something right.

5. **Be sure to tell subordinates what they are doing wrong.**
   If a manager withholds rewards from subordinates without telling them
   why, it will result in confusion and uncertainty in their later behavior.
   Just as telling people when they have done something right, informing
   them when they haven't performed properly will improve motivation.

6. **Use punishment wisely.**
   Two points are key. First, use punishment as soon after the poor performance as possible for quick correction. Second, don't punish in public.
   A public reprimand often humiliates the subordinate in front of his or
   her peers, causing embarrassment to the subordinate or, possibly, increased resentment toward the manager. The effect on others (an avoid-

ance reinforcement) of a private reprimand will still be present. Either the person will tell others, or the "grapevine" will pass on the information. Most people know what is going on when a person is called into the supervisor's office, without actually being there to see and hear.

Although reinforcement theory has many positive implications for managers, some nagging problems persist.[16] First, critics point out that the theory may oversimplify behavior. In particular, it does not take into account important individual characteristics such as needs. Second, others claim that it is not really reinforcement that occurs, but manipulation and control. This, critics say, has tones of inhumanity. Third, with its heavy emphasis on extrinsic rewards, the theory may ignore the fact that some employees can be motivated by the job itself (as discussed earlier, the job can be a powerful motivator).

Finally, there is the issue of what rewards are available to the manager to administer. While an organization's reward system may contain pay, advancement, praise, and recognition, not all these rewards are available to every manager. For example, promotions may not be within the responsibility of the manager. Thus, the manager is left with a reward package that is less than effective in motivating subordinates. The only reward that many managers can offer is recognition, which will only go so far with most people.

MANAGERIAL APPROACHES TO MOTIVATION

In the first sections of this chapter, we focused on theoretical presentations of the content and process theories. In this section, we show how some managers have applied these theories to motivate employees. Two approaches have been singled out for presentation: job design and behavior modification.

Job Design—Domestic and International Approaches

It has only been within the last few decades that the job as a motivational influence has gained the attention of management practitioners and scholars. Previously, most job design programs were guided by the principles of scientific management. As discussed in chapter 3, adopting a scientific management perspective meant that jobs were designed to be as efficient as possible (i.e., narrowly defined, routine, with short work cycles), where monetary incentives were used to motivate workers.

This managerial attitude began to change in the 1950s as more and more workers began to voice displeasure with jobs that were boring, routine, and mundane. As this feeling among workers grew more intense, organizations began to see increases in turnover, absenteeism, grievances, work slowdowns, and so on. This forced management to reevaluate its thinking about what motivates workers and, in particular, what role the job plays in this process.

Early Approaches. Two of the earliest managerial approaches, or reactions to this worker dissatisfaction, were job rotation and job enlargement.[17] *Job rotation,* very simply, involved moving workers between a series of jobs within a particular unit. For example, a worker on an auto assembly line assigned to the interior of the car would work one week installing seats, followed by two weeks assembling dashboard components, and so on. Unfortunately, this approach did not solve worker mo-tivational problems, since it became clear that all that was done was subject the worker to a series of boring tasks, not just one. As we saw in chapter 10, job rotation has also assumed a role as an effective training method.

Job enlargement was the first approach that involved a change in the job. The change—or enlargement—entailed giving the worker more to do by increasing the work cycle (i.e., providing the worker with more job variety).

Applications of job enlargement have met with more success in or-ganizations than have applications of job rotation. Many organizations, including IBM, Ford, and Maytag, adopted job enlargement programs to help solve worker problems. For example, at Maytag the job of assembling the washing machine pump was a focal point of one study.[18] Prior to enlargement, the task involved six operators assembling the pump on an assembly line. After enlargement, the work previously done on the as-sembly line, or conveyor belt, was done at four one-person benches.

Some job enlargement programs have shown improvements in work-er morale, production costs, and product quality. A number of problems have also arisen, including: some workers did not have the necessary skills and abilities to handle an enlarged job; because workers were asked to do more, they wanted more pay; and finally, since fewer workers were required to accomplish the tasks, layoffs resulted, creating tension be-tween workers and management. Adjusting wage levels and keeping the work force size steady not only took away some of the strong features of the approach, but it became clear that job enlargement was not the only way to motivate workers through changes in the job. This led managers to consider the approach known as job enrichment.

COMMENTS ON THE PRACTICE OF MANAGEMENT
(See p. 404)

> The Practice of Management introduction, "Two Views of Motivation," provides contrasting experiences of the job as a motivator. For George Sampson, the job in the electronics plant offers a high degree of challenge and an opportunity to satisfy higher-level needs (e.g., creativity). As a result, he feels he is contrib-uting to the organization. Since he is rewarded, he continues to exert effort toward successful performance.
>
> Sandy Jenkins, on the other hand, looks at her secretarial job as anything but motivational. The boring work, coupled with the tight control exerted by supervisors, leads to increasing dissatisfaction and emotional fatigue. She seeks to make a contribution to the firm, but finds instead that she is motivated to perform more out of a need for job security. The influence of her father and the inability to become an airline stewardess are also key expectation factors in her motivational profile.

Job Enrichment. Job enrichment as a managerial tool was founded on Herzberg's two-factor theory of motivation.[19] As noted earlier in this chapter, the theory stresses the concepts, or motivators, of challenge, achievement, autonomy, and responsibility. Applying job enrichment to organizations involves two important factors: giving employees more va-riety in their work, and also giving them more authority and responsibility for their work. In other words, job enlargement is part of a job enrichment strategy.

To illustrate this job-related approach to motivation, consider a technologist in a hospital pathology laboratory. Prior to enrichment, the job of the technologist involved analyzing a set of patient blood samples according to standard procedures and reporting the results on the patient's record.

How could the technologist's job be enriched? The following changes, involving Herzberg's motivators, could be considered:

1. *Responsibility.* Increase the level of responsibility by making the individual responsible not only for daily productivity, but also quality control over his work and the scheduled maintenance on the blood analysis equipment.

2. *Decision making.* Increase the technologist's authority and autonomy through setting productivity standards per shift, controlling the pace of the work, and removing some supervisory controls.

3. *Feedback.* Provide direct feedback to the technologist by making productivity data available to him. In some cases, permit the technologist actually to collect and maintain such data.

4. *Personal growth and development.* The above points provide new learning experiences for the technologist, such as becoming acquainted with quality control and maintenance procedures. Also, permit the technologist to offer suggestions concerning any improvements that can be made to the analysis system. In addition, the manager could structure training programs or career paths beyond the present job that are dependent on the level of performance.

5. *Achievement.* By increasing such aspects as responsibility, autonomy, and feedback, a sense of accomplishing something worthwhile could develop for the technologist.

Since its introduction, job enrichment has found its way into a variety of organizations, such as utilities (AT & T), insurance (Traveler's), investments (Merrill Lynch), financial (Chemical Bank), airlines (American Airlines), and manufacturing (Texas Instruments, Polaroid, and Bosch).[20] Applications are also found in all parts of the globe.

At Texas Instruments, a group of employees who had been assembling radar equipment according to specifications drawn up by the engineering department was given the responsibility for developing its own methods, manufacturing processes, and production goals.[21] After job enrichment, not only had the total time for assembling a unit been reduced from 136 hours to 36 hours, but it was determined that the number of supervisors could be reduced since the workers exercised a high degree of self-control.

At Bosch, a large German electronics manufacturer, two units reported successes with job enrichment.[22] The automobile radio assembly unit of sixty employees was redesigned so that each worker does the entire assembly job, resulting in greater flexibility, elimination of rigid time frames, and improved worker morale. In the autospeaker unit, the employees were broken down into five three-person groups, with each group building the entire unit. Each worker was required over time to learn all the individual tasks, providing an excellent training and learning opportunity.

Whether job enrichment is a consistently successful mechanism for improved motivation and performance is unresolved.[23] Some applications have been successful; others, however, have resulted not only in high implementation costs, but resistance from workers—particularly older workers—has caused the program to be terminated. This points out the need for the development of diagnostic skills before the enrichment program begins, and the need for the use of conceptual skills in evaluating the success of the program's implementation progress.

Job Redesign—Need Satisfaction and Job Characteristics. The successes and problems managers have experienced with job rotation, enlargement, and enrichment identify at least two important points that must be considered in any job design program. First, there needs to be the recognition that not all people will react favorably to a job that has been changed. There are many workers at all organizational levels who are quite happy and satisfied working on routine and repetitive jobs. This may be the result of a self-selection process in which certain workers seek out routine jobs because they want only the satisfaction of lower-level needs (e.g, pay, employee benefits, job security) from their jobs. They may seek fulfillment of higher-order needs outside work through hobbies, participation in civic activities, and so on. An attempt to "enrich" jobs for these workers would probably be met with resistance and possible failure.

Second, a closer analysis and diagnosis of particular jobs is needed. A job should be looked at from the basis of strengths and weaknesses for employee motivation. In other words, a job may not need to be enriched with increased responsibility, decision making, feedback, and so on, if some of these components are already at acceptable levels. Changing all of these components at the same time (the shotgun approach), when only one or two need enriching, is both unnecessary and costly. What is needed are better ways of analyzing jobs in order to identify what can and should be changed.

An approach that incorporates both of these points was developed by J. Richard Hackman and his associates.[24] Shown in exhibit 12-9, this approach to job redesign emphasizes four specific points. These points, translated into managerial questions, are as follows:

1. **What are the desired outcomes from work?**

   The identified outcomes—motivation, performance, satisfaction, turnover, and absenteeism—focus on aspects that relate not only to the improved effectiveness of the organization, but the satisfaction of individual needs. In other words, the organization *and* the worker should benefit from job redesign.

2. **What psychological states are important to job redesign?**

   Three key psychological states are identified: the experienced meaningfulness of the work, the experienced responsibility for work outcomes, and the knowledge of the results from the work. A manager needs to carefully analyze specific jobs for these key states to see which are missing

EXHIBIT 12-9
A Job Redesign
Model

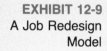

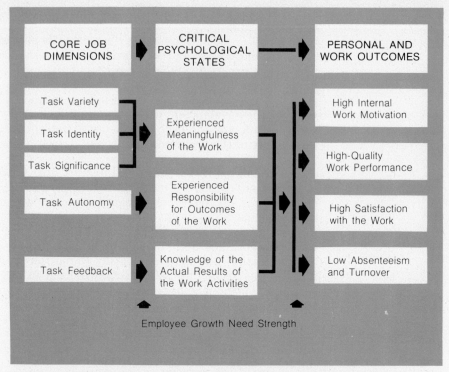

Source: J. R. Hackman and G. R. Oldham, "Development of the Job Diagnostic Survey," Journal of Applied Psychology (1975): 159–70. Copyright 1975 by the American Psychological Association. Reprinted by permission.

and, more importantly, which can be changed within the constraints of the work.

3. **What important job characteristics are involved?**

Five important characteristics of the job are noted.[25] These are: (a) *task variety*—the degree to which a job requires employees to perform a wide range of operations in their work; (b) *task identity*—the extent to which employees do an entire or whole piece of work and can clearly identify with the results of their efforts; (c) *task significance*—the degree to which employees feel that they are contributing something worthwhile to the organization; (e) *task autonomy*—the extent that employees have a major say in scheduling their work, selecting the equipment they will use, and deciding the procedures to be followed; and (f) *task feedback*—the degree to which employees receive information as they are working that tells them how well they are performing on the job.

For effective job redesign, the manager must link the psychological states with the core job characteristics. That is, if a job is found to lack "experienced responsibility," the Hackman approach suggests that increased emphasis on task autonomy would be effective. Thus, the "shotgun" approach of job enrichment can be decreased.

4. **What is the level of employee growth need strength?**

Possibly the most important component of the approach, this factor really asks how ready employees are for a change in jobs. This relates to the concept of growth need strength, which is similar to a combination of Maslow's ego and self-actualization needs. In essence, it is suggested that workers with high growth needs will react more favorably to job design efforts than employees with low growth needs.

Once the manager has identified the right people for job redesign and diagnosed the task, there are a number of factors that can be altered to change the required job characteristics. For example, if there is a need to improve the "meaningfulness" of the job, the manager can implement such programs as combining tasks (enlargement), assigning natural units of work methods, and permitting self-paced control. Improved "responsibility" can result from the creation of autonomous work groups and greater worker participation in decision making. Finally, increasing the "knowledge of actual results" can occur through making production data available to the worker, holding frequent meetings between superiors and subordinates (see chapter 11), or setting up self-evaluation programs.

Since this approach is relatively new, there have been few direct tests of its validity or applicability. However, there are a number of indirect applications by organizations. Among the most interesting are found in General Motors and in Volvo of Sweden.

At G. M.'s assembly plant in Tarrytown, New York, job-related problems among workers had reached a critical stage in the late 1960s and early 1970s.[26] Operating costs were high, frustration, fear, and mistrust of management reigned, absenteeism and turnover were dramatically high, and over 2000 labor grievances remained unresolved.

To help solve some of these problems, both management and labor began a program designed to give workers greater participation in deciding the makeup of their tasks. The program began with a request by management to have workers comment on a revised layout for two departments. Surprising management, the workers came up with ideas that made the transition and revised operations more efficient. Since then, the program has expanded to include more than 3500 workers. Workers have a greater say in the design of jobs; in addition, more data on their performance are being fed back to employees, and there is greater emphasis on communication between superiors and subordinates. During the eight years since the program's inception, the plant has gone from one of the worst performers to one of the best, quality has improved, and turnover, absenteeism, and grievances have declined.

Some words of caution should be mentioned about the Tarrytown project. First, the situation prior to the job redesign was so bad that something had to be done. Thus, both management and labor were more accepting of change. Second, the program did not result in overnight improvement. In fact, many years passed before positive results were found. Finally, the program did not supersede the goal of economic performance. During the time of the program's development and introduction, there were significant layoffs due to an economic decline, plus the speed of the assembly line was increased from fifty-six to sixty cars per hour. It was a credit to the people involved that even under such trying times, the program continued to exist.

In Sweden, Volvo faced many of the problems of the G. M. Tarrytown plant—turnover exceeded 50 percent per year and absenteeism approached 20 percent.[27] One important difference between the two organizations was that Volvo was also facing a significant cultural problem. In particular, only four out of ten students graduating from high school in Sweden indicated a willingness to take rank-and-file jobs. This resulted not only in increased difficulty in filling factory jobs, but also increased dependence on foreign workers (58 percent of the work force was foreign).

Among the many projects begun by Volvo to counter this problem was the assembly plant at Kalmar.[28] The plant contained many job redesign features including compartmentalized workshops with large windows, employees who worked in teams and could vary the work pace or change teams as they wished, instant productivity data provided by a computerized display screen, and individual autos mounted on trolleys that rolled 90 degrees on the side and permitted work to be done in a less fatiguing manner.

While this job redesign program has proven to be successful for Volvo, there are a few cautionary notes. First, from a survival and societal view, the company had to do something. The country's present and future work force was highly educated, possibly indicating that routine and mundane jobs were no longer attractive (i.e., a high growth need). Second, as discussed in earlier chapters, worker participation is accepted in Sweden. Thus, worker involvement in job redesign efforts did not meet much resistance. Finally, the plant layout, with holding stations, trolleys, and flexible schedules, was easily adapted to a product that was essentially high cost and low volume. If the Kalmar plant were to be adopted in the U. S. with present costs and production rates, the plant would cost from 10 to 30 percent more to build than a normal plant.

These examples of job design (see also the General Foods case at the end of the chapter) indicate that the redesign of jobs can contribute significantly to the motivation of workers. An important fact is that job redesign is not for every organization. It works when there is a definite need, when the key factors have been clearly diagnosed, and when it has been properly planned and implemented.

Behavior Modification

Earlier in this chapter, we discussed reinforcement theory as a process motivation approach that depends heavily on the use of extrinsic rewards. One of the formats for reinforcement theory in organizations has been termed *behavior modification*.[29]

In the use of behavior modification by managers with subordinates, positive reinforcement is stressed heavily. The reason is that research findings suggest that positive reinforcers are more effective than punitive reinforcers (i.e., punishment) in achieving *lasting* changes in behavior. Contrary to the belief of many managers, all that punishment does is buy the manager a little time (you have told the subordinate what not to do) but you still need to strengthen behavior; that is, what should be done.

Behavior modification also emphasizes that rewards should be administered as close in time to the actual behavior of the employee as possible. This is probably one of the reasons why pay (salary or hourly wage rate) is considered a hygiene factor by Herzberg: pay is a reward the employee receives long after the occurrence of the desired behavior. For example, in most organizations, employees receive a pay raise once a year, usually after the yearly performance review. It is hard for the person to relate pay to performance when the reward represents twelve months' worth of activities. Because of the time lag between the desired behavior and a reinforcer such as money, many managers and behavioral scientists recommend the use of such reinforcers as praise, recognition, compliments, and other verbal approaches. They are easier to apply and can be administered soon after the desired behaviors. Monetary reinforcers in the form of incentive pay or bonuses, if available, can also be used as positive reinforcers.

EXHIBIT 12-10

Behavior
Modification
Program

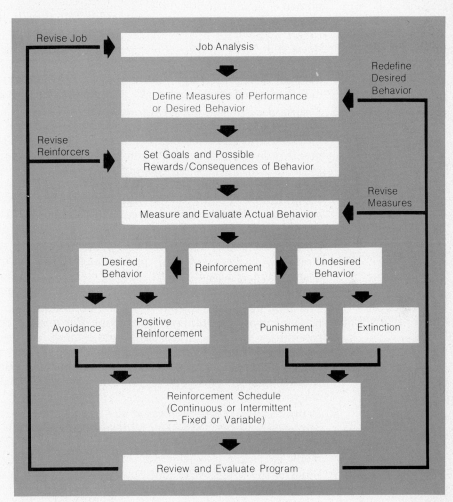

Exhibit 12-10 shows the sequences involved in a typical behavior modification program in an organization. As an illustration, consider a manager of the receiving and marking department in the warehouse operations of a large retail chain. The manager supervises a group of fifteen subordinates who are responsible for unloading, inspecting, pricing, and distributing women's fashions to the organization's five branch stores. How can behavior modification help this manager motivate his or her subordinates to higher productivity? Let's follow the steps in exhibit 12-10:

1. *Job analysis* is the process of defining the requirements of the job, the areas of responsibility and authority, and so on. Since everyone in our example performs the same task (unload, inspect, price, and distribute), this step can be accomplished easily and quickly.

2. *Defining performance measures* is defining the criteria for job performance. This may be difficult for organizations that use subjective, or qualitative factors to measure performance (e.g., cooperativeness and ability to get along with others, as opposed to number of units produced), or those that have no formal performance evaluation system at all. In the warehouse example, three criteria may be chosen: number of units handled per day, percentage rejects from branch stores (i.e., clothing that is defective or missing price tags), and monthly absenteeism.

3. *Setting goals* is the important step of stating what is (or is not) desired behavior of the subordinates. For example, goals for the warehouse employees could be: (a) 500 units processed per day; (b) store rejects held at monthly levels of 4 percent; and (c) no absences per month. *Identifying rewards/consequences of behavior* entails informing the employees what they will receive for their performance. Examples include praise and recognition (e.g., awards for high performance or just a simple "thank you"), a major input into the yearly performance review, a year-end bonus, or an extra day off.

4. In *measurement of actual behavior,* the manager or the employee keeps a record of daily and monthly performance data. This can be done through observation or actual record keeping. Having the employee keep a performance record has the added effect of a self-feedback mechanism.

5. The *reinforcement* stage involves the administration of a reinforcer dependent upon the employee's behavior. For desired behavior, praise and recognition could be given daily, while more lengthy good performance could result in more formal recognition and possibly monetary rewards. Undesired behavior would result in some form of punishment (i.e., reprimand initially, followed by termination if the undesired behavior is not corrected).

6. *Reinforcement schedules* concern the timing of the reinforcer. Continuous reinforcement can be used for undesired behavior (after each occurrence), while a fixed or variable schedule may be used with positive reinforcement.

7. Finally, the program is continually *reviewed and evaluated.* If the program is successful, little or no change may be needed. On the other hand, a review of the program may require a change in any of the individual components. For example, the warehouse manager may want to revise the output goal to reflect the differences in inspecting and marking women's coats as opposed to blouses or scarves (i.e., coats take much longer to process).

The important aspect for managers to recognize about a behavior modification program is that it is a *continuous* program, not a one-shot deal.
For maximum effectiveness, the program must be revised and strengthened as needed.

Since the initial applications, the list of organizations using behavior modification has grown steadily with positive and interesting results.[30]
For example, Emery Air Freight has been using a positive reinforcement
program for over ten years to improve productivity and the quality of
service.

While the program resulted in a cost savings of over $2 million per
year, Emery's management noticed a major flaw in their program: praise
was overused as a reward, dulling its effect as a reinforcer through sheer
repetition, even to the risk of making praise an irritant to employees.

To counter this, Emery managers were trained and encouraged to
expand their reinforcers beyond just praise. The reinforcers now include
a public letter or a letter home, being given a more enjoyable task, invitations to business luncheons, delegating responsibility and decision
making, and special time off for good performance. In a similar manner,
Connecticut General Life Insurance Company uses positive reinforcement in the form of an attendance bonus system for its clerical personnel.
Employees receive one extra day off for each ten weeks of perfect attendance. As a result of the program, chronic absenteeism and lateness
have been dramatically reduced.

Additional successes have been reported in other companies. For
example, Weyerhaeuser uses a cash bonus (over and above regular salary)
for tree planters who exceed production goals. The sanitation department
of Detroit used a positive reinforcement system with its refuse collectors.
The plan provided for sharing the savings from productivity improvement
with workers. General Electric used a behavior modification program—
positive reinforcement and feedback—in training employees. The initial
program centered on teaching male supervisors how to interact and communicate with minority and female employees and teaching minority
and female employees how to become successful by improving their self-
images. Using a format similar to behavior modeling (see chapter 10),
the program stressed the use of role playing and videotape feedback.

It is apparent that behavior modification use will continue to expand, probably taking various forms in different organizations. The same
criticisms as noted for reinforcement theory in general hold for behavior
modification, so its acceptance should be made with caution.[31] Overall,
however, it should be clear to managers that tying rewards to performance is a powerful approach to motivating employees.

MOTIVATION, PERFORMANCE, AND THE MANAGER'S JOB

Motivation is one of the key concepts that organizations and managers
use to make the most effective use of human resources. It is, however,
still an elusive concept that may mean different things to different people.
The experiences of many managers reveal certain keys to success that
may be helpful to other managers.

Keys to Success with Motivation

1. **There is no universal theory or approach to motivation.**

   While each of the discussed motivation theories has a certain degree of intuitive appeal to managers, none of them can be accepted as the one best way. For the most effective results, the manager must be able to diagnose each situation and apply the various motivation principles as required.

2. **Motivation is a complex process.**

   Motivation involves at least an analysis of needs, behavioral choice, ability, actual behavior, performance evaluation, rewards, and satisfaction. Beyond this apparent complexity, there are two key points for managers to consider. First, individuals differ in what motivates them—some value money highly, others look more toward the nature of the job, while still others are motivated by a combination of factors. This difference in individuals is crucial for a manager to recognize. Second, motivation is essentially a process of learning; as such, the manager should not expect overnight results in attempting to motivate subordinates. Motivation is a continuous activity by managers.

3. **The organization's reward system is a powerful motivation mechanism.**

   Rewards are a key motivator because people generally exert as much effort as they get in return—in other words, "what they get for what they do." While we have noted the importance differences between intrinsic and extrinsic rewards in motivation, the manager should not depend solely on one or the other. Just as a challenging job will eventually prove to be dissatisfying without proper monetary benefits, a highly paid job that is boring will prove to be troublesome to motivation. The manager must learn to blend the use of intrinsic and extrinsic rewards.

4. **The manager is the key element in the motivation process.**

   The manager can influence each stage of a person's motivation process. Managers identify the key motivating needs, help in directing motivated behavior and choice, assist in training subordinates to improve their skills and abilities to perform, evaluate performance, and reward (or punish) behavior. Not only must managers recognize their important role in this process, but they must be effectively trained in individual stages—from learning how to recognize what motivates subordinates to the proper way to conduct a performance evaluation session (see chapter 16).

   As more research and applications involving motivation theories and techniques become available, managers will increasingly come to understand the motivation process. Even with the many unknowns, today's managers are in a much better position than their predecessors to understand what makes a subordinate a high performer or a low performer.

Motivation and the Manager's Job

Motivation is one of the important factors in the manager's leadership function. There also are important implications for the skills and roles associated with the manager's job. While motivating employees involves a high degree of *human* skills, the other managerial skills are equally important. Before managers can motivate employees they need to know what makes the people "tick" and what they can do to motivate them to high performance. This involves both *diagnostic* and *conceptual* skills.

From a managerial role perspective, the manager motivates through performance in the *leader* role. It is through this authority position that the manager directs and rewards high performance. Through the *informational* roles, the manager gathers information on what motivates subordinates, what rewards are available to be administered, and what changes in jobs can be implemented. Finally, the *decisional* roles, particularly the resource allocator, are the key roles in which the manager's reward power comes to play. In the resource allocator role, the manager decides what rewards can be given, to whom, and in what manner.

SUMMARY FOR THE MANAGER

1. Motivation is a complex process that involves unsatisfied needs, direction of behavior, actual effort, evaluation of performance, and the resulting rewards. While no single motivation theory has yet been developed that encompasses all components of the motivation process, it is helpful to classify the various motivation theories by focus (content approach or process approach).

2. Maslow's need hierarchy theory was one of the first scientifically based approaches to the study of motivation in organizations. It is a content theory that considers unsatisfied needs to be arousal or behavior-energizing factors. People are motivated to satisfy these needs. The five levels of needs—physiological, safety, social, ego, and self-actualization—indicate to the manager how mature an individual's motivation process is at that time. While it is not a complete motivation theory, it strongly suggests that managers must be aware of employee needs because these elements usually *start* the motivation process.

3. Another content theory, Herzberg's two-factor theory, suggests that needs can be classified as hygiene factors or motivators. Aspects such as pay, fringe benefits, and working conditions do not motivate employees; only those factors that relate to the job—challenge, responsibility, and advancement—act as motivators. A manager accepting this approach would try to improve motivation by making changes in the employee's job. However, a number of significant shortcomings exist in the theory, which make its acceptance by managers a tenuous proposition.

4. Expectancy theory, classified as a process theory, stresses the importance of both arousal factors *and* analyzation of the direction of motivated behavior. According to the theory, employees will be motivated to adopt behavior that will lead to valued rewards. By clarifying and strengthening effort-to-performance, and performance-to-reward relationships, the manager can have a significant impact on a worker's behavior.

5. Reinforcement theory emphasizes that motivation is a *learned* behavior. If a valued reward is given for following a managerial directive, then the employee will probably repeat that motivated behavior the next time a similar directive is given. Positive reinforcement coupled with a variable schedule of reinforcement has been found to influence motivation the strongest. Punishment, when used properly, can eliminate undesired behavior; however, the employee must be told what to do right, not just what was done incorrectly.

6. One of the main applied-motivation techniques is job design. Job design focuses on altering the employee's job so that it is challenging and intrinsically rewarding. A variety of approaches, including job rotation, enlargement, enrichment, and job redesign, have developed. For best results, the manager must recognize that not all employees will react favorably to a more challenging job. In addition, the success of these programs is highly dependent on how well the manager has diagnosed what changes are needed, what the potential side effects are, and what level of management commitment has been given to the program.

7. Behavior modification, which is based on reinforcement theory and heavily stresses the use of extrinsic rewards, is another popular applied-motivation technique. In a number of organizations, behavior modification has improved employee motivation. Managers, however, must recognize the importance of measurable behavior, the proper use of rewards, the value the subordinate places on the reward, and what rewards the manager can offer.

8. While motivating employees is an important human skill, conceptual skills and diagnostic skills are also important. In much the same manner, motivation heavily involves the leader role, but the informational and decisional roles also play important parts. Overall, the manager is the key element in motivating subordinates. The manager assigns the work, recognizes the needs of subordinates, guides the work, evaluates it, and rewards it—all of which involve the motivation process.

QUESTIONS FOR REVIEW AND DISCUSSION

1. Compare the need hierarchy and expectancy theory approaches to motivation. What are their similarities and differences?
2. How can a manager influence an employee's perceptions of expectancy (effort-to-performance) and instrumentality (performance-to-reward)?
3. Discuss the advantages and disadvantages of reinforcement theory in organizations.
4. How would you present expectancy theory to a group of managers?
5. Why is Herzberg's two-factor theory so popular among managers, even though the many criticisms are significant?
6. Why has job rotation been considered only a short-term job design strategy to counter worker morale problems?
7. Why is feedback an important element in any job design program?
8. Discuss the impact of cultural differences on job design programs.
9. Why do some workers resist having their jobs made more challenging?
10. What is the difference between intrinsic rewards and extrinsic rewards?

NOTES

1. "Managing Motivation," *General Electric Monogram* (November–December 1975): 2–5.

2. M. R. Jones, ed. *Nebraska Symposium on Motivation* (Lincoln: University of Nebraska, 1955).

3. A. H. Maslow, *Motivation and Personality* (New York: Harper & Row, 1954).

4. See J. M. Ivancevich, "Perceived Need Satisfactions of Domestic versus Overseas Management," *Journal of Applied Psychology* (August 1969): 274–78; and D. Serota and J. M. Greenwood, "Understand Your Overseas Work Force," *Harvard Business Review* (January–February 1971): 53–60.

5. L. W. Porter, *Organizational Patterns of Managerial Job Attitudes* (New York: American Foundation for Management Research, 1964).

6. E. E. Lawler III and J. L. Suttle, "A Causal Correlational Test of the Need Hierarchy Concept," *Organizational Behavior and Human Performance* (April 1972): 265–87.

7. D. T. Hall and K. E. Nougaim, "An Examination of Maslow's Need Hierarchy Concept," *Organizational Behavior and Human Performance* (February 1968): 12–35.

8. F. Herzberg, B. Mausner, and B. Snyderman, *The Motivation to Work,* 2nd ed. (New York: Wiley, 1959).

9. R. J. House and L. Wigdor, "Herzberg's Dual-Factor Theory of Job Satisfaction and Motivation: A Review of the Empirical Evidence and a Criticism," *Personnel Psychology* (Winter 1967): 369–80.

10. V. H. Vroom, *Work and Motivation* (New York: Wiley, 1964).

11. R. J. House, H. J. Shapero, and M. A. Wahba, "Expectancy Theory as a Predictor of Work Behavior and Attitudes: A Re-examination of the Empirical Evidence," *Decision Sciences* (July 1974): 481–506.

12. See F. Schmidt, "Implication of a Measurement Problem for Expectancy Theory Research," *Organizational Behavior and Human Performance* (April 1973): 243–51; and J. M. Feldman, H. J. Reitz, and R. J. Hilterman, "Alternatives to Optimization in Expectancy Theory," *Journal of Applied Psychology* (December 1976): 712–20.

13. See B. F. Skinner, *Contingencies of Reinforcement* (New York: Appleton-Century-Crofts, 1969); and R. M. Tarpy, *Basic Principles of Learning* (Glenview, Ill.: Scott, Foresman, 1974).

14. F. Luthans and R. Kreitner, *Organizational Behavior Modifications* (Glenview, Ill.: Scott, Foresman, 1975).

15. W. C. Hamner, "Reinforcement Theory and Contingency Management in Organizational Settings," in *Orga-*

nizational Behavior and Management: A Contingency Approach, H. L. Tosi and W. C. Hamner, eds. (Chicago, Ill.: St. Clair, 1974), pp. 86–112.

16. Ibid., pp. 104–08.

17. See A. D. Szilagyi and M. J. Wallace, *Organizational Behavior and Performance,* 2nd ed. (Santa Monica, Calif.: Goodyear, 1980), pp. 149–57.

18. M. D. Kilbridge, "Reduced Costs through Job Enlargement: A Case, *The Journal of Business* (October 1960): 357–62.

19. F. Herzberg, "The Wise Old Turk," *Harvard Business Review* (September–October 1974): 70–80.

20. R. Ford, "Job Enrichment Lessons for AT&T," *Harvard Business Review* (January–February 1973): 96–106.

21. M. S. Myers, *Every Employee a Manager* (New York: McGraw-Hill, 1970).

22. Ohio Human Relations Commissions, *World of Work Report I* (May 1976).

23. See J. R. Hackman, "Is Job Enrichment Just a Fad?" *Harvard Business Review* (September–October 1975): 129–39; and M. Fein, "Job Enrichment: A Re-evaluation," *Sloan Management Review* (Winter 1974): 69–88.

24. J. R. Hackman, G. Oldham, R. Janson, and K. Purdy, "A New Strategy for Job Enrichment," *California Management Review* (Summer 1975): 57–71.

25. H. P. Sims, A. D. Szilagyi, and R. T. Keller, "The Measurement of Job Characteristics," *Academy of Management Journal* (June 1976): 195–212.

26. R. H. Guest, "Quality of Work Life—Learning from Tarrytown," *Harvard Business Review* (July–August 1979): 76–87.

27. See W. F. Dowling, "Job Design on the Assembly-Line: Farewell to the Blue-Collar Blues?" *Organizational Dynamics* (Spring 1973): 51–67; and P. Gyllenhammar, *People at Work* (Reading, Mass.: Addison-Wesley, 1977).

28. J. M. Roach, "Why Volvo Abolished the Assembly-Line," *Management Review* (September 1977): 50.

29. W. C. Hamner and E. P. Hamner, "Behavior Modification on the Bottom Line," *Organizational Dynamics* (Spring 1976): 2–21.

30. Ibid., p. 4.

31. E. A. Locke, "The Myths of Behavior Mod in Organizations," *Academy of Management Review* (October 1977): 543–53.

ADDITIONAL REFERENCES

Blood, M. R., and Hulin, C. L. "Alienation, Environmental Characteristics, and Worker Responses." *Journal of Applied Psychology* (1967), pp. 284–90.

Davis, L. E., and Cherns, A. B., eds. *The Quality of Working Life.* New York: Free Press, 1975.

Deci, E. L. *Intrinsic Motivation.* New York: Plenum, 1975.

Dunnette, M. D. *Work and Non-Work in the Year 2001.* Monterey, Calif.: Brooks-Cole, 1973.

Fein, M. "Motivation for Work." In R. Dubin, ed., *Handbook of Work, Organization, and Society.* Chicago: Rand McNally, 1976.

Gooding, J. "It Pays to Wake Up the Blue-Collar Worker."

Fortune, July 1970, pp. 133–39.

McClelland, D., and Winter, D. G. *Motivating Economic Achievement.* New York: Free Press, 1969.

Staw, B. "Motivation in Organizations: Toward Synthesis and Redirection." In B. M. Staw and G. R. Salancik, *New Directions in Organizational Behavior.* Chicago: St. Clair, 1977, pp. 55–96.

Turkel, S. *Working.* New York: Avon Books, 1974.

Yukl, G. A.; Latham, G. P.; and Pursell, E. L. "The Effectiveness of Performance Incentives Under Continuous and Variable Schedules of Reinforcement." *Personnel Psychology* (1976), pp. 221–31.

A CASE FOR ANALYSIS

General Foods

In 1968, General Foods was considering the construction of a plant in Topeka, Kansas, to manufacture pet foods. Because of continuing problems at their existing plants—product waste, sabotage, frequent shutdowns, and low morale—the management of General Foods wanted to try a set of innovative motivational techniques at this new plant. The basic design of the new plant was oriented around the principles of skills development, challenging jobs, and teamwork:

1. *Autonomous work groups.* The work force of seventy employees was divided into teams of seven to fourteen employees. Three types of teams were created: processing, packaging, and shipping. These teams were self-managed by the workers: they were involved in making work assignments, screening and selecting new

members, and the added responsibility of the decision making for large segments of the plant's operations.

2. *Challenging jobs.* The basic design of each job was developed to eliminate the boring and routine aspects as much as possible. Each job—whether on the manufacturing line or in the warehouse—was designed to include a high degree of variety, autonomy, planning, liaison work with other teams, and responsibility for diagnosing and correcting mechanical or process problems.

3. *Job mobility and rewards for learning.* Because each set of jobs was designed to be equally challenging, it was possible to have a single job classification for all operators. Employees could receive pay increases by developing new skills and mastering different jobs. Team members were, in essence, paid for learning more and more of the plant's operations.

4. *Information availability.* Unlike most manufacturing plants, the operators at this new plant were provided the necessary economic, quantity, and quality information normally reserved for managers.

5. *Self-government.* Rather than working with a set of predetermined rules and procedures, such policies were developed as the need arose. This resulted in fewer unnecessary rules to guide the work. Only critical guidelines or rules were developed, and generally these were based on the collective experience of the team.

6. *Status symbols.* The typical physical and social status symbols of assigned parking spaces, wide variations in the decor of offices and rooms, and separate entrance and eating facilities were eliminated. There existed an open parking lot, a single entrance for both office and plant workers, and a common decor throughout the entire plant.

7. *Learning and evaluation.* The most basic feature of the plant was the commitment to evaluate continually both the plant's productivity and the state of employee morale. Before any change was made in the plant, an evaluation of the impact on both productivity and worker morale was made.

As in any major redesign program, management at the new plant was faced with a number of implementation problems. First, tension among employees developed concerning pay rates. There were four basic pay rates in the plant: (1) starting rate; (2) single rate (mastery of one job); (3) team rate (mastery of all jobs within the team); and (4) plant rate (mastery of all operator jobs within the plant). Because the decision on pay rates was primarily the responsibility of the team leader, certain questions about the judgment of job mastery and whether workers had an equal opportunity to learn jobs developed.

Second, because the management philosophy at this particular plant was quite different from that at the other plants, difficulties arose whenever employees of the new plant interacted with other General Foods personnel. Problems of resistance and a lack of acceptance and support developed.

Finally, the expectations of a small minority of workers did not coincide with the new teamwork concept of the plant. Certain employees resisted the movement toward greater responsibility. Again, individual differences among employees was shown to be important to the job redesign movement.

Was the new plant successful with its innovative work arrangement? A review after eighteen months of operation suggested positive results. For example, fixed overhead costs were 33 percent lower than in order plants, quality rejects were reduced by 92 percent, and the safety record was one of the best in the company. Focusing on the human resource side, morale was high, absenteeism was 9 percent below the industry norm, and turnover was far below normal.

The plant was widely heralded as a model for the future, and General Foods claims that it still is. In fact, GF has applied a similar system at a second dogfood plant in Topeka and at a coffee plant in New Jersey. And it says it may eventually do the same at two plants in Mexico and among white-collar workers at its White Plains headquarters.

But management analysts and former employees tell a different story. And General Foods, which once encouraged publicity about the Topeka plant, now refuses to let reporters inside. Critics say that after the initial euphoria, the system, faced with indifference and outright hostility from some GF managers, has been eroding steadily.

"The system went to heck. It didn't work," says one former manager. Adds another ex-employee: "It was a mixed bag. Economically it was a success, but it became a power struggle. It was too threatening to too many people." He predicts that the plant will eventually switch to a traditional factory system. In fact, he says, the transition has already begun.

The problem has been not so much that the workers could not manage their own affairs as that some management and staff personnel saw their own positions threatened because the workers performed almost too well. One former employee says the system—built around a team concept—came squarely up against the company's bureaucracy. Lawyers, fearing reaction from the National Labor Relations Board, opposed the idea of allowing team members to vote on pay raises. Personnel managers objected because team members made hiring decisions. Engineers resented workers doing engineering work.

From the standpoint of humanistic working life and economic results, you can consider it a success. But a former employee at the Topeka plant does not see it that way. "Creating a system is different from maintaining it," he says. "There were pressures almost from the inception, and not because the system didn't work. The basic reason was power. We flew in the face of corporate policy. People like stable states."

Consequently, critics say, there has been a stiffening of the Topeka system: more job classifications, less participation, more supervision. GF has added seven management positions to the plant, including controller, plant engineering manager, and manufacturing services manager. GF says these were necessary because of a plant expansion. When GF geared up a plant adjacent to the first one to produce Cycle, a canned dog food, it introduced the Topeka process but deferred several elements of the system.

While the system has not lived up to the goals of many of the managers involved, and while it seems to be deteriorating, it nevertheless has led to a productive working atmosphere and has met many of the goals set for it. The big question is whether it will renew itself or continue to erode, fulfilling the prediction of one manager that "the future of that plant is to conform to the company."

Suggested from R. E. Walton, "How to Counter Alienation in the Plant," Harvard Business Review (November–December 1972); and Business Week, "Stonewalling Plant Democracy" (March 26, 1977): 78–82.

Questions for Discussion

1. What basic motivational principles were involved in the General Foods Topeka plant?
2. Initially, why did the job redesign program work effectively?
3. What were some of the reasons for the slow decline in the commitment by managers to the program?
4. What can other managers learn from the Topeka experience?

EXPERIENTIAL EXERCISE

Motivation Factors

Purpose

1. To examine the application of motivation approaches to organizations.
2. To understand the relationship between motivation and differences in individuals.

Required Understanding

The student should have a basic understanding of the different approaches to motivation.

Instructions for the Exercise

Exhibit 12-11 presents a list of ten job-related factors that can be found in most organizations. Examine these ten factors and *rank-order* from 1 (most influential to motivation) to 10 (least influential to motivation). (No ties, please.) Three rank-orders are required:

1. *Self-rating:* A rank-order of the factors as evaluated by yourself.
2. *Non-supervisory, assembly-line worker:* Rank-order the ten factors as you believe a nonsupervisory employee working on an assembly line would do.
3. *Middle-level manager:* Rank-order the ten factors as you believe a middle-level manager would do. *Note:* The instructor may wish to narrow this requirement somewhat by specifying a particular industry or organization.

When completed, the rankings will be compared with a set of comparative data that has been made available to the instructor. The differences in the rankings, if any, should be discussed, particularly between the different jobs.

EXHIBIT 12-11   Motivation Factors

FACTOR DESCRIPTION	Self	RANKINGS Nonsupervisor Assembly Line	Middle-Level Manager
1. *Recognition:* Receiving recognition from peers, supervisors, and/or subordinates for good work performances.			
2. *Pay:* A wage that not only covers normal living expenses but provides additional funds for certain luxury items.			
3. *Sense of Achievement:* The feelings associated with successful completion of a job, finding solutions to different problems, or seeing the results of one's work.			
4. *Supervision:* Working for a supervisor who is both competent in doing his or her job and looks out for the welfare of his or her subordinates.			
5. *Advancement:* The opportunity for advancement or promotion based on ability.			
6. *Job Itself:* Having a job that is interesting, challenging, and provides for substantial variety and autonomy.			
7. *Job Security:* Feeling good about security within the company.			
8. *Working Conditions:* Safe and attractive conditions for doing work.			
9. *Fringe Benefits:* A substantial fringe benefit package covering such aspects as personal protection.			
10. *Personal Development:* The opportunity to develop and refine new skills and abilities.			

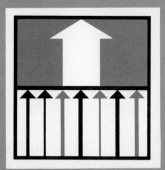

13

Leadership

CHAPTER OUTLINE

KEY POINTS IN THIS CHAPTER

1. Leadership in organizations is a process in which influence is founded on the strength of the leader's power base.

2. Trait theories of leadership attempt to identify certain managerial characteristics that can be used to distinguish successful from unsuccessful leaders.

3. Behavioral theories of leadership concern the leader's style or behavioral patterns. An attempt is made to identify the best style of leadership.

4. Fiedler's contingency model, the first situational approach to leadership, relates certain situational factors to the leader's style in order to develop the most effective match.

5. The path-goal theory, based on expectancy theory, is a situational approach that seeks to improve employee motivation through the use of different leader behaviors.

6. A manager's needs and preferred leadership style are influenced by cultural factors.

7. Leaders influence superiors and peers as well as subordinates.

8. Leadership is a learned skill that can be acquired through a variety of mechanisms, including experience, observation, and training programs.

THE PRACTICE OF MANAGEMENT

Marisa Bellisario of Olivetti America

Olivetti America, the largest of the Italian-based Olivetti Corporation's thirty worldwide subsidiaries, is a troubled organization. It has been battering its head against the gates of the U. S. market for over twenty years since it bought out the Underwood typewriter company, always with the same dismal results (e.g., a $39 million loss in 1978). Four Italian executives had been sent over to New York to try to solve the many problems, but each returned to Irves in Italy with mission unaccomplished. Finally, Carlo De Benedetti, Olivetti's new chief executive, reached out for one of his toughest managers, Marisa Bellisario, and charged her with the task of turning the U. S. operations into a profitable company. He gave her three years to do the job.

On her first day in New York, Bellisario laid down the law to her staff. Her aim was to create a new Olivetti. It would be a well-controlled, well-disciplined company, concentrating on a limited number of products in the American market. Employees would be expected to work hard and the company would have to be profitable. Those who did not want to be part of the new Olivetti were invited to seek other employment.

Bellisario made it to the top on her own. She had been willing to submit to the discipline a management career demands: long hours, complete dedication to the job, and personal sacrifices. Her sacrifices include seeing only rarely her husband, Lionello Cantoni, professor of applied mathematics at the University of Turin, whom she left at home in Italy. She relishes her chance to run a company on her own, to have the responsibility for everything in a dynamic market such as the U. S.

She joined the computer division of Olivetti shortly after receiving her degree in economics from the University of Turin. She stayed with the division as it was sold to G. E. and then to Honeywell. Looking back on the six years she spent with the two American firms, Bellisario concluded that it was a fruitful part of her career from a professional point of view. She learned about American marketing and management, about strategic planning and the need for strong financial reporting systems. She returned to Olivetti in 1972 to head up the data-processing division.

In Italy and the U. S., Bellisario gained a reputation for making excessive demands, both on herself and on her subordinates. Among the confident and enthusiastic New York staff, there is often exasperation at the boss's expectations. For example, the salesperson who sells a product only to report it cancelled the next month gets docked as though he or she had lost three orders, instead of one. The service division, once so obliging as to repair the competition's products, now sticks to Olivetti's only. In addition, after one of her long working days, Bellisario frequently leaves handwritten notes of instruction on chairs, ready for a manager's early-morning arrival.

There is no let up, even when she makes her monthly visit to Italy for budget sessions. She returns Monday mornings on the Concorde, flying at mach two in order to put in a ten-hour day. One vice president stated that had Mrs. Bellisario been given the job, Rome probably would have been built in a day.

Suggested from Eleanor J. Tracy, "She Has Three Years to Turn Olivetti America Around," Fortune *(October 22, 1979): 87–90.*

13

Leadership is considered by both practicing managers and management scholars as one of the most important factors affecting organizational performance. For the manager, leadership is directing employees to work toward the accomplishment of goals. From a human resource point of view, the actions of the leader also have a significant effect on the behavior, attitudes, and performance of employees.[1]

We will discuss the concept of leadership in organizations in three major parts. The foundations of leadership will be established first, with a discussion of the definition of leadership and the basic elements that make up its content. Second, the three major approaches to the study of leadership—trait, behavioral, and situational—will be presented. Finally, we will discuss a number of contemporary issues in leadership and end the chapter with an analysis of leadership, performance, and the manager's job.

THE DEFINITION OF LEADERSHIP

If a group of people was asked to give a one- or two-word definition of what leadership means to them, it is likely that words such as *direction, example, powerful, motivator, control, authority, reinforcer,* and *delegator* would be mentioned. Leadership probably involves each of these words. The one word, however, that seems to encompass the major focus of leadership is *influence.* With this word, we will define leadership as follows:

> Leadership is a process involving two or more people in which one attempts to influence the other's behavior toward the accomplishment of some goal or goals.

There are at least three important implications of this definition. First, leadership is a *process* engaged in by certain individuals. That is, it is an ongoing activity in an organization. Second, leadership involves *other people,* usually in the form of subordinates. By their willingness to be influenced by the leaders, subordinates formalize the leader's authority and make the leadership process possible. Finally, the outcome of the leadership process is some form of *goal accomplishment.* This suggests that the leader's attempts at influence are directional, aimed at some level of achievement.

Manager and/or Leader?

Management and leadership are not synonymous. A person can be a leader without being a manager. For example, in sports, Willie Stargell (baseball), "Mean" Joe Greene (football), and Gordie Howe (hockey) were leaders of their respective teams without being the managers. That is, they did not plan, organize, or control the activities of the team, nor did they have this responsibility. Through their superior performance and example, however, they often influenced the behavior of other team members.

On the other hand, a person can be a manager without also being the leader. People are managers by virtue of the authority in their positions as given by the organization (see chapter 8). They have the *right* to influence because of their positions, but they may not choose to exercise this right, or subordinates may choose to be influenced by other individuals or factors. For example, a head nurse in a hospital is technically the manager over a group of floor nurses. Yet frequently the behavior of the floor nurses is influenced by the directives of the physician or by the nurses' own knowledge of what to do for a patient.

Informal Leaders

A second way to approach the manager versus leader issue is to discuss *informal* leaders. For example, consider a group of clerical personnel who are responsible for maintaining customer charge accounts for a large retail store. The question, "Who is your leader?" may draw different responses. A typical response might be, "Well, my direct supervisor is Emily, but Julie is really the leader of my group. Emily gives directions and orders and generally tells us what to do. She is the 'organization's person,' and we go to her with problems concerning rules, procedures, and policies. Julie, on the other hand, has the same clerical job as we do, but has worked here longer than any of us. You might say she 'knows the ropes.' Julie helps us with our work by showing us the best methods for doing the job in the most efficient manner. Everyone feels good that Julie is around—she helps us build confidence in our work and is a real morale booster."

This example draws attention to two important sources of influence and leadership. Emily is the *formal* supervisor, and as such, exercises formal influence. Leadership, however, can be *informal,* such as the type of influence exerted by Julie. This type of leader is referred to as the informal, emergent, or peer leader.

While not prescribed by the organization, informal leaders can significantly influence the behavior of other organizational members. Informal influence originates not from the position held by the individual, but from some special quality, ability, or skill of the informal leader that is wanted by the group. In Julie's case, this influence is based on her work experience and willingness to help her co-workers.

In some situations, only a formal leader will exist. In our clerical example, if Emily performed her formal leadership role and also provided the support her subordinates needed and had the necessary skills, then an informal leader probably would not emerge. Julie held her informal leadership role because Emily's behavior was not satisfying the work-related needs of the workers.

Informal leaders can play a very valuable role in organizations if their behavior and influence are congruent with the goals of the organization. If the informal leader influences the other workers to perform their work more efficiently and effectively, then he or she is acting in support of the organization's purposes. But if instead of offering assistance in work-related problems, Julie supported lengthy lunches and frequent "gab" sessions around the coffee pot, or refused to work overtime, she would be acting incongruent with the organization's purpose.

FOUNDATIONS OF LEADERSHIP

Two factors are foundational elements of our discussion of leadership in organizations. These are an analysis of the concept of power and identification of the process of leadership.

Power in the Leadership Position

As noted in chapter 8, the concepts of influence and power are closely related. In particular, power has been defined as the "capacity to influence another through the control over needed resources." It is important for the manager to understand that power to influence can originate from a variety of sources. In the example of clerical personnel, Emily's power came from her positional authority, while Julie's originated from certain skills and abilities. In other words, power in organizations includes positional and personal attributes.

One of the most widely used descriptions of organizational power was proposed by John R. P. French and Bertran Raven.[2] They stated that there are five different forms of power a leader may possess.

1. *Legitimate power* is given the manager by the organization because of the manager's position in the hierarchy. The organization usually sanctions this form of power by titles such as manager, director, or supervisor.

2. *Reward power* is based on the ability of the manager to control and administer rewards to others (money, promotions, praise) for compliance with the leader's orders or requests.

3. *Coercive power,* on the other hand, is based on the manager's ability to use punishment on others (reprimands, termination) for noncompliance with the manager's orders.

4. *Expert power* is derived from some special ability, skills, or knowledge exhibited by the individual. In our clerical example, Julie had expert power, which was used to influence her peers.

5. *Referent power* can be shown in at least two forms in an organization. First, it can be based on a certain attractiveness or appeal of one person to another. A person may be admired because of certain characteristics or traits that inspire or attract followers (e.g., charisma). For example, President John Kennedy and General George Patton were said to have had charisma, which permitted them to have followers both inside and outside their realms of authority. Referent power may also be based on a person's connection or relationship with another powerful individual. For example, the title "assistant to . . ." has been given to people who work closely with others with substantial power (see chapter 8). Although the assistant to the vice president may not have legitimate, reward, or coercive power, other individuals may perceive that this person is acting with the consent of the vice president, resulting in the assistant's power to influence. Before he became secretary of state, Henry Kissinger was President Nixon's national security advisor. That being a staff position, Kissinger had little organizationally based power. When he spoke in meetings, however, people assumed that he spoke for the president.

The manager should recognize that legitimate, reward, and coercive power are given to the manager by the organization and are based on the control of important organizational resources. Expert and, to some extent, referent power are based on the characteristics of the individual and may or may not be given by the organization.

Many times, managers find that they lack certain organizationally based power components. For example, managers may have legitimate power because of their positions, but decisions on pay raises or reprimands may be limited by organizational rules or procedures (e.g., union contracts). Thus, some of the manager's ability to influence others has been taken away. When faced with this frequent situation, many managers seek to improve their ability to influence others by strengthening an individually based power component. They accomplish this usually by becoming "expert" in their particular areas of responsibility. The important factor is that the stronger the manager's power base, the greater the chance that influence attempts will be successful. When certain power bases are missing—particularly organizationally based power—the manager may seek to compensate by strengthening individually based power.

A Basic Leadership Model

With the preceding foundation, we can now present a basic model of the leadership process. As shown in exhibit 13-1, the model consists of three major parts.

1. Power is the *basis* of the leadership process.

2. There is a series of four process factors, or *leader behaviors,* which serve as the main influence elements. The first stage, *assignment,* is leader behaviors that start the influence, or goal-achievement, activities. Included are planning, directing, instructing, and so on. The second stage, *implementation,* is the leader's activities that guide, monitor, delegate, and support subordinates in their work. The *evaluation* stage is the leader activities that evaluate and control the work. Finally, in the fourth stage, *rewards,* the leader rewards, revises, and feeds back information regarding the degree to which the workers' performance has achieved the stated goals. Consider the manager of quality control in a farm equipment manufacturing plant who wants to put into operation a new quality control technique. At the beginning, the manager instructs his or her subordinates in how to use the new technique (assignment stage). As the subordinates begin using the technique, the manager makes sure that it is being used properly (implementation stage). As time passes, the manager

EXHIBIT 13-1
**A Basic
Leadership Model**

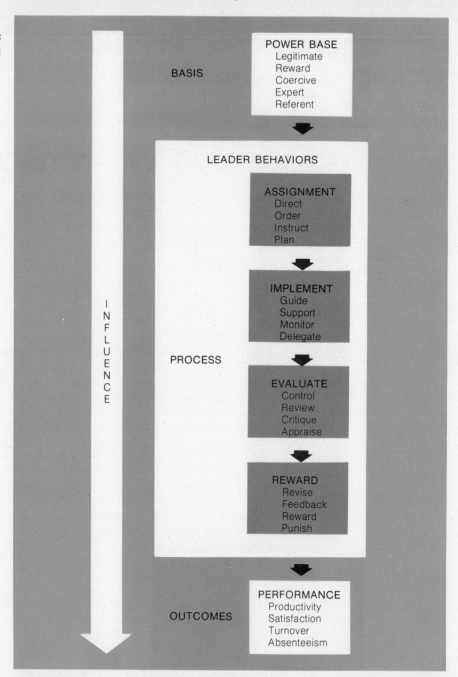

evaluates how the technique has worked, how the subordinate technicians have adapted to it, and so on (evaluation stage). Finally, when
sufficient data have been collected, the manager revises certain procedures associated with the technique, feeds this information back to the
subordinates, and rewards them for their performance (reward stage).

3. The third major part of the model is the *outcomes* of the leadership process. Outcomes can include increased productivity, increased satisfaction, or decreased turnover and absenteeism.

Approaches to the Study of Leadership

With the basic leadership model, we can examine the various approaches to leadership. Three broad approaches have characterized the study of leadership during the last forty years: trait theories, behavioral theories, and situational theories.[3]

The early *trait theories* studied leadership by attempting to answer the question, "In terms of managerial characteristics, who are the most effective leaders?" Following the early trait theories came *behavioral theories,* in which researchers and practicing managers altered their approach from an emphasis on the characteristics of the leader to a concern for the style of leadership exhibited by the leader. The key question asked was, "Is one leadership style more effective than any other leadership style?" In terms of the basic leadership model, the focus was actually on the leadership process itself. In other words, attention shifted from a concern of "who the leader is" to "what the leader does."

Finally, contemporary management scholars developed what we will call *situational theories*. These approaches expanded on our basic leadership model by considering leadership to be a complex process that involves the leader, subordinates, and the nature of the situation. These management scholars were directed by the belief that "effective leadership is a function of the characteristics of the leader, the style of leadership, the characteristics of the subordinates, and the situation surrounding the leadership environment." We will begin our discussion of the various approaches to the study of leadership with a brief analysis of the trait theories.

THE SEARCH FOR LEADERSHIP TRAITS

One of the first scientific efforts to study and understand leadership was directed at identifying the important characteristics of leaders. This research, which began in earnest after World War II, attempted systematically to analyze something that many of us have observed: there is some quality in military heroes, movie heroes and heroines, successful politicians, executives, and some everyday people that makes these people seem naturally more intelligent, braver, more decisive, more articulate, and more loyal than anyone else.

One of the most interesting discussions of this special quality was presented by Tom Wolfe in *The Right Stuff,* which describes the behind-the-scenes selection and training of the first American astronauts. Wolfe defines "the right stuff" as follows:

> Herein the world was divided into those who had it and those who did not. This quality, this *it*, was never named, however, nor was it talked about in any way. As to just what this ineffable quality was . . . well, it obviously involved bravery. . . . The idea here seemed to be that a man should have the ability to go up in a hurtling piece of machinery and put his hide on the line and then have the moxie, the reflexes, the experience, the coolness, to pull it back in the last yawning moment—and then to go up again the next day, and the next, and every next day, even if the series should prove

infinite. . . . The idea was to prove at every foot of the way that you were one of the elected and anointed ones who had *the right stuff* and could move higher and higher and even—ultimately, God willing, one day—that you might be able to join that special few at the very top, that elite who had the capacity to bring tears to men's eyes, the very Brotherhood of the Right Stuff itself.[4]

This "right stuff" of the first astronauts, much like the traits of leaders, was recognized by most people but proved difficult to study and measure.

Research on Leader Traits

The trait approach to leadership began with the following question: Can a set of finite traits be found that can distinguish effective from ineffective leaders, such that the results can be used to select new leaders? This new approach to managerial selection was supposed to be the major contribution of the trait theories.

EXHIBIT 13-2   Examples of Studied Leader Traits

PHYSICAL CHARACTERISTICS	SOCIAL BACKGROUND	INTELLIGENCE
1. Age	1. Education	1. Ability
2. Weight	2. Mobility	2. Judgment
3. Height	3. Social status	3. Decisiveness
4. Appearance	4. Family background	4. Fluency of speech
PERSONALITY	**TASK-RELATED CHARACTERISTICS**	**SOCIAL CHARACTERISTICS**
1. Independence	1. Achievement need	1. Administrative ability
2. Self-confidence	2. Initiative	2. Attractiveness
3. Dominance	3. Persistence	3. Cooperativeness
4. Aggression	4. Responsibility need	4. Interpersonal skills

Exhibit 13-2 presents a list of example traits that have been investigated. The results of the many research studies indicated that there was a *tendency* for leaders (emergent and effective leaders) to be taller, more intelligent, self-confident, extroverted, and more effective in their communication (see chapter 11).[5] In a study of Fortune 500 executives, it was found that a high percentage (but not a majority) of them came from a middle-class background, held Protestant or Episcopalian religious beliefs, identified with Republican or independent political stands, and had fathers who were professional or business executives.[6]

Edwin E. Ghiselli performed one of the most famous studies of managerial effectiveness.[7] He examined thirteen personality and motivational traits of managers to determine how these traits related to managerial success. The results are summarized in exhibit 13-3.

1. Supervisory ability—the capacity to direct the work of others and to organize and integrate their activities and behavior toward goal accomplishment—was the most distinguishing trait of managerial success.

EXHIBIT 13-3 Importance of Leader Traits to Managerial Effectiveness

VERY IMPORTANT TO MANAGERIAL EFFECTIVENESS	MODERATELY IMPORTANT TO MANAGERIAL EFFECTIVENESS	LITTLE IMPORTANCE TO MANAGERIAL EFFECTIVENESS
Supervisory ability	Lack of need for security	Lack of need for high financial rewards
Occupational achievement	Working class affinity	Need for power over others
Intelligence	Initiative	Masculinity-femininity
Self-actualization		
Self-assurance		
Decisiveness		

2. Next in importance is a cluster of five traits: the need for (occupational) achievement, intelligence, the need for self-actualization, self-assurance, and decisiveness. This suggests two things: (a) successful leaders have the need to achieve, have the drive to act independently, and are self-assured in their work; and (b) leadership ability is strongly associated with good judgment (see chapter 7) and proven communication skills (see chapter 11).

3. The results suggest that intelligence is an accurate predictor of managerial success within a certain range of intelligence. At the extremes of this range—very high or very low intelligence—the chance of successful performance decreases. Ghiselli's findings imply that the leader's intelligence should not be too different from that of the subordinates. In other words, the leader who is too smart or not smart enough may lose the respect of subordinates and, hence, lose the ability to influence their behavior.

4. A number of traits were identified as contributing little to managerial success. The low level of importance given to the need for power and wealth points to a theory Y orientation of these managers, rather than a theory X philosophy.

   Acceptance of Ghiselli's findings should be tempered not only due to the small sample size, but also because the traits are not totally independent of each other. Nevertheless, his work was a major addition to the study of managerial success from a trait point of view.

Issues and Implications of Trait Theories

Even with these sometimes interesting results, the general view was that trait research did not provide an accurate analysis of the leadership process. First, the list of studied leader traits was not finite in number, but approached the many hundreds. Thus, the application of the findings to managerial selection in organizations was tenuous. Second, there were inconsistent findings across organizations. That is, the discriminating traits that were found in one organization frequently did not apply to other organizations. Third, there was the recognition that some of these identifying traits may have been *learned* while a person performed a leadership role. For example, people in leadership positions may recognize that in order to improve their performances, they need to become more assertive, more decisive, and stronger in the ability to communicate. During this process, their levels of self-confidence may also increase.

Finally, there was the belated understanding that effective leadership depends not so much on *who* the leader is but on what the leader does and how well the leader adapts to the varying requirements of different situations. This led researchers to an examination of the behavior or styles of the leader.

THE BEHAVIORAL APPROACH TO LEADERSHIP

Dissatisfaction with the trait approach motivated management scholars to refocus their attention on the study of actual behaviors. This approach has been termed the behavioral or leadership-style approach. Unlike trait theories, the behavioral approach emphasized what leaders do, not who they are in terms of individual characteristics. Similar to trait theories, however, the behavioral approach sought the "one best" style of leadership that would be effective in all situations.

Research on the Behavioral Approach

A number of definitions of leadership styles were developed from the various behavioral theories of leadership. As we will see, although many terms were assigned to the different leadership styles, two dimensions were stressed in each theory: task orientation and employee orientation. *Task orientation* is the emphasis the leader places on getting the job done by such actions as assigning and organizing the work, making decisions, and monitoring and evaluating performance. *Employee orientation* is the openness and friendliness exhibited by the leader and the concern shown for the welfare of subordinates.

In exhibit 13-4, the two orientations have been presented in a two-dimensional framework. This framework reflects the notion that a leader's behavioral style can vary along each of the dimensions, resulting

EXHIBIT 13-4
Dimensions of
Leadership Style

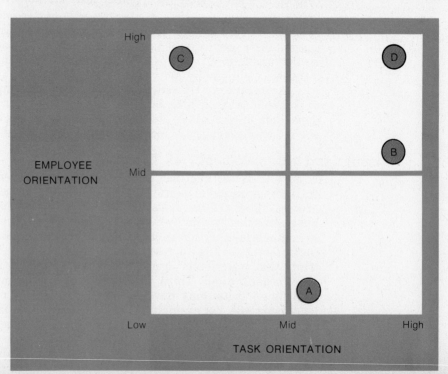

in a great array of possible leader styles. For example, point *A* represents a manager whose style is moderate on task orientation, but low on employee orientation. Similarly, manager *B* is shown to exhibit a high degree of task orientation and a moderate degree of employee orientation, while manager *C* is depicted as low on task orientation but high on employee orientation.

Two research groups were most noted for work on leadership styles: Ohio State University and the University of Michigan. At Ohio State, the two leader dimensions were named *initiating structure* (task orientation) and *consideration* (employee orientation).[8] Much of the early work was conducted with the belief that the most effective leadership style was one that was high on both initiating structure and consideration (manager *D* in exhibit 13-4). It was assumed that leaders using this style would be associated with groups of subordinates who were high performers and had equally high levels of job satisfaction. However, in numerous studies in such organizations as a petroleum refinery, a business machine manufacturer, an aircraft manufacturer, and military groups, no single leadership style emerged as being the most effective. In certain organizations, a high initiating structure and high consideration style was found to be most effective; in others, a low initiating structure and high consideration style was best; while in still others, a high initiating structure and low consideration style was associated with high subordinate performance.[9]

In the University of Michigan studies, the dimensions of task orientation and employee orientation were called *job-centered* and *employee-centered* styles. In a major study that characterized much of their work, Michigan researchers compared the effectiveness of two units in a large corporation. The prevailing leadership style in one unit was highly job-centered, while a highly employee-centered style was dominant in the second unit. The study found that production increased in both units; however, the attitudinal and behavioral relationships among the study participants were quite different. In the unit with leaders exhibiting high employee-centered styles, satisfaction increased, while turnover and absenteeism decreased; the high job-centered style unit reported decreased satisfaction and higher turnover and absenteeism.[10]

The main conclusion reached from this and similar studies by the Michigan group was that the effectiveness of a leadership style should not be evaluated solely by productivity measures. Other measures of organizational performance, such as employee job satisfaction, turnover, and absenteeism, should be carefully considered (see chapter 2). In the University of Michigan framework, the results would support a conclusion that employee-centered leader behavior would be the most effective and appropriate.

The Managerial Grid®

The work of Robert R. Blake and Jane S. Mouton has also been identified with studies that adopted the task-orientation/employee-orientation approach to leadership styles.[11] Using *concern for production* and *concern for people,* Blake and Mouton created the "managerial grid." Shown in exhibit 13-5, the grid focuses on five main leadership styles:

1. *The 9, 1 style,* termed task or authoritarian management, stresses a high concern for production and efficiency but a low concern for employees.

EXHIBIT 13-5
The Managerial Grid

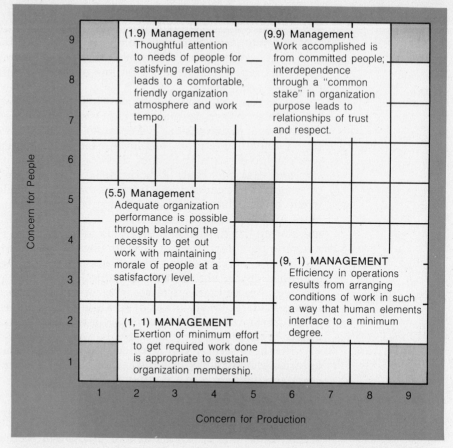

The Managerial Grid figure from **The New Managerial Grid,** by Robert R. Blake and Jane Srygley Mouton. Houston: Gulf Publishing Company, Copyright © 1978, page 11. Reproduced by permission.

2. *The 1, 9 style* is the country-club management style, where there is a high concern for employees but a low concern for production.

3. *The 1, 1 style* is termed impoverished or laissez-faire management because of the low concern on both style dimensions.

4. *The 5, 5 style* is called middle-of-the-road management due to the intermediate emphasis placed on concerns for production and employees.

5. *The 9, 9 style,* termed team or democratic management, expresses a high concern for both production and employees.

The managerial grid is related to both the Ohio State and Michigan studies. Similar to the Ohio State work, the 9, 9 style (called high initiating structure and high consideration in the Ohio State framework) was suggested as the most effective leadership style. Like the work at the University of Michigan, Blake and Mouton propose that the outcomes of the leader's influence attempts should include increases in both productivity and satisfaction.

Subsequent research on the grid resulted in only moderate support for the superiority of the 9, 9 style. As we will see later in this chapter, other management scholars and practicing managers believe that the 9, 9 style tends to oversimplify the complexities of the leadership process. The growing belief was that situational factors surrounding the leadership environment would have to be considered much more thoroughly before a better understanding of leadership could emerge.

Issues and Implications of the Behavioral Approach

There are a number of important managerial implications that can be derived from an analysis of the behavioral approach to leadership:

1. **Leadership style is a multidimensional concept.**

   At least two different leadership styles have been identified and studied: task orientation and employee orientation. The important implication for managers is that varying one's style along each dimension will result in a significant number of leader behaviors available to the manager.

2. **A manager's leadership style is flexible.**

   Contrary to what was initially believed, there is no one best style of leadership that consistently leads to high levels of performance. There are too many complex relationships in leadership to make possible a single most effective style. One of the many situational factors—one that we discussed earlier in this chapter—is the power base of the leader. As shown in exhibit 13-6, the stronger the leader's power base (legitimate, reward, and coercive), the greater the ability of the leader to use a task-oriented style.[12] Conversely, the weaker the leader's power base, the more the leader will depend on an employee-oriented style.

EXHIBIT 13-6   Power Base and Leadership Styles

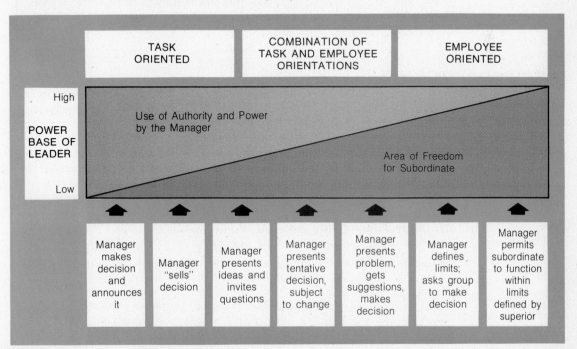

Adapted from Robert Tannenbaum and Warren H. Schmidt, "How to Choose a Leadership Style," Harvard Business Review (May–June 1973): 162–80.

3. **Leadership style is a learned managerial skill.**

The ability of a leader to use task-oriented and employee-oriented styles is probably acquired through experience. Managers not only recognize what works for them in various situations, but they usually carefully observe what leader behaviors work for other managers.

The various theories that helped build the behavioral approach to leadership made a large contribution to the study of leadership. While the main proposition that there was one best leadership style that was most effective in most situations was not supported by research, the recognition that other factors must be considered was very important.

COMMENTS ON THE PRACTICE OF MANAGEMENT
(See p. 441)

The Practice of Management section, discussing the Marisa Bellisario episode at Olivetti America, is a good illustration of the various approaches to leadership. From a trait theory viewpoint, she recognized not only that the attribute of decisiveness was required for success, but her own needs for achievement and challenge played an important role. From a behavioral theory viewpoint, Bellisario's style of leadership was very clearly learned from her experiences in Italy, and in the U. S. with G. E. and Honeywell. Finally, from a situational framework, she understood early that a tough, task-oriented style of leadership was required in the troubled situation that she was put into. She diagnosed the situation well, and adapted her style and behavior accordingly.

Two other aspects should be pointed out. First, her power base to turn the company around was quite strong. She not only had the blessings of the top management in Italy, but being the main Olivetti executive in the U. S., she was the focal point of all U. S. activities. The other point not to be lost is the fact that being a woman apparently had little to do with her selection for the job or her success to date. Good management and leadership skills are not the sole possession of any sex.

SITUATIONAL APPROACHES TO LEADERSHIP

The limitations of the trait and behavioral approaches to leadership led researchers to refine and refocus their efforts on the study of leadership in organizations. The result was an increased emphasis on the important situational factors that affect the leader's attempts at influence. There was the significant recognition that effectiveness in leadership is highly dependent on being able to diagnose and adapt to the dynamics of the particular situation.

This emphasis on diagnosis requires the leader to examine at least four factors. As shown in exhibit 13-7 (which is a revision of exhibit 13-1), the four factors are managerial characteristics, subordinate characteristics, task requirements, and organizational characteristics.

1. Inclusion of the *managerial characteristics* factor in the diagram recognizes that what the manager brings to the leadership situation is very important. In essence, consideration of managerial characteristics is an application of findings of the trait theories. Important characteristics to consider are the leader's personality, needs, past experience and reinforcement, and expectations. For instance, a manager with high safety and security needs may use a different leadership style than a manager

EXHIBIT 13-7 Situational Factors Affecting Leadership

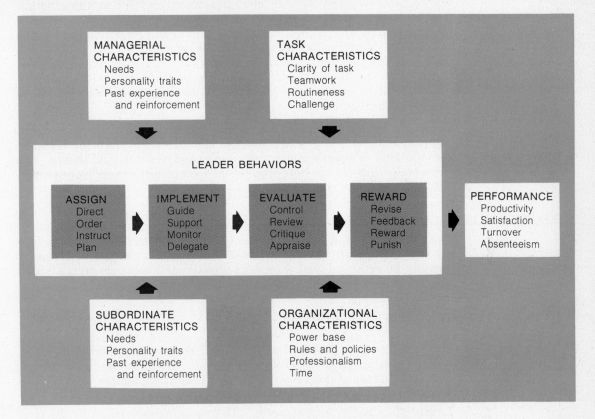

with high self-actualization needs, even though they may hold similar positions within the organization.

2. *Subordinate characteristics* is an important situational concept that was missing from the trait and behavioral approaches. This factor is what subordinates bring to the situation in terms of personality, needs, past experience and reinforcement, and expectations. Consider, for example, the supervisor in the x-ray unit in an outpatient clinic. One of the technicians under the supervisor always exhibits a high level of self-confidence, while another frequently behaves in a manner that suggests a low level of self-confidence. Situational approaches to leadership would indicate that the supervisor would be correct in using different leader behaviors with the two technicians.

3. *Task characteristics,* or the nature of the subordinate's job requirements, will also affect the way the leader behaves. For example, the use of a high task-oriented style of leadership would be more appropriate in jobs that require exact and detailed instructions (e.g., assembling a pocket calculator), than jobs that require more freedom (e.g., research chemist). Similarly, one would expect that a high employee-oriented style would be better for situations that require a high degree of teamwork (e.g., physical therapy in a hospital) than situations where there is a high degree of independence (e.g., sales representative).

4. *Organizational characteristics* are aspects within the organization that may alter or constrain the leader's influence attempts. Examples include the leader's power base, the degree to which the organization operates on strict rules and procedures, and the level of professionalism of the employees. Many union contracts, for example, limit the supervisor's ability to reward, punish, or instruct workers. In a similar manner, because of their education, professional employees such as accountants, nurses, and engineers may require less direction than workers on an assembly line.

This list of situational factors, although not exhaustive, should point out that leadership is indeed a complex process. In the following sections, two theories—Fiedler's contingency model and the path-goal theory—are presented, illustrating how situational factors have been incorporated into the study of leadership.

FIEDLER'S CONTINGENCY MODEL

Fred E. Fiedler was one of the first to develop a situational approach to leadership.[13] In the contingency model (known also as the contingency theory), he proposed that a leader's effectiveness depends on the interaction between the leader's behavior and certain situational factors.

Contingency Theory Components

Five factors are the major components of Fiedler's model: (1) leadership style assessment; (2) task structure; (3) leader/member relations; (4) the leader's position power; and (5) effectiveness. The first identifies the *motivational* aspect of the leader, while the remaining factors relate to the *situational favorableness* for the leader.

Leadership Style Assessment.   The main variable used in the contingency model to assess leadership style is called the least preferred co-worker (LPC). With the use of a questionnaire, the leader is asked to describe the person with whom he or she has worked least effectively on a recent task. The model suggests that a low LPC score—an unfavorable evaluation of the least preferred co-worker—indicates that the leader is ready to reject those with whom he or she has difficulty working. Therefore, the lower the LPC score, the greater the tendency for the leader to be *task oriented*. On the other hand, a high LPC score—a favorable evaluation of the least preferred co-worker—indicates a willingness to perceive even the worst co-worker as having some positive characteristics. Thus, the higher the LPC score, the greater the tendency for the leader to use an *employee-oriented* style.

Task Structure.   This first situational factor concerns the nature of the subordinate's task. It measures the degree the task is routine (structured) or complex (unstructured). For example, an accounting clerk in a retail store may work on a fairly structured task, while the manager of planning for a health maintenance organization probably works on an unstructured task.

Leader/Member Relations.   As the second situational factor, this variable measures the relationship between the leader and subordinates. It is the degree of confidence, trust, and respect subordinates have in the leader. It is evaluated along a continuum of good to poor, and the main idea is that the better the relationship between leader and subordinate, the easier it will be for the leader to exercise influence. When the relationship is poor, the leader may have to resort to special behaviors or favors to get good performance.

Leader Position Power.   The final situational factor concerns the extent of the leader's power base. As discussed earlier in this chapter, this variable refers to the degree that the leader possesses, through legitimate, reward, and coercive power, the ability to influence the behavior of the subordinate. According to Fiedler, position power can vary from strong (vice president of manufacturing) to weak (committee chairperson).

Effectiveness.   The major outcome variable in the contingency theory is effectiveness. In other words, the focus of this situational approach is on task or goal accomplishment, as opposed to issues of worker job satisfaction.

Contingency Theory Framework

The various components of the contingency theory have been combined into a situational framework, which is shown in exhibit 13-8. The combination of the three situational factors—task structure, leader/member relations, and leader position power—leads to an examination of an eight-cell framework that varies along a continuum of *situational favorableness.*

As exhibit 13-8 indicates, the recommended leadership style also varies with the certainty of the situation. According to the model, a task-oriented leadership style will be more effective than an employee-oriented style under extreme conditions—that is, where the situation is either highly certain or highly uncertain. For example, a task-oriented style

EXHIBIT 13-8   Fiedler's Contingency Model

	CELL	1	2	3	4	5	6	7	8
SITUATIONAL FACTORS	Leader/Member Relations	Good	Good	Good	Good	Poor	Poor	Poor	Poor
	Task Structure	Structured	Structured	Unstructured	Unstructured	Structured	Structured	Unstructured	Unstructured
	Leader Position Power	Strong	Weak	Strong	Weak	Strong	Weak	Strong	Weak
SITUATIONAL FAVORABLENESS		Favorable			Moderately Favorable			Unfavorable	
SITUATIONAL CERTAINTY		Very Certain Situation			Moderately Certain Situation			Very Uncertain Situation	
RECOMMENDED LEADERSHIP STYLE		Task	Task	Task	Employee	Employee	Employee	Task	Task

Adapted from Fred E. Fiedler, *A Theory of Leadership Effectiveness* (New York: McGraw-Hill, 1967), p. 37.

would be recommended for a manager of a large restaurant (cell 1). The tasks are highly structured for the waiters, waitresses, chefs, and support staff. Moreover, if the owner backs the manager's decisions (or if the manager is the owner), the position power is strong. Finally, if the manager gains the respect and trust of the subordinates through fair treatment and is able to gain significant pay increases, the leader-member relations may be good. Under these conditions, a task-oriented style is preferred to an employee-oriented style in order to achieve high performance.

An employee-oriented style is more appropriate for moderate levels of certainty and situational favorableness. For example, in many research laboratories, the tasks of the scientists are quite unstructured and the leader may have weak position power, but leader-member relations are good (cell 4). Since research scientists prefer to follow their own creative tendencies as opposed to being told what to do by the research director, an employee-oriented style would be recommended.

Issues and Implications with the Contingency Model

Possibly the most important managerial implication of the contingency model is the relationship between the leader and the situation. On one hand, the leadership style of the manager is not only considered to be unidimensional, but because it is part of the leader's characteristics, the leadership style is a rigid behavioral quality. This has led supporters of Fiedler's model to suggest that leader effectiveness is a function of fitting the manager to the job. In other words, since the leader's style is rigid, for the highest level of effectiveness one must first diagnose the situation and then select the manager whose style fits the favorableness of that situation. Thus, task-oriented leaders would find themselves placed in situations represented by cells 1, 2, 3, 7, and 8 in exhibit 13-8, while employee-oriented leaders would be selected to manage in situations represented in cells 4, 5, and 6.

Since its introduction, Fiedler's model has been the subject of a growing body of research.[14] As one would expect, a number of significant criticisms have developed.[15] These include questions of whether managerial style is indeed unidimensional and rigid and what the LPC scale really measures. In addition, there is concern over the lack of attention to the interaction between leadership style and the situation. For example, it is highly probable that an employee-oriented style can change leader-member relations from poor to good. If this happens—as in cell 5—the situation can change to one represented by cell 1. Cell 1, however, requires a task-oriented style. Managers with the employee-oriented style would, thus, have worked themselves out of their jobs! According to the model, they must be moved to other situations where their style would be more appropriate.

Even with these and other major concerns, Fiedler's contingency model has proven to be a significant addition to the study of leadership in organizations. With its emphasis on diagnosing the leadership situation, the model has drawn attention to the importance of considering other factors that can affect the leader's attempt to influence the behavior of subordinates.

EXHIBIT 13-9   Path-Goal Theory of Leadership

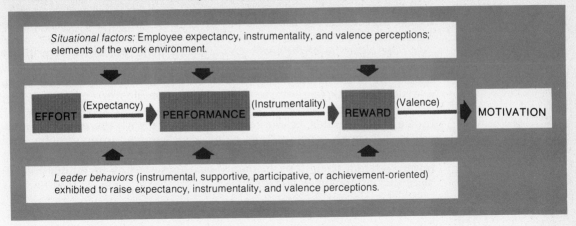

Situational factors: Employee expectancy, instrumentality, and valence perceptions; elements of the work environment.

EFFORT —(Expectancy)→ PERFORMANCE —(Instrumentality)→ REWARD —(Valence)→ MOTIVATION

Leader behaviors (instrumental, supportive, participative, or achievement-oriented) exhibited to raise expectancy, instrumentality, and valence perceptions.

A PATH-GOAL THEORY OF LEADER EFFECTIVENESS

A second situational approach to leadership was recently developed from the work of Martin G. Evans and Robert J. House.[16] Named the path-goal theory, the model attempts to study leadership effectiveness in a variety of situations. In brief, the model suggests that leaders are effective by means of their impact on employee motivation. It is termed path-goal because it focuses on how the leader influences the perceptions of work goals or rewards of subordinates and also focuses on the paths, or behaviors, that lead to the successful accomplishment of work goals.

Path-Goal Components

As shown in exhibit 13-9, the expectancy theory motivational approach is the foundation for the path-goal theory. From our discussion in chapter 12, recall that the expectancy theory suggests that employees will be motivated to perform on the job when (1) they believe they can accomplish a specific task (expectancy); (2) rewards are given that relate to the person's level of performance (instrumentality); and (3) the rewards are of value to the person (valence). Path-goal theory states that certain situational factors can adversely affect the employee's perceptions of expectancy, instrumentality, or valence. When this happens, motivation is reduced. If the leader, through the use of various behaviors, can help remove, or clarify, these perceptions, then motivation will improve, along with increased effectiveness.

Beyond the expectancy theory variables of expectancy, instrumentality, and valence, there are three main components of the path-goal approach: situational factors, leader behaviors, and outcomes.

Situational Factors.   Two situational factors are considered important in path-goal theory: subordinate characteristics and elements of the work environment. The key *subordinate characteristics* include ability, self-confidence, and needs. In the theory's framework, ability is the degree to which the person believes he or she can do the work (expectancy), self-confidence concerns the degree to which the employee believes that he or she has control over what happens to himself or herself (instrumentality), and needs are the internal wants and desires of the individual (valence).

The *elements of the work environment* involve such factors in the organization as the employee's task, relationships with co-workers, and the nature of the reward system. For example, an employee working on a structured task (e.g., nurse's aide) may have clearer expectancy perceptions than one performing on an unstructured task (e.g., physicist). In the same manner, co-workers who interfere with the employee's activities—through constant goofing-off and frequent interruptions—can lower expectancy and instrumentality perceptions. Finally, a complete reward system that is performance-based can result in higher instrumentality and valence perceptions.

THE MANAGER'S JOB
Fletcher Byrom of Koppers

Fletcher Byrom is a man of many titles, which, in turn, bespeak a diversity of interests and accomplishments: chairman of the board and chief executive of Koppers, chairman of the President's Export Council, chairman of the Committee for Economic Development, trustee of Allegheny College and the Carnegie Mellon University, and director of Mellon National Bank and the Ralston Purina Company.

Titles, however, are not specific. They indicate that their possessor is a high achiever, an unordinary man. In reading about Byrom, in reading what he has written, one gets an idea about his leadership philosophy. He is a man convinced that the key role of the chief executive of any organization is to act as a role model for other managers to follow. His role model consists of the following "commandments":

1. Hang loose.
2. Listen for the winds of change.
3. Increase the number of interfaces, both within and outside the organization.
4. Keep your intuition well lubricated, but . . .
5. Make sure you know where the information is buried.
6. Use growth as a means of getting and keeping good people, and use those people as a means of achieving continued growth.
7. Avoid like the plague those specialists who are only specialists.
8. Set your priorities in terms of the probable, rather than the merely possible; but . . .
9. Make sure you generate a reasonable number of mistakes—learn from them.

Adapted from William F. Dowling, "Conversation with Fletcher Byrom," Organizational Dynamics *(Summer 1978).*

Leader Behaviors. One of the major contributions of path-goal theory has been the identification of a more complete set of leader behaviors. In particular, four, not two, leadership styles have been most frequently studied through path-goal theory: instrumental, supportive, participative, and achievement-oriented.

1. *Instrumental* behavior is the planning, task assignment, monitoring, and control aspects of the leader's behavior. It is similar to the traditional

dimension of task orientation in that the leader's style emphasizes letting subordinates know what is expected of them. An instrumental leadership style can be used to increase an employee's effort-to-performance perception (expectancy) that had been low due to ability problems or because of an ambiguous or unstructured task.

2. *Supportive* behavior includes giving consideration to the needs of subordinates, displaying concern for their well-being and welfare, and creating a friendly and pleasant work environment. For instance, employees with high social needs (valence) may relate more positively to a supportive leadership style. Or, in a boring-type task such as janitorial services, the leader can make the path from performance-to-rewards (instrumentality) easier to travel by being supportive of subordinates.

3. *Participative* behavior, like supportive behavior, can be considered within the larger classification of employee-oriented leadership style. It is characterized by the sharing of information, emphasis on working with subordinates, and use of their ideas in making managerial decisions. A subordinate who exhibits ability to do the work and/or is highly self-confident (high expectancy) will probably react more favorably to a participative style by the leader than an instrumental style.

4. *Achievement-oriented* behavior is setting challenging goals, expecting subordinates to perform at the highest levels, and continually seeking improvement in performance. The leader wants good performance—a task-oriented type of leader behavior—but at the same time displays confidence in the ability of the subordinates to do a good job. An achievement-oriented style would work well with employees who have high ego needs (valence). On the other hand, this style can help clarify an employee's low performance-to-reward perception (instrumentality), by working with him or her to seek high goal accomplishment.

EXHIBIT 13-10   Examples of Path-Goal Theory of Leadership

SITUATION	IMPORTANT EXPECTANCY-THEORY PERCEPTIONS	RECOMMENDED LEADERSHIP STYLE FOR HIGH PERFORMANCE
1. Employee with low ability to perform	Low expectancy	Instrumental style
2. Highly capable employee	High expectancy	Supportive style
3. Employee exhibiting low self-confidence	Low instrumentality	Instrumental and supportive styles
4. Employee exhibiting high self-confidence	High instrumentality	Participative style
5. Employee working on an unstructured task	Low expectancy and instrumentality	Instrumental and supportive style
6. Employee working on a structured task	High expectancy and instrumentality	Achievement-oriented and supportive style
7. Employee with a low achievement need	Low valence	Achievement-oriented and participative style

Outcomes.   Unlike Fiedler's model, the path-goal approach stresses the concern for outcomes that benefit the organization (productivity) and the employee (job satisfaction). Because of this emphasis on multi-outcome measures, the path-goal approach is a much more complete—and, maybe, more realistic—situational theory of leadership than the contingency model. Exhibit 13-10 presents a set of typical situations.

Issues and Implications of the Path-Goal Theory

Even though the path-goal theory of leadership is of recent vintage, it has made a number of contributions to both the study and practice of management.[17] The more important implications for the manager include the following points:

1. **A manager's leadership style may include more than just two dimensions.**

   The results of the behavioral approach suggested that a manager's leadership style was multidimensional, involving the dimensions of task orientation and employee orientation. Path-goal theory, however, promotes the position that leadership style is even more complex than first thought. Indeed, instrumental, supportive, participative, and achievement-oriented leader behavior not only are distinct dimensions, but they are styles that most managers understand and use. The important factor for managers to consider is that their style of leadership is neither unidimensional and rigid as proposed by Fiedler, nor as simple as being task and/or employee oriented. The manager's leadership style consists of a complex array of different behaviors.

2. **Effective leadership is a function of proper situational diagnosis.**

   By far the most important implication of path-goal theory is that before leaders use a particular style of leadership, they must diagnose the situation. Since improved effectiveness comes from increasing the motivation of subordinates, the manager should first analyze the factors that enhance or constrain the level of motivation of the subordinate. The manager can then choose and exhibit the necessary behavior. More than any one aspect, this recognition helps to refute the "one best way" approach to leadership.

3. **The leader is not the only source of influence on the subordinate.**

   The classical or traditional view of leadership has suggested ways in which the leader can influence the subordinate toward goal accomplishment.[18] Path-goal theory also supports this notion, but adds that other sources of influence exist in the work environment. For example, individuals who exhibit high levels of self-confidence and/or have the necessary ability to do the job effectively, may not need much guidance from the leader. In essence, they are self-motivated to perform at high levels. Similarly, highly skilled or trained employees, such as nurses and research personnel, depend more on their education and experience to influence their work than the behavior of the leader. In these and similar examples, path-goal theory would suggest the use of supportive and/or participative behavior by the leader. These behaviors do more to establish a climate for high performance than actually to influence workers in what they should do and how they should do it.

Managers should act with caution in adopting the path-goal approach. For one, due to the relatively recent introduction of the theory, there is a lack of supporting research.[19] In addition, because path-goal theory uses expectancy theory as a basis, the criticisms of expectancy theory, discussed in chapter 12, still apply. Yet, overall, path-goal theory should be examined carefully by managers, if for no other reason than it has identified key leadership styles and suggested when and how these behaviors should be used.

CONTEMPORARY ISSUES IN LEADERSHIP

The study of leadership in organizations has made significant strides during the last twenty years. Much of this progress is the result of both management scholars and practicing managers recognizing and emphasizing the important factors that can lead to improved effectiveness.

As in the case of many scientific fields, there exist a number of contemporary issues to which the various theoretical approaches can be applied. These applications include leadership in the international realm, relationships with superiors and peers, and learning how to be a leader.

Leadership in the International Realm

As illustrated throughout this book, management must be considered as *international,* not something mature and vital only in the United States. Given this, one must be cognizant of the impact of cultural differences in leadership situations. Culture influences people and their needs, wants, aspirations, and behavior whether they are managers or not.

In a recent study of the cross-cultural aspect of management involving over 3000 managers in 12 countries, some interesting findings were reported on the motivating needs of managers and their leadership style preferences.[20]

1. Even with the supposed vast differences in cultures, there is a remarkable consistency across the different countries concerning many of the needs.

2. What are the dominant motivating needs of these managers? Clearly the higher-level needs—particularly self-actualization and independence—are most salient. This supports Ghiselli's findings discussed earlier in this chapter.

3. What needs are of less importance to the managers? Again, there is some consistency which suggests that the lower-level needs related to wealth, security, and affection (social) are of less importance.

4. The need for leadership, which may be considered as an ego, status, esteem need in Maslow's framework, is of moderate importance to the sampled managers. It appears that achieving a leadership position is not an end in itself, but a means whereby the more important self-actualization and independence needs get satisfied.

While these findings represent only a small sample, they do suggest some important differences and similarities that should be considered by managers and future managers.

What are the leadership styles preferred by managers in different countries? A common stereotype is that German managers use more task orientation than their U. S. counterparts. In fact, the opposite is true:

German managers are not only less task oriented than U. S. managers, but they exhibit greater employee orientation also.

The reasons for this focus on the German concept of collective responsibility. Under German law, nonmanagement personnel have equal representation on two management boards: the board of directors and the board of managers. Because of this, German managers are more concerned with the views of their workers and are more sympathetic to workers' efforts to assert their rights. Having representation on boards and being better informed about the organization may be a partial reason why strikes and walkouts are not as common as in the U. S.

Also, German managers, because of their attitudes toward authority, are able to issue an order and assume it will be carried out without close monitoring. In the U. S., we tend to place more emphasis on individual capabilities and independence: consequently, U. S. managers are more inclined to be more task oriented—to monitor the behavior of subordinates and use monetary incentives (or punishment) more frequently to insure compliance.

Japanese managers report a leadership style profile that is similar to German managers', but for different reasons. In Japan, there is a greater emphasis on achieving harmony, cooperation, and teamwork than in most countries. Because of this, managing in Japan is rarely accomplished with the use of high task-orientation. Instead, consultation, with emphasis on getting the opinions of most workers, is stressed to the point that even low-level supervisors get involved in the planning and policy formulation processes. Getting everyone involved before actions are taken results in less conflict and resistance to change. Such a process, however, is time consuming and may result in decision delay.

Another important factor is the state of economic development. In developed countries, because individual initiative is such a dominant assumption, task orientation need not be heavily used by managers. This may explain why managers in such developing countries as India and those in Latin America place a strong emphasis on a continued high use of task orientation. Managers in these countries may feel that subordinates have less ability and little to offer other than muscle. Initiative, therefore, comes from the task orientation of the leader.

This discussion should not suggest that any one leadership style is better than any other. What is important is what fits and works within a particular culture. Successful managers in the U. S., Germany, and Japan are those individuals who have correctly diagnosed and adapted to their situations.

Relationships with Superiors and Peers

Throughout this chapter, the emphasis has been on how managers can influence the behavior of subordinates toward better performance. While this is certainly one of the manager's major roles, of equal importance are the manager's relationships with superiors and peers. The key question is how can managers influence the behavior of people they do not supervise?

The response to this question is complex and can involve many different approaches. For our purposes, we will focus on influence from personal and positional sources. *Personal* sources of influence concern interpersonal relationships with superiors and peers, or, more simply, how the manager may satisfy important needs of others such that improved interpersonal relations result.

Drawing on motivational theories, managers should consider at least four need-satisfying behaviors. First, the manager can get work done or help a superior or peer solve a difficult problem. This not only establishes the manager as a dependable person, but also satisfies certain *physiological/safety needs* of the other person. Second, the manager can get to know the superior or peer, in both formal and informal activities, resulting in the satisfaction of *social needs*. Third, the manager can treat the other person with respect, which can raise the person's *esteem need* satisfaction. Finally, by observing and interacting with superiors and peers, the manager can learn effective behaviors. This activity will help in satisfying the other person's *self-actualization needs*.

A manager can also influence the behaviors of superiors and peers because of the importance of his or her *position* in the organization. This positional influence can originate from at least three sources: controlling uncertainty, substitutability, and centrality.[21]

No one likes to be taken by surprise, including managers. Surprise (i.e., *uncertainties*) can create disruptions, confusion, and lower performance. If a manager can control the effects of uncertain events so that they do not affect others, he or she can be accorded a significant level of influence. Examples include the maintenance manager who can prevent costly plant shutdowns through an effective preventative maintenance system, the market research or planning manager who can successfully detect and monitor environmental events, and the manager in personnel or the legal department who can shield line managers from constant governmental intervention.

Another source of positional influence is the lack of *substitutability*—that is, the manager controls activities or resources that no one else in the organization can. In such situations, the manager can have a tremendous effect on the performance of other units. For example, purchasing managers control the purchase of raw materials and equipment for a manufacturing plant, and the director of the x-ray unit in a hospital has control over this much-needed diagnostic activity. The x-ray unit director can affect the activities of physicians, nurses, and even the accounting department.

The final source of positional influence concerns the degree to which the manager's activities are interlinked into the organization. This *centrality* relates to how important the manager is in producing the products and services of the organization. The more central the activity, the greater the level of influence. For example, a hospital cannot operate for long without nurses, nor can a manufacturer of pocket calculators function without computer chips.

Keys to Success with Superior/Peer Relationships. A number of guidelines for success can be developed from the experiences of managers in all types of organizations in relationships with superiors and peers. The most important include the following:

1. **There are important similarities and differences in relations with superiors and peers.**
   While the above points have applicability to relationships with both

groups, there are important differences. For example, superiors control a person's work assignments and rewards, whereas peers generally do not. Therefore, superiors must be treated with more attention. On the other hand, relations with peers are usually not clearly defined with respect to authority and responsibility. This puts a premium on good interpersonal relationships.

2. **Interact with superiors and peers frequently.**

Continued interaction with these individuals will not only affect social needs, but managers can learn others' problems and understand where they can make an impact. Frequent interaction will also improve the flow of information, which is an important part of the manager's informational roles.

3. **Build coalitions or alliances with important superiors and peers.**

Many times, managers will find themselves in situations where a combined effort is required for effective performance. Coalitions will also establish relationships for future interactions when these individuals can be counted on to be on your side. In other words, "you scratch my back, and I'll scratch yours."

4. **Be careful not to alienate an important colleague.**

Embarrassing a colleague may have short-term benefits for the manager in accomplishing a particular task: in the long-run, however, it may come back to haunt the manager. Remember that it is better to have people indebted to you, not out for your hide.

5. **There is a distinction between influence and politics.**

One of the most important, yet least understood, activities in organizations is political behavior. In our framework, managers engage in influence attempts with superiors and peers primarily to improve their personal status when politics is involved. Examples include such activities as isolating a colleague, trying to "show-up" others, establishing rules and procedures that favor your unit over your peer's, and interfering with normal communication. The manager would be well advised to concentrate on influence attempts directed at task accomplishment, not personal gratification. "Goal displacement" (personal goals over organizational goals) can eventually result in lower overall performance for everyone.

Learning to Be a Leader

Throughout this chapter, we have suggested that leadership is primarily a learned quality. Given this situation, how can the aspiring manager learn to become a more effective leader? The experience of many managers suggests that four points should be studied carefully:

1. **Learn from experience, practice, and observation.**

If leadership is primarily a learned quality, then it benefits the manager to participate in as many learning experiences as possible. Examples include mentoring (see chapter 2), practice, and observation of the behavior of other leaders. Through these and other learning experiences, the manager can develop knowledge in the important interpersonal, informational, and decisional roles performed by effective leaders.[22]

2. **Learn from continuing education and training and development programs.**

In-house or outside programs, coupled with job rotation (see chapter 10), provide an opportunity to develop many of the technical, human, conceptual, and diagnostic skills required of a leader.

3. **Learn from subordinates.**

For too long, management scholars assumed that the influence process in leadership was one-way—from the leader to the subordinate. In reality, the influence process is two-way; subordinates can significantly influence the behavior of the leader.[23] The use of punishment is a clear-cut situation in which the behavior of the subordinate influences what the leader does. There are at least two ways the manager can learn from subordinates. First, make note of what behaviors are effective, not only in different situations, but with different subordinates. The situational approaches have stressed this point strongly. Second, continually viewing employees from a theory X framework ignores the fact that many times subordinates are equally, if not more, skilled in the work being performed than the manager. If given the opportunity, employees can teach the manager better ways of performing the department's work, which may lead to greater effectiveness.

4. **Know yourself.**

Many times, behavior as a manager is influenced by personal characteristics. For example, in the last chapter, we emphasized the importance of needs as energizing factors in motivation. This framework would be just as valuable a mechanism for self-analysis as it is for understanding the behavior of subordinates. A manager with high social needs—one who is seeking respect and friendship from others—may use a different style of leadership than a manager with high ego needs—one who strives for recognition and status. We will cover this point in greater detail in chapter 20.

These points are by no means all-inclusive. The key point is for the manager always to be aware of learning experiences. With today's complex environments and organizations, managers can ill afford to stand pat in their approach to leadership.

LEADERSHIP, PERFORMANCE, AND THE MANAGER'S JOB

Leadership is one of the central functions of management. It is through leadership activities that the manager assigns, motivates, directs, controls, and rewards subordinates for achieving organizational goals. Similar to motivation, leadership is a far more complex activity than most people realize. Many theories, approaches, and prescriptions have been developed about how employees will respond to different leader behaviors.

Keys to Success in Leadership

While it would be difficult to summarize all that we know (or don't know) about leadership, certain keys to success can be offered that have proven helpful to many managers:

1. **The manager must understand the strengths and limitations of his or her power base.**

   The ability to influence others is founded on the strength of the leader's power base. A leader who functions with all five power factors—legitimate, reward, coercive, expert, and referent—is in the best position to influence subordinates. Such a situation may be more ideal than real, however. Most leaders find themselves in managerial situations in which they must influence with a limited power base. For example, the head nurse in a hospital may have legitimate power, but little in the way of reward or coercive power. Similarly, the manager in a liaison or committee-head role may only have weak referent power to influence others. A good rule to follow is that when you have only limited power, try to *strengthen what you have,* and *acquire power* from other sources.[24] The head nurse may improve the situation by becoming expert in her area, while liaison managers may ask for a formal title (i.e., legitimate power) to increase their ability to influence others.

2. **Leadership effectiveness depends heavily on developing diagnostic skills.**

   The various approaches to leadership have shown that there is no one best way to lead. We know that leadership involves a complex interaction among personal, task organizational, and environmental forces and conditions. This says two things to managers: (a) they must accurately diagnose these conditions and (b) their leader behavior must be both multidimensional and flexible enough in the particular conditions in order to achieve a level of acceptable performance.

3. **A manager's style of leadership is not infinitely flexible.**

   In the last point above (and throughout the last part of the chapter), we suggested that managers should attempt to adapt their behavior to the conditions of the situation. This, however, does not suggest that successful managers can adapt to *every* situation that confronts them. The fact is that most managers have leadership styles that can be adaptable to many situations, but not *all* situations. In other words, a manager usually has a preferred *set* of behaviors that can be used—using behaviors not within this set would be difficult. For example, using the managerial grid framework, a typical manager may easily exhibit 9, 1; 9, 9; or 5, 5 styles. If a situation demands a 1, 9 or a 1, 1 style, it not only would be a problem to exhibit one of these styles (since they are not within the preferred set of behaviors), but it would be recognized by everyone that the manager was "acting strangely." Influence would, therefore, be significantly constrained. The key point is that leadership styles are fundamentally interpersonal or *human skills* that, at least partially, were shaped at an early age and have been with the manager most of his or her life.[25] By adulthood, these skills are as much as part of a person as facial features. To *radically* change these preferred styles or behaviors would be as troublesome as continually agonizing over them. Training and experience can help managers expand their sets of behaviors. It is, however, improbable that a manager can exhibit a total range of styles. Stated differently, it is probably as incorrect to believe in a "one best way" as it is to think that a manager can be "all things to all people."

4. **Leader behavior includes both style and reward components.**
Over the years, the practitioner literature and the formats for various managerial training programs have emphasized the study of a manager's leadership style. As we have seen, style is an important part of the influence process. It does not, however, totally define all leader behaviors available to the manager (see exhibit 13-7). Leader style involves a number of activities, from task assignment to task accomplishment. From the previous chapter, however, we know that what comes *after* task accomplishment—rewards—is equally, if not more, important to future subordinate motivation. In other words, the manager must think of leader behavior in terms of *both* style and reward activities.

5. **The manager and his or her subordinates are a team.**
The manager/subordinate unit establishes the organization's most basic mechanism for goal achievement. In recognizing that they are members of an important team, subordinates will accept the leader's influence attempts when it will lead to valued rewards. The key aspect for managers to remember is that there is a major difference between influence and manipulation. Both may lead to goal achievement in the short run: in the long run, continued manipulation will destroy the team concept, and hence, lead to performance problems.[26]

6. **The manager should look at each task, project, or position as a new learning experience.**
The manager or future manager should view new activities and experiences for their long-term learning impact, not so much from the perspective of the short-term problems that must be faced. Most managers can recall as many boring and routine assignments in their careers as assignments that were challenging and exciting. It is a rare manager, however, who would say that he or she didn't learn something useful from both assignments. The key is this: don't go into a new job with a preconceived notion about what you will face and how you will react—keep an open mind and be willing to adapt, because this is when the greatest learning occurs.[27]

Leadership and the Manager's Job

Managerial skills and roles play an important part in the manager's leadership activities. In managerial *skills,* technical skills are related to many parts of the leadership process, particularly the assignment stage. Human skills are required throughout, especially in relationships with subordinates, superiors, and peers. Conceptual and diagnostic skills are highlighted in the situational approaches, where there is an emphasis on identifying the important elements of a situation and adapting one's style to it.

From a managerial *role* perspective, leadership focuses on the important interpersonal roles. Informational roles are equally important because the manager must learn how to use and transmit information through the organization. In decisional roles, the emphasis is on how managers assign and evaluate tasks and task performance, the manner in which rewards and resources are allocated, and what changes are required in the unit or the entire organization.

SUMMARY FOR THE MANAGER

1. Leadership involves the process of influencing others toward goal accomplishment. The most important aspect for managers is that leadership is an ongoing, everyday activity that involves power, desired outcomes, and other people. It should also be recognized that a person can be a leader without being a manager, and vice-versa. To be both a manager and a leader, the person needs to be given the title by the organization and must be able to influence subordinates through behavior.

2. Influence in leadership is based on the concept of power. The power to influence can originate from organizational sources (legitimate, reward, and coercive) or from the individual's particular characteristics (expert and referent). The key point is that the greater the leader's power base, the greater the capacity to influence others. Leaders who recognize that their organizationally based power is not as strong as desired may attempt to compensate by acquiring power in other areas. In most cases, leaders attempt to become expert in their fields to enhance their power bases.

3. Trait theories, which were the first real scientific analyses of leadership, sought to determine if there are any individual characteristics or traits that distinguish successful from less successful leaders. If these select traits exist, then they could be used in future managerial selections. The results suggested, albeit weakly, that successful leaders are more intelligent and decisive, report higher achievement and self-actualization needs, and have good communication skills. These results, however, were not consistent across different organizations, which decreased the importance of trait theories in the study and practice of leadership.

4. Behavioral theories came after the trait approach, and emphasized what the leader does in a leadership situation—leadership style. While at first the one best leadership style was sought, it became clear that no such style exists. For the manager, the behavioral approach made three important contributions: (a) leadership style is multidimensional; (b) style is flexible; and (c) styles of leadership are learned behaviors.

5. Fiedler's contingency model, the first of the situational approaches to leadership, analyzed the relationship between leadership style and three situational factors: task structure; leader-member relations; and position power of the leader. Task-oriented style was suggested as more appropriate when the situation is either good or poor, while employee-oriented style is best when the situation is only moderately good for the leader. Fiedler's suggestion that a manager's leadership style is both unidimensional and rigid subtracted from the usefulness of the theory.

6. The path-goal theory, based on the expectancy theory of motivation, was a more complex framework to study the interactions between the leader, the subordinate, and the situation. It is important for managers to understand that one of the main functions of the leader is to motivate subordinates. Path-goal theory suggested that if the leader, through style, can remove some of the barriers to motivation, enhanced performance will result.

7. Culture is an important consideration in leadership. Across a number of countries, there are more similarities than differences in what motivates managers. In particular, higher-level needs (ego and self-actualization) are more important contributors to managerial motivation than the lower-level needs (social and safety/security).

8. Relationships with superiors and peers require influence attempts by managers. Two approaches are most widely used: personal (interpersonal relationships with others that result in satisfying an important need of the other person), and positional (controlling uncertainty, substitutability, and the centrality or importance of the position).

9. Effectiveness as a leader depends on the ability of the manager to learn new skills and roles from a variety of sources, including experience, practice, observation, training programs, subordinate activities, and self-knowledge. Since managers can learn from exciting jobs as well as boring ones, they must keep an open mind and be adaptable.

QUESTIONS FOR REVIEW AND DISCUSSION

1. Discuss the relationship between power and influence.
2. Under what conditions can the behavior of an informal leader be dysfunctional to the organization?
3. Why was trait theory unsuccessful in predicting leadership effectiveness?
4. What is the relationship between the style dimensions of task and employee orientation and McGregor's theory X and theory Y?

5. According to Fiedler, how can the organization engineer the job to fit the manager?

6. Is a manager's leadership style flexible or rigid?

7. How does mentoring relate to learning to be a leader?

8. Besides the leader's behavior, what organizational factors can have a significant influence on the employee's performance?

9. Why must one study the leader's reward behavior in any analysis of leadership?

10. Why is it important for the manager to develop good diagnostic skills in order to become an effective leader?

NOTES

1. R. M. Stogdill, *Handbook of Leadership* (New York: Free Press, 1974).

2. J. R. P. French and B. Raven, "The Bases of Social Power," in *Group Dynamics,* 2nd ed., D. Cartwright and A. F. Zander (Evanston, Ill.: Peterson, 1960), pp. 607–23.

3. A. D. Szilagyi and M. Wallace, *Organizational Behavior and Performance,* 2nd ed. (Santa Monica, Calif.: Goodyear, 1980), p. 275.

4. Tom Wolfe, *The Right Stuff* (New York: Farrer-Strauss-Giroux, 1979), p. 24.

5. See R. M. Stogdill, "Personal Factors Associated with Leadership: A Survey of the Literature," *Journal of Applied Psychology* (January 1948): 35–71; and Stogdill, *Handbook of Leadership,* pp. 74–75.

6. C. G. Burck, "A Group Profile of the Fortune 500 Chief Executive," *Fortune* (May 1976): 172–77.

7. E. E. Ghiselli, *Explorations in Managerial Talent* (Pacific Palisades, Calif.: Goodyear, 1971), p. 165.

8. E. A. Fleishman, "Twenty Years of Consideration and Structure," in *Current Developments in the Study of Leadership,"* E. A. Fleishman and J. G. Hunt, eds. (Carbondale, Ill.: Southern Illinois University Press, 1973), pp. 1–37.

9. See R. J. House, A. C. Filley, and S. Kerr, "Relation of Leader Consideration and Initiating Structure to R and D Subordinates' Satisfaction," *Administrative Science Quarterly* (March 1971): 19–30; and A. K. Korman, "Consideration, Initiating Structure, and Organizational Criteria—A Review," *Personnel Psychology* (Winter 1976): 349–61.

10. R. Likert, *The Human Organization* (New York: McGraw-Hill, 1976).

11. R. R. Blake and J. S. Mouton, *The New Managerial Grid* (Houston: Gulf Publishing, 1978), p. 11.

12. R. Tannenbaum and W. H. Schmidt, "How to Choose a Leadership Pattern," *Harvard Business Review* (May–June 1973): 162–80.

13. F. Fiedler, *A Theory of Leadership Effectiveness* (New York: McGraw-Hill, 1967).

14. See G. Graen, J. B. Orris, and K. W. Alvares, "Contingency Model of Leadership Effectiveness: Some Experimental Results," *Journal of Applied Psychology* (June 1971): 196–201; and J. T. McMahon, "The Contingency Theory: Logic and Method Revisited," *Personnel Psychology* (December 1972): 697–710.

15. See J. Stinson and L. Tracy, "Some Disturbing Characteristics of the LPC Score," *Personnel Psychology* (1974): 477–85; and R. Vecchio, "An Empirical Examination of the Validity of Fiedler's Model," *Organizational Behavior and Human Performance* (June 1977): 180–206.

16. See R. J. House, "A Path-Goal Theory of Leader Effectiveness," *Administrative Science Quarterly* (1971): 321–32; and M. G. Evans, "The Effects of Supervisory Behavior on the Path-Goal Relationship," *Organizational Behavior and Human Performance* (May 1970): 277–98.

17. See R. J. House and T. R. Mitchell, "Path-Goal Theory of Leadership," *Journal of Contemporary Business* (Autumn 1974): 81–98; and A. D. Szilagyi and H. P. Sims, "An Exploration of the Path-Goal Theory of Leadership in a Health Care Environment," *Academy of Management Journal* (December 1974): 622–34.

18. S. Kerr, "Toward a Contingency Theory of Leadership Based Upon Consideration and Initiating Structure Literature," *Organizational Behavior and Human Performance* (1974): 62–82.

19. House and Mitchell, "Path-Goal Theory of Leadership."

20. B. M. Bass and P. C. Burger, *Assessment of Managers—An International Comparison* (New York: Free Press, 1979).

21. D. J. Hickson, D. S. Pugh, and D. C. Pheysey, "A Strategic Contingencies Theory of Intra-organizational Power," *Administrative Science Quarterly* (1971): 216–27.

22. T. Levitt, "The Managerial Merry-Go-Round," *Harvard Business Review* (July–August 1974): 120–28.

23. See C. N. Greene, "The Reciprocal Nature of Influence Between Leader and Subordinate Performance," *Journal of Applied Psychology* (April 1975): 187–93; and A. Lowin and J. Craig, "The Influence of Level of Performance on Managerial Style," *Organizational Behavior and Human Performance* (1968): 440–58.

24. J. P. Kotter, "Power, Dependence, and Effective Management," *Harvard Business Review* (July–August 1979): 125–36.

25. C. Argyris, "Leadership, Learning, and Changing the Status Quo," *Organizational Dynamics* (Winter 1976): 29–43.

26. N. C. Hill, *Increasing Managerial Effectiveness* (Reading, Mass.: Addison-Wesley, 1979), pp. 84–100.

27. Argyris, "Leadership, Learning, and Effective Management," pp. 32–34.

ADDITIONAL REFERENCES

Bartol, K. M. "The Sex Structuring of Organizations: A Search for Possible Clues," *Academy of Management Review,* October 1978, pp. 805–15.

Fiedler, F. E. "The Leadership Game: Matching the Man to the Situation." *Organizational Dynamics,* Winter 1976, pp. 6–16.

Greiner, L. E. "What Managers Think of Participative Leadership." *Harvard Business Review,* May–June 1973, pp. 111–18.

Hunt, J. G. and Larson, L. L., eds. *Leadership: The Cutting Edge.* Carbondale, Ill.: Southern Illinois Press, 1977.

Jay, A. *Management and Machiavelli.* New York: Holt, Rinehart and Winston, 1967.

Kotter, J. P. "Power, Success, and Organizational Effec-tiveness." *Organizational Dynamics,* Winter 1978, pp. 26–40.

McClelland, D. C. and Burnham, D. H. "Power Is the Great Motivator." *Harvard Business Review,* March–April 1976, pp. 100–10.

Salancik, G. R. and Pfeffer, J. "Who Gets Power—And How They Hold on to It: A Strategic-Contingency Model of Power." *Organizational Dynamics,* Winter 1977, pp. 2–21.

Vroom, V. H. "Can Leaders Learn to Lead?" *Organizational Dynamics,* Winter 1976, pp. 17–28.

Yukl, G. A. "Toward a Behavioral Theory of Leadership." *Organizational Behavior and Human Performance,* 1971, pp. 414–40.

A CASE FOR ANALYSIS

The Computer Software Department

Jill Prince is manager of software systems for a large international manufacturer of plastic products. Jill's department consists of eighteen computer programmers and systems analysts responsible for developing computer application systems (i.e., payroll, accounting, and financial systems) for the corporation's many divisions. All of Jill's subordinates are college degreed and classified as professional. Jill has undergraduate and graduate degrees in computer science and has been with the company for over six years.

It was almost 7 p.m. on a Friday evening in late December, nearly two hours past her usual time to go home. In her office, she sat looking out the window with a very concerned look, trying to piece together what had happened over the past two months. She kept trying to understand why the performance of her unit had dropped off so dramatically during this time.

Her first thoughts recalled a three-day management training seminar she attended, sponsored by the company, but led by a well-known behavioral consultant. The most vivid experience involved a session on leadership style where she completed a self-report questionnaire that was supposed to measure her style of leadership on two dimensions: task orientation and employee orientation. The results—she scored high on task orientation but very low on employee orientation—were a surprise to her. She had always thought of herself as very people oriented with her subordinates. She remembered that the seminar leader suggested that the most effective leadership style was one that was high on both task and employee orientation.

The timing of the leadership seminar was of particular importance to Jill due to the problems she was having with a number of people in her department. The busy year-end season was at hand, which meant a big push by the divisions to have new analyses programs on-line. Many of her problems centered on the performance of her subordinates. She felt that she could divide her people almost equally into two groups: those who consistently performed above standard, and those whose work was usually late and/or done poorly.

She looked at two subordinates as illustrative of the behaviors of the two groups. First, there was Jack Domec, who had worked as a systems analyst for the past three years. Jack was dependable, quality conscious, and one Jill could count on to put out 110 percent effort if needed. On the other hand, there was Art Roman, a computer programmer who had been working a little over two years. In Jill's opinion, Art spent too much time goofing off when work needed to be done, was overly concerned with socializing with fellow workers over coffee, and was usually the first one out the door at quitting time each day. Because Art's performance rarely reached standard, Jill warned him many times about his performance and the effect on his yearly evaluation and potential for advancement. These warnings usually had an effect on him for a few days, but his old habits returned.

The management training convinced Jill that what she needed to do to improve the performance of people like Art was to increase her employee-oriented behavior toward them—in other words, to conform to the ideal of being high on both leader style dimensions. As a result, she made a special effort to be more open and friendly to people like Art, to take more interest in their personal lives, and to try to be more sympathetic about the constant pressures for more work out of the department.

As Jill sat looking out the window, she was both upset and puzzled. Her attempt at being more employee oriented was a flop. Not only had Art's performance not changed, but many high-performing subordinates, including Jack, were showing dramatic drops in their quality and quantity of performance. The drop in performance couldn't have come at a worse time. Her direct supervisor, and many of her divisional contacts, were on her back to improve her unit's performance. She sat there wondering what to do next.

Questions for Discussion

1. Evaluate Jill's experience at the management training program.
2. Why was her attempt to be more employee oriented a failure?
3. What change in Jill's behavior is needed to improve the performance of the unit?

EXPERIENTIAL EXERCISE

Situational Factors and Leadership Styles

Purpose

1. To examine the relationship between leadership styles and situational factors.
2. To further develop diagnostic skills.

Required Understanding

The student should have a basic understanding of the behavioral and situational approaches to the study of leadership.

How to Set Up the Exercise

The exercise can be conducted with students in groups, or with students individually making the necessary decisions.

Instructions for the Exercise

Six different situations are given on the next page. Put yourself in the position of the manager described in the situation. Using the five leadership styles shown in the grid, choose that style (or styles) of leadership that you believe will lead to improved or continued high *performance* by the manager's subordinates. The decisions should then be discussed by the entire class.

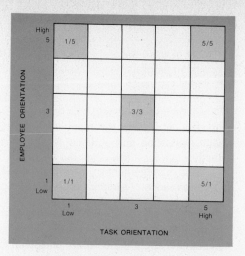

1. *Situation 1:* Jane Holman is the head nurse on the late night shift in the trauma ward (emergency room) of a large metropolitan hospital. It's Friday night, about 11:30 p.m., and not only are all treatment rooms full, but there are two ambulances arriving shortly with seriously ill or injured patients. How can she influence her subordinate nurses to perform at high levels? *Style* _____

2. *Situation 2:* As an auditing group leader for a medium-sized accounting firm, Bill Taylor supervises six staff accountants. Two new employees, recently graduated from well-known universities, are joining the group tomorrow. Neither of the new accountants has worked fulltime in an accounting firm. What style of leadership should he use with the new employees during their first few weeks on the job? *Style* _____

3. *Situation 3:* Paul Polaski, superintendent of maintenance for a large chemical plant, is about to have a meeting with his maintenance supervisors. He wants to pass on information from a recently completed quarterly report which shows that maintenance expenses are not only running 30 percent over budget, but only one out of three projects is being finished on schedule. He wants to get to the heart of the problem (or problems) quickly, so that any remedies can be instituted as fast as possible. What style of leadership should he exhibit at the meeting? *Style* _____

4. *Situation 4:* Janice Edwards is the political campaign manager for a congressional representative who is up for reelection. The election is five weeks away and the race is considered a toss-up by a number of pollsters. What style of leadership should she exhibit during the remainder of the campaign to get the volunteer workers to perform at higher levels? *Style* _____

5. *Situation 5:* As director of research for a large international electronics firm, Dr. Aubrey Holloway is about to meet with his four project directors to discuss next year's budget. He knows that each director will be asking for more money and manpower to conduct expanded projects. He also knows from his recent meeting at the home office that his unit has been allocated essentially the same level of resources as this year. In what manner should he behave in the meeting—what style of leadership—in order to maintain his unit's high performance? *Style* _____

6. *Situation 6:* Harry Thompson is the loan officer for a small savings and loan association in Florida. The association is a highly centralized organization with essentially all power to make decisions—major loan approvals, merit pay increases, organizational policies—residing with the association's president. Harry's group has exhibited a declining level of performance along with an increase in employee turnover. Harry doesn't see a dramatic change in this centralized power situation. How can he lead or influence his subordinates to higher levels of performance? *Style* _____

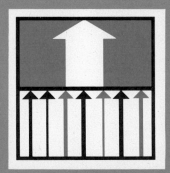

14

Managing Groups

CHAPTER OUTLINE

KEY POINTS IN THIS CHAPTER

1. Groups exist in a variety of types and for a number of purposes in organizations. Since the manager spends a great deal of his or her time in some form of group activities, a good knowledge of group behavior is necessary for improved performance.

2. Groups develop in stages; the early stages focus on learning to perform, while the latter stages actually concern performance activities. Groups can revert back to an earlier stage for a variety of reasons.

3. Group norms—behavioral and performance norms—not only can influence the level of performance, but nonadherence to norms can mean rejection by the group for a member or members.

4. Status systems exist in all types of groups. It is the concept of status congruence, however, that is important to managers because it strongly affects group performance.

5. Lack of clarity of one's responsibilities in a group (role ambiguity), and multiple demands on a member (role conflict) can adversely influence the level of group performance.

6. Group solidarity, or cohesiveness, is a significant determinant of group performance. Groups that are highly cohesive and set high performance norms usually perform at high levels.

7. The uses of groups in organizations include the typical superior-subordinate group, committees and task forces, decision-making groups, the group manager concept, and venture groups.

8. With respect to the manager's job: group behavior relates to the leading function; effective group activities involve all the managerial skills, especially human and diagnostic skills; and leading, transmitting information, and making allocation (resource) decisions concern the concept of managerial roles.

THE PRACTICE OF MANAGEMENT

Group Decision-Making at Yellow Freight Lines

Consensus is defined as agreement by all parties involved in some decision or action; it occurs only after deliberation and discussion of the pros and cons of the issues, and when many of the group members are in agreement. In other words, each member must be satisfied as to the ultimate course of action to be taken.

Decision making by group consensus has been practiced at Yellow Freight Lines since the present management assumed control of the company in the early 1950s. Consensus decisions at Yellow Freight can be illustrated by the following examples:

1. Company officers and division managers decide jointly each year the goals and plans for the company during the coming year.

2. When deciding on the opening of a new terminal, the division manager seeks opinions from at least the regional and branch managers. At issue is whether there are sufficient data available that indicate the existence of significant consumer demand.

3. Personnel promotions and lateral employee moves at all levels of the company involve consensus decisions. When a new branch manager, for example, is being selected, the president and the vice president of sales and operations generally get involved.

4. When a new account is obtained, the branch manager involves several people in the decision-making process. In deciding how this account should be handled, the branch manager involves the salesperson, the dispatcher, and the operations manager in all aspects of the new account.

When dock foremen and dispatchers are working with nonmanagement groups, it is not always possible or practical to strive for decision making by consensus. However, they can allow union employees to participate in the implementation measures relating to the decision. For example, a dock foreman can utilize participative management. If a terminal wants to increase its load average by 500 pounds, the foreman can involve his crew; since the dock workers will actually be loading the trailers, they probably will have a number of suggestions about how to increase the load average.

Effective work groups of supervisors and subordinates should be able to make good decisions through participation and to reach decisions on a consensus basis. Managers and employees are committed to decisions when they have helped make decisions. Managers must make every effort to establish effective work groups at the top organizational levels; once these groups have been established, others can be set up throughout the organization.

Adapted from Jack J. Holder, Jr., "Decision Making by Consensus," Business Horizons *(April 1972): 47–54.*

14

Many assume their first managerial positions expecting that much of their time will be devoted to independent thought, planning, decision making, organizing, and the like. For the vast majority, these expectations are proven false. The newly appointed manager is often amazed by the enormous amount of time and energy that is devoted to managing groups, including participating in task forces and committees. In fact, some have estimated that a manager spends as much as 50 percent of his or her time in one form of group activity or another. In this chapter, we will examine how groups fit into the manager's job.

The chapter is divided into four main sections. First, we will investigate the basic elements, functions, and types of groups. This will be followed by an important discussion of the key characteristics of groups in organizations; an understanding of these characteristics is crucial to the manager because they strongly relate to organizational performance. In the third section, we will examine the salient uses of groups in organizations; emphasis will be placed on committees, group decision-making, the group manager, and venture groups. Finally, our discussion will conclude with a presentation of the relationship between performance, groups, and the manager's job.

GROUPS IN ORGANIZATIONS

Management scholars and practicing managers have provided numerous, varied, and sometimes overlapping definitions of a group.[1] This is because these individuals are studying different aspects that are related to the same phenomena—namely, groups and the management of groups. For our purposes, we offer the following definition:

> A group is a collection of two or more individuals who are interdependent and interact with one another for the purpose of performing to achieve a common goal.

The main characteristics of this definition—goals, interaction, and performance—are critical to management effectiveness. These characteristics also distinguish a group from a collection of people attending a baseball game or waiting for a bus.

The Importance of Groups

The study of groups is important to the manager for a number of reasons. First, the group is a key element in the social order of our culture. Groups serve not only as the focal point of social life, but they provide an important source of direction to individuals for understanding social values and norms. Second, through participation in groups, individuals may satisfy important economic, status, safety, security, and friendship needs. Finally, the behavior and performance of groups provide a major mechanism for the achievement of organizational goals. Lack of group direction, a tense and stressful climate, continual conflict, and a lack of employee need satisfaction all can contribute to the performance or lack of performance of the group. Thus, the importance of groups and their strong link to performance are sufficient reasons why they should be carefully studied and understood by managers in all types of organizations.

THE MANAGER'S JOB
Fred T. Allen of Pitney Bowes, Inc.

Fred T. Allen, chairman and president of Pitney Bowes, Inc., believes in laying it on the line, especially when it comes to the firm's employees. To him, well-informed and involved employees are the most productive ones.

Among his greatest contributions have been the formation of the Council of Personnel Relations (CPR) and the company's annual jobholders reports and jobholders meetings. Both enable Pitney Bowes management and employees to voice mutual views and concerns. the CPR is a monthly forum where representatives of management and the employees meet to discuss mutual problems and opportunities. Employees air their complaints or suggestions to their council representatives, who bring them to management's attention. Management, at the same time, communicates its policies and ideas to employees.

To employees, jobholders reports and jobholders meetings are the equivalent of annual reports and meetings of shareholders. Employees receive copies of the company's annual report along with a jobholders report describing such topics as new products, new benefit programs, and an overview of pay scales. Ideas and/or problems brought out in both these groups are then used to form problem-solving task forces where the issue is discussed further.

Suggested from Stanley Modic, "Profile of a Winner," Industry Week *(October 29, 1979):* 53–55.

Types of Groups

There are at least two ways of classifying groups in organizations: by purpose and by orientation.[2] As shown in exhibit 14-1, classification by *purpose* involves three types of groups:

1. *Functional or command groups* are the most frequently occurring groups because they are specified by the structure of the organization—in other words, a combination of the chain of command and span of control identifies superior/subordinate relationships. Examples include the dean of a school of education with his or her group of administrators (i.e., department chairpersons), and the director of hospitals of a medical center with subordinate administrators at the various center hospitals.

2. *Task or project groups* relate to problem solving—employees are brought together to accomplish a specific task. For example, a divisional manager of a manufacturing company may establish a task force to study the problem of why so many customers are receiving products in damaged condition.

3. *Interest and friendship groups* are groups that develop in organizations to satisfy employee needs that are not satisfied by normal organizational means. Company baseball teams and weekend poker clubs are examples. One may even classify the beginnings of unions as this type of group because they form to present a united front to management.

EXHIBIT 14-1 Types of Groups in Organizations

GROUP TYPE	CHARACTERISTICS	EXAMPLES
Functional Groups	1. Member relationships specified by the structure of the organization. 2. Involves a superior-subordinate relationship. 3. Involves the accomplishment of ongoing tasks. 4. Generally can be considered a formal group.	1. Head nurse supported by registered nurses, practical nurses, and nurses' aides. 2. Manager of accounting supported by staff accountants, financial analysts, computer operators, and secretaries.
Task or Project Groups	1. Member relationships established for the accomplishment of a specific task. 2. Can be short-term or long-term duration. 3. Can involve superior-subordinate relationship. 4. Generally can be considered a formal group.	1. Project-planning teams. 2. Committees. 3. Special task forces.
Interest and Friendship Groups	1. Member relationships formed because of some common characteristic such as age, political beliefs, or interests. 2. Generally can be considered a formal or informal group. 3. Can have goals that are congruent or incongruent to the goals of the organization.	1. Trade unions can also be a functional group. 2. Social groups. 3. Recreation clubs.

Classifying groups by *orientation* makes the important distinctions between formal and informal groups. *Formal* groups exist in organizations to carry out the purposes and goals of the organization. Groups that are classified as functional and/or task and project groups when classified by purpose are usually considered formal groups when classified by orientation. Because of the influence of the structure of the organization, all employees belong to one or more formal organizational groups. As shown in exhibit 14-2, managers are the "linking pins" that integrate the various formal groups in the organization.

Informal groups generally are considered interest and friendship groups because employees are brought together for a common interest or because of their proximityy of interaction.[3] It is important for managers to recognize that informal groups can support *or* oppose the purposes of the organization. Recreational clubs, for example, strengthen the employees' ties with the organization. On the other hand, since there can be a strong bond among members of an informal group, they may object to or oppose the setting of high production goals by management. For example, workers on assembly lines, such as on automobile lines, often object and work against the management's goal of increasing the speed of the line.

Besides supporting the goals and policies of the organization, informal groups offer other benefits.[4] First, they can provide status and social satisfaction that members might not otherwise enjoy. In many large organizations, there is the probability that the individual employee could feel just like another anonymous "small cog in a big wheel." Within the confines of a small, informal group, however, the employee can enjoy recognition for good work or gain valued friendships. Second, informal groups can help the communication system. As discussed in chapter 11, the "grapevine," an informal group component, can improve the effectiveness of the overall communication networks.

EXHIBIT 14-2

The Linking Pin Concept of Groups

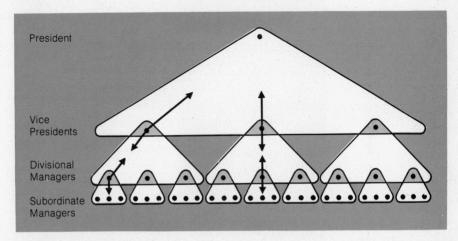

Source: Rensis Likert, New Patterns in Management *(New York: McGraw-Hill, 1961), p. 113. Used with permission.*

Some important disadvantages to informal groups can also be identified. First, as noted previously, such groups can oppose the goals of the organization, or simply resist change. Most groups develop norms, or standards of behavior, that guide the behavior of members. For example, a clerical group may develop an informal norm for dress that is more casual than the organization wants. The imposition of a formal dress code by the organization may be resisted by the informal group.

Another problem is communication systems that go awry because of the influence of informal groups. That is, there is a fine line of distinction between a "grapevine" and a "rumor mill," and the latter essentially transmits incorrect information. When employees are not well-informed on organizational matters, there is the tendency to spread false rumors that may prove damaging to the morale of the organization. For example, when pay raises are awarded, unless the organization has an open-information pay system, informal groups tend to pass on data on pay raises that significantly inflate the actual amounts.

The various types of groups in organizations have been studied by management scholars for a number of years. In the next section, we will focus on the key characteristics of groups and how these characteristics relate to performance.

GROUP CHARACTERISTICS AND PERFORMANCE

Groups in organizations, whether formal or informal, develop certain characteristics or structural components that govern the behavior of their members. These are shown in exhibit 14-3. At least five characteristics have been identified: group development stages, norms, status, roles, and cohesion.

EXHIBIT 14-3
Groups in
Organizations

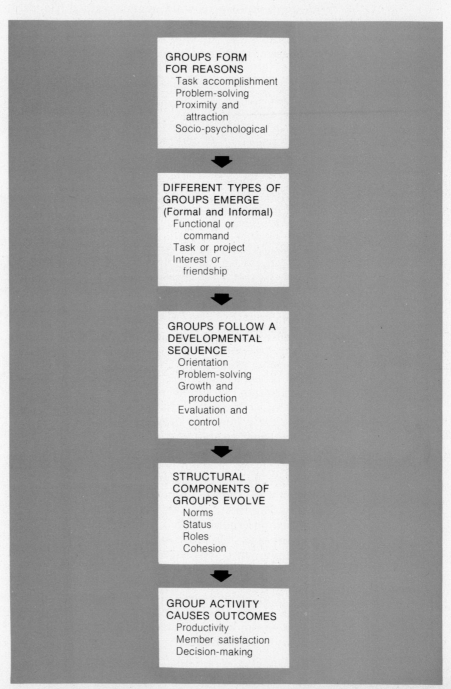

GROUPS FORM
FOR REASONS
   Task accomplishment
   Problem-solving
   Proximity and
     attraction
   Socio-psychological

DIFFERENT TYPES OF
GROUPS EMERGE
(Formal and Informal)
   Functional or
     command
   Task or project
   Interest or
     friendship

GROUPS FOLLOW A
DEVELOPMENTAL
SEQUENCE
   Orientation
   Problem-solving
   Growth and
     production
   Evaluation and
     control

STRUCTURAL
COMPONENTS OF
GROUPS EVOLVE
   Norms
   Status
   Roles
   Cohesion

GROUP ACTIVITY
CAUSES OUTCOMES
   Productivity
   Member satisfaction
   Decision-making

EXHIBIT 14-4
Stages of
Group
Development

STAGE	GROUP ACTIVITY
Orientation	1. Establishment of structure, rules, and communications networks.
	2. Clarifying relations and interdependencies among group members.
	3. Identification of leadership roles and clarification of authority and responsibility relationships.
	4. Developing a plan for goal accomplishment.
Internal Problem-Solving	1. Identification and resolution of interpersonal conflict.
	2. Further clarification of rules, goals, and structural relationships.
	3. Development of a participative climate among group members.
Growth and Productivity	1. Group activity directed toward goal accomplishment.
	2. Development of data-flow and feedback systems for task performance.
	3. Growing cohesion among members of the group.
Evaluation and Control	1. Leadership role emphasizes facilitation, feedback, and evaluation.
	2. Roles and group interdependencies are renewed, revised, and strengthened.
	3. Group exhibits strong motivation toward goal accomplishment.

Group Development Stages

The performance capacity of a group does not emerge with the group's formation, but develops over time.[5] Group members must get to know one another, they must resolve internal problems, and goals and procedures must be established before the group can devote its attention to accomplishing a task. This is the concept of group formation and development stages. While it is sometimes difficult to identify where a group is in its developmental sequence, it is important for the manager to help the group move quickly through these stages, particularly the early stages, because performance is highly dependent on what stage the group is in.

As shown in exhibit 14-4, group development usually consists of four stages: orientation, internal problem-solving, growth and productivity, and evaluation and control. As an illustration, consider the fire department of a medium-sized city that has decided to form a new arson investigation unit. The group will consist of six experienced firemen—one will be director, and the others will be investigators. This group is a formal, task or command group that has been charged with investigating the origins of fires within the confines of the city.

1. *Orientation* concerns the various activities that occur when a group gets together for the first few times. In our fire department example, this stage is such activities as establishing the structure, rules, and procedures of the group, clarifying member relations and interdependencies, and developing a plan of action. In other words, the emphasis is on who are members of the group, what it is to do, and what it needs to do it.

2. *Internal problem-solving* relates to problems that would bar goal accomplishment. Usually, the problems develop because some factors were not adequately covered in the orientation stage. For example, in the arson unit, problems could arise over who takes over when the director is out of town, how arson reports should be presented, or personality conflicts between group members.

3. *Growth and productivity* is one of the most important stages because it is at this time that many of the group's internal problems have been solved and all member activities can be devoted to accomplishing the assigned task. Member relations in the arson unit at this stage would be characterized by increased closeness, sharing of ideas and approaches, providing and receiving feedback, and exploring better ways of doing the job.

4. *Evaluation and control* concerns activities as the group approaches the conclusion of its task, or after the group has been in existence for a time. The fire department unit would be involved in such activities as review of procedures, revising, reporting, and public communication programs.

An important aspect is that a group can revert to an earlier stage at any time. A new task, a new leader, or the addition or replacement of members can be the cause. For example, a revision of the purpose of the fire department arson unit can cause it to revert back to the orientation stage. In addition, a new member with a different background or expectations can force the group back into the internal problem-solving stage. Consider what has happened over the past few years in organized baseball with the emergence of highly paid free agents. The free agent, usually a high performer with another team, is added to a new team through a lengthy bidding process. Problems have occurred—internal problem-solving—when existing team members become upset over the large salary that the free agent is receiving.

Group Norms and Norm Conformity

Steve Hightower works in the purchasing department of a large regional supermarket chain. Steve is responsible for the purchase of all food products related to breakfast consumption (e.g., cereals). As such, a great number of food product sales representatives call on him each day. With Christmas less than a week away, Steve, who has been in the purchasing department less than a year, is called into his boss's office (the purchasing agent) for a discussion.

In a straightforward but nonpunitive manner, the purchasing agent informs Steve that he is doing two things wrong on his job that he does not realize. First, he has accepted a number of Christmas gifts (e.g., a pen-and-pencil set, an ashtray, a box of cigars) from some of the sales representatives who have called on him recently. Gifts that are offered during a presentation should be refused, he is told. Gifts received through the mail will be returned. Second, while going to lunch occasionally with an important supplier is acceptable, Steve is told he should suggest going to a close-by restaurant instead of frequently going across town to a more fancy food establishment. The reason is that eating at the nearby restaurant will allow him to be back on the job sooner.

This illustration is an example of the function of *group norms* in organizations.[6] Norms are defined as *standards or rules of behavior* that are established by formal and/or informal group members to provide some *order* to individual and group activities. If individuals in a group were permitted to act, interact, or perform their functions as each saw fit, the result would be increased anxiety, stress, conflict, and chaos, along with decreased performance.

Two important aspects of group norms are types of norms and norm conformity.

Types of Norms.   There are basically two types of group norms in organizations. First are *behavioral* norms, which relate to specific behaviors of the person. For example, in the purchasing department illustration, Steve Hightower did not adhere to the behavioral norm of refusing Christmas gifts from suppliers. Since this norm is also a formal rule of the organization, there is added impact.

The second type of group norm is the *performance* norm. In Steve's case, by taking long lunches, he was not in his office performing his assigned work. The key aspect of performance norms is their relation to the productivity of the group.

It should be understood by managers that group norms can either support or oppose the purpose or goals of the organization. In Steve's situation, the established norms were congruent with the organization's purpose, since they emphasized both high productivity and ethical behavior. On the other hand, if buyers were permitted both to accept gifts and take lengthy lunch breaks, then the performance of the group and the organization might suffer. It thus is an important activity of the manager to understand the norms of the group and to evaluate their contribution to the organization. The manager can do little to stop the formation of norms—such qualities have existed in different societies for centuries. The manager, however, can alter certain norms—through direct orders or within a participative environment—that are deemed unproductive.

Norm Conformity.   Group norms, whether congruent or incongruent with the goals of the organization, are a powerful influence on members' behaviors. In essence, to be considered a member of a group, one must follow and adhere to the established norms. This *norm conformity* is important for managers to understand, because group members will attempt to enforce adherence to group norms on nonadhering members.[7]

For example, consider a group of workers responsible for the total assembly of a pocket transistor radio. Through lengthy interaction, group members have established an informal performance norm that they will assemble no more than eighteen units per hour. The group established this norm because it provided a level of productivity that was acceptable to the organization and did not push the group members to work so hard as to be fatigued at the end of a typical day.

A new worker is added to the group and immediately begins assembling at the rate of twenty-five units per hour. Since this behavior is contrary to the group performance norms, how will the group react? Generally, a three-phase reaction will be shown. First, select group members (usually the informal leader) will inform the new member of the norms of the group and suggest that they be followed. If this comment is ignored by the new employee, the reactions of the group become less friendly. They may speak quite directly and forcefully to him, indicating what he is doing wrong, or in isolated situations attempt to sabotage his work. Finally, if the above two behaviors do not work, the individual is ostracized—no one will talk to him, eat at the same lunch table, help him fix a flat tire on his car, and so on.

Such activities are not uncommon in many positions in organizations. It is incumbent on the manager not only to recognize when such a situation is occurring, but to understand whether or not the enforced group norm is actually beneficial to the organization.

Status Systems

Status is a social ranking within a group, and it is given to persons because of their positions in the organization or important individual traits. Status can be a function of the title of the individual, wage or salary level, mobility, seniority or expertise.

By far the most important factor is job title. A plant manager holds greater status than a supervisor. Likewise, the supervisor has greater status than a machine operator. Another important factor is seniority and/or expertise. For example, the oldest nurse in a pediatric ward may enjoy higher status in her group because of age, tenure, or expertise.

Like norms, status systems have positive and negative aspects. The positive aspects are the clarification of relationships, authority, and responsibility. On the other hand, an overemphasis on status can reduce both the frequency of interaction among members and their level of communication.

Status systems have a direct influence on group performance through the concept of *status congruence*, which is the agreement among group members on the level of status accorded to each member. When there is full and clear agreement on status levels (status congruence), the group can spend its time concentrating on task accomplishment. However, when there is disagreement on status levels (status incongruence), some group activity is diverted from task accomplishment and directed toward resolving the conflict.

As an illustration, consider a branch manager of a savings and loan association who attends a week-long training seminar out of state. The manager assumes, through the authority and status system, that the assistant branch manager will take over the responsibilities of running the branch. However, the head teller believes that because he has been with the branch longer than the assistant branch manager (ten years compared to six months), he should take charge in the manager's absence. Imagine the resulting performance of the branch personnel with two people giving conflicting orders. The branch manager may have to return early to try to salvage the organization!

Groups and Member Roles

In chapter 2, we introduced the concept of roles when we discussed the main managerial roles—interpersonal, informational, and decisional. In essence, everyone in an organization, and in a group, has a role or roles that he or she must perform. The administrator of a hospital is expected to organize and manage the overall operations of the hospital; the director of nursing is expected to oversee the total activities associated with the nursing function; while the head nurse in the intensive care unit is expected to organize and manage the activities of that important unit.

Managers need to understand two key characteristics of roles in groups: sources of roles, and the existence of multiple roles.[8] First, with regard to sources, there are a number of *sources* in organizations that formulate an employee's role, be he or she a manager or nonmanager. These include the considerations of the organization (e.g., job descriptions), the group (e.g., group norms), and the individual (e.g., expectations based on values and attitudes). For example, a newly hired computer programmer in a bank develops an understanding of his role from job descriptions and communication with superiors (organizational sources), from observing and talking to colleagues as he works (group norm sources), and from his own perceptions about the work, perceptions which have developed from educational training and his value systems (individual sources).

The second key characteristic of roles is *multiple roles*—the fact that most people perform many roles during a typical day. For example, the owner of a small suburban hardware store may be the principal manager of the store, along with being the president of the local chamber of commerce and co-chairperson of the area United Appeal. Of course, there are important family roles that this person must also play. The more involved the person's work, the more complex the person's *role set*.

These two characteristics of roles give rise to two major role problems in organizations.[9] These role problems are important for managers because they have a direct impact on the performance of the individual and hence, the group. First, when the person's role is unclear, due to lack of clarity from the sources of roles, a state of *role ambiguity* is created. If a manager is experiencing role ambiguity, he is unsure and/or unclear what he should do, what is expected of him by the group and organization, and so on. For example, consider the dilemma that many professionals— engineers, accountants, and medical personnel—face when they move into managerial positions. An engineer may be highly trained and experienced in the design of electrical circuitry for computers, but this may not prepare him to perform adequately as manager of the Circuit Design Department. He may come to the recognition early that there is an important difference between being a technical/professional person and being a manager. Because of this lack of clarity, this engineer functions in a state of role ambiguity, which may result in both lower performance and satisfaction for the person and the group.

The second role problem is the situation in which there are multiple roles and/or role sources that conflict. This is *role conflict*. Consider the case of production supervisor in a plant manufacturing fertilizers. How would you react if, on any given day, the following happened to you in this position? (1) The production manager wants you to increase production to 98 percent of rated capacity; (2) the maintenance supervisor wants you to shut the plant down for thirty-six hours to repair a poorly functioning piece of equipment; (3) the quality control manager informs you that during the past three days, quality rejects of batched product have increased 20 percent; and (4) a product manager calls and wants you to switch the plant's production to manufacture a special grade of product for a good customer as quick as you can. Where can you turn and what should you do first? Needless to say, if this situation was allowed to continue, it would be detrimental to the unit's performance and the supervisor's morale.

What can managers do if they recognize either of these role problems? For role ambiguity, the resolution may be as simple as asking for a clarification of one's role, or as complex as added managerial training for the newly appointed computer design manager. In the case of role conflict, a quick solution would be to appeal to a higher authority (see chapter 8). In the production supervisor's situation, he should immediately go to his direct manager (the production manager) and ask for direction. In the case of matrix designs (see chapter 9), however, such conflict is built into the relationship because of the dual-authority system. Resolution, therefore, may not be that easy.

Role problems are common occurrences in many organizations. The important aspect for managers to consider is that high levels of either role ambiguity or role conflict will lead to performance and morale problems among group members. It is, therefore, important for the manager to recognize these problems, their causes, and the possible solutions.

Group Cohesiveness

Each one of us at one time or another has observed or participated in groups that possessed a degree of closeness or solidarity that made working with the group a pleasure. This closeness, termed *group cohesiveness,* is a structural characteristic where the factors acting on group members to remain and participate in the group are greater than those acting on members to leave it.[10]

Group cohesiveness presents at least two important implications for managers. First, cohesiveness is an important indicator of the degree of *influence* the group as a whole has on individual members—the greater the cohesiveness, the greater the group's influence on members. This is because highly cohesive groups generally have adopted strong behavioral and performance norms. Group members are not likely to violate the norms of the group to which they are strongly attached.

Second, highly cohesive groups are usually characterized by good feeling among members and an absence of tension, hostility, and major conflicts. For this reason, highly cohesive groups are potentially better performers than noncohesive groups. We will discuss this point further at the end of this section.

If we initially assume that group cohesiveness is a positive factor that can lead to improved performance, then it is important for managers to understand what they can do to increase a group's cohesiveness. The manager should consider at least five different mechanisms or strategies. As an example, examine the propulsion group in mission control for NASA's space shuttle program.

1. *Group goal achievement.* If the group agrees on the purpose and direction of its activities (i.e., to monitor, direct, and advise on the propulsion systems of the shuttle), this binds the group together for better performance.

2. *Frequency of interaction.* When group members have the opportunity to interact frequently with each other, the probability for cohesion to develop will increase. For the shuttle group, the group manager may want to schedule a number of meetings (formal and informal), and possibly, physically design the office layout so that offices are close together.[11]

3. *Personal attractiveness and dependence.* Cohesiveness is increased when members are attracted to one another, creating a state of mutual trust

and support. This can be accomplished by adding members who get along well with other people, and who have the expertise to perform at high levels. What the group stands for and what it does—its norms, friendship bonds, communication networks—are bonds that attract the individual to the group.

4. *Evaluation as a group.* While it is important that individual performance be evaluated and rewarded (see chapter 12), cohesion can be increased by evaluating the group as a whole. NASA and other decentralized management structures in many organizations have used this technique to draw attention to the group as an important unit. It also is a mechanism that brings the group together to achieve a common purpose.

5. *Group prestige and status.* Cohesion can increase by according the group some prestige or status—in other words, aspects that make existing group members feel good that they are members and that cause other employees to want to become members. This can be done by openly recognizing the excellent performance of the group, frequently rewarding or promoting group members, stressing the important skills and abilities required for group membership, or allowing great independence of action among group members. During the Mercury, Gemini, and Apollo manned spacecraft programs, NASA began an extensive program of giving achievement awards to groups for outstanding performance. Such awards create prestige, which further strengthens cohesiveness and supports continued outstanding performance.

EXHIBIT 14-5
Norms, Cohesion
and Group
Performance

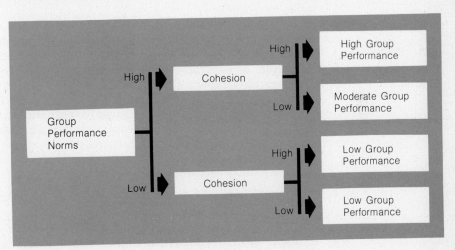

Group Cohesiveness and Performance.   Even though we have suggested that the manager should be aware of the positive relationship between cohesiveness and group performance, our examination would be incomplete without also looking at the influence of group norms. That is, because group members highly value the membership in a cohesive group, we would expect that the individual would be more responsive to the demands and norms of the cohesive group. If this assumption is correct, two things should be apparent: (1) the major difference between high and low cohesive groups would be how closely members conform to group norms; and (2) group performance would be influenced not only by cohesion, but by the type or strength of group norms.

As shown in exhibit 14-5, research has supported the assumption that group performance is a function of both norms and cohesion—that is, the highest performance levels are found in groups that are highly cohesive and maintain high performance norms. As an example, consider two highly cohesive groups of machine operators. The first group has established a high and challenging performance norm of sixty units per day for each group member. Due to the high cohesion, we would expect that group members would work hard to conform to this norm. On the other hand, the second group has set a markedly lower performance norm (i.e., forty-five units per day for each member), which also would be adhered to by the members because of the level of cohesion.

It is, therefore, important for managers to understand that cohesiveness by itself will not guarantee high performance. One must not only work to increase the group's cohesion, but also insure that group norms are at a level that contributes to the overall good of the organization.

USES OF GROUPS IN ORGANIZATIONS

Organizations have found a number of ways to use groups. The most obvious use is the superior/subordinate relationship, or the task or command group. Beyond this most frequent application, four other uses of groups have been selected for discussion here: committees, decision-making groups, the group manager, and venture groups.

Committees in Organizations

To many managers, committee membership is a symbol of status; to others, it is considered a plague. Whatever the view, being a member of a committee, or committees, is necessary for most managers. Surveys of managers have reported that (1) they are members of an average of three committees; (2) about four hours per week are spent in committee meetings, with another four hours required for preparation before the meeting; and (3) the number of committees a manager is a member of increases as one goes up the organizational hierarchy.[12]

In organizations, committees can serve one or more purposes. The most frequently identified purposes include:[13]

1. To provide managers with an opportunity to exchange information and differing views on a variety of subjects
2. To generate ideas or solutions to organizational problems
3. To make recommendations to higher-level management
4. To actually make decisions

The specific purpose of a committee depends on a number of factors. For example, the more decentralized the organization, the greater the decision-making authority that is given to a committee (see chapter 8). In a similar manner, the greater the problems of coordination between different units, the higher the probability that a committee, or committees, will be formed.

As a special form of groups, committees share many of the key characteristics inherent in group behavior. As shown in exhibit 14-6, committees can exhibit a number of important assets and liabilities.[14]

EXHIBIT 14-6
Assets and
Liabilities of
Committees and
Decision-Making
Groups

ASSETS	LIABILITIES
Greater knowledge and information	Premature decisions
More approaches to a problem	Excessive conformity to the group norms
Increased acceptance of solution	Individual domination
Better understanding and comprehension of the decision	Conflicting interests
Improved communication and cooperation	Excessive idle chatter; time and manpower commitments

Adapted from Norman R. F. Maier, "Assets and Liabilities in Group
Problem Solving," *Psychological Review* (July 1967): 239–49.

While these advantages and disadvantages are not all-inclusive, they
should be recognized by all managers as factors that can enhance or
retard the committee's performance.

Types of Committees. Committees differ in purpose, membership,
decision-making authority, and frequency of meetings. In general, four
types of committees can be identified:

1. *Task forces,* as discussed in chapter 8, are formed to deal with a specific
purpose or problem. They exist until the problem is solved, and then the
members return to their normal duties. For example, in developing a new
aircraft design, the Boeing Company, which is functionally organized,
establishes a number of task forces to facilitate the coordination of these
large projects. The task forces deal with various parts of the new plane.
For example, a wing task force has members from the design, construction, quality control, and flight-test functions. Other task forces exist for
the interior, the flight cabin, the engines, the tail section, and so on.
When the particular plane has been completed, the members return to
their original functions.

2. *Permanent committees,* sometimes called standing committees, remain
in existence to deal with a continuing organizational issue. Examples
include a curriculum development committee in a college of business, a
new product review committee in a consumer products company, or a
budget review committee in a hospital. These committees can make recommendations to higher management, or they may have the authority
to make decisions.

3. *Boards* are groups that have been given the charge of managing an
organization. They can exist in either public or private organizations,
and the members are appointed or elected. Examples include the board
of directors for a corporation, a school board, or a hospital board. The key
feature of boards is that they frequently have a great deal of decision-
making authority. Corporate boards of directors establish stock dividend
policies and capital funding programs and select high-level executives.
School boards hire superintendents, raise revenue through taxes, and
approve textbook selection procedures.

4. *Commissions* are similar to boards in that they can have broad decision-
making authority. The main difference is that the members usually are

appointed by officials to carry out administrative duties. Examples include such government commissions as the Federal Trade Commission and the Securities and Exchange Commission.

These committees differ in a number of dimensions: temporary or permanent, elected or appointed members, and advisory or decision-making authority. Another important dimension is who the committee is responsible to. Task forces and permanent committees generally are internal groups that are responsible to a higher-level manager. Boards and commissions usually have an external focus and are responsible to the public. For example, a corporate board is responsible to stockholders, a school board to the community, and a commission to the general public.

Guidelines for the Effective Committee.

In a corporate meeting room high up in the New York headquarters of International Telephone & Telegraph, a number of executives sit around a long, felt-covered table. There, from all over the world, they are reporting to Harold S. Geneen, ITT's combative, contentious chairman who sits at the center of the table.

"John," says Geneen, speaking to one of the executives, "what have you done about that problem?"

Leaning forward, John responds, "Well, I called the manager, but I couldn't get him to make a decision."

"Do you want me to call him?" is Geneen's response.

"Gosh, that's a good idea. Would you mind?"

"I'll be glad to," says Geneen. "But it will cost you your pay check."

"Never mind," says a flustered John. "I'll call him again myself."[15]

This illustration of a high-level management meeting is used not so much to suggest how a committee meeting should be run as to show the management style of one of today's most interesting executives, Harold Geneen. While we may or may not agree with his handling of this particular situation, Geneen obviously has gotten what he wants—executive action.

Because committees play an integral role in the management of organizations, it is important for managers to learn how to use committees more effectively. In this regard, we will offer three broad guidelines, corresponding to *what to do before the meeting,* the *role of the chairperson,* and the *role of the participant.*[16] The discussion will focus on committees whose purpose is to gather or exchange information, to generate solutions to organizational problems, and to make recommendations to higher-level management. The decision-making group will be the subject of the next section.

There are a number of *guidelines to follow before the committee convenes for the first time:*

1. **The purpose of the committee should be clearly defined.**
The appointing body, usually higher-level management, should insure that the committee members know what is the purpose of the group. This includes the specific charge (the goals), the level of authority (e.g., how far the committee can go in gathering information), and the time frame (e.g., when the committee is to finish its business). Without a clearly stated purpose, the committee may spend endless hours going in circles.

2. **Give the composition of the committee close consideration.**

There's another meeting in five minutes, Ed. Did you hear me, Ed? Ed?

Any group or committee can be doomed without the right people as members. Three guidelines are important: (a) try to keep the number of members at a manageable size, usually five to seven—large-sized committees are difficult to coordinate, plus there is the increased probability of cliques; (b) make sure you have some experts on the committee who are familiar with the problem or issue; and (c) keep status differences between members at a minimum—this will facilitate information exchange and reduce chances of domination by a single person.

3. **Develop a habit of working from an agenda.**

Knowing what is to be done at each meeting of the committee will help eliminate idle chatter and keep the group on track toward goal accomplishment.

4. **Choose the meeting site carefully.**

To remove outside influences, some managers have found it useful to hold committee meetings at neutral sites, such as conference rooms away from the major activities of the organization. In addition, the meeting room should be set up so that there is face-to-face interaction among members. Since sitting next to the committee chairperson can be considered a status position, it may be a worthwhile strategy for the chairperson to rotate his or her seat around the table.

5. **Provide information on the committee's charge to the members before the meeting.**

This strategy will allow the members to become familiar with the problem before the meeting is held and will help to get the committee off on the right foot.

If there is a single key to the success of a committee, it is probably the way the committee chairperson runs the meetings. The chairperson's role involves the way committee members are handled and the particular procedures that are used. The *chairperson's role in handling committee members* involves the following guidelines:

1. **Encourage the participation of all members.**

   Since one of the major advantages of a committee system is the pooling of ideas and expertise, the committee chairperson should attempt to get everyone involved in the process. This means, for example, that one member should not be permitted to dominate the discussion, the silent types should be encouraged to participate (e.g., ask them for their opinions to get the discussion started), and status differences should not be allowed to discourage junior members from sharing their ideas.

2. **Don't compete with the committee members.**

   One easy way for the chairperson to disrupt a meeting is to state his or her opinion on a subject at the beginning of a session. When this happens, some group members may unconsciously favor your opinion for the good of the group's solidarity (i.e., cohesion), resulting in an inhibited discussion. Chairpersons should express their opinions at other times, such as during an explanation of another's point, or after all ideas have been presented.

3. **Go to the most senior people or higher-status members last.**

   Similar to the last point, this will encourage other members to participate and state their views without the adverse effect of organizational influences.

4. **Use committee experts wisely.**

   Experts not only bring valuable information to the meeting, but can act as sounding boards for newly generated ideas. When the group is moving toward a solution, watch the expert's reaction carefully. Encourage experts to speak out whether they agree or disagree with an idea.

   In a similar manner, the chairperson has an important role in the *procedures that are followed by the committee.* The most important guidelines include the following:

1. **Become knowledgeable in the committee's subject.**

   With whatever time is available, the chairperson should acquaint himself or herself with the major issues of the committee's subject and charge. This will not only allow the group to move toward successful task accomplishment much easier, but will put the chairperson in a better position when the committee's findings are presented to higher management.

2. **Keep the group's energy level high.**

   Effort should be directed to keep the committee moving and not allow it to bog down in circular discussions. Many managers have found it valuable to not only keep the number of committee meetings to a minimum, but unless absolutely necessary, to prohibit overly lengthy meetings.

3. **Avoid premature solutions.**

   Sometimes, committees can act like a runaway freight train when they believe they are near a solution. This phenomenon, sometimes called group locomotion, occurs when a group that has been floundering around on a particular problem sees a potential solution and rushes toward it.

At this time, the chairperson should bring the group to a halt by throwing out pointed questions, encouraging opposing views, or even adjourning the meeting to another day when cooler heads may prevail.

4. **Place importance on the wrap-up of the meetings.**

After each meeting, the chairperson should attempt to summarize the points or conclusions that were reached and what is expected for the next meeting. Minutes of each meeting should be prepared and follow-up discussions between meetings should be encouraged.

COMMENTS ON THE PRACTICE OF MANAGEMENT
(See p. 477)

The Practice of Management section provided an example of how one company, Yellow Freight Lines, uses group decision-making and subordinate participation in making decisions. At least two factors should be derived from this illustration. First, the different decision-making groups occur at all levels in the organization, from company president on down to the shipping supervisor. In other words, group decision-making in this organization is found not just at the managerial and executive level. Second, the various decision-making groups are formed with employees who have both an interest and some expertise in the subjects to be discussed. Decision-making in this manner can not only bring most of the important information to the members' attention, but participation in the group can develop commitment among members to the resulting decision.

Much like guidelines for the chairperson, there are *guidelines that can be suggested for committee members*. The most important include the following:

1. **State your point clearly and logically.**

All members are entitled to state their views on any issue facing the committee. For maximum impact, these views should be presented in a straightforward manner. Defend your views, but also listen to and carefully evaluate the opinions of the other members.

2. **Carefully examine each potential solution.**

Each view or potential solution should be evaluated on its merit. In order to achieve this situation, committee members should avoid win-lose situations as well as yield on a point for the sake of the harmony of the group.

3. **Try for consensus decisions, not majority votes.**

One of the most damaging procedures that can be used by groups is to take a vote on an issue. This will divide the group into opposing sides and will inhibit further interaction. Seeking a consensus will also avoid the common problem of the "I gave in to you last time, now it's my turn" approach.

With the growing complexity of today's organizations, coupled with the rapid rate of change of the external environment, it appears that organizations will continue to require the information pooling, expert evaluation, communication, and coordination benefits that can be provided by the committee structure. There are many disadvantages to the use of committees, but with proper procedures and leadership, these can be far outweighed by the advantages.

Decision-making Groups—Domestic and International

In many types of organizations, groups exist that, more than advisory capacity, have actual decision-making authority. Examples include school boards, the Civil Aeronautics Board, executive committees in corporations, and so on. In these cases, the group analyzes the problem and various alternative solutions and then makes the decision.

Benefits of Group Decision-Making.   The major benefits of group decision-making can be expressed by the following formula:[17]

$$
\begin{array}{ccccc}
\text{Group} \\
\text{Decision-Making} & = & \text{Sum of Independent} & + & \text{Assembly} & - & \text{Process} \\
\text{Effectiveness} & & \text{Individual Effort} & & \text{Effect} & & \text{Losses}
\end{array}
$$

Sum of independent individual effort is a positive feature, reflecting that there is better information when more people are involved. In other words, two heads are better than one. *Assembly effect,* a second positive feature of group decision-making, represents what some have called a "synergy" effect. In essence, the interaction of individuals with varied views can result in a decision that is better than a single individual's. In other words, "2 + 2 = 5." *Process losses* is a negative feature of group decision-making that reflects two important aspects. First, groups take more time to make a decision than does an individual. When faced with severe time constraints, many organizations prefer not to use groups. Second, there are certain motivational effects. In essence, some group members may choose to be "hidden" in the group and not be committed to the decision—a "let George do it" philosophy.

Types of Decision-Making Groups.   Three general types of decision-making groups can be found in organizations: the interacting group, and the nominal and Delphi groups that were discussed in earlier chapters. Exhibit 14-7 compares these three groups.

1. *Interacting groups* are the typical committees, where there is face-to-face interaction. Such decision-making groups are usually formed to solve a particular problem, can be highly flexible in their approach, and can generate a moderate number of possible solutions. Consensus decisions are sought, but dominance and movement toward group norm conformity can be problems. Decisions can be made relatively quickly, but can be costly in the combined amount of time by members.

2. *Nominal groups* are highly oriented toward idea generation and evaluation. They are more proactive in their orientation (i.e., forward looking), decisions can be made in a moderate amount of time, and the effects of conformity and member dominance can be reduced through procedural means. Because of the structured nature, however, there is little flexibility in the approach.

3. *Delphi groups* can only be considered pseudo groups because members do not physically interact. As a result, idea generation and evaluation is high and the effects of group conformity have been minimized. Such groups are highly inflexible, majority votes are sought, but they can be both time-consuming and costly.

EXHIBIT 14-7   Comparison of Interacting, Nominal, and Delphi Groups

DIMENSION	INTERACTING GROUPS	NOMINAL GROUPS	DELPHI GROUPS
Example	A product development task force	A group attempting to resolve intergroup conflict	A group attempting to forecast environmental events for the next ten years
Overall Methodology	Unstructured, face-face group meeting High flexibility High variability in the behavior of groups	Structured, face-face group meeting Low flexibility Low variability in the behavior of groups	Structured series of questionnaires and feedback reports Low flexibility Low variability in respondent behavior
Relative Quantity of Ideas	Moderate	High	High
Search Behavior	Reactive, sometimes short-term focus	Proactive, long-term focus	Proactive, long-term but controlled focus
Conformity	High	Moderate	Low
Equality of Participation	High chance for member dominance	Member equality in search and choice activities	Respondent equality in pooling of independent opinions
Method of Problem Solving	Individual-centered Possible win/lose, smoothing, and withdrawal	Problem-centered Confrontation	Problem-centered Majority rule
Resources Utilized	Low administrative cost and time High participant cost and time	Medium administrative cost, time, and preparation High participant cost and time	High administrative cost and time Moderate participant cost and time
Time to Obtain Group Ideas	One to five hours	Three hours to two days	Three to five months

Adapted from A. Van de Ven and Andre Delbecq, "The Effectiveness of Nominal, Delphi, and Interacting Group Decision-Making Processes," *Academy of Management Journal* (1974): 605–21.

As the exhibit indicates, each type of decision-making group has advantages and disadvantages. The manager should recognize these points when appointing these groups or participating in them.[18] Some rules may be helpful to follow: (1) Use interacting groups in attempting to solve an immediate problem that needs fairly quick solution; (2) nominal groups are good for idea generation or for resolving intergroup problems such as conflict; and (3) use Delphi groups when idea generation is desired and when the experts are physically dispersed.

Cross-Cultural Differences in Group Decision-Making

Research into cross-cultural differences has drawn the attention of many management scholars and practicing managers.

A number of points of interpretation can evolve from an analysis of this research.[19] First, as we have discussed previously, in Japan the participatory style of decision making is heavily rooted in culture and history. Japanese managers are expected to seek the opinions of others, including subordinates, in making decisions.

Second, while U. S. managers tend slightly to prefer a participatory approach to group decision-making, the strong orientation toward individualism and independence acts as a constraint to being overly participative. A key differentiating factor is that most U. S. managers are evaluated heavily on their *individual* performance, whereas when they are evaluted, Japanese managers place greater emphasis on the performance of the *team*.

Third, managers in many of the underdeveloped countries (India, Chile, and many of the African states) seem to prefer a less participatory orientation. This again indicates that these managers feel that their subordinates have little to offer, perhaps because of the low education and skill levels of workers.

Finally, research has shown that there are differences in the nature of formal and informal participation in group decision-making across cultures. For example, U. S. managers prefer to use an informal participation style rather than a formal one. On the one hand, in Germany, Sweden, and Yugoslavia, formal rules exist requiring subordinate participation in decisions, while in Israel, both formal and informal approaches are used in group decision-making.

Problems with Decision-Making Groups.   Despite the potential advantages of group over individual decision-making, a number of management scholars and practicing managers have pointed out some important disadvantages to group decision-making. Perhaps the most notable of these is the phenomenon of *groupthink* as discussed by Irving L. Janis.[20] In studying several major governmental fiascos involving high-level decisions (e.g., the Bay of Pigs incident of the Kennedy administration, the Johnson administration decision to escalate the Vietnam War, the failure to be prepared for the attack on Pearl Habor, and the stalemate of the Korean War during the Truman era), Janis concluded that group processes actually prevented effective decision-making.

Groupthink usually occurs in highly cohesive groups where the strength of the need to conform to group norms pressures group members toward consensus. One way for the manager to recognize if groupthink is occurring is to look for some of the following symptoms:

1. *Invulnerability*. Do group members develop an illusion of invulnerability that leads them to ignore obvious dangers or warnings? This may lead to becoming overly optimistic and possibly to taking unnecessary risks.

2. *Rationale*. Closely related to a feeling of invulnerability, group members develop rationalizations to discount sources of information that contradict to the group's thinking. Usually the source is discredited as unreliable.

3. *Morality*. The closeness of the group may lead to the raising of the group's moralistic level. In other words, the group members strongly believe that they are morally right in what they do.

4. *Stereotypes.* If someone external to the group doesn't go along with the group's views, he is discredited, or sometimes viewed as ignorant. The group's view is, "Who could not possibly understand the logic of the group's position."

5. *Pressure.* If any member doubts the position of the group, he is branded as subverting the welfare of the group, or even banished.

6. *Self-censorship.* Members who hold doubts about the group's views restrain themselves from expression. Janis cites several examples of individuals who regretted, after an erroneous decision by a group, not having spoken up and expressed doubts or opposite positions. This self-censorship is seen as a response to the pressure to conform to group norms.

7. *Unanimity.* Self-censorship leads to the illusion of unanimity of opinion within the group. The false assumption is that anyone who remains silent is automatically in favor of the decision.

8. *Mindguards.* Members affected by groupthink appoint themselves as "mindguards"—people who have the duty to protect the leader and other group members from adverse information about the group's position. As an example, Janis cites the instance of Attorney General Robert Kennedy warning Arthur Schlesinger not to share his doubts about the Bay of Pigs invasion with the President, because the President's mind was already made up.

If the manager recognizes some of these groupthink symptoms in his or her policy-making group, what can be done to reduce the adverse impact of this phenomenon? To illustrate some of the strategies that the manager can employ, consider a problem found by the tire and rubber companies a number of years ago. Most of the major tire companies were located in Akron, Ohio, known as the tire capital of the world. Akron was not only the site of the headquarters of these companies, but most of the manufacturing facilities were also located there, employing many thousands of workers. Rapidly decreasing profit margins—the result of antiquated equipment and costly union contracts—forced the executives of many of the companies seriously to consider moving some or all production capacity to certain southern states where newer, more cost-efficient equipment could be used and a nonunionized work force could be employed.

If you were the chairperson of a high-level policy-making group in one of the companies—a group that would make the decision on any manufacturing move out of Akron—and you recognized a number of groupthink symptoms developing in the group, the following strategies would be helpful in reducing the groupthink problem:[21]

1. **Appoint an individual to act as a critical evaluator and/or a devil's advocate.**

Since it is difficult for opposing views to be brought out in a groupthink situation, the chairperson should appoint (on a rotating basis) individual group members to act as critical evaluators during group discussions. In the tire company example, the group may move swiftly to a tentative decision to pull 50 percent of the manufacturing capacity out of Akron. A critical evaluator would be one to ask pointed questions about the economic impact on the city, possible legal implications, and so on. This may force the group to slow down and rethink its options.

2. **If the group is large enough, break it up into subgroups for discussions.**

In groups of ten or larger, it is easy for information or opinions to be withheld by members (i.e., self-censorship). Breaking up into smaller subgroups will usually create a better climate for discussion. In the example, the group chairperson could establish subgroups to investigate the following alternatives: (a) total manufacturing movement to the South; (b) partial manufacturing movement; or (c) no movement out of Akron.

3. **Seek out opinions from qualified people outside the group.**

To prevent an insulation of the group from the outside, it may be worthwhile to discuss the group's deliberations (confidentially) with trusted colleagues, or to invite external experts to the group's meetings. In this manner, new information can be gathered, which may challenge the group's position. During the Iranian and Cuban crises of 1979, President Carter brought in outside experts, such as Henry Kissinger, to present their views on the situation.

4. **Allot specific time for the group to discuss contingency plans.**

As we pointed out in chapter 6, situations arise that can make the best-laid plans obsolete. In order to alleviate the invulnerability, morality, and rationality groupthink symptoms, the chairperson should force the group to consider seriously "what if" the decision is not accepted. In the tire company example, the group should spend time discussing possible warning signals from the unions, the Akron community, the state government, and so on.

5. **Hold second-chance meetings.**

When it becomes clear that the group has made a decision, many managers have found it to be a good policy to hold "second-chance" meetings, at which time members are expected to express as vividly as they can all their residual doubts and to rethink the entire issue before making a definite choice. As stated by Alfred P. Sloan, former chairman of General Motors, "I take it we are all in complete agreement on the decision here. . . . Then I propose we postpone further discussion of this matter until our next meeting to give ourselves time to develop disagreement and perhaps gain some understanding of what the decision is all about."

Managing the effective decision-making group is not an easy task. There are many forces, both internal and external to the group, that the manager must understand and learn to adapt to. In other words, it would behoove managers to develop diagnostic skills that will enable them to adjust to the situation.

The Group Manager

John Agal is forty-two years old, prosperous, and by most measures a clear success. John, his wife, and their three children live in a large home in a suburban community, where they enjoy many of the pleasures of the good life, brought about through John's substantial income.

Even with this seemingly positive situation, John's wife has seen him become increasingly discontented, frustrated, and irritable. He complains about a lack of any sense of accomplishment, a growing sense of isolation from both his peers and subordinates, and nagging doubts about his own self-worth.

John's problem traces back to over a year ago, when he received his most recent promotion at AMT Industries, a manufacturer and distributor of a variety of industrial machinery. For five years, he was the successful divisional manager of specialty molded machinery for AMT. This performance led to his advancement to group manager of industrial products, where he has four divisional managers reporting to him. Even though he has advanced up the hierarchy, he feels he is no longer in the middle of the action. On one hand, he sees the exciting activity below him at the divisional level, and above him at the executive level. On the other hand, he is frustrated because his management role is unclear, his decision-making latitude appears to be narrower, not broader than before, and his direct authority over the divisions is questionable. He finds himself in the role of thinker, planner, and director, yet confronted with the responsibilities of a doer.

This hypothetical situation is reality to many individuals who hold what has become a popular organizational position—*the group manager.*[22] As shown in exhibit 14-8, the group manager position is the result of the growth and complexities of many of today's organizations. In its most basic form, the group manager position is created in multiproduct or multiservice organizations when it is recognized that a single executive can no longer handle the growing span of control. In response to this situation, a new layer of management is established and a group of product or divisional managers reports to the new group manager. For example, as group manager of industrial products, John Agal may have divisional managers reporting to him who are responsible for specialty machinery, numerical control equipment, food processing equipment, and industrial cleaning machinery.

Group managers usually identify three factors that can lead to feelings of frustration, stress, and lack of accomplishment. First, the group manager is neither a super-divisional manager nor a higher-level executive, but one who is sandwiched between these two organizational levels. As in John's case, the group manager position rarely carries either the *operational* decision authority of a divisional manager or the *strategic* decision authority of an executive. Thus, the group manager is neither fish nor fowl, which is frustrating for one who wishes to "run the whole show." This problem, then, is one of *role definition.*

Second, the group manager's position often lacks the mechanisms or resources to contribute much to the performance of the divisions or to the overall direction of the organization. Group managers usually have few if any staff resources of their own and too little organizational staff support to help them participate effectively in either division or corporate affairs. The end result is a group manager who really has no true "group," but a collection of rather independent subordinate managers. They find themselves as little more than administrators, consolidators of numbers, information conduits, or liaison persons (see chapter 8).

EXHIBIT 14-8
The Group
Manager Position

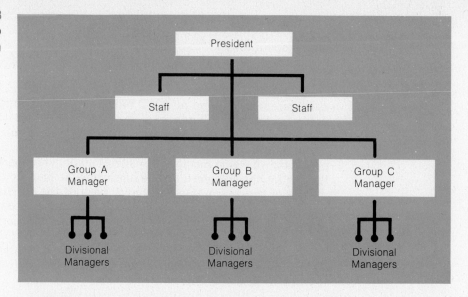

Finally, there is the issue of motivation and rewards, where a paradox exists. On one hand, the group manager's income and bonus is directly tied to the collective performance of his or her divisions. On the other hand, the group manager has little direct impact on the division's year-to-year performance. This reward paradox not only leads to concern over the stability of one's income, but questions of prestige and achievement arise when the group manager attempts to identify his or her particular contributions.

Given this all-too-frequent situation, one might argue that the group manager concept is a failure and ought to be eliminated. Unfortunately, no alternative is available for diversified organizations that require a management layer between the executive and the numerous operating divisions. Somehow these sometimes-diverse organizational activities must be grouped into a manageable number of units. Enter the group manager.

How can the group manager position be made more meaningful and useful? A number of organizations have experimented with one or all of the following concepts:

1. **Alter authority, responsibility, and power relationships.**
The first issue to attempt to change is the "person in the middle" problem. Two approaches have been tried. If the organization has adopted a centralized management philosophy, then the group manager should be given greater control over his or her divisions—in other words, create a true task group (i.e., group manager and subordinate divisional managers). In highly decentralized organizations, the group manager should be given more executive responsibility and authority for the strategic management of the divisions and major input into the total organization.

2. **Revise the reward system for the group manager.**
In a centralized structure, the group manager should be evaluated and

rewarded on the performance of the collective divisions. For the decentralized approach, the financial reward system should reinforce the group manager's top management strategic role. Compensation should be tied, not to the performance of the divisions, but to the group manager's contribution to the long-term performance of the total organization.

3. **Pick the right people for the group manager position.**

In choosing a person to be a group manager, at least three factors should be considered. First, the group manager should be an effective team player—that is, be able to work effectively with peers and staff units over which he or she may not have direct authority. Second, rather than a narrow experience profile, managers with wide industry and functional experience often make the best group managers. Finally, the group manager must have shown the skill to communicate well with the external public—stockholders, security analysts, government agencies, and the like.

Despite its faults and potential frustrations, the group manager concept will probably continue to be an integral part of the organizational world for some time to come. The basic fact is that in many diversified, multiproduct or multiservice organizations, this new layer of management is needed. For the future manager, the group manager position should be looked on not negatively, but as a challenge. It should be viewed as another opportunity to develop the skills necessary to become an effective manager. The group manager concept is also important in that it highlights the need for the person to develop a "general manager" as opposed to a "specialized manager" philosophy. We will cover this point in more depth in chapter 19.

Venture Groups

In many of today's organizations, the dynamic and shifting needs of the market are frequently constrained by the complexity, size, and bureaucracy of the organization's structure and process. In essence, the organization's activities can act as a barrier to innovation and new ways of conducting a business.

One new approach that seems partially to eliminate some of these barriers is venture management or venture groups. A *venture group* is an entrepreneurial concept that enjoys remarkable freedom from typical corporate restraints in seeking out growth opportunities and in preparing to capitalize on them.[23] Venture groups are springing up in many corporations and also in a variety of smaller, highly dynamic organizations. They are raising new problems for management, but they are also raising new opportunities for small-group planning, radical new product development, new market or service penetration, and the profitable extension of organizational capabilities in both the near and distant future.

Dow, General Electric, Monsanto, Westinghouse, Celanese, and Union Carbide are some of the many organizations in which venture groups are an established method of planning entry into new businesses. At Minnesota Mining and Manufacturing, at least two dozen ventures have been in operation at one time, and 3M reports that six of its current divisions have grown out of its venture group concept. Du Pont is also committed to the venture method, where as many as thirty to fifty new development teams can be operating at one time. And at General Mills, the venture operating philosophy has been incorporated into company structure as a New Ventures Department, which is responsible for investigating, innovating, and developing new business opportunities.

There are at least four distinguishing characteristics of venture groups.[24] First, most venture groups focus on this single, unifying goal: to plan their organization's profitable entry into a new business or service area. Second, most, if not all venture groups are formed by taking skilled experts and managers from the various functional areas of the organization and putting them under a single head. As shown earlier in exhibit 14-8, the groups generally have few members, and the manager of the group reports only to a higher-level executive. This establishes the all-important autonomy of the group.

Third, venture groups offer a number of distinct advantages to the organization. These include the following:

1. A venture group is *unidirectional*. It is chartered for a single purpose. In other words, it always knows what business it is in.

2. A venture group is *multidisciplinary*. It contains representative skills from the marketing sciences, research and development, finance, and manufacturing. It thus has an external opportunity orientation and an internal cost orientation.

3. A venture group is *eclectic*. It enjoys relative freedom in probing market and service needs that offer opportunities to the organization. Its tendency to be innovative is unimpeded by being held hostage to traditional ways of doing business.

4. A venture group is a good *management training ground*. Because of the freedom of activities coupled with a clear-cut purpose and written plan, venture groups offer a unique opportunity for the development of future managers.

5. A venture group is *action oriented*. It is dedicated to change, which becomes expected of it. Standing ready to fill new needs, its justification for existence lies in doing something innovative.

The final important characteristic is the eventual disposition of the venture group. Most venture groups are temporal groups in that they are established for a specific purpose and a particular length of time. Once a venture group has completed its charge (e.g., to plan and introduce a new product into the market), at least three actions can be taken with the group. First, the individual members can go back to their original functional departments. Second, they can go on to become members of new venture groups. Or third, the most frequently occurring alternative, the group stays together and forms the nucleus of a new division responsible for the newly developed product or product line. This alternative is preferred by organizations because the expertise in the venture group allows the new product to get off on the right foot. It also provides for the important movement of managers and employees into more challenging and responsible positions.

Venture groups are not without some significant criticisms. Some of the negative comments range from claims that venture groups tie up too many valuable people, to accusations that they create a "prima donna" environment or that many of the generated ideas have little or no commercial application.

By far the most severe criticism that has been directed at venture groups concerns organizational spinoffs. Frequently, members of venture teams get an idea for a new product or service, and instead of developing it for the mother organization, they decide to leave and form their own company. This has been a particular problem for high technology companies, such as Texas Instruments, which has seen more than a half-dozen new companies form in the last ten years from the ideas of former TI employees.[25] While there are certain legal considerations that can be brought to bear to help eliminate such unhealthy (for the organization) spinoffs, it is clear that the entrepreneurial drive—the belief that you can do something better by yourself in your own organization—is a powerful motive for many managers.

GROUPS, PERFORMANCE, AND THE MANAGER'S JOB

Groups have been the subject of study for many years by a number of behavioral scientists. The combined knowledge of these scholars and that of the practicing manager has yielded a number of keys to success in working with groups. Some of the more important keys are discussed below.

Keys to Success with Groups

1. **Learn to live with group activities.**

   Almost everyone at one time or another has had a bad experience working in a group. These experiences can range from a group project in a class to a formal task force in an organization. These bad experiences, however, should not cause managers to shy away from all further group activities. On the contrary, because of the nature of today's organizations, participation in some form of group interaction is almost inevitable. The manager should not only learn to live with groups, but to recognize the important advantages and disadvantages they offer. Pooling of knowledge and expertise is a powerful performance feature that groups can offer the organization.

2. **Informal groups can contribute much to the organization.**

   Many managers take the view that informal groups subvert or at least deter goal achievement in organizations. On the contrary, many informal groups add a great deal to the organization's performance. It is incumbent on the manager, however, to identify the group's norms and purpose. An informal group that has norms and a purpose that are congruent with the organization can improve communications, enhance interpersonal relationships, and generally help the manager and the organization.

3. **Achieving high group performance involves many factors.**

   It is frequently a false assumption that if members of a group or committee get along with each other, they will perform at high levels. This belief is far too simplistic. Managing a high-performing group usually involves the following factors: (a) successful movement of the group to the latter stages of group development; (b) challenging and organizationally congruent norms; (c) clarity of responsibilities and a minimum of conflict; and (d) a cohesive environment.

4. **The chairperson holds a key role in a task force or committee.**

The leadership exhibited by the chairperson of a group is one of the main keys to success in task forces and committees. The chairperson must not only recognize and influence important structural components (norms, status congruence, cohesion, roles), but he or she must learn to guide the group effectively toward task accomplishment. The most important factor—frequently the most difficult to understand and internalize—is that in a chairperson role, the manager represents not so much his or her functional area or unit, but, rather, the *total* organization. This global, as opposed to narrow, viewpoint enables the group to investigate and discuss issues from a more constructive framework than does adopting a self-serving, short-term attitude of protecting one's own unit. Win-lose problems should be put aside and replaced with an objective of promoting the good of the entire organization.

Groups and the Manager's Job

In our manager's job framework developed in chapter 2, group behavior and the management of groups was shown as an important component of the managerial function of *leading*. In its most basic sense, the management of groups is where the manager probably has his or her greatest impact on the performance of employees. Groups, no matter whether they are task or command groups, task forces or committees, are an integral part of the manager's job.

The development and exercise of *managerial skills* is also closely related to group activities. Technical skills are enhanced by such activities as establishing standards and rules during the orientation stage of group development, learning to follow an agenda and other procedural details in committees, and so forth.

By far the most important managerial skills involving group activities are the *human skills*. Groups consist of people who must be motivated, led, guided, and rewarded, all of which involves careful consideration of the material in the previous two chapters on motivation and leadership.

A manager's *conceptual skills* come to the forefront when visualizing where the group fits into the framework of the total organization. As noted in the previous section, this is particularly important in the committee chairperson role.

Finally, *diagnostic skills* gain prominence when, for example, the manager is attempting to pinpoint group performance problems. Issues of where the group is in its development stage, the quality of norms and cohesion, and the impact of status systems and role definition problems relate to the formation and exercise of diagnostic skills.

From a *managerial role* perspective, a manager's *interpersonal roles* become salient. In leading a group, the manager must act as a figurehead, leader, and liaison person to the total organization. Informational and decisional roles are also stressed in such activities as transmitting information to and from the group, making resource allocation decisions, resolving conflicts, and leading task forces to effective decisions.

SUMMARY FOR THE MANAGER

1. Groups in organizations serve many functions—from task accomplishment to socio-psychological satisfaction—and exist in a number of forms—functional groups, project groups, and interest groups. Since managers can spend a great deal of time in such group activities as leading subordinates and participating in committees and task forces, it is important for them to understand the key concepts that can lead to higher group performance.

2. Groups develop in stages, involving orientation, internal problem-solving, growth and productivity, and evaluation and control. Groups can develop naturally through the stages or revert back to an earlier stage due to the introduction of a new task, a new leader, or new members. It would behoove the manager to recognize where his or her group is in its developmental sequence because groups tend to perform better in the latter stages. If a group remains in its early stages of development, much of the members' time and energy is directed toward clarifying relationships, goals, and procedures, and resolving conflict—time and energy that could have been more constructively used in working on a task.

3. Norms, which have both behavioral and performance components, are one of the strongest factors in determining group performance. Norm conformity can be considered a ticket to group acceptance. Since norms will form in most groups that interact over a period of time, the manager needs to know what the norms are and at what level they operate. This is where some of the manager's diagnostic skills come into play.

4. Status systems, much like norms, are an almost inevitable occurrence in organizational groups and committees. Job titles, seniority, and expertise can all lead to some form of status within the group. What is important to the manager is to insure that there is agreement among group members on individual status levels (i.e., status congruence). Without such agreement, confusion, conflict, and misdirected energies will develop, which will subtract from the group's purpose.

5. Roles represent what is expected of the individual in the group concerning his or her duties, authority, and responsibilities. Problems with roles—either role ambiguity or role conflict—can be barriers to high performance. Role ambiguity—the lack of clarity with respect to what one is supposed to do—can be countered through additional training and experience, or by directly asking for clarification from a higher authority. Role conflict—originating from multiple demands on one's time—can be alleviated by appealing to a higher authority or by ranking activities by priority.

6. Cohesion is one of the most powerful determinants of group performance. The group solidarity associated with a cohesive environment creates a unity of purpose that is a positive influence on performance. While there are a number of ways a manager can increase the cohesiveness of a group, the most important factor to understand is that high performance is the result of the combined effect of both cohesion and norms. That is, higher-performing groups exhibit high cohesion *and* high group performance norms. Most other combinations will usually result in lower performance.

7. Groups have found wide application in many organizations. Examples include information exchange (as in committees), decision making (as in boards or commissions), planning new market and service activities (venture groups), and strengthening the managerial hierarchy (the group manager concept).

8. Groups influence many aspects of the manager's job. Groups are a focal element of the manager's leadership function, whether it is leading subordinates or chairing a committee. Following procedures and agendas, resolving conflict, identifying the group's contribution to the total organization, and pinpointing group problems all involve important managerial skills. In much the same manner, being the group leader, acting as a communication and information transmitter, and making resource allocation decisions concern managerial roles.

QUESTIONS FOR REVIEW AND DISCUSSION

1. Describe the possible conditions that would cause a group in the control stage to revert to the internal problem-solving stage.
2. Can you identify particular jobs, occupations, or organizations in which group behavior is not important?

3. Discuss the development of trade unions in terms of type of group and stages of group development.

4. When a manager believes his or her group has set performance norms well below what they are capable of attaining, what can be done to raise these norms?

5. Under what conditions can status incongruence develop?

6. Can the manager control the composition of the group he or she manages?

7. Describe some sources of role ambiguity and role conflict.

8. Is cohesiveness a more important aspect of group performance for functional groups than of task or project groups?

9. How may the manager increase the frequency of group interaction to increase cohesiveness?

10. Would it be a sound managerial policy to break up a highly cohesive group that has low performance norms?

NOTES

1. See M. E. Shaw, *Group Dynamics: The Psychology of Small Group Behavior,* 2nd ed. (New York: McGraw-Hill, 1976).

2. See D. Cartwright and A. Zander, eds., *Group Dynamics: Research and Theory,* 3rd ed. (New York: Harper & Row, 1968).

3. R. Likert, *New Patterns in Management* (New York: McGraw-Hill, 1961).

4. K. Davis, *Human Behavior at Work,* 5th ed. (New York: McGraw-Hill, 1977), pp. 274–76.

5. W. Bennis and H. A. Shepard, "A Theory of Group Development," *Human Relations* (Summer 1963): 414–57.

6. See P. C. Andre de la Porte, "Group Norms: Key to Building a Winning Team," *Personnel* (September–October 1974): 60–67.

7. H. T. Reitan and M. E. Shaw, "Group Membership, Sex Compositions of the Group, and Conformity Behavior," *Journal of Social Psychology* (October 1969): 45–51.

8. R. Kahn, D. Wolfe, R. Quinn, and J. Snoek, *Organizational Stress: Studies in Role Conflict and Ambiguity* (New York: Wiley, 1964).

9. See C. N. Greene and D. W. Organ, "Role Ambiguity, Locus Control, Role Dynamics, and Job Satisfaction," *Journal of Applied Psychology* (December 1973): 101–02; and A. D. Szilagyi, "An Empirical Test of Causal Influences Between Role Perceptions, Job Satisfaction, Performance, and Organizational Level," *Personnel Psychology* (1977): 375–88.

10. A. J. Lott and B. E. Lott, "Group Cohesiveness as Interpersonal Attraction: A Review of Relationships and Antecedent and Consequent Variables," *Psychological Bulletin* (October 1965): 259–309.

11. A. D. Szilagyi, W. E. Holland, and C. Oliver, "Keys to Success with Open Plan Offices," *Management Review* (August 1979): 26–28, 38–41.

12. R. Tillman, Jr., "Committees on Trial," *Harvard Business Review* (May–June 1960): 6–7.

13. "Committees: Their Role in Management Today," *Management Review* (October 1957): 4–10.

14. N. R. F. Maier, "Assets and Liabilities in Group Problem Solving," *Psychological Bulletin* (July 1967): 239–49.

15. "They Call It Geneen U," *Forbes* (May 1, 1968).

16. See R. A. Golde, "Are Your Meetings Like This One?" *Harvard Business Review* (January–February 1972): 68–77; A. Jay, "How to Run a Meeting," *Harvard Business Review* (March–April 1976): 43–57; and G. M. Prince, "How to be a Better Meeting Chairman," *Harvard Business Review* (January–February 1969): 98–108.

17. Shaw, *Group Dynamics,* p. 35.

18. See A. Van de Ven, A. Delbecq, and D. H. Gustafson, *Group Techniques for Program Planning* (Glenview, Ill.: Scott-Foresman, 1975).

19. See B. M. Bass and P. C. Burger, *Assessment of Managers* (Chicago: Free Press, 1979).

20. I. L. Janis, "Groupthink," *Psychology Today* (November 1971).

21. I. L. Janis, *Victims of Groupthink* (New York: Houghton-Mifflin, 1972).

22. J. H. Ransom, "The Group Executive's Job: Mission Impossible?" *Management Review* (March 1979): 9–14.

23. See K. H. Vesper, *New Venture Strategies* (Englewood Cliffs, N.J.: Prentice-Hall, 1980).

24. M. Hanan, "Corporate Growth Through Venture Management," *Harvard Business Review* (January–February 1969): 43–61.

25. D. Clark, "Texas Instruments and Its Breakaway Offspring," *Texas Business* (September 1979): 36–41.

ADDITIONAL REFERENCES

Bion, W. R. *Experiences in Groups.* New York: Basic Books, 1959.

Collins, B. E. and Guetzkow, H. A. *Social Psychology of Group Processes for Decision Making.* New York: Wiley, 1964.

Davis, J. H. *Group Performance.* Reading, Mass.: Addison-Wesley, 1969.

Gibbard, G. S., Hartman, J. J., and Mann, R. D. *Analysis of Groups.* San Francisco: Jossey-Bass, 1974.

Hackman, J. "Group Influences on Individuals," in *Handbook of Industrial and Organizational Psychology,* edited by M. D. Dunnette. Chicago: Rand McNally, 1976.

Holander, E. P. *Leaders, Groups, and Influence.* New York: Oxford University Press, 1964.

Homans, G. C. *The Human Group.* New York: Harcourt, Brace & World, 1950.

Katz, D. and Kahn, R. L. *The Social Psychology of Organizations,* 2nd ed. New York: Wiley, 1978.

McGrath, J. E. and Altman, J. E. *Small Group Research.* New York: Holt, Rinehart & Winston, 1966.

Mills, T. M. *The Sociology of Small Groups.* Englewood Cliffs, N.J.: Prentice-Hall, 1967.

A CASE FOR ANALYSIS

Committees for Computer Management

Few people would deny that data-processing technology has revolutionized almost every aspect of the operation of a business. Yet even the strongest proponents of that revolution concede that the computer equipment in place at most companies has grown in sophistication much faster than the managerial capability for directing its use.

Although they possess strong technical expertise, the computer specialists who supervise data-processing systems at most companies often lack the business background that is needed to determine just how those systems can best be used to improve the operation of their companies. In recent years nearly 100 major companies have filled that void by taking computer management out of the hands of technicians and putting it into the hands of computer management teams, headed by high-ranking executives who are just as comfortable talking about profits and losses as they are about bits and bytes.

Partly because of a lack of computer executives who understand both technical systems and management needs, many companies have recently formed steering committees, composed of top corporate officers, to ride herd over computer operations. These are distant cousins to the old steering committees that were often established when companies made their first computer acquisitions and that were usually disbanded several years later when the communications gap between the computer managers and the line managers was discovered to be too vast.

The reasons behind the committees are multifold. First, they are ruling a far more costly roost than their predecessor groups: The per-capita white-collar investment in computers and information systems has doubled during the 1970s to about $5000 today, and that figure is expected to hit $20,000 in the 1990s.

Essentially, these committees try to improve the company's use of computers for everything from strategic planning to production control. Instead of letting computer technology determine how the company operates, which experts warn can happen without sufficient corporate oversight, the steering committees see to it that the needs of the business dictate how the computer is used.

For example, at Security Pacific National Bank in Los Angeles, the administrative planning committee formally reviews plans for information systems and resources every ninety days, just as it does for marketing and production. Among other things, it determines how the bank's computer equipment can support new banking services or speed up operations at the bank's branches.

Similarly, at Massachusetts Mutual Life Insurance Co., all divisions that use computer services are represented on the steering committee, which develops a plan that relates data processing to broader corporate goals. Each year the plan is presented to Mass Mutual's three top corporate officers for approval.

In determining how to fit computers to the company's operation, the committees also oversee the purchasing of computer hardware and software, limiting purchases to what is really necessary. With computer technology speeding ahead far more rapidly than management can absorb it in daily use, self-restraint is considered vital by many executives who worry that their companies might wind up with a lot of sophisticated equipment that does not get used. At Industrial Valley Bank & Trust Co. in Philadelphia, for example, a committee of senior executives helps put the brakes on managers who want too much too soon by reviewing requests from division managers for additions to the bank's computer system.

Aside from avoiding waste in purchasing new equipment, the steering committees usually try to increase the efficiency of the computers the company already has. That often requires them to arbitrate among the demands of competing division heads for computer time. At Inland Steel Co., the systems review committee, which consists of seven executives of vice-presidential rank or higher, decides the computer priorities among corporate sales, finance, and manufacturing.

Even when companies eventually hire a computer executive capable of making both systems-oriented and business-oriented decisions, the steering committee that had been filling that void seldom disbands. Although corporate executives may have been searching desperately for a sophisticated computer chief, they are keenly aware that such an individual, once he joins the company, has the tools to be a formidable force.

Indeed, at Chicago-based Kraft Inc., the data-processing department completely changed the modus operandi of the sales force at the company's food service division by equipping it with hand-held computer terminals that are used to transfer sales information instantly via telephone lines to a central computer in Chicago. Result: The division reduced the time between the placement and delivery of an institution's food order from seventy-two hours to only twenty-four hours. The process also allowed Kraft to triple its institutional food offerings while eliminating three hours of daily paperwork for each salesperson. Partly because of the new system, orders jumped to 100,000 a day from 30,000 in 1972.

The potential for such a significant impact on the bottom line explains why companies are anxious to hire top-flight computer managers on the one hand and yet continue to oversee the operation of their departments closely on the other. As long as they are included as key members of senior management, however, the new computer executives seem content to share their power with the steering committee.

Adapted from Business Week, *"Solving a Computer Mismatch in Management" (April 2, 1979): 73–76.*

Questions for Discussion

1. What type of group is represented in this case? Why was it formed?
2. What functions does the computer management group serve?
3. What problems have arisen, or could arise, with this form of management by group?
4. What are the keys to success with the computer management group?
5. When will the computer management group not be needed (under what conditions) in most organizations?

EXPERIENTIAL EXERCISE

The Desert Survival Situation

Purpose

1. To examine the process of group decision-making.
2. To investigate and experience some of the benefits of group decision-making in comparison with individual decision-making.

Required Understanding

The student should have a basic understanding of the components of group structure and the elements of group decision-making.

How to Set Up the Exercise

Groups of between four to eight persons should be established for the 45–60-minute exercise. The groups should be physically separated and members asked to converse only with their own group members.

The Situation

It is approximately 10 a.m. in mid-August and you have just crash-landed in the Sonora Desert in the southwestern United States. The light twin-engine plane, containing the bodies of the pilot and co-pilot, has completely burned. Only the air frame remains. None of the rest of you have been injured.

The pilot was unable to notify anyone of your position before the crash. However, he had indicated before impact that you were 70 miles south-southwest from a mining camp which is the nearest known habitation, and that you were approximately 65 miles off the course that was filed in your VFR flight plan.

The immediate area is quite flat and except for occasional barrel and saguaro cacti, appears to be rather barren. The last weather report indicated the temperature would reach 110 degrees that day, which means that the temperature at ground level will be 130 degrees. You are dressed in light clothing—short-sleeved shirts or blouses, pants, and street shoes. Everyone has a handkerchief. Collectively, your pockets contain $2.83 in change, $85.00 in bills, a pack of cigarettes, and a ballpoint pen.

Instructions for the Exercise

Before the plane caught fire your group was able to salvage the fifteen items shown in exhibit 14-9. Your task is twofold:

1. *Individually,* rank order the fifteen items from 1, the most important, to 15, the least important. Do not discuss the situation or problem until each member has finished the individual rankings. Take approximately ten minutes.
2. *As a group,* perform the same task of ranking the fifteen items. Once the group discussion has begun, do not change your individual rankings. You have forty-five minute to perform this phase of the exercise.

You may assume the following:

1. The number of survivors is the same as the number on your team.
2. You are the actual people in the situation.
3. The team has agreed to stick together.
4. All items are in good condition.

All ranking should be placed on exhibit 14-9. An expert's evaluation of this situation will be provided by your instructor.

EXHIBIT 14-9 Ranking for the Desert Survival Exercise

ITEMS	STEP 1 YOUR INDIVIDUAL RANKING	STEP 2 THE TEAM'S RANKING	STEP 3 SURVIVAL EXPERT'S RANKING	STEP 4 DIFFERENCE BETWEEN STEP 1 & STEP 3	STEP 5 DIFFERENCE BETWEEN STEP 2 & STEP 3
flashlight (4-battery size)					
jackknife					
sectional air map of the area					
plastic raincoat (large size)					
magnetic compass					
compress kit with gauze					
.45 caliber pistol (loaded)					
parachute (red and white)					
bottle of salt tablets (1000 tablets)					
1 quart of water per person					
a book entitled *Edible Animals of the Desert*					
a pair of sunglasses per person					
2 quarts of 180-proof Vodka					
1 topcoat per person					
a cosmetic mirror					
			TOTALS (the lower the score the better)	Your Score Step 4	Team Score Step 5

Source: "The Desert Survival Situation," Human Synergistics (1974). © 1974 by Experiential Learning Methods. Used with permission.

15

Improving Job Performance

CHAPTER OUTLINE

KEY POINTS IN THIS CHAPTER

1. Improved job performance involves the consideration of individuals and individuals in groups. The focus on job performance is twofold: planning for improved job performance and removing the barriers to effective job performance.

2. In an increasingly dynamic environment of change, the process of creativity and innovation gains significantly in importance. In many cases, the organization's survival will depend on the degree to which it can come up with new products and services.

3. The key factor in facilitating creativity and innovation is not the size of the firm nor the industry it is in, but the quality of the environment established by the manager.

4. Management by objectives is basically a reflection of the total management process. It concerns planning, organizing, leading, control, and change.

5. MBO has been shown to improve a manager's performance significantly. However, this result is highly dependent on such factors as top management commitment to the program, proper training and diagnosis, consistent reinforcement, and so on.

6. Conflict can be caused by a number of factors, including goal incompatibility, availability of resources, performance expectations, and the organization's structure.

7. Avoidance, defusion, and confrontation are possible conflict resolution strategies. Confrontation is preferred because it attempts to get at the source of the conflict.

8. Excessive on-the-job stress is of concern to the manager because it can lead to psychological and physical problems, along with a decline in performance. Some stress, however, can be expected in all managerial jobs.

THE PRACTICE OF MANAGEMENT

Using Brainstorming Groups

U. S. productivity is sagging, and the blame has been placed on everything from governmental regulation to declines in business investment. To change that, more and more U. S. companies are returning the responsibility for solving factory floor problems to the factory floor itself. On the premise that the workers often know best, the firms are forming "quality circles." These are groups of five to thirteen employees who volunteer to gather, for perhaps an hour each week on company time, in brainstorming sessions that focus on what can be done to improve output per hour worked. Supervisors lead the discussions and help put the recommendations into practice. The result: Bonuses and more job satisfaction for workers plus higher profits and productivity for firms.

The idea is hardly new. The Japanese developed circles after World War II, borrowing ideas from U. S. business theorists, and such groups are considered to be an important contribution to Japan's productivity. Among the U. S. corporations now using quality circles are General Motors, Ford, American Airlines, 3M, and Martin Marietta.

At Westinghouse, workers have christened their circles with such acronyms as VIPS (Volunteers Interested in Perfection), IMPS (Improved Methods and Products Seekers), and TOPS (Turned Onto Productivity and Savings). By any name, they have already generated savings of at least $800,000. Examples:

—A group of people who use the wire-bonding machines suggested that if a single worker came in fifteen minutes early each morning to warm up all the machines, all the others could start work as soon as they arrived. The saving: about $22,000 a year.

—Another circle, of people who use color-coded tapes to assemble transformers for radar systems, recommended that each worker be given his or her own tape machine rather than sharing on a three-for-one basis. The twelve extra machines cost $174, but the company saves some $11,000 a year in production time.

—A purchasing department circle noted that when supplies were ordered, many vendors routinely sent more than requested. The company either paid the bill or shipped the parts back at its own expense. The group tallied all the overcharge costs and found them startling. The solution was to inform suppliers that the company would either keep the extra material or charge for returning it. The saving: $636,000 a year.

Westinghouse claims that the circles motivated people—they provide an environment of participation. In essence, the workers have all become minimanagers.

Suggested from "The Workers Know Best," Time *(January 28, 1980): 65.*

15

In this last chapter of part IV, we will complete our discussion of the function of leading by presenting selected managerial techniques that have shown some success in improving job performance. Our definition of job performance is broad in nature in order to include the performance both of individuals and of groups.

Our discussion of improving job performance will concern three main areas. First, we will present a basic format for discussion. This will be followed by a presentation of four selected techniques—creativity and innovation, management by objectives, conflict, and managerial stress. Third, the chapter will conclude with an analysis of improving job performance and the manager's job.

In this chapter, we have chosen to present four different approaches that can be placed into two broad classifications. First, we will discuss two approaches that emphasize *planning for improved job performance*. Within this classification, we will discuss the creative and innovative processes and the popular management-by-objectives technique. Second, two approaches will be presented that emphasize the process of *removing the barriers to effective job performance:* conflict resolution and managerial stress.

It should be noted that these four techniques do not represent the only approaches to improve team performance that are available to managers. While a great variety of techniques are available, these four techniques have been chosen because of their popularity and frequency of reported successes.

PLANNING FOR IMPROVED JOB PERFORMANCE: CREATIVITY AND INNOVATION

In a world dominated by turbulence and change, management cannot afford to stand still and expect to survive in the long run. Faced with increasing competition, scarcity of all types of resources, international opportunities and threats, and ever-increasing labor and raw material costs, anything that can lead to more efficient and effective operations will be welcomed by most managers. The high-performing manager is one who can continually come up with new approaches to planning, decision-making, structuring organizations, and selecting and motivating employees. High performance is not only being creative and innovative in managerial work, but also encouraging creativity and innovation in subordinates.

Examples of the impact of creativity and innovations in organizations abound. Xerox saw the novel promise of Chester Carlson's copying machine; IBM initially rejected it. Edward Land recognized the need for instant photography, enabling Polaroid, through protective patents, to exclude competition, especially giant Kodak, from the market for years. R.C.A. was able to envision the innovative opportunity in radio; the

Victor Talking Machine Company did not. Henry Ford saw the promise of the automobile; yet it was General Motors that recognized the need to segment the market by price and performance components. Marshall Field understood the unique opportunities of installment buying in retailing; Endicott Johnson ignored it. And today, Texas Instruments developed the integrated circuit with such speed that it caught the entire electronics industry by surprise, enabling TI to jump into a significant competitive lead.

Creativity and Innovation

In studying the dynamics of change in organizations, many people conclude that creativity and innovation are related but distinct factors. For our purposes, we will define *creativity* as the process of generating a new idea, while *innovation* involves the translation of the idea into a new product or service.[1]

This distinction has significant implications to managers. Creativity abounds all around us, whether we are working in an organization or not. We can all point to people we interact with each day who are virtual idea-generation machines. True innovation in organizations is much rarer because it involves taking an idea and finding a *useful* application for it. The effective manager is one who recognizes not only the difference between these two factors, but understands that an organization needs both creative *and* innovative employees to achieve its goals. An organization full of creative people may never get a product or service to the marketplace, while a heavy innovative orientation would be ineffective without someone to generate ideas.

The creative and innovative process is shown in exhibit 15-1. Two major features are salient in this exhibit. First, creativity and innovation are sequentially related to each other. Second, the innovation step may require far more time and organizational resources than the creative stage. Let us examine the components of creativity and innovation.

The Creative Process. Creativity, contrary to the belief of some people, is not simply the sudden feeling of "Eureka, I've found it." It is, in fact, a process that involves a number of distinct steps.[2]

1. *Identification.* The individual selects or identifies a problem to concentrate on. Usually the issue arises because of some difficulty the person is having doing his or her normal work. This step can occur in all jobs.

2. *Preparation or immersion.* After selecting a problem, the individual immerses himself or herself in collecting information and data, recalling certain situations, or just "getting dirty" in the issue. Illustrations include the extensive preparation George C. Scott put in for his movie role as General Patton; in baseball, Lou Brock and Rod Carew studied films of various pitchers to develop their basestealing and hitting skills; anthropologist Leakey worked the Olduvai site for years before he made some of his initial discoveries.[3]

3. *Incubation.* A little-understood but extremely important part of the creative process is the time the individual relaxes or stands back and mulls

EXHIBIT 15-1
The Creativity and
Innovation
Process

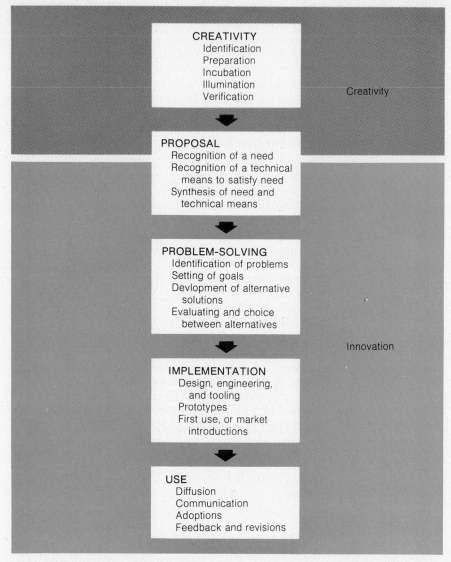

Adapted from James M. Utterback, "The Process of Technological Innovation within the Firm," Academy of Management Journal (March 1971): 83.

over (consciously and/or subconsciously) the collected information. What may look like daydreaming or idle time is actually being used to arrange, integrate, and make sense of the information.

4. *Insight or illumination.* Insight or illumination occurs when the individual first becomes aware of the value of a new idea or association. It is the solving of the problem, the breakthrough that has been sought. Insight can appear in many forms, such as Newton's inspiration (a gradual awareness growing out of research or hard work), or by accident (as in the discovery of the vulcanization process in rubber manufacturing).

5. *Verification.* Verification is the process the individual uses to prove, through logic or experiment, that the idea is of value and can be implemented. In its most basic form, verification is the cutting, polishing, and

knocking off the rough edges of an idea. It may come from continued individual work on an idea, or in seeking the options of other people.

The Innovation Process. Exhibit 15-1 suggests that the process of innovation involves three separate steps. These steps are the proposal, problem-solving, and implementation stages.[4]

1. *Proposal.* The proposal stage is probably the most important of the entire creativity-innovation process because it involves the "go/no-go" decision the organization must make of whether the idea has application merit. It involves the recognition of a *need,* the recognition of the *technical* means to satisfy the need, and the *synthesis* of the need and technology for the further development of the idea. In essence, this stage suggests an analysis of the following questions: (a) Who is interested in our idea? (b) Can the idea be translated into a product or service? and (c) Can the product or service be efficiently and effectively produced and successfully marketed?

   The studies over the past two decades on this part of the innovation process have yielded some interesting findings. First, most of the information leading to innovations in many industries comes from *outside* any given firm. This has been found in such diverse industries as textiles, machine tools, steel, railroads, housing supplies, and computer equipment. For example, of Du Pont's twenty-five major product and process innovations over the last fifty years, nearly 60 percent had their origins in external sources. Du Pont, in essence, was more a developer than an innovator.[5]

   Second, the size of the firm has little effect on its relative ability to originate innovations. For example, of the seven major innovations in the aluminum industry, only one was initiated by a primary producer, such as Alcoa. There is, in fact, some evidence that in certain mature industries such as textiles and machine tools, innovations are more likely to come from smaller new firms than older and larger organizations.

   Finally, a number of studies have shown that there may be a specific sequence of steps in the innovation proposal stage. In particular, in over two-thirds of the cases studied, successful innovations begin with a recognition of a need, followed by search for a technical means to meet the need.[6]

   These findings and others suggest that innovation is a wide-open process that can occur in all types of organizations. In other words, innovation is more a function of the individual and his or her immediate surroundings than it is a function of the size of the organization, or even what industry the organization is in.

   There are many classic examples where an individual (or individuals) formed a new company that was based on an idea with strong technical qualities, but the new company soon folded because no one was interested in buying the evolving product or service. Even well-established companies fall victim to failing to link a need with a technical means. For example, in an attempt to diversify itself out of the highly competitive writing instrument industry, Scripto began development on a new high-resolution camera. The camera, which was the idea of one of the company's engineering executives, was initially thought to have some military and commercial applications. After years of development, and the use of a large amount of the organization's resources, the camera project was dropped—no one could be found who would buy it!

2. *Problem Solving.* Once the idea has received the support of the organization, the innovation process is concerned with setting product or service goals, resolving the many problems, and evaluating design priorities and policies. This stage not only relates to the previously discussed process of decision making (see chapter 7), but as we will soon show, the different roles people perform (see chapters 2 and 14) and the strength of the internal and external communication systems (see chapter 11).

3. *Implementation.* This stage involves an emphasis on the manufacturing, engineering, tooling, and plant start-up required to bring the prototype product or service to its first use or market introduction. While implementation generally involves greater commitment and expenditures by the firm than the other innovation stages, the technical uncertainties are usually less than those of the earlier stages. Implementation also concerns projections of economic or market success, testing, acceptance, and an increased emphasis on internal and external communication.

An Illustration—the Polaroid SX-70.   In the early 1970s, Edward Land and Polaroid took one of the biggest gambles ever made on a consumer product: the eight-year program to bring out the SX-70 camera and film. Although the company never officially revealed the project's cost, Land has frequently referred to the SX-70 as at least a half-billion dollar investment.[7]

From the point of view of creativity and innovation, SX-70 provides some interesting insights. Creatively, Land's background and experience in optics and chemistry led him to the idea of the fast-developing film in the late 1940s. In the SX-70, his idea focused on the idea of "complete one-step" photography in a single instrument.

The difficulties were dismayingly evident, and some of the technical staff seriously doubted the feasibility of the idea. From past experience, it is known that when Land feels strongly about a project, he can and will force it through. Land exhibits some interesting characteristics of a creative person. As some of his colleagues have noted, when he is doing something "wild and risky" (i.e., creative), he'll not only lock himself in the laboratory for days, but he is careful to insulate himself from anyone who would be critical of his idea. He strongly believes that it is very easy in the early stages of creativity to have a dream explode.

Innovatively, a number of important issues were faced. First, Polaroid needed to know if anyone would be willing to purchase such a camera, especially at the high price (recognition of a need). After some study, the company felt that they could sell at least 6 million SX-70s during the first few years after introduction—a figure that justified its further development. Second, significant breakthroughs in chemistry, optics, and electronics needed to be made before the camera became reality (recognition of a technical means). Finally, assuming the breakthroughs could be made, there remained the issue of whether the camera could be made within certain cost constraints (synthesis of needs and technical means).

The problem-solving stage presented the most difficult issues. The film posed the most serious problems. The initial requirements of the film included a bright, clear, self-developing picture; long shelf-life; significant anti-fade qualities; and no "garbage" (no sheet to tear off and throw away). To compound the problems in developing this entirely new film, Polaroid decided to manufacture its own negatives, a process they had subcontracted to other manufacturers for years.

Electronically, the SX-70 needed sophisticated miniaturized circuitry that up to that time was only on the drawing boards. The development of the computer chip by Texas Instruments—there are six in each camera—solved this problem. The camera also needed a completely redesigned lens system with a complex sequence of exposure and development. On top of all this, Land insisted that the camera look modern and be able to fold up to fit into a man's coat pocket or a woman's small purse.

The implementation phase of the SX-70 innovation was also troublesome. First, new expertise had to be developed quickly in mass-producing negatives. Their success was nothing short of phenomenal—useable negatives were produced on the second production run. Considering that the plant was extremely complicated (it was almost totally run by computers and had a surgically clean environment with prodigious amounts of purified air and water) and most operations were conducted in the dark, Polaroid's success was amazing. Second, quality-control problems with the battery in the film package and the sequencing of the circuitry had to be solved. Finally, to introduce the product, Polaroid spent over $9 million on advertising, and enticed Sir Laurence Olivier (for a reported sum of $250,000) to make his first sales pitch. To help move the cameras, Polaroid began an innovative bonus program with their distributors, in which the sales outlet could receive a substantial sales bonus for selling the camera, film, and expertise on the camera.

Even with the introduction of a competing product by Kodak, the SX-70 is a success. While issues remain of whether Polaroid can remain a one-product company, and what (if anything) can top the SX-70 (is it the ultimate?), the Polaroid example provides an interesting illustration of the creative and innovative processes at work.

Managing Creativity and Innovation

Effectively managing the creative and innovative processes in organizations requires a recognition of at least three points: What are the significant barriers to creativity and innovation?, what elements can function as aides?, and what is a good organizational climate for creativity and innovation and how can be it be created?

Barriers to Creativity and Innovation.   The field of psychology contains numerous studies that identify characteristics of creative people (e.g., intelligence, family background, age, nonconformity, and personality factors). Creative behavior, however, is not simply a matter of the proper selection, training, and placement of employees. The organization itself can facilitate or impede the creative and innovative processes. At least four factors can be considered:[8]

1. *Excessive pressure to produce.* Creativity and innovation can be impeded when the organization imposes excessive pressures to produce. This can create a state of fear, anxiety, and defensiveness among employees. This "crisis management" mode can result in the solution of many short-term problems, but long-term opportunities suffer.

2. *Fear of evaluation.* Creativity and innovation can be high risk activities. A great deal of time and effort can be devoted to an idea that eventually may have no market potential. The individual may go through this

THE
MANAGER'S
JOB
Barry Diller of
Paramount
Pictures

To Barry Diller, head of Paramount Pictures, managing people in the so-called creative industries—moviemaking, recording, publishing, and the like—simply calls for different rules. These are industries where computerized market research does little good, where an idea session generally occurs in someone's living room not a laboratory, and where long-term growth and sales projections are often no better than a shot in the dark.

Diller cites some prerequisites for the successful manager in the creative industries:

—Don't make people in the creative end of the business feel that Big Brother is watching.

—Have the courage to act on your intuition and gut feelings.

—Develop the ability to praise people whose egos are outsized, and whose work habits are peculiar at best.

—Be willing to persuade, rather than order, creative staffers to follow a profitable path.

—Possess strong business sense that can attend to details such as keeping warehouse costs down, improving distribution, and holding budgets in line, without interfering with the creative process.

Suggested from "Mastering Management in Creative Industries," Business Week *(May 29, 1978): 86–88.*

process a number of times before a successful innovation is developed. If the employee fears criticism for his or her initial failures, personal security issues tend to take precedence over creativity.

3. *Cultural or group factors.* Some researchers have suggested that certain cultural and/or group norms can inhibit creativity and innovation. While studies in this area are few, we know that norms and norm conformity can be powerful determinants of human behavior.

4. *Organizational structure.* In chapter 8, it was pointed out that the structure of an organization consists of grouping, influence, and coordinative components. Certain factors of these components, especially in a bureaucratic organizaton, can significiantly impede creative and innovative activities. This can include the excessive use of rules, procedures, policies, schedules, and so on.

Aids for Creativity and Innovation.   Organizations can use other means to facilitate creative and innovative activities. First, as discussed in the last chapter, special units or task forces can be established (i.e., venture groups) to investigate an idea or problem. Second, two group processes can be utilized—brainstorming and synectics.[9]

Brainstorming in groups involves six to twelve persons who get together to search for solutions to a problem. It was used many years ago in its initial application to help solve advertising problems for a commercial food-products company. Since then it has received wide application. The main idea is to have group members produce as many solutions to an issue or problem as they can without permitting judgments or criticisms to inhibit the free flow of ideas. Due to the freewheeling environment, brainstorming groups can come up with a wide range of useable ideas. As with any group, the composition is of great importance—that is, a major part of the group should consist of experts or people who are familiar with the issue at hand.

Synectics, developed by the Arthur D. Little Inc. consulting firn. not as known or widely used as brainstorming. Two major characteristic are inherent in synectics teams. First, the group members are chosen only after thorough testing and screening of potential members. This selection process results in a tailor-made team composed of individuals best equipped intellectually and psychologically to deal with problems unique to their organization. Second, only the group leader knows the exact nature of the problem. The group members are given a very broad description of the issue and then allowed to talk out loud about a variety of issues related to the broad issue. For example, management at Kellogg's may be interested in developing new breakfast cereals for children.[10] In the synectic team, the group leader suggests that the initial discussion center on the issue of "breakfast." After a number of give-and-take sessions, the group leader might focus the discussion on other breakfast cereals that it might be possible to produce and market. In reality, Kellogg's used this process not only to develop new cereals for children that were lower in presweetened qualities (i.e., sugar content), but a whole new line of cereals for health-conscious young adults.

These are some of the many mechanisms that organizations can use to facilitate the creative and innovative process. The key factor is that the organization takes an active role in providing the means and resources to further these important activities.

The Organizational Climate for Creativity and Innovation.   The truly creative and innovative organization is, unfortunately, found only infrequently. The reasons are many but generally focus on the type of people that are employed and the nature of the organization's structure and procedures. If a manager is seriously interested in establishing a creative and innovative environment in his or her unit, what are some of the necessary elements? The following factors may give that person at least a good start:[11]

1. *Permit open communications and interaction.* As the discussion on roles suggested, the successful idea and innovation is highly dependent on the free flow of information and data. By allowing employees to communicate and interact more freely, the chance that an idea can be generated is increased. The manager can facilitate this by holding frequent meetings, physically moving the employees closer together, or evaluating the communication between employees not as a waste of valuable time and effort, but as a constructive activity.

2. *Encourage new ideas.* Managers should welcome new ideas and approaches. Rather than hastily evaluating an idea as "it won't work, now go back to work" or enforcing strict rules, the manager should encourage experimentation and informal brainstorming sessions. Giving a new idea a "fair hearing" may prove to be a most profitable activity.

3. *Provide clear goals and guidelines.* Creativity and innovation can be stimulated when employees have at least a minimum idea of purpose and direction. The manager, however, should be careful not to set a too-strict time schedule. This may hinder rather than encourage creativity. A "ball park" or extended time frame is preferred.

4. *Tolerate failures.* Every new idea will not reach the final stages of the innovation process. In fact, only about one out of fifty ideas ever gets past

the proposal stage. If new ideas are rejected, the persons should feel that they should continue their activities, and not be worrying about whether this rejection will affect their career growth or security in the organization.

5. *Constantly reinforce.* Creative and innovative people are motivated not only by intrinsic means (the feeling of accomplishment), but also by extrinsic means. If it's nothing more than a pat on the back or a simple "thanks for your effort," the manager will see many benefits. Of course, bonuses, significant pay increases, or advancement are important to creative individuals, but the basic recognition that they are doing well can be a strong motivator to continue their activities.

6. *Consider the use of outside help.* Many times, the creative and innovative process can be stimulated by bringing in or using people outside the confines of the organization. This may simply take the form of talking over an idea with a neighbor, friend, or colleague in another company. A short conversation with another person may prove to be a significant cerebral-massage technique. On a more formal basis, many organizations have been turning to other organizations specializing in creative or innovative thinking. For example, the well-known management consulting firm Booz-Allen & Hamilton has a unit that specializes in innovation consulting. Booz-Allen lays claim to innovative assistance in developing aerosol shaving foam, latex paint, frozen pizza, and other consumer products.

One last factor—the influence of the external environment—should be carefully considered by the manager.[12] The strictness of governmental regulatory bodies, antitrust laws, the availability of venture capital, and the influence of international competition all have a tremendous impact on the creative and innovative processes. Many people believe that the 1980s can be an era of great innovation much like the 1950s and 60s. What is needed to achieve this are a number of factors, including federal policies that bolster innovation, a revision of thinking inside the organization that will move it away from the need to upgrade short-term earnings, greater risk taking, and more long-range planning and thinking. This is a significant challenge to the managers of the 1980s.

COMMENTS ON THE PRACTICE OF MANAGEMENT

(See p. 515)

The Practice of Management section at the beginning of the chapter provides an example of the use of brainstorming groups in organizations. The manager should recognize a number of important items in this illustration. First, brainstorming groups can be used in all types of organizations, at many levels in the organization, and across different cultures. Second, the results of these groups not only benefit the organization through improved productivity, but can improve the morale and performance of the individual employee. Last, brainstorming groups can create a climate of commitment and participation that has a long-term impact on the organization.

PLANNING FOR IMPROVED JOB PERFORMANCE: MANAGEMENT BY OBJECTIVES

One of the most popular and frequently used approaches to effective team management—one that is used in at least one-half of the business organizations in the United States—is *management by objectives* (MBO). In its most basic form, MBO is defined as:

A process whereby the superior and subordinate managers of an organization jointly identify common goals, define each individual's major areas of responsibilities in terms of the results expected of them, and use these measures as guides for operating the unit and assessing the contribution of each of its members.[13]

In essence, MBO is an applied managerial technique that not only stresses the importance of mutual understanding between a superior and a subordinate, but is concerned with initiating and stimulating better performance through a "proactive" as opposed to a "reactive" style of managing.

The idea of giving employees a specific amount of work to be accomplished—a task, a quota, a performance standard, a deadline, or a goal—is not new to the management profession. The task concept and performance standards were well-founded over seventy years ago with Taylor's scientific management (see chapter 3). As we discussed, Taylor used the system to increase the productivity of first-line workers. It was not until about twenty years ago that the idea of goal setting reappeared under a new name, management by objectives. This time, however, the technique was designed for managers.

The Foundations and Process of MBO

MBO has evolved in many organizations because it addresses certain important factors inherent in a person's job:

1. Employees can perform better when it is clear to them not only what is expected of them, but how their individual efforts contribute to the overall performance of the organization.

2. Employees usually want to have some say in the particular results that are expected of them.

3. While performing, employees have a need to know how well they are doing.

4. Employees want to be rewarded (e.g., money, recognition, opportunities for growth, and a sense of achievement) in line with their levels of performance.

These foundational elements have been translated into operational terms. As shown in exhibit 15-2, an operational MBO process usually involves at least eight steps:

Step 1—Diagnosis. This first step concerns the preliminary activities that are directed toward an understanding of the important employee needs, jobs, technology, and issues in the organization.

Step 2—Planning. Involved in this MBO step are issues related to the overall goals and strategies of the organization, receiving management commitment to the MBO process, and training and development in learning how to use the technique.

Step 3—Defining the Employee's Job. Possibly one of the most difficult steps, the employee is required to describe his or her particular job, its content, duties, requirements, and responsibilities. The important aspect of this step is that before individual goals can be set, one must know what work is being done.

Step 4—Goal Setting. The employee initiates the superior-subordinate interaction by developing a set of goals for the upcoming period, usually one year. Concern is shown for the type of goal (maintenance, project, and development—see chapter 2), setting priorities, target dates, and methods of measurement.

EXHIBIT 15-2   The MBO Process

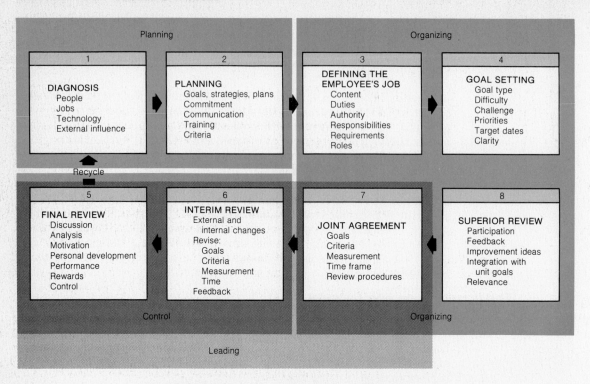

Step 5—Superior Review. The employee's superior reviews the initial goals, offers suggestions for improvement, and so on.

Step 6—Joint Agreement. Steps 4 and 5 are repeated until both the employee and the manager agree on the established set of goals for the period.

Step 7—Interim Review. During the period of evaluation, the employee and manager get together to review the progress toward goal accomplishment. These meetings can be scheduled for once, twice, or more during the year. The focus of these interim reviews is not only to see what progress has been made, but to adjust the goals should new information or changing environmental events become important.

Step 8—Final Review. At the end of the goal-setting period, the employee and manager formally get together to review the results. Emphasis is placed on analysis, discussion, feedback, and input to the next MBO cycle. At the end of this step, the cycle is repeated for the next period.

As noted in exhibit 15-3, the MBO process is closely related to the major functions of management. That is, the *planning* function deals with steps 1 and 2; *organizing* concerns steps 3 through 6; *leading* relates to steps 6 through 8; and *control* concerns steps 7 and 8. Managerial change relates to the recycling of the process.

This direct relationship to managerial functions has resulted in the fact that organizations sometimes use MBO for different purposes. Some organizations use MBO to clarify the employee's job (planning and organizing); others use it to motivate employees (leading); while still other organizations apply MBO as a performance control mechanism to check performance and to adapt to new conditions (control and change).

Nowhere is this difference in application more pronounced than in

EXHIBIT 15-3   Goal-Setting (MBO) Plan for a Production Supervisor

RESPONSIBILITIES (Major headings of job responsibilities.)	PERFORMANCE FACTORS AND/OR RESULTS TO BE ACHIEVED (A more specific statement of the employee's key responsibilities and/or goals employee can reasonably be expected to achieve in the coming period. Indicate how results will be measured. When specific quantitative indicators are not possible, state what conditions will exist when a job is well performed.)	PRIORITY AND/OR TARGET
Production	93% of all job lots delivered on time.	A
	90% of all orders delivered on time.	A
	Improve utilization of key equipment from 86% to 91%.	9/1/19—
	Production rate will meet monthly efficiency plan.	A
Quality	Finished product will meet standards within ± .5 of specification. No justifiable customer complaints attributable to my department.	A
Maintenance	Scheduled downtime will be utilized for preventive maintenance. No downtime will result from inadequate spare parts availability.	B
Employee Relations	Grievances processed and disposed within specified contract period.	B
Safety	No more than 2 disabling injuries in my department.	B
Affirmative Action	Increase minority employee percentage to 19%.	6/30/19—
Personal Development	Complete Preventive Maintenance Engineering Course with at least 85% average.	10/31/19—

INTERIM REVIEW: CHANGES IN THE PLAN

Quality	Finished product standards changed to ± .07 of specifications (by product engineering).	A

how organizations use the results of the MBO process (step 8). Some organizations tie the MBO process results directly into the merit review process (see chapter 16). In this way, the employee sees a direct monetary impact of MBO on his or her salary. Other organizations use MBO to improve job-related performance, with little or no tie into the merit review process. Finally, still other organizations use MBO to identify managers for development and future advancement. There is no best application of MBO. The organization generally identifies its own needs and then adapts the MBO process to them.

Exhibits 15-3 and 15-4 show how MBO can be used for a production supervisor's job. Exhibit 15-3 represents the result of the objective setting process (step 6), while exhibit 15-4 is the final outcome at the end of the process period (step 8). In exhibit 15-4, note that the type of goal varies by maintenance ("90 percent of all orders delivered on time"), project or improvement ("increase minority employee percentage by 19 percent"), and personal development ("complete preventive engineering correspondence course with at least an 85 percent average"), and that some of the goals have been prioritized (A equaling the highest priority, B being the next-highest priority), or assigned target dates, depending on the goal.

MBO Applications

Because of its popularity, MBO has been the subject of many organizational applications and studies. Among the most notable studies include those conducted at General Electric, Wells Fargo, Purex, Weyerhaeuser, and Black and Decker. These studies have revealed the following:[14]

EXHIBIT 15-4 Superior's Evaluation of Production Supervisor's Goal Achievement

(SUPERIOR'S EVALUATION) LEVEL OF ACTUAL ACHIEVEMENT	ADDITIONAL SIGNIFICANT ACCOMPLISHMENTS

(SUPERIOR'S EVALUATION)
LEVEL OF ACTUAL ACHIEVEMENT

Job lot deliveries averaged 92.6%. Orders delivered, averaged 91.1%.

His study of key equipment utilization in cooperation with our I.E. staff caused production planning change which has improved his utilization rate to 87.8% (the best we've ever done).

Monthly efficiency plan standards were within ± 1% of average expected.

Product engineering changes these specs. during the year. He ran consistently at ± .06%.

He received two (2) customer complaints during the year compared to his predecessor's average of 7/year.

He developed a "preventive maintenance program schedule" which permitted maximum use of downtime. We're using it in other control.

Spare parts availability did not cause any downtime within his control.

He had a real problem with one overtime grievance which is now in arbitration (due to advice of corporate labor relations).

His department had two disabling injuries, which I consider were within his control.

Minority employees now average 23%. He is our best supervisor from an affirmative action standpoint.

He completed this course on July 1 with an 89% average.

ADDITIONAL SIGNIFICANT
ACCOMPLISHMENTS

Served as "United Way" chairman for our plant and brought in our best pledge record to date.

CONTINUING RESPONSIBILITIES Indicate additional responsibilities whenever they have had a significant positive or negative effect on the overall results achieved.

As "energy control coordinator" for his department, he achieved a 1% reduction from last year.

RELATIONSHIP WITH OTHERS — (JOB RE-LATED) Give significant positive or negative influence this employee has had on the results achieved by other employees.

He and the safety director are "polarized." I feel it is affecting his safety judgment and his record.

OVERALL RATING

Review actual level of achievement against overall performance plans. Consider performance in key results areas: that is actual performance against important priorities, dates, amounts and other factors listed above. Check the definition which best describes the employee's overall performance.

☐ Results achieved were unsatisfactory — performance did not meet expectations and must improve.

☐ Results achieved were adequate — performance met expectations in most key areas.

☐ Results achieved were satisfactory — performance exceeded expectations in a few key results areas.

☒ Results achieved were above average — performance exceeded expectations in many key results areas.

☐ Results achieved were outstanding — performance exceeded expectations in most key results areas.

1. Setting clear and specific goals has a greater positive effect on performance improvement than does the "do the best you can" approach.

2. Employee goals that are perceived to be difficult but achievable tend to lead to better performance than do easy goals, so long as the goals are accepted by the individual.

3. Superior-subordinate participative goal-setting has been shown to improve performance more than superior-assigned goal-setting.

4. The use of frequent performance feedback in the MBO process results in higher performance by individuals than when feedback is not used.

5. There is growing evidence that unless successful goal achievement is reinforced, the performance levels of individuals will begin to decline.

So as not to mislead the reader, these and other studies have pointed out a number of important criticisms in the use of MBO. The most prominent complaints include:

1. The program was used as a whip by management to get employees to do what management wanted them to do, not what the employee felt was best.

2. The program significantly increased paperwork in the organization.

3. The program not only failed to reach the lower managerial levels, but staff positions were frequently excluded, creating a problem of the "haves and have nots."

4. There was an overemphasis on achieving quantitative results. This ignores some of the more important aspects of a manger's job that can only be assessed through qualitative or subjective means.

5. Rewards for good performance did not equal either the level of subsequent performance or the efforts put in by employees in the MBO program.

In essence, these negative feelings and findings are viewed as indicators that despite some initial performance improvements, the MBO programs may have produced some important side-effects that developed into serious problems.

Keys to Success with MBO

MBO has been known and used by managers for more than two decades. What have these managers learned from its use and results? Although not exhaustive, the following list can be looked upon at least as a start to determining some keys to success with MBO.

1. *Top management support,* commitment, and involvement is mandatory. Without it, MBO will probably slowly decline in usage and effectiveness.

2. MBO should be *integrated* into the normal, everyday activities of the manager. Managers must accept it as part of the total management system, not just something they pull out of their desks once a year.

3. MBO should emphasize goals that when achieved can benefit the organization and the manager. In other words, *personal development goals* must be included in an MBO program.

4. Organizational resources (time and people) should be devoted to the important *diagnostic and training* activities. A firm foundation of goals, plans for implementation, and trained personnel make later activities flow smoother.

5. Recognition of *differences* in units, departments, and functions in an

organization is essential. Forcing a standardized program on units that involve different processes, methods, and constraints may meet with resistance and possible failure. Slight modifications to an MBO program at the unit level can prove to be quite valuable.

6. Overemphasis on *quantitative* goals (e.g., dollars, time) can undermine success. Because managerial jobs are inherently ambiguous and difficult to evaluate and measure, *qualitative* goals can be equally useful.

7. *An MBO system need not generate too much paperwork.* An effective program can be conducted without the massive use of forms, memos, reports, and the like. Remember, the key aspect of MBO is the interaction between the superior and the subordinate, an interaction that need not be spelled out on paper every time.

8. Great emphasis should be placed on *evaluation.*

9. *Overnight results* should not be expected. Because of its complex nature and time frame, past experience has shown that concrete results probably will not be seen until eighteen to twenty-four months into the program. In other words, don't abandon the program after only one year.

10. Finally, a *flexible and adaptable MBO system* should be a goal in itself. As the system is used, new and different factors are learned and evaluated. Be prepared to add or delete certain components of the system.

The work on MBO evaluation and application is really just beginning, despite over twenty years of study. There will undoubtedly be more work on the process of MBO, the impact of MBO on minority employees, the training requirements of MBO, and so on. The work to date has shown that MBO can result in improved performance, but in doing so it requires careful diagnosis, training, implementation, and reinforcement. These results clearly indicate that although MBO appears to be quite simple on paper, it is a complex process and difficult program to make work at any level in any organization.

REMOVING BARRIERS TO IMPROVED JOB PERFORMANCE: CONFLICT

Because an organization is complex and dynamic, the various subunits and groups that make up its character develop different and sometimes highly specialized ways of doing their work. When these individuals, groups, and subunits interact, these differences can lead to conflict. For our purposes, we will define conflict as the disagreement between two or more organizational members concerning the manner to be used to achieve certain goals.

The ways in which organizations view and treat conflict have changed greatly during the last decade. Two major views of conflict are most prominent: traditional and contemporary. The traditional approach views conflict as something to be avoided, caused by personality conflicts or a failure of leadership, and resolved by physically separating the conflicting parties or by direct managerial intervention. The contemporary approach, on the other hand, views conflict as an inevitable consequence of everyday organizational life, caused primarily by the complexities of our internal system. Through such mechanisms as problem-solving approaches, the resolution of conflict can lead to positive organizational change.

Types of Conflict

At least five types of conflict are found in organizations:

1. **Conflict within the individual.**

   This is a special form of conflict which does not exactly fit our definition. It is basically a situation where a person feels uncertain about himself, his ability to perform, and the demands put on him by the organization. Examples include the individual who questions his capability to handle a difficult project, and the individual who questions whether what the organization wants him to do is ethically right.

2. **Conflict between individuals.**

   This form of conflict is the most frequent in organizations. It concerns the quality of interactions between two organizational members. In the past, many managers felt that it was caused by severe personality differences between the parties. However, as we discussed earlier (and will expand on in the next section), most of these problems are role related. For example, a maintenance supervisor may tell the manufacturing supervisor, "The quality control problems we're having are not due to defective equipment, but to your sloppy operating procedures."

3. **Conflict between individuals and groups.**

   This type of conflict typically occurs when a member resists the influences of the group to conform to certain practices. As we discussed in chapter 14, acceptance into a group implies that the individual also accepts the norms of the group. Lack of acceptance can lead to conflict and deviate behavior.

4. **Conflict between groups.**

   Usually termed intergroup conflict, this is a frequently occurring problem facing managers in diverse and complex organizations. As presented in the next section, this type of conflict is related to such factors as groups fighting for scarce resources, differences of opinion about the way a unit should be managed, and the dependence of one group on another. For instance, in building a new manufacturing facility, the production group may want a plant that permits long manufacturing runs that can provide greater cost efficiencies, while the marketing group would like a plant that is flexible to customer needs and can be changed quickly to produce a different product.

5. **Conflict between organizations.**

   Conflict is built into many economic systems through the competitive motive. Such conflicts result in new products, services, technologies, and innovations. On the other hand, organization-to-organization conflict can occur when, for example, there is a disagreement on procedures and practices. Illustrations include the interaction between federal regulatory agencies and business on safety, investment issues, prices, and employment discrimination.

   In the following sections, our focus will be on conflicts between individuals, conflicts between individuals and groups, and intergroup conflict. A special case of conflict within the individual—stress—will be presented later in the chapter.

EXHIBIT 15-5   Sources and Resolution of Conflict

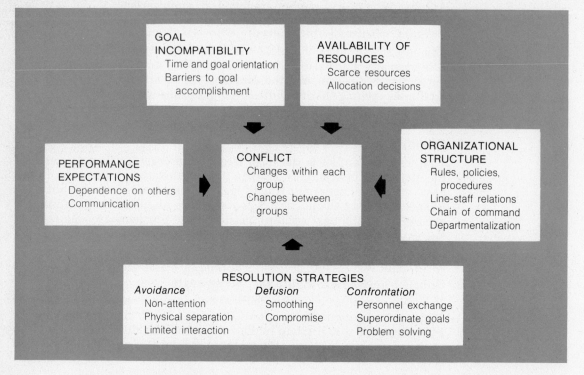

Sources of Conflict

To illustrate the potential sources of conflict, throughout this section we will be considering a high-level policy-making task force in a large domestic airline. The task force consists of managers from operations, maintenance, scheduling, engineering, finance, and flight services and is charged with recommending to top management which new wide-bodied aircraft to purchase for their fleet—the existing European Airbus A-300 or the developmental Boeing 757/767. The task force is given six months to make its choice.

There are at least four major sources of conflict among and between groups: (1) goal incompatibility; (2) availability of resources; (3) performance expectations and (4) organization structure. These sources are shown in exhibit 15-5.

Goal Incompatibility.   Goal incompatibility, which is defined as lack of agreement concerning the direction of group activity and the criteria for evaluating task accomplishment, is probably the most frequently identified source of conflict. Two elements contribute to the existence of goal incompatibility. First, as discussed in chapter 8, individual members bring with them different time and goal orientations, which creates a state of high differentiation. For example, deliberations in the airline task force may become conflictful when the maintenance and operating representatives evaluate the alternative aircraft from a short-term, cost, and efficiency orientation, while the engineering member believes the two planes should be looked upon from a more long-term, technical superiority point of view.

Another source of goal incompatibility is barriers to goal accomplishment, where the goal attainment by one group or member is seen as preventing the others from achieving their goals. In our illustration, the scheduling and operations representatives may lean toward the Airbus because its immediate availability will enable them to put the plane on routes where competition already is using wide-body aircraft. On the other hand, maintenance may prefer the Boeing plane because it is less costly to operate and maintain, even though the plane's delivery time is twice as long as the Airbus.

Availability of Resources.   Another frequent contributor to conflict concerns the availability of resources, particularly when there are limited resources to go around. Managers must divide limited financial, physical, and human resources among different groups in what they believe is the most efficient and equitable manner. However, what is perceived as equitable by one group may not be perceived in a similar manner by other groups. A group that believes it is not receiving a fair share of organizational resources often becomes antagonistic toward the organization and toward other groups. This conflict can result in withholding of information, disruptive behavior, and similar actions.

In our airline example, the finance representative may push for the Airbus because he knows that, it being a European-made plane, the company can receive better long-term financing for the purchase of a fleet of planes from European banks. The flight-service representative, however, recognizes that the Airbus will cost more per plane than the Boeing counterpart. Because of this added cost, he believes that the organization would not look favorably on his future request for capital to build a new flight-training facility.

Performance Expectations.   The third source of conflict is activity or performance of one group or member that affects the subsequent performance of other groups. In other words, one person's work cannot begin until another person provides some needed information.

For example, in examining the differences between the two planes, the finance member is charged with putting together a cost analysis on each plane. To do this, he asks the maintenance representative to provide cost information on the repair frequencies and parts costs of each plane; similarly, the representative from operations is requested to collect comparative operating efficiency (fuel) data on each plane. When one or both members are late in providing this information to the finance representative, a conflict can arise.

Organizational Structure.   In many organizations, the structure is a potential source of conflict. There can be function-to-function conflict in a functional structure, division-to-division conflict in a product structure, and function-to-division conflict in a matrix structure.

The most visible conflict caused by an organization's structure is the relationship between line and staff.[15] The heart of the conflict lies in the line and staff members' different viewpoints of each other and their roles in the organization. In essence, these viewpoints have their foundation in the aforementioned causes of conflict—that is, line and staff members have different time and goal orientations, they compete for the same resources, and so on. Because of these multiple sources, the conflict between line and staff members can become heated and be detrimental to the overall performance of the organization.

How does line and staff conflict develop? For example, consider the relationship between the manufacturing (line) group and the personnel department (staff) in a plant producing heavy industrial equipment. The manufacturing manager may view the personnel department in the following way:

1. *Staff members interefere with normal operations.* The activities of the personnel department can be considered an intrusion into the daily operations of the manufacturing area. For example, manufacturing may want to promote an hourly worker to a salaried supervisory position as soon as possible; the personnel department may take three weeks to approve the promotion.

2. *Staff members don't understand what is going on in line functions.* Because they are not involved in the everyday activities in the manufacturing area, there is the claim by certain line managers that the ideas and decisions made by the personnel function are not realistic. The manufacturing manager may request the hiring of six new maintenance workers for an additional maintenance crew. Personnel, however, may only authorize four new hires, not knowing that six people make up a crew.

3. *Staff members rarely take the blame for their mistakes.* "When they make a suggestion that proves to be successful, personnel tries to grab all the glory. When one of their ideas results in a failure, all personnel does is hide behind their staff doors and claim that they had no control over what manufacturing does."

On the other hand, the manager of personnel may make the following statements about the manufacturing function:

1. *Line managers don't use staff functions properly.* Due to many of the reasons noted above, line managers are reluctant to contact staff experts on an issue. For example, in promoting a particular hourly worker to a supervisory position, personnel did some close checking and found that not only would the person's fringe benefits be different, but there was a stipulation in the latest union contract which stated that the worker with the greatest seniority must be offered the job first.

2. *Line managers resist the ideas of staff members.* While they may not be knowledgeable in the total expertise of the line positions, staff members are experts in their own areas. For example, the approval to hire only four new maintenance workers may have originated not only from human-resource budget considerations, but the latest industry data suggest a four-person maintenance crew may be able to perform the needed work as effectively as a larger crew.

3. *Line managers think of staff positions as being "excess" baggage.* Line managers frequently develop the view that anything or anyone not directly involved with the product or service is not contributing to the overall performance of the organization. Personnel managers, for instance, can point out that every manufacturing manager and supervisor could not become totally expert in the growing body of legislative and judicial acts and positions on the handling of human resource problems. A specialized staff position is needed to handle this issue.

These four major sources of conflict are not all-inclusive. They are, however, the most frequently reported and most serious situations. In the next section, we will discuss the effects of conflict in the special case of the relationship between two or more groups.

Strategies for Resolving Conflict

Because intergroup conflict is inherent in the nature of today's complex organizations, it is necessary that management be capable of resolving this conflict before the dysfunctional consequences affect organizational performance. The ability to minimize and resolve conflict successfully is an important skill that managers must develop. The various strategies for minimizing and resolving intergroup conflict can be classified into three categories: avoidance, defusion, and confrontation.[16]

Avoidance.   The avoidance strategy involves a general disregard for the causes of the conflict by enabling the conflict to continue only under certain controlled conditions. Three separate methods prevail under an avoidance philosophy: nonattention, physical separation, and limited interaction.

Nonattention is the manager totally avoiding or ignoring the dysfunctional situation. The manager "looks the other way" or disregards hostile actions in hopes that the situation will resolve itself in time. Because the sources of conflict are not identified by this method, it is likely that the situation will continue or worsen with time.

Physical separation involves actually moving conflicting groups physically apart from each other. The rationale for this strategy is that if the groups cannot interact, conflict will diminish. The disadvantages of this strategy are that not only have the sources of the conflict not been identified, but if the groups are highly interdependent, physical separation will adversely affect the overall effectiveness of the organization. It is at best only a stopgap measure and may eventually require more organizational resources for continuous surveillance to keep the groups separate.

Limited interaction is not an all-inclusive strategy, as is physical separation, because conflicting parties are permitted to interact on a limited basis. Interactions are permitted generally under only formal situations, such as a meeting at which a strict agenda is followed. The same disadvantages caused by physical separation (i.e., sources of conflict still prevail, problems of high interdependency, and future dysfunctional consequences) can result.

Defusion.   Defusion strategy attempts to buy time until the conflict between two groups becomes less emotional or less crucial. It involves solving minor points of disagreement, but allows the major points to linger or diminish in importance with time. Two particular methods are classified as defusion strategies: smoothing and compromise.

Smoothing is a process of playing down the differences between two groups while accentuating their similarities and common interests. Identifying and stressing similarities and common interests between conflicting parties can eventually lead to the groups realizing that they are not as far apart (e.g., goal incompatibility) as they initially believed. Although building on a common viewpoint is preferable to an avoidance philosophy, the sources of conflict have not been fully confronted and remain under the surface. Sooner or later, the central conflict issues will surface, possibly creating a more severe situation then.

Compromise is a "give and take" exchange, resulting in neither a clear winner nor loser. Compromise can be utilized when the object, goal, or resource in conflict can be divided in some way between the competing groups. In other cases, one group may yield on one point if it can gain something in exchange. Some types of management-labor negotiations can be viewed as compromise. For example, management will agree to a cost-of-living pay increase if labor will guarantee productivity increases. Compromise is generally effective when the conflicting groups are relatively equal in strength. However, in situations where one of the groups is significantly stronger or in a better position than the second group, a compromise strategy would probably not work because the stronger group would hold out for a one-sided solution.

Confrontation.   This final conflict resolution strategy differs from avoidance and defusion in that the sources of conflict are generally identified and discussed, which emphasizes the attainment of the common interests of the conflicting groups. Three techniques are categorized as confrontation methods: mutual personnel exchange, emphasis on a superordinate goal, and problem-solving or confrontation meetings.

Mutual personnel exchange involves increasing the communication and understanding between groups by exchanging personnel for a time. The assumption underlying this strategy is that the exchanged personnel can learn about the other group and communicate their impressions to their original group. For example, a common practice among manufacturing firms is to have shipping supervisors and sales representatives exchange roles. During the short exchange period (usually three to six weeks), it is hoped that each will gain an appreciation for the other's job. This approach is limited because it is only a temporary solution mechanism. In addition, on their return to their permanent groups, the exchanged personnel may be treated as outsiders, which may result in their knowledge and opinions not being fully utilized.

Superordinate goals are common, more important goals on which the conflicting parties can focus their attention. Such goals are unattainable by one group alone and generally supersede all other goals of each group. A common superordinate goal could be the survival of the organization. Petty differences are considered unimportant when the survival of the overall organization is in question.

Problem solving involves bringing together conflicting groups in order to conduct a formal confrontation meeting. The objective of this approach is to have the groups present their views to each other and work through the differences in attitudes and perceptions. Issues of who is right or wrong are not allowed; only the identification of problems and possible solutions is permitted. This technique is most effective when a thorough analysis of the problem and identification of points of mutual interest can be made and alternatives can be suggested. A problem-solving approach, however, requires great time and commitment and usually is ineffective when the source of conflict originates from value-laden issues.

REMOVING BARRIERS TO IMPROVED
JOB PERFORMANCE: JOB STRESS

It is well-established that most organizations place a high value on the members of their management team. An organization's set of human resources, especially managers, provide the direction, motivation, leadership, and control that leads to profitability, growth, and survival.

Until recently, organizations have stressed the development and retention of management through selection, training, varied job assignments, and an effective reward system. This level of emphasis and resources given to management development, however, can go up in smoke when promising, effective managers are stricken with heart attacks or other physiological disorders. It is because of this situation that many organizations are placing an increased emphasis on understanding and reducing a primary factor in such physiological and health problems—job stress.

Stress, which we will define as an internal experience or position creating a physiological or psychological imbalance within the individual, has been addressed in both the medical and management literatures.[17] It is only recently that the two literatures have been combined to form a more comprehensive framework of the relationship between organizational stress and physiological disorders. In general, a review of the two literatures suggests that:

1. A great variety of organizational and environmental conditions are capable of producing stress.
2. Different individuals respond to the same conditions in different ways.
3. The intensity and extent of stress within the individual are difficult to predict.
4. The consequences of prolonged stress may include behavioral issues, such as increased absenteeism, or a chronic disease, such as coronary heart disease.

In order more fully to understand job stress, a framework for analysis is presented in exhibit 15-6. Five major categories are included in the framework: stressors, stress moderators, actual stress, the outcomes of stress, and possible stress reducers.

Stressors

Exhibit 15-6 identifies three main stressor categories: environmental factors, organizational factors, and individual factors. Stressors are essentially the sources of stress, or factors that facilitate the development of job stress.

Environmental factors relate to the general environmental situation and its impact on the organization and individuals. Such concerns as the state of the economy (e.g., inflation, recession, unemployment rate, increasing competition), uncertainties in the political arena (e.g., how will new mayors, senators, governors, and other representatives vote on important issues?), and the general quality of life (e.g., pollution, decline of the importance of family, rising crime) all can create a state of stress.

Many of the organizational factors have been discussed in previous chapters, including the three levels of analysis we have discussed throughout. At the *organizational level,* stress can be induced by an in-

EXHIBIT 15-6   Job Stress Analysis Framework

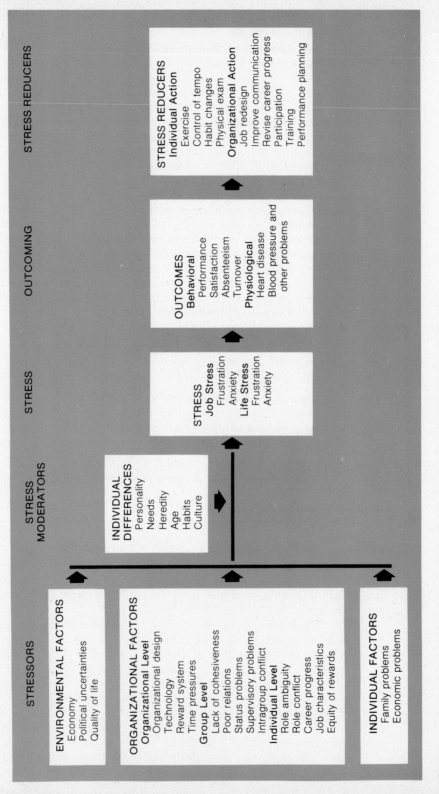

Suggested from J. M. Ivancevich and M. T. Matteson, "Managing for a Healthier Heart," Management Review (October 1978): 17.

effective organizational design (e.g., too much emphasis on rules, procedures, and control systems) or from a less-than-satisfactory reward system. *Group-level* stressors include problems related to low cohesion, conflict, or a coercive supervisor. At the *individual* level, the emphasis is on dysfunctions associated with role (e.g., role ambiguity and role conflict), jobs that are either too routine and boring or too complex to handle, or a lack of career progress.

Individual factors concern such stressors as family (e.g., illness or divorce), economic difficulties (e.g., rising household and mortgage costs), and issues of mobility (e.g., disruption of family life with a transfer to another state).

Stress Moderators—Personality and International Factors

It is suggested that certain of the variables—singly or in some combination—are moderators that either accentuate or diminish the impact of stressors. Some researchers have suggested that personality differences are important stress moderators, involving such concepts as self-esteem, self-confidence, and aggressiveness. The most frequently cited is the work of Friedman and his associates, who are responsible for the development of the type A and type B personality taxonomy.[18] According to their approach, individuals exhibiting aggressive, hard-driving personality characteristics (type A) are more susceptible to heart disease than are their more relaxed counterparts (type B). Other more demographic variables have been shown to relate to stress and physiological disorders. Included are such variables as heredity, age, exercise, diet, and alcohol and tobacco use.

Culture can also be viewed as a moderator of stress. For example, in a recent study comparing U. S. and Canadian managers, some interesting similarities and differences were found.[19] The findings indicated that managers in both countries felt that lack of clarity in one's job was an important stress inducer. On the other hand, Canadian managers reported that a great deal of their stress was caused by the use of inappropriate organizational design, while U. S. managers felt that high stress was more the result of the great pressures put on them for effective decision-making.

Stress

We identify stress—perceived and/or actual—as involving two categories. *Job stress* is associated with organizational causes; *life stress* concerns individual and/or family causes. For each stress category, two components of stress are noted: frustration and anxiety. First, frustration applies to any obstruction or barrier between behavior and its goal. Frustration can occur from a change, delay, or lack of reinforcement for certain behaviors (e.g., not receiving a sales contract even though all preparatory factors were done correctly); or simple obstructions (e.g., rules or procedures that prevent the adoption of a new work technique). Whereas frustration is blockage or interference with behavior, anxiety is the feeling of not having the appropriate response, or feeling a lack of preparation for some activity. Examples could be taking a CPA exam, conducting a performance evaluation, or presenting a marketing plan to the board of directors while not feeling confident in so doing.

"I don't like to seem pushy, but it has been some time
since we've heard an 'eureka' in this research lab."

Stress Outcomes

Stress can be costly to an organization. For instance, recent figures from
the U. S. National Clearing House for Mental Health Information show
that stress resulted in a $12 billion decrease in the productive capacity
of U. S. industrial workers. This includes excessive absenteeism ($5.5
billion), excessive unemployment ($2.7 billion), and inefficiency on the
job ($1.9 billion). Startling as these figures are, they represent only stress
that has resulted in mental problems. Excessive stress that has resulted
in psychosomatic and/or physical disorders may even have a bigger impact
on organizational performance.[20]

In our framework, the outcomes of stress are shown as relating to
both physiological and behavioral factors. A number of studies have
shown the potential link between stress and such dysfunctional physiological outcomes as heart disease. Similarly, stress and such behavioral
outcomes as work dissatisfaction, decreased performance, and increased
absenteeism have been reported. There is also some research that suggests that behavioral and physiological outcomes are related; in particular, job and life satisfaction may be related to heart disease.

Stress Reducers

Because excessive stress can be related to both organizations and individuals, it is important for managers to understand the causes and reactions to stress and understand potential methods of stress reduction.

As shown in exhibit 15-8, stress reducers include individual and
organizational actions.[21]

Individual Actions.   First and foremost, a physical exam conducted by
a doctor is almost a prerequisite to any stress-reduction program. Knowl-

edge about one's physical condition, smoking and drinking habits, coronary history, and heredity all help in understanding the causes of stress and its potential effects. Other individual actions include increasing exercise, changing habits, and learning to control the tempo of the day's work through relaxation exercises or meditation.

Organizational Factors.   The responsibility for stress reduction also falls on the organization. Because many stressors are related to ambiguous or conflicting job activities, the organization may take such steps as improving communications, redesigning jobs to decrease boredom or remove unnecessary demands, revising career paths to be more realistic, increasing participation in decision making, training in stress causes and reduction procedures, or performance planning (e.g., MBO).

Overall, although we have emphasized the negative effects of stress, let us not overlook one very important aspect: stress is and will continue to be a daily fact of working in contemporary complex organizations. Some managers, in fact, thrive and are most effective under stressful conditions. The key point, however, is that managers must recognize that reduction of the dysfunctional consequences of stress is strongly determined by the degree of understanding of stressors and the ability to diagnose their existence and causes.

IMPROVED JOB PERFORMANCE AND THE MANAGER'S JOB

In this chapter, we have focused our attention on improving job performance. The four selected techniques—the creative and innovative process, MBO, conflict, and stress analysis—were chosen not only because of their popularity and number of reported successes, but because they represent two views of management: planning for improved job performance, and removing the barriers to effective job performance.

There are a number of managerial skills and roles that are related to these performance techniques. With creativity and innovation, *human* and *conceptual* skills are most salient. Human skills concern the manner in which the manager establishes the climate for creative and innovative activities to occur. The success of the innovative proposal stage is determined to a great extent by a manager's conceptual skills—the degree to which the need and technology can be synthesized. Managerial roles are also closely involved with creativity and innovation. The manager's *liaison* interpersonal role and all the *informational* roles are important because of their emphasis on communication and information flow, which are so crucial to the innovation process. The manner in which the manager performs his or her *entrepreneurial* and *resource allocator* roles helps to move the creative and innovative process toward a successful conclusion.

All four of the managerial skills are involved in MBO. *Technical skills* relate to how the manager follows the MBO process steps; *human skills* concern the important interactions between the manager and subordinate; *conceptual skills* come to the forefront when the manager links the performance plans of the subordinates to the total organization; and *diagnostic skills* relate not only to analyzing the particular jobs, but especially to the interim review stage when internal and/or external changes force a revision of an employee's goals and plans. From a managerial role perspective, the manager's interpersonal *leader* role and all the *informational* roles also are important to the MBO process.

Human and *diagnostic* skills are the most important managerial skills in the resolution of organizational conflict. That is, diagnostic skills relate to the process of identifying the sources of conflict, while human skills become salient in the interpersonal activities in the resolution process. Successful conflict resolution is also related to the performance of the manager in a *leader* role and in the *disturbance handler resource allocator* and *negotiator* decisional roles.

Finally, in identifying the sources of stress, the manager's *conceptual* and *diagnostic skills* come into action. Managers must also recognize if their performance in the *leader* and *resource allocator* roles is contributing to excessive stress among and between employees. In reducing stress, managers emphasize their *human skills* and *informational* roles.

SUMMARY FOR THE MANAGER

1. The theoretical material on motivation, leadership, and group behavior can be integrated into an applied framework directed at improving job performance. Understanding this framework is important because a manager, in order to reach high performance levels, must be able to motivate and lead individuals and individuals in groups.

2. Two of the most important factors in facilitating the creative and innovative process in organizations are improving information flow and creating a climate for innovation. A lack of information flow coupled with a coercive team environment will deter the development of new ideas, new products, and new services.

3. A key factor for managers to understand is that creativity and innovation are functions more of the immediate environment than functions of the size of the organization or industry. The organization can provide the needed resources for creativity and innovation to occur; however, one-on-one relationships are the real heart of this process.

4. In its most basic form, management by objectives is really a simplified expression of the total management process. It involves planning (describing and analyzing one's job, setting goals, and so on), organizing (establishing action plans), leading (joint agreement and review), control (interim and final results evaluation), and change (recycling the process).

5. The manager can use MBO to achieve a number of purposes. Examples include clarifying the subordinate's job, establishing a unified effort among members, enhancing the planning process, improving the merit review process, or identifying high-performing managers for future advancement. Not only should this purpose be made clear to the employees, but it is essential that the manager receive top management support and commitment to the use of MBO. Properly implemented, MBO can be a powerful performance determinant; improperly used, it can be looked upon as an unnecessary chore.

6. Managers must recognize that conflict is a common occurrence in most organizations. The crucial factor for managers with respect to conflict is to develop the skills to properly diagnose the sources of conflict. These sometimes complex sources relate to goal incompatibility, allocation of resources, performance expectations, and the organization's structure.

7. Once the sources of conflict have been identified, the resolution process can begin. Managers who choose an avoidance or defusion approach to conflict resolution must understand that these approaches rarely get at the heart of the conflict. As a result, it can return, often in a more severe form. The confrontation approach is much more complicated and time consuming; however, because it emphasizes source identification, the chances for effective resolution significantly improve.

8. Dynamic external environmental changes and growing internal complexity, coupled with personal issues, have catapulted the concern for managerial stress to the forefront in the managerial literature. While stress has been shown to relate to psychological and physical disorders, it is important for the manager to understand that stress is part of every job, whether managerial or nonmanagerial. The key factor is excessive stress and methods of reducing it to manageable proportions.

9. The methods of reducing managerial stress are just beginning to develop. The current emphasis is placed on identifying and controlling organizational factors that contribute to excessive stress, and on using individual methods such as changing habits and reducing the tempo of one's job.

10. The successful use of techniques to improve job performance is closely related to the managerial skills and roles, especially human skills, conceptual skills, and informational roles.

QUESTIONS FOR REVIEW AND DISCUSSION

1. Why is creativity a crucial part of the manager's job?
2. What is the difference between creativity and innovation?
3. Why is it said that many new ideas for products or the formation of new companies fail because they have not successfully passed through the innovation proposal stage?
4. What are the similarities and differences between MBO and the management process?
5. What are the different functions or purposes that can be served by MBO in organizations?
6. Why is it important to have top management commitment and support for an MBO program?
7. Under what conditions can the organization's structure cause conflict?
8. Why is a confrontation approach to conflict resolution preferable to either an avoidance or defusion approach?
9. Why do some managers believe that some stress has a positive influence on a manager's performance?
10. What techniques or practices can the individual adopt to help reduce excessive stress on the job?

NOTES

1. L. B. Mohr, "Determinants of Innovation in Organizations," *American Political Science Review* (1969): 112.

2. G. F. Kneller, *The Art and Science of Creativity* (New York: Holt, Rinehart and Winston, 1965).

3. H. J. Reitz, *Behavior in Organizations* (Homewood, Ill.: Irwin, 1977), pp. 235–242.

4. J. M. Utterback, "Innovation in Industry and the Diffusion of Technology," *Science* (February 15, 1974): 620–26.

5. J. M. Utterback, "The Process of Innovation," *NAECON Record* (1970): 19–26.

6. Ibid., p. 21.

7. D. Cordtz, "How Polaroid Bet Its Future on the SX-70," *Fortune* (January 1974): 82–86.

8. Reitz, *Behavior in Organizations*, pp. 242–48.

9. I. Summers and D. E. White, "Creativity Techniques: Toward Improvement of the Decision Process," *Academy of Management Review* (April 1976): 99–107.

10. "Kellogg—Still the Cereal People," *Business Week* (November 26, 1979): 80–93.

11. R. E. Dutton, "Creative Use of Creative People," *Personnel Journal* (November 1972): 818–22.

12. See J. D. Hlavecek and V. A. Thompson, "Bureaucracy and Venture Failures," *Academy of Management Review* (April 1978): 242–48; and "Vanishing Innovation," *Business Week* (July 3, 1978): 46–54.

13. G. S. Odiorne, *Management by Objectives* (New York: Pittman, 1965), p. 8.

14. A. D. Szilagyi and M. Wallace, *Organizational Behav-*

ior and Performance, 2nd ed. (Santa Monica, California: Goodyear, 1980), p. 136.

15. M. Dalton, "Conflicts Between Staff and Line Managerial Officers," *American Sociological Review* (June 1950): 243–51.

16. R. T. Golembieski and A. Blumberg, "Confrontation as a Training Design in Complex Organizations," *Journal of Applied Behavioral Science* (October 1967): 525–47.

17. M. T. Matteson and J. M. Ivancevich, "Organizational Stressors, Physiological and Behavioral Outcomes and Coronary Heart Disease: A Research Model," *Academy of Management Review* (July 1979): 347–58.

18. M. Friedman and R. Roseman, "Overt Behavior Pattern in Coronary Disease," *Journal of the American Medical Association* (1960): 1320.

19. R. E. Rogers, "Executive Stress," *Human Resource Management* (Fall 1975): 21–24.

20. Rogers, "Executive Stress," p. 21.

21. J. C. Quick and J. D. Quick, "Reducing Stress Through Preventive Management," *Human Resource Management* (Fall 1979): 15–22.

ADDITIONAL REFERENCES

Abend, C. J. "Innovation Management: The Missing Link in Productivity." *Management Review* (June 1979): 25–28.

Dryer, W. G. *Team Building.* Reading, Mass.: Addison-Wesley, 1977.

Keller, R. T. and Holland, W. E. "Technical Information Flows and Innovative Processes." Final Report on the National Science Foundation Grant PRA76-18441, October 1978.

Latham, G. P. and Locke, E. A. "Goal Setting—A Motivational Technique that Works." *Organizational Dynamics* (Autumn 1979): 68–80.

McGaffey, T. N. "New Horizons in Organizational Stress Prevention Approaches." *The Personnel Administrator* (November 1978): 26–34.

Pierce, J. L. and Delbecq. "Organizational Structure, Individual Attitudes and Innovation." *Academy of Management Review* (January 1977): 27–37.

Raia, A. P. *Management by Objectives.* Glenview, Ill.: Scott, Foresman, 1974.

Robertson, T. S. *Innovative Behavior and Communication.* New York: Holt, Rinehart, and Winston, 1971.

Rogers, E. M. *Diffusion of Innovations.* New York: Free Press, 1962.

Schmidt, S. M. and Kochan, T. A. "Conflict: Toward Conceptual Clarity." *Administrative Science Quarterly* (September 1972): 359–70.

A CASE FOR ANALYSIS

McDonnell-Douglas

Shortly after Sanford N. "Sandy" McDonnell was named chief executive of McDonnell-Douglas Corp. in 1972, he got into a mild dispute with his predecessor, James S. "Mr. Mac" McDonnell, who is his uncle and the company's chairman. When the elder McDonnell insisted on having his way, Sandy objected: "But Mr. Mac, you and the board made me president last year, and you've just made me chief executive officer." "That's right," the senior McDonnell responded. "You're the CEO, and I'm the boss."

The chairman's influence, for example, was sharply reflected in the company's agonizing decision to abandon development of so-called "new-generation" jetliners in the mid-size, medium-range class to compete with Boeing and Europe's Airbus Industrie. In accord with Mr. Mac's well-known bent for frugality and prudence, McDonnell-Douglas is concentrating on derivative designs of the DC-9 and DC-10.

Suggested from "Where Management Style Set the Strategy," Business Week (October 23, 1978): 88–99; and Rush Loving, Jr., "Unraveling the Riddle of the DC-10," Fortune (July 16, 1979): 54–61.

rather than launching costly new development programs to meet the new boom in airline buying.

The chairman's ultraconservative style also shows up clearly in a corporate diversification strategy that continues to limit new ventures to natural outgrowths of the company's existing aerospace, electronics, and related high-technology operations. McDonnell-Douglas is not—and never has been—interested in acquiring companies in general industrial fields, although such deals are brought regularly to its attention.

Now Mr. Mac is finally showing signs of pulling back from running the company he built. McDonnell-Douglas has thrived consistently on a steady flow of military aircraft orders and has become celebrated as one of the Pentagon's most proficient and lowest-cost producers. And unlike Boeing, whose backlog of defense orders has shriveled, McDonnell-Douglas has never lacked for new work to replace expiring contracts.

McDonnell-Douglas has prospered in the defense market because of superior technical talents (it was a pioneer in computer-aided design and automated manufacturing techniques), a prodigious skill in controlling costs and meeting schedules, and an uncanny ability to anticipate military needs. What sets them apart is the meticulous personal management attention from the top that is given to detail.

Despite his advancing age, the chairman is alert, energetic, and in good health. Trim and fit, he looks like a man in his early sixties and comes into his office nearly every morning. He presides over meetings of the company's board, division presidents, and the executive committee, and pokes into any matter that attracts his attention.

McDonnell-Douglas is a prototype for proprietary-style management. The chairman's reluctance to give up the managerial reins and the long drawn-out transition at the top are probably endemic in such an environment. The company is one of the very few giant corporations in which the founder is still actively on the premises. Mr. Mac has run the St. Louis–based company with a firm hand and has taken a fierce personal pride in its success as a frontrunner in one of the most competitive and technologically advanced industries.

In few, if any, companies its size has a single man's influence been so pervasive. In style and tone, McDonnell-Douglas directly mirrors Mr. Mac's personal characteristics. A brilliant engineer and aircraft designer, he has built a company that is exceedingly inbred, paternalistic, dominated by engineers, and infused with a penchant for penny-pinching—except when parsimony interferes with the chairman's passion for technology. The company has never stinted on spending for research and for the most advanced plant and equipment.

Most of the company's top- and middle-level managers have never worked anywhere else, and outsiders are rarely recruited for important jobs. Half the company's stock is owned by employees, including 20 percent in the hands of the elder McDonnell and his two sons.

The word "employee" is rarely used at McDonnell-Douglas. In company regulations, correspondence, and even in conversation, people on the payroll are normally referred to as "teammates." Says an executive: "Mr. Mac would have preferred to call them 'comrades,' except that the Communists have usurped the word."

The chairman's frugality and engineering orientation were both displayed many years ago in what has become a bit of corporate folklore: At an office Christmas party he used a slide rule to figure out how much whiskey to put into the punch bowl. More recently, his concern about obesity and heart disease induced him to introduce a low-calorie, low-cholesterol diet in the executive dining room. He personally calculated the calories, protein, and cholesterol content of major food items—including "1 slice of corned beef $3 \times 2 \times \frac{1}{4}$ in."—and attached file cards to the menus to specify the ingredients down to the decimal point.

The management style at McDonnell-Douglas is the strategy. Measuring every risk carefully, being highly conservative, and being dedicated to technical approaches produce a strategy without debating it around a table. Right away, you rule out a lot of strategies because they don't fit the character.

As the company crew from a very modest start into a giant corporation, "Mr. Mac always liked to look at it as a gathering of his friends," says a veteran executive. This was once demonstrated in such practices as gifts of baby shoes to new fathers. Such managerial folksiness, of course, is more difficult to display with a payroll that now numbers 65,000. But the president is trying to retain as much of a family-style atmosphere as possible. Like his uncle, who regularly used the plantwide public address system to inform employees of new contract awards and other vital company news—greeting them crisply with "this is Mac calling the team"—Sandy also takes to the microphone to keep in personal contact. He comes on with a more diffident salutation: "May I please have your attention? This is Sandy McDonnell."

In this highly personalized type of environment, McDonnell-Douglas has developed what can be called an avuncular form of management. There is, for example, a preoccupation with face-to-face meetings and only a minor regard for the organizational protocol that more institutionalized corporations possess.

In addition to the regular meetings in which Sandy McDonnell and his uncle sit down with the operating divisions and the company's executive committee, the president meets weekly at separate conferences with the treasurer and controller. Daily at 8:20 a.m., he holds what are commonly called "standup meetings" with his vice presidents. These usually last only ten to fifteen minutes—long enough for major problems and routine situations to be discussed. "No one sits," says one vice president, "because once you get on your butt, you might stay too long." Similar types of "standup meetings" are held daily in the operating divisions and in the offices of project managers throughout the company.

But no one interprets this informality as a license for untrammeled free will at the operational level. The company has a tightly centralized management reporting and financial controls system. In an appraisal that applies to the entire company, a Douglas Aircraft executive stresses that "there are no free-thinkers or wheeler-dealers around here."

As Sandy McDonnell assumes increasing influence, some executives observe signs of a transition from paternal management to a modernized management structure. In essence, they mean a switch to major decision-making that is based more on the input of others than on the thinking in the head of a single individual, Mr. Mac.

Questions for Discussion

1. How does McDonnell-Douglas approach the creative and innovative processes?
2. When Mr. Mac is gone, would you expect conflict and stress to increase? Why?
3. Why has Mr. Mac's approach to job performance been so successful to date?

EXPERIENTIAL EXERCISE

Conflict

Purpose

To study the causes and possible resolution strategies for conflict in teams.

Required Understanding

The reader should be familiar with the issues and concepts relating to conflict.

How to Set Up the Exercise

Set up groups of four to eight students for the forty-five to sixty-minute exercise. The groups should be separated from each other and members asked to converse only with their group members. Before forming the groups, participants are asked to complete the exercise by themselves and then to join the group and reach a decision.

The Situation

Assume that you are employed by a larger corporation specializing in the manufacture and marketing of commodity and specialty chemicals. Your particular position is manufacturing manager—plastics. You report to the vice president of manufacturing, who, in turn, reports to the divisional vice president.

Currently, your firm is experiencing a relatively high growth rate in sales and profits due to the recent introduction of new product lines; your products represent a major portion of this high growth rate. In order to provide better coordination of new-product development and marketing efforts, the president of your firm decided to establish product-planning teams for each new product or product lines. Each team is responsible for the effective planning and coordination of efforts necessary to bring the new product through the pilot, plant construction, and initial marketing phases.

Last year, a product-planning team was established to coordinate the introduction of a new, extremely durable, but expensive plastic to be used in the electronics industry. The team consists of yourself and representatives from engineering, research, and marketing departments. The representative from engineering has been appointed as chairperson of the planning team. Pilot plant studies have been concluded, and the team will be meeting shortly to discuss the various aspects of construction of the new plant.

This morning, the planning team conducted a meeting at which you presented a plan for the construction of the new plant. The plan contained material, equipment, and capacity details and a proposed construction time-schedule. Incorporated in your plan was the use of new processing equipment that will provide considerable manufacturing cost savings over existing equipment. The delivery time of this newer equipment, however, is estimated to be twelve months longer than equipment that is currently available.

During the team meeting, the marketing representative voiced strong opposition to your plan, indicating that the primary emphasis should be on placing this new product on the market as soon as possible. You, however, pointed out that the long-term benefits of your plan, in terms of manufacturing cost savings, outweigh short-term marketing considerations. The discussion became increasingly heated and tense as each of you became further entrenched in your positions. In addition, the engineering representative believed that you have the most valid point, and decided to go along with the original plan. The research representative, however, agreed with the marketing representative, which resulted in a stalemated meeting with no decision being made.

After the meeting, as you reflect on what has happened, you are clearly upset and disturbed. You are aware that the views expressed by you and the marketing team member represent not only your personal views, but the positions of the total manufacturing and marketing departments. Because you believe that this is a serious problem between the two departments, you decide that something must be done quickly to insure the success of the project. You see the alternatives as follows:

1. You can rework your plan to go along with the objections of the marketing representative, and do the best you can with the long-term manufacturing cost considerations of the plan.
2. You can have a meeting with the marketing representative at which you stress the positive aspects of the project and point out that the new equipment will make the company the foremost producer of the product in the world.
3. You can send a letter to the president resigning your position on the team.
4. You can tell the marketing representative that if he goes with your position now, you will give full support to his new marketing plan that is to be presented to the team in the near future.
5. You can go to the divisional vice president and request that he intercede for you.
6. You can ask the marketing representative to meet with you for a full day the next week in order to work out your differences and come up with an alternative solution.
7. You can ask a member of the divisional vice president's staff to sit in on all team meetings and act as the new chairperson and arbitrator of all problems.
8. You can send the marketing representative a letter (with copies to all team members, the divisional vice president, and the president) indicating that his opposition to your plan is holding up a potentially profitable project.
9. You can ask the divisional vice president to attend the next team meeting in order to stress the importance of this project to the continued growth of the company.
10. You can immediately walk into the marketing representative's office and ask him to justify his position to you.

Instructions for the Exercise

1. Individually, group members should:
   a. Identify the cause(s) of the present conflict situation.
   b. On exhibit 15-7, identify the type of conflict resolution and rank-order each of the ten possible alternatives from 1 (the most desirable) to 10 (the least desirable).
2. Form into the preassigned groups and answer question 1 as a group. Fill in the group responses on exhibit 15-7.
3. A spokesperson from each group should give the instructor the group's decision and a rationale for that deicion.

EXHIBIT 15-7   Intergroup Conflict Exercise

CONFLICT-RESOLUTION ALTERNATIVE	INDIVIDUAL		GROUP	
	Type of Resolution	Rank	Type of Resolution	Rank
1.				
2.				
3.				
4.				
5.				
6.				
7.				
8.				
9.				
10.				

V

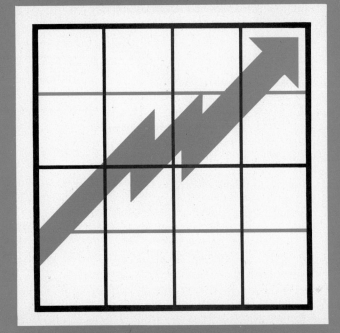

Evaluating Performance
Performance
– Control –

16

Control Elements and Behavioral Control Systems

CHAPTER OUTLINE

KEY POINTS IN THIS CHAPTER

1. Control is a managerial function that assures that actual activities conform to planned activities. Three types of control are found in most organizations: input controls, process controls, and output controls.

2. Performance evaluations in organizations vary by approach and method. The most popular methods include rankings, ratings, critical incidents, BARS, and MBO.

3. The appraisal interview is the heart of the evaluation process. Learning how to conduct this interview effectively is a crucial skill for managers.

4. Pay—which can involve base pay, pay increase methods, and supplemental pay—is one of the organization's most powerful reward system components.

5, Promotion programs in organizations are moving toward more openness. This includes an emphasis on job postings and improved communication with employees.

6. Employee benefits can be quite costly to an organization. Cafeteria plans and the use of executive perks are gaining in popularity.

7. Employee terminations are originated by the organization or by the individual. The latter, employee resignation, has multiple sources, some of which are uncontrollable.

8. A control system involves the use of many managerial skills and roles.

THE PRACTICE OF MANAGEMENT

Integrating Planning and Control: Emerson Electric

When a young management consultant named Charles F. Knight took over as chairman of St. Louis's Emerson Electric Company a few years ago, Wall Street had some doubts about the future of the company. The doubts soon faded as Knight took charge and quickened Emerson's growth pace.

Emerson's net profit of nearly 8 percent is well above the industry average of 4.6 percent, and its 18 percent return on capital compares with an estimated industry average of 12.5 percent. The company's success is attributed to the unique way it has engineered and managed that impressive record. Maintaining the flexibility usually associated with a small company, it has flourished through a meticulously orchestrated growth plan and a management control system that is considered one of the best in industry.

Widely diversified, Emerson produces hundreds of electrical and electronic components and related products for commercial and industrial use, consumer markets, and the government. This diversification, as well as its broad customer base, has long been considered one of the company's major strengths.

Emerson is decentralized by product lines into thirty-five divisions, each of which makes its own operating decisions and is run pretty much as an independent company. Knight keeps as much decision making as possible at the operating level because he feels that division managers are in the best position to respond quickly to the marketplace and determine what steps can be taken at the lowest cost in keeping with efficiency and product quality.

Emerson's growth plan calls for both internal expansion and external expansion through acquisitions. At the same time, Knight has developed a sophisticated system of internal management controls that allows Emerson, which operates in markets where price competitiveness is often of top priority, to build sales by consistently underpricing the competition and yet maintain high quality and profit margins.

Planning and control start at the division level, where each manager must come up with detailed growth projections (one year and five year) for every product line—showing how much growth will come from acquisitions, internal sales, new product development, and overseas and government business. The priorities and strategies for attaining the next year's goals are refined in a corporate planning conference that top management holds with division managers. What emerges is a written plan of action and control systems for achieving the goals, product by product, with subordinate managers made responsible for dozens of lesser goals. That manual becomes the bible for every manager.

Emerson also motivates its managers through an incentive system that pays bonuses of up to 40 percent of salary for meeting goals. But most important, Knight believes, is the commitment of all managers to meet those goals. "There are a lot of companies that have systems to control profits," he says, "but what most of them lack is the dedication and commitment that goes down six and seven levels." Knight believes that the reason planning and cost control work better at Emerson is the flexibility, incentives, and discipline incorporated into their system.

At the operating level, Emerson eschews the giant factories favored by such competitors as General Electric. Few Emerson plants employ more than 600 workers. At this smaller size, Knight feels that management can maintain personal contact with individual employees. Emerson puts heavy stress on those personal contacts with employees, spending thousands of dollars every year on personnel surveys, employee communications, and periodic performance reviews with each worker. In addition, Emerson pays prevailing wages in localities where it operates, as opposed to inflexible corporate-wide wage schedules. Even employee benefits such as medical and pension plans are negotiated at the plant level.

Adapted from "Emerson Electric: The Unique Manager," Dun's Review *(December 1977):* 52–55.

16

With this chapter, we begin a three-chapter sequence dealing with the important managerial function of control. We will be concerned with those managerial activities that assure that both the actual operations and the final products or services of an organization conform to stated goals and plans. As noted in many of the earlier chapters (especially chapter 3), the control function is not only well-founded in management history, but it continues today to be a most crucial management activity.

In this first chapter, the discussion will focus on two aspects of control. First, the foundational elements of control, including the process of control and the various types of control, will be presented. The second part of the chapter will be devoted to an analysis of the control function as it applies to the behavior of employees.

ELEMENTS OF CONTROL

The control function is one of the major guiding principles of the entire management process. Control of activities is found in all types of organizations. For example, Teledyne won't invest in a new project unless it can return 20 percent on assets; Polaroid not only wanted a debris-less film, but a camera that could fit into a man's coat pocket; Kellogg's will introduce a new cereal if it can capture at least 1 percent of the market; the Cleveland Clinic limits the number of research assistants that are hired in relationship to the amount of grant money that is available.

Managers themselves have their own philosophy of control, which not only guides their behavior, but influences the behavior of those around them. For instance, consider the case of Harry Gray, the hard-driving chairman of United Technologies.

> Gray considers himself a prototype of the corporate generalist. He is as interested in financial management as he is in marketing, and he has introduced exceptionally tight-fisted financial controls on both operating expenses and capital investment. To generate more cash flow, he has reduced "days outstanding" on accounts by as much as 40 percent and has increased "turnover of inventories" significantly.
>
> Gray is also a very tough taskmaster. There has been a steady exodus of managers who have failed to meet his profit targets and controls. "Harry is a helluva driver who demands constant attention to detail," says a man who once worked for him. "Although he delegated responsibility, he wanted to be part of the process. He wanted to know what every one of his people was doing every minute of the day. Some people wouldn't go to the bathroom without calling Harry."[1]

While this example may illustrate the extremes of behavioral control, it does suggest that control is an integral part of every manager's job.

Planning and control work hand-in-hand in organizations. For example, consider the interrelationships among the concepts of direction, resources, problems, and performance:

Planning		*Control*
Provides a sense of direction and attention to goals	DIRECTION	Guides activities toward organizational ends
Allocates the resources of the organization	RESOURCES	Insures the effective utilization of organizational resources
Anticipates problems	PROBLEMS	Corrects problems
Motivates employees to achieve organizational goals	EMPLOYEE	Rewards employees for goal achievement

More than anything else, these interrelationships should suggest to the student that the elements of the management process must be integrated in order to achieve some level of acceptable performance.[2]

The Control Process

Control, like many managerial functions, is a process that involves a number of steps. As shown in exhibit 16-1, there are usually four steps in the control process:

1. *Establish performance standards.* Standards are reference points to which actual performance can be compared. In their most basic form, standards are the various goals and subgoals that have been set by the organization. Examples include load factors and seat-miles by airline companies, and sales per square foot in department stores.

2. *Measure performance.* Measuring performance has at least two aspects. First, what *methods* will be used to measure the level of performance. As discussed in chapter 2, quantitative measures, qualitative measures, or a combination of both can be used. For example, a manager's performance can be measured according to the unit's profit contribution to the organization (quantitative measure) and the superior's evaluation of such subjective measures as the manager's initiative and ability to get along with others (qualitative measures). The second major consideration is *time*—when will the activity be measured? As pointed out in chapter 12 in the discussion of reinforcement schedules, at least two time-frames can be used—continuous or intermittent. The former concerns measures of activities that occur on each unit, such as quality-control checks on tractors manufactured by John Deere. The latter involves measures of activities at specified time intervals, such as a manager's yearly merit review or the bi-monthly evaluation of inventories by a business supply distributor. The important consideration for managers in choosing the time interval is that it should not be so short as to incur excessive control costs, nor so long such that performance problems are not detected.

3. *Compare the performance to the standard.* As shown in exhibit 16-1, this step involves a decision by the manager. If performance meets the standard, the control process returns to the measurement stage. On the other hand, if performance does not meet the standard, some form of corrective action may be required.

4. *Corrective action.* Corrective action by the organization and/or the manager is required when the performance and performance standard do not match. This deviation between performance and standard can be favorable or unfavorable to the organization. For example, a department store may establish a standard of $20 sales per square foot of store space for

EXHIBIT 16-1
Steps in a Control
Process

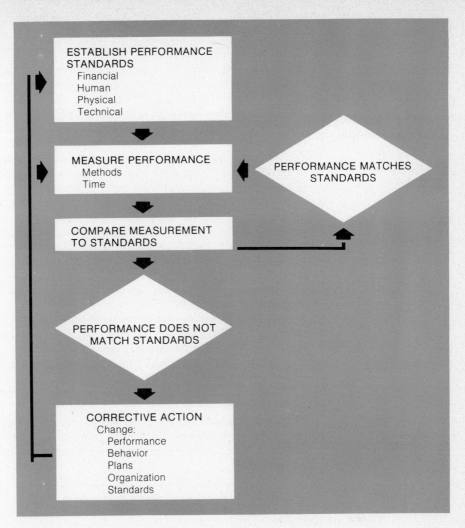

each store. If a particular store reports sales of $24 per square foot, no corrective action may be needed, since the deviation is favorable to the organization. In the long run, the standard may be revised upward, or it might be determined that this store offers an opportunity for expansion. In contrast, consider a domestic airline in the monthly process of evaluating the performance of its individual routes. If a particular route is operating at only 45 percent of aircraft seat capacity (when 65 percent is the stated standard), the airline may contemplate such corrective measures as added promotion, fare decreases, or even discontinuation of the route. Corrective action can thus change the performance of the unit, or force a re-evaluation of the standard and its associated goals and plans.

As this brief discussion of the control process indicates, control is an important function that is performed by managers in all types of organizations. Control involves such aspects as financial performance, inventory cost control, sales force performance, absenteeism and turnover, employee productivity, safety, market share, and the like. It is, therefore, found throughout an organization.

THE
MANAGER'S
JOB
Victor Rice of
Massey-Ferguson
Ltd. (Canada)

Massey-Ferguson Ltd., the large Canadian farm equipment multinational, has earned praise from many analysts for rebounding from an operating loss of $132.5 million in 1978 to a $30.2 million operating profit in 1979. Much of the credit for this turnaround goes to Mr. Victor Rice, president and chief operating officer, and his tightening of organizational controls. But the praise may be premature. Among the many problems now facing Rice are high interest rates, declining farm income, and currency fluctuations. For instance, over $1 billion of the company's debt is made up of short-term variable interest loans that jump in tandem with every movement of the U. S. prime rate. The company's interest expense is thus staggering. Largely because of rising fuel and fertilizer costs, the net income of U. S. farmers is expected to decline between 15 and 20 percent from 1979 to 1980. For Massey, which drew 28 percent of sales from the U. S. in 1979, such figures are ominous. On top of this, almost all of Massey's engines are made in Britain. Appreciation of the British pound has raised costs and cut heavily into profits.

To counter these trends, Rice has instituted a number of additional control strategies. These include:

—Selling a variety of overseas subsidiaries including money-losing Massey-Ferguson Hanomag, Inc., a West German construction equipment producer, and a 37 percent share in Spain's Motor Iberica.

—Reducing the number of manufacturing plants from seventy to forty-six, idling more than 20,000 workers.

—Further tightening Massey's inventory control procedures and speeding up collections.

Rice is slowly running out of internal control strategies to improve his company's position. He hopes that the external environment—particularly the stabilizing of worldwide economies—will provide him with some good news in the near future.

Adapted from "Massey-Ferguson: On the Razor's Edge," Business Week *(April 21, 1980): 74.*

Types of Control

Consider the position of director of area blood banks for a large metropolitan hospital district. As manager of the central source of blood units for the county health care institutions, the director is concerned with a number of control factors. Among the most important are acquiring sufficient supplies of blood from various blood donation programs, making sure that the units have been properly analyzed and stored, and keeping the departmental operating costs within budgetary limits. As shown in exhibit 16-2, three major types of control have been identified: input controls, process controls, and output controls.[3]

1. *Input controls.* Sometimes called steering controls, input controls detect deviations from a standard or goal so as to permit correction *before* the major activity has begun. In the blood bank example, the director may compare present and planned inventories with planned surgery schedules and trends in emergency room usage. As noted in exhibit 16-2, other examples include analyzing job descriptions, selection and placement activities, raw material inspection, budget requirements, and training needs.

2. *Process controls.* This type of control acts as a *screening* process, so that the main activity may not continue if the standard has not been met. In

EXHIBIT 16-2
Types of Control

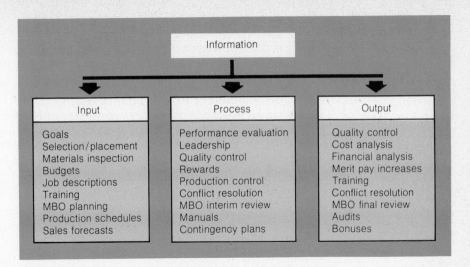

Information		
Input	**Process**	**Output**
Goals	Performance evaluation	Quality control
Selection/placement	Leadership	Cost analysis
Materials inspection	Quality control	Financial analysis
Budgets	Rewards	Merit pay increases
Job descriptions	Production control	Training
Training	Conflict resolution	Conflict resolution
MBO planning	MBO interim review	MBO final review
Production schedules	Manuals	Audits
Sales forecasts	Contingency plans	Bonuses

other words, it determines whether a unit in process is either acceptable or unacceptable. Production and process quality control activities are the most prevalent forms of process controls. In the blood bank illustration, determining the blood type of each unit and maintaining adequate inventories are examples of process controls.

3. *Output controls*. As the name suggests, this type of control concerns those activities that analyze the final product or service. The monthly cost analysis by the blood bank director is an example.

This discussion and exhibit 16-2 suggest at least three key aspects for the manager to consider. First, each type of control has its own process—that is, there are standards, measurement activities, and possible corrective actions involved in all three types. Second, certain control activities occur across the three types of controls. For example, quality control deals with raw material inspection (input), ongoing examination of the operations (process), and analysis of the final product (output).

Finally, each of the control types and their inherent processes involve a rather detailed communication or information system. Standards must be communicated, the results need to be passed on to the involved parties, and information about corrective actions must be forwarded.

Keys to Success with Control Systems

At this point, even though we have not discussed specific control systems, there are certain keys to success that can be derived from a general perspective and can apply to most control types and systems. The following are some of the more important suggestions:

1. **Control systems must be accurate, timely, and economical.**
This is an all-encompassing suggestion that highlights some of the core concerns that managers have with control systems. In essence, the effective control system measures the right things at the proper times, and does so without incurring excessive costs.

2. **Don't overlook the value of control systems to anticipate problems.**
Control systems—whether of the input, process, or output type—can be quite valuable if the manager uses them not only to evaluate "after-the-fact" activities (feedback controls), but to look closely at the information

for its predictive power (feedforward controls), much the same as leading economic indicators are used to anticipate changes in the economy.

3. **Evaluate control data from an integrative viewpoint.**

Managers should not look at quality control information, cost analyses, or employee productivity data as separate, unrelated pieces of data. Instead, they should be evaluated as part of a larger information system. For instance, a manager of data processing may be concerned about the decline in productivity and increases in absenteeism and turnover among data entry personnel (e.g., keypunch operators). Rather than investigate these problems separately, it might be of value for the manager to ask if the data are related.

4. **Control systems should not only indicate deviations, but what corrective actions may be needed.**

Many managers view control systems and control managers as if they are the organization's internal "police" department. Policing—that is, pointing out errors and deviations—is an important function of control systems. Equally important is the function of indicating "where we go from here"—what can be done to correct the deviation. In this way, control systems support operating managers, not work against them.

5. **Present control information clearly and concisely.**

As we have discussed throughout this book, a frequent complaint by managers is that they do not have enough time to complete their duties—they are overloaded with information and have insufficient time to review it all. For control information to be of maximum value, it should be presented to the manager concisely and clearly so that it can be easily understood and acted upon.

6. **Keep control systems flexible.**

Control systems are not the final word, but they should be flexible enough to adapt to changing conditions. For example, a brewery may institute a control procedure on the purchase of new equipment that requires the signatures of six executives before it can be processed. This procedure may introduce so much time-consuming activity that the organization will miss a purchase deadline that would have provided an attractive discount. Instead, a procedure that varies the number of signatures by the value of the equipment (e.g., two signatures for purchases under $10,000, three signatures for equipment purchases between $10,000 and $30,000, and so on) may result in added benefits.

CONTROL IN THE INTERNATIONAL ENVIRONMENT

Controlling resources and operations in order to achieve organizational goals is just as important in the international environment as it is in the home country of the parent organization. The managerial control process in international operations, however, is complicated by a number of unique factors. The most important include consideration of distance, outside ownership interests, diversity, uncertainties, and host country goals.[4] Both the cultural and geographic distance separating countries will increase the time, expense, and possibility of error for the organization in international control. Not only may control systems not be fully understood by the organization's foreign managers, but the time and expense of gaining verification may make the control systems worth less than their cost.

Many multinational organizations frequently have subsidiaries in which outside ownership interests are significant. Control becomes a problem when goals and strategies are not shared by the organization and the local partners. The diversity among countries in accounting procedures and economic, political, and cultural features complicates the task of setting standards, evaluating performance, and designing effective corrective actions. Uncertainties arise about the accuracy and completeness of economic and industry data across different countries. In addition, political and economic conditions can change rapidly from the basis on which global planning was established. Finally, in some countries—particularly the less developed ones—the organization's goals and methods of control may be on a collision course with host country goals.

To highlight these factors, three control system elements now will be briefly discussed. These are evaluation measures, control reporting techniques, and possible corrective actions.

Evaluation Measures.   The previously mentioned factors create a situation in which the evaluation of performance of a unit in international operations is quite difficult. Consequently, many organizations have adopted systems of evaluation that depend on a number of different performance indicators. The measures most frequently used include market share, quality of distribution, new product development, productivity changes, product quality, profitability, output per worker, plant utilization rates, and prices relative to foreign competing firms. In situations in which the foreign operation is a joint venture or subsidiary (i.e., the organization may not have a 100 percent interest), each of the owners may want a different set of evaluation measures computed and analyzed. This can further complicate and confuse the control process.

One of the biggest problems of evaluation is comparability. As we will discuss in chapter 18, an organization may produce a similar product in two countries but use two different processes. For example, International Harvester may produce farm tractors in the U. S. with highly automated equipment, while producing the same product in South America with the use of more labor and fewer automated machines. A comparison of output per worker, labor costs, volume, maintenance expenses, and so on may prove to be of little value. In these situations, organizations usually separate the different operations for comparison purposes, or group operations by the similarity of the process. International Harvester may compare U. S. operations with those in Europe, while grouping South American and African facilities together for analysis.

Control Reporting Techniques.   Timely reports from all operating units of an international organization are needed so that management can allocate resources properly, make corrections in plans, and reward employees for their performance. Not surprisingly, several studies of reporting systems used in international organizations confirm that those used for foreign operations are essentially the same as those used domestically.[5] The reasons for this include the economies of carrying the same types of reports, the strong possibility that what is effective in the home country will prove the same overseas, and the fact that, where possible, comparability is enhanced.

The manager should recognize two important elements of international reporting systems: method and the type of information that is transmitted. Essentially, there are at least eight methods of sending control information: mail, telephone, cable, radio, telex, leased channel, alternate voice data, and travel. Because these methods vary considerably in cost, the choice in specific situations depends on message frequency, average length, destination, urgency, and ease of personal communication.[6] In terms of the type of control information sent, the largest information flow is in the form of standardized reports, followed by finance, market, technical, and environmental information. The fact that environmental information is fourth in volume confirms a point made earlier in this book that the manager on the spot can better utilize environmental information than can management at corporate headquarters.

Enforcing Corrective Actions.   Valid control standards and accurate reporting information are of little use when the organization is limited in its ability to implement corrective actions. The important factors to consider include the degree of ownership of the foreign operation, the legal structure of the countries involved, and the national interest as perceived by political leaders.

In cases where the foreign operation is wholly owned, the use of corrective measures is simplified. This assumes that such corrective actions as worker layoffs, financial restructuring, or facility shutdowns are permissible under the country's legal system. However, what happens if a foreign operation is a joint venture, is substantially independent financially (that is, it generates its own operating funds), is managed by foreign nationals, or is not selling to or buying from the parent?

In these situations, the headquarters management can maintain control over some valued asset, such as patents, brand name, or raw materials. It can also separate equity into voting and nonvoting stock, or as in the case of Westinghouse in Mexico, set up an operating committee in which its minority interest has a majority representation.[7]

BEHAVIORAL CONTROL SYSTEMS: PERFORMANCE EVALUATION

The appraisal and evaluation of employee performance is one of the most important, yet perplexing, aspects of the manager's job. On one hand, management literature has touted its importance for years as a basic management function. It has been mentioned repeatedly in terms of contributing to employee development, identifying employee potential, aiding in human resource planning, determining employee compensation, and improving the performance of the employee and the organization. On the other hand, managers involved in employee performance evaluation have voiced concerns about its objectivity, relevance, and validity. The most frequently heard complaint is that the appraisal system simply does not work. In this section, we will point out both the benefits and problems associated with employee performance evaluation as a control system.

Performance evaluation can mean different things to different people. For example, consider the case of a major league baseball pitcher:

You could always tell how you were doing by the way the pitching coach said good morning. If he said, "Well, now, good morning Jimsie boy," that meant that you'd won your last two or three games and were in the starting rotation. If he nodded his head to you and said, "Jimbo, how are you doin'?" you were still in the starting rotation, but your record probably wasn't much over .500. If he said, "Mornin'," that meant you were on your way down, that you'd probably lost four out of five and it was doubtful if you would be getting any more starts. If he simply looked at you and gave you a solemn nod, that meant you might get some mop up work, or you might not, but you definitely weren't starting anymore. . . . And if he looked past you, over your shoulder as if you didn't exist, it was all over and you might as well pack your bags because you could be traded or sent down to the minors at any moment.[9]

In most organizations, however, the process is much more complicated.

For our purposes, employee performance evaluation or appraisal is the process of identifying, measuring, and developing human performance in organizations. An effective performance evaluation system must not only accurately measure current performance levels, but also contain mechanisms for reinforcing strengths, identifying weaknesses, and feeding such information back to the employees in order that they may be able to improve future performance. In the most basic terms, performance evaluation answers the following questions about an employee: "What is he doing?", "How well is he doing it?", and "What can be done either to maintain what he is doing well or improve on what he is doing less well?"

Our definition of performance evaluation implies three major functions:

1. *Observation and identification* refers to the process of viewing or scrutinizing certain job behaviors. It concerns the process of choosing what behaviors to observe (e.g., the number of computer cards punched by a keypunch operator), as well as how often to observe them.

2. *Measurement* occurs after managers choose what behaviors to examine. It relates to the comparison of this information about the behavior against a set of organizational goals or standards. The degree to which the observed behavior meets or exceeds the standards determines the level of performance it reflects (e.g., excellent or acceptable level of performance).

3. *Development* refers to performance improvement over time. A performance evaluation system must be able to point out deficiencies and strengths in people's behavior so they can be motivated to improve future performance.[10]

These broad-based functions of a performance evaluation system can be translated into specific purposes. The most important include the following:

1. Feedback for employees regarding how the manager and organization view their overall performance

2. Promotion, separation, and transfer decisions

3. The identification of criteria to allocate organizational rewards

4. Criteria to evaluate the effectiveness of selection and placement decisions

5. Ascertaining training and development needs along with criteria to evaluate the success of training and development decisions

The important point for managers to remember is that the performance evaluation process is at the focal point of the entire behavioral control system. That is, it not only evaluates the employee's behavior, but also initiates any corrective activities.

EXHIBIT 16-3 Steps in the Performance Evaluations for a Quality-Control Manager

Job Analysis	Performance criteria	Measuring Instruments	Performance Standards	Appraisal	Corrective Action
Develop, maintain and revise Q/C standards	Specifications and testing	Records	Prepare specs on products by April 1	Product specs developed on all products	None
Supervise Q/C technicians	Supervision (performance, absenteeism, etc.)	Rating scales	Maintain 90% inspection rate	92% inspection rate maintained	None
			Reduce absenteeism and turnover by 20%	Absenteeism and turnover increased by 10%	Formal analysis of causes
Work within a budget	Cost control	Budget and cost data	No excess costs during 19____	No excess costs	None
Respond to customer complaints	Quality rejects	Correspondence	Reduce complaints by 10% by year end—respond within 30 days	Complaints reduced by 3%	Discussions with manufacturing manager
Monitor air pollution	Environmental control standards	Records and data	Meet local, state and federal standards	Air pollution emission standards met only 45% of the time	Examine testing equipment
					Form air pollution task force

The Performance Evaluation Process

To illustrate the typical performance evaluation process, consider the job of quality-control manager for a medium-sized manufacturer of home appliances. The manager's job consists of the following responsibilities: develop, maintain, and revise quality-control standards for the firm's products; supervise a group of four quality-control technicians who perform tests; maintain quality-control costs within budgetary constraints; respond and act upon customer complaints; monitor the plant's air pollution emissions; and so on.

The steps in a performance evaluation of the quality-control manager are shown in exhibit 16-3 and discussed below.[11] Note by examining exhibit 16-3 that there is great similarity between this process and MBO. Two points should be made about these two processes. First, the similarity between MBO and performance evaluation is why many organizations tie the two processes together, especially for wage and salary considerations. Since many of the same points are covered, they can sometimes be merged into a more comprehensive system. Second, performance evaluation covers more of a person's job than does MBO. MBO is usually concerned with "key results" areas—those aspects of a job that are deemed most important to the individual and to the organization. MBO generally covers somewhere between 50 and 75 percent of a person's job. Performance evaluation, on the other hand, deals with the total job. These are the steps in performance evaluation, shown in exhibit 16-3:

Step 1: Job analysis. As discussed in chapter 10, job analysis is an examination of the elements that make up a job. For the quality-control manager in our example, these elements include such duties and responsibilities as cost control, quality testing, supervision, customer complaints, and so on.

Step 2: Identify performance criteria. This step concerns the question, "What are the important elements of performance?" For example, for the quality-control manager, the cost control responsibility would concern the criteria of running the unit within the budget and the expenses incurred in developing a new test.

Step 3: Develop measuring instruments. Two aspects are related to this step: what is a valid representation of each criterion; and, what is a reliable gauge of each measure? As discussed in chapter 2, most performance is measured using either (or both) quantitative and qualitative measures. For example, the number of customer complaints is a quantitative measure, while the evaluation of the quality-control manager's supervisory performance is determined by the use of a subjective or qualitative measure.

Step 4: Establish performance standards. This step defines good performance. Responding to customer complaints within 30 days, the reduction of product reject rates by 15 percent, or developing a new air pollution emissions test by October 1 are examples for the quality-control manager.

Step 5: Performance appraisal and interview. This is one of the most important steps because it concerns how the manager evaluates a subordinate's performance and the manner in which this evaluation is communicated. Of importance are the content of the interview, its frequency and timing, and the quality of interaction between superior and subordinate.

Step 6: Intervention or corrective action. The level of performance will determine the nature of the activities in this step. If the performance of the subordinate is less than satisfactory, some form of corrective action or adjustment may be required. If the performance is satisfactory or exceeds standards, some form of positive reinforcement or plan for continued high performance would be discussed. We will present this step in greater detail when reward systems are discussed in the next part of the chapter.

We have selected two of the steps of the performance evaluation process for further discussion in the next sections: developing measuring instruments (step 3), and the performance appraisal interview (step 5). These two steps have been chosen because of their centrality to the success of the evaluation and behavioral control system.

Selecting Measuring Approaches and Instruments

Assume you are the store manager in a branch of a large retail department store. You have a total of ten department managers reporting to you (e.g., men's, women's, and children's clothing, appliances, garden shop, and so on), along with a support staff (e.g., two assistant store managers, personnel, accounting, maintenance, security). If you are interested in evaluating the performance of the department managers, there are at least two issues you must consider with respect to measurement: the approach and the method.

Performance Evaluation Approaches. The performance evaluation approach concerns the issue of *who* evaluates the performance of the department manager. Let us assume we are evaluating the performance of the manager of children's clothing. There are at least five appraisal approaches that can be used. The first, the *superior evaluating the subordinate,* is the most common in organizations. In other words, the subordinate department manager would be evaluated solely by the store manager.

Second, a number of organizations have opted for a *group of supervisors evaluating a subordinate.* The idea is that a better appraisal can be obtained if more than one individual contributes to the evaluation. In a matrix structure, this approach is frequently found. In our example, the department manager could be evaluated by the store manager and the two assistant store managers. A major problem is that this approach assumes that all the evaluators have knowledge of the manager's performance. In addition, this approach can be time consuming and may dilute the subordinate's feelings of influence and accountability to the immediate superior.

A *group of peers evaluating a colleague* is the third approach. In the department store, a number of other department managers who understand the work of the children's clothing department would be asked separately for an evaluation. This is a common approach used in the military and by scientists in research institutions. It is a less common approach in other organizations because competition among peers for merit pay increases and/or promotions may bias their evaluations.

The fourth approach is *subordinates evaluating their superior.* Examples include student evaluations of a professor's teaching performance, or the appraisal of the performance of the department manager by the sales staff. While this is becoming a more frequently used evaluation approach, managers must make sure that subordinates are capable and trained in evaluation procedures.

Finally, in some cases organizations ask for a *self-evaluation*. Usually this approach is used as a supplement to the other approaches, rather than used alone. Some managers are concerned that if it is the only evaluation approach used, there is too great a tendency for positive bias to become a problem (e.g., if you had a choice between giving yourself a C or an F in this course, which one would you choose?).

Because of the growing complexities of organizations and of the manager's job, a number of organizations have chosen to use a *combination approach*. For example, to evaluate the performance of the department manager, the store manager initially performs an appraisal. In addition, separate evaluations from the assistant store managers are provided, along with a number of one-on-one interviews with the manager's subordinates. Though this can become a time-consuming process, the cross-section of opinions may prove valuable, especially if the store manager is thinking of promoting the department manager to a more responsible position.

Performance Evaluation Methods.   There is a wide variety of methods for performance evaluation. The five most popular are global ranking, trait-based rating scales, critical incidents, behaviorally anchored rating scales (BARS), and effectiveness-based (objective) measure.[12]

Global ranking is a simple unidimensional rank order that involves a manager's *overall* estimate of performance of a group of subordinates without distinguishing between important job factors. For instance, in the earlier department store illustration, with a ranking method the store manager would take the ten department managers and rank order them from 1 (highest performer) to 10 (lowest performer). While this approach has the advantage of being fairly easy and quick to conduct, there are a number of serious disadvantages. The negative features include the problem of reducing performance to a single index, the inability to distinguish between different levels of performance (e.g., is the difference in performance between the third and fourth best performers the same as the difference between the seventh and eighth?), and questions as to the legality of the method (performance evaluation methods that are not based on a job analysis may be open to discrimination claims).

Trait-based rating scales are probably the oldest and most frequently used methods for evaluating employee performance. They are distinguished from ranking scales by at least three factors: (1) job performance is recognized as consisting of different dimensions, such as quality, dependability, cooperativeness, knowledge of work, and initiative; (2) each dimension is broken down by different levels of performance, usually on a five-point scale (e.g., 1 (low performance) to 5 (high performance), or poor to outstanding); and (3) the meaning of the dimensions and the level of evaluation is clear to the rater and ratee, making feedback much easier. Some examples of different ratings scales are shown in exhibit 16-4. Rating scales are generally preferred over rankings; however, there still are a number of weaknesses that the manager should carefully consider. Two weaknesses are most salient. First, the meaning of the dimensions must be clear and unidimensional—for example, being rated low on "dependability" or low on "personal relationships" may not only mean different things to different people but these words themselves may have

EXHIBIT 16-4 Examples of Rating Scale Items

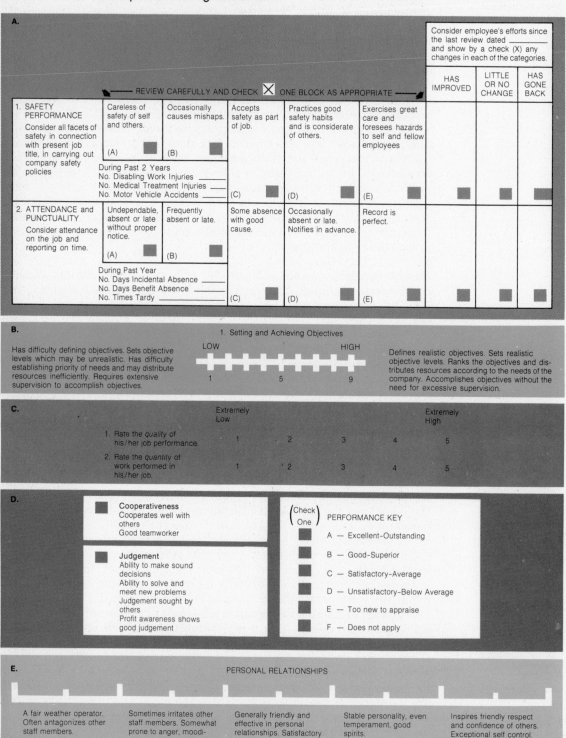

A.

	Consider employee's efforts since the last review dated _____ and show by a check (X) any changes in each of the categories.		
←— REVIEW CAREFULLY AND CHECK ☒ ONE BLOCK AS APPROPRIATE —→	HAS IMPROVED	LITTLE OR NO CHANGE	HAS GONE BACK

1. SAFETY PERFORMANCE — Consider all facets of safety in connection with present job title, in carrying out company safety policies

| (A) Careless of safety of self and others. ▨ | (B) Occasionally causes mishaps. ▨ | (C) Accepts safety as part of job. ▨ | (D) Practices good safety habits and is considerate of others. ▨ | (E) Exercises great care and foresees hazards to self and fellow employees ▨ | ▨ | ▨ | ▨ |

During Past 2 Years
No. Disabling Work Injuries _____
No. Medical Treatment Injuries _____
No. Motor Vehicle Accidents _____

2. ATTENDANCE and PUNCTUALITY — Consider attendance on the job and reporting on time.

| (A) Undependable, absent or late without proper notice. ▨ | (B) Frequently absent or late. ▨ | (C) Some absence with good cause. ▨ | (D) Occasionally absent or late. Notifies in advance. ▨ | (E) Record is perfect. ▨ | ▨ | ▨ | ▨ |

During Past Year
No. Days Incidental Absence _____
No. Days Benefit Absence _____
No. Times Tardy _____

B.

1. Setting and Achieving Objectives

Has difficulty defining objectives. Sets objective levels which may be unrealistic. Has difficulty establishing priority of needs and may distribute resources inefficiently. Requires extensive supervision to accomplish objectives.

LOW |—+—+—+—+—+—+—+—| HIGH
1   5   9

Defines realistic objectives. Sets realistic objective levels. Ranks the objectives and distributes resources according to the needs of the company. Accomplishes objectives without the need for excessive supervision.

C.

	Extremely Low				Extremely High
1. Rate the *quality* of his/her job performance.	1	2	3	4	5
2. Rate the *quantity* of work performed in his/her job.	1	2	3	4	5

D.

▨ **Cooperativeness**
Cooperates well with others
Good teamworker

▨ **Judgement**
Ability to make sound decisions
Ability to solve and meet new problems
Judgement sought by others
Profit awareness shows good judgement

(Check One) PERFORMANCE KEY

▨ A — Excellent-Outstanding

▨ B — Good-Superior

▨ C — Satisfactory-Average

▨ D — Unsatisfactory-Below Average

▨ E — Too new to appraise

▨ F — Does not apply

E.

PERSONAL RELATIONSHIPS

| A fair weather operator. Often antagonizes other staff members. | Sometimes irritates other staff members. Somewhat prone to anger, moodiness or nervousness. | Generally friendly and effective in personal relationships. Satisfactory self control. | Stable personality, even temperament, good spirits. | Inspires friendly respect and confidence of others. Exceptional self control. |

separate subdimensions. Second, some of the performance dimensions may not have applicability to the specific job and person being evaluated. For example, the performance dimension "ability to work independent of supervision" would be closely aligned with a sales representative's job; on the other hand, evaluating a research physicist's "quality of work" may be questionable.

The critical incidents method attempts to use illustrations of actual behaviors to determine an evaluative rating.[13] For example, one of the assistant store managers in the department store illustration may have prepared an excellent quarterly sales report for the store's different departments. The store manager may make a written note of this behavior and place it in a file maintained on each subordinate. At the time of the yearly performance review, the file is examined and used to determine the final evaluation. While managers who use the critical incidents method like its behavior-specific and good feedback qualities, the time-consuming nature of the method, particularly when a manager has many subordinates, has been a significant deterrent to its use.

Behaviorally anchored rating scales (BARS) have been gaining in popularity. They are called behaviorally based measures of job performance because they focus on detailed evaluation of *specific* acts or behaviors, rather than global aspects.[14] The development of a behaviorally anchored rating scale depends upon the judgment of those employees and managers who are closest to the job itself—those individuals who will be the ones using the final instrument or receiving feedback from it. The development of one of these scales involves at least the following steps:

1. Expert judges—those closest and most familiar with the job—are interviewed and asked to make two kinds of judgments about the job. First, they are asked to identify the basic task dimensions of the job (e.g., setting and achieving goals, developing subordinates). Second, they are asked to relate specific illustrative behaviors of either effective or ineffective activities with respect to each dimension.

2. Several other groups of expert judges are asked to evaluate the illustrations generated by the initial group. They are asked first to assign each illustration to a particular task dimension. Second, they are requested to rate the behavior in the illustration in terms of how effective or ineffective it is in accomplishing the task dimension.

3. Based upon the judgments of the second step, items or behavioral illustrations are retained only if there is substantial agreement among the judges as to the dimension of the job to which they refer and its effectiveness in terms of success on that dimension. Items on which there is disagreement are thrown out.

The result of an analysis carried out according to these three steps is a pool of every job-specific item describing effective and ineffective behavior in the language of those closest to the job—raters and ratees. Exhibit 16-5 presents one of ten behaviorally anchored performance dimensions for the job of a design engineer. Note that the evaluator does not have to rely on general adjectives such as "outstanding" or "poor" in evaluating an engineer's performance. Instead, the evaluator can concentrate on specific job behaviors on the right side of the scale in deciding how effective the engineer was during the review period.

EXHIBIT 16-5   A BARS Performance Dimension for a Design Engineer

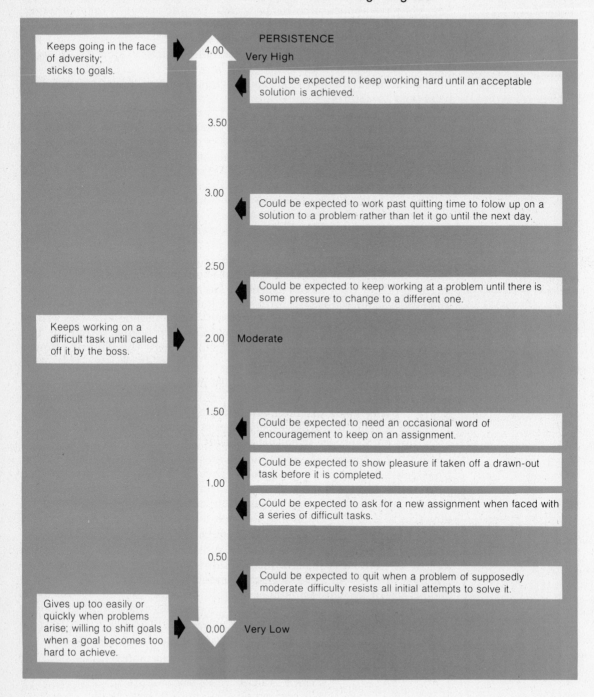

EXHIBIT 16-6   Evaluation of Performance Evaluation Methods

METHOD	PERFORMANCE EVALUATION PURPOSES					Resources Needed to Develop	Degree of Job Speci-ficity
	Feedback/ Development	Promotion, Separation, Transfer Decision	Reward Allocation	Selection, Placement Decision	Assessing Training Needs		
1. Global Ranking	Poor	Poor	Poor	Poor	Poor	Low	Low
2. Trait-Based Rating Scales	Fair	Poor to Fair	Fair	Poor to Fair	Fair	Low	Low to Moderate
3. Critical Incidents	Fair to Good	Fair	Fair	Poor to Fair	Fair	Moderate	Moderate
4. BARS	Good to Very Good	Very Good	Very Good	Very Good to Outstanding	Very Good	High	High
5. Effective-ness-Based Measures	Fair to Good	Good	Very Good to Outstanding	Good to Very Good	Good	High	High

Adapted from C. E. Schneier and R. W. Beatty, "Integrating Behaviorally-Based and Effectiveness-Based Methods," *The Personnel Administrator* (July 1979): 68.

The behaviorally anchored scale is clearly a superior method of evaluating the performance of an employee. Not only does this development process identify important job dimensions, but since many employees are actually involved in developing the scale, they may become more committed to its use. On the other hand, this type of evaluation method is quite time- and resource-consuming. Being job specific, a scale developed for design engineers may not be totally transferable to the job of construction engineer. Thus, the development process must be conducted for each different job or job classification.

Effectiveness-based measures depend heavily on objective measures of performance. MBO (see chapter 15) can be an effectiveness-based measure in which there is an emphasis on such quantitative or objective measures as time, costs, and sales.

Exhibit 16-6 presents an evaluation of the five methods according to the degree to which they accomplish the main goals of the performance evaluation process, along with the amount of resources (time, human, and administrative) needed to develop the method and the degree to which the method is job specific. As the exhibit indicates, behaviorally anchored scales and effectiveness-based measures (MBO) achieve the goals of the performance evaluation process better than the other measures because they are more job specific. On the other hand, these methods consume a large amount of organizational resources in their development, which to many managers is a deterrent to their frequent use.

Elements of the Evaluation Interview

Even when managers use the most appropriate approach and the most valid method, the entire performance evaluation process can prove disastrous if the actual evaluation interview is conducted poorly. Many reasons can be given for this problem. The most prevalent include: the manager is not prepared or does not understand the important performance-related data for a particular subordinate; the manager is not properly trained to conduct a performance evaluation interview; or the manager does not do well in one-on-one interactions and, as a result, either offers undeserved praise, focuses too much on the negatives of the individual's performance rather than equally on the positives, or tries to finish the interview as quickly as possible.

While describing the proper way to conduct an evaluation interview can take up an entire chapter, we have selected three broad areas for discussion: what to do before the interview, what to stress during the interview, and what to do after the interview.[15]

Preparing for the Evaluation Interview.   There are at least three factors in a manager's preparation for an evaluation interview with an employee. First, the manager should decide how *often* the appraisal will be made. Most organizations make a choice between either a standard review cycle, such as every twelve months, or an evaluation at "natural" points, such as the completion of a project. In some rare situations, the employee requests the appraisal. The appropriateness of these alternatives depends upon the nature of the work and the skills of the employee. For example, if the tasks are relatively simple and standard (e.g., janitors or clerical personnel) and/or the subordinates have minimal job-related skills, a standard review cycle is usually preferred. If subordinates are highly skilled professionals, and/or tasks do not follow standard cycles (e.g., accountants, scientists, or engineers), it probably would be better if the review followed shortly after the completion of a unit of work. For example, an accountant may work on three major projects during a twelve-month period—a performance appraisal, therefore, may occur after each project has been completed. Many organizations are moving toward the "natural" point review because of its motivational value— that is, according to reinforcement theory, if the appraisal and rewards follow closely on the actual performance, the chance that desired behavior will continue is enhanced.

Second, the manager should spend some time and *prepare* for each subordinate's review. This entails gathering and reviewing all the important information and identifying the major points of discussion.

Finally, the manager should *set aside enough uninterrupted time* for the interview to cover all the key points. This means that phone calls and other visitors are held until later. The subordinate must recognize that this is his time, not to be shared with other people.

The Evaluation Interview.   If the actual performance evaluation interview could be reduced to its simplest components, it would involve the responses to these two questions for the subordinate: *How well am I doing?* and *Where do I go from here?* The first question generally involves the issues of maintaining or improving successful performance or correcting unsuccessful performance. In the case of a subordinate who is performing at or above acceptable standards, the manager should discuss why the performance is at that that level, in order to insure that these same elements are in existence in the future. For example, a high-performing nurse may indicate that the main reason for her current level of performance is her recent transfer to a position as a surgical nurse— a job which offers more challenge and an opportunity to use her training and experience. The manager conducting the appraisal may conclude that

EXHIBIT 16-7   General Guidelines for Performance Evaluation Interviews

AVOID	TRY
Focus on the person and personalities.	Focus on the behavior.
Be judgmental.	Be descriptive.
Use negative words or too many criticisms.	Reassure the subordinate by building on strengths, giving confidence.
Use a "you vs. me" attitude.	Use a "we" attitude when discussing problems.
Give insincere or undeserved praise.	Be specific when discussing the positive and negative features of the performance.
Dominate the interview.	Draw employees out by asking questions, listening, and then reflecting on their responses.
Be a nit-picker.	Counsel, don't advise.
Appear bored or hurried.	Summarize, plan for improvement, write down results, close properly.

the nurse should be allowed to continue in this position.

With a low-performing subordinate, the process of identifying the contributing factors becomes more important. At least four factors should be considered by the manager in these situations: (1) Does the person have sufficient job-related knowledge and skills to perform effectively?; (2) Has the person been equitably rewarded in the past for his performance?; (3) Does the present job satisfy his job-related needs (see chapter 12)?; and (4) Are there certain extraneous factors, such as poor co-worker relationships or inadequate working conditions, that are adversely affecting his performance? In the example of the nurse above, she may have performed less than satisfactorily in her previous position because her knowledge and skills were not being effectively used.

The second question ("Where do I go from here?") involves discussing career interests and developmental needs. This topic relates to our discussion of training and development activities in chapter 10 and the subject of managerial career development, which will be discussed in detail in chapter 20.

The success of the evaluation interview hinges on the environment that is established by the manager. Exhibit 16-7 lists a set of points to *avoid* and to *try*.

After the Evaluation Interview.   Shortly after the evaluation interview, there are at least three activities that the manager should do. First, the subordinate's file should be up-dated with all the information regarding the present period's performance. It may be helpful for the manager to write a brief report that summarizes all the activities, including the discussion in the appraisal interview. Second, the manager should begin the next period's evaluation profile with a summary of the present report and any goals and/or plans for the period. This would also be a good time to begin using the critical incidents method. Finally, in an informal way, the manager should let the employee know from time to time that he is interested in frequent progress reports on the person's performance, particularly if new data or changes are noted. The key point is not to appear to be nagging, but to let the subordinate be the one to initiate such informal progress reviews. In this manner, the two-way exchange of ideas and feelings has been enhanced.

Keys to Success with Performance Evaluations

There are a number of keys to success with performance evaluations that have been gathered from the experiences of many managers. The most important include the following:

1. **Focus on the behavior, not the person.**

   The issue at hand is what the person did, not who he is. By focusing on the behavior, confusing and conflicting personality differences can remain out of the evaluation meeting.

2. **Try not to be influenced by status differences.**

   Managers may be influenced by the position, seniority, title, or wage level of the person being evaluated. For various reasons, managers frequently assign higher ratings to persons who are older or have more seniority. These ratings often are independent of the actual quality of work being performed. This tendency sometimes can be attributed to a manager's fear of recrimination or reprisal on the part of the person being evaluated, or other individuals who may have a vested interest in the appraisal. Whatever the source of bias, a manager can err in the appraisal process.

3. **Try to avoid making rating errors.**

   There are at least three types of rating errors the manager can make. Leniency error is where the manager evaluates all subordinates highly; strictness error concerns the opposite—where all subordinates are rated only "poor to fair"; finally, the error of central tendency concerns the situation where the rateees are all evaluated at about the mid-point, or average performance. This doesn't mean that the manager should try to develop a perfectly normal distribution; it means that a certain spread of ratings from poor to outstanding should appear. It might be a beneficial practice for the manager to plot the ratings given to the subordinates and determine the form of the distribution.

4. **Be an active listener.**

   Becoming an active listener means that the manager has mastered many of the components of the communication process (see chapter 11). This means that the manager should give full attention and not make snap decisions, avoid interruptions, be patient, listen for meanings, and avoid expressing personal feelings or opinions.

5. **Seek out multiple sources of employee performance information.**

   Even though an organization may use a rating scale for performance evaluation, this should not stop the manager from seeking out other information. In the department store illustration earlier, the store manager could use observations and interviews with other managers and selected subordinates in order to get a fuller picture of a particular employee's performance activities. A key is the more sources of information, the better the position of the manager in the performance evaluation interview.

6. Performance evaluation is an ongoing process.

While the major portion of this discussion has centered on how to conduct periodic reviews of subordinates, the manager should not be lulled into believing that evaluation is a once-a-year activity. If only informally, the manager should be continually involved in an evaluation-reward process with subordinates. If employees are doing well, tell them now—don't wait until the formal review time. In the same manner, don't wait until the end of the review period to inform subordinates that they are doing something incorrectly. Activities of this sort may well serve to improve the motivation and performance of the employee.

COMMENTS ON THE PRACTICE OF MANAGEMENT
(See p. 552)

The Emerson Electric example provides a rich illustration of management in a successful organization. First of all, we see how planning and control systems work hand-in-hand—managers know not only what to do, but they have developed methods of finding out how well they are doing. Second, we see the use of incentive pay as a reward in the behavioral control system. More importantly, the way in which Emerson has developed its control system does not force people to do what they don't want to do, nor is it used in a police-like manner. Managers are *committed* to its use because they have helped in its development and its successful functioning will benefit both themselves and the organization.

BEHAVIORAL CONTROL SYSTEMS: REWARDS

Each day, week, month, or year, organizations distribute a variety of rewards to employees. These rewards may be as simple as a verbal "thank you" to an employee for a job well done, or as complex as a promotion program; they may be closely tied to performance, such as pay systems, or generally unrelated to performance, such as employee benefits; they may have special meaning to a few individuals, as with status symbols, or have a meaning and value to all employees, as with a profit sharing program. Whatever the focus, rewards can have both a short- and long-term impact on the organization's performance and survival.

Rewards serve a variety of purposes and have different requirements depending on whether they are seen from an individual viewpoint or an organizational viewpoint.[16] Individual employees generally seek rewards that satisfy their basic needs (*reward level*), are given to them in line with their level of performance (*internal equity*), are comparable with similar jobs in other organizations (*external equity*), and offer a variety of reward types to satisfy the complex needs of the individual (*individuality*).

Organizations, on the other hand, want the reward system to facilitate the process of people joining the organization (*membership*), to be at such a level as to enhance the probability of employees coming to work (*attendance or absenteeism*), to relate rewards to performance (*motivation*), and to vary the distribution of rewards so as to reinforce the differences in managerial levels and in the importance of different jobs (*structure*).

Our discussion of organizational reward systems will cover three major points. First, a basic rewards system model will be presented which links the previous discussions on motivation (chapter 12) and performance evaluations. Second, because of their importance and frequency of use, pay systems, promotions, and employee benefits have been singled out for separate discussions. Finally, we will offer certain keys to success with rewards in organizations.

A Basic Reward System Model

A basic model of an organization's reward system is shown in exhibit 16-8. For managers, there are at least four points of importance that can be derived from an analysis of this model. First, the exhibit represents an expansion of our basic motivation model (see chapter 12). That is, it links the concepts of motivation, performance, performance evaluation, rewards, and satisfaction. Second, the centrality of the performance evaluation process is again highlighted. In other words, the absence of a valid and accurate evaluation system will not only hamper the equitable distribution of rewards, but later motivation may be adversely influenced.

Third, we have again made a distinction between intrinsic and extrinsic rewards. Recall from chapter 12 that *intrinsic* rewards are those rewards that the individual receives from doing the job (e.g., achievement, pride, autonomy, and personal growth and development). *Extrinsic* rewards are those rewards that are given to the individual by someone else. Included are pay increases and bonuses, promotion, recognition and praise, and employee benefits. Since the topic of intrinsic rewards was covered in the job design discussion in chapter 12, we will concentrate on an analysis of extrinsic rewards in the remainder of this chapter.

EXHIBIT 16-8 A Basic Reward System Model

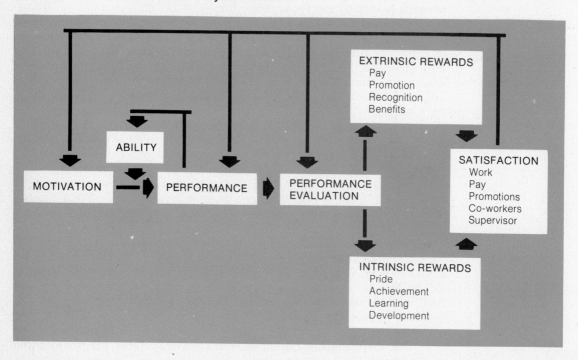

© 1980 by NEA, Inc. T M Reg U S Pat Off

Finally, the feedback from performance and satisfaction to motivation again emphasizes the importance of rewards and performance levels to subsequent motivation. In essence, managers must recognize that administering rewards is a continuous process.

Approaches to Pay as a Reward

There are many approaches through which an organization can use pay as a reward. Most of these approaches can be categorized as base pay, increases in base pay, and supplemental or incentive pay systems.[17]

Base Pay. Base pay is that level of compensation that serves as the foundation of the employee's wage or salary level. Four major approaches can be used: job evaluation, skill evaluation, piece-rate or commission, or the all-salaried workforce.

1. *Job evaluation* as a base pay approach consists of describing the job and then assessing its important characteristics. This flows from a job analysis and makes distinctions of organizational level and the amount of authority, responsibility, and accountability. Once a job has been evaluated, it is compared to what other organizations pay for similar jobs and pay is set at a level that is in line with the outside market and internal characteristics.

2. *Skill evaluation* pays employees according to what they *can do* rather than what they *actually do*—that is, in terms of their abilities rather than their level of performance. This type of pay program first came into prominence in Norway and has since spread to such organizations as Procter and Gamble and General Foods (see the General Foods case in chapter 12). While the idea of stressing learning new skills is a popular one, there is the significant problem of an employee "topping out"—that is, learning all the jobs with no place to go from there. As a result, the skill evaluation plan is more appropriate for newer plants than older plants, because in new plants there is an emphasis on the acquisition of new skills.

3. *Piece-rate or commission* is based on the amount of work that a person does. Examples include paying a certain rate for each unit produced or a commission for a sales representative (i.e., 2 percent of every sale). Because this approach depends on identifying a particular unit of work, its applicability has been limited.

4. The *all-salaried workforce* attempts to eliminate some distinctions between managerial/professional and nonsupervisory employees. The idea

is that by paying everyone the same way, improved loyalty, teamwork, and commitment and a decrease in administrative costs can result. IBM and Gillette are two of the many organizations that have certain units that have gone to the all-salaried plan. In addition, the United Auto Workers (UAW) has raised the issue of all-salary plans in negotiating with the big-three auto makers. Opponents of the plan claim that absenteeism and tardiness will increase with this plan because no time clock is used. Unfortunately, no solid research exists to support either the benefits or problems of the all-salary plan.

Increases in Base Pay.   In most organizations, employees rarely stay at their base pay for an extended period of time. Because of an employee's level of performance, changes in the nature of the job, or external conditions (e.g., inflation), organizations have developed methods of increasing the pay level of employees. We will discuss four of the most popular approaches to increasing pay: merit increases, lump-sum payments, cost of living increases, and bargaining.

1. *Merit increases* is a performance-based approach—that is, the higher the performance, the greater the pay increase. This is the most popular approach in organizations for salaried personnel. It assumes, however, that a valid and accurate performance evaluation system exists that can distinguish between different levels of performance. Since the use of a merit pay system not only rewards past performance but seeks to maintain or improve future performance, organizations attempt to tie performance and rewards as closely as possible. This means that high performers receive significant rewards, while low poor performers may receive no increase in pay.

2. *Lump-sum payments* attempt to make the manner in which the pay increase is given more flexible. For example, consider a media relations specialist working in the public affairs department of a large organization. If the person is making $18,000 per year and receives a 10 percent merit increase ($1800), the traditional method is to increase the employee's salary check by $150 per month. In a lump-sum program, the employee is given the $1800 in total at the first of the year (or anniversary date of employment). Employees, and some organizations, like the lump-sum plan because it gives the employee a large amount of money at one time (for possible purchases of large goods or services), it gives visibility to the organization's merit pay program, and it generally involves little or no cost to the organization. A major problem is what happens if the person leaves the organization before the year has passed? In these cases, the lump-sum is treated as a loan and any excess is paid back.

3. *Cost of living increases* entail the adjustment in pay due to changes in external conditions, such as inflation or increases in pay levels for a comparable job in other organizations. Cost of living increases due to inflation are given so that the employee's basic financial needs are covered, while adjustments due to changes in the external job market are made to keep the organization competitive for skilled people.

4. *Bargaining* is the process whereby a group of employees negotiate for wage increases. This is most frequently found in the relationship between management and labor groups.

Supplemental or Incentive Pay. Among all types and levels of employees, one of the most popular pay approaches is that of supplemental or incentive pay. Supplemental pay is usually based on the level of the individual's performance, or in some cases, on the level of performance of the group or organization. Typically, such compensation is given as a one-time award, but the person is eligible for the supplement during the next period. We will discuss two broad supplemental approaches: bonuses and profit sharing.

1. *A bonus* is a form of supplemental pay that is given to employees for meeting or exceeding a particular goal set by the organization. Examples include sales representatives who exceed a sales goal or obtain a large customer contract, or in baseball when a pitcher wins eight games in a row including a no-hitter. In many organizations, higher level executives are frequently eligible for bonuses based on their unit's performance.

2. *Profit sharing* is quite popular with many workers because they can share in the successes of their organizations. There are a number of forms of profit sharing in existence, but usually they are related to the distribution of income over a certain after-tax profit. In addition, the amount of money received by the employee is based on that person's level in the organization and on his particular level of performance. A popular approach is the Scanlon Plan, which has been in existence since the 1930s.[18] It can take the form of straight profit sharing, as in the above case, or be based on labor cost efficiency. In the latter case, a base rate is established at the beginning of a period with respect to the ratio of total sales volume to total payroll expenses. At the end of the period, any money savings resulting from improvements over the base rate are shared equally by all workers.

While many managers and nonmanagers recognize the importance of pay, there are two practices in many organizations that may act to reduce its impact. First, many organizations prefer to review an employee's performance once per year, resulting in a yearly pay increase. Under such a system, it is difficult for the employee to make the connection between pay and performance, since the year is made up of many performance-related activities. In essence, the individual is rewarded on the basis of an *average* performance level.

Second, another way for the employee to make the connection between pay and performance is to have some knowledge of what other employees have received. Yet, most organizations function with a secret pay program; that is, there is a lack of knowledge among employees (nonunion) about their respective pay levels.

Managers in favor of an open pay system claim that employees engage in a comparison process with other employees no matter what type of pay system exists. Research has shown that in a secret pay system, employees tend to overestimate the pay of individuals at their same organizational levels and those below them, but underestimate the pay of people above them. With an open system, a person can make accurate comparisons, which may lead to clearer performance-reward beliefs. An open system also contributes to improved trust in the organization because it communicates to employees that the organization has nothing to hide.

Managers favoring a secret pay plan point out that secrecy gives pay administrators more freedom in administering pay, because they do not have to explain their actions. They suggest that certain pay inequities will always exist in most organizations because of differences in such aspects as demand for jobs and experience and expertise levels of employees. For example, in such professional occupations as accounting, finance, and engineering, the demand for these jobs may put the recent graduate and the organization in a difficult position. The young accountant may join a firm with a salary of $14,000 per year. After one year, good performance yields a 10 percent merit increase to $15,400. That same year, the tight market for accountants forces the firm to increase starting salaries to $15,000. If an open pay system existed in this firm, consider the morale problems among accountants as described above when they realize that after a year of good performance they are making only $400 per year more than the newly hired, inexperienced accountant.

In addition, secret pay proponents not only claim that it would be extremely difficult to communicate to employees all the details of a pay plan, but also that in reality there is no great demand by employees that pay raises be made public. This, however, is a questionable assumption.

The debate over secret versus open pay plans will no doubt continue for some time to come. It seems that most organizations will adopt a system that best fits their particular climate. Authoritarian or democratic organizations, for example, may require different pay systems. The latter can easily tolerate openness about pay and the basing of pay on performance. It is much less clear that openness can be accepted fully in an authoritarian organization.

Promotions

Promotions, because of their impact on the development of the individual and the organization, are some of the most important long-range decisions that managers make in the human resource area. Ideally, one would like to see a promotion program that is fair, free from bias and discrimination, and performance- or merit-based. In some organizations, these objectives are met; in others, they are not.

Promotion programs in organizations can take many forms and involve different processes. We have selected for discussion two promotion programs—noted as Plan A and Plan B—that may be considered at the extremes of existing programs.

Plan A is characterized by both openness and an emphasis on an analysis of the needs of the organization and the abilities and skills of the person. Among the most frequently used techniques in Plan A are human resource planning and assessment centers (see chapter 10), MBO (see chapter 15), career pathing (see chapter 20), and a comprehensive performance evaluation system. The result is a fairly steady stream of capable, skilled, and high-performance managers who are available for frequent movement throughout the organization.

Plan B at the other extreme, is based on secrecy and a minimum understanding by the employee of the ongoing process. Because promotions are regarded as so important to the organization, the decisions about who will be moved where and when are made by managers who are at least one managerial level above both the position that is being filled and the individuals who are being considered to fill it. The whole process is kept secret; often even the people being considered for a position are not aware of the fact. Sometimes they are not even aware that a position is open, or about to be open. It is not uncommon, for example, to find that top management has a secret manning chart (i.e., human resource plan) that shows the back-up people for all positions in the organization. The use of this type of promotion plan sometimes results in a lack of understanding about the kinds of career paths and plans that are available to managers, and a decrease in morale when managers are by-passed for promotions and they feel they are more qualified than the person who fills that position.

While most organizations have adopted a promotion program that is somewhat between the Plan A and Plan B extremes, it appears that the movement is more toward the acceptance of a Plan A approach. The clarity and openness not only contributes to improved motivation, but the emphasis on analysis can help identify and select the managers with the greatest potential to handle the increasing complexity of today's and tomorrow's organizations.

An element of this movement toward more openness is the practice of posting the availability of jobs and inviting individuals to nominate themselves. Job posting is a common practice in many government organizations and such companies as Xerox, Texas Instruments, Tenneco, and Procter and Gamble.

Open posting often entails some additional administrative work; on the other hand, it may lead to better promotion decisions. For one thing, open posting helps ensure that all qualified applicants who want to be considered are considered. Often when jobs are being filled, the individuals who make promotion decisions are not aware of who is available or who can do the job, especially in large organizations. A possible negative feature of the open posting system is that by publicly declaring interest in a different job, people may unknowingly be sending a signal to their superiors that they are dissatisfied with their present situations. If the promotion is not received, in isolated instances, repercussions may occur.

Employee Benefits

Compensation and promotion make up the major reward systems in organizations. However, these components do not represent the total cost to the organization for services performed by the employee. Today a variety of benefits, referred to in the past as fringe benefits, supplement the wages that are paid directly to employees. These benefits include vacations, holidays, retirement pensions, unemployment benefits, social security, and a variety of insurance benefits. While it is beyond the scope of this book to cover fully the subject of employee benefits, two important trends will be pointed out that may have a significant impact on managers: cafeteria plans and executive perquisites.

Cafeteria Plans.   Employee benefits are not only one of the most costly employee-related activities for organizations, but these costs have increased dramatically over the last two decades. For example, in 1955 organizations on the average devoted approximately $1000 per employee for benefits, which equated to 25 percent of total payroll costs. In 1975, these figures increased to nearly $5000 per employee and over 40 percent of total payroll costs.[19]

Even with these impressive figures, research has clearly shown that there is a wide variety in benefit satisfaction among employees; a benefit that is valued by one employee sometimes is not valued by another. These programs end up costing an organization a great deal of money for benefits that are not valued by many employees and therefore, do not contribute fully to either their satisfaction or to their motivation to perform effectively.

One way that organizations have attempted to overcome this problem is through the use of a cafeteria plan.[20] This plan involves telling employees just how much the organization is willing to spend on their total pay package and then giving them the opportunity to spend this money as they wish. A younger employee, for example, can take the majority of money in cash, another employee may decide to devote more money to medical insurance to cover family expenses, while an older employee may choose to emphasize retirement benefits. This type of plan makes it clear to employees how much the organization is spending to compensate them, and it assures that the money will be spent on the benefits the employees really want.

Executive "Perks."   Throughout the world, in all types of organizations, executives receive special perquisites because of their positions. Known as "perks," they tend to be used more in Europe than in the United States because such extras are frequently taxed as income in this country. Examples include the following:

1. *Income or Insured Benefits*—Income deferral, supplemental retirement benefits, supplemental life insurance and disability insurance, liability insurance, profit sharing, and stock purchase plans.

2. *Special Privileges*—Financial counseling services, company loans for stock option exercise, home purchase, education, or personal investment, company cars, paid memberships to clubs, liberal expense accounts, company housing, first-class airfare and hotel suites, employment contracts, second office in home, executive medical examinations, and a special office decorating allowance.

3. *Expense Privileges*—Tuition assistance and scholarships for children, discounts on company products, services and facilities, and uncovered family medical expenses.

The popularity of perks is increasing in organizations; however, their exact meaning and contribution to organizational effectiveness is relatively unknown. From Maslow's motivation framework, one may conclude that the big, nicely furnished office contributes to satisfying ego and recognition needs. The use of a company car, club memberships, financial counseling, and so on can be viewed also as a status-related need. On the other hand, the emphasis on deferred income and supplemental insurance policies is clearly related to safety and security needs.

One thing is clear: the use of perks will continue to spread in all types of organizations. The competition for proven management talent across organizations almost requires the use of perks to acquire, reward, and retain this talent. The growth in the use of perks, however, may decline as more and more of them become taxable.

Perks have also found their way into professional sports. We all have read of the large contracts signed by such stars as Earl Campbell, Reggie Jackson, and Larry Bird. A three-year contract for $4 million may seem large, but this money is spread out over as many as twenty years.

Keys to Success with Reward Systems

The reward program is one of the most important and costly control systems in any organization. Reward systems have also become much more complex, and hence require the increased attention of managers. Given this situation, certain keys to success that have worked for a number of managers may help the future manager.

1. **Maintain flexibility in a reward system.**

The need for flexibility means a system that includes a variety of approaches (e.g., merit and incentive pay, job postings, cafeteria plans), and a system that adapts to changing conditions by adopting or dropping various approaches. The key is to have a base program that covers all employees equally, but includes enough flexibility to meet the differences in employee needs and changes in external conditions.

2. **There must be a balance between function and cost.**

While the major focus of a reward system should be on rewarding performance, managers must carefully and quickly recognize that the more flexible a performance-based reward system is, the greater the costs will be. Therefore, managers may face a trade-off between costs and a performance-contingent reward system.

3. **Reward and performance evaluation systems go hand-in-hand.**

Stated differently, a reward system is only as good as the accuracy and validity of the performance evaluation approach. If performance is to be highly rewarded, then managers must be confident that high performance actually occurred.

4. **Effectively communicate components of the reward system.**

Employees must know that performance is rewarded by the organization in order that continued high performance is to be achieved. This means that employees must know and understand how the reward system works and what they need to do to improve their performance. Secrecy in a reward system may shield managers from short-term criticism; it also opens the door to misperceptions and problems of morale.

BEHAVIORAL CONTROL SYSTEMS: TERMINATIONS

As we are all aware, situations arise in many organizations where the employee is separated from the organization. These *terminations* result from at least four circumstances: (1) termination by the employer with due cause (theft, incompetence, wrongdoing, etc.); (2) termination by the employer without due cause (layoff, plant closing, and so on); (3) voluntary termination by the employee (resignation or turnover); and (4) termination in the event of death, disability, or retirement. For our purposes, we will focus only on termination by the organization.

Termination by the Organization

Throughout this book, we have stressed methods of improving or maintaining high performance levels among all employees. There are many situations, however, in which an employee continually proves to be ineffective in a given position. At least four options are available to organizations under these circumstances. First, the person can be *transferred* to another position, one where there is a better match between the requirements of the job and the skills and abilities of the person. This strategy, however, requires careful selection and a willingness by the employee to make the move.

Second, the employee can be *re-trained* through extensive training and development programs. This can be a costly process that assumes not only that the person can be re-trained, but that the organization wants it. Third, an infrequently used strategy is to *demote* the person to a less responsible position. With a demotion, the employee may find it hard to maintain relationships with former superiors, peers, and subordinates. Sometimes a demotion can take the form of a lateral transfer or the creation of an impressively titled job, but one that involves much less responsibility.

Finally, the employee may be *fired.* In terminating an employee the organization must be careful not to leave itself open for claims of discrimination. It is wise to back up a termination with a file on the person's performance, or economic and resource justifications for the termination. Gaining popularity is out-placement counseling, in which the organization helps the terminated employee find another job or pays to have the person re-trained. This "easing out" process may limit the shock of losing a job.

Terminating a number of employees to control or reduce costs can have its drawbacks. Consider the case of Ed Hennessy who, in 1979, became president of the financially troubled Allied Chemical Company:

> The painful job of making [personnel] cuts fell to Hennessy himself. The corporate staff was hardest hit, the census declining from 1600 to 450. Many people were fired and others were transferred to jobs in the operating companies. . . . One result will be a $30 million annual savings in overhead. . . . Hennessy made at least one serious tactical mistake. When the pink slips were handed out in mid-September, he was on a long-scheduled visit to Allied's operations in the North Sea. He acknowledged that he should have been on the firing line in Morristown. When he returned to the office, he was accompanied for a week, on the advice of his "out-placement" consultants, by a bodyguard.[21]

This example and others suggest that the process of termination—whether of one manager or a large group—should be carefully planned and carefully implemented.

Termination Costs

Rarely is a manager or nonmanager terminated by an organization without being provided some form of termination or severance pay. This extra pay can range from less than a month's to more than a year's salary. As shown in exhibit 16-9, severance pay varies by termination reason and by country. For example, in Venezuela, severance pay is provided for all terminations, while in Australia, no severance pay is ever given.

Termination by the organization is an emotionally difficult, but many times necessary, decision. It should be pointed out, however, that termination does not always equate to employee incompetence. A personality conflict with one's superior, the phasing out of a product line or plant, or the merger with another company can result in the elimination

EXHIBIT 16-9   Severance Pay by Termination Reason for Different Countries

COUNTRY	TERM- INATION WITH CAUSE	TERMINATION WITHOUT CAUSE	VOLUN- TARY TERMINATION	RETIRE- MENT	DEATH	DISABILITY
LATIN AMERICA						
Argentina	–	×	–	–	–	–
Mexico	–	×	×	×	×	×
Puerto Rico	–	×	–	–	–	–
Venezuela	×	×	×	×	×	×
EUROPE						
Austria	–	×	–	×	×	×
Denmark	–	×	–	–	–	–
Italy	×	×	×	×	×	×
England	–	×	–	–	–	–
MIDDLE EAST/ NORTH AFRICA						
Egypt	–	×	×	–	–	–
Israel	–	×	–	×	–	–
Saudi Arabia	–	×	×	×	–	–
ASIA/PACIFIC						
Australia	–	–	–	–	–	–
India	–	×	×	×	×	×
Japan	–	×	×	×	×	×
Singapore	–	–	–	–	–	–
Taiwan	–	×	–	–	–	–

Adapted from J. C. Roberts, "Termination Indemnities Around the World," *The Personnel Administrator* (June 1979): 75–80.

of a job, even though the employee has performed effectively. The literature is full of instances where managers have been terminated by one organization, only to become a success in another. Consider the case of W. Michael Blumenthal, whose successes as chairman of Bendix Corporation led to his appointment as treasury secretary in President Carter's cabinet. Unfortunately, his corporate successes did not carry over into governmental activities—he was one of a number of cabinet members who abruptly left (or were fired?) during 1979. Since leaving government, Blumenthal has once again achieved success, this time as president of Burroughs Corporation.[22]

CONTROL AND THE MANAGER'S JOB

Control, and particularly behavioral control systems, is a managerial function which assures that actual organizational activities conform to planned activities. Since control cuts across almost all the operations and activities of an organization, there is a high degree of managerial involvement and use of managerial skills and roles.

From a managerial role viewpoint, control is an important activity. In their *interpersonal* roles, managers provide much-needed guidance and direction. The manager looks for operations that are going wrong, problems in need of attention, and subordinates who require encouragement or criticism. The managers' *informational* roles also are important because through these roles, managers must be alert to the various operations in the organization. Acting as monitor, disseminator, and spokesperson, the manager receives, aggregates, and transmits information concerning the performance of individuals and units. Finally, in their *decisional* roles, managers must make decisions to ensure the achievement of organizational goals. This can include identifying and resolving interpersonal conflict, making sure that organizational resources are allocated properly and used effectively, and negotiating with labor groups on pay increases.

Managerial skills are also closely tied to control systems. *Technical* skills enable the manager to understand the particular elements of his or her unit, especially those where control is important. *Human* skills relate strongly to the way in which performance evaluations are conducted. As we mentioned earlier, the interpersonal exchange during an appraisal interview is frequently more important than the method of evaluation. *Conceptual* skills come to the forefront when the manager recognizes the tie between control and the other managerial functions, particularly planning. In addition, the manager must develop *diagnostic* skills accurately to identify why certain deviations from plans have occurred and what corrective actions are needed. For example, managers at Eastern Airlines diagnosed early that the dramatic rise in fuel costs would have an adverse effect on profitability. In order to control costs, they retired older equipment, dropped many routes, and suggested that their planes fly at higher altitudes where the fuel usage is lower due to less drag from the atmosphere. Eastern also attempted to cut some of the weight off their planes. In order to cut over 250 pounds off the jet's weight, Eastern has stripped the white paint off its fleet, revealing the silvery, polished metal underneath. The fuel savings from this weight loss: almost $1 million per year.[23]

SUMMARY FOR THE MANAGER

1. Control is a managerial function that assures that actual organizational activities conform to planned activities. For managers, two aspects are important. First, control activities occur at all stages or steps in producing the organization's products or services—from input (raw material inspection), through the process (production control, contingency plans), to output controls (audits, cost analysis). Second, control is closely tied to the other managerial functions, especially planning. Good plans, in fact, have detailed control systems built into them.

2. An integral part of a behavioral control system is the process of performance evaluation. The manager should recognize that performance evaluation serves many purposes: appraising employee performance, identifying training needs, providing information for selection, placement, and termination decisions, and providing information for reward allocation.

3. Performance evaluations in organizations can vary by approach and method. While a number of different approaches can be used by the manager to evaluate an employee's performance (superior, peer, subordinate, or self-evaluation), the wise manager seeks multiple inputs, as opposed to a single source of information, in order to ensure validity and accuracy.

4. Performance evaluation methods, such as global ranking, trait-based rating scales, critical incidents, BARS, and effectiveness-based measures can be used to evaluate a subordinate's performance. It is crucial for the manager to understand the strengths and weaknesses of each of these methods. For example, rankings are quick, but can be quite inaccurate: BARS and effectiveness-based measures are job specific, but extremely time consuming.

5. The appraisal interview can make or break the

performance evaluation process. It is important that the manager understands the employee's performance data, establishes a positive climate for the interview, focuses on the behavior, not the person, and ends the interview so that the employee knows how well he has done and what he should do next.

6. Pay is one of the organization's most powerful reward components. Many forms of pay exist, including base pay, increases in base pay, and supplemental pay. Whatever the organization chooses, it is important that the employees connect the level of their performance and the amount of their pay.

7. Promotion and employee benefits are two other reward system components. In promotion programs, one of the most important approaches that the manager should consider is the openness of the program. This includes job postings and open knowledge of career paths and how promotion decisions are made. In employee benefit plans, the manager should be aware of the importance of cafeteria plans and the selective use of executive perks. Cafeteria plans allow the individual employees to tailor the benefit plan to their needs. Executive perks are becoming more and more popular because of the scarcity of good executive talent.

8. A behavioral control system also includes the process of terminating employees. Termination can occur as a result of due cause (e.g., theft), organizational reasons (e.g., plant or office closings), voluntary termination (turnover), death, retirement, or disability. The key factor is that effort should be given not only to justifying the termination, but if the plan involves more than one employee, it must be well-planned and implemented, involving even finding the person a job.

9. Such factors as distance, outside ownership interests, diversity, uncertainties, and host-country goals must be taken into account when an organization develops and implements a control system for international operations. Additional problems include the development of evaluation standards, using the most effective control reporting techniques, and attempting to enforce corrective actions in foreign operations that are not wholly owned by the organization.

10. Control involves many managerial roles and skills. The manager must gather information on an activity, diagnose the sources of any problems, recognize the importance of the activity to the total organization, and take corrective actions to bring the activity back to its planned level.

QUESTIONS FOR REVIEW AND DISCUSSION

1. Why is it suggested that planning and control are closely related?
2. Name key differences between input controls, process controls, and output controls.
3. How important are communication networks to the success of a control system?
4. Why is it recommended that a manager should use multiple sources or approaches in evaluating the performance of subordinates?
5. What are the major differences between trait-based rating scales and BARS?
6. Why is it important for the manager to establish a good climate in the performance evaluation interview?
7. What are some of the advantages and disadvantages of having yearly performance evaluations and pay increases?
8. If you had a choice between working for an organization with a secret pay and promotion program and one where there was more openness in the reward program, which would you choose and why?
9. Why are executive perks becoming so popular and important to organizations?
10. Under what conditions would a termination benefit the manager and the organization?

NOTES

1. "What Makes Harry Gray Run?" *Business Week* (December 10, 1979): 80.

2. R. J. Mockler, *The Management Control Process* (Englewood Cliffs, N.J.: Prentice-Hall, 1972).

3. W. Newman, *Constructive Control: Design and Use of Control Systems* (Englewood Cliffs, N.J.: Prentice-Hall, 1975).

4. J. D. Daniels, E. W. Orgram, and L. H. Radebaugh, *International Business: Environments and Operations,* 2nd ed. (Reading, Mass.: Addison-Wesley, 1979), p. 389.

5. See F. Hawkins, "Controlling Foreign Operations," *Financial Executive* (February 1965); and J. M. McInnes, "Financial Control Systems for Multinational Operations: An Empirical Investigation," *Journal of International Business Studies* (Fall 1971): 11–28.

6. R. D. Robinson, *International Business Management* (Hinsdale, Ill.: Dryden, 1973), p. 624.

7. Daniels, et al., *International Business*, p. 408.

8. Robinson, *International Business Management*, p. 518.

9. C. E. Schneier and R. W. Beatty, "Integrating Behaviorally-Based and Effectiveness-Based Methods," *The Personnel Administrator* (July 1979): 65–76.

10. Ibid., p. 66.

11. J. M. McFillen and P. G. Decker, "Building Meaning Into Appraisal," *The Personnel Administrator* (June 1978): 75–84.

12. R. M. Guion, *Personnel Testing* (New York: McGraw-Hill, 1965), p. 90–95.

13. H. Levinson, "Appraisal of What Performance?" *Harvard Business Review* (July–August 1976): 30–48.

14. See J. P. Campbell, M. D. Dunnette, R. D. Arvey, and L. W. Hellervik, "The Development and Evaluation of Behaviorally Based Rating Scales," *Journal of Applied Psychology* (February 1973): 15–22; and D. P. Schwab, H. G.

Henneman III, and T. A. DeCotiis, "Behaviorally Anchored Rating Scales: A Review of the Literature," *Personnel Psychology* (Winter 1975): 549–62.

15. R. Henderson, *Performance Appraisal: Theory and Practice* (Reston, Va.: Reston, 1980); and N. R. F. Maier, *The Appraisal Interview* (La Jolla, Calif.: University Associates, 1976).

16. Schneier and Beatty, "Integrating Behaviorally-Based and Effectiveness-Based Methods," p. 66.

17. This section draws heavily from E. E. Lawler III, "Reward Systems," in J. R. Hackman and J. L. Suttle, *Improving Life at Work* (Santa Monica, Calif.: Goodyear, 1977), pp. 163–226.

18. See R. J. Schulhof, "Five Years with a Scanlon Plan," *The Personnel Administrator* (June 1979): 55–62.

19. W. F. Glueck, *Personnel* (Dallas: Business Publications, 1978), p. 456.

20. Lawler, "Reward Systems," pp. 180–81.

21. P. W. Bernstein, "The Hennessy Hurricane Whips Through Allied Chemical," *Fortune* (December 17, 1979): 101.

22. A. L. Porter, "The Myth of Managerial Tenure," *Human Resource Management* (Summer 1977): 2–16.

23. "Fuel Takes Off," *Time* (March 10, 1980): 71.

ADDITIONAL REFERENCES

Anthony, R. N. and Dearden, J. *Management Control Systems,* 3rd ed. Homewood, Ill.: Irwin, 1976.

Cammann, C. and Nadler, D. "Fit Control Systems to Your Managerial Style." *Harvard Business Review* (January–February 1976): 65–72.

Cathey, P. "How to Hang On to the Right Employees." *Iron Age* (September 17, 1979): 35–38.

Deci, E. L. "The Hidden Cost of Rewards." *Organizational Dynamics* (Winter 1976): 61–72.

Harrison, E. L. "Discipline and the Professional Employee." *The Personnel Administrator* (March 1979): 35–38.

Kearney, W. J. "Improving Work Performance Through

Appraisal." *Human Resource Management* (Summer 1978): 15–23.

Kellogg, M. *What To Do About Performance Appraisal.* New York: AMACOM, 1975.

Koontz, H. and Bradspies, R. W. "Managing Through Feedforward Control." *Business Horizons* (June 1972): 25–36.

Kuzmits, F. E. "How Much Is Absenteeism Costing Your Organization?" *The Personnel Administrator* (June 1979): 29–34.

Todd, J. "Management Control Systems: A Key Link Between Strategy, Structure and Employee Performance." *Organizational Dynamics* (Spring 1977): 65–78.

A CASE FOR ANALYSIS

The Singer Company

Late in 1975, the board of directors of Singer Company brought in Joseph Flavin to replace a chief executive who was seriously ill and had let the enterprise run out of control. The choice seemed inspired. Widely respected, Flavin had spent the first fourteen years of his career rising to controller of IBM World Trade Corporation and the last eight at Xerox, where he became an executive vice president. When he took the helm at Singer, he confidently predicted, "This company can be turned around." Within a month, he took a $411-million write-off, sweeping away a legacy of sick operations left by his predecessor.

The new CEO had the take-charge air of a man who could not falter. But when Singer stunned the business world with its second announcement of a $130-million write-off, the news raised serious questions about Flavin's stewardship. Unlike the earlier write-off, this one struck at the vitals of the enterprise that is synonymous with the corporate name. And Flavin admits that, for two full years, he didn't know how bad the sewing-machine business really was.

Singer has nothing in common, except for the fame of its great trademark, with the solidly staffed and professionally managed companies Flavin came from. He inherited a management so weakened that he has not been able to find the talent to fill the vacancy in the president's job. Nevertheless, sounding as confident as ever, he is again saying that Singer can be turned around.

Flavin's write-off gave the public its first look at how bad the situation really was. The day before, following a long session with Singer's board, Flavin took an overnight flight to Glasgow where he met with a delegation of Scottish trade unionists to deliver some very bad news: Singer would close down its ninety-three-year-old Clydebank plant by June of next year. The factory employs 3000 workers, nearly a third of the total force at Singer's seven sewing-machine plants in Europe and North America.

Singer's top brass was woefully late to grasp what was happening. When Flavin was brought in, most outsiders—and, apparently, Singer insiders as well—were convinced that the sewing-machine business was basically sound. But in fact the U.S. market for sewing machines had peaked in 1972, and the European market had stopped growing in 1974, a year before Flavin came to Singer's rescue.

The trend line in the U.S. was dropping like an anchor when Flavin arrived in December of 1975, but Singer's executives blamed their own sales slowdown on the recession. Though the trouble was more fundamental, they had no way of knowing that. The company's market research was, at best, primitive. Singer had never gone in for polling its customers, as many appliance manufacturers do. And it suited the company fine that no trade association existed to collect market information; Singer executives arrogantly assumed that the gathering of data could be valuable only to competitors.

In 1977, Flavin belatedly commissioned a study to get at why the market in the U.S. was in such a disturbing decline. Prepared by economist Norma Pace, it pointed out the obvious: women between the ages of sixteen and twenty-nine, Singer's great potential market, did not have a consuming interest in sewing or, for that matter, in possessing a sewing machine. "The downward trend is so strong," wrote Pace, "that it indicates only 18 percent of females in the sixteen to twenty-four ages will own machines in 1985, compared with an estimated 46 percent in 1970. The drop in the twenty-five to twenty-nine-year-olds is even more dramatic, with only 31 percent owning machines in 1985 in these age brackets, as compared with 79 percent in 1970."

On top of this, it was gently hinted that the working women of America (now 41 percent of the working population) had many alternative ways to fill their leisure time. Concluded Pace, "The high skill level that is required for sewing apparel stands out as a major barrier in a consumer world where many competing activities vie for the available time; an imperfect skill is quickly revealed and has a stigma. A poor tennis player is subject to less ridicule than an amateur sewer."

Though the decline in Europe began shortly after Pace delivered her analysis of the U.S. market, no one at Singer could accept the idea that European women were so quickly falling into step with their American counterparts. One Singer executive admitted, "Whenever we had trouble, the motto was 'This too shall pass.' "

As 1978 unwound, Flavin finally woke up. The entire market for consumer sewing machines dropped dramatically on both continents, pulling Singer's unit sales down with it. For the first time in memory, Singer's U.S. operations lost money: $21 million. But the European operations stayed well in the black, so that the combined businesses eked out a $5-million operating profit on $701 million in sales. Gradually, the rot worsened. In the first half of 1979, the combined operations lost $6.8 million.

In announcing the write-off, Singer blamed most of its problems on a single devastating fact: the U.S. market for sewing machines has been cut in half since 1972. But the company's troubles really go back much further than that. The sewing business is international, and Singer has been attacked since the fifties in almost all markets. The Japanese came first, and they were followed by other Asian manufacturers. Though the company has shifted some of its production to low-cost locations such as Brazil, Mexico, and Taiwan, it has been unable to hold the more aggressive competitors at bay.

In many respects, the operations in Clydebank are symbolic of Singer's anguish. The nearly century-old plant is appallingly antiquated, with manufacturing operations on several floors and a casting process that would be out of date in Chungking. Productivity has been so low in recent years that even the unions have conceded that, in its present shape, the plant is incapable of competing with anyone, much less the producers on Taiwan. Over 90 percent of Clydebank's shipments go to Europe or North America, where they compete with lower-cost models. A competitor's machine comparable to one that costs Singer $123 to make at Clydebank can be turned out for $65 in Taiwan.

The closing of Clydebank is but the first of a series of efforts planned to treat Singer's numbing wounds. Flavin knows he has to batten down operations in Europe and North America to provide protection from the worst possible scenario, including a long and deep recession, a reduction in real purchasing power, and continued inroads by low-cost manufacturers.

For years Singer acted as if the sewing-products operation could run without a coherent business plan. Extraordinary latitude was given to the top managers. Small empires were created in this hands-off atmosphere, with scant communication among the emperors.

A very frank and downhearted Singer executive, looking back on the littered landscape, offers this summary: "What happened is not at all mysterious. We had no control systems. It's a classic case that will be studied for a long time to come."

The decision Flavin faced would test the mettle of any man. No one likes firing people, and Flavin is going to have to let thousands of workers go. "Most people need a lot of love," he said recently, "but here there is necessarily anger and hurt." Though his self-confidence appears to be intact, his own share of responsibility for Singer's predicament cannot have escaped him. He was late to diagnose the situation when he arrived, and now, assuming he survives as chief executive, he will have to live with it for some time to come.

Questions for Discussion

1. Discuss the elements of the control system operating at Singer before the arrival of Flavin.

2. What type of control system does Singer need now and in the future?

3. Discuss the relationship between planning and control as it functioned in the case.

4. What are the corrective actions that Flavin is taking to reverse Singer's problems?

Adapted from Thomas O'Hanlon, "Behind the Snafu at Singer," Fortune (November 5, 1979): 76–79.

EXPERIENTIAL EXERCISE

Merit Pay Increases

Purpose

1. To examine the application and problems of merit pay increases
2. To consider the impact of multiple performance criteria in managerial decision making.

Required Understanding

The student should understand the different methods in performance evaluation.

How to Set Up the Exercise

Set up groups of four to eight students for the forty-five to sixty-minute exercise. The groups should be separated from each other and asked to converse only with members of their own group. The participants should then read the following:

Coastal Instrument Corporation is a small manufacturing company located in San Jose, California. The company is nonunionized and manufactures laboratory analysis equipment for hospitals.

Approximately one year ago, the manager of the assembly department established three manufacturing goals for the department. The goals were: (1) reduce raw material storage costs by 15 percent; (2) reduce variable labor costs (i.e., overtime) by 20 percent; and (3) decrease the number of quality rejects by 15 percent. The department manager stated to the six unit supervisors that the degree to which each supervisor met or exceeded these goals would be one of the major inputs into their merit pay increases for the year. In previous years, merit increases were based on seniority.

The six department supervisors worked on separate but similar production lines. A profile of each supervisor is as follows:

Jim Owens: black, age twenty-four; married with no children; one year with the company after graduating from a local college. First full-time job since graduation from college. He is well-liked by all employees and has exhibited a high level of enthusiasm for his work.

Mary Beck: white, age twenty-eight; single; three years with the company after receiving her degree from the state university. Has a job offer from another company for a similar job that provides a substantial pay increase over her present salary (15 percent). Coastal does not want to lose Mary because her overall performance has been excellent. The job offer would require her to move to another state, which she views unfavorably. Coastal can keep her if it can come close to matching her salary offer.

Jack Turner: white; age thirty-two; married with three children; three years with the company; high school education. One of the most stable and steady supervisors. However, he supervises a group of workers who are known to be unfriendly and uncooperative with him and other employees.

Joseph Koch: white; age thirty-four; married with four children; high school equivalent learning; one year with the company. Immigrated to this country ten years ago and has recently become a U. S. citizen. A steady worker, well-liked by his coworkers, but has had difficulty learning the English language. As a result, certain problems of communication within his group and with other groups have developed in the past.

Maria Juarez: Hispanic; age twenty-nine; divorcee with three children; two years with the company; high school education. Since her divorce one year ago, her performance has begun to improve. Prior to that, her performance was very erratic, with frequent absences. She is the sole support for her three children.

Frank Wedman: white; age twenty-seven; single; two years with the company; college graduate. One of the best-liked employees at Coastal. However, has shown a lack of initiative and ambition on the job. Appears to be preoccupied with his outside social life.

Exhibit 16-10 presents summary data on the performance of the six supervisors during the past year. The data include current annual salary, performance level on the three goals, and an overall evaluation by the department manager.

The new budget for the upcoming year has allocated a total of $114,400 for supervisory salaries in the assembly department, a $10,400 (or 10 percent) increase from last year. Top management has indicated that salary increases should range from 4 percent to 12 percent and should be tied as closely as possible to performance.

In making the merit pay increase decisions, the following points should be considered:

1. The decisions will likely set a precedent for future salary and merit increase considerations.

2. Salary increases should not be excessive, but should be representative of the supervisor's performance during the past year.

3. The decisions should be concerned with internal equity; that is, they ought to be consistent with each other.

4. The company does not want to lose these experienced supervisors to other firms. Management not only wants the supervisors to be satisfied with their salary increases, but also to further develop the feeling that Coastal Manufacturing is a good company for advancement, growth, and career development.

Instructions for the Exercise

1. Each student should individually determine the dollar amount and percentage increase in salary (4 percent, 8 percent, or 12 percent) for each supervisor. Individual decisions should be justified by a rational or decision rule.

2. After each individual has reached a decision, the group will convene and make the same decision as in (1) above.

3. After each group has reached a decision, a spokesperson for each group will present the following information to the class:
   a. The group's decision concerning merit pay increases for each supervisor (percentage)
   b. The high, low, and average individual decisions in the group
   c. A rationale for the group's decision

EXHIBIT 16-10   Individual Performance for the Six Supervisors During the Past Year

| | | GOAL ATTAINMENT[a] | | | MANAGER'S EVALUATION[b] | | | |
SUPERVISOR	CURRENT SALARY (000s OMITTED)	Storage Costs (15%)	Labor Costs (20%)	Quality Rejects (15%)	Effort	Dependability	Ability to Work Independently	Knowledge of Job
Owens	$16.5	18%	19%	17%	Excellent	Excellent	Good	Good
Beck	$18.0	18%	21%	16%	Excellent	Excellent	Excellent	Excellent
Turner	$18.0	12%	8%	3%	Good	Excellent	Good	Good
Koch	$16.5	10%	10%	12%	Excellent	Good	Fair	Fair
Juarez	$17.5	16%	15%	10%	Good	Fair	Fair	Good
Wedman	$17.5	12%	16%	3%	Fair	Fair	Fair	Fair

[a]Numbers designate actual cost and quality reject reduction   [b]The possible ratings are poor, fair, good, and excellent

17

Financial and
Information Control Systems

CHAPTER OUTLINE

KEY POINTS IN THIS CHAPTER

1. Control indicates how effective the other management functions—planning, organizing, and leading—are performing.

2. Operating and financial budgets are important parts of the manager's job.

3. Those managers who are responsible for working within a budget should have some say in its development—this is the bottom-up approach.

4. Financial statements determine the state of the organization's financial resources during or at a particular time period.

5. Financial ratios are used to analyze the organization's current financial position and identify important trends.

6. External financial audits—usually performed by professional accounting firms—and internal audits are used to verify the organization's financial position and the validity of its financial statements.

7. A management audit includes an evaluation of the organization's goals, strategies, policies, and so on.

8. Financial statements, financial analyses, and audits vary greatly across countries.

9. MIS can improve the organization's early-warning and decision processes.

10. A MIS-oriented decision-support system enables the manager to make improved decisions with the integration of management science models, the computer, and interactive terminals.

THE PRACTICE OF MANAGEMENT

Management Information Systems and the Railroad Industry

The railroads in the U. S. are beginning to rely increasingly on a new type of weapon in the fight to get back the freight business they have lost to the truckers and barges. Their strategy hinges not only on shiny new rolling stock and faster train schedules, but also on information processing technology that will enable them to make the most of the equipment they already have.

Although computers and information systems have been a part of railroad operations for the past twenty years, only recently have they been upgraded to do more sophisticated tasks of keeping track of cars and locomotives and scheduling loaded cars on trains. The Association of American Railroads (AAR) is planning to expand its nationwide computer bank that provides up-to-the-minute data on the location of some 2.2 million freight cars. Known as "car service directives," they tell railroads how to move rolling stock from one region to another when a car shortage develops.

Within individual companies, information systems are beginning to pay off in more efficient use of cars and locomotives, less costly maintenance efforts, and better long-range planning. The Atchison, Topeka & Santa Fe, for example, has completed a central computerized information file, or data bank, that contains information on everything from car movements to finances. The system is sophisticated enough to handle such jobs as calculating payrolls for train crews, along with car movements and scheduling. Although the Santa Fe spends millions of dollars annually on information systems, it has already resulted in significant cost savings.

The Santa Fe's biggest cost savings to date are coming from the computer's ability to keep tabs on the whereabouts of every freight car and locomotive on the line. Each time a car pulls into a rail yard, a Santa Fe clerk enters its identification number into a central computer file. When a shipper requests a freight car, the computer locates the nearest suitable one in a matter of seconds and sends dispatching instructions to the yard. Similar systems are being used by the Missouri Pacific and the Southern Pacific railroads.

One failing in such systems, however, is that all data on rail car locations must be keypunched manually into the computer file. An earlier attempt to read the identification numbers with trackside optical scanners ended in failure in 1978 because the scanners could not read the bar code on dirty cars. A new type of automatic reading equipment using television cameras has been developed, but the once bitten railroads are reluctant to try it.

Even so, the present systems are a far cry from the days when computers were limited only to accounting functions. Before the Missouri Pacific computerized its dispatching, a shipper had to call one of the company's 300 freight stations and wait while an agent made an often lengthy search for available cars. By keeping track of the rolling stock, the new information systems have resulted in a 10 percent improvement in car utilization, which in turn has led to an annual cost savings that went beyond the company's expectation of $8 million. According to Missouri Pacific managers, the new system has paid for itself several times over.

These efforts could become even more vital to rail operations if Congress deregulates the railroads as it did the airline industry. Now, months elapse between the time that rate changes are announced and the time they take effect. But if rates are deregulated, they could change overnight. The computerized information system would be the only way to extract and analyze the information and react successfully.

Adapted from "Data Processing: A Bigger Load for Rail Computers," Business Week *(February 4, 1980): 89–90.*

17

The objective of managerial control systems is to ensure that the resources of the organization are used wisely and efficiently. The last chapter dealt with controlling human resources, while the next chapter looks at production and operations control. In this chapter our attention will focus on controlling the important financial and information resources of an organization.

The chapter is divided into three main sections. First, the characteristics of an organization's financial control system will be discussed. This will include presentations on the topics of budgets, financial analyses, and audits. The second part deals with the important topic of information systems. In this section, a basic understanding will be developed of the function of management information systems (MIS) in organizations. Finally, we present a discussion of the relationship between financial and information control and the manager's job.

FINANCIAL CONTROL SYSTEMS: BUDGETS

In previous chapters it was noted that there is a wide variation in the way managers emphasize and apply the tools and techniques associated with management functions. Some managers believe strongly in the use of contingency planning, while others hardly plan at all; an executive may require strict adherence to a formal chain of command, while another executive may prefer a more informal approach; one manager may insist on the use of objective, quantifiable data in employee performance evaluation, while a second manager may believe that subjective, qualitative performance data are sufficient, and so on. One area where there is a great deal of similarity is the emphasis given to a knowledge of the expenses, revenues, and profits for a period of time—the budget.

Budgets are formal statements of future expenditures, revenues, and expected profits developed to control the use of the financial resources of an organization. Budgets form the last link in the management process chain that began with goals and strategies. Thus, they are the most detailed management practice used to ensure that an organization's goals are achieved.

Budgets are important to the manager for a number of reasons.[1] First, they aid in *planning* in that they force management to develop achievable goals and basic plans and policies associated with these goals. In other words, budgets set a standard of production (the budgeted amount of output). From an *organizing* point of view, budgets assist in clarifying responsibilities among organizational members. This is particularly important in coordinating the activities of the organization. The interaction between managers and subordinates that occurs during the budget development process helps define and integrate performance-related activities. By specifying what resources are to be used, budgets help in achieving goals through the successful implementation of the organization's strategies. This is an important part of the *leading* function. Finally, from a *control* view, budgets lead to the efficient use of resources, assist in preserving valuable resources, and establish a mechanism for periodic organizational analysis.

More than anything, budgets are important and so widely used because they are stated in monetary terms. Dollar figures are a common denominator among managers across a wide variety of organizational activities, including the purchase of raw materials and equipment in manufacturing, selling and advertising expenses in marketing, hiring and training of employees in personnel, and so on. Since profits are expressed in monetary terms, budgets are a main mechanism used by profit-oriented firms in estimating and guiding activities.

The Budgeting Process

Budgets can be prepared by at least two procedures: top-down or bottom-up.[2] In the top-down approach, a budget is almost totally developed by executive management and then imposed on lower management levels without much consultation on their part. These budgets are usually prepared by the chief financial officer, such as the vice president of finance or the controller. While lower-level managers can sometimes offer counter-proposals on budgets sent to them by superiors, their major duty is to implement the budget.

Most organizations, however, are beginning to follow a procedure in which the budgets are prepared by the managers who are responsible for their implementation. This bottom-up procedure offers a number of advantages, including: (1) lower-level managers have a more realistic view of their requirements, needs, and constraints; (2) there is less chance that important elements will be overlooked; and (3) these managers are more motivated to work toward good performance when they have had a voice in developing the budget.

Managers, however, should recognize some of the problems that could arise with the bottom-up approach.[3] First, increased political behavior may develop when a number of managers are competing for scarce resources: being overly friendly with superiors, talking down the skills and abilities of other managers, and attempting to discover the secret details of other managers' budgets through covert information systems are examples. Second, in order to ensure proper funding, many managers overstate their financial needs.

The budgeting process for a bottom-up approach includes the following key steps:

1. *Statement of goals* is the communicating of the organization's goals and strategies for the coming budget period. Included are many important forecasts of economic and competitive activity and a timetable for preparing and implementing the budget.

2. *Budget preparation* is the responsibility of lower-level managers. Budgets are prepared with respect to resource acquisition, utilization, and time requirements.

3. *Review and approval* brings top management back into the budget process, usually in the form of a budget committee or department. These

managers review the individual budgets for their anticipated revenues, expenditures, and resource utilization, and integrate them into the organization's strategies and goals.

4. Budget *evaluation and revision* occurs as the unit performs during the specified period. Unit managers are encouraged to meet the budget, and if a unit's performance is less than satisfactory, the manager is asked to take corrective action. This performance is then used as an input into the next budget period.

Budgets must be a flexible managerial instrument. Similar to forecasts—which budgets really are—there must be provisions for unforeseen events. For this reason, formal updating periods may be established at intervals.

Types of Budgets

The overall budget for an organization is a composite of budgets for departments, divisions, and other organizational units. Three budget types are most frequently found in organizations: operating budgets, financial budgets, and variable versus fixed budgets.[4]

Operating Budgets.   Operating budgets, as shown in exhibit 17-1, are those that indicate the raw materials, goods, or services the organizational unit expects to *consume* during the budget period. For a wood products company such as Boise Cascade, this includes the cost of the raw lumber, manufacturing expenses in converting the lumber into such products as plywood boards, and the revenue generated from the product's sale. Operating budgets can be best analyzed from the basis of responsibility centers: expense centers, revenue centers, and profit centers.

Expense or cost centers are those units in which the budget relates to the efficiency of the operations. These budgets—sometimes called "engineered" budgets—are typically used in manufacturing units where there is a concern for material and labor costs, as well as estimated overhead costs. Exceeding the budget is an indication that costs are higher than they should be and a certain level of inefficiency exists. Expense center budgets can be used in departments such as personnel, legal, and research and development, where the measurement of output is difficult. Termed "discretionary" cost budgets, the concern is not so much with efficiency as it is with controlling the number of tasks performed.

Revenue centers are concerned with outputs, as opposed to costs or expenses for inputs. An example would be a regional sales office of an organization as it prepares sales budgets for each product and salesperson. Revenue budgets are less precise than expense budgets, since managers lack control over the elements that determine their levels of effectiveness, such as products out of stock, rapid swings in the economy, or unforeseen decisions by competitors (e.g., a price cut).

Profit centers combine expense and revenue budgets into one statement. These budgets are usually found at the divisional level in an organization, where the manager is responsible for the best combination of costs and revenues. The goal is to maximize the bottom line—profits.

Profit centers are one of the foundational elements of the planning and control system of BankAmerica Corporation, the largest financial institution in this nation. All operating authority is in the hands of unit

EXHIBIT 17-1   Types of Budgets in a Manufacturing Firm

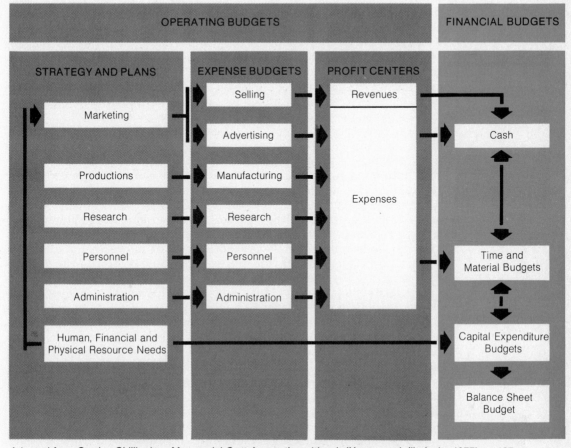

Adapted from Gordon Shillinglaw, Managerial Cost Accounting, *4th ed. (Homewood, Ill.: Irwin, 1977), p. 137.*

managers at some 150 profit centers around the world, while headquarters retains control of capital and major credit decisions.

Overall planning starts with BankAmerica's research policy council (i.e., top management), which early each year comes up with a list of economic assumptions likely to affect the bank over the coming five years. The list goes to the manager of each profit center, who must then turn the assumptions into a business plan. The plan—highly detailed for the next year, less so for the following years—charts such items as basic operating strategies, new services, and new market opportunities. Later in the year, the manager develops a detailed financial plan showing how the profit center will use the funds available to it. These two plans form the basic operating program for every profit center.

To measure financial performance of the profit centers, the bank relies on an elaborate control system, called the "building blocks," which features a method of pricing money transfers. Simply put, each profit center is credited for the funds it generates and is charged for the funds it uses. The result is one of the most efficient and lowest-cost operations in the banking industry.[5]

Financial Budgets. Financial budgets deal with how the organization intends to spend money during the particular period. Cash budgets, capital expenditure budgets, time and material budgets, and balance sheet budgets are financial budgets.

Cash budgets are a projection of revenues and expenses for the budget period. A cash budget will give the manager information about the amount of cash flowing through the organization and the pattern of cash disbursements and receipts. This information will tell the manager when excessive cash is available for short-term investments, or when a cash shortage may require some internal corrective actions.

Capital expenditure budgets describe the future investments of the organization in such physical resources as buildings, property, and equipment. Because of their importance to the future of the organization and their infrequency, capital expenditure budgets are developed only after careful study. A major issue with capital expenditure budgeting is that money is being committed for several years in advance. Thus, this type of budget must be integrated with forecasts and long-range planning.

Capital expenditure budgets are made with a careful analysis of the external environment and the probability of certain events. For example, in 1975 Dow Chemical Company recognized during their long-range planning activities that funds for new plant construction would be needed in approximately two years. To most companies, this would have meant that they could wait at least a year before attempting to acquire capital money from investors in the form of stocks or bonds. Dow's management, through a detailed financial analysis, projected that interest rates on bonds would probably rise dramatically in the following years. With this information in mind, Dow sold over $200 million in bonds during 1975 at an interest rate of 8.5 percent. Even though the money was not needed immediately, this decision proved to be correct because when the money would have been needed, the interest rates had climbed more than 2 percent. Dow will save nearly $40 million over the thirty-year term of the bonds.[6]

Time and material budgets deal with the resources needed to produce a good or service. A time budget involves a forecast of labor costs, while a materials budget concerns the amount of material required to achieve an end result, such as producing a product or constructing a plant.

Finally, a *balance sheet budget* is a composite of all other financial budgets and shows the relationship between assets, liabilities, and equity at some future point in time. Usually called a pro forma balance sheet, it indicates the expected financial status of the organization at a future time if the various budgets are met.

Flexible Budgets. The previously discussed budgets are developed with the assumption of a single level of output. They are called *fixed budgets*. Included are the labor and material costs for that level of output plus the associated property taxes, depreciation, insurance, and administrative costs.

Situations arise, however, in which the level of output can vary significantly. In these cases, a *variable budget* is required. Costs for materials, labor and certain maintenance, energy, supplies, and selling based on output must be considered. Costs, such as advertising, are semi-variable and must be included in the variable budget.

The combination of variable, semi-variable, and fixed costs and revenues makes it almost impossible for the manager to prepare a simple graph or table of results. Computer simulations, however, are gaining in popularity in organizations for use in these situations.

Contemporary Budgeting Approaches

In recent years, many profit and not-for-profit organizations have adopted new approaches to budgeting. Among the most popular are the Planning-Programming-Budgeting System and Zero-Base Budgeting.

Planning-Programming-Budgeting System.   During the Kennedy administration, a new approach to budgeting known as Planning-Programming-Budgeting System (PPBS) was introduced in the Defense Department. The system was designed to identify and eliminate costly program duplications within the Defense Department and integrate these programs into a more accurate overall budget.

The following steps are generally involved in a PPBS approach:[7]

1. State and analyze the basic goals of a program or activity.
2. Analyze the output of the program in light of its stated goals.
3. Measure the total program costs for several years, not just one year.
4. Compare and choose the alternative that best achieves overall goals.

By analyzing each program from a basis of its impact on the total system, it was hoped that the organization would use its resources more efficiently.

Unfortunately, PPBS never was fully implemented in the federal government. Two reasons appear to be most important. First, many agencies and units resisted its use because they saw little benefit from it and because it was being forced upon them without consultation. Second, the insistence by President Johnson that PPBS be put into use immediately resulted in different versions being developed, improper instructions and procedures, and generally poor communication and implementation efforts.

Zero-Base Budgeting.   In traditional budgeting exercises, managers generally start with the existing year's budget and then make adjustments for changing conditions. In other words, it is assumed that past expenditures are appropriate and should be continued. The manager's attention is directed, therefore, to justifying added expenditures for the coming year.

In zero-base budgeting, no such assumption is made. With each new budget preparation period, managers must justify every dollar expenditure as if they started from scratch, or a "zero base."[8] For example, a manager of marketing research who is developing a new budget must justify funds for any new market studies *and* those that are carried over from the previous period.

Zero-base budgeting, which is extensively used in such organizations as Xerox and Texas Instruments and was instituted in the federal government under President Carter, stresses three basic steps. First, activities are broken down into "decision packages" that include all the information needed to evaluate and compare the benefits, costs, and purpose of a program or activity. In the market research example, each project would be considered a decision package. Second, the individual decision packages are ranked according to their benefit to the organization during the budget period. Unit rankings are then given to higher-level management, who develop a rank order for the total organization. Finally, resources are allocated to the individual programs according to rank in the organization.

Zero-base budgeting offers advantages and disadvantages to managers. On one hand, it forces managers to scrutinize each program carefully, eliminating low-priority programs and possibly developing more effective activities. On the other hand, some managers are reluctant to give up pet projects, possibly forcing them to inflate their importance at the expense of better projects. Because it takes a total organizational viewpoint and stresses both the efficient and effective use of resources, zero-base budgeting is being used in a growing number of organizations.

Keys to Success with Budgets

Because all managers develop and must operate within budgets, learning to work effectively with a budget is a key to successful managerial performance. The following are guidelines for managers.

1. **Stress participation of lower-level managers in budget preparation.**

A frequent error made by higher-level managers is to impose a budget on managers who have had little or no say in its development. Participation of lower-level managers in budget preparation not only provides more accurate information, but it improves their commitment to the budget.

2. **Budgets should be viewed as flexible, not ends in themselves.**

Budgets should not be considered as inflexible laws of organizational activities. On the contrary, they should guide managerial actions and be adaptable to changing internal and external environmental conditions.

3. **Avoid an overemphasis on short-run results.**

Managers must give consideration to elements that may occur after the budget period. To meet a current budget, managers may lay-off workers, only to rehire them a short time later; a piece of equipment may be purchased quickly, only to have it become inefficient with the introduction of a newer model; or, assets may be sold to meet a budget, only to find that in the next period, they are needed. Such actions are taken with blinders on. Managers must always look ahead to potential side-effects and benefits.

4. **Be aware of any backscratching or horsetrading.**

In budget preparation, some managers negotiate with other managers on budget elements. This backscratching or horsetrading may result in an inefficient use of resources. For example, a maintenance manager in a manufacturing plant may suggest to the production manager that they will budget for an increase in the number of maintenance employees if the production manager will budget for an increase in the time allotted for maintenance repairs. For the production manager, the benefit of an increased maintenance work force is faster repair, while for the maintenance manager, the increased time will result in less idle time by workers. For the organization, the result will be increased expenses in both departments.

5. Don't overlook the motivational value of budgets.

Budgets are really nothing more than standards of performance. Adherence to budgets should, therefore, be tied to the organization's evaluation and reward system. When managers perform within budget constraints, they should be rewarded, increasing the budget's motivational value. The key is to establish difficult but achievable budgets.

THE MANAGER'S JOB
Don Nyrop of
Northwest Airlines

Like a bronco rider of old, Donald W. Nyrop, chairman of Northwest Airlines, is willing to dig in his spurs and take his lumps in order to stay on top of everything that affects his beloved bottom line. He strongly believes that a key to success in the highly competitive deregulated airline industry is the effective control of company resources. His tight-fisted approach to business and his constant delving into the minutest details have given rise to a lean and trim, but highly profitable enterprise. Examples of Nyrop's concern over control include:

—Northwest's offices are in a dowdy, hangarlike building at the Minneapolis–St. Paul airport. There are no windows, no pictures on the walls, and all offices are small. The lease on the building costs Northwest $1.75 per square foot, compared with the $10 or more that most of its competitors pay for offices.

—Advertising is kept to a minimum and free flights by company personnel are prohibited.

—The management team is small in size, meaning that there are fewer assistant vice presidents and fewer secretaries. When outside meetings are required, managers go one at a time, not in groups.

—New planes are purchased through retained earnings and the sale of stock, rather than costly debt issues.

—Northwest operates with only two basic engines and three fuselages—the 727, 747, and DC-10.

—Planes are traded-in frequently. For example, a 727 which cost Northwest $4.6 million five years ago can be sold for $4 million today. The capital goes to purchasing new planes.

The results of these and other cost control measures have been impressive over the past few years. For example:

—While Northwest is seventh in size of revenues, it is first in return on sales (i.e., approximately 8 percent).

—At $91,000, its revenue per employee is the highest in the industry.

—It operates one of the safest, most modern fleets in the industry. In addition, its breakeven load factor is one of the lowest.

—Northwest's financing and maintenance policies have resulted in impressive savings in interest payments and spare parts.

This management philosophy of tight control is not without its drawbacks. Northwest is known for its sluggish onboard service, its slow moving ticket lines, and the long waits for passenger baggage.

Adapted from Hugh D. Menzies, "Don Nyrop Keeps a Tight Rein on Northwest," Fortune (August 14, 1978): 142–46.

FINANCIAL CONTROL SYSTEMS: FINANCIAL ANALYSES

Budgets, as discussed in chapter 16, are primarily input controls—that is, they are established generally before any organizational activities have begun. During or after an operation, the manager's attention switches to other financial matters. These include financial statements, ratio analyses, and human resource accounting.

Financial Statements

Financial statements present an analysis of the use of organizational resources and the flow of goods, money, and services to, within, and from the organization.[9] The purpose of financial statements is fourfold:

1. To determine the long-term and short-term financial condition of the organization
2. To analyze the manner in which resources are being utilized
3. To determine the liquidity of the organization
4. To ascertain the profitability of the organization over a period of time

Financial statements are usually prepared to indicate what financial events occurred since the presentation of the last statement, usually covering a twelve-month period. In our framework, the various types of financial statements can be considered a form of output controls.

It is beyond the scope of this book to cover in detail the different types of financial statements. A brief summary of the three main types—balance sheet, income statement, and cash flow statement—is provided. As an illustration, exhibits 17-2 and 17-3 present a company's balance sheet and income statements for 1979.

Balance Sheet.   In simple terms, a balance sheet indicates what the organization "owns and owes" at a particular point of time. What the organization owns are its assets, such as cash, land, inventories, and receivables. Its liabilities are what it owes: accounts payable, debts, and leases. A balance sheet also shows the organization's net worth—that amount that represents stockholders' equity (common stock, preferred stock, and retained earnings) (see exhibit 17-2).

Income Statement.   As shown in exhibit 17-3, an income statement shows how much money an organization has made over a period of time. It starts with the firm's sales or revenues and then subtracts all costs, expenses, and taxes. The remaining amount—net income—can be distributed as stockholders' dividends or reinvested in the organization.

Cash Flow Statement.   A cash flow statement, or sources and uses of funds statement, shows where cash or funds come from (sales, receivables, or sale of property) and where they are used (equipment purchases, reducing payables, or distributing dividends). Similar to the income statement, a cash flow statement concerns financial activities over time.

While financial statements are used primarily for internal control purposes, they may have significant external applications. For example, financial statements are used by bankers and other investment institutions in deciding whether or not to loan or invest money in the organization. In addition, it is a wise practice by managers (and future managers) to study a firm's financial statements before they decide to be employed there.

EXHIBIT 17-2 Consolidated Balance Sheet

	YEAR ENDED 12/31/79
ASSETS	
Current assets:	
Cash, including time deposits	$ 520,296
Marketable securities at cost, which approximates market	548,553
Accounts and notes receivable	1,636,274
Inventories	719,109
Total current assets	3,424,232
Investments and advances	217,327
Long-term receivables	121,213
Property, plant, and equipment, at cost, less accumulated depreciation, depletion, and amortization	
Owned	5,120,313
Leased under capital leases	227,907
	5,238,220
Prepaid and deferred charges	200,179
	$9,311,171
LIABILITIES AND STOCKHOLDERS' EQUITY	
Current liabilities:	
Notes payable	$ 79,225
Accounts payable	1,359,748
Accrued taxes, including income taxes	656,768
Other accrued liabilities	330,800
Long-term debt due within one year	49,250
Capital lease obligations due within one year	15,526
Total current liabilities	2,491,317
Long-term debt	1,367,392
Capital lease obligations	254,253
Minority interest in subsidiaries	284,797
Deferred credits and other liabilities:	
Income taxes	716,597
Employee benefits	260,418
Other	153,286
	1,130,301
Stockholders' equity	
Preferred Stock	502
Common Stock	566,469
Capital surplus	532,310
Retained earnings	2,715,296
	3,814,577
Less Common Stock in treasury	31,466
Total stockholders' equity	3,783,111
	$9,311,171

EXHIBIT 17-3 Statement of Consolidated Income and Retained Earnings

	YEAR ENDED 12/31/79
REVENUES:	
Sales and services (including excise taxes)	$12,851,369
Interest and other income	231,515
	13,082,884
COSTS, EXPENSES, AND TAXES:	
Costs and operating expenses	7,835,780
Selling, general, and administrative expenses	862,614
Depreciation, depletion, and amortization	398,308
Interest and debt expense	167,020
Income and other taxes	2,952,853
Minority interest in subsidiaries' net income	50,949
	12,267,524
NET INCOME	815,360
RETAINED EARNINGS:	
Balance at beginning of year	2,083,131
	2,898,491
Dividends paid:	
Common Stock (1979—$1.70 per share)	182,870
Preferred Stock ($2.00 per share)	325
	183,195
Balance at end of year	$2,715,296
NET INCOME PER SHARE OF COMMON STOCK	$7.58

Ratio Analysis

Ratio analysis is performed by most organizations in evaluating the organization's financial condition. This activity basically involves taking figures from the financial statements and computing ratios or percentages for analysis. The evaluation of these results can involve at least two purposes: (1) comparison of the ratio over time within the organization, or (2) comparison of the calculation to similar organizations at one point in time or over a period of time.

The most commonly used ratios can be divided into a number of different categories. We have chosen four major categories for a brief discussion—liquidity, leverage, operating, and profitability ratios.[10] Exhibit 17-4 presents the method of calculating these ratios for the data presented in exhibits 17-2 and 17-3.

Liquidity ratios measure the organization's ability to meet its maturing financial obligations. In essence, an analysis of liquidity responds to the question, "Does the organization have sufficient cash and quickly convertible securities on hand to meet short-term obligations and still remain financially solvent?" The standard of acceptability is usually based on the organization's characteristics and the nature of its industry.

Leverage ratios compare the contributions of financing by owners to the financing by creditors. Leverage refers to the influence of the fixed costs of the debt on profits or losses. Leverage ratios vary significantly by industry. For example, the debt-to-equity ratio for utility companies can run as high as 1.00, while for retail firms it can be as low as 0.20.

Operating ratios (activity ratios) indicate how effectively an organization is using its resources. By comparing sales or revenues to expenses used to generate them, the effectiveness of the operation can be established. As shown in exhibit 17-4, most operating ratios concern the relationship among sales and assets, inventory, and net working capital.

Profitability ratios measure the organization's success in achieving desired profit levels. In a profit-making firm, profitability ratios are used as a measure of the company's efficiency and effectiveness of operations. Exhibit 17-5 presents profitability ratios for a number of well-known organizations.

Human Resource Accounting

The basic idea behind human resource accounting is that employees have a quantifiable value to an organization which should be considered in managerial decision-making. Effective human resource management is important because employees are the resource that produces profits; the other resources, financial and physical, merely facilitate profit-making capabilities. Proponents of this concept point out that if we can dramatize the importance of human resources to the organization, greater attention will be given to the way that they are managed.

A number of techniques have been formulated for evaluating human resources.[11] Four are most prominent: historical costs, replacement costs, economic value, and present value. With the *historical cost* method, the recruiting, training, and other acquisition costs incurred for each employee are recorded, capitalized, and amortized over the employee's expected tenure or some other time period. When the employee leaves the

EXHIBIT 17-4 Financial Ratio Analysis

RATIO	CALCULATION	MEASURES	EXAMPLE	
Liquidity Ratios:				
1. Current ratio	$\dfrac{\text{Current assets}}{\text{Current liabilities}}$	Indicates the extent to which the claims of short-term creditors are covered by assets that are expected to be converted to cash.	$\dfrac{\$3,424,232}{\$2,491,317}$	= 1.37
2. Quick ratio (or acid-test ratio)	$\dfrac{\text{Current assets—inventory}}{\text{Current liabilities}}$	A measure of the organization's ability to pay short-term obligations without the sale of its inventories.	$\dfrac{\$2,705,127}{\$2,491,317}$	= 1.08
3. Inventory to net working capital	$\dfrac{\text{Inventory}}{\text{Current assets—current liabilities}}$	A measure of the extent to which the organization's working capital is tied up in inventory.	$\dfrac{\$719,109}{\$932,315}$	= 0.77
Leverage Ratios:				
1. Debt to assets ratio	$\dfrac{\text{Total debt}}{\text{Total assets}}$	Measures the extent to which borrowed funds have been used to finance operations.	$\dfrac{\$5,526,060}{\$9,311,171}$	= 0.59
2. Debt to equity ratio	$\dfrac{\text{Total debt}}{\text{Total stockholders' equity}}$	Another measure of the funds provided by creditors versus the funds provided by owners.	$\dfrac{\$5,526,060}{\$3,783,111}$	= 1.46
3. Long-term debt to equity ratio	$\dfrac{\text{Long-term debt}}{\text{Total stockholders' equity}}$	Measures the balance between debt and equity in the firm's overall capital structure.	$\dfrac{\$1,367,392}{\$3,783,111}$	= 0.36
4. Times-interest-earned (or coverage ratios)	$\dfrac{\text{Profits before interest and taxes}}{\text{Total interest charges}}$	Measures the extent to which profits can decline such that the organization becomes unable to meet its interest expenses.	$\dfrac{\$3,986,182}{\$\ 271,369}$	= 18.33
Operating Ratios:				
1. Inventory turnover	$\dfrac{\text{Revenue}}{\text{Inventory}}$	Indicates the number of times inventory is replaced during the period.	$\dfrac{\$13,082,884}{\$\ 719,109}$	= 18.19
2. Net working capital turnover	$\dfrac{\text{Revenue}}{\text{Net working capital}}$	Measures the degree to which working capital is used effectively.	$\dfrac{\$13,082,884}{\$\ 932,315}$	= 14.03
3. Total asset turnover	$\dfrac{\text{Revenue}}{\text{Total Assets}}$	Measures the relationship between sales and the assets needed to reach this level of sales.	$\dfrac{\$13,082,884}{\$\ 9,311,171}$	= 1.41
Profitability Ratios:				
1. Operating profit margin	$\dfrac{\text{Profits before taxes and before interest}}{\text{Revenues}}$	Measures the organization's profitability from current operations without regard to interest charges.	$\dfrac{\$\ 3,986,182}{\$13,082,884}$	= 0.30
2. Profit margin	$\dfrac{\text{Net income}}{\text{Revenue}}$	Measures profits per dollar of sales.	$\dfrac{\$\ 815,360}{\$13,082,884}$	= 0.06
3. Return on total assets	$\dfrac{\text{Net income}}{\text{Total assets}}$	A measure of the return on total investment in the enterprise.	$\dfrac{\$\ 815,360}{\$\ 8,311,171}$	= 0.09
4. Return on net worth	$\dfrac{\text{Net income}}{\text{Total stockholders' equity}}$	Measures the rate of return on stockholders' investment in the organization.	$\dfrac{\$\ 815,360}{\$\ 3,783,111}$	= 0.22
5. Earnings per share	$\dfrac{\text{Net income—preferred stock dividends}}{\text{Number of shares of common stock outstanding}}$	Shows the earnings available to the owners of common stock.	$\dfrac{\$\ 815,035}{\$\ 6,177,965}$	= \$7.58

EXHIBIT 17-5
Selected Financial
Ratios for
Example
Companies
(1979)

Company	Profit Margin	Return on Net Worth	Earnings per Share
A. U.S. INDUSTRIAL COMPANIES			
Anheuser-Busch	7.1%	21.6%	$4.34
Boeing	6.2	27.4	7.88
Chrysler	(9.1)	—	—
Coca-Cola	8.5	21.9	3.80
DuPont	7.5	17.7	6.42
Exxon	5.4	19.0	9.74
General Electric	6.2	19.1	6.20
General Motors	4.9	15.1	10.04
Goodyear Tire	1.8	1.8	2.02
IBM	13.1	20.1	5.16
Kodak	12.4	18.6	6.20
Procter & Gamble	6.2	17.9	6.99
Schlitz	(5.7)	—	—
Texas Instruments	5.4	18.1	7.58
Time, Inc.	5.8	18.1	5.15
Uniroyal	(4.6)	—	—
U. S. Steel	(2.3)	—	—
Westinghouse	(1.0)	—	—
Whirlpool	4.8	16.5	3.06
Xerox	8.1	17.5	6.69
B. INDUSTRIAL COMPANIES OUTSIDE U. S.			
Bayer (Germany)	1.7	8.5	—
Bridgestone Tire (Japan)	5.0	18.5	—
Montedison (Italy)	0.3	2.9	—
Hitachi (Japan)	3.8	13.4	—
Indian Oil (India)	2.4	18.3	—
Michelin (France)	2.0	6.6	—
Nestlé (Switzerland)	3.7	10.5	—
Shell (Netherlands-Britain)	10.9	28.0	—
Volkswagen (Germany)	2.2	11.2	—
Volvo (Sweden)	1.7	15.7	—
C. U. S. RETAILING & TRANSPORTATION COMPANIES			
American Airlines	2.7	11.1	2.63
Federated Stores	3.5	12.4	4.21
J. C. Penney	2.2	9.7	5.52
K Mart	2.8	16.4	2.84
Kroger	0.9	14.0	3.13
Pan Am	3.1	10.5	1.07
Santa Fe Industries	8.9	11.0	8.08
Sears, Roebuck	4.6	10.8	2.54
UAL	(1.9)	—	—
United Parcel Service	2.5	16.1	1.97
Yellow Freight	2.4	9.5	1.45

organization, the unamortized balance of the investment is written off as a loss in the period of separation. The *replacement cost* method assumes that an employee should be valued according to the incurred expenses that would be needed to replace him or her. Costs include not only recruiting and training expenses, but also the costs of not having a capable replacement for a period of time. The *economic value* method usually uses salary as a measure of the individual's value to the firm. The assumption is that employees are compensated according to their worth to the organization. Finally, the *present value* method analyzes the stream of net future contributions of the employee to the organization. This method uses expected salary, probability of separation (i.e., turnover), and future productivity.

Human resource accounting is still very much in its infancy as a managerial tool, and as the description of the methods for calculation show, there are too many estimates and "rough edges" that must be overcome before the tool becomes widely used. Nevertheless, the concept draws much-needed attention to the fact that an organization's employees are important assets.

FINANCIAL CONTROL SYSTEMS: AUDITS

To most people, "audit" means the process whereby one party attempts to determine if a second party has done something wrong. Governmental audits of the work of defense contractors such as Lockheed's C-5A airplane, or of political campaign contributions during the Watergate investigation, have turned up surprising information. Even a letter from the IRS indicating their desire to audit your tax returns is interpreted negatively.

While the discovery of misdeeds is a purpose of an audit, it is surely not its only purpose. An audit is basically an investigation of an organization's activities for purposes of analysis, verification, and correction. An audit may just as well be oriented to validating the honesty and fairness of an organization's financial statements—in fact, this is by far the main purpose of an audit.

Two basic types of audits are found in organizations. First are the external and internal audits, which deal with financial data. Second, the management audit is an evaluation of various management practices and policies.

External audits are independent evaluations of the organization's financial statements, usually by public accounting firms. The task of the auditors is not to prepare the financial statements, but to verify that the organization has followed generally accepted accounting principles in valuing its assets and liabilities.

There are a number of advantages to organizations in the use of external audits. First, because public accounting firms are independent organizations, there is a high degree of objectivity in their analyses. They are required by professional accounting standards to report the financial conditions and practices of the audited organization *as they exist*. Second, because the staffs of the accounting firms are highly skilled professionals, the audit can be useful in diagnosing problems involving the financial activities of the organization. Finally, because the external audit verifies that the financial statements were prepared and verified according to standard accounting principles, interested banks and investors are assured of the validity of the information.

In addition to external audits, many organizations use their own personnel to conduct ongoing *internal* audits. The purpose is the same—to ensure that the organization's financial statements accurately and honestly reflect the true financial condition of the organization.

On the plus side, because internal audits are made by internal employees, the knowledge of the inside operations of the organization allows them to go into more depth in their analysis. In addition, such audits can occur throughout the year as opposed to once a year with external auditors. Thus, problems can be identified early. On the negative side, internal audits can not only be costly, but they may require hiring highly skilled professionals to develop the reports. A frequently occurring problem with internal audits is that some managers view them as a "police" action, rather than a constructive activity. Unless internal audit personnel are skilled in interpersonal relations, the audited managers may resist cooperating with them because they are afraid of the repercussions if some error, even minor, is found.

A *management audit* involves an evaluation and assessment of the operations of the total organization.[12] Financial data can be analyzed, but this type of audit is not limited to that type of investigation. In particular, a management audit evaluates the organization's goals, strategies, plans, policies, resources (i.e., strengths and weaknesses), and future opportunities. The areas of investigation could include:

1. What market share should the organization strive for in each product line?
2. How effective are the key managers? How effective are the directors on the board?
3. Are the financial policies sound?
4. What is the state of the organization's research and development?
5. What environmental threats should the organization investigate?
6. Is the organization using the most effective structure?
7. What is the relationship between the organization and its stockholders?
8. How efficient are the organization's manufacturing operations?
9. Should the compensation system be revised?
10. How effective are the employment policies?

Management audits can be conducted by internal personnel, external consultants, or both. A growing trend by public accounting firms is to provide a management audit service to organizations. The rationale is that since the accounting firm knows about the strengths and weaknesses of the organization on the financial side, it could expand to include the entire operations of the organization.

FINANCIAL CONTROL IN THE INTERNATIONAL REALM

One of the more complex problems the manager operating in the international realm has to face is financial control. Financial statements, financial analyses, and audits will be briefly discussed to highlight this problem.

Financial Statements.   The preparation of detailed and standardized financial statements is an accepted way of life for organizations operating in the U. S., but in overseas operations, a great variety of practices are followed. For example, the accounting profession in the U. S. has developed a set of "generally accepted accounting practices" (GAAP). Similar situations exist in Canada, the United Kingdom, and the Netherlands. In other countries, few standard practices exist, making the development and analysis of financial statements difficult.[13]

Another problem is currency. The problem is not so much translating other currencies into dollars, but that the exchange rate may vary widely and change rapidly. An exchange rate change can have a significant effect on a company. For example, when the dollar was devalued in 1971, many firms holding debt in stronger European currencies suffered large losses. Exxon alone suffered exchange losses of $70 million related to long-term debt it held in Europe.[14] To counter currency problems, many international organizations prepare two sets of financial statements: parent and consolidated. The parent books reflect the organization's operations in the headquarters country, while the consolidated or combined books blend all operations into one set of financial statements.

Some standards have been set by the Financial Accounting Standard Board (FASB) with regard to financial disclosures. At minimum, the following information is now required to be disclosed for both domestic and foreign operations in the aggregate or by geographic area: revenue, sales to unaffiliated customers and between geographic areas, operating profit or loss or net income, and identifiable assets.

The Foreign Corrupt Practices Act of 1977 has had an effect on the way some organizations prepare their financial statements (see chapter 4). With the passing of the act, organizations can no longer "hide" bribes to foreign officials in their books. For example, prior to the act, the American Hospital Supply Corporation paid a 10 percent "commission" to certain officials to obtain a contract to sell hospital equipment to Saudi Arabia for the new King Faisal Specialist Hospital. The price of the equipment was increased to include the kickback, thus overstating revenues. The kickback was then recorded as a consulting fee, even though no such services were performed. This allowed the kickback to become a deductible expense and made the cash payment appear to be legitimate. Such activities are no longer permissible.[15]

Financial Analyses.   If the organization can overcome some of the problems discussed above, the analysis of financial performance still remains complicated. For example, a comparison of financial ratios across different foreign operations may lead to incorrect conclusions. An operation in one country that is run with highly automated equipment and few skilled workers is not equivalent to one where a large labor force is used with fewer automated machines. The assets and operating expenses are different; hence, the calculation of certain ratios will also be different.

Organizations have worked around this problem in two ways.[16] First, a comparison of ratios is permitted between similar countries, such as the United Kingdom and Germany. The second and most popular approach is to use budget performance as the main measure of financial effectiveness. Since the budget is stated in local currencies, budget performance (actual versus predicted) can be a significant performance criterion.

Audits.   The independent external auditor is relied upon heavily in many countries to verify the information in financial statements. Auditing standards, however, vary considerably among different countries, as do qualifications for becoming an auditor.

For instance, in some countries all aspects of auditing are determined by the accounting profession itself, while in other countries the government determines who can perform the audit and the manner in which it is done. In many European countries, an audit merely states that financial statements were prepared in adherence to the procedures of the *organization*. At the other extreme, such as in the U. S. and the United Kingdom, there is greater reliance on GAAP from independent standards boards.[17]

As to the auditor himself or herself, in West Germany, for example, it takes several years of study and practice and a difficult series of examinations before one is allowed to perform an audit. In Peru, on the other hand, a person need only graduate from a recognized university with an accounting major and receive an easy-to-get license from the government.

In response to the needs of organizations for consistency in auditing, many large U. S. independent accounting firms have established foreign offices or formed partnerships with local accounting firms. In some cases, the foreign government will accept the more detailed audit of these U. S. firms; in other cases, these firms have to perform a second audit in conjunction with the audit approved by the government.

MANAGEMENT INFORMATION SYSTEMS

Throughout this book we have emphasized the importance of information as a resource and in organizational communication. Information is important to managers in analyzing the external and internal environment, in developing and implementing strategies and plans, in making decisions, in coordinating the work of departments and units, in evaluating the performance of employees, in controlling resources, and so on.

Information systems to assist managers in their work are not new innovations. As we pointed out in chapter 3, accounting systems were one of the first managerial information systems. Financial information, however, is one of many information sources that managers need. In recent years, the manager's job has been enhanced by the development of *management information systems* (MIS). For our purposes, an MIS is a formalized and structured activity of individuals, machines, and methods for providing information to managers on a regular basis to assist in planning, allocating resources, controlling activities, and making decisions.

Purpose of MIS

The purpose of MIS in organizations is fourfold.[18] First, an MIS provides a basis for analyzing *early warning signals* that can originate both external and internal to the organization. Proper information to managers prevents a long-term gap between plant capacity and the demand for the firm's products, averts surprises due to technological breakthroughs affecting the firm's products and services, and maintains an awareness of top-management succession problems.

Second, MIS is an important aid in *managerial decision-making*. A way to identify the specific information requirements of managers is to isolate the nature, frequency, and interrelationships of the major decisions. This requires analysis of responses to the following questions:

1. What decisions are made and/or need to be made?
2. What factors are important in making these decisions?
3. How and when should these decisions be made?
4. What information is useful in making these decisions?

Examples include supplying financial trends and ratios, inventory reports, and market share information, and providing models and computer hardware that will answer managers' "What if . . . ?" questions on profits, costs, and combinations of products and services.

Third, MIS can assist managers in making *programmed decisions*. As explained in chapter 7, decisions that are relatively simple and are made on a routine basis are programmed decisions. Examples include assigning orders to machines, scheduling orders or services, allocating advertising expenditures to different media sources, and ordering supplies and raw materials. Since these are straightforward decisions, much of the work can be performed by the MIS.

Finally, MIS can be used to *automate* routine clerical operations. Such activities as preparing payrolls, inventory reports, and transportation system records are quite adaptable to automation. Automation can save the organization a great deal of money because less personnel are needed and the turnaround time is much quicker.

As shown in exhibit 17-6, the purposes of an MIS are related to the different types of information found in organizations. The information types include planning, management control, and operational control.[19]

Planning information concerns the process of formulating goals, strategies, and plans, the resources needed to achieve these goals, and the policies that direct their use (see chapter 6). Because this information forms the input to top management for these nonprogrammed decisions, there is great emphasis on the early warning signal capability of an MIS.

Management control information aids managers in making decisions that are consistent with the efficient use of organizational resources. Used primarily by middle-level managers, the information is usually internal and concerns many of the factors discussed earlier in this chapter (i.e., budgets, financial analysis, and so on).

Finally, *operational control information* is normally used by first-line managers for decisions that are highly programmed—that is, the manager can build a program that identifies the time at which a decision is needed, the alternatives available, and the criteria for selecting the best alternative under different conditions.

Using this framework as a base, an analysis of an organization's decision-making patterns in strategy, managerial control, and operational control draws out the specific information requirements for the critical areas of the organization. Some examples of the information needs for an airline, a department store, and a savings and loan are also shown in exhibit 17-6.

Emergence of MIS

The emergence of MIS in organizations can be traced to at least two causes. First, as pointed out in chapters 1 and 2, the manager's job has become increasingly complex. The external environment facing many organizations has become more dynamic and turbulent. Managers need information regarding technological trends and developments, the activities of competitors, the needs of customers, and so forth. In addition, the internal environment of organizations is increasingly complex. Complicated resource allocation decisions, the need to coordinate units better, and the growth in the use of technical specialists all contribute to the need for accurate and timely information for managers.

EXHIBIT 17-6 MIS Purposes and Example Information Needs

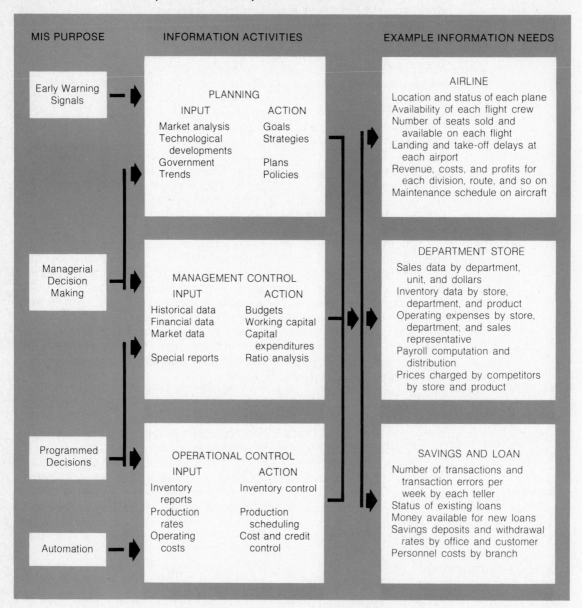

The second factor in the emergence of MIS is the computer. Computer usage in organizations has developed in stages.[20] Initially, computers were based on vacuum-tube technology and were costly to purchase and operate. Because of this, organizations used computers only for such time-consuming functions as payroll processing and customer billing. This stage was followed by a generation of computers that used transistors, which permitted larger data storage capacity and faster computing time. The uses of computers in information processing extended to such applications as airline reservations, and policy data on policies for insurance companies.[21]

In the third stage, the development of integrated-circuit technology enabled computers to not only accept and process data more than ten times as fast as before, but they could store much more information. This generation of computers saw the emergence of remote terminals for data entry and analysis, which were tied to large centrally located computers. Managers were not only capable of performing a wide variety of tasks by computer, but the computing time and cost had decreased significantly. For example, a typical calculation that took forty-seven seconds and cost $2.48 in 1960 would take five seconds today and cost 20 cents.[22]

It should be pointed out that some people may confuse MIS with electronic data processing (EDP). They are not really the same—in reality, EDP is merely an element of MIS. EDP deals with computers and their operations, while MIS involves much more than computers. MIS is a total information system that includes such aspects as accounting data, market research information, and production reports, some of which can be computerized.

The combination of the changing nature of the manager's job and the development of different generations of computers has resulted in the emergence of MIS in four distinct stages.[23] As shown in exhibit 17-7, stage one, *initiation,* generally involved accounting applications of the operational and management control types. Top management saw the goal of MIS as a decrease in costs associated with personnel and computation time. The MIS unit was usually staffed by technical personnel and was embedded in the accounting department. To most managers, MIS was an unknown area involving a "black box." This uncertainty

EXHIBIT 17-7   Emergence of MIS in Organizations

	STAGE ONE Initiation	STAGE TWO Growth	STAGE THREE Moratorium	STAGE FOUR Integration
Application focus	Accounting and cost reduction	Expansion of applications in many functional areas	Halt on new applications; emphasis on control	Integrating existing systems into the organization; decision support systems
Example applications	Accounts payable, accounts receivable, payroll, billing	*Stage one plus:* cash flow, budgeting, forecasting, personnel inventory, sales, inventory control	*Stage two plus:* purchasing control, production scheduling	*Stage three plus:* simulation models, financial planning models, on-line personnel query system
MIS staffing	Primarily computer experts and other skilled professionals	User-oriented system analysts and programmers	Entry of functional managers into MIS unit	Balance of technical and management specialists
Location of MIS in structure	Embedded in accounting department	Growth in size of staff; still in accounting area	Separate MIS unit reporting to head financial officer	Same as stage three, or decentralization into divisions
What top management wants from MIS	Speed computations with a reduction in clerical staff	Broader applications into operational areas	Concern over MIS costs and usefulness	Acceptance as a major organizational function; involved in planning and control
User attitudes	Uncertainty; hands-off approach; anxiety over applications	Somewhat enthusiastic; minimum involvement in system design	Frustration and dissatisfaction over developed systems; concern over costs of developing and operating systems	Acceptance of MIS in their work; involvement in system design, implementation, and operation

Adapted from Richard L. Nolan, "Controlling the Costs of Data Services," *Harvard Business Review* (July–August 1977): 114–24.

developed into a hands-off philosophy by managers who did not have extensive computer knowledge.

As the use and value of MIS increased, stage two, the *growth* stage emerged. MIS applications expanded significantly beyond accounting into production and marketing. It still involved the main use of operational and managerial control information. MIS personnel became highly specialized in their skills and the entire unit sometimes became separate from accounting, usually reporting to the controller. Stage three emphasized a *moratorium* on the growth in use of MIS. Top management became concerned that the purpose of MIS and its integration into the total organization was being clouded by a proliferation of larger computers and a lack of user awareness of the potential of MIS.[24]

The fourth stage, *integration,* stressed the acceptance of MIS as a major management activity that must be integrated into the total organization. MIS was being used with all types of information (strategic, management control, and operational control), and with a new generation of computers. In addition, the use of portable, interactive terminals enabled managers to have better access and hence, more involvement in the system. The MIS unit was staffed not only with highly skilled technical people, but management specialists from other areas began working their way into operating the unit. This latter point may have been the most important because the combination of technical and management functional specialists allowed MIS to be applied in everyday activities.

Integrating MIS into management activities can occur *across* organizations as well as within. For example, travel agents have long eyed the computer as a way to link up with airlines, hotels, and the rest of the travel business to improve their productivity and sales. A system developed by American Express appears to be one that can satisfy this need. The system will do everything from booking a flight, hotel room, and rental car, to using a videodisk player to show television pictures of resorts and hotel rooms to prospective travelers.[25]

MIS evolved into a separate unit in the structure of many organizations in stages three and four. Exhibit 17-8 shows the MIS unit for Kraft, Inc. Note the various activities depicted in the exhibit, from computer systems development and applications to telecommunications. This again emphasizes that MIS involves much more than just EDP systems.

Applying MIS: Personnel Systems

MIS applications can be found in many organizational functions, including manufacturing, marketing, accounting, and personnel. Consider the activity shown in exhibit 17-9, which depicts a portion of the human resource process. Three major subprocesses are shown in the exhibit: (1) determining human resource needs; (2) interviewing and hiring new employees to meet these needs; and (3) preparing and distributing detailed data on the state of human resources in the organization.

The system shown in the exhibit provides an example of the application of the systems approach to MIS design and implementation. The systems approach views ongoing operations or functions within a transformation framework; that is, inputs are transformed by a process (or processes) into outputs. The systems approach is illustrated in the exhibit in the following manner:

EXHIBIT 17-8   MIS Structure in Kraft, Inc.

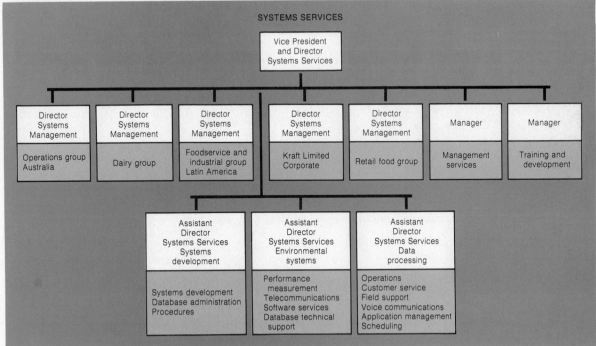

1. *Inputs.* Three major inputs are shown. First, the human resource plan originating from the goals and strategies of the organization serves as the main input to the process of determining human resource needs. Second, area employment data not only act as inputs to the human resource needs and employee hiring processes, but also feed information to the human resource inventory file. Finally, wage and salary structure data are major inputs into the employee interviewing and hiring process.

2. *Process.* Transforming inputs into outputs is the role performed by process activities. In the illustration, the process is really a collection of decision-making activities. For example, in hiring a new employee, management takes information from the human resource plan, data on area employment activities, and the organization's wage and salary structure and makes such decisions as searching for qualified employees, screening candidates, and making the offer.

3. *Outputs.* There are two kinds of end products of the process. First, an output can be in the form of a statement such as a written offer for employment or a set of job descriptions. Second, it can take the form of a series of reports that are given to managers for analysis. This latter is illustrated by the various types of reports on payroll, turnover, and position openings that are provided by the human resource inventory file.

   An important part of the human resource system illustration are the two files that maintain organizational and human resource inventory information. These two files collect and distribute data on various jobs and personnel to management. In the past, these files were cumbersome and costly to maintain. With the advent of computer usage, the value of the file system has increased significantly.

EXHIBIT 17-9   Information System Flow Chart for Personnel MIS

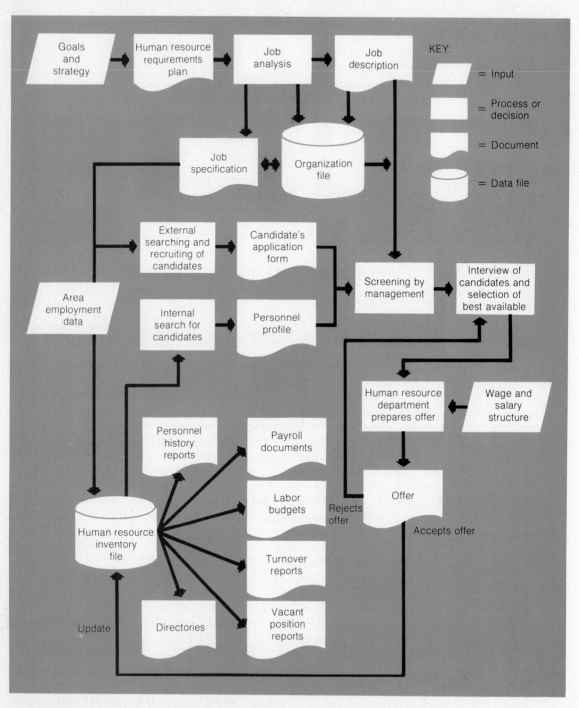

Adapted from Robert G. Murdick, MIS: Concepts and Design, © *1980, p. 88. Reprinted by permission of Prentice-Hall, Inc., Englewood Cliffs, N.J.*

**COMMENTS ON
THE PRACTICE
OF
MANAGEMENT**
(See p. 593)

The Practice of Management introductory section provided an illustration of the current uses of MIS in the railroad industry. A number of benefits can be noted. First, from a planning point of view, the various MIS operations have provided management not only with a better way of scheduling shipments, but, for example, a shortage of cars and locomotives can be easily discovered, indicating when new equipment should be purchased. Second, MIS enables management to provide more effective control on available resources by knowing where rolling stock is at all times. Third, customers are served quickly and more efficiently than in the past. This would probably have a positive effect on future revenues. Finally, the MIS gives management an improved tool to make better decisions. These decisions not only include rolling stock allocations, but improvements in decision making in the areas of accounting, payroll accuracy, and human resource needs. The manager should make careful note that such information systems are not cheap and are only as good as the accuracy of the data and the programming. With proper data and operations, and with capable people managing the system, the payoffs can be significant.

Contemporary Issues in MIS

During the past decade, the development and use of MIS has reached into all types of organizations and influenced the work of many managers. With the increasing complexity of the manager's job and the continuing introduction of new information and computer technology, we can expect this trend in MIS usage to continue. To illustrate this trend, we have selected two contemporary issues in MIS: decision support systems and distributive processing.

Decision Support Systems.   Consider the case of Mr. Charles Fry, manager of material analysis and planning for Shaklee Corporation, a large California producer of food supplements, cosmetics, and household cleaners.[26] While sales had increased to $350 million in 1979—more than a thirtyfold increase in just ten years—Fry was concerned that top management was making many strategic and policy decisions less on objective information and more on a subjective and political basis.

To improve this situation, Fry's unit fed data on plant locations, products made, costs per unit, and production capacity for its three facilities and twenty contract manufacturers. It also stored details on more than 500 line items, 360 customers, and its 100 distribution centers. The first task was finding the best way to reduce delivery times to customers without increasing production or distribution costs. The newly developed decision support system calculated the impact that various delivery requirements would have on transportation costs, the cost of operating distribution centers, and the cost of carrying inventories. In the end, Shaklee found a way to speed up deliveries to customers and save money at the same time. The new system also allowed the company to develop a comprehensive information and data base that it could use to analyze other operating problems.

This and other illustrations are examples of a special type of information system that has begun to appear in many organizations: a *decision support system* (DSS), considered by many managers to be a highly advanced MIS.

A number of factors characterize a DSS in an organization. First, an MIS is found that has been in operation for some time. Thus, there already exist sufficient computer hardware and software packages and experienced personnel to develop the system. Second, the salient design feature of a DSS is the integration of management science models (see chapter 7), a comprehensive data base, and a skilled decision-maker usually working from an interactive computer terminal. Finally, rather than a series of scheduled reports, a DSS supplies analyses as demanded by the manager. In operation, the manager identifies a problem, enters information usually with the use of the terminal, and interacts with the information and the system's management science models until the desired results are obtained.

The nature of the DSS depends on the type of problem and the complexity of the needed models. The approach can range from straightforward problems, such as the use of simple statistical analysis models, to "what if . . ." contingency-type problems. For example, National Airlines (now part of PanAm) kept its flights on schedule during 1979 fuel shortages, while compensating for fluctuating supplies and rising costs, with a DSS.[27] The airline's system stores data on fuel prices and availability, along with storage costs and fuel capacity at each of the thirty cities it serves. The performance and tentative monthly itinerary are also included for each of its fifty-six aircraft. In just fifteen minutes the DSS produces a list of the best fueling stations and vendors for each flight, something that usually took a month to compute manually. Management runs the system three times a week, resulting in a fuel cost savings of 2 cents a gallon. Since the airline uses 25 million gallons per month, the savings is $500,000.

On the other hand, American Can Company faced a contingency-type problem when it recently planned to install a $50 million production system at one of its plants in the Pacific Northwest. When management used its DSS to investigate thirty-two alternative locations, they decided instead to locate the new system in a Southeastern plant.[28] If manufacturing had had its way, it would have cost the company an additional $7 million a year in distribution costs.

A DSS is not something management can plug in and start running right away. Designing and implementing a DSS can be time consuming and costly. The Shaklee system, for example, took six months and $250,000 to develop, plus approximately $50,000 a year to operate. If the wrong model or inaccurate information is used, the result can be the well-known phenomenon to computer users called GI-GO—garbage in, garbage out. Collecting appropriate and accurate data is the biggest obstacle to developing a sound DSS.

Even with these problems, development and use of DSS is expected to continue at a growing rate. The main reason is that DSS fits well into the integration stage of MIS development. Integrating computer technology and management science models, and providing the functional manager with "hands-on" experience can result in improved managerial decision-making and performance.[29]

EXHIBIT 17-10
MIS Distributive Processing

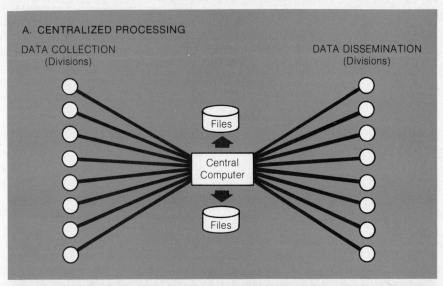

A. CENTRALIZED PROCESSING

DATA COLLECTION
(Divisions)

DATA DISSEMINATION
(Divisions)

Files

Central
Computer

Files

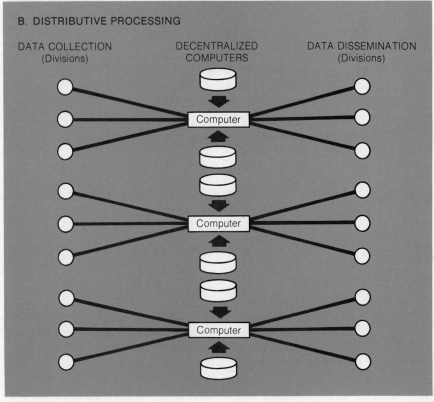

B. DISTRIBUTIVE PROCESSING

DATA COLLECTION
(Divisions)

DECENTRALIZED
COMPUTERS

DATA DISSEMINATION
(Divisions)

Computer

Computer

Computer

Distributive Processing

In MIS-user organizations during the 1970s, a mature MIS usually involved a large centralized computer supported by a substantial professional staff (the growth and moratorium stages of the emergence of MIS). This is shown in exhibit 17-10a. This centralized approach offered benefits and limitations. On the plus side, the organization can maintain efficiencies of scale (i.e., cost control) and acquire the latest and most advanced large computer system. On the other hand, the use of centralized computers often leads to data input bottlenecks and lengthy delays in feedback of information.

For the user manager, the problems of a centralized system are particularly troublesome. The manager generally wants information and analysis reports returned quickly, accurately, and at minimum costs. What can happen is that the manager's problem is only one of many problems to be solved by the MIS unit, resulting in lengthy delays. In addition, the MIS output may be inappropriate because of a lack of knowledge of the manager's situation by the MIS specialist. Finally, the manager must pay for MIS services, not only in direct costs, but also in incremental costs to cover MIS overhead charges.

In order to eliminate some of these problems, many organizations are moving to a distributive processing approach to MIS.[30] As shown in exhibit 17-10b, distributive processing is a decentralized approach that involves the use of smaller, self-contained MIS units that can be found within the divisional structures of the organization. With this approach, the user manager is brought closer to the actual computations, and hence to greater involvement in the analysis. Several technological developments have contributed to the adoption of distributive processing:

1. *Superchip*. This remarkable development in computer processing, which can put the computer's heart and brains on a slice of silicon no bigger than a pencil eraser, is a key to processing at an extremely low cost. Products using the computer-on-a-chip include digital watches, postage scales that compute postage rates when zip codes are keyed in, and mobile telephones that can store up to ten numbers and automatically dial any one of them.

2. *Advanced teleprocessing*. New communication networks and technology are now capable of moving data at high speed and diminishing costs.

3. *Improved hardware and software*. New programming philosophies, translated into widely applicable systems, can effectively handle the complexities of data transmission, dispersed files, and the interconnection of units. In addition, a wide variety of terminals is available for data collection, report printing, visual display, and direct translation of data into information that can be easily interpreted by the user manager.

The ability of user managers to get closer to their analyses is an important benefit to the use of distributive processing. A major problem faced by organizations wishing to go this route is what to do with the large centralized computer systems and associated personnel. Management must face the problem of selling the large computers and the resistance by personnel to relocate to the decentralized sites before distributive processing reaches its full potential.

Keys to Success with MIS

Management information systems is an area of management that is in its infancy. Because of this, it can be extremely exciting, challenging, and a worthwhile career choice—it can also involve many frustrating moments and times of temporary failure. The growing literature and experience in MIS suggest that there are important keys to success. Some of the more salient keys are discussed below:

1. **The user manager should be involved in MIS design and implementation.**

   This point, more than any other, has been the impediment to MIS success. The main reason is that many MIS managers not only fail to identify the user manager's information needs, but also there is insufficient recognition given to the fact that managers' jobs are different. User managers must be involved in just about all facets and steps of MIS design and implementation. Remember a key point: the user manager is *paying* the MIS unit to develop an information system: therefore, give the user manager something that is useful. User managers are not going to be coming back for new systems if the last time you charged for a Mercedes and all they wanted was a Chevette.

2. **A well-designed MIS doesn't automatically mean that better decisions will be made.**

   Decision making is a matter of judgment and choice. Two managers given the same information may come up with completely different actions to take. MIS must, therefore, be considered an *input* into the managerial decision-making process. Managers make decisions—an MIS does not.

3. **Proper staffing of the MIS unit is important to success.**

   As noted earlier, since MIS involves highly technical work, there has been the tendency by organizations to staff MIS units with highly technical people—what some have called "number crunchers." Such individuals, while quite skilled in their own areas, are sometimes unable to understand the information needs of functional managers. At the same time, user managers do not always know what information they really need. Most successful MIS units are staffed with people whose backgrounds are a blend of technical and functional management skills and expertise. In this way, there is an effective combination of the theoretical and the applied. Many organizations, in fact, have appointed heads of MIS units whose computer experience is minimal, but whose functional knowledge (e.g., accounting, production, and marketing) is great. In this way, the unit is given strong integrative direction from the top.

4. **More information is not necessarily better information.**

   An MIS should present the user manager with enough information to make an informed decision. Too much information—information overload—can only confuse managers and prohibit them from sorting the important information from a mass of irrelevant data and figures. User managers should be given information that they *can* use, not what they *might* eventually use.

5. **Information in MIS should be treated confidentially.**

"We need the order-entry tracking system by the 1st. The budget consolidation in two weeks. The sales forecast next week. And the seating arrangement for my daughter's wedding by tomorrow."

Courtesy of General Electric Information Services Company.

Most of the data and information generated by an MIS are not for the public. For example, a personnel MIS can contain a great deal of information on each employee. While personal background data are important for such functions as insurance plans, pensions, and tax deductions, it need not be available to the employee's direct manager. Information of this type should be made available only on a "need to know" basis. Confidentiality, privacy, and security should be watchwords.

6. **MIS should be integrated into management activities.**

For long-term MIS success, this is probably the most important point. Managers must view MIS as an important tool to achieve high performance in their jobs. To do this, there must be a concerted effort by all to get people to understand and properly use the generated systems. This means proper education, training, design, and implementation of all involved people *over the long-term*, not just a once-over-lightly. It might be beneficial for managers to work initially with one functional area (e.g., accounting or personnel) in developing information systems for their use. Once the "bugs" have been worked out, applications in other functions (e.g., production or marketing) can be contemplated. If MIS is not integrated, it can become a short-lived phenomenon.

FINANCIAL CONTROL, MIS, AND THE MANAGER'S JOB

Throughout this chapter, we have emphasized that while control is the last of the four management functions (planning, organizing, leading, and control) it is the function that makes the entire process tick. Control indicates how well the plan is being achieved; it indicates whether the organizational structure is facilitating or impeding performance of individuals, groups, or departments; it provides an evaluation of the effectiveness of leadership; and it identifies possible corrective action, should it be needed.

Finance and information are important organizational resources that must be controlled effectively for the organization to achieve its goals. For the manager, there are important skills and roles involved in this activity. From a managerial skills perspective, *technical skills* are crucial in the process of developing budgets and financial statements, and in operating an MIS. These skills are far from routine; highly professional activities are involved in each.

Human skills in financial and information control can focus on the participative process between managers and subordinates. The bottom-up approach to budgeting requires that the higher-level manager allow lower-level personnel to participate in development of the budget.

With respect to *conceptual skills,* a number of activities are involved. For example, a manager preparing a budget for a profit center needs to know the impact on costs and revenues of each involved unit or person; in MIS, the movement toward integrating MIS into the other managerial functions stresses the fit of the concept with the total organization; distributive processing emphasizes the impact of MIS at the different levels and between the various divisions of an organization; finally, in ranking projects within a zero-base budgeting approach, the ability to pick the right projects involves conceptual skills.

Successful financial and information control also stresses the development of *diagnostic skills*. For instance, the manager must recognize in the budget process that striving for successful short-term performance may lead to long-term problems. In addition, ratio analysis and the auditing procedures figure strongly in the development and use of diagnostic skills, much the same as managing the early warning signal capacity of MIS involves the same skills.

From a managerial role viewpoint, the interpersonal *liaison role* and the *monitor, disseminator,* and *spokesperson* informational roles are not only required in collecting and analyzing financial data, but they are important roles in MIS. Finally, occupying the *decisional roles* involves the *resource allocator* in making decisions from a financial analysis, and in being an *entrepreneur* with the use of decision support systems.

These are only some of the many possible examples of the application and development of managerial skills and roles in this important control process. By now it should be apparent that the practice of management is indeed a complex activity—one that requires not only knowledge of the salient functions, but also requires ways of developing skills and using them in the important managerial roles.

SUMMARY FOR THE MANAGER

1. Budgets are one of the most detailed and important parts of the manager's job. One of the keys to successful budget performance is permitting the participation of lower-level managers in its development. These managers not only have greater knowledge of the concerned operations, but since they will be responsible for its performance, they may be more motivated to work within its structure.

2. Budgets are not rigid, inflexible financial instruments. On the contrary, they must be flexible to the variable costs of the unit and to changes in the

environment. It is also important for managers to recognize that short-term successful budget performance does not necessarily guarantee improved long-term performance. Cutting corners, for example, at the end of a budget period may allow managers to meet their current budget goals; it may, however, also have an adverse effect on the next period's performance.

3. Financial statements present the status of the organization's financial resources at a particular point in time. In addition, they are valuable to the person interested in investing in the organization, as well as to the individual contemplating employment with the firm.

4. Financial ratios are used to examine the current state of the organization and to analyze any important trends that have developed over years. The manager's diagnostic skills are particularly important in this analysis.

5. Financial audits verify the organization's financial statements. A trend in organizations is to form an internal auditing department to conduct ongoing audits. This permits the identification of problems much earlier than with the sole use of external auditors.

6. Management audits analyze the entire management process—from goals, strategies, and plans to control procedures. Whether performed by the professional accounting firm or a consulting organization, management audits help pinpoint external opportunities and threats, and internal strengths and weaknesses.

7. In international operations, the manager must recognize that currency differences, exchange rates, and disclosure policies can affect the preparation of financial statements. Likewise, these differences make financial ratio analyses difficult.

8. MIS can facilitate the information and decision processes in organizations. Successful MIS design and implementation is dependent on a number of factors, the most important of which is integrating MIS into the total management system of the organization. A "tacked on" MIS will be short-lived. Integration involves combining technical and functional managers into the structure of the MIS unit and getting the user manager involved early in the system design process.

9. Decision support systems and distributive processing are some of the many new applications of MIS. The manager should be cautioned that decision support systems do not necessarily make for better decisions—managers make decisions, not the MIS. In addition, distributive processing is not for every organization. It is particularly applicable to complex organizations with many divisions or product lines or with widely dispersed units.

10. The development of managerial skills and their use in the performance of managerial roles is also important to financial and information control. Preparing budgets (technical skills), allowing lower-level management participation in the budget process (human skills), integrating MIS into the total organization (conceptual skills), and analyzing financial ratios (diagnostic skills) are examples of the importance of managerial skills.

11. The manager's informational and decisional roles are stressed in financial and information control. Managers must gather, analyze, and disseminate information and base resource allocation decisions upon it.

QUESTIONS FOR REVIEW AND DISCUSSION

1. What organizational units are usually associated with each of the budget responsibility centers?
2. Discuss the benefits and limitations of bottom-up budgeting.
2. What are the differences between cash, capital expenditure, and balance sheet budgets?
4. What are the main reasons PPBS has been unsuccessful in the federal government?
5. What role do financial ratios play in financial control systems?
6. What is the purpose of a management audit?
7. What is the difference between EDP and MIS?
8. What is meant by the "early warning signal" purpose of MIS? Give examples.
9. Why was the moratorium stage of MIS development so important to its current use?
10. What types of organizational structures would be best for a distributive processing approach?

NOTES

1. R. N. Anthony and J. Dearden, *Management Control Systems,* 3rd ed. (Homewood, Ill.: Irwin, 1976), p. 453.

2. Ibid., p. 475.

3. H. L. Tosi, "The Human Effects of Budgeting Systems on Management," *MSU Business Topics* (Autumn 1974): 53–63.

4. G. Shillinglaw, *Managerial Cost Accounting,* 4th ed. (Homewood, Ill.: Irwin, 1977), p. 137.

5. R. F. Vancil, "What Kind of Management Control Do You Need?" *Harvard Business Review* (March–April 1973): 75–86; and "Banking's Aggressive Conservative," *Dun's Review* (December 1976): 47–49.

6. "The Financial Chemistry at Dow," *Dun's Review* (December 1975): 50–57.

7. A. Schick, "A Death in the Bureaucracy: The Demise of Federal PPBS," *Public Administration Review* (March–April 1973): 146–56.

8. L. M. Cheek, "Zero-Base Budgeting in Washington," *Business Horizons* (June 1978): 24.

9. W. F. Frese and R. K. Mautz, "Financial Reporting—by Whom?" *Harvard Business Review* (March–April 1972): 6–21.

10. J. C. Van Horne, *Financial Management and Policy,* 4th ed. (Englewood Cliffs, N.J.: Prentice-Hall, 1977), pp. 672–89.

11. See R. B. Frantzreb, L. T. Landau, and D. P. Lundberge, "The Valuation of Human Resources," *Business Horizons* (June 1974): 73–80; and M. M. K. Fleming, "Behavioral Implications of Human Resource Accounting: A Survey of Potential Problems," *Human Resources Management* (Summer 1977): 24–29.

12. R. B. Buchele, "How to Evaluate a Firm," *California Management Review* (Fall 1962): 5–16.

13. W. P. Hauworth, "Problems in the Development of Worldwide Accounting Standards," *International Journal of Accounting* (Fall 1973): 24.

14. J. D. Daniels, E. W. Ogram, and L. H. Radebaugh, *International Business: Environments and Operations* (Reading, Mass.: Addison-Wesley, 1979), p. 446.

15. J. C. Taylor, "Preventing Improper Payments Through Internal Controls," *The Conference Board* (August 1976): 17–18.

16. S. M. Robbins and R. B. Stobaugh, "The Bent Measuring Stick for Foreign Subsidiaries," *Harvard Business Review* (September–October 1973): 85.

17. L. D. Tooman, "Starting the Internal Audit of Foreign Operations," *The Internal Auditor* (November 1975): 56–62.

18. R. G. Murdick, *MIS: Concepts and Design* (Englewood Cliffs, N.J.: Prentice-Hall, 1980), p. 253.

19. W. M. Zani, "Blueprint for MIS," *Harvard Business Review* (November–December 1970): 100.

20. F. G. Withington, "Five Generations of Computers," *Harvard Business Review* (September–October 1972): 105.

21. "Insurance Agents Go Electric," *Business Week* (November 19, 1979): 142–43.

22. Withington, "Five Generations of Computers," p. 106.

23. R. L. Nolan, "Controlling the Costs of Data Services," *Harvard Business Review* (July–August 1977): 117.

24. J. F. Rockart, "Chief Executives Define Their Own Data Needs," *Harvard Business Review* (March–April 1979): 81–93.

25. "Computer Rescue for Travel Agents," *Business Week* (April 7, 1980): 81–82.

26. "What If Help for Management," *Business Week* (January 21, 1980): 73–74.

27. Ibid., p. 74.

28. Ibid.

29. S. L. Alter, "How Effective Managers Use Information Systems," *Harvard Business Review* (November–December 1976): 97–104.

30. F. Kaufman, *Distributive Processing* (New York: Coopers & Lybrand, 1977).

ADDITIONAL REFERENCES

Buchanan, J. R. and Linowes, R. G. "Understanding Distributed Data Processing." *Harvard Business Review* (July–August 1980): 143–53.

Cowen, S. S. and Dean, B. V. "Zero-Base Budgeting as a Management Tool," *MSU Business Topics,* Spring 1978, p. 23–29.

Emery, J. C. *Organizational Planning and Control Systems.* New York: Macmillan, 1969.

Gibson, C. F. and Nolan, R. L. "Managing the Four Stages of EDP Growth." *Harvard Business Review* (January–February 1974): 76–88.

Lawler III, E. E. and Rhode, J. G. *Information and Control in Organizations.* Santa Monica, Calif.: Goodyear, 1976.

McFarlan, F. W. "Management Audit of the EDP Department." *Harvard Business Review* (May–June 1973): 131–42.

Morton, M. S. *Management Decision Systems.* Cambridge, Mass.: Harvard University Press, 1971.

Strassmann, P. A. "Managing the Costs of Information." *Harvard Business Review* (September–October 1976): 133–42.

Strong, E. P. and Smith, R. D. *Management Control Models.* New York: Holt, Rinehart and Winston, 1968.

"How Not to Exploit the Hardware." *Business Week* (March 24, 1980): 90–91.

A CASE FOR ANALYSIS

Johns Hopkins University Hospital

Inflation and its effects on operating costs have raised havoc with many an organization's budget. The influence of inflation is felt by profit and not-for-profit organizations alike, including hospitals. Between 1975 and 1979, the rate of cost increases in U. S. hospitals has averaged over 15 percent per year. At Johns Hopkins University Hospital in Baltimore, however, the rate of cost increase has been declining during this period, from 16.4 percent to less than 8 percent in 1978. Hospital administrators point to a combination of decentralized management and a comprehensive system of monitoring costs as the main reasons for their success.

At Johns Hopkins, most of the credit for what has happened goes to two determined men who took over the leadership of the hospital in 1972. One of them is Robert M. Heyssel, who became hospital director, a position comparable to chief operating officer. Heyssel speaks in the quiet, firm manner of one who assumes his orders will be carried out. The call name of the CB radio in his car, "Bottom Line," is evidence of his obsession with cost control.

The other key figure is William E. McGuirk, Jr., who is chairman of Mercantile Bankshares Corp., a Baltimore bank holding company. McGuirk, who had served as a hospital trustee for fifteen years, became chairman of the board of trustees in 1972. A graduate of the U. S. Naval Academy who also serves on the boards of Dun & Bradstreet and several other companies, he has the tough, direct manner of a shipboard officer. He is also a longtime believer in the decentralized form of management.

When Heyssel and McGuirk took over, Johns Hopkins was already coming under pressure to get its financial house in order. Costs were rising by more than 14 percent annually, and operating deficits over the previous six years had totaled $7.6 million. McGuirk, a one-time manager on Wall Street, was already worrying that, because of its deficits, the hospital would have trouble selling bonds to finance a proposed building and renovation program. Meanwhile, the Maryland legislature had just created a commission to hold down hospital costs, and this had intensified the pressure to do something.

It had become clear that the hospital's management control system was outmoded for a large institution with 1100 beds, over 4000 employees, more than 20 clinical and service departments, and a total budget then approaching $60 million. In some ways, Hopkins resembled feudal England. The clinical departments, such as surgery, medicine, and neurosciences, were commonly called "fiefdoms," and when the medical chiefs of the departments got together, it was referred to as "a meeting of the barons." Since a department's power and prestige were measured in large part by its accumulation of assets, from beds to tongue depressors, there was open competition for resources and personnel. At that time, Blue Cross and other third-party insurers were reimbursing the hospital on a cost-plus basis, which gave little incentive for the "barons" to economize.

The hospital's accounting system was in worse shape. Lacking detailed cost information, central management had no effective way of imposing fiscal restraint on the departments. Even the department chiefs didn't always know where the money was going.

What McGuirk and Heyssel did was to wheel Hopkins into the operating room, where they implanted a new form of organization that had become widespread in industry. Most of the hospital was reorganized into fourteen autonomous clinical departments that function under their own budgets, subject to the control of the central administration. Excluded from the new system are departments whose services are provided more efficiently on a centralized basis, e.g., housekeeping, food services, and security. An elaborate, computerized cost-information system was set up, enabling the newly autonomous departments to see where the money was going, and to buy goods and services from each other in "intracompany" transactions.

It was no easy task to persuade the doctors to assume the added managerial responsibilities that the new system required. McGuirk explained the setup late in 1972 at a meeting of the physician department heads, many of whom were world-renowned experts in their fields. When he finished, one of the chiefs rose from his seat in an obvious challenge to McGuirk's authority. What would happen, the doctor wanted to know, if he wasn't able to hold his department to its budget. McGuirk's face clouded ominously. Staring back at the doctor, he drew his index finger across his throat with a flourish.

Each department was set up to run, in most respects, like a small business with its own "profit-and-loss" statement (Hopkins has long used the term profit and loss, even though, like most hospitals, it is a nonprofit institution). In charge of each department is the physician medical director, who has the traditional responsibilities of patient care, teaching, and research, as well as accountability for budgetary results. Two executives are directly under him: a nonphysician administrator concentrates full-time on the business and financial details and draws up the annual budget, while the nursing director manages the unit's nursing staff, a term which includes paraprofessionals.

Before decentralization, the hospital's clinical departments directly controlled only 30 percent of their costs. The rest was allocated from the budgets of the central service departments. The picture is much different today: each clinical department controls about 85 percent of its costs. This includes the cost of laboratory tests, X rays, and medicine purchased from other departments.

To help implement decentralization, several young executives from private industry were brought in. Among the most important is Irving Kues, who was formerly the chief operating officer of a data-processing and computer-services subsidiary of Commercial Credit Co. Kues is the hospital's vice president for finance and management systems; he developed the cost information system, which meticulously breaks down costs by department, hospital floor, and even individual physician.

The hospital's resemblance to a decentralized corporation has its limits. In private industry, division executives who flout their fiscal responsibilities can be summarily fired. Heyssel, on the other hand, does not have the average chief executive's power to enforce compliance with budgets. A hospital's free-spending clinical director may just happen to be a leading brain surgeon who must be handled with delicate diplomacy.

Heyssel is able to use financial incentives to get his way. Departments that perform well are given extra points in the competition for approval of new programs, equipment, and personnel. Since money for new programs no longer flows freely, as it once did, that extra edge can be important.

Hopkins has been saving money in all sorts of ways by placing fiscal accountability at the level at which hospital services are performed. Under decentralization, the physicians who actually prescribe diagnosis and treatment have had to keep an eye on their departments' budgets with costs to worry about. The chiefs of the hospital's autonomous units have been much more willing to part with unused beds, some of which have been reassigned to other departments that really need them. When Hopkins opened its new cancer center in 1977, it transferred sixty beds that had gone unused elsewhere. Partly because beds are more intelligently distributed, the hospital's overall occupancy rate—a critical measure of efficiency—has risen from 76.6 percent in 1972 to 82 percent in 1979. Some of the most dramatic savings have been achieved within Hopkins's individual departments. The activities of these autonomous departments, and hence the ways in which they have cut costs, vary greatly.

The Department of Medicine, which includes such specialties as cardiology, hematology, and internal medicine, has had remarkable success in reducing the laboratory tests for which hospitals have become almost notorious. Although the department's admissions were up 13.8 percent in 1979, the use of lab procedures had risen only 2.2 percent. This makes Medicine a kind of pacesetter compared with the hospital as a whole, in which tests are still increasing faster than the number of patients even though the rate of increase has slowed. Several years ago, tests were increasing so rapidly that the hospital seemed on the verge of becoming an auxiliary of the laboratory.

The Department of Medicine's clampdown on tests began in May 1978, when the department's administrator began circulating lists of lab-test charges and copies of patients' bills to the physicians who ordered the tests. The department's clinical director goes beyond the mere transmittal of copies of bills. He often sits down with individual doctors to review their recent lab tests.

The Department of Gynecology and Obstetrics has had a much different problem: how to drum up the added business it needs to climb out of the red. When the new clinic director took charge in 1971, the cries of newborn babies were becoming much fewer. Deliveries had fallen to 1900 babies a year from almost 3400 in 1958. This was due both to a declining birthrate and to an aging physical plant that expectant mothers were beginning to shun. Women in labor would actually come up to the entrance and refuse to go in.

To cut operating costs and attract customers, the hospital replaced its aging Women's Clinic in 1977 with a new facility, containing only 96 beds instead of the previous 133. In the new order of things, excess beds represented a cost drain, not a source of power. To bring in more business, they designed a special pregnancy-care program for unwed adolescents in the inner-city neighborhoods surrounding Hopkins, and expanded a pre-natal diagnostic center that attracts women with early pregnancy problems. As a result of all this effort, deliveries are currently running at 2800 a year.

The department has chalked up some impressive savings. In the case of childbirth, the average length of stay has dropped in three years from 4.4 days to 4.1, and in high-risk cases from 11.6 days to 7.4. The department has achieved this reduction by performing more pre- and post-natal care on an outpatient basis.

Whether Johns Hopkins's approach to financial control is a long-term solution or just a stop-gap measure is a subject open to much debate. Hospital costs jumped from a 7.9 percent increase in 1978 to 9.7 percent increase in 1979, reflecting the growth in the nation's inflation rate. Expansion plans have also been slowed because of the high interest rates that must be paid on construction bonds. In the future, the hospital may have to face a national health insurance along with the possibility of a federal cost containment act. The problem for hospital management is that the former will probably increase costs, while the latter may require cost containment or cuts. No one knows if the current control system will work in this new environment.

Adapted from Stephen Solomon, "How One Hospital Broke Its Inflation Fever," Fortune *(June 18, 1979): 148–54.*

Questions for Discussion

1. What general principles of management control are illustrated in this case?
2. What are the main differences between the control system in this not-for-profit organization and a profit-making organization?
3. What are the elements that would motivate hospital personnel to follow the current control system policies?
4. Do you think that an approach that emphasizes a decentralized form of management coupled with a comprehensive control system will be successful in the future?

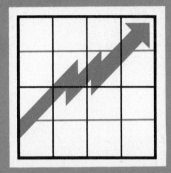

18

Production and Operations Control

CHAPTER OUTLINE

KEY POINTS IN THIS CHAPTER

1. The elements of production and operations control involve consideration of selection, production design, production planning, and production evaluation.

2. Facilities layout, a component of production design, concerns the overall arrangement of equipment, people, materials, storage, and service operations.

3. Material requirements planning is a computer-based approach to production planning that is gaining in popularity among production managers.

4. Quality control is involved in the total production process—from input to output control. Acceptance sampling and process control charts are statistical approaches to quality control.

5. An important key to success in production and operations control is for the manager to ensure that it is integrated into the total organizational system.

6. EOQ, PERT, linear programming, and queuing models are four of the many quantitative aids available to managers.

7. Production and operations in foreign countries require a careful analysis of the differences in the control elements.

8. Managerial skills, and the use of these skills in managerial roles, are found throughout the production and operations control system.

THE PRACTICE OF MANAGEMENT

Production and Operations Control: Pasta and the Airline Industry

To the casual observer, there is probably little relationship between an Italian woman's pasta making and the function of production and operations control. If your name is Marcella Vitalini Aitken, the relationship is significant. Thanks to Mrs. Aitken, passengers on major U. S. airlines are saying arrivederci to meat and potatoes and benvenuto to some tasty lasagne, cannelloni, and fettuccine. Because of an efficient production plant, Mrs. Aitken has turned a small operation into a $6 million per year enterprise.

Vivacious, talkative, and as Italian as pasta itself, Mrs. Aitken is best known for her Miami, Florida restaurants, Marcella's and Cucino Mia. Two years ago Marcella—as everyone calls her—sold Eastern Air Lines on the idea of serving pasta prepared according to her own recipes. Since then she has signed on National, Western, and Ozark, and is negotiating with nine other airlines, including Continental and US Air. Soon she will be feeding airline passengers as many as 25,000 meals per day.

The basis of pasta power is cost. It costs Marcella a mere 33 cents to prepare a meal of say, crêpes Florentine. The airlines, which normally pay about $1.50 for a steak dinner, are more than willing to pay that much for a pasta meal. In just two years, Eastern's purchases have gone from 15,000 trial servings to over 150,000 per month.

Marcella had to enlist the help of her entire family—including her ninety-three-year-old mother—to produce pasta. As the Eastern business increased, she decided to automate. Putting up $400,000 herself, and borrowing the rest from local banks, she invested $1 million in new equipment, including five pasta-making machines.

Her four-room factory, which is housed in a one-story building that connects with both her restaurants, turns out 25,000 meals every day—lasagne, Swiss crêpes, ravioli, cannelloni, and fettuccine Alfredo. In one room, dough is turned into various kinds of pasta. In another, sauces bubble in huge vats. In a third room it all comes together, as sauces and pasta move along a production line. Each serving—six or eight ounces in a plastic tray—is then flash-frozen with liquid nitrogen in a fourth room, boxed, and sent off in refrigerated trucks.

Marcella recently took delivery on a $55,000 versatile Italian pasta-making machine from Milan. The only one of its kind in the U. S., it mixes the ingredients, kneads the dough, and turns out everything from fettuccine to macaroni. The machine then cooks the pasta, dries it, stuffs it with meat, cheese, or vegetables, and cuts it into portions. The new pasta maker will double capacity and reduce labor costs by two-thirds.

Marcella says that management success is just like cooking. She claims that you have got to have a good factory, a good product, good people, and good customers. Couple this with a management style that involves tenacity, patience, and a "never give up" attitude, and you have all the ingredients for success.

Adapted from Susie G. Nazem, "Mamma Marcella Takes to the Air with Pasta Power,"
Fortune (August 27, 1979): 118–19.

18

In this last chapter on the control function, our attention will focus on production and operations activities. The emphasis will be on controlling the physical resources of the organization; however, as we will see, in the control of physical resources, managers must include consideration of human, information, and financial resources.

The chapter has been divided into five major sections. The first discusses the key elements of production and operations control. This includes an introduction to the elements of selection, production design, production planning, and production evaluation. Second, three of the production and operations control elements—production design, production planning, and production evaluation—are singled out for a separate discussion. The third section highlights some of the issues managers must consider in international production. The fourth section presents certain quantitative aids in production and operations control. These aids include economic order quantity (EOQ), linear programming, program evaluation and review technique (PERT), and queuing models. Finally, the relationship between production and operations control and the manager's job is discussed in the last section.

ELEMENTS OF PRODUCTION AND OPERATIONS CONTROL

Production and operations control is a subset of a larger and growing area of study termed production and operations management (POM), production and logistics management (PLM), or just operations management (OPS Management). Whatever terminology, the concern is a variety of concepts and approaches to improve the overall operating performance of an organization. The most frequently studied topics include the management of materials, products, equipment, and work force used in producing the products and services of an organization.

Exhibit 18-1 depicts a production and operations system for a typical manufacturing organization. As the exhibit suggests, a discussion of production and operations control should consider the elements of selection, production design, production planning, and production evaluation.[1]

Selection identifies those factors that are necessary to establish the foundation of the production and operations control system. The system begins, as in most other organizational activities, with a statement of the organization's *goals and strategies*. This identifies what the organization wants to produce, where, and with what type of process and work force. This is translated into decisions on *products and processes,* the *site* of the producing facility, and the selection of a *work force*. Work force was discussed in detail in chapter 10.

Production design concerns the design of products, processes, services, jobs, wage and salary structure, and control systems. In conjunction with our discussion in chapter 16, the major focus is *input controls*. The

EXHIBIT 18-1
An Example
Production &
Operations
System

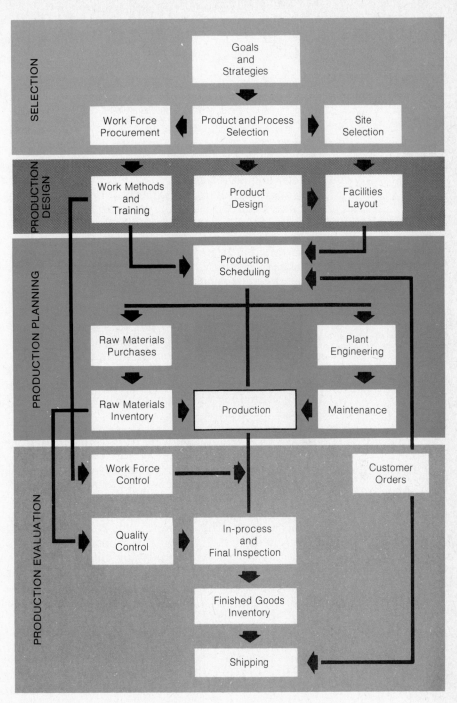

main functions include *product design, plant design engineering* (i.e., layout) and *training* the work force to use the newly developed *work methods* and procedures properly. The material in chapters 5, 8, and 10 has provided a discussion of this last topic.

Production planning involves those activities that are related to the actual production of the product or service. Attention is given to the important functions of *production scheduling,* material and equipment *purchases,* raw materials *inventory,* and *maintenance* procedures. A later discussion of this element will introduce the important topics of master production scheduling and material requirements planning. The main focus is on *process controls,* as discussed in chapter 16.

Production evaluation concerns possible revisions to the production and operating system in light of the discovery of new products and services and technological breakthroughs, and also concerns work force control and problems with existing products and services. Of particular concern are *quality control,* finished product *inventories,* and employee *performance evaluation* (see chapter 16). We defined these earlier as *ouput controls.*

An Illustration. Emphasis on production and operations control by managers exists in all types of organizations. Many of the elements presented for a manufacturing company are closely related to those found in banks, government offices, restaurants, and other service organizations.

Consider the case of a county hospital commission in a large, growing urban area. The commission is responsible for the construction, operation, and maintenance of tax-supported health care institutions in the surrounding area. After analyzing data on population trends and movements, citizen needs, and the area's tax base, commission members have decided to build a new county hospital in one of the fastest growing parts of the county. From a production and operations viewpoint, what elements should the members consider?

In terms of *selection,* the decision to build the hospital is in response to the goals and strategies of the commission. This is followed by a concern for the site of the hospital, including evaluation of various pieces of land according to such criteria as cost, citizen accessibility, and availability of utilities. Product and process selection would involve decisions on the size of the hospital, the types of services that will be offered (such as the comprehensiveness of the emergency room), and the degree of emphasis given to such specialties as surgery, pediatrics, and out-patient care. This will lead to the selection of a work force that will fit the choices on products and services.

The initial decision on *production design* concerns the layout of the hospital—designing the physical layout of the hospital production system such that the most efficient flow of materials and people is achieved. The specific work methods are chosen with regard to the type of work force that is hired and the nature of the hospital's physical layout.

In *production planning,* hospital administrators would be concerned with purchasing fixed equipment such as x-ray machines, equipping the pathology laboratory and surgical ward, and periodically purchasing supplies such as linens, drugs, and the like. In addition, emphasis must be given to scheduling employees to tasks and maintaining an efficient inventory of needed materials. As noted in the Johns Hopkins University Hospital case at the end of chapter 17, managers must develop an effective balance between material and product availability and the significant costs of having these inventories on hand.

The final element, *production evaluation,* concerns the development of accurate employee performance evaluation and reward systems so that the most effective work force is retained (see chapter 16). A second concern, which we will discuss later in this chapter, is quality control. The hospital management must give attention to the accuracy of laboratory tests, the quality of x-rays, the control of unit costs, and so on.

As this and other examples illustrate, production and operations control is an integral part of the manager's job. It is not only a function that translates goals and strategies into action, but it is clearly the place where the manager is "on the firing line" for the performance of the organization.

In the following sections, we will discuss three elements of production and operations control in greater detail: production design, production planning, and production evaluation.

PRODUCTION DESIGN: FACILITIES LAYOUT

Facilities layout is the overall arrangement of equipment, people, materials handling, storage, and service operations required to ensure efficient operation of the production system. The way the facilities of an organization are laid out can have a significant impact on overall performance. Machines and people scattered about in a haphazard fashion add valuable time to the production process and can result in higher costs.

Goals of Facilities Layout

Production and operations managers suggest that a production system with the following layout characteristics will enhance performance:

1. Materials handling and internal transportation requirements that reduce the costs and time needed to move materials through the production process.
2. Floor space requirements that eliminate floor congestion and bottlenecks, resulting in a maximum return on the fixed investment in facilities.
3. Minimizing the distance workers must move to obtain materials, tools, and supplies, resulting in improved labor efficiency.
4. Providing for employee convenience, safety, and comfort.
5. Providing flexibility for expansion caused by growth, new products, and/or new processes.

As an example, consider the Burger King division of Pillsbury.[2] Like many other organizations, this fast-food restaurant is faced with rising costs from land, labor, and raw materials (e.g., beef) that can adversely affect the division's profitability. To counter this trend, Burger King's management started a productivity improvement program, part of which is aimed at better facilities layout. Time is money to Burger King: therefore, if ways can be found to reduce the time between the customer's order and when they receive the food—while maintaining high food quality—the organization's performance should improve.

Burger King's work on facilities layout involves both major and minor improvements. For example, the bell hose that rings when a car is in the drive-in lane was moved back ten feet from the remote order entry device. This distance allows workers to be ready to take the customer's order immediately after the car brakes for a stop. The time savings permits an extra thirty cars per hour to be handled. Similarly, to keep Whoppers hot without warming the iced drinks stationed next to them, the company installed a sheet metal plate between the products to concentrate the heat on the burgers.

On the major improvement side, the company is experimenting with a new cash register that performs multiple functions. Besides calculating the customer's bill, the machine electronically transfers food orders to cooks on a computerized readout terminal. The cooks make fewer mistakes and as a result don't waste as much food. The new cash registers are also being adapted to activate a machine that mixes, pours, and caps soft drinks automatically. In a further improvement, management of Burger King studied traffic flow and customer movements in its restaurants with a computer simulation program. The analysis resulted in a reduction in the number of floor plans from five to two—one for small towns and one for larger volume stores.

While Burger King's profit margin is less than McDonald's (12 percent versus 18 percent), it has increased over 30 percent in the last five years—a figure that is twice as large as McDonald's. The division is already Pillsbury's fastest-growing unit.

Layout Patterns

In visiting a number of factories, hospitals, or department stores, a manager can identify a great variety of production layouts. Most layouts, however, are based on three distinct patterns. As shown in exhibit 18-2, the three basic patterns are process, product, and fixed position.[3]

A *process* layout is one where similar processing components and equipment are grouped together in one area on the basis of the function they perform, without regard to the product. This pattern is preferred when the number of products is many and high flexibility is desired. Examples include department stores, hospitals, and manufacturing job shops.

When production components are arranged according to the steps required in producing a product, this is termed a *product* pattern. Product layouts are used in continuous production systems where the number of different products is small, the volume is high, and the parts are highly standardized and interchangeable. Automobile assembly lines, food processing plants, and appliance manufacturers are illustrations.

EXHIBIT 18-2 Layout Patterns

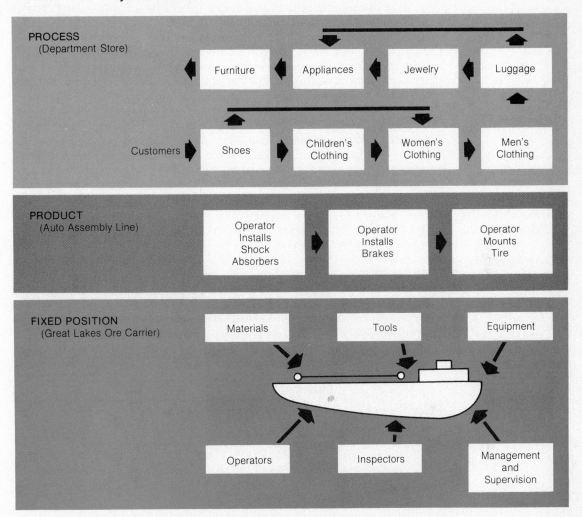

A *fixed-position* layout is where the product remains in one position because of its bulk and weight, and workers, materials, and tools are brought to it. This pattern is normally used in producing such products as ships, airplanes, locomotives, and large pieces of equipment.

Layout Pattern Comparisons

Each of the layout patterns offers distinct benefits and limitations. For the process layout, flexibility allows work to be shifted between machines when one breaks down. In a similar manner, since sequencing of operations is not a problem, equipment that is noisy or gives off irritating fumes can be located in another area. Since the pace of the work is determined by the person, not the machine, incentive pay systems can be used. However, complex production planning is required to control materials flow, inventory storage, and scheduling. The main key to success with the process layout is materials handling.

With the product layout, materials handling is simplified by means of conveyor systems. With this layout, production control and employee training are easier; less inspection is required on the final product; and since there is less work in process and smaller aisles and storage are required, the useful floor area is more productive. Conversely, production equipment usually requires a higher capital investment; there are greater problems when work stoppages occur; the highly repetitive nature of the workers' jobs creates motivation and morale problems; and the inflexibility of the layout makes it costly when product or process design changes are implemented. Above all, the key to success with the product layout is balancing the production steps—each step in the process must be provided with enough capacity so that material flow will be uninterrupted. This is *line balancing*.

COMMENTS ON THE PRACTICE OF MANAGEMENT
(See p. 531)

> The Practice of Management introductory section on Mrs. Marcella Aitken's entry into the airline food business makes a number of important points of how production efficiency can lead to improved organizational performance. First, the raw material cost for pasta provides an edge for the company over other foods used by airlines. Second, the newly purchased pasta machine simplifies production while simultaneously reducing labor costs. Finally, even though it is a relatively small operation, the nature of the product layout allows the company to reap significant savings. In summary, Marcella was able to produce a product that the marketplace demanded with a cost structure that benefited not only Marcella, but the airlines as well.

The fixed-position layout eliminates costly and space-consuming materials-handling equipment. This layout pattern is also popular with workers because they can move about freely and are not restricted to a particular area. On the other hand, fixed-position layouts require large and costly working areas, especially if more than one unit, such as at a G.M. locomotive assembly plant, is being worked on at the same time. In addition, highly skilled workers are needed to perform the jobs. This places a great deal of emphasis on the hiring and placement process. (For example, in gearing up to design and produce its new 757 and 767 model aircraft, Boeing was forced to advertise for skilled workers across the entire U. S.) One of the major keys to success with this layout is material availability. Parts must be stored close to the product, to reduce the travel and idle time of the highly paid worker. This may require large and space-consuming storage areas.

In actual operations, most organizations combine layouts to produce a product. For example, the parts of an automobile (e.g., doors, frames, and engines) are manufactured with a process layout, while the actual assembly uses a product layout.

The crucial factor in production layout is cost—fixed and variable. With a high-volume product, product and process layouts are preferred; a low-volume, high-cost product is amenable to a fixed-position format. This is why Volvo and Saab can afford to use a combination of product and fixed-position layouts (low-volume, high-priced product).

PRODUCTION PLANNING: MATERIAL REQUIREMENTS PLANNING

One of the most difficult problems facing production and operations managers over the years is how to plan and control production and materials flow effectively. In essence, the manager must be able to juggle product design changes, purchasing needs, production rates and schedules, and inventories such that costs are controlled and the customer is provided with the right product on time.

Until recently, managers have attacked this problem with an assortment of tools and techniques. However, a number of organizations, beginning with Black and Decker, Xerox, Steelcase, Hewlett-Packard, and Abbott Laboratories have begun to apply computer technology to the problem of production planning.[4] The rationale for using the computer in production planning was the favorable cost balance—computer computation costs were decreasing (see chapter 17), while production costs, especially raw materials and inventories, were rising. What has evolved is a new approach to production planning: material requirements planning (MRP) systems.

For our purposes, material requirements planning is a computer-based system that develops schedules for the specific parts and materials required to produce a product, the particular numbers that are needed, and the dates when orders for these materials should be processed and be received.[5] In application, the purposes of an MRP are to *control:* (1) inventory levels (order the right part, in the right quantity, at the right time), (2) priorities for materials (order with a valid due date), and (3) capacity planning (plan for complete and accurate production rates).[6]

The logic of MRP is that demand for materials and parts and fluctuations in inventories are a direct function of demand for the end product. This logic is described in exhibit 18-3. The exhibit illustrates the five core components in an MRP system: the master production schedule, the bill of materials file, the inventory file, the MRP computer program, and the various output reports.

Master Production Schedule.   The master production schedule is the major input into the MRP system. Three elements make up the schedule. First are firm orders for products by customers—orders of known quantity and delivery time. For example, an electric utility company may have a long-term contract with a coal company to purchase a minimum number of tons of coal per year. The second element is forecasts of consumer demand (see chapter 4), including demand for both regular and replacement products. For instance, a producer of automobile spark plugs should forecast demand for installation in new cars and demand for spark plugs for older cars brought in for tune-ups.

The final element is data on the production capacity of the unit. It is important for the manager to know if the demand will exceed or be less than existing capacity. Such information will show when idle capacity exists or when an increase in capacity is needed. For example, during the late 1970s and early 1980s the demand for small, fuel efficient cars far exceeded the plant capacities of General Motors and Chrysler to produce these cars. At the same time, the plants assembling the large-sized cars for each of these companies lay partially idle.[7]

EXHIBIT 18-3 Material Requirements Planning

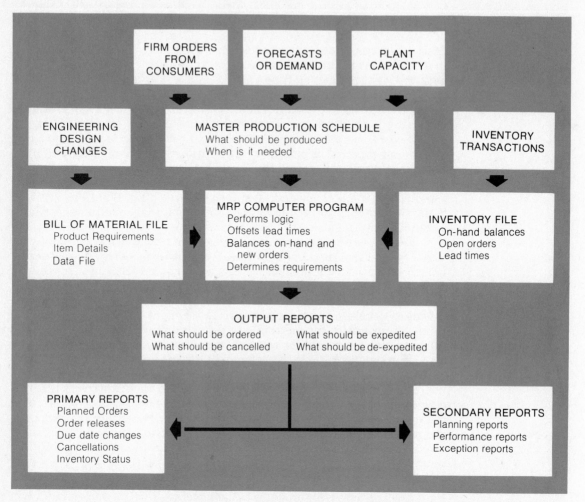

Adapted from Jeffrey G. Miller and Linda G. Sprague, "Behind the Growth in Material Requirements Planning," Harvard Business Review (September-October 1975): 84.

A master production schedule, which evaluates demand for products and available capacity of the production unit, means that many decisions can be faced in planning rather than in a crisis. Instead of waiting (or hoping) for all production elements to fall together in the right order, managers can ensure that these elements indeed fall together correctly. Budgets and other organizational plans can be more accurately developed and related to end products.

Bill of Materials. The bill of materials file (B/M) is usually developed by design engineers from product specifications. It lists all items, including quantities of each, required to produce one unit of finished product. Bills of materials can vary greatly by product. For example, for a non-refillable pen, there are three pieces (i.e., plastic barrel, ink cartridge, and plastic cap with a clip) and a 747 requires thousands of pages to present the bill of materials.

THE
MANAGER'S
JOB
William Lord of
Crompton
Company

To Bill Lord, head of Crompton Company, a New York–based manufacturer of corduroy and velveteen, success—and even survival—in the textile industry is highly dependent on the efficiency of the production plant. With this emphasis on efficiency, coupled with an aggressive exporting strategy, Crompton is one textile company that has not been beaten to death by inexpensive imports.

Crompton's keys to success are three major strategies. First, to push the efficiency of its weaving equipment as high as possible, the company keeps the machines running 24 hours a day, 350 days a year. New export markets provide the customers to buy the extra output produced by the nonstop operations. Over one-third of Crompton's sales in the last three years came from overseas markets. In the textile industry, a plant running at 88 percent of capacity is considered inefficient—Crompton consistently operates over 92 percent.

Second, Lord determined that rising quality defects was more a people problem than a machine problem. Low pay and erratic work schedules created morale, absenteeism, and turnover problems which were themselves related to quality rejects approaching 10 percent of total production. To counter this trend, Crompton instituted a three-day, twelve-hour work schedule that gives the mill hands a full week off once every eight weeks. In addition, not only were pay rates increased, but to decrease absenteeism Lord paid a bonus for employees who stay on the job; they are paid for forty hours if they complete the required thirty-six. Labor turnover at Crompton is only 9 percent, an impressively low figure in an industry where the average rate is over 50 percent.

Third, Lord promotes the use of engineering—sometimes of the bubble-gum and paper clip variety—to improve the efficiency of his equipment. Some of the results haven't been worth the effort. For instance, Crompton tried out a complicated new piece of equipment to replace the workers who change the bobbins on spinning machines; but, Lord noticed that the contraption had to be constantly attended by three engineers, so he got rid of it. On the positive side, Crompton's engineers were dissatisfied with a spring-steel blade machine used to cut the tiny grooves that give velveteen its plushness. The unit didn't keep a sharp edge, so the engineers substituted ordinary razor blades and got a 60 percent boost in efficiency.

Company-wide, the emphasis on productivity has yielded an annual increase of 8 percent in output per labor-hour since 1974. This is well above the average for the textile industry and more than five times the average for the U. S. labor force as a whole.

Adapted from Edward Meadows, "How Three Companies Increased Their Productivity," Fortune *(March 10, 1980): 92–101.*

Inventory File. The inventory file contains information on at least two factors. First, there is information on the three major types of inventories: raw materials and supplies, in-process, and finished products. Second, the lead times required between submission of the order for a raw material and date of receipt are needed. For Paper Mate, for example, it is important to know that the lead time for plastic pen barrels is ten days, but twenty-five days for ink cartridges.

Without inventories, organizations could not produce goods (raw materials), maintain stable production rates (in-process), or sell to customers (finished products). If they were not costly, most organizations would keep very large inventories on hand to maintain a smooth-running operation. However, inventories quite often represent a significant percentage of an organization's current assets, as much as 20 to 30 percent. Inventory cost categories include storage costs, insurance, inventory and property taxes, spoilage, obsolescence, and opportunity costs. Since these costs can amount to a significant sum, managers need to develop techniques to balance smooth-running production runs with inventory costs. One approach to this problem, the economic order quantity (EOQ), will be discussed later in this chapter.

MRP Computer Program.   The heart of the material requirements planning system is a computer program that operates on the inventory file, the bill of materials file, and the master production schedule. Most programs that are available commercially or can be developed by the organization operate in the following manner. First, information from the master production schedule (list of items needed by time period), the bill of materials file (description of the materials and parts needed to make each item), and the inventory file (number of units of each item and material currently on hand and on order) is placed in the system. Second, the program manipulates the inventory file while frequently referring to the bill of materials file to calculate the quantity of each item. Third, the number of units of each item required is corrected for on-hand amounts and net requirements are recomputed to allow for the lead time needed to obtain the material. Finally, the manager operating the program feeds in the different components of the master production schedule in an iterative manner. Each time the program is run, the output is compared with the production capacity of product demand characteristics of the production schedule. The master schedule is adjusted to try to correct for any imbalances and then the program is executed again. This process is repeated until a satisfactory output is obtained.

Output Reports.   The various data that flow from the MRP system are combined into reports that focus on the following questions: (1) What items should be ordered and when?; (2) what items should be expedited?; (3) what orders can be cancelled?; (4) when can deliveries be stretched out?; and (5) when can the customer be realistically told the product will be received? As shown in exhibit 18-3, the reports from an MRP system can be classified as either primary or secondary.[8]

Primary reports are the main reports used for production, operations, and inventory control. The most frequently developed primary reports include

1. *Planned orders* to be released at a future time
2. *Order release* forms to execute the planned orders
3. *Changes in due dates* of open orders due to rescheduling
4. *Cancellations or suspensions* of open orders
5. *Inventory status* data

Secondary or optional reports that can be generated by an MRP system include

1. *Planning reports* that can be used in forecasting inventory and specifying requirements over a particular time frame
2. *Performance reports* to identify the existence of inactive items and determine the agreement between actual and programmed lead times and between actual and programmed usage and costs
3. *Exceptions reports,* which identify serious errors such as late or overdue orders, excess scrap, or out-of-range operations

The main beneficiaries of the output reports are production and purchasing managers. The MRP does the detailed scheduling and monitoring to ensure that work is being completed on time. Priorities for purchases are maintained and can be used for changing due dates or quantities. Feedback from these two functions is important because it can be used to revise inputs into the MRP system.

PRODUCTION EVALUATION: QUALITY CONTROL

Product quality is a claim advertised by organizations. We are confronted daily with claims of 99 and 44/100 percent pure Ivory Soap, seemingly indestructible Maytag products, the perpetual life of Volvo automobiles, and the "100 percent pure beef" used in hamburgers by many fast-food chains. Quality has also been one of the major rallying cries of environmental and consumer interest groups. These and other groups point to quality problems such as flammable clothing and harmful toys for children, cars that fall apart after only a few thousand miles, and manufacturing plants that pollute the air and water.

Quality is a term that means different things to different people. To the consumer, quality means that a product or service performs according to manufacturing claims or to the consumer's expectations. On the other hand, the production and quality control managers speak of quality in terms of the manner in which product specifications are met within certain cost constraints. For our purposes, quality is a characteristic of a product or service that determines its value in the market and how well it will perform the function for which it was designed.

In most organizations, quality of a product is usually expressed in terms of a standard; therefore, the role of quality control is to ensure that there is an acceptable degree of conformance with the standards set for the product or service. Our discussion of quality control will be presented in three parts: the dimensions of quality control, types of quality control, and statistical quality control methods.

Dimensions of Quality Control

Product quality is viewed by most organizations as multidimensional. The frequently used dimensions of quality include the following:[9]

1. *Function* refers to whether the product or service actually performed its purpose when put into use. Does a light bulb work when placed in a socket?, does a new car achieve its designated M.P.G.?, does the automatic-erasing capability of a typewriter function correctly?
2. *Reliability and durability* refer to the length of time that the product will perform its function. Will a new auto tire actually wear for over 50,000 miles?, will a spotlight last for 1000 hours of continual use?, or, even if

the odometer of a Mercedes-Benz automobile can register to 999,999 miles, will the car last that long?

3. *Esthetic characteristics* concern the physical appearance of the product. Are scratches and chips absent from the new dining room table?, is the new dress in style?, or does the shape and color of the new refrigerator fit with the decor of the kitchen?

4. *Safety* refers to whether the product will perform its function without unnecessarily endangering the user. Does the microwave oven emit dangerous microwaves?, does the new roofing material resist fire?, or does the food product contain foreign material?

In responding to these quality dimensions, one of the most important parts of a manager's job is to balance the marketability of high-quality products with the costs of achieving this high quality. Contrary to certain claims, it is rare that a company can "produce the highest quality product at the lowest possible cost." High quality usually entails greater costs. For example, the average television set has an approximately eight-year service life. If a manufacturer offers a set that lasts twenty years but costs nearly 50 percent more, how many customers would be interested in buying? The price, which contains the extra costs for higher quality, may not only be out of the expected price range of the typical buyer, but in twenty years the technology used in the set may be obsolete.

Types of Quality Control

As an illustration, consider a brewing company such as Coors, Miller, or Anheuser-Busch. In producing a particular beer, the quality control manager at each of these companies would be concerned with at least three different types of quality control.

First is concern for the quality of the input materials, sometimes called *feedforward* control. This type of quality control focuses on the quality of purchased materials (hops, grain, and so forth) and other raw materials (water). The objective is to inspect before costly operations have been conducted on items that are defective.

The second type of quality control, also *feedforward,* is evaluation of the *work in process*. In a brewery, the quality of the product is checked before and after each of the ingredients is placed in the batch reactor. In other industries, for example, the metal finish of new automobiles is checked for foreign matter or rough surfaces; before clothing products are sent to branch stores, the distribution operation of department stores quality checks goods for defects; and in hospital pathology laboratories, a standard blood, urine, or tissue sample is placed in the sample flow from time to time to check the accuracy of the equipment and techniques.

Finally, a quality check is made on the final product. Termed *output* quality control or *feedback* control, this type of quality control insures that the product satisfies the original design specifications. Brewers not only check the product as it is placed in barrels for storage, but from time to time the products are checked in storage to insure that the quality is maintained. In some organizations, another form of feedback quality control involves investigating and responding to customer quality complaints. A bad-quality product means a dissatisfied customer, which can cause bad publicity and possible lower sales. For example, recent surveys indicate that one reason U. S. customers purchase Japanese cars is the perception that Toyotas, Datsuns, and so on are better quality cars than their American counterparts. The problem for U. S. automakers is that while these perceptions may develop quickly, they can take a long time to change.

Statistical Quality Control

Since quality control implies the existence of a standard, that standard must be stated in some measurable terms if it is to be enforced. Measurement can be by variables or by certain attributes. *Variable* measurement usually involves some form of physical measurement—height, weight, diameter, tensile strength, and so on. For example, tires are checked for tread width, tread depth, diameter, circumference, weight, and so forth.

An *attribute* approach ascertains whether some characteristic is present or absent from the product. Examples include whether or not flights arrive within ten minutes of the scheduled arrival for airlines, all buttons are on each shirt for a clothing manufacturer, and digital watches perform correctly for Timex.

Variable and attribute measures can be used with a variety of statistical quality control procedures. Two of the most frequently used are acceptable sampling procedures and process control procedures.

Acceptance Sampling Procedures.   Acceptance sampling is a quality control procedure used to predict the quality of a batch, stream, or large number of products from an inspection of a sample or samples from the larger production run. This procedure is preferred by many organizations for these reasons: (1) from a cost perspective, it would be unrealistic to test each unit—it would be costly for McDonald's to test each batch of french fries or for Kellogg's to check each box of corn flakes; (2) inspection of each unit may result in the destruction of that unit—one cannot take a bite out of each Big Mac, or test each G.E. flash bulb or each match from the Diamond Match Company; and (3) sampling allows management to check the product's quality more quickly than if each unit were tested.

Different forms of acceptance sampling can occur within the same department. For example, at one of GM's four-cylinder engine plants, 400 engines are assembled per day. Acceptance sampling involves three stages: (1) each engine is visually inspected to see that all parts have been assembled; (2) approximately one-fourth of the engines are "hot tested"—actually started and allowed to run for a period of time; and (3) twice a day, an engine is totally disassembled by a quality control technician and checked for proper assembling and operating characteristics.

In nonmanufacturing, acceptance sampling is also used, but less widely than in manufacturing enterprises. Earlier, we mentioned how hospital laboratories use standard samples to check for equipment and operator accuracy. Many labs augment this with frequent double checking on a patient's sample. For example, the lab supervisor may ask another technologist to perform the same blood analysis on a sample as was performed by a first technologist. At insurance companies such as Prudential or State Farm, samples of newly written policies are checked by a quality control unit for accuracy. In retail stores, control managers frequently check random customer accounts for proper credit calculations and balances. In many of these organizations, the unit performing the acceptance sampling is within the internal audit department (see chapter 17).

Process Control Procedures.　Acceptance sampling can be used in feedforward and feedback types of quality control. Process control, on the other hand, focuses almost exclusively on testing products in process so that adjustments can be made to the production process itself before poor-quality items are produced.

For example, consider a dinnerware manufacturing plant of Corning Glass. One of the many variable measures of quality control is the diameter of the plates as they leave the forming oven. Process control occurs as follows:

> Right in the center of the plant are three big sets of traffic lights hanging from the ceiling. A green light means a production line is running smoothly; amber advertises the fact that a line needs close supervision because defects (diameter of plates) were found in some of its dinnerware. Red is shutdown. The signals are regulated by quality inspectors, who used to check each plate, but who now take a sampling. The new method had led to better quality control. It is also much faster.[10]

Note in this sample that sampling is also an integral part of process control.

The major tool of process control is a process control chart. An ex-

EXHIBIT 18-4
Process Control
Chart for
Monitoring
Corning Dinner
Plates

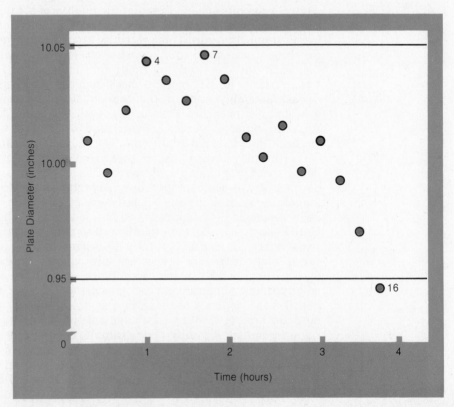

ample for a Corning Ware dinner plate is shown in exhibit 18-4. The first step is the use of a process control chart is to establish quality standard for comparison. For a dinner plate, the diameter standard is set at 10.0 inches ± 0.05 inches. Next, the frequency of sampling is determined. If the oven produces 1000 plates per hour, a sample every fifteen minutes, or after each 250-plate unit has passed, would be an example. Finally, the results of the quality control checks are plotted on the control chart and analyzed. In the example chart, samples 4 and 7 would necessitate an amber warning light; sample 16 would result in a red light. All other samples would cause a green light to be shown.

INTERNATIONAL ISSUES IN PRODUCTION AND OPERATIONS CONTROL

With the growing importance of international trade and business, many organizations are taking a serious look at operating production facilities in other countries. This includes U. S. firms operating overseas and foreign organizations producing in the U. S. (see the Honda case at the end of the chapter). While it is beyond the scope of this book to cover all issues, three major issues have been chosen for discussion: plant acquisition or construction, site selection, and production design.

Plant Acquisition or Construction.   If an organization decides to market products and services in another country, the question arises as to whether a production facility should be constructed from scratch, or an existing production plant purchased. For example, how important is it to acquire management, a labor force, or access to otherwise closed channels of distribution? As we have discussed, the availability of key managers and skilled labor is a significant problem in many countries. In addition, will acquisition allow early market entry?; will acquisition preempt purchase of facilities by a competing firm?; will construction allow the organization to build-in the latest technological advances?[11]

The political factor is, in most cases, the most important. Past experiences by organizations have shown that the acquisition of locally owned firms and their physical resources can generate more political problems than a decision to construct a new facility. Such countries as Canada, Japan, Australia, France, and the United Kingdom have exhibited opposition to takeovers by U. S. firms. The reverse is also true. If a foreign firm is a member of a cartel, U. S. antitrust laws may become a factor. Restraint of trade must also be considered. For example, when British Petroleum acquired a significant interest in Sohio, the U. S. Justice Department looked carefully at whether the acquisition would adversely affect competition in this country.

Beyond the resistance by governments to foreign takeovers, an equally important factor is the price set by the owner for the organization. The demand for the foreign operation coupled with the nontaxation of capital gains in some countries has created an inflated price for acquisition. Because of these and other issues, the movement is more toward construction of new facilities rather than acquisition. However, construction is fraught with problems.

Site Selection.   Once the decision has been made to construct production or service facilities in another country, management can concern itself with site selection. One of the first issues that must be confronted is the slowness of governmental bureaucracies. Since most land acquisitions require governmental approval—especially if the land is owned by the state, as it is in many cases—the organization may be in for a long wait. For example, it may take as long as a year to acquire a site in Indonesia. Rarely can this process be speeded up, so management must build this time into their plans.

The actual selection process varies by organization and country. A simple evaluation scheme is shown in exhibit 18-5, which presents a weighting scheme for seven important variables. Of the six sites analyzed, A, E, and F would be worth investigating further for legal, engineering, and economic feasibility.

One of the major drawbacks of an analysis as shown in exhibit 18-5 is that in many countries markets can change rapidly. Power, resources, community development, and environmental issues can develop at a rate much faster than in the U. S. For example, the recent concern over the pollution of the Mediterranean Sea has forced many countries to revise their environmental regulations for facilities that border the sea or are located on rivers that discharge into it.

The key for managers is to consider site evaluation and selection as a *dynamic* as opposed to a *static* process. Site selection evaluation must be conducted continuously, so that sensitive issues are identified early.

Production Design.   The production design decision in foreign operations must consider the type of equipment and the local labor environment and determine the desired balance between machine skill and labor skill, given relative capital and labor costs. In other words, if only low-skilled labor is available, should the organization invest in highly automated equipment?; or, if skilled labor can be hired, is it better to use multipurpose equipment which requires this type of labor? Managers must recognize that automated equipment generally requires long production runs to bring down unit costs, while multipurpose equipment

EXHIBIT 18-5   Site Selection for an International Facility

CRITERIA	MAXIMUM VALUE ASSIGNED	SITES					
		A	B	C	D	E	F
Living conditions	100	70	40	45	50	60	60
Accessibility	75	55	35	20	60	70	70
Industrialization	60	40	50	55	35	35	30
Labor availability	35	30	10	10	30	35	35
Economics	35	15	15	15	15	25	25
Community capability and attitude	30	25	20	10	15	25	15
Effect on company reputation	35	25	20	10	15	25	15
Total	370	260	180	165	225	280	265

Source: E. S. Groo, "Choosing Foreign Locations: One Company's Experience," *Columbia Journal of World Business* (September–October 1971): 77.

requires closer quality control, which in many developing countries is hard to come by.

To illustrate the need to adapt to the local environment, consider the following two examples. In the oil-producing Middle Eastern countries, there is a high percentage of low-skilled labor. Because of this, many of the oil companies have opted for highly specialized, narrowly defined jobs, thereby simplifying employee training. With a few highly skilled troubleshooters, automated equipment can be used effectively. In Western Europe, on the other hand, Gillette decided to use multipurpose equipment with the available skilled work force.[12]

Success in international business requires a careful balance between volume, labor, and capital equipment costs. This further illustrates the importance of an effective link between an organization's planning and control systems.

PRODUCTION AND OPERATIONS CONTROL: KEYS TO SUCCESS

Production and operations is the heart of the organization's daily activities. It is "where the action is" because it is the focal point where planning, organizing, leading, and control come together. From the experiences of practicing managers, there are a number of keys to success that should be carefully studied by future managers.

1. **Production and operations control is most effective when it has been integrated into the other organizational systems.**

   In much the same manner as recommended for MIS, production and operations control needs to be fully integrated into the organization before its full potential is realized. A "tacked-on" production and operations control system will only lead to it being considered a "police" function. Managers in this area need to be consulted frequently throughout the entire management process. Without their input, goals, strategies, plans, structure, communications systems, and the like may not be effective.

2. **Careful attention should be given to staffing the production and operations control area.**

   Almost all successful MRP implementations are led by a senior manager, backed up by a well-selected team of key production people, not computer specialists. Managers who know the ins and outs of operating systems must be the ones who work continuously to keep the formal system up to date. In much the same manner, it would be wise to staff the quality control area with managers and supervisors who have had operating experience in production. The technical skills associated with quality control are not overly difficult to master. A key to success for quality control managers, however, is the development of conceptual and diagnostic skills in integrating quality control with the total system.

3. **Develop observational skills in analyzing production activities.**

   As we will discuss in the next section, a number of management science models have been extensively used in production and operations control. Identifying production problems can be quite effectively done with proper observation by the manager. Observing idle or broken-down equipment, parts and materials stored in aisles, lack of cleanliness throughout the plant, slow repair by maintenance crews, and absenteeism problems are just as effective in pinpointing production difficulties as the most sophisticated computer program or statistical procedure.

4. Production criteria should be broad in scope.

Many production and operations managers believe that their main objective is to produce a product or service at the lowest possible cost. This may be fine, but one main element is missing—namely, such a product or service may have characteristics that are not desired by the consumer. A much more appropriate objective is to produce a product that satisfies the needs of the consumer and can be produced within an acceptable cost range.

5. Be attentive to feedback on your own operations.

The primary goal of production and operations control is to evaluate a unit's performance and to recommend corrective actions, if needed. The reverse holds for the management of production and operations control. Managers in this area must evaluate their units' performance and also take corrective action, if needed. Examples include inadequate reporting procedures to other functional departments and high sampling costs.

6. International environments require careful planning.

It may be a serious mistake for managers to believe that an organization can totally transfer production equipment, technology, and knowledge to an operation in another country without serious problems. Countries differ not only in cultures, but in size of markets, governmental processes and laws, availability of labor, and so on. Successful production and operations control clearly requires an emphasis on front-end planning to adjust to these national differences.

AIDS IN PRODUCTION AND OPERATIONS CONTROL

The management science school has contributed a number of quantitative techniques that have improved the way managers perform. Some of these techniques were introduced in chapters 3, 6, and 7. We will continue this presentation with a discussion of four techniques that have been successfully applied in many production and operations control activities. The four are economic order quantity models (EOQ), program evaluation and review technique (PERT), linear programming, and queuing models.

A detailed discussion of each decision-aid technique is beyond the scope of this book. We have, however, selected one well-used technique for each of the four application areas.

Economic Order Quantity (EOQ)

Managers in all types of organizations are often faced with the problem of maintaining adequate inventories. A hospital is concerned with supplies of blood plasma, a clothing store with sweaters and pants, a grain elevator with wheat, or an Internal Revenue office with forms. The problem facing managers is to minimize the costs of maintaining the inventory without jeopardizing service to the customer, client, or patient.

The inventory decision problem involves at least two fundamental issues: the size of the order and the point at which this order should be placed.[13] The main factors that determine the responses to these issues are two cost calculations: order cost and carrying cost.

Order cost refers to all the costs of procuring the material for the inventory. These costs, which are incurred each time an order is placed, include expenses for time needed to prepare bids and evaluate cost es-

EXHIBIT 18-6
Inventory Cost
Analysis

NO. ORDERS PLACED	ORDER QUANTITY	ORDER COSTS ($1000)	CARRYING COSTS (25 PERCENT)	TOTAL COSTS
1	20,000	$ 1,000	$100,000	$100,000
2	10,000	2,000	50,000	52,000
4	5,000	4,000	25,000	29,000
8	2,500	8,000	12,500	20,500
16	1,250	16,000	6,250	22,250
20	1,000	20,000	5,000	25,000

timates, clerical expenses, telephone costs, and transportation expenses.

Carrying costs of an item include physical storage, interest, taxes, insurance, spoilage, and internal handling. An exact figure for carrying costs is difficult to determine. Since these costs generally vary in direct proportion to the price paid for the item, most organizations express carrying costs as a percentage of the total price paid during some period.

Consider the case of Robinson Machine Company, a manufacturer of commercial business machines. For its large business calculator, the company purchases a total of 20,000 keyboards per year to be used in the final assembly of the product. The cost for each order is $1000, while the purchase price for the keyboards is $40 per unit. The inventory manager has determined that the inventory carrying cost for the keyboards is 25 percent of the inventory value. Exhibit 18-6 presents an analysis relating orders, quantities per order, and the various costs.

To minimize inventory costs, the manager must attempt to minimize both ordering and carrying costs by proper ordering of the keyboards— the *economic order quantity* (EOQ). However, as the number of orders increases, ordering costs increase while carrying costs decrease. This relationship is shown in exhibit 18-7.

To calculate the order quantity that will minimize inventory costs, managers can use two methods. First, they can use the information shown in exhibit 18-7 to determine that the economic order quantity is somewhere between 2500 and 1250 units and 9 and 12 orders per year. The visual method is acceptable in simple cases; however, when inventory costs run into the hundreds of thousands of dollars, a more precise method of determining EOQ is desirable.

A more precise means of determining the EOQ is to derive it algebraically. To begin with, we can describe the various factors in the calculation as follows:

D = total annual demand for the keyboards = 20,000 units

Q = quantity per order

O = ordering costs = $1000 per unit

V = value of the item = $40 per unit

C = carrying costs, expressed as a percentage of average inventory value = 25 percent

If we assume a constant rate of inventory usage, then the average quantity in inventory at any one time is half the order quantity, or $Q/2$. If we also note that the relationships are linear, then setting carrying

EXHIBIT 18-7
Inventory Cost
Relationships

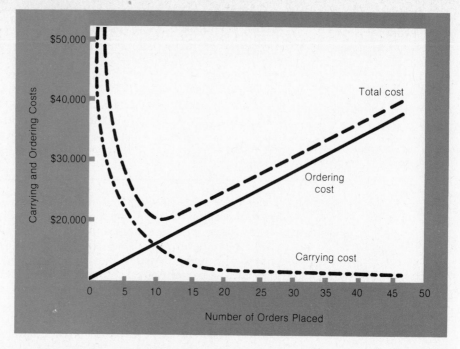

costs equal to ordering costs, we get:

$$\frac{Q}{2}(V)(C) = \frac{D}{Q}(O)$$

(carrying costs)   (ordering costs)

Solving for Q yields:

$$Q = \sqrt{\frac{2DO}{(VC)}}$$

This final equation is commonly known as the EOQ formula, and can be used to solve our business machine by board problem. Using the collected data, we get:

$$Q = \sqrt{\frac{2(20,000)(\$1000)}{(\$40)(0.25)}} = \sqrt{\frac{\$40,000,000}{\$10}} = \sqrt{4,000,000} = 2000 \text{ units}$$

With the use of this formula, we can see that with an EOQ of 2000 units, the optimum number of orders per year is ten, which is a more precise way of calculation.

The simplicity of this method should not lull the manager into total acceptance. Note that two of the most important inputs into the equation are *estimates*—demand and carrying costs. A slight variation in either variable can dramatically change the calculation. Shortages, seasonal variations, transportation problems, and cost changes all must be monitored carefully by the manager.

Program Evaluation and Review Technique (PERT)

During the late 1950s the U. S. Navy was faced with the crucial task of developing and deploying the Polaris ballistic missile program for our submarine fleet. This was no small task since time and coordination were of prime concern. On one hand was the need to make the missile fleet operational as soon as possible. On the other hand, to complete the program would necessitate coordination of efforts among 250 prime contractors, over 9000 subcontractors, and many thousands of individuals. To accomplish this task, the navy developed a network planning technique known as Program Evaluation and Review Technique—PERT for short.[14] Not only did PERT help the navy put the Polaris missile fleet into operation two years ahead of schedule, but since then many other projects, both within and outside the armed services, have adopted PERT in their planning programs.

PERT is termed a network planning model because it deals with a series of interrelated steps and activities. The key objective of the technique is to complete a project with a high degree of coordination. PERT facilitates the planning function through controlling the element of time (and in some cases, cost).

To illustrate PERT, consider the problem of introducing a new consumer product into the market. Past experience has shown that such a venture requires the planning and coordination of at least the manufacturing and marketing functions of an organization. The PERT analysis of this problem is shown in exhibits 18-8 and 18-9. The process elements of PERT are as follows:

1. *Events and activities.* An activity is defined in terms of the time and resources required to complete a specific task. An event is the actual completion of that task. As shown in exhibit 18-8, activity 1—modifying the manufacturing plant—results in event A—completion of plant modifications.

2. *Develop the PERT network.* The activities and events are ordered in terms of occurrence—that is, even G must happen before H. Wherever possible, two or more activities can occur at the same time. For example, while quality control procedures are being developed (activity 4), the plant work force can be trained (activity 5). As noted in exhibit 18-9, the result is a network of activities and events.

3. *Estimate the time required between events.* The third step is to estimate the time required to perform an activity, resulting in the occurrence of an event. Three time estimates are prepared: (a) *optimistic* or minimum time for completion, (b) *most likely* time for completion, and (c) *pessimistic* or maximum time for completion. The three time estimates are combined to compute the expected time (t_e), which is a more realistic time estimate since it is based on three, not one estimation. In computing the expected time, the three time estimates are combined in the following equation, which is based on a Beta distribution:

$$\frac{\text{Optimistic} + 4\,(\text{Most likely}) + \text{Pessimistic}}{6} = t_e$$

Exhibit 18-8 shows the optimistic, most likely, pessimistic, and expected time for each activity.

4. *Identify the critical path.* The critical path in a PERT network is the series of activities and events that results in the *longest* time to complete the project. It is termed the critical path because a delay in completing any of the activities will result in a delay of the entire project. For our example, the critical path is the following: A-C-G-H-K-O-P, which re-

EXHIBIT 18-8   Activities, Events, and Expected Time of PERT

Activity	Event	TIME Optimistic	Most Likely	Pessimistic	t_e
(1) Modify plant	(A) Plant complete	18	24	30	24
(2) Design packaging	(B) Packaging design complete	5	8	11	8
(3) Acquire raw materials	(C) Raw materials received	2	3	4	3
(4) Develop quality controls	(D) Quality control complete	1	3	5	3
(5) Train work force	(E) Work force trained	3	4	6	4
(6) Study price	(F) Price set	1	2	3	2
(7) Production trials	(G) Plant ready	3	6	9	6
(8) Study product specs	(H) Set product specs	1	1	1	1
(9) Develop promotion plan	(I) Promotion set	3	4	6	4
(10) Finalize packaging	(J) Package set	1	2	3	2
(11) Produce inventory	(K) Inventory ready	1	3	6	3
(12) Train sales force	(L) Sales force ready	4	8	12	8
(13) Study transportation	(M) Transportation ready	1	1	1	1
(14) Seek customer orders	(N) Customer orders ready	2	4	6	4
(15) Prepare shipments	(O) Shipments prepared	1	2	3	2
(16) Finalize shipments	(P) Ship	1	1	1	1

quires forty weeks for completion. In other words, this path is the most appropriate time network in which the project can be completed.

5. *Slack time.* The slack time in a particular network is the amount of *extra* time that can be spent without delaying the entire project. For example, the slack times for three of the many networks in exhibit 18-9 are as follows:

A-D-G-H-K-O-P   (40 weeks – 36 weeks =   4 weeks slack time)

B-I-L-N-P   (40 weeks – 25 weeks = 15 weeks slack time)

F-J-K-O-P   (40 weeks – 12 weeks = 28 weeks slack time)

Slack time allows management to "fine tune" particular activities until they are at their optimum value.

Evaluation of PERT.   Since its introduction more than twenty years ago, applications of PERT have grown significantly. Uses can be found not only in plant construction and new product development, but in research and development programs, maintenance projects, development of new processes, or other complex projects with many interrelated and interdependent activities. In some cases, certain federal agencies doing business with contractors require them to plan with PERT.

A number of advantages can accrue to the organization when it uses PERT. First, it draws attention to ways of preventing delays in projects. The manager must now think in terms of time, cost, and interrelationships of events. Second, slack time allows the manager to divert resources to critical areas without endangering the project's progress. Finally, PERT has proven to be an excellent communications tool among man-

EXHIBIT 18-9   PERT Chart for Introducing a New Product

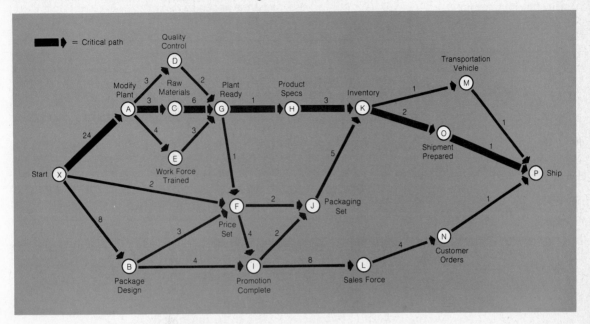

agers. PERT provides a way of better communicating the roles of managers and subordinates involved in a project. In addition, there are the intangible benefits of being able to provide a clear and easily understood picture of the entire project to everyone involved.

Three points of caution should be made regarding PERT. First, PERT is only as good as the information used to develop the network. Thus, managers should evaluate their estimates of time, the interrelationships among events, and so on. Second, any reallocation of resources from slack time adjustments may actually change the critical path. Finally, many of the PERT networks being developed today are far more complicated than our example, In other words, the use of the computer may become a necessity, as such complex networks are beyond the skills of one person to develop or manipulate.

Linear Programming

Consider a problem faced by your author when he worked as a manufacturing manager in a chemical plant. One area of his responsibility was the production of two pigment-type products, one used in the manufacture of paper products (X_1), and the other in the manufacture of paints (X_2). The two products, which are silica based, are essentially the same, except the product used in the manufacture of paper contains less water (i.e., is a dryer product).

Three production stages are required for each product: chemical reaction, drying, and packaging. The chemical reaction time for each 100 pounds of product is identical for X_1 and X_2; however, X_1 takes longer in the drying stage, while X_2 requires slightly more time to package. Because of limited production capacities at the three stages, the products are given only a certain number of minutes per day in each stage. Product X_1 contributes $40 profit per 100 pounds sold, while X_2 contributes $30

EXHIBIT 18-10
Manufacturing
Data

MANUFACTURING PROCESS STAGES	MINUTES REQUIRED PER 100-POUND UNITS		TOTAL MINUTES AVAILABLE
	Product X_1	Product X_2	
Chemical reaction	6	6	960
Drying	8	4	720
Packaging	5	4	600

per 100 pounds. These data are shown in exhibit 18-10. The problem for the manufacturing manager is to allocate the production equipment within the production time constraints, such that profit is maximized.

This problem can be solved using a *linear programming model*.[15] Linear programming is a method that has the purpose of maximizing some goal such as profits, or minimizing some goal such as costs, within certain constraints. The model is termed *linear* because the variables under study are directly and precisely proportional to each other. The linear programming model is particularly useful when the manager must find an optimal way to allocate scarce or limited resources to achieve some goal.

In developing a linear programming model to solve our manufacturing example, two factors need to be discussed:

1. *Objective function.* The objective or goal of our example is to maximize profits for the two products within the time constraints of the production equipment. Mathematically, this can be expressed as:

Maximize Profit $(P) = \$40\ (X_1) + \$30\ (X_2)$

In other words, we need to determine what combination of production of products X_1 and X_2 (in 100-pound units) will yield the highest profits.

2. *Constraining functions.* As expressed in the example, there are a number of constraining factors. First, there are time constraints associated with each production stage—chemical reaction, drying, and packaging. Mathematically, these constraints can be shown as follows (note: $\leq$ means "less than or equal to"):

$6X_1 + 6X_1 \leq 960$ minutes (chemical reaction stage)

$8X_1 + 4X_2 \leq 720$ minutes (drying stage)

$5X_1 + 4X_2 \leq 600$ minutes (packaging stage)

where X_1 and X_2 stand for the amount of product—in 100-pound units—that can be manufactured.

In addition, since it is required that an amount of each product must be produced, this is another constraining function. This can be expressed as follows (note: $>$ means "greater than"):　$X_1 > 0$　$X_2 > 0$

An easy way of solving simple problems as presented here is with graphs. The solution is shown in exhibit 18-11. The graphical solution to the problem requires two steps:

1. *Graph constraining functions.* Each of the first three constraining functions can be graphed through a simple process. For example, if we take the drying stage function, the process is as follows:

$$8X_1 + 4X_2 = 720$$

Setting X_1 equal to 0, we get:

$$8(0) + 4X_2 = 720$$

or X_2 equals 180 100-pound production units. Similarly, setting X_2 equal to 0, we get:

$$8X_1 + 4(0) = 720$$

or, X_1 equals ninety 100-pound units. This result is then plotted on the graph shown in exhibit 18-11.

   Using a similar methodology we can solve and plot the linear relationships for the other two constraint functions.

2. *Solve for maximum point.* The possible solutions to this production problem are contained within the shaded area bounded by the linear constraining functions. This is called the "feasibility space or polygon." The maximum profit will occur at the extreme point of the feasibility space. Visually, this point is located at $X_1 = 40$ and $X_2 = 100$.

   We can also solve the problem mathematically without a graph. Since the first constraining function does not enter into the solution, we

EXHIBIT 18-11
Linear
Programming
Graphical Solution

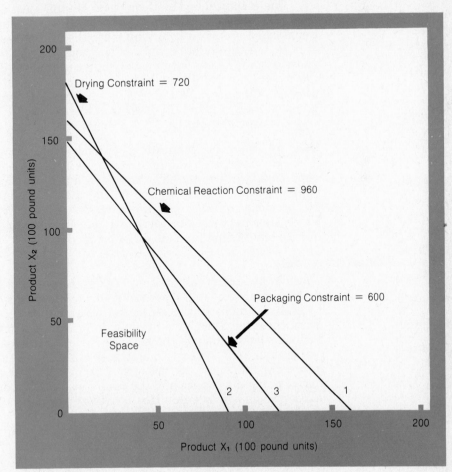

can solve the remaining equations simultaneously by (a) multiplying the third function by -1 and adding the functions together

$$(8X_1 + 4X_2 = 720) = 8X_1 + 4X_2 = 720 \qquad \text{Drying function}$$

$$-1(5X_1 + 4X_2 = 600) = \underline{5X_1 + 4X_2 = 600} \qquad \text{Packaging function}$$

$$3X_1 \qquad\qquad = 120 \qquad \text{or } \underline{X_1 = 40}$$

(b) substituting 40 for X_1 in the third function

$$5(40) + 4X_2 = 600$$

$$4X_2 = 200 \quad \text{or} \quad \underline{X_2 = 100}$$

(c) returning to the objective function and substituting the values for X_1 and X_2

$$\text{Maximum Profit} = \$40(40) + \$30(100) = \$4600$$

In other words, if we produce 4000 pounds of product X_1 (or 40 100-pound units) and 10,000 pounds of product X_2 (or 100 100-pound units), the company can make a total of $4600 profit per day on production.

The graphical and mathematical solutions just described are special cases of the *general* simplex method of linear programming. For more complicated problems involving more than four constraints, it is necessary to use the *iterative* simplex method. This is also a mathematical method which begins with identifying an initial solution that satisfies all the constraints. Modifications are made to the initial solution and incorporated into a second feasible solution. This is repeated until the maximum solution is found. In other words, each step or iteration brings us closer to the final solution.

Uses of linear programming.   Linear programming can be used in most situations where limited resources must be allocated to optimize some objective function. The objective functions can maximize profits, minimize costs, and so on. Uses of linear programming include product mix problems, minimizing transportation costs of shipping products from warehouses to customers, assigning personnel to projects, and allocating limited advertising funds to different products.

Queuing Models

Consider an airline reservations desk with several ticket agents, a bank with a number of teller positions, an automobile service station with several gas pumps, or a supermarket with a number of checkout counters. What these facilities have in common is that each provides service to a customer who demands the service at random times. When customers arrive to find all the service activities busy, they join a waiting line, or *queue*. For the manager, these situations involve two opposing costs: the cost of providing service and the cost of waiting for service. The decision to be made is how to minimize these two costs while still providing effective service.

Queuing problems have different levels of complexity. Exhibit 18-12 shows four examples of structural configurations of queuing systems,

EXHIBIT 18-12
Different Queuing
Model Structures

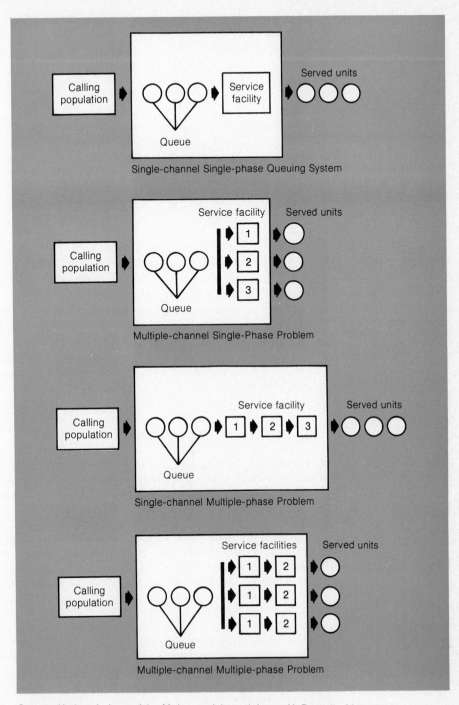

Single-channel Single-phase Queuing System

Multiple-channel Single-Phase Problem

Single-channel Multiple-phase Problem

Multiple-channel Multiple-phase Problem

Source: Herbert L. Lyon, John M. Ivancevich, and James H. Donnelly, Management Science in Organizations *(Santa Monica, Calif.: Goodyear, 1976), pp. 286–87.*

as defined by the type of service facility. Beyond the structural complexity of the servicing unit, queuing systems can vary along several dimensions. The most important include the following:[16]

1. *Population source.* The servicing population can be *finite,* such as employees using an elevator in a large building, or *infinite,* such as people attending a concert.

2. *Arrival characteristics.* Variations of arrival characteristics can include *pattern* (controllable, as in students going to lunch in an elementary school, or uncontrollable, such as the use of a refreshment stand at a football game), *size of arrival* (single, as in a car wash, or batch, such as passengers arriving on an airplane), *time of arrival* (constant, as in an assembly line, or random, such as an emergency room at a hospital), and *degree of patience* (patient, such as trucks waiting to be unloaded, or impatient, as in waiting to cash a check during lunch hour).

3. *Physical features of the queue.* The features of the queue can vary by *length* (infinite, as in waiting for gas for a car, or finite, such as patients in a physician's office) and *number* (single lines, such as golfers waiting to tee off at the first tee, or multiple, such as placing an order at McDonald's).

4. *Selection from the queue.* A number of possibilities exist, including *first come, first serve* (checkout counter in a supermarket) or reservations and emergencies first (a restaurant or an emergency room in a clinic).

5. *Service rate.* The service rate can vary at a *constant* rate, as in a car wash, or by some *mathematical* function, such as customers leaving cars off for repair.

6. *Exit characteristics.* Once a customer or unit is serviced, it can have a low probability of *reservice,* as in a toll station on a turnpike, or a certain frequency of reservice, such as an aircraft scheduled for maintenance.

As one might discern, the development and analysis of queuing systems can become a quite complex activity. Consider the truck unloading dock in a large manufacturing firm. One crew of four employees is responsible for unloading incoming trucks, which are bringing in raw materials to be used in production. As shown in exhibit 18-12, this system may be considered a single-channel, single-phase queuing system. Assume that members of the unloading crew are each paid $6 per hour, with an overtime rate of one and one-half the normal pay scale. The truck drivers earn $10 per hour. During the normal day shift (8 a.m. to 4 p.m.), trucks can be unloaded at a constant rate of thirty minutes per truck, but the trucks are arriving at a constant rate of one every twenty minutes.

The manager of shipping and receiving is concerned with the costs associated with this arrangement. This is apparent since sixteen trucks can be unloaded per eight-hour shift, but a total of twenty-four trucks have arrived, and to service the trucks, a considerable amount of overtime has been paid.

An analysis of this problem using queuing models can proceed as follows. Assume that the first truck arrives a 8 a.m. and is unloaded by 8:30 a.m. with no excess wait time by the driver. The second truck arrives at 8:20 a.m. and is unloaded by 9 a.m., with thirty minutes of unloading time and ten minutes of waiting in the queue. Continuing, the sixteenth truck arrives at 1 p.m. but is not unloaded until 4 p.m., resulting in a

EXHIBIT 18-13   Queuing Cost Analysis

UNLOADING CREWS	REGULAR UNLOADING COSTS ($6/HR × 4 PERSONS)	OVERTIME UNLOADING COSTS ($9/HR × 4 PERSONS)	REGULAR TRUCKERS COSTS ($10/HR)	EXCESS TRUCKER WAIT COSTS ($10/HR)	TOTAL COSTS
One crew	$192	$144	$120	$455	$911
One-and-one-half crews	$288	$0	$120	$0	$408

thirty-minute unloading time, but a three-and-one-half-hour wait (assume that unloading continues through the lunch hour with a replacement unloading crew). Finally, the twenty-fourth truck arrives at 3:40 p.m., but does not leave until 8 p.m. The unloading time is still thirty minutes, but the queue wait is three hours and forty minutes, plus overtime for the unloading crew.

Mathematically, the manager can calculate the amount of time in minutes that the truck drivers spend in the queue as:

$$\sum_{i=2,24}^{N} [(n_i - 2)10 + 40]$$

where n_i is the arrival number of the truck.

Since the first truck has no time in the queue, twenty-three trucks incur an amount of waiting time during the regular shift plus overtime. The calculation reveals a total of 3450 minutes, or 57.5 hours total time in the queue for the truck drivers. Since 12 hours (24 trucks times 30 minutes) is allocated for unloading, a total of 45.5 accumulated hours are incurred by the drivers in waiting to be unloaded. A cost analysis of this problem, shown in exhibit 18-13, indicates that $911 is paid out by the organization in wages for the unloading crew and truck drivers. Of this amount, $599 or 65 percent is expended for problems due to queue wait time and overtime for the unloading crew.

As shown in exhibit 18-13, a solution to the cost problem is to use a second unloading crew to work half-time on the loading dock and the other half on the unloading side. With a second crew, the costs are $408, a significant reduction from the original situation.

The example, while admittedly simple, is not unlike many queuing problems experienced by managers in organizations. In more complicated situations, the use of complex equations may be necessary. The more elaborate queuing models become fairly cumbersome and difficult to develop and understand. In such cases, a different aid, such as simulation, may provide better information.

PRODUCTION AND OPERATIONS CONTROL AND THE MANAGER'S JOB

The skills and roles associated with the management of production and operations control present a number of important implications for the manager's job. From a *managerial skills* perspective, the application of technical skills is found throughout the production and operations control system. Using quantitative models, analyzing quality control and plant layout information, and collecting and analyzing inventory data and purchasing information all involve the development and use of this management skill.

Human skills are important in a number of ways. For example, the nature of the quality control function requires the manager to be well-versed in interpersonal relations. Such information must be presented in a factual, straightforward, and nonoffensive manner if it is to be useful to the receiving manager. Similarly, since many production and operations managers are on the "firing line," human skills are important when crisis situations develop. Managers must be able to keep their cool and lead employees to the solution of problems.

Managerial *conceptual skills* are especially crucial in recognizing where production and operations control fits into the total organizational system. For example, MPR and quality control will not have their maximum effect on organizational performance until they are integrated with the other planning, organizing, leading, and control functions. In addition, diagnostic skills are highlighted in determining the meaning of quality control data, the future impact of layout decisions, and the proper scheduling of production.

The application of these managerial skills in the different roles that managers perform has significant implications for production and operations control. For example, performing in the *interpersonal roles,* production and operations managers act as leaders of their function in exchanges with other functional managers; they must select and train employees to staff important positions in design, scheduling, and quality control; and they must act as liaisons with the external environment in identifying important trends and developments with new production techniques and processes.

The *informational roles* provide another perspective for the production and operations manager. For example, the production planning manager and the quality control manager must monitor and disseminate information about production schedules, inventory levels, and product quality problems. Through the purchasing function, managers communicate with suppliers concerning material and equipment needs. Finally, the major role of production and operations managers is that of *resource allocators*—they must allocate scarce physical and human resources to crucial production activities. They also must be *negotiators* in representing management in labor interactions, act as *disturbance handlers* when transmitting control data to other functional managers, and perform an *entrepreneurial* function when attempting to improve the various steps in the production process.

SUMMARY FOR THE MANAGER

1. Production and operations control, sometimes referred to as production and operations management (POM) is the focal point where planning, organizing, leading, and control come together. The four major elements of production and operations control are selection, production design, production planning, and production evaluation.

2. One of the major components of production design is facility layout—the overall arrangement of equipment, people, materials, storage, and service operations required to produce a product or service. The three main layout patterns—process, product, and fixed position—differ in their keys to success. The process layout is a flexible pattern that requires complex materials flow, storage, and production scheduling, along with a high percentage of highly skilled workers. Because of the sequential nature of a product layout, the balancing of production systems is of prime importance. Finally, the fixed-position layout requires a large work area that places a high degree of emphasis on material flow and availability.

3. One of the fastest-growing approaches to production planning is material requirements planning (MRP). It is a computer-based approach to scheduling that integrates information forecasts of demand, product specifications, and inventory data to produce output reports that can help in material purchases, inventories, and capacity planning, along with a stream of important control data.

4. Quality control is one of the main functions of the production evaluation element. Quality control pervades the entire production process in manufacturing and nonmanufacturing organizations alike. Quality control involves all three types of management controls: input (inspecting incoming raw materials and equipment), process (evaluating work-in-process), and output (checking the quality of the final product).

5. The measurement of quality can involve evaluation by variable or by attribute. The former concerns some form of physical measurement and the latter involves the presence or absence of some characteristic. Acceptance sampling and process control charts are two of the most frequently used statistical control methods.

6. The major keys to success in production and operations control are integrating its components

with the total organizational system, giving attention to the proper personnel staffing of the production units, complementing quantitative analysis with observational skills, adopting a broad-based approach to the measure of performance, and accepting feedback as well as giving it to other units.

7. Four popular quantitative aids in production and operations control were presented. EOQ attempts to minimize inventory costs by investigating the size and cost of an order along with what time an order should be placed. PERT is a technique that has been extensively used in both planning and control functions. As a network model, it develops the best approach to project completion by analyzing the time needed at each stage of the project. Linear programming has been frequently used in resource allocation decisions where knowledge of certain constraints is critical. Finally, queuing models focus on scheduling and sequencing decisions that concern the management of the waiting times of units, equipment, or people in the production process.

8. Production and operations in foreign countries requires an analysis of the potential differences that may exist in such elements as site selection, production design, and construction versus acquisition. Careful and detailed planning is needed before operating and control decisions are made.

9. The skills and roles of the manager's job are as important to this management function as they are to the other functions. Development and use of managerial skills are important in collecting and analyzing production data (technical skills), in the interpersonal exchange involving presentation of quality control data to area managers (human skills), in integrating MRP and quality control with other organizational systems (conceptual skills), and in determining the future impact of layout and production scheduling decisions (diagnostic skills). These skills are used by managers in performing their various roles. Production and operations managers act as leaders of their areas (interpersonal roles), monitor and disseminate information throughout the entire organization (informational roles), and make allocation decisions regarding physical, financial, and human resources (decisional roles).

QUESTIONS FOR REVIEW AND DISCUSSION

1. What is the difference between production design and production planning?
2. Why do managers and economists look at aggregate inventory figures as a sign of an upcoming recession?
3. What is the difference between PERT and MRP?
4. What elements should the manager be concerned with in international site selection?
5. Identify the keys to success for each of the three facility layout patterns.
6. What is the relationship between master production scheduling and MRP?
7. What are the differences between feedforward and feedback control?
8. List some products for which you would insist on a 100-percent quality inspection.
9. How can an airline company use production and operations control to select a particular aircraft—727 or DC-10—for a route?
10. In a bank, where is inventory control important? In a hospital?

NOTES

1. R. B. Chase and N. J. Acquilano, *Production and Operations Management* (Homewood, Ill.: Irwin, 1977), p. 31.

2. E. Meadows, "How Three Companies Increased Their Productivity," *Fortune* (March 10, 1980): 92–101.

3. Chase and Acquilano, *Production and Operations Management,* pp. 157–58.

4. E. W. Davis, ed., *Case Studies in Materials Requirements Planning* (Washington, D.C.: APICS, 1978).

5. J. G. Miller and L. G. Sprague, "Behind the Growth in Materials Requirements Planning," *Harvard Business Review* (September–October 1975): 83–91.

6. R. W. Hall and T. E. Vollmann, "Planning Your Material Requirements," *Harvard Business Review* (September–October 1978): 115–12.

7. "An Unemployment Wallop," *Time* (May 12, 1980): 54–55.

8. Chase and Acquilano, *Production and Operations Management,* p. 425.

9. H. E. Fearon, W. A. Ruch, P. G. Decker, V. G. Reuter, and C. D. Wieters, *Fundamentals of Production/Operations Management* (St. Paul, Minn.: West, 1979), p. 141.

10. Meadows, "How Three Companies Increased Their Productivity," p. 94.

11. R. D. Robinson, *International Business Management* (Hinsdale, Ill.: Dryden, 1973), p. 143.

12. J. Baranson, "Automated Manufacturing in Developing Economies," *Finance and Development,* vol. 8, no. 4 (1971): 12–17.

13. See R. G. Brown, *Decision Rules for Inventory Management* (New York: Holt, Rinehart & Winston, 1967).

14. R. E. Schellenberger, *Managerial Analysis* (Homewood, Ill.: Irwin, 1969), p. 313.

15. See R. I. Lewin and R. Lamone, *Linear Programming for Management Decisions* (Homewood, Ill.: Irwin, 1969); and H. M. Wagner, *Principles of Operations Research* (Englewood Cliffs, N.J.: Prentice-Hall, 1975).

16. H. L. Lyon, J. M. Ivancevich, and J. H. Donnelly, *Management Science in Organizations* (Santa Monica, Calif.: Goodyear, 1976), ch. 13.

ADDITIONAL REFERENCES

Berry, W. L., Vollmann, T. E., and Whybark, D. C. *Master Production Scheduling.* Washington, D.C.: APICS, 1979.

Bishop, J. E. "Integrating Critical Elements of Production Planning." *Harvard Business Review* (September–October 1979): 154–60.

Blank, L. and Solorozano, J. "Using Quality Cost Analysis for Management Improvement." *Industrial Engineering* (February 1978): 46–51.

Francis, R. L. and White, J. A. *Facility Layout and Location: An Analytical Approach.* Englewood Cliffs, N.J.: Prentice-Hall, 1974.

Hayes, R. H. and Schmenner, R. W. "How Should You Organize Manufacturing?" *Harvard Business Review* (January–February 1978): 105–19.

Juran, J. M. and Gryna, F. M. *Quality Planning and Analysis.* New York: McGraw-Hill, 1970.

Mosca, S. "Changing Approaches to Plant Location in Europe." *Worldwide P & I Planning* (September–October 1967).

Orlicky, J. *Material Requirements Planning.* New York: McGraw-Hill, 1975.

Skinner, W. *American Industry in Developing Countries.* New York: Wiley, 1968.

Vinson, W. D. and Heany, D. F. "Is Quality Out of Control?" *Harvard Business Review* (November–December 1977): 114–22.

Honda Motor Company

Near Nagoya, Japan, Honda Motor Company's biggest domestic factory will soon begin an expansion to boost auto production by one-third. But the company will succeed only through excruciating effort. Surrounded by residential housing instead of the farm fields that existed when the plant was built in 1960, the facility will have to squeeze out more cars by further crowding the motorcycle production space that used to dominate the 870,000-square-meter complex. Already, conveyor belts are moving up and down as well as horizontally.

The production pinch in Nagoya hints at a key reason behind Honda's announcement that it will sink $200 million into a new auto production plant in Marysville, Ohio—the first Japanese car assembly plant in the U. S. Yet that is not the only reason, nor likely the central one. The company's decision to build cars in Ohio comes in the face of mounting political pressure in the U. S. to restrict imports of Japanese automobiles, which now command nearly 20 percent of the American new-car market, up from 6.3 percent in 1973, the year before a fourfold increase in oil prices suddenly made Japan's small cars fashionable.

With 353,000 cars sold in the U. S. in 1979, Honda ranks third among Japan's auto makers in the American market; Toyota Motor Co., with 508,000 cars sold in the U. S. is first, just ahead of Nissan Motor Co., which sold 472,000 of its Datsuns in the U. S. in 1979. Still, Honda has good reason to be even more sensitive to the threat of trade barriers because its U. S. sales have grown 134 percent since 1976, compared with 46 percent for Toyota and 75 percent for Nissan. Furthermore, Honda relies on exports for 68 percent of its car sales—compared with 40 percent for Toyota and 44 percent for Nissan—and with 43 percent of its overall car sales coming from the U. S., it is more dependent on the American market than any other foreign auto maker.

But it was Honda's pressing need for new production capacity that tipped the balance in favor of building a new U. S. plant. Not only is the company running out of space at its two auto plants in Japan, but industrial land prices there have zoomed.

Strong demand for Honda cars is not limited to the U. S., and the company's new Ohio plant represents only part of a new worldwide expansion strategy. In addition to the Marysville facility, which will abut an existing Honda motorcycle plant, the company has completed a licensing agreement with British auto maker BL Ltd. to manufacture in Britain a new Honda model in 1981 for the European market. And Honda estimates that during the next four to five years Honda will spend another $130 million to build additional foreign auto and motorcycle plants. Honda also has reportedly agreed to a joint venture with its Yugoslavian distributor, Standard Metalska Industrija, to manufacture nonautomotive engines, and has received preliminary approval to make gasohol-powered motorcycles in Brazil.

For the moment, however, it is the Marysville plant that has impressed the U. S. business community. Auto executives in Detroit applaud the proposal because they have long hoped to see their Japanese competitors endure the same higher production costs—especially for labor—that U. S. companies face. Detroit also has been protesting the 15 percent to 20 percent commodity tax that must be paid on American cars sold in Japan, compared with the 3 percent duty on Japanese cars imported to the U. S.

However, it is far from certain that Honda's much larger Japanese rivals will also enter the U. S. market. They have been studying a production move to the U. S. for years, but Detroit is not yet convinced the Honda move will spark them to action. Toyota and Nissan officials in the U. S. are noncommittal on the subject. Observers in Japan suggest that the U. S. investment could solve Honda's U. S. sales capacity problem and at the same time give the company a potentially significant edge over the other Japanese auto makers. If Honda's investment is not enough to solve strained U. S.-Japanese trade relations, Washington could still establish import restrictions that would penalize Toyota and Nissan much more harshly.

Adapted from "Honda: Building Overseas to Meet Demand Diplomatically," Business Week *(January 28, 1980): 112–17.*

Questions for Discussion

1. What is Honda's strategy for building production facilities overseas?
2. What are the elements or criteria in Honda's site selection strategy?
3. What production and operations problems do you think Honda will face in the U. S. that it does not face in Japan?

A CASE FOR ANALYSIS

Maytag

Mention the name Maytag to a group of people and most times the word "quality" comes to mind first. A growing number of consumers clearly believe in the superiority of Maytag appliances, which have won wider market shares in recent years. The most complicated product, the automatic clothes washer, commands a premium of roughly $70 at retail. Its sales are only one-fourth as large as Whirlpool, the major competitor. However, Maytag's return on equity of over 25 percent is nearly 50 percent more than Whirlpool.

Many people deserve laurels for Maytag's performance, not least its management team who exalts quality and abhors wasteful model changes, and a research department that quietly goes on modifying product designs "under the hood" to lessen vibration, wear, and breakdown. The chief defender of Maytag's reputation, however, is the man in charge of turning laboratory prototypes and books of specifications into gleaming appliances mass-produced at a rate of hundreds per hour. Appliances that will perform so well in millions of homes that at least some Maytag repairmen will really lead the homely lives celebrated in television commercials. That crucial person is Maytag's vice president for manufacturing, Sterling Swanger.

Swanger puts on no airs and sits in a windowless office with desk drawers full of gears and other appliance innards that looks like that of someone two levels further down in the organization. He is a manager of great staying power who can gently monitor, decide, or put the pressure on, if necessary.

Swanger has held the line on quality in an era of widespread temptation to do otherwise. Like many appliance makers, in fact, Maytag is producing a more reliable machine than ever. In the mid-1950s, when the company's late president, Fred Maytag II, laid down a standard of ten years' trouble-free operation, the company's average automatic clothes washer was three years short of the target. Today, grueling "lifetime" tests show a typical machine leaving the loading platform should run fourteen years without serious trouble.

At the same time, the manufacturing division has chipped away at production costs. The plastic top of the water pump in a clothes washer, for example, was formerly put in place with thirteen screws, now it is quickly sealed with the application of heat. In 1979, the division beat its goal of $4 million worth of money savings changes in methods and materials. Such savings, of course, cannot make up for the ever-rising prices of purchased materials or for increases in wages. Along with Frigidaire, Maytag has the highest wages in the industry.

Maytag's Newton, Iowa production plant, with extensive automation and twenty-five miles of overhead conveyors, is awesomely intricate and vulnerable to stoppage at dozens of points. But Swanger has the plant running with the dependability of—well, a Maytag washer. The worst production loss in the past three years occurred when a freak accident in a big press forced a brief four-hour shutdown of the clothes-washer line.

The Iowa location is fertile soil in which someone like Swanger can thrive. The whole organization, most of it right in Newton, has the sort of productive attitude that the founders of work teams dream about. The top people are obsessed with the patient, painstaking pursuit of better products and production methods.

The new products come forth only when Maytag is good and ready. The company's first automatic clothes washer did not appear until 1949, a decade behind the nation's first "home laundry." Since then Maytag washers have gone on to outsell every competing make except Whirlpool (whose sales include the Kenmore line produced for Sears) and General Electric. Maytag has slowly brought out other appliances, but only when it was sure that they could win a place at the top of the market. Since the product mix is limited and model changes are rare, the manufacturing people can concentrate on honing the production process.

As Swanger moved higher with successive promotions, his time-consuming involvement in projects like these came to an end. Today he functions mainly as a maestro, coaxing the best possible performances out of seven department heads who report to him. One of them, Gene Nicol, runs the actual assembly lines and operates largely on his own; on a typical day he spends only a half hour with Swanger, going over production reports. Swanger spends far more time on the other aspects of manufacturing, each of which has some special Maytag touches.

Quality control, for example, is strongly based on the premise that reliability cannot be "inspected" into a product. There's inspection aplenty, of course. Every Maytag appliance is operated just before it is packed for shipment. Clothes washers are hooked up on a slowly revolving "merry-go-round" and run through every function in a fifteen-minute test. Machines that don't work perfectly go to the "boneyard" for repair or dismantlement. (Whirlpool and G.E. also make a final test of every function on each machine and say that their tests, while shorter, are just as good as Maytag's.)

Long before the machines reach the final testing stage, inspectors from the 177-person quality-control department have watched them take shape at critical points on the assembly lines, and before that have sampled and tested the purchased materials and parts that went into them. Maytag is very fussy with suppliers, and in recent years has been working with them to improve the quality of such potentially troublesome components as motors and timers. Thanks to this effort, Swanger says, Maytag repairmen are sending back fewer defective motors and timers than ever.

The real key to quality control, however, is the attitude of the individual Maytag worker. The main role of inspectors, Swanger says, is to "audit" a quality control job that must be done by everybody. Pride helps.

His mission, Swanger observes, is to get people enthusiastic about keeping costs down and quality up, right down to the assembly line. Like any top executive, Swanger must also spend a good deal of his time preparing for Maytag's future. Promising young executives must be groomed for higher posts, and Maytag must be kept informed of new manufacturing technology.

Maytag is unique among manufacturers, particularly in this era of rising costs and the influx of cheap imports. Whether the company can retain its small-company atmosphere, high-quality products, and increasing market shares is a point that only time will decide.

Adapted from Edmund Faltermayer, "The Man Who Keeps Those Maytag Repairmen Lonely," Fortune (November 1977): 192–97.

Questions for Discussion

1. Discuss the key points of Maytag's quality control philosophy and process.
2. What important managerial skills does Swanger exhibit in the case? Do they work for him?
3. What internal and external threats should Swanger carefully consider that may adversely affect the company's high level of success? Do you think Maytag can survive in its present form in the future without major changes?
4. How important is the site of the plant (in a rural Iowa setting) and the type of people who live there, to the quality control function?

VI

The Adaptive Organization and Manager
– Change –

19

Adapting to Change

CHAPTER OUTLINE

KEY POINTS IN THIS CHAPTER

1. Change can be proactive in nature (initiated by the organization) or responsive in nature (where the organization adapts to change).

2. Increased international competition, population shifts, marketplace changes, increased business-government interaction, and new technologies are some of the major external forces for change.

3. Internal forces for change include work-force changes, need for improved productivity, the quality of working life concept, and the availability of resources.

4. The planned change process includes diagnosis, establishing program goals, identifying constraints, selecting a change strategy, implementation, and evaluation.

5. Improved environmental monitoring, increased scope of organizational goals, new strategies and plans, and different approaches to decision making are some of the changes that are occurring in the planning function.

6. Major changes now occurring in the organizing function include the development of the office of the president, continued use of the group manager concept and temporary teams, and new selection, training, compensation, and benefit plans.

7. The need for better productivity measurement, more flexible leadership styles, the ability to adapt to the growing numbers of knowledgeable workers, and the emphasis on a generalistic orientation are some of the changes now occurring in the leading function.

8. The control function is seeing an increased emphasis on budgetary procedures, the continued use of computers in all operations, and the growth of production sharing in international operations.

THE PRACTICE OF MANAGEMENT

The Los Angeles Dodgers

The Los Angeles Dodgers baseball team is one of the most successful organized sports teams, both on and off the field. Good players coupled with attendance figures that approach or pass 3 million each year equate not only to an outstanding won-lost record, but a bottom-line profitability that is the envy of teams in all sports.

How do they do it? A consistently competitive team (only four times in twenty-two seasons in Los Angeles has it lost more games than it has won), excellent weather (only nine rainouts at home in that time), and a market of more than 10 million potential fans to draw from are some easily identified reasons. There are other reasons that are equally if not more important than the above.

First, the owners, the O'Malley family, instilled strong management principles into the Dodger organization, establishing departments for group sales, marketing, and novelties. Another reason is full-time ownership. The O'Malleys and Calvin Griffith of the Minnesota Twins are the only major league baseball team owners who have devoted all their business energies to the sport.

A third important Dodger management principle is personnel stability. Former manager Walter Alston was skipper under twenty-three one-year contracts, a longevity unheard of in the insecure world of the sports manager. Al Campanis, vice president of player personnel, has been with the club for thirty-nine years. In addition, the club builds loyalty with generous salaries and healthy employee benefits, including a profit-sharing plan for nonplayers.

Perhaps the major key to success of the Dodger organization is management's ability to both create and successfully adapt to change. The boldest and most significant change was the transfer of the team from Brooklyn to the untested Los Angeles market in 1958. It also built and totally owns one of the most beautiful stadiums in all organized sports, its facility in Chavez Ravine.

Further proof of Dodger daring is the team's impressive list of baseball firsts: first commercial television broadcast, first pay-TV broadcast, first Spanish-language radio broadcast, and first to buy its own jet. The team also pioneered in baseball instruction as well. It was the first to bring both major and minor leaguers to one spring training site, thus making it easier to track players' progress. It was likewise first to standardize instruction methods throughout its organization. Al Campanis's 1954 book, *The Dodger Way to Play Baseball,* has been printed in several languages. The Dodgers were also the first to promote games by giving away free merchandise throughout the season, including t-shirts, caps, helmets, and bats.

Like any organization, however, resistance to change is also visible. For example, the team has steadfastly refused to accept the designated-hitter rule, along with vetoing any move to permit interleague play between the American and National Leagues. Tight control is also imposed on players, especially those who don't fit the "Dodger Blue" image—generally pictured as clean-cut men who don't make waves. Maury Wills, Dick Allen, and Elias Sosa went to the press with their team problems—they were traded quickly. As team management states, the Dodgers are a business and, like any other, it must act like a business. Players are assets that can be developed or sold.

In the past two plus decades of financial success, the Dodger image has not changed much, according to team announcer Vin Scully. But in the early days in Brooklyn, the Dodgers were "the Bums," who were one step ahead of foreclosure. Few people refer to them as bums anymore.

Suggested from Hal Lancaster, "Los Angeles Dodgers, Again Seeking Pennant, Keep on Winning Fans," Wall Street Journal *(October 5, 1978).*

19 ⬇➡

In his thought provoking book *Future Shock,* Alvin Toffler argues that the environment is—and will continue to be—so dynamic and complex that it threatens people and organizations with "future shock."[1] Future shock occurs when the nature, types, and speed of introduction of change overpower the individual's ability and capacity to adapt. He dramatically illustrates this situation by pointing out that much of what we use daily has been developed within our own lifetime.

No one can escape change, particularly managers. This is why it must be stressed that managers need to be skilled in ways to respond to change to insure the survival of organizations. We will call this *planned change,* because it is a conscious attempt to modify or change certain operations, functions, or processes. Planned change can be of two types: *proactive,* where the change is initiated by the organization, and *responsive,* where managers develop policies or programs (such as contingency plans) to enable organizations to respond quickly and effectively to change that was not planned.

This chapter begins a two-chapter sequence on the challenges to organizations and managers. We will focus on the challenges to *organizations* in this chapter and continue the theme with a focus on the challenges to *managers* in the next chapter. This first chapter is divided into three major sections. First, we will identify some of the major forces for change, including those with external and internal origins. Second, the process of planned change will be discussed. Finally, we will end the chapter with a presentation of the impact of change on the management process.

ELEMENTS OF ORGANIZATIONAL CHANGE

Change can affect all types of organizations, from IBM and the Mayo Clinic, to a small machine-tool manufacturer and a social service agency. Even the neighborhood drugstore is not immune to the effects of change. For instance, the snowballing demands from insurance companies and government legislation have created a paper blizzard so fierce that the very survival of many drugstores is at stake. Pharmacists are spending nearly 40 percent of their time on paperwork, and the resulting squeeze on profitability has helped drop profit margins for the average store by 30 percent over the past decade.[2]

In response to these problems, many pharmacists are turning to time-sharing computers for help. The main advantage of these devices is that they can not only store a great deal of information, but they can quickly calculate many different transactions. Users of time-share computers in drugstores report that the benefits include an increase in filled prescriptions from twenty to fifty per hour, more accurate files on customer needs, increased knowledge of the availability of generic drugs, better control of drug prices, and significant clerical savings. The computer is not without drawbacks: new skills are required of the pharmacist in operating the system, and computer systems can cost as much as $30,000 per store to install.

This example illustrates the main elements of change in organizations. As shown in exhibit 19-1, three major elements have been identified. First is the recognition of certain forces for change. These forces can be of external origin—such as insurance company and governmental requirements in the drugstore example—or internal—such as the drugstores' increase in paperwork and lower profitability. Second, in response to the forces of change, managers are required to diagnose the situation and choose strategies to control the effects of the change. Finally, the change process can influence the way managers perform their functions. In the case of a drugstore, not only are new skills required, but a totally new operating system of files and clerical support is created. In the following sections, we will discuss each of these change elements.

EXHIBIT 19-1
Elements of
Organizational
Change

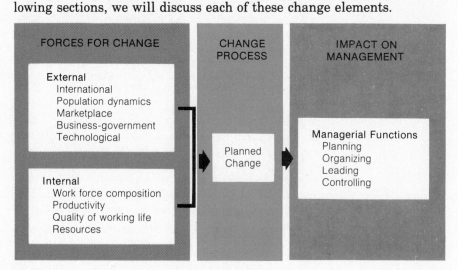

EXTERNAL AND INTERNAL FORCES FOR CHANGE: DOMESTIC AND INTERNATIONAL

In chapter 4, we pointed out important trends and developments that can influence management and performance. This section will continue that theme by highlighting some of the more important forces for change. As before, we will classify these as external and internal forces.

External Forces for Change

The list of forces in the external environment influencing organizations and managers is large and complex. Their effect also varies across industries; for example, forces that affect the airline industry are quite different from those that affect the health-care industry. While not all-inclusive, the following paragraphs describe a number of external factors that are affecting or will soon affect a wide variety of organizations.

International.   Among the most important external forces for change are the effects of managing in the *international* arena. As we have seen, there are as many differences as there are similarities in operating in other countries. Organizations must contend with and adapt to differences in culture, communication patterns, work ethics, and operating procedures before desired levels of performance can be achieved. There is also the increasing occurrence of foreign companies operating in the U. S. While this is in recognition of the stability and growth potential of the U. S. market, it adds to the already heavy competition across many product lines and services.

One movement within the international environment is the growth of *transnational organizations*.[3] The 1960s and 1970s saw the emergence of organizations with operations (production, sales, and/or distribution) in a number of countries—the multinational company. In the 1980s and beyond, the notion of a more integrated world economy may take hold. This will mean not only more specialization of operations within a country, but these operations will be given more autonomy in developing and implementing strategies. With the Ford Fiesta car, the British-French Concorde plane, and Massey-Fergusson tractors we already see products that have major parts manufactured in a variety of countries and assembled in another. We will speak more on this issue later in this chapter when we introduce the concept of production sharing.

Population Dynamics.   A second important external force for change is the changing nature of *population dynamics*. At least three factors are important for managers to consider. First, as we discussed in chapter 10, the decline in the birth rate in developed countries is resulting in a definite shift in the age distribution of the population. This will mean not only visible shortages of skilled and capable people in many professions, but also that we will have to manage with a number of "labor forces" rather than a single "labor force" in mind. Second, the changing age distribution of the population will accentuate different lifestyles that are adopted by people. Finally, geographic movement of people, particularly in the U. S., will force managers to re-think their marketing strategies and plans. The movement of individuals and families from the northeast to sunbelt cities, for example, is already forcing organizations to change the nature of their job offerings, products, and services.

The Marketplace.   For a variety of reasons—some noted above—the *marketplace* in the latter part of this century will be in a dynamic state. Among other things, competitors will introduce new products, improve advertising, reduce prices, or improve services more frequently than in the past. The introduction of light beers, Pepsi's mass advertising campaign against Coke's dominant market position, "super saver" fares on airlines, and the growth of international competition are some examples.

A second point related to the marketplace is the effects of greater complexity in the nature of consumer markets. In the automobile industry, for example, segmentation of markets was initially accomplished by responding to differences in socio-economic class. Different income groups wanted different cars—hence the popularity of the distinctions between Chevrolet, Pontiac, Oldsmobile, Buick, and Cadillac, which are all made by General Motors. Later came the emergence of segmentation by lifestyles. Car and price or status were no longer closely correlated, but car and lifestyle were. Examples included the Mustang, Corvette, and Thunderbird—models that reflected the buyer's lifestyle, not his or her income. Finally, in the 1970s, came market segmentation by population dynamics. The emergence and popularity of such cars as the Eldorado, Volvo, Monte Carlo, and various pickup trucks and vans reflect a more complex distinction among consumers. Young professionals and young marrieds want a particular kind of car, recreation-oriented families want another type, older families and couples desire another model, and so on. A close observation of other products reveals the same type of segmentation. Examples are fast-food and other restaurants, travel, transportation, home preferences (e.g., condominium, apartment, patio home, or single-family dwelling), choice of higher-education institutions, and the like.

Business and Government.   The continuing and growing relationship between *business and government* is another important external force for change. Included are not only issues of regulation-deregulation and the increasing number of employee-related legislative acts, but also concerns over the complex relationships between foreign governments.

The importance of business-government relations has given rise, at least in part, to a new type of manager in the 1970s. Characterized by such executives as Irving Shapiro of Du Pont, Reginald Jones of G. E., Clifton Garvin of Exxon, Thomas Murphy of G. M., John deButts of A T &T, and Walter Wriston of Citicorp, these managers have become activists in society and politics.[4] The main reason is that they recognize that no organization can survive as an island; none can be totally successful without a sound economy and good government-business-society relations. As stated by Shapiro:

> In the past, businessmen wore blinders. After hours, they would run to their club, play golf with other businessmen, have a martini—and that was about it. They did not see their role as being concerned with public policy issues. In a world where government simply took taxes from you and did not interfere with your operations, maybe that was sensible. In today's world, it is not. I'm more interested in what a U. S. Senator thinks than what some businessmen think.
>
> Most of the new executives understand the outside world, and they can deal with policy issues in America and abroad. If I were choosing a chief executive, I would not be overly concerned with his/her education or specific background. I would ask if he/she relates to the larger world as opposed to knowing how to produce widgets and nothing else.[5]

Shapiro's description of the need for an integrated view of business-government-society is clearly an important concept for future managers to understand.

Technological.   Finally, there is the issue of rapid *technological* change, involving change in the tools, equipment, processes, and knowledge used to produce a product or service. The main impact of technological change has been to shorten the life of many products and services to the point where nearly 60 percent of the products used today were not even available ten years ago. Developing new technologies is a high-cost, high-risk activity for organizations; ignoring technological development is even more risky, many times even putting the survival of the organization at stake.

Examples of technological change are all around us:

Microwave ovens, video-recorders, and solid-state televisions, so accepted today, were in but a few homes ten years ago.

Popular automobile models in 1970 included the small but powerful Pontiac GTO and Oldsmobile 442, convertibles, and large six-passenger sedans; today, most of these have been replaced by compact, fuel-efficient models.

An entire industry of energy-saving appliances and building materials emerged during the decade of the 1970s.

Quartz and digital technologies have all but totally changed the timepiece industry.

Disposable lighters and pens have almost entirely replaced their more permanent counterparts.

A number of informed sources have predicted that the era of the 1980s will see great emphasis being placed on innovation processes in organizations. To managers, this means that change will probably occur even more rapidly than in the past decade.

Internal Forces for Change

Organizations and managers must also contend with internal sources of change. These forces can originate primarily from internal operations, or be the result of the impact of external changes. For example, changes in the *composition of the work force* are, in part, the result of changes in population characteristics of the external environment.

Work Force Composition. A number of factors are involved in the anticipated changes in an organization's work force. First, as pointed out earlier, the age distribution in the U. S. population will create some interesting problems for the organization. As shown in exhibit 19-2, it is anticipated that there will be a dramatic increase in the number of managers in the 30-to-40-year-old age group. This, coupled with a decrease in the number of older executives, means that not only will there be a large group of individuals competing for a few high management posts, but there will be a shortage of older executives to train these younger, career-minded managers. A major project for management will be to develop methods to identify the young men and women with the greatest potential and then place them in an accelerated career path.

EXHIBIT 19-2
Age Group Trends
—1976–1985

1976 AGE GROUP	1976 TOTAL POPULATION (IN MILLIONS)	PERCENT INCREASE OR DECREASE	
		To 1980	To 1985
30–34	13.8	+26	+42
35–39	11.6	+20	+49
40–44	11.1	+ 4	+23
45–49	11.8	− 8	− 3
50–54	11.8	− 3	−10
55–59	10.6	+ 6	+ 3

Second, the numbers of women entering the ranks of management will increase significantly. This situation has been brought on in part by stricter enforcement and adoption of antidiscrimination practices by organizations, increased educational achievement, greater emphasis on growth and self-development by women, and more favorable attitudes toward women as colleagues and managers by men. Additional changes in the work force include such trends as hiring the handicapped and the hardcore unemployed, the movement toward temporary employment, dual-career couples, and the increase in the number of white-collar, professional, or knowledge workers.

As Drucker states, the growth in knowledge workers creates the problem for management of the "double-headed monster." Illustrated by the saying "one cannot run a hospital with doctors, and one cannot run one without them," this situation applies to nearly all modern organizations. The "double-headed monster" is where the organization depends on the performance of professionals—such as doctors, lawyers, engineers, and technologists—who are as strongly dedicated to their discipline as they are to the organization. In other words, professional employees seek both acceptance by their profession and high performance levels in their organization position—the problem, as in the case of some university professors, is that these two roles may compete against each other.[6]

Productivity.   Another important force for change—which is both external and internal in origin—is increased emphasis on improving the *productivity* of the worker. In most discussions today, productivity is defined as the amount of goods or services produced per worker or per dollar invested. By most measurements, productivity in the U. S. is significantly lagging behind the rest of the world. (See exhibit 19-3.) Government statistics have revealed that productivity of the American worker has risen one percent or less per year over the last five years. This is a problem for the organization and the country as a whole for at least two reasons. First, if productivity rises as fast as wages, there will be enough goods around to soak up the extra money; but if wages rise faster, there is more money chasing fewer goods—the classic definition of inflation. Second, America's ability to compete in the world market is measured by the unit costs of its goods—how much each unit costs to make. If wages and other costs rise faster than output, American goods will be more expensive abroad.

For example, Japanese productivity increased by 8 percent in 1978, while wages rose 6.1 percent. That gave Japan a 1.9 percent decrease in unit costs. In the U. S., wages outstripped productivity by nearly 8 percent during the same period. The message to managers is clear: U. S. goods and services will become less competitive unless productivity of workers improves. This problem is becoming acute for such U. S. industries as autos, steel, televisions, and textiles.

As shown in exhibit 19-3, although productivity rates are growing faster in other countries, the U. S. still leads overall. On the average, each American still produces more than the individual Japanese or German worker, for example, The gap is narrowing, but as these nations become more service-minded, a slowing down of their productivity increases could result.[7]

EXHIBIT 19-3   Productivity: How U.S. Compares Against the World

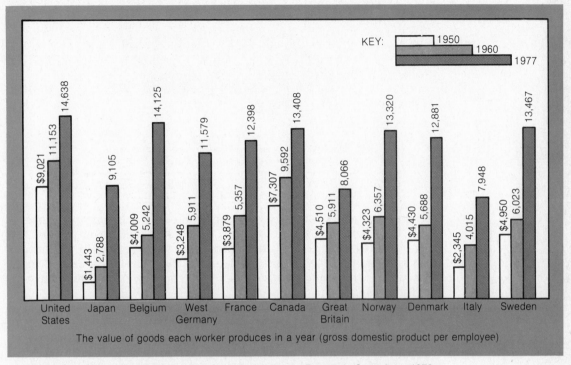

KEY: 1950 1960 1977

United States: $9,021 / 11,153 / 14,638
Japan: $1,443 / 2,788 / 9,105
Belgium: $4,009 / 5,242 / 14,125
West Germany: $3,248 / 5,911 / 11,579
France: $3,879 / 5,357 / 12,398
Canada: $7,307 / 9,592 / 13,408
Great Britain: $4,510 / 5,911 / 8,066
Norway: $4,323 / 6,357 / 13,320
Denmark: $4,430 / 5,688 / 12,881
Italy: $2,345 / 4,015 / 7,948
Sweden: $4,950 / 6,023 / 13,467

The value of goods each worker produces in a year (gross domestic product per employee)

Source: Bureau of Labor Statistics and Congressional Joint Economic Committee, 1979.

Quality of Working Life. A third major force for change—also one that has both internal and external origins—is the growing popularity of the *quality of working life* concept. For years, people have been concerned about work as a means for earning a living, as an outlet for creativity, as a framework for group interaction, as a means of attaining profits, and as a contribution to a viable society. These broad factors include the many facets of the needs, ambitions, and goals of people, organizations, and different cultures and societies.

Because people spend a high proportion of their waking hours on activities associated with their work, it is not surprising that management scholars and practitioners have become increasingly interested in the conditions of the workplace. Given the broad title of the "quality of working life," the focus of interest has centered on such questions as:[8]

1. What are the major elements and causes of employee dissatisfaction?
2. What are an individual's important needs? How do they change with increased material well-being and with personal development? How are they affected by changes in the work environment and changes in the external environment?
3. To what extent are the conditions of work determined by the technology of production and the organization's structure?
4. How can the quality of work affect organizational performance and societal benefits?

Al, do whatever you have to do to increase productivity.
Threaten, cajole, fire at will. Have fun.

5. Is there a conflict between economic performance of an organization and the quality of working life of the individual worker?

These and other questions have been studied by such organizations as G. M., Shell Oil, Xerox, Nabisco, and Cummins Engine over the last few years. The key feature of this movement is strongly related to the concern over worker productivity; that is, can organizations improve the conditions under which most people work such that an improvement in productivity results?

Resources.   Finally, a major concern for managers is the changing nature and availability of needed *resources* to produce products and services. As we have already seen, the changing nature of the work force relates to the issue of human resources. Other resources will also change the management environment in the future.

For example, during the last two decades, world fuel consumption has tripled, oil and gas consumption quintupled, and electricity use increased nearly sevenfold. Worldwide energy shortages have become an almost yearly occurrence, which has affected our daily lives. The availability of gasoline, for instance, has altered significantly the travel and recreational patterns of many Americans. In a similar vein, many knowledgeable people are predicting that during the latter part of this century, water for human and manufacturing consumption will become scarce.

The process of managing limited natural resources is an important responsibility for all in the future, especially managers. Ineffective management can result in continued productivity losses, elimination of product lines, shortages, and general decline in the standard of living of persons all over the globe.

These external and internal forces for change are just some of the many factors that will influence the practice of management in the future. The important key to managerial success is learning how to adapt and live with change. A crucial part of this way of life is understanding and practicing the process of planned change—the subject of the next section.

THE PROCESS OF PLANNED CHANGE

The process of planned change involves a number of distinct steps or subprocesses. The model shown in exhibit 19-4 consists of six basic steps

EXHIBIT 19-4
Process of
Planned Change

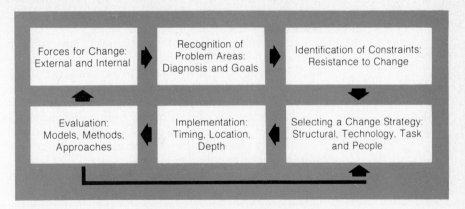

that are linked in a logical sequence. The process begins with the identification of the forces for change, which were presented in the previous section. The remaining steps are discussed below.

Recognition of Problem Areas: Diagnosis and Program Goals

The flow of accurate information from outside and inside an organization is the basis upon which managers are made aware of problems that require some form of change. Internally, an organization generates reports on resource utilization, human resource development, morale, absenteeism, and other areas of interest. The external data base includes information on competitive actions, customer or client demand, governmental regulations, and the public's attitude toward or impression of the organization. By combining internal and external information, managers are able to detect actual or potential problems. The more accurate the information, the more knowledge the manager has to assess the need for change.

A need for change is obvious when key personnel are quitting in alarming numbers, or market share is rapidly declining, or executives are indicted for price collusion. The less catastrophic problems are those that demand managerial attention in the form of careful monitoring of information systems and the use of diagnostic procedures.

In essence, the job of a manager *always* involves diagnosis, whether the focus is on motivation, job design, leadership, or any other managerial topic; it involves diagnosis or study of the properties of interest in a systematic and valid manner. In this case, performing a diagnosis of potential problem areas requires that a manager focus on a number of issues. Some of these are:

1. Determining the specific problems that require correction
2. Deciding or considering the potential determinants or forces causing these problems
3. Deciding what needs to be changed and when to change it to resolve the problems
4. Determining what the goals are for the change and how goal accomplishment will be measured

Answers to these crucial issues are difficult to generate because managers are typically overextended in their workload and do not have time to perform the necessary diagnostic work.

A variety of diagnostic techniques are employed to determine answers to the four issues cited above. Organizations use committees, reports, consultants, task forces, interviews, questionnaire surveys, informal discussion groups, and other information-generating techniques. The central issue is not which technique or combination of them to utilize, it is the gathering of reasonably valid information. Without good or representative information, a change strategy is virtually worthless because it is blindly based. Thus, a thorough diagnosis is important to the success of organizational change efforts.

Toward what ends an organization should be changed and developed is also a necessary question that diagnosis can help answer. For example, is the organization interested in high production at any cost, or does it want a happy work force? The amount of performance that will be sacrificed for morale is basically a goal decision. The goals of organizational change can be made specific enough so that a decision can be reached about whether or not they are being achieved. Therefore, specifications that consider operationalization, constraints, costs, and consequences are a desired result of the diagnosis and evaluation steps in our model.

COMMENTS ON THE PRACTICE OF MANAGEMENT
(See p. 672)

> The Los Angeles Dodger baseball illustration shows that change can occur in all types of organizations, even organized sports clubs. Three particular points should be drawn from the illustration. First, change can be proactive in nature, where the organization actually creates change. Media broadcasts, promotional efforts, and new training techniques that are taken for granted today in baseball were pioneered by the Dodgers. Second, even though change may occur frequently, most successful organizations adapt from a sound foundation. This is brought forth in the stability of Dodger management and its formal structuring. Finally, the examples of interleague play, the designated hitter rule, and the profile of the "Dodger Blue" player draw attention to the fact that organizations successful at change can also resist change.

The Constraints

There are numerous constraints to change that need to be considered. These constraints, which affect any type of change, include leadership climate, formal organization, and individual characteristics.[9]

Leadership climate is the atmosphere in the work environment that results from the leadership style and administrative practices of superiors. The climate is set by the leaders, who can influence subordinates to accept or reject changes implemented from the top executive group. The leader's values, attitudes, and perceptions are all constraining forces.

The *formal organization design* must have some compatibility with the proposed change. For example, attempting to implement a goal-setting program or participative decision-making practices in a rigid and bureaucratic organization is somewhat unrealistic and displays a lack of understanding. There must be some congruence between the program of change and the design of the system if the change is to be effective.

The *individual characteristics* that are important to change programs include learning abilities, attitudes, personality, and expectations.

If employees do not have the ability to utilize computer information, then it makes little sense to introduce highly sophisticated and expensive computer technology. Managers need to continually consider individual characteristics when analyzing potential constraints of a particular change strategy.

Although change is a recurring feature of organizational life, people tend to resist it. Resistance in the form of sabotaging performance standards, absenteeism, filing unfounded grievances, and reducing productivity regularly occurs in organizations. The resistance may be overt, such as slowing down production, or implicit, such as feigning illness so that a new machine does not have to be faced on a particular day.[10]

Employees typically like to have some control over their work environments, the pace of their work, and the manner in which the job is accomplished. When management suddenly announces a change in work design, personnel, equipment, or work flow, there are usually some people who want to have an opportunity to participate in these decisions. In addition, some changes are of such magnitude that they frighten employees because of the uncertainties associated with them. For example, the elimination of an entire layer of the management hierarchy or the closing of a plant and the reassignment of personnel can make the reassigned employees uncertain about their new jobs, supervisors, and colleagues. To understand why people resist, we need to focus on some of the causes from individual and group sources.

Fear of Economic Loss.   Any change that creates the feeling that some positions will be eliminated and employees laid off or terminated is likely to meet with resistance because of the consequential loss of earning power. In a society that requires employment to earn a living, the fear of losing a job is serious. Management would have a difficult time minimizing this fear and would need to make employees believe that job reductions will not follow a change. This involves communication to the work force on why the change is necessary. If employees need to be terminated, the rationale and procedures should be explained. This is not to say that the reduction will be accepted, but a better understanding may result in less disruption in the work process.

Potential Social Descriptions.   By working with each other, employees develop comfortable patterns of communication and interaction. This comfort makes work more enjoyable and permits friendships to develop. Almost any change in structure, technology, or personnel has the potential to disrupt these comfortable interaction patterns or ties.

Inconvenience.   The introduction of a new procedure for handling a job or a new machine to produce units more efficiently may disrupt the normal routine of performing a job. Any change that interferes with the normal patterns of work will generally be resisted.

Fear of Uncertainties.   By establishing a normal routine in performing a job, employees learn what their range of responsibilities are and what the supervisor's reaction to their behavior will be in certain situations. Any change creates some potential unknowns. Employees, before and after changes, speculate about what their modified roles will be and about how their supervisors will respond to them and the changes. This speculation focuses on uncertainties that did not exist prior to the change and results in some resistance to the change.

Resistance from Groups.   Groups establish norms of behavior and performance that are communicated to members. This communication establishes the boundaries of expected behaviors. Failure to comply with such norms can result in ostracism, lack of respect, or restriction of desirable rewards such as praise and recognition. The more attractive or cohesive the group is to its members, the greater the influence that the group can exert on the membership. A group is attractive to the extent it satisfies the needs of its members. If management initiates changes that are viewed as threatening to a group's norms, they are likely to meet with resistance. The more cohesive the group, the greater its resistance to change.

Any change program needs to pay attention to the needs of both the organization and the individual in order to reduce resistance to change. Thus, the individual must be able to perceive personal benefits to be gained by the change. These benefits and potential problems need to be communicated so that an atmosphere of trust is created.

In some cases individuals or groups want to share in planning, analyzing, and coordinating the change effort. This participation may improve an employee's understanding of the need for change and result in a minimization of resistance. The knowledge of how the change program is progressing is also important to many participants. By receiving knowledge of results, an individual has a better grasp of the problems, responses, and future of the change program. Employees like to have this feedback so that some of their questions can be answered and some of their fears reduced.

Strategies for Change

The next step in the planned change process is the identification and choice of change strategies. Exhibit 19-5 identifies four major change strategies—structure, technology, task, and people—while exhibit 19-6 provides some examples of individual change approaches.

Structural change involves, among other aspects, the three dimensions of organizations—grouping, influence, and coordination—discussed in chapter 8. Examples include a large, centralized organization that decentralizes decision making, a change from a functional to a product structure, revising lines of authority and responsibility, and setting up

EXHIBIT 19-5
Organizational
Change Strategies

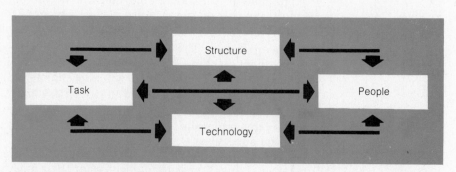

Source: Harold Levitt, "Applied Organizational Changes in Industry: Structural, Technological, and Humanistic Approaches," in *Handbook of Organizations,* ed. James G. March (Chicago: Rand McNally, 1965): 1145.

EXHIBIT 19-6 Examples of Change Strategies

STRATEGY	EXAMPLES	STRATEGY	EXAMPLES
Structure	Matrix organizational designs Decentralization Task forces and teams Socio-technical systems	People	Managerial grid Career planning Training and development Coaching and counseling Survey feedback Confrontation meetings Conflict resolution Management by objectives
Task	Job rotation Job enlargement Job enrichment Job redesign	Technology	Computer systems Production designs Automation Production tools, equipment, and methods

a number of task forces to assist in coordinating the organization's activities.

Technology changes concern the impact of new work methods, processes of production, and improved work flow and information systems. In the automobile industry, the increased use by U. S. manufacturers of automated equipment and the modular assembly revisions instituted by Volvo are some examples of technology change.

Task changes are some of the most frequently used change strategies by managers because of their ease of implementation. Job enlargement, job enrichment, and job redesign, along with an emphasis on team development, fall within the task change category.

Finally, *people changes* attempt to modify the attitudes, values, behavior, interpersonal skills, and potential for advancement of employees. Classroom and on-the-job training programs, external management development programs, behavior modeling approaches, career planning, and behavior modification efforts are aimed at people changes.

One of the most important aspects illustrated by exhibit 19-5 is the interrelated nature of the change strategies. That is, the implementation of any one change strategy can cause a change in one or more of the others. A movement toward decentralization, for example, will not only result in a change in the way work is performed, but may also change the attitudes of employees toward their work. Identifying potential side effects of change is an important management diagnostic skill.

Implementation

The implementation of any organizational change effort has three important dimensions: timing, location, and depth. *Timing* refers to the when of the effort: When is the best time to begin implementation? Two important issues are the organization's operating cycle and the completion of necessary preparation. If the operating cycle is at its peak and if preparation, such as informing those to be affected, has not been completed, timing has not been properly handled. Of course, if an organization is fighting for survival and cannot wait, survival takes precedence over any timing consideration.

Managers involved in implementing change must decide where (i.e., *location*) to initiate the change. Many organizational change scholars believe change should be initiated from the top-management level to the lower-management or operating-employee level.[11] These individuals believe that for change efforts to accomplish their goals, top management must display active support for the program. If top management does not show support and commitment, there is a tendency for others in the organization to essentially "go through the motions," but if top management is supporting a program and participating in it, there seems to be more enthusiasm and interest among subordinates to follow their example.

There is, however, some support for bottom-up or middle-level initiation of programs. Work design changes through a job enrichment technique are usually initiated lower in the organization. Top management may allow these changes to occur, but they are not necessarily involved in them. Thus, for some change efforts, top-management commitment would be displayed through active involvement; in others, it would entail just allowing middle- and lower-level managers and nonmanagers to work out the details and follow through for change. The three locations for implementing organizational change are illustrated in exhibit 19-7.

The *depth* of the implementation involves the issue of target groups. Should the change program be directed at the total organization, units, groups, or individuals? In general, target growth involves not only the particular change strategy that is chosen, but the anticipated side effects of change.

EXHIBIT 19-7
Three Potential Locations for Implementing Organizational Change

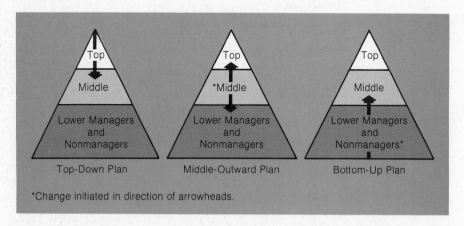

Top-Down Plan   Middle-Outward Plan   Bottom-Up Plan

*Change initiated in direction of arrowheads.

Evaluation

The final segment of our model in exhibit 19-4 is evaluation. It is only recently that scientifically based studies have evaluated the effectiveness of change efforts. Much of the literature on the evaluation of organizational change is based on enthusiastic testimonies by advocates of a particular technique, approach, or model. Fads have resulted in extravagant claims of the superiority of a particular program. The reasons for the abundance of testimonial support and the dearth of scientifically based studies of organizational change and development are clear.

First, it is difficult to conduct field studies over a period of time without the occurrence of major, uncontrollable changes, which contaminate the results of the planned change program and discourage many researchers from becoming involved in the necessary longitudinal studies. Second, it is difficult for those with research skills to gain entree into organizations to perform sound evaluations. Practitioners are concerned, rightfully so in some cases, about the disruption of normal operations when their organizations are intruded upon by researchers, who sometimes refuse to discuss problems in terms that are understandable and application oriented. Finally, many practitioners are not certain about the intent of a particular change effort because the objectives of the effort are not clearly stated.

Despite these problems, there are signs that more refined and valid research on organizational change is occurring. The literature is beginning to indicate that practitioners and researchers are starting to work together more intensely to improve the organizational change programs being implemented. Only through evaluation can feedback be provided that can result in needed improvements.

Evaluation involves the use of interviews, self-report questionnaires, observation, records, or reports of critical incidents. If at all possible, it seems that a combination of these methods needs to be used to acquire a valid picture of the results of the efforts. The feedback received from the evaluation is returned to the forces-for-change stage and to the change strategy phase in our model. This link is essential for assessing any changes that have occurred in an organization, group, or individual. It aids the manager in reaching a conclusion about whether the change was effective in accomplishing desirable goals.

THE MANAGER'S JOB
Frank Borman of Eastern Airlines

For Frank Borman, West Point graduate, fighter pilot, Air Force colonel, and astronaut on Gemini 7 and Apollo 8, taking the chief executive job at Eastern Airlines in 1975 may have been his most challenging task. He took over an airline that was losing money, was heavily in debt, and had developed a reputation among travelers as a discourteous and inefficient company.

In typical Borman fashion, he jumped in with both sleeves rolled up. He quickly cut back on personnel, eliminated expensive executive frills such as limousines and frequent business lunches, instituted new training programs to help employees relate better to passengers, and moved the company's headquarters from lush Rockefeller Center in New York to a plain office building in Miami. He not only persuaded union and non-union employees to take a pay cut, but on one particularly busy weekend he even helped unload baggage at the Miami airport. Within a year, the airline posted record profits and employee morale had increased dramatically.

Borman's key to successful change was simple: get people involved, from the top to the bottom of the organization. He believes that a manager must first understand people and then apply the proper motivational, organizing, and communication techniques. Most importantly, the manager must be committed and involved in the effort from beginning to end.

CHANGES IN THE MANAGERIAL PROCESS

Some of the major changes or situations that will affect the organization and its managers in the future were pointed out earlier in this chapter. The effects of these changes, along with the adequacy of the planned change program, are likely to vary from organization to organization. For example, the effects of changing population dynamics and the emphasis being placed on productivity are applicable to most organizations. On the other hand, the growing complexity of the marketplace may be of more concern to an IBM or a General Foods than it would be to a small-town hospital. This is another example of the contingency approach to management (see chapter 3).

In a general sense, however, we may speculate what the manager of the future will face. Our discussion will focus on some of the changes one might expect to find in the functions of planning, organizing, leading, and controlling.

Changes in Planning

Part II of this book, "Developing the Framework for Performance," concerns the managerial activities analyzing the external and internal environment, organizational goals, strategies and plans, and decision making. These planning activities can be expected to undergo significant changes in the future.

First, one can expect that the dynamic external environment will force many organizations into more extensive and formal *environmental monitoring* and *scanning activities*. While existing market and economic monitoring procedures will be strengthened, the most significant growth will be in monitoring and scanning political activities. A variety of approaches are already being used, including formal committees, paid consultants, and computer simulations.

For example, Behtel Corporation, a large construction company, lost a significant amount of money and assets as a result of the Iranian revolution. Since then, the company has used consultants, such as Richard Helms, former director of the Central Intelligence Agency, to check out political climates in foreign countries. Some major manufacturers such as Caterpillar and General Motors have formed advisory councils of prominent foreign managers and retired governmental officials. Henry Kissinger, for instance, serves as a paid advisor to Merck, the pharmaceutical company, and Goldman-Sachs and Chase Manhattan Bank in the financial sector. On the other hand, Gulf Oil uses an internal four-person international-studies unit to analyze foreign activities, while American Can, General Telephone and Telegraph (G T & E), and United Technologies have developed computer programs to study international situations. The computer analysis, made up of economic, financial, and questionnaire data from overseas managers, provides executives with an assessment by a large number of knowledgeable people.[12]

Managers can also expect to see the *goals* of their organizations change in the future. One of the major changes will be in broadening the scope of an organization's goals. In manufacturing firms, for example, one may expect to find goals that reflect entry and expansion in international markets and a growing concern for the social responsibilities of the organization. A change in the scope of goals for hospitals is already seen. The early goals of taking care of the poor and sick have been transformed into an emphasis on preventative medicine. In the future, the growth of specialized clinics and health-care facilities may force the large community hospital into a further refinement of goals.

The area where the most significant changes will occur is *strategies and plans*. From a strategic point of view, at least two developments will have a major impact. First, many management scholars and practicing managers are forecasting a knowledge and innovation expansion similar to what happened during the 1950s and 1960s. New or totally revamped industries dealing with communications and more technologically oriented health care, manufacturing, and banking are expected to develop.

Due in part to technological change, the second major strategic issue in the future is the definition of "market leadership." In the past, an organization could be expected to survive and be successful if it was one of the top two or three in market share or profitability in the particular industry. Now, many managers are looking to a twofold redefinition of market leadership: being the market leader in a *broad* market such as food products, or a leader in a *narrow* market such as specialized medical diagnostic equipment.[13] These changes are already visible. For example, the number of profitable brewers has declined dramatically in the past two decades to the point where such well-known companies as Schlitz and Strohs are in danger of consistently operating at a loss, or being taken over by a larger organization. On the other hand, while the major domestic airlines are fighting for fewer and fewer long-distance travelers, the regional, intercity, or intrastate airlines are in a boom cycle.

Translating new strategies into action—planning—will require new approaches and skills from managers. The dynamic nature of the external environment will probably require managers to use contingency planning more frequently than in the past. In addition, a new type of planning—entrepreneurial planning—may become more important. The major function of entrepreneurial planning is to search out new opportunities that will enhance the growth of the organization. Venture groups, as discussed in chapter 14, are a preliminary form of this type of planning. As more and more organizations seek to take advantage of new technologies and/ or achieve a market leadership position, entrepreneurial planning can be expected to grow in importance.

Finally, one of the consequences of revised goals, strategies, and plans will be a change in the way *decisions* are made. In particular, new technologies in the computer systems, electronic communication, and management information systems areas will enable managers to convert many decisions from nonprogrammed to routine-programmed decisions. The complexity and dynamic nature of the environment will also see a rise in different types of nonprogrammed decisions, particularly in the strategy formulation and contingency planning functions.

Future managers will probably face the same number of programmed and nonprogrammed decisions as their current counterparts; however, the types of each decision will change dramatically. For example, the availability of computer software and time-sharing packages have already converted some nonroutine decisions to those that are programmed. Stock investment decisions, medical diagnoses, and store locations for retailers have now been at least partially programmed by some organizations.[14]

Changes in Organizing

A wide variety of structural arrangements will be available to organizations in the future. No one structure will dominate as bureaucracy did earlier in this century. Functional, product, mixed, and matrix designs will be just as prevalent tomorrow as they are today. This situation is due, in part, to the recognition by managers that the most appropriate structure is the one that evolves from an analysis of the goals, strategies, and technology of the organization.

At least three major trends in organizational *structure* should become more widely adopted in the future. First, the single chief executive notion is being replaced by a concept known as the "office of the president." The volume of work and numbers of new and complex problems, coupled with the demand for different talents and skills, are issues that are almost impossible for one person to handle. As shown in exhibit 19-8, the duties of the president can be divided among a group of managers, including the president and four executive vice presidents. Each of these individuals is given specific responsibilities for a segment of the operations; thus, the typical hierarchy is replaced with a peer group or coalition of executives.

Exhibit 19-8 also shows the second major trend; that is, the continued movement toward the use of group managers under the office of the president. As discussed in chapter 14, group managers are responsible for particular segments or product lines of the organization. The major change in this concept is that the use of computers and other sophisticated information systems will permit a greater centralization of certain functions. For example, the centralization of such activities as purchasing, personnel, budgeting, planning, and transportation will enable the group manager to maintain greater control, and hence, provide more time to lower-level managers for innovative activities.

The third development in the organizing function will be more frequent use of temporary groups such as task forces or venture groups to do much of the opportunity finding, contingency planning, and innovative problem-solving which, in the past, were infrequently delegated to individual managers.

The combination of changing population dynamics and complex employee needs will have a major impact on the *human resource* policies of organizations. Selection procedures, for example, must adapt to the changing population mix. In addition to the typical high school and college graduate, the labor force (or labor forces) will contain a significant number of people who seek second careers, mature women who want to work after raising their children, and individuals who choose to work instead of retire. All of these people will be competing for similar jobs.

Given this diversity in the labor force, managers will need to take a second look at training programs. Instead of throwing these people into a training program geared for the unskilled worker, for example, it may be wise to ask them: "What can you do?" Mature workers bring with them expertise that the organization needs to recognize. The post-retire-

EXHIBIT 19-8   Office of the President

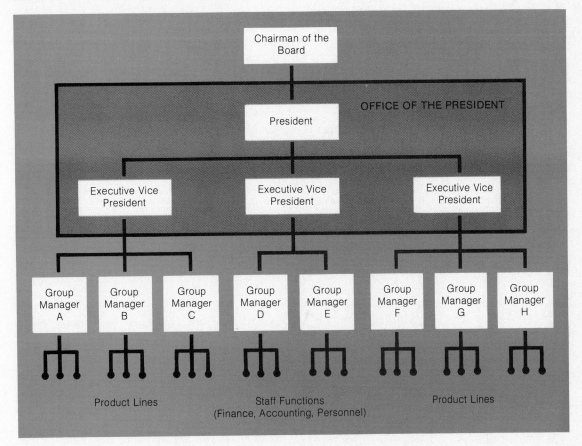

ment-age worker knows *how* to work, and women who enter the work force after years of raising children have really been the "chief executives" of their homes. This knowledge, maturity, and experience must be used by organizations.

Compensation and employee benefit programs will also undergo many changes. The movement toward individuality in these programs will continue. Included will be the greater use of merit pay systems, modified workweeks, and cafeteria benefit plans in which each employee is given a set of options from which he or she can choose the package that gives him or her the most for the money available.

As Peter Drucker states:

> The employer of tomorrow will have to learn to use full-time people and part-time people, men and women, people past retirement age and people who are interested only in working in one functional or technical skill (such as computer specialists) and who move on to a different employer once they have finished their particular assignment. Whether university, hospital, or business, the employer will have to move from managing personnel to managing people.[15]

Changes in Leading

The growing emphasis on productivity and productivity improvements will affect the leading function in a number of ways. First, there will be an increased effort to develop better ways of *defining and measuring productivity*. Before managers can successfully influence others to perform, they must have a clear understanding of what it is they are to achieve. In many cases, managers will be faced with more complex goals and productivity standards (e.g., quantity, quality, morale, employee retention, employee welfare).

Second, because of major changes in the organization's strategies, managers will need to carefully evaluate the *allocation and use of resources*. For example, a strategy of market leadership through specialization will require high concentration of resources in a particular area. In essence, this is what has happened to Chrysler and, to some extent, Ford: Chrysler's financial troubles in the late 1970s forced it to adopt a strategy of concentrating on a particular model of car (small, gas efficient) for a more specialized market. Throughout the entire management hierarchy, managers must make important decisions regarding where the physical, financial, and human resources of the organization will be allocated. Some of these decisions will result in layoffs, plant closings, and product-line eliminations. When the survival of the organization is at stake, the manager must take the lead and the responsibility.

The diversity of the work force will force managers to be more *flexible* in their styles of leadership. Besides leading a work force made up of many older workers, women, and part-time and temporary employees, one of the more interesting leadership issues will be directing the work of the professional or "knowledge" worker. The ranks of such knowledge workers as accountants, engineers, systems analysts, health-care technologists, and service personnel will increase significantly during the latter part of this century, as shown in exhibit 19-9.

This situation will create at least two problems for managers. First, because knowledge workers are potentially the most productive, but also the most expensive, managers need to know the types of tasks best suited for the worker's skills. In other words, management must learn to assign the right people to a task where the potential for improved productivity is greatest. As the complexity of professions increases, this will become a most demanding part of the manager's job.

Second, managers need to understand that the knowledge worker is likely to know more about the way to perform a task than the manager. This means that the manager must be willing to ask employees about the task and the best way to perform it and, most importantly, listen to what they say. Theoretically and practically, this means that a portion of the manager's ability to influence is taken away.

We can see this situation today. For example, most laboratory technologists in hospitals have achieved an education level equivalent to a master's degree. The lab supervisor does not have to tell the technologist how to analyze a patient's blood sample. What the supervisor can do to insure high performance is to make sure that the right person is on the task, all the equipment is functioning well, and working conditions and procedures do not interfere with the successful completion of the work. For future success, managers must recognize that as the number of knowl-

EXHIBIT 19-9 Percentage Change in Employment: 1972–1985 (Projected)

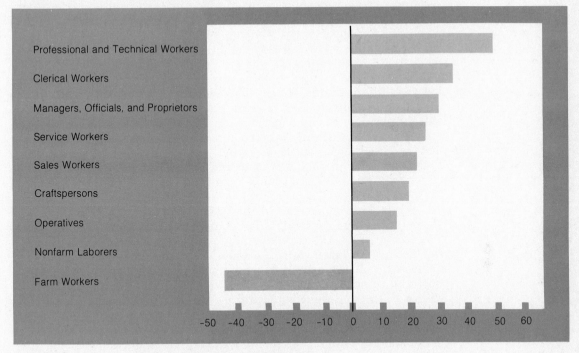

From U. S. Department of Labor, 1977.

edge workers increases, so will the number of "substitutes for leadership" in the form of rules, higher education and training, and peer groups. Adapting to this situation is another important part of managing.[16]

The final change in the leading function is a paradox. On one hand, we anticipate that the number of professionals, specialists, and knowledge workers will increase. On the other hand, the people who manage these workers will increasingly need to be *generalists*. Improved productivity in groups, departments, divisions, or organizations will require managers who are able to *integrate* the various specialized tasks into a unified whole. In other words, the manager is not expected to actually perform the specialized task, but he or she must be able to pull the different tasks together into a smooth-running unit. This means that a premium will be placed on the development of important conceptual skills. We will discuss this issue further in the next chapter on career planning.

Changes in Controlling

Various aspects of the control function will also undergo changes in the future. For instance, with the increased attention expected to be given to the allocation of scarce resources to more specialized strategies, managers can also anticipate greater emphasis on control through budgetary procedures.

In addition to operational budgets, a second type of budget will require the time and attention of managers—the opportunities budget.

Whereas the operational budget concerns acquisition and allocation of resources over a particular period of time, the opportunities budget looks at what resources will be needed in the long-term to take advantage of an anticipated opportunity. Many organizations such as Xerox, IBM, Gulf Oil, and John Deere are already building opportunities budgets into their long-range, entrepreneurial, and contingency planning processes.

Advanced computer systems can also be expected to make further inroads into the manager's job. This will not only include the use of the computer to solve complex problems, but also interactive terminals, which will increasingly be found in the manager's office. Through these devices, managers will tie directly into the organization's information systems for instant data analysis and information. As we noted earlier, increased use of the computer to handle routine and nonroutine decisions will enable managers to devote more time to long-range planning, innovative activities, and the like.

Finally, developments in the international area will provide both opportunities and constraints for management. In the developed countries of the West, the costs of traditional manufacturing activities will rise because of labor costs and labor shortages. In other words, those industries that are heavily labor intensive (e.g., automobiles, construction, and so on) will increasingly become noncompetitive. The opposite will occur in the developing countries, where industries are needed that will provide work for their surplus of labor.

One response to this problem and to the development of the transnational organization is *production sharing*. In production sharing, manufacturing a product can involve operations in more than one country.[17] The capital intensive part of the production process may occur in one of the developed countries, while the labor intensive portion will move to one of the developing countries.

Some examples can even be found today. Men's shoes, for instance, begin with the hide of an American cow; the hide is tanned in Brazil; the soles are made in Haiti; the uppers are put together in the British Virgin Islands; and, finally, the uppers and soles are sent to Puerto Rico or Jamaica for assembly and sent back to the U. S. as a finished shoe. Similarly, Japanese pocket calculators begin with an electronic chip manufactured in the U. S.; the chips are shipped to Singapore, Malaya, or Nigeria where they are assembled with steel components that were made in India. The finished unit is then sent to Japan where the "Made in Japan" label is applied.

Production sharing will place different demands on management. Not only will there be an increased emphasis on production design, quality control, and marketing, but managers must learn how to sharpen their managerial skills. More importantly, managers will be faced with decentralized control that will require the development of new integrating and coordinating methods and techniques. Unless new methods are developed, consumers will be faced with frequent product quality problems, costs will rise, and productivity will suffer.

Summary

The points discussed in this section are some of the many potential changes that managers are expected to face in the future. They are not all-inclusive, nor are they guaranteed to occur. Some are anticipated, while others are already visible. Overall, the most important factor is that change will occur in one form or another. The job of the manager will involve not only diagnosing what these changes are, but also what the appropriate responses should be to insure continued or improved performance. These changes and their suggested impact on the manager's job are shown in exhibit 19-10.

EXHIBIT 19-10   Impact of Change on the Manager's Job: Summary

	CHANGE ELEMENT	IMPACT ON THE MANAGER'S JOB
PLANNING	Increase in Environmental Monitoring and Scanning	New methods and approaches, both formal and informal, need to be developed. Strengthening of technical and diagnostic skill required. Informational roles will be emphasized.
	Revised Organizational Goals	Broadening scope of goals will require improved knowledge of internal and external affairs. Conceptual skills will be stressed.
	New Strategies and Plans	Ability to understand market leadership concept. Redefinition of keys to success for performance. Capacity to conduct both entrepreneurial and contingency planning. Strong emphasis on technical and diagnostic skills and decisional roles.
	New Approaches to Decision Making	Ability to convert nonprogrammed decisions to programmed decisions with computer technology. Recognition of the emergence of new types of nonprogrammed decisions. Technical and conceptual skills stressed along with informational and decisional roles.
ORGANIZING	Different Structural Arrangements	Teamwork and cooperation required by the Office of the President concept. Wider range of skills and roles required to perform in a group manager's position. Increased use of temporary groups and task forces. Strengthening of human and conceptual skills along with interpersonal and decisional roles.
	New Human Resource Requirements	Changing population characteristics will require new approaches to selection, placement, and training. Compensation and benefit programs need to be developed around the merit and individuality concepts. Further emphasis on human and diagnostic skills in addition to interpersonal roles.
LEADING	Revised Leadership Approaches	Changing measures of performance will require new ways of influencing others. More flexible leadership styles will be required. Human skills and interpersonal roles stressed.
	Growth in the Number of Knowledge Workers	Improved mechanisms to integrate the professional needs of the individual with the performance requirements of the organization. Better understanding of the influence of leadership substitutes for knowledge workers. Human and conceptual skills required along with an emphasis on interpersonal roles.
	Need for Generalists	Greater emphasis on managing people rather than being an expert in a field. Strengthening of all skills and roles.
CONTROLLING	New Control Approaches	Increased emphasis on resource allocation procedures. Development of more accurate performance evaluation methods. Improved knowledge and understanding of computers. Technical human and diagnostic skills and decisional roles stressed.
	Production Sharing	Development of new plant location and design approaches. Increased knowledge of international operations. Improved management of decentralized operations. All skills and roles will be emphasized.

SUMMARY FOR THE MANAGER

1. Change is an inevitable consequence of operating in a dynamic environment. For managers, it is important to recognize that change can be initiated by the organization (proactive) or be a reaction by the organization (responsive).

2. The major external forces for change include increased international competition, population characteristic changes, marketplace shifts, increased business-government interaction, and continued technological change. A major key to success with external change forces is being able to identify the elements and develop programs such that the organization is not taken by disruptive surprise.

3. Internal forces for change can originate within the organization, or be caused by external forces. Among the most important forces include changes in the composition of the work force, increased emphasis on improving productivity, the development of the quality of working life concept, and the availability of needed resources.

4. Whether change is proactive or responsive in nature, it is most successful when the organization adapts with a planned approach. The important planned change process elements include diagnosis and program goals, identification of constraints, selection of the proper change strategy,

consideration of timing, location, and depth during implementation, and use of proven evaluation mechanisms.

5. Change can be expected to alter the managerial process. In planning, increased emphasis will be placed on improving environmental monitoring and scanning approaches, revising the scope of organizational goals, developing new strategies and plans, and changing the way decisions are made.

6. Changes in organizing will see new structures, including the office of the president, increased use of group managers and temporary teams and task forces, and new approaches to human resource management.

7. The leading function in the future will see greater concern over productivity measurement, better ways of allocating resources, more flexible leadership styles, concern over the growing number of knowledge workers, and need for a generalist orientation.

8. Changes in the control function will be significant. For example, budgetary procedures will be strengthened, use of computers in control will increase, and new production designs and systems will be needed if the concept of international production sharing continues to grow.

QUESTIONS FOR REVIEW AND DISCUSSION

1. What major forces for change are operating on a state university? A medical clinic?
2. Why is improved productivity such an important issue for all types of organizations?
3. What is the difference between proactive change and responsive change?
4. Discuss the differences between task and technology change strategies. How can one affect the other?
5. What methods can managers use to evaluate a change program?
6. In what ways will the computer affect the manager's job in the future?
7. Why is it important for managers to develop conceptual and diagnostic skills?
8. Why does the increase in the number of knowledge workers pose a problem for future managers?

NOTES

1. A. Toffler, *Future Shock* (New York: Random House, 1970).

2. "Saving Druggists in a Paper Storm," *Business Week* (June 2, 1980): 84.

3. P. F. Drucker, *Managing in Turbulent Times* (New York: Harper & Row, 1980), pp. 103–10.

4. W. Guzzardi, Jr., "A New Public Face for Business," *Fortune* (June 30, 1980): 48–52.

5. M. Loeb, "The Corporate Chiefs' New Class," *Time* (April 14, 1980): 87.

6. Drucker, *Managing in Turbulent Times,* pp. 130–34.

7. "How to Promote Productivity," *Business Week* (July 24, 1978): 146–51.

8. S. Eilm, "The Quality of Working Life," *Omega* (1976): 367–73.

9. N. M. Tichy, "Agents for Planned Social Change: Congruence of Values, Cognitions, and Actions," *Administrative Science Quarterly* (March 1974): 164–82.

10. E. F. Huse, *Organizational Development and Change* (St. Paul, Minn.: West, 1975), p. 113.

11. See W. G. Bennis, *Organizational Development: Its Nature, Origins, and Prospects* (Reading, Mass.: Addison-Wesley, 1969); and R. Beckhard, *Organizational Development: Strategies and Models* (Reading, Mass.: Addison-Wesley, 1969).

12. L. Kraar, "The Multinationals Get Smarter About Political Risks," *Fortune* (March 24, 1980): 85–100.

13. Drucker, *Managing in Turbulent Times,* pp. 62–64.

14. W. Liechel, III, "Everything You Always Wanted to Know May Soon Be On-Line," *Fortune* (May 5, 1980): 226–40.

15. Drucker, *Managing in Turbulent Times,* p. 130.

16. S. Kerr, "Toward a Contingency Theory of Leadership Based Upon the Consideration and Initiating Structure Literature," *Organizational Behavior and Performance* (October 1974): 62–82.

17. Drucker, *Managing in Turbulent Times,* p. 95.

ADDITIONAL REFERENCES

Carlson, H. C. "Measuring the Quality of Work Life in General Motors." *Personnel* (November–December 1978): 21–26.

Heenan, D. A. and Perlmutter, H. V. *Multinational Organizational Development.* Reading, Mass.: Addison-Wesley, 1979.

Hill, C. T. and Utterback, J. M. "The Dynamics of Product and Process Innovation." *Management Review* (January 1980): pp. 14–20.

Kahn, H.; Brown, W.; and Martel, L. *The Next 200 Years.* New York: Morrow, 1976.

Lawler, E. E., III. "The New Plant Revolution." *Organizational Dynamics* (Winter 1978): 2–12.

Levinson, H. *Organizational Diagnosis.* Cambridge, Mass.: Harvard University Press, 1972.

Pascarella, P. "Bottom Line No Longer Priority." *Industry Week* (October 1, 1979): 73–76.

Stead, B. A. *Women in Management.* Englewood Cliffs, N.J.: Prentice-Hall, 1980.

Van Dam, A. "The Future of Management." *Management World* (January 1978): 3–6.

White, B. J. and Ramsey, V. J. "Some Unintended Consequences of Top Down Organizational Development." *Human Resource Management* (Summer 1978): 7–14.

A CASE FOR ANALYSIS

AT & T

AT & T has been anything but a marketing company. Growing as a monopoly, it was required to do little more than wait for its customers to call. Change, however, was forced upon it by an onslaught of competition. Over the last decade, technological advances combined with regulatory and judicial decisions cracked open more and more of Bell's protected markets. Home telephones, complex communications equipment for business, private transmission lines—all of these are monopolies no more.

In response, Bell's top managers threw their weight behind transforming the corporation from a monopolist, intent on preserving its privileges, into a marketing company, responsive to customers and capable of thriving on competition. Since 1973, marketing expenditures for the Bell System have more than doubled, to about $2.1 billion. More than 1,500 managers a year from the operating companies have passed through special marketing courses arranged by headquarters. AT & T has also recruited over a hundred systems analysts from IBM, Litton, Xerox, and elsewhere—an earthshaking event in an enterprise that has always promoted from within in the belief that nobody can understand the System who hasn't grown up with it.

One of those outsiders is Archie J. McGill, a director of market management and development, who at thirty-three was the youngest vice president in IBM's history and directed strategic planning for computer systems. McGill calls AT & T's attempt to become a marketing company "the greatest challenge in American business." He may not be exaggerating. The change will require Bell System executives to rethink the fundamental goals of their business, to examine anew their corporate ideology.

Competition began seeping into residential telephone service back in 1968 with the Supreme Court's famous Carterfone decision, which for the first time allowed Bell customers to attach "foreign" (read non-Bell) devices to the network. For years, AT & T threw up barriers that retarded competitors' progress in the "interconnect" market. But other companies have gradually carved out profitable market niches by selling automatic answering machines and a wide variety of telephone sets that offer styling or special features usually unavailable with standard-issue telephones.

Bell responded four years ago by launching its Design Line of decorator telephones, many of which it buys from outside suppliers. The company also began to open retail Phone Stores for the new line and will have about 1,800 locations by the end of the year. For the short term, AT & T is trying to get more phones into the nation's living rooms. And since in any one month 30 percent of AT & T's residential customers make no long-distance calls, the company is striving to increase usage by advertising the warmth and family solidarity long-distance calls can create.

The basis of Bell's marketing thrust was a study by McKinsey & Co. commissioned back in 1972, mainly out of concern about the System's ability to respond to growing competition. The study found that AT & T lacked internal systems for addressing customer needs, ensuring that new products and services reflected those needs, and delivering individualized solutions to its customers' problems. McKinsey recommended, among other things, that AT & T set up a new marketing department at headquarters under a senior executive, zero in on particular markets where Bell was under strongest attack, and dramatically upgrade the quality of its sales force, which was hardly more than a bunch of order-takers.

Archie McGill, one of the main marketing managers hired by AT & T, left IBM to set up a consulting firm that worked with Japanese corporations and the Soviet Union. He brought to AT & T not only a thorough grounding in IBM's market-planning methods and a number of friends from his alma mater, but a direct personal style guaranteed to fluster Bell managers unused to critical analysis.

McGill's market managers concentrate on anticipating customer needs rather than simply reacting to market developments, as AT & T too often has done in the past. For the first time, AT & T has performed classic analyses, segmenting business customers into more than fifty industry classifications and studying each segment to determine how communications affect profit and loss. The aim of the exercise is to increase the amount of money corporations spend with the Bell System by finding ways the corporations can use communications to fatten their profits—for example, by cutting down on travel.

Based on their studies, the market managers make formal product requests, describing the general characteristics of the products or services they think their industries need. Then a product manager takes over to make sure the market research is translated into new offerings. The product managers carry out analyses to determine whether there will be enough demand for a new product or service to make money on it; if it proves out, they oversee its development. Once the new entry is in the field, the product manager leads a team of functional specialists in such areas as repair, installation, and accounting who keep track of its costs. All this attention to costs and profits might seem second nature for Procter & Gamble, but it is a history-making development at Ma Bell.

The cutting edge of the marketing system is the Bell System sales force, which AT & T has decided to reorganize strictly along industry lines. But it is here where problems have arisen. The plan is laid out in a document that may be the crowning intellectual achievement of the AT & T staff. Called "Bell Marketing System Business Guidelines," it describes in fifty-two pages the philosophy behind the system and exactly how operating companies must structure their sales organizations.

Account executives are to be assigned to various markets, finely segmented according to the federal government's Standard Industrial Classification, and are to be held responsible for all of the customers in that particular industry. The account exec is supposed to be the single Bell "problem solver" for each of his customers.

The kind of "systems selling" AT & T envisions is a far cry from its traditional sales approach. For one thing, the guidelines ask line marketing executives to treat their operating costs not as expenses to be kept down but as investments that will produce revenues and that therefore may have to be increased to get new business. And the marketing manager's performance won't be measured by the host of indices and productivity measures Bell has used in the past—e.g., net service order measurement, which kept track of the number of orders obtained but not the revenue. Now he will be judged only by how much revenue he brings in and how much he has to spend to get it. In short, the new system requires the companies to abandon many of the habits that have grown up around the goal of universal monopoly service—including the emphasis on efficiency for efficiency's sake, and the tendency to wait for a customer to state his needs rather than taking the initiative to serve him.

But there are signs that, for all of McGill's efforts, the system has run into resistance in the operating companies, where such specialists as installers and engineers cling to their old ways of doing business. There has been a tendency for some of the telephone companies, dissatisfied with the plans handed down from AT & T, to thoroughly rewrite them, which undermines systemwide coordination and blocks implementation for months. Only about half of the operating companies have assigned salesmen to S.I.C. segments. Most of them still have the salesmen reporting to the vice president of operations, as in the past, rather than to the vice president for marketing, who remains only a staff officer. Some of Bell's largest customers say that they have no single account exec with whom to work but still must deal with a bewildering array of salespeople.

Moving the marketing system out of the holding company and into the field will take longer, for many of AT & T's salesmen are unqualified to do systems selling, and simply trying to retrain them may not be enough. Some of the people Bell has have been yanked out of mechanical and clerical positions and given a few weeks of training, and they don't even know what a WATS line is.

If it is to be successful, the Bell System sales force will have to change the way its customers think. Many corporate communications managers still focus on cost control rather than looking at communications services as a way to improve their own company's profitability. They won't accept higher communications bills unless there is a lot of sophisticated cost-effectiveness analysis to justify them. And they resent account execs who try to do systems selling without enough experience.

Developing a sales force that can do the job, AT & T executives and customers agree, will take many years. By then, Bell will indeed be the "different business." It will have been driven by competition to adopt a new organizational structure, new management methods, and a new line of products and services. It will have all the outward appearance of a marketing company more than capable of dealing with the likes of ITT and IBM. But whether these changes will be more than window dressing—the illusion without the reality—is still uncertain.

Adapted with permission from "Selling Is No Longer Mickey Mouse at AT & T," Fortune (July 17, 1978).

Questions for Discussion

1. Identify the forces for change at AT & T.
2. What were the findings of AT & T's diagnostic efforts? Identify the goals of change.
3. What were the sources of resistance to change? Why did they resist?
4. What is AT & T's plan for implementation?
5. What are the keys to success that management at AT & T recognizes in order for its change plan to work?

20

Careers in Management

CHAPTER OUTLINE

KEY POINTS IN THIS CHAPTER

1. Job opportunities exist in a number of areas, including health care, engineering, computer analysis, and the service sectors.

2. Today's executives are highly educated, tend to be born in the Midwest, have fathers who are professionals or businessmen, and have worked for three or less organizations during their careers.

3. A concern for results and people and a desire for achievement and responsibility are keys to successful managerial careers.

4. Lessons from the first job concern unrealistic expectations, the first supervisor, confronting politics, and anxiety and stress.

5. Career planning has at least two elements: organizational career planning and individual career planning.

6. Career pathing involves vertical, lateral, and downward moves.

7. Individual career planning concerns and resource analysis, a preference analysis, and a series of career goals.

8. Dual career couples and the mid-career plateau are two of the many current issues in managerial careers.

THE PRACTICE OF MANAGEMENT

Konosuke Matsushita of Matsushita Electric Company

Amid the reserved company men who usually head Japan's big corporations, Konosuke Matsushita has long been an outspoken exception. The son of a poor rice dealer, he founded the Matsushita Electric Company as a three-person shop in 1918 and built it into one of the world's largest producers of consumer electronic goods. In the U. S. and other foreign markets, the firm sells its products under the Panasonic, Technics, Quasar, and National Brand names.

He uses his prestige to expound opinions on everything from nuclear power to management's role as the servant of society. In 1973 he retired, but only to become more active in other fields. Matsushita wrote books, gave frequent lectures, and published the upbeat magazine called PHP—Peace and Happiness Through Prosperity—in Japanese and English.

Recently, he founded the Matsushita School of Government and Management, located southwest of Tokyo. The five-year program is designed to mold Japanese leaders for the twenty-first century. He believes that the next century will be crucial to the survival of the Japanese society, a fact that he feels has escaped his country's political leaders.

The new school, into which Matsushita has already invested $28 million of his own money, attacks the problem of developing managers for the future head-on. Students are given free tuition, room, and board and a $600 per month stipend. The first year 904 applicants were processed, but just 24 passed the grueling written and oral examinations. Matsushita himself participated in some of the screening interviews to select the most suitable candidates to enter the institute.

The scholars, all college graduates, will study under a total of forty-four visiting lecturers, including John Kenneth Galbraith, science fiction writer Sakyo Komatsu, and Matsushita's electronics competitor Masaru Ibuka, founder of Sony Corporation. After three years, students will be dispatched to a variety of organizations and will be sent for six months to a foreign country to gain further experiences.

The curriculum emphasizes foreign languages and physical conditioning, including swordsmanship. But nearly everything that could be taught at a regular college is out. The dominant lecture themes attempt to define the essential qualities of human beings and the disciplines that help a society endure.

More than any other Japanese company, Matsushita Electric reflects the management philosophy of its founder. When a young Japanese manager joins the firm, he soon realizes that he is acquiring more than a job—he is being inoculated with a daily dose of "Matsushitaism." That's best defined by Mr. Matsushita himself: "The purpose of an enterprise is to serve for the benefit of society and to the people of that society."

Adapted from Mike Tharp, "A Talk With a Famed Japanese Entrepreneur," Wall Street Journal (September 21, 1979): 21; and "Leaders for the 21st Century?" Time (April 28, 1980): 81.

20

In recent years, management scholars and practicing managers have given increased attention to assisting individuals and organizations develop career plans and effective career planning programs. This interest originates from the dynamic forces affecting organizations—population characteristics, changes in business patterns, and the growth of international organizations—and because many people are seeking the challenges that are part of a management job. Effective career planning requires knowledge of the needs of individuals and organizations, and an understanding of the forces in the environment.

This chapter has five sections. First, we will identify job opportunities in the 1980s. Second, to assist managers and organizations, we will summarize the results of studies that have developed profiles of the effective managerial career. Third, we will focus on the manager's initial job assignments and the challenges that are faced. Fourth, the elements of a career planning program will be developed. Finally, we will discuss the important keys to success in managerial careers.

JOB OPPORTUNITIES IN THE 1980s—DOMESTIC AND INTERNATIONAL

Managerial careers in the 1980s, like organizations themselves, will be influenced by internal and external forces. In choosing a management career, it is important to recognize these forces (see chapter 10) and be selective in the choice of job and industry.

Many attempt to forecast future job opportunities. This activity, like forecasting sales, is full of many unknowns and uncertainties, yet it is necessary for human resource planning. A summary of these forecasts, identifying the ten most and least promising opportunities through 1985, is shown in exhibit 20-1.

EXHIBIT 20-1
Most and Least Promising Professions through 1985

MOST PROMISING PROFESSIONS	LEAST PROMISING PROFESSIONS
1. Systems/computer analysts	1. School teachers
2. Engineers	2. Librarians
3. Doctors	3. Clergymen
4. Geologists	4. Foresters
5. Health care specialists (nurses, technologists, etc.)	5. Newspaper reporters
6. Accountants/financial analysts	6. Hotel managers
7. Human resource personnel	7. College professors
8. Dentists	8. Military officers
9. City managers	9. Biologists
10. Pharmacists	10. Lawyers

Source: Bureau of Labor Statistics, 1978.

These opportunities reflect important trends that were discussed in the last chapter. First, the high rating given to systems analysts and computer specialists is due to the rapid technological advances expected to occur. Engineers will also benefit from this trend, especially energy specialists, as more and more countries face significant energy shortages. Second, emphasis on productivity will increase demand for jobs related to the managerial control function. This is why accounting rates as a promising profession. Third, future challenges in labor relations, recruitment, affirmative action, compensation, benefits, and changing population characteristics are reflected in the anticipated demand for human resource managers.

Job Opportunities in Industries

A second way of looking at future job opportunities is to analyze employment growth by industry. One analysis is shown in exhibit 20-2. At least three major points can be derived from this information. First, the greatest growth in employment opportunities will be in service industries, particularly the medical field. This confirms the data in exhibit 20-1, where four of the top ten job opportunities were health care related.

Second, significant employment growth will occur in banking, insurance, real estate, and government. Combined with point one, this shows that in a developed country such as the U. S., an increasing number of jobs will be in the nonmanufacturing sector. In developing countries, such as Latin America, Africa, and India, growth in employment in these industries would be much lower. Finally, the growth in employment in the traditional trade, manufacturing, and construction industries is forecast to be lower than the above industries. It should be pointed out, however, that these industries employ a significantly greater number of people than the health care field. This means that while the growth may be slower, the actual number of job opportunities may be much greater.

What does this information mean to managers? Overall, it points to significant opportunities in management. These opportunities will develop not only in the traditional manufacturing industries, but also in the service, financial, and public sectors.

MANAGERIAL PROFILES

In discussing future careers of managers, it may be helpful to look at elements of careers of existing managers. We may be able to learn about key factors that have led to managerial success. In this section, we will summarize recent studies investigating characteristics of managers.

We should caution the reader on two points. First, the majority of the data were collected from middle and executive management levels. Thus, extrapolation to lower managerial levels should be made cautiously. Second, having these characteristics does not necessarily mean that the individual will be a successful manager. Similar to the trait theories of leadership (see chapter 13), success as a manager involves a number of factors, including individual characteristics, the nature of the task, the characteristics of the subordinates, and situational factors.

Background Factors

Fortune magazine recently surveyed top management in the 500 largest industrial companies and the 50 biggest commercial banking companies,

EXHIBIT 20-2   Employment Growth and Opportunities through 1985

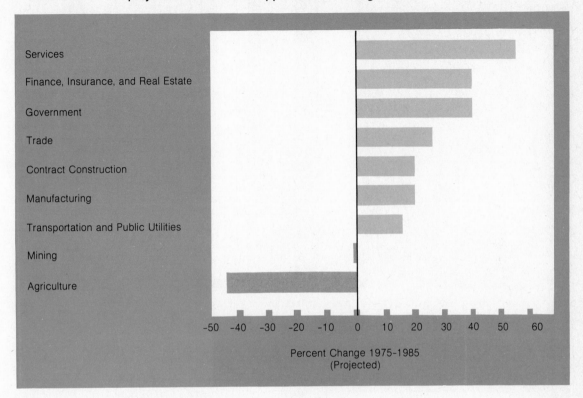

Services

Finance, Insurance, and Real Estate

Government

Trade

Contract Construction

Manufacturing

Transportation and Public Utilities

Mining

Agriculture

-50 -40 -30 -20 -10 0 10 20 30 40 50 60

Percent Change 1975–1985
(Projected)

Source: Bureau of Labor Statistics, 1976.

insurance firms, retailers, transportation companies, and utilities.[1] Among the most interesting findings were responses to questions on the executives' personal backgrounds (see exhibit 20-3). A number of important points can be derived from this information:

1. Confirming recent trends, the data indicate that executives have high levels of educational achievement. Not only are more than 86 percent college graduates, but nearly 40 percent have received graduate degrees. This reflects the growing importance of the M.B.A.

2. The number of high-level executives who come from middle-class backgrounds has swelled, while the proportion from rich families has declined significantly. More executives than ever before grew up in blue-collar households. Yet, it is still striking that nearly 10 percent run large corporations previously headed by their fathers.

3. The Middle West is the breeding ground for high-level executives. Even though it accounts for only 27 percent of the U. S. population, fully 40 percent were born there. It is interesting to note that in the thirty years that *Fortune* has been conducting this type of survey, the number of executives from the Midwest, Far West, and South have all increased, while the number from the Northeast has declined. This reflects, in part, the movement of the population to the Sun Belt states.

EXHIBIT 20-3   Managerial Profile: Background Factors

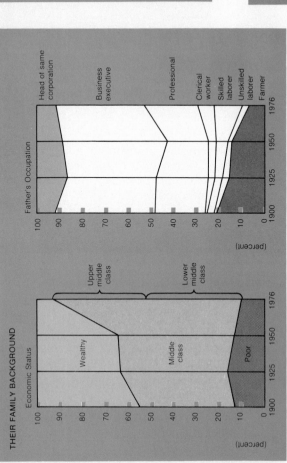

THEIR FAMILY BACKGROUND

Economic Status

Wealthy

Upper middle class

Lower middle class

Middle class

Poor

(percent)

1900 1925 1950 1976

Father's Occupation

Head of same corporation

Business executive

Professional

Clerical worker

Skilled laborer

Unskilled laborer

Farmer

(percent)

1900 1925 1950 1976

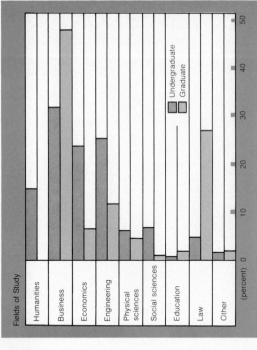

HOW THEY WERE EDUCATED

Highest Level Attained

Attended graduate school

Graduated college

Attended college

(percent)

1900 1925 1950 1976

Fields of Study

Humanities

Business

Economics

Engineering

Physical sciences

Social sciences

Education

Law

Other

(percent)   0   10   20   30   40   50

Undergraduate

Graduate

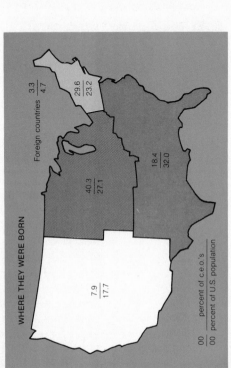

WHERE THEY WERE BORN

Foreign countries   3.3 / 4.7

29.6 / 23.2

40.3 / 27.1

18.4 / 32.0

7.9 / 17.7

00 / 00   percent of c.e.o.'s / percent of U.S. population

Source: Charles G. Burck, "A Group Profile of the Fortune 500 Chief Executive," Fortune (May 1976). Adapted from graphs by Joe Argenziano for FORTUNE Magazine, 1976.

EXHIBIT 20-4   Managerial Profile: Career Factors

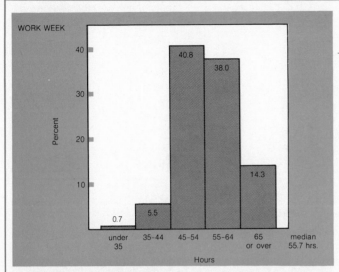

YEARS EMPLOYED BY PRESENT COMPANY		
Number of Years	Times Mentioned	Percent
Under 3	81	4.7
3–5	167	9.8
6–10	267	15.6
11–15	212	12.4
16–20	204	11.9
21–25	232	13.6
26–30	262	15.3
31–35	128	7.5
36 and over	133	7.8
No response	22	1.3
TOTAL	1708	100.0
Average: 19 years		

WORK WEEK

Percent — Hours

under 35: 0.7
35–44: 5.5
45–54: 40.8
55–64: 38.0
65 or over: 14.3
median 55.7 hrs.

PRIMARY CAREER EMPHASIS OF CEO's

(percent)

Financial	19.5
Administrative/ General Management	16.4
Marketing	13.7
Legal	12.0
Production/ Operations	10.7
Technical	10.7
Banking	9.4
Founder	5.1
Other	2.4

NUMBER OF COMPANIES WORKED FOR DURING CAREER		
Number of Companies	Times Mentioned	Percent
1	445	26.0
2	426	24.9
3	413	24.2
4	215	12.6
5	80	4.7
6 and over	81	4.7
No Response	48	2.8
TOTAL	1708	100.0
Average: 3 companies		

Source: Charles G. Burck, "A Group Profile of the Fortune 500 Chief Executive," Fortune *(May 1976); "How Much Does Your Boss Make?"* Forbes *(June 11, 1979); and John A. Sussman, "Making It to the Top: A Career Profile of the Senior Executive,"* Management Review *(July 1979).*

Career Factors

In addition to the *Fortune* study, a number of other investigations have been conducted on the managerial profile. A more recent study of nearly 2000 top executives revealed interesting findings concerning managerial career activities.[2] These results, shown in exhibit 20-4, include:

1. Concurrent with the view of many people, executives devote a great deal of their time to work-related concerns. The executives' median workweek of 55.7 hours can be translated into over 11 hours per day for a five-day workweek, or about 9 hours if Saturdays are included.

2. What is the path to the executive suite? Nearly one in five executives

EXHIBIT 20-5
Managerial Profile:
Career Success
Factors

FACTOR	PERCENT MENTIONED	PERCENT MENTIONED AS MOST IMPORTANT
Aggressiveness	36.2%	3.6%
Ambition, desire to achieve	38.1	9.4
Appearance	14.8	2.1
Concern for people	49.2	9.0
Concern for results	73.7	17.5
Creativity	44.7	2.8
Desire for responsibility	57.8	14.3
Integrity, honesty	66.3	3.6
Intelligence	19.5	2.8
Education	30.5	3.3
Loyalty	23.4	3.2
Professional or technical competence	34.3	2.5
Timing—being in the right place at the right time	22.4	4.5

Adapted from John A. Sussman, "A Career Profile of the Senior Executive," *Management Review* (July 1979): 19.

came from a primary career in finance, followed closely by general management and marketing. Yet, aspiring corporate executives should be cautioned against choosing a financial specialization solely because it is the leading background of today's executives. Twenty years ago the dominant career areas were production and operations, while in the mid-1970s, it was marketing. Current thinking suggests that by the late 1980s, a general management main career emphasis will be dominant, followed by legal, which reflects the growing concerns over federal, state, and local legislative and regulatory activities.

3. Frequent job hopping is not a characteristic of top-level managers. Over three-fourths of the sampled executives have been with three or less companies during their careers. These data are most interesting, given the widely held view that the senior-level executive will move easily if opportunities for advancement are not available at the present employer.

Career Success Factors

What factors do successful managers believe were most important to their achievement? The opinions of executives are shown in exhibit 20-5.

From these results, a profile of the successful manager looks as follows: he or she is concerned with achieving high performance levels (the theme of this book!), and accomplishes this through integrity, responsibility seeking behaviors, creativity, and concern for the people around him or her. At the other end, general appearance, intelligence level, and being in the right place at the right time are of lesser importance than some may believe.

Do these findings fit both male and female managers? Other studies suggest that they do.[3] While women managers are only now reaching the executive suite, recent findings suggest that they have reached the higher management levels through hard work, persistence, and concern for performance. Whether this will prove valid in the future remains to be answered. The major point, however, is that an emphasis on seeking high performance levels through drive, hard work, and persistence is a key to managerial advancement.

LESSONS FROM THE FIRST JOB

A manager's career begins with the first job out of school. Usually, this initial position makes a deep and lasting impression. It can be a rapid learning experience in the ways of organizations, especially where the reward system and personal relationships are different from those experienced in school.

Because those first few years in an organization are so important to future success, it is worthwhile to discuss what the manager can expect to find. Expectations, initial job experiences, political processes, and coping with anxiety and stress will be discussed in this section.

Expectations

Many young managers enter their first job with the expectations that they will immediately take on significant responsibilities, be challenged daily with new experiences, have subordinates reporting to them, and earn a substantial salary. Unfortunately, these same young managers become disillusioned in the first few weeks or months on the job. Their first job is usually routine and boring, they supervise no one, and they find that the first paycheck—after taxes, social security, and other deductions—will not cover payments on a new car, an expensive apartment or home, or a new wardrobe. We are talking about a frequent phenomenon—unrealistic expectations.[4]

These unrealistic expectations have multiple origins. The most formative one is the college education process itself. In school, students become accustomed to studying large organizations and high-level managers who encounter problems or issues that demand the integration of many functional areas. The problems are interesting, challenging, and thought provoking. Unfortunately, students are led to believe that all problems that they will face in years to come will be of the same caliber. The education process has thus prepared the student to perform effectively in *later* positions, but not for the initial assignment out of school.

A second source of unrealistic expectations was discussed in chapter 10—the recruiting process. Company recruiters frequently overstate the attractiveness of the job and the organization to secure a sufficient number of candidates. The candidates are also guilty of inaccuracies when they inflate their abilities or understate their needs in order to improve the chances of being selected. The result is a mismatch between the individual and the job.

Finally, the young manager's family can be a source of unrealistic expectations. As shown in exhibit 20-3, the percentage of managers whose fathers are professional or managerial is increasing. Thus, the conversation at home may not prepare the individual for on-the-job experiences. The young manager whose father is an executive may hear about situations faced by a high-level manager, not the person on the first rung of the managerial career ladder.

What can be done to reduce unrealistic expectations? First, the young recruit should find out what the organization expects of him or her.[5] These expectations are often some of the following:

1. *Competence to get a job done*—to identify the problem and see it through to solution.

2. *Ability to accept organizational "realities"*—to grasp organizational goals, recognition of group loyalties, internal power arrangements, office politics, and the like.

3. *Ability to generate and sell ideas*—including translating technical solutions into practical terms, diagnosing and overcoming resistance to change, patience and perseverance in gaining acceptance of new ideas.

4. *Loyalty and commitment*—to place the goals of the organization ahead of individual motives.

5. *Personal integrity and strength*—to stick to one's point of view without being a rebel.

6. *Capacity to grow*—to learn from experience and to demonstrate ability to take on increasing responsibility and mature in the handling of interpersonal relationships.

Second, beyond participating in realistic job interviews and being honest about one's abilities and needs, it would behoove the young manager to seek out as much information as possible about the company and the job. This can be done by reading current literature and reports on the organization (e.g., *Business Week, Fortune,* and annual reports) and talking to people who are employed by the firm. If this is accomplished *before* the recruiting process begins, the young manager can be in a much better position to discuss important issues.

Initial Job Experiences

During the first few months in the new job, young managers are confronted with many different experiences and activities, all of which contribute to their learning. Among the most important concern the manager's first supervisor, the performance evaluation process, and the challenge of the initial job.

The First Supervisor.   The first supervisor can significantly influence subsequent performance of the new manager. The first supervisor is the initial contact the new employee has with the mentoring process.

Two general types of first supervisors are encountered. First, the supervisor can act with patience, understanding, and insight in directing new managers. He or she can insure that the new managers do the right things at the right time and, if not, that they learn from their mistakes. Consider the case of Russell Banks, founder of Metropolitan Telecommunications Corporation and later president of Grow Chemical Company. According to Banks, the first gap in his education turned out to be that he had not been taught much about analysis of financial statements. But his boss was sympathetic and helpful.

> He gave me a great deal of authority in the beginning and therefore I got into the analysis and preparation of financial statements to a degree most young people couldn't. I became very inquisitive and he responded to every question so that I was able to understand the various systems people would be using and why. . . . He also taught me something about accuracy. When I reconciled a bank's annual statement to within 10 cents, I was proud. But my boss was not. "Russ," he said, "it's not 99 percent correct here, as it is in school. It's either 100 percent or nothing."[6]

On the other hand, the first supervisor can perceive the new recruit as a threat to his or her own position. Not only may the new manager come to the job with more up-to-date technical skills and techniques, but he or she may also enter at a salary that is comparable (or greater) to the supervisor's. Because of this, the relationship between the new manager and the first supervisor may become strained and never develop its full potential.

Performance Evaluations.   In chapter 16, we discussed the performance evaluation process. While we described how the process *should be* done, frequently just the opposite occurs. Young managers expect that feedback on their performance will be frequent and developmental. What can occur is that the performance review must be asked for and, when given, is done poorly. Young managers are left in a state of confusion not only about how well they are doing, but what they can do to improve.

Job Challenge.   We stated earlier that young managers usually find that their first job lacks challenge. Yet, there are ways that they can make their jobs more challenging. For example, they can ask the supervisor for more to do or actually develop new ways of doing the job. Young managers may be too accustomed to having everything presented to them, as in school. The new employee needs to take the initiative by taking a more active role in defining the job. Remember a credo: a job is *what you make it,* not something defined by a job description or the previous job-holder.

Confronting Organizational Politics

One of the most difficult lessons a young college graduate must learn is that there are behind-the-scenes activities in organizations that often supersede more rational processes. Young managers cannot understand, for example, why hard work and long hours haven't paid off in a promotion, why a seemingly straightforward decision took so long to make, and why a supposedly innovative idea was flatly turned down by higher management. These behind-the-scenes activities are well-known to experienced managers as *organizational politics*.

As discussed in chapter 13, a manager's ability to influence others is strongly based on his or her power base. Managers will usually try to improve their power bases in as many ways as possible. This power-seeking behavior can focus on improving one's position (legitimate power), gaining control over important reward system components (reward and coercive power), and becoming skilled in a particular area (expert power).

Another important base is created when managers form political alliances with other managers—that is, when they gain the cooperation of peers and superiors. Such alliances can be used to resolve an issue more quickly than when more formal mechanisms are used. It is a "give and take" process among managers that can have short- and long-term effects on the organization.

What is difficult for the young manager to understand is that a new idea, for example, should not only be considered on its own merits, but also for the impact it has on other systems. For instance, a young sales representative may suggest the use of an improved packaging design for a product. This person may only see the merits of the new packaging design from the view of consumer response. The sales representative's superior, however, may recognize that the new design will disrupt the production process of the manufacturing manager. When the idea is turned down, the sales representative may fail to look beyond the packaging design itself to the more important elements of the "big picture." In other words, the sales manager and manufacturing manager had developed a political alliance over time that had resulted in a smooth-running operation for both.

There are some other important features of organizational politics. One discussed in chapter 9 was position protection. That is, managers seek power through political processes for no other reason than to have power to protect their jobs. They can influence others without exercising that power—just having the power is enough to get what they want. For example, an office manager of a large building complex may have obtained control over the budget for office equipment and must approve all office moves. Other managers may recognize this power base and how important it is for their own expansion plans. Therefore, in order to get what they want (new offices, new furniture, or an increase in word-processing equipment), they quickly form a cooperative alliance with the office manager. In this way, all get what they want—the functional manager receives the needed equipment and the office manager has protected his or her job. As an executive acquaintance of your author once said: "He who controls the gold, makes the rules."

Anxiety and Stress

Anxiety and stress are factors that all managers face in their careers. The young manager is anxious over whether he or she will be able to adapt to organizational practices and perform effectively. As their assignments grow more challenging and demanding, more mature managers question their ability to handle these jobs. Similarly, older managers are concerned about demands of the job, growing competition from young, better-educated managers, and possible conflicts between the job and the family.

As discussed in chapter 15, anxiety and stress are part of every manager's job. On the positive side, stress can motivate, stimulate, and challenge the manager. Some people in fact believe that too little stress on the job can be harmful since the individual loses his or her mental acuity and can become open to other ailments. On the other side, excessive stress, especially when coupled with smoking and poor diet, can result in elevated blood pressure and the increased probability of heart disease.

If stress is excessive, what can the manager do to reduce it?[7] Chapter 15 presented a number of techniques currently used in organizations. It is important for the manager to recognize that stress prevention can originate from the organization or from the individual.

Interviews with top executives show that many of them know how to take stress in stride. Many of these same executives believe that a person cannot reach the top unless he or she knows how to handle stress. Perhaps John Zimmerman, vice president of employee relations for Firestone Tire and Rubber, said it best: "Stress is what you make of it, and that can be the difference between coping and collapsing."[8]

CAREER PLANNING

Increasingly, management scholars and practitioners are turning their attention to assisting employees to plan their career goals and steps in a manner that satisfies developing and changing needs. These attempts reflect a recognition of the increasing importance of career development in people's lives and reflect the increased effectiveness of the organization. The topic that encompasses these issues is known as career planning.

Our coverage of career planning will focus on career stages, organizational career planning, individual career planning, and current issues in career planning.

Career Stages

Most management scholars define a career as a sequence of jobs that unfolds over time. In addition to moving from one job to the next, an individual moves through identifiable occupational and life stages. As shown in exhibit 20-6, there are four distinct career stages.

Stage I concerns the individual's first job in the organization. The main role is one of a trainee who seeks assistance and direction from others. Socialization and group acceptance processes are strong, and the individual concentrates on settling down and learning.

In *Stage II*, the first real managerial position is accepted. The individual begins to make his or her initial contribution to the organization. Job rotation is frequent, as are learning and skills development activities.

Stage III finds the manager at mid-career, where he or she has taken on more responsibility. Leadership roles include not only directional activities, but also mentorship and the training of others. Frequent job changes, sometimes cross-functional, add to the manager's skills.

EXHIBIT 20-6 Managerial Career Stages

| | CAREER STAGES | | | |
	I	II	III	IV
POSITION	Trainee, novice	Manager	Middle manager	Senior manager or Executive
PRIMARY RELATIONSHIPS	Apprentice	Colleague	Mentor	Sponsor
MAJOR ACTIVITIES	Helping, learning, following directions	Independent contributor	Training, interfacing with others	Shaping the direction of the organization
FOCUS OF TASK	Dependence, varied job activities, self-exploration and settling down, initial job choices	Independence, developing competence in an area, creativity and innovation, job rotation	Assuming responsibility, developing skills in training and coaching others, rotating into new jobs requiring new skills	Exercising power, identifying successors, long-range planning, increased outside activities
ORGANIZATIONAL PROCESSES	Training, indoctrination, socialization, acceptance as a group member, conferring of status	First testing of capacity to function, granting of real responsibility, preparation for bigger jobs, further education	Increased leadership activities, movement across functional boundaries	Key communication link, respected member, expert power, preparation for exit

Adapted from E. Schein, "The Individual, the Organization, and the Career," Journal of Applied Behavioral Science *(1971); D. T. Hall and M. Morgan, "Career Development and Planning," in W. C. Hamner and F. Schmidt, eds.,* Contemporary Problems in Personnel, *rev. ed. (Chicago: St. Clair Press, 1977); and G. W. Dalton, P. H. Thompson, and R. L. Price, "The Four Stages of Professional Careers,"* Organizational Dynamics *(Summer 1977).*

Finally, in *Stage IV,* managers find themselves with at least two major job responsibilities. First, now at the higher-management levels, they are responsible for setting the future direction of the organization. They are in their most powerful position, where there is a high degree of control over important organizational resources. Managers in this career stage find that contact with people and organizations outside their own has increased significantly. The second major responsibility of Stage IV is the preparation for exit. This includes not only identifying and grooming possible successors, but preparing oneself for retirement years and the major adjustments that must be made. With recent changes in retirement laws, however, many executives are staying on beyond age sixty-five, either as executives or in an important advisory capacity.

A second way of looking at career stages is to recognize that some careers may be independent of the person's age. One way of depicting this situation is shown in exhibit 20-7, where the two major dimensions correspond to the manager's performance and advancement potential or promotability.[9] The *learner* is a manager who exhibits high promotability, but is performing at a low level. This can be the new management recruit or the person who has recently taken a new position, but has not had time to master it. The *star* is an individual who is doing outstanding work and has the potential to advance further in the organization. *Rocks* are managers who are consistent high performers, but may have plateaued in advancement. These managers provide the solid foundation for the organization's activities and may very well be chosen as mentors. Finally, *deadwood* is a manager whose performance and promotability are low. He or she is making little or no contribution to the organization and could be let go, moved to an unimportant job, or retrained.

The key feature of this approach to describing career stages is that a manager can move *between* the stages, unlike approaches that emphasize the manager's age and the sequential development of the stages. For example, a manager in a high-level manufacturing position may be considered a rock by the organization. Because the manager is a consistently high performer, top management may laterally move him or her to a

EXHIBIT 20-7
Career Stress:
Performance and
Promotability

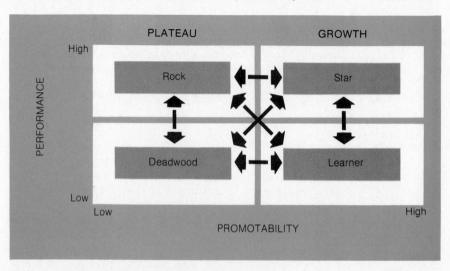

Adapted from T. P. Ference, J. A. F. Stoner, and E. K. Warren, "Managing the Career Plateau," Academy of Management Review *(October 1977).*

newly created position in personnel in an important subsidiary. The transfer essentially moves the manager from the rock category to that of a learner. The hope is for the manager to learn and grow again into a star. Similarly, organizations frequently use extensive training programs to move managers from the deadwood stage to the learner position.

Elements of Career Planning

Even with the growing popularity of the concept there is great confusion concerning the focus and definition of career planning. The literature is full of such terms as manpower planning, career counseling, career pathing, achievement programs, and career development. We believe that a better approach is to look at career planning as consisting of two major elements, as shown in exhibit 20-8: organizational career planning and individual career planning.[10]

EXHIBIT 20-8
Career Planning Elements

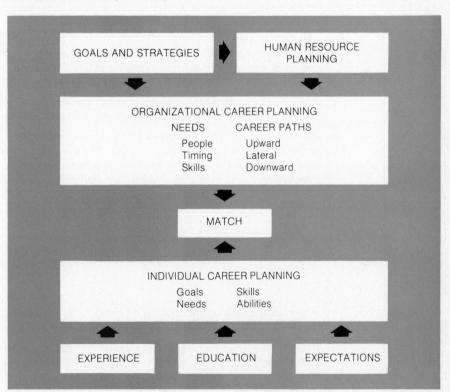

Organizational career planning integrates human resource needs and a number of career activities, emphasizing career ladders or paths. Human resource needs are an important component of the human resource planning process (see chapter 10), while career paths are sets of connecting job families within the organization.

As shown in exhibit 20-9, available career activities or programs are numerous, including career counseling, career pathing, human resource inventories and information systems, and training. Various organizations stress different components or programs.[11] For example:

1. *General Electric* begins with an extensive set of manuals. They are: (a) Career Dimensions I—a workbook for the employee's initial exploration

EXHIBIT 20-9
Specific Career
Activities

CAREER COUNSELING

Career counseling during the employment interview.

Career counseling during the performance appraisal session.

Psychological assessment and career alternative planning.

Career counseling as part of the day-to-day supervisor/subordinate relationship.

Special career counseling for high-potential employees.

Counseling for downward transfers.

CAREER PATHING

Planning job progression for new employees.

Career pathing to help managers acquire the necessary experience for future jobs.

Committee performs an annual review of management personnel's strengths and weaknesses and then develops a five-year career plan for each.

Plan job moves for high-potential employees to place them in a particular target job.

Rotate first-level supervisors through various departments to prepare them for upper-management positions.

HUMAN RESOURCES

Computerized inventory of backgrounds and skills to help identify replacements.

Succession planning or replacement charts at all levels of management.

CAREER INFORMATION SYSTEMS

Job posting for all nonofficer positions; individual can bid to be considered.

Job posting for hourly employees and career counseling for salaried employees.

MANAGEMENT OR SUPERVISORY DEVELOPMENT

Special program for those moving from hourly employment to management.

Responsibility of the department head to develop managers.

Management development committee to look after the career development of management groups.

In-house advanced management program.

TRAINING

In-house supervisory training.

Technical skills training for lower levels.

Outside management seminars.

Formalized job rotation programs.

Intern programs.

Responsibility for manager for on-the-job training.

Tuition reimbursement program.

SPECIAL GROUPS

Outplacement programs.

Minority indoctrination training program.

Career management seminar for women.

Preretirement counseling.

Career counseling and job rotation for women and minorities.

Refresher course for midcareer managers.

Presupervisory training program for women and minorities.

Source: M. A. Morgan, D. T. Hall, and A. Martier, "Career Development Strategies in Industry: Where Are We and Where Should We Be?" *Personnel*, March–April 1979, (New York: AMACOM, a division of American Management Associations, 1979).

of life issues that affect career decisions; (b) Career Dimensions II—a career-planning workbook for the employee; (c) Career Dimensions III—a guide to help the manager have effective career conversations with employees; and (d) Career Dimensions IV—a handbook for those who design and conduct career planning workshops and seminars. These manuals and workshops provide a background for career planning and career management.

2. *Syntex's* interest in career planning evolved from a need to improve management selection and development. Their system uses three elements: an assessment center, a career planning workbook for all employees, and a series of regularly scheduled seminars designed for different level employees.

3. *Crocker Bank* developed a career planning program that emphasizes career counseling, workshops, workbooks, job posting, and integration of career planning with the bank's human resource planning system.

4. At *IBM*, the focus of career planning is the interaction between superior and subordinate. The employee, through descriptive brochures and cassettes, is encouraged to do some precounseling planning by preparing answers to a series of questions. These questions are analyzed with the superior, and a career plan is developed.

As the reader may have surmised, there is no one best approach to career planning. Organizations select those approaches that work best for them and refine them over time.

THE MANAGER'S JOB

Lewis Lehr of 3M Company

Lewis W. Lehr started his career at Minnesota Mining and Manufacturing (3M) shortly after the Second World War, testing competitor's tapes in the laboratory. He claimed it was one of the dullest jobs around, but stuck it out and recently was named chairman of the company.

The comings and goings of top executives spin tales of corporate intrigue at CBS, R.C.A., and Pillsbury—but not at 3M. Its management is one of the most inbred in the U. S., and it has long turned its back on job jumpers—executives who frequently move from one company to another.

According to Lehr, the foundation of this philosophy is an extensive career planning system. The key elements are as follows:

—A strong belief in promotion from within.

—An overall communication program featuring meetings, informal referrals, and communication to increase the awareness of career opportunities.

—A career information center with information about company jobs and career paths, current literature on career planning, and self-development programs.

—An extensive career counseling program.

—Career growth workshops to aid in assessing oneself and one's current job as a base for growth.

—Assistance in making job transfers.

Lehr believes that 3M's approach is to provide support services that make one's current job a continuing base for growth, increase personal satisfaction, and offer the opportunity for increased effectiveness.

Adapted from Lawrence Ingrassia, "3M Uses Promote-From-Within Policy to Breed Managers Like Chairman Lehr," Wall Street Journal (July 7, 1980): 13.

EXHIBIT 20-10
Schein's Cone
Model of Career
Development

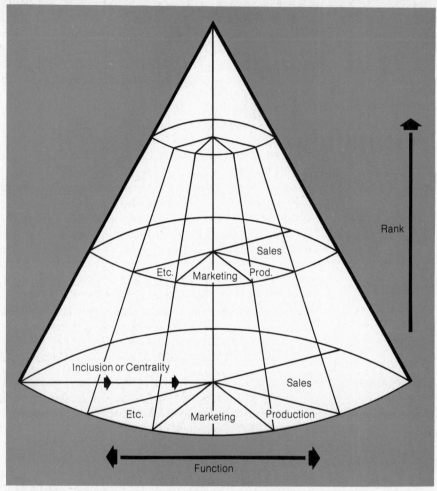

Reproduced by special permission from The Journal of Applied Behavioral Science, *"The Individual, the Organization, and the Career: A Conceptual Scheme," by Edgar Schein, vol. 7, no. 4, p. 404. Copyright 1971, NTL Institute.*

Individual career planning differs philosophically and procedurally from organizational career planning. This type of career planning focuses on individuals and their wants, skills, and desires. Most importantly, individual career planning involves procedures and diagnostic exercises to assist the person determine "who am I?" in abilities and potential. These procedures involve a "reality check" to help the individual toward a meaningful identification of his or her strengths and weaknesses, and encouragement to lead from strength and to correct weaknesses. This "self-assessment" aspect will be developed later in this chapter.

The key to career planning is the match between organizational career planning and individual career planning. The organization has as much to gain as the individual in identifying resource needs and creating and maintaining career paths that move people through talent-challenging experiences.

ORGANIZATIONAL CAREER PLANNING: CAREER PATHING

Career pathing, an important component of organizational career planning, has its origins in the writings of many management scholars. One approach that has had a major impact is the work of Edgar Schein.[12] His model focuses on the career as a set of attributes and experiences of the individual who joins, moves through various jobs, and finally leaves the system. The appropriate career path is defined by the organization after consideration of whom to move, when, how, and how often.

The Cone Model

Schein's *cone model* (exhibit 20-10) indicates that career paths can proceed in at least three directions:

1. *Vertically,* which involves increasing or decreasing one's role in the organizational hierarchy. We have come to know this as moving from first-line management, to middle-management, to the executive level.
2. *Radially,* which is increasing or decreasing one's importance or centrality in the organization. This can mean moving from line to staff positions, or movement toward or away from the organization's "inner circle."
3. *Circumferentially,* which involves moving from one functional area to another in the organization. In other words, managers are moved from, say, production to marketing, from marketing to personnel, and so on.

Schein suggests that with each move, or combination of moves, the organization will attempt to influence the individual, and the individual will attempt to influence the organization in return. The influence of the organization on the individual can occur in two ways. First, in moving vertically or radially, the manager is subjected to different *socialization* attempts by members of the new unit. This is considered an important concept because acquiring new attitudes and values is necessary for high performance. For example, it must be made clear to a manager that in moving from the middle-management to the executive level, not only are different managerial functions emphasized (see chapter 2), but new ways of thinking—as in going from short-range to long-range planning—are needed.

Second, a circumferential move will require additional *training* for the manager. For instance, if a manager moves from a job in production to one in personnel, there will be a need to acquire new skills and knowledge of the different roles that must be performed. The combination of socialization and training prepares the manager to not only perform effectively in the new position, but the new attitudes, values, and skills are added to the manager's qualifications for future moves.

The way the individual influences the organization is through the *innovation* process. While vertical, radial, and circumferential movements force managers into new learning situations, managers also have ideas and approaches of their own. As we have all experienced, sometimes it takes a "new face" in our group to cause change, leading to improved effectiveness. Before a new manager can innovate, or cause change, he or she must be accepted into the group and be recognized for some expert skill or valuable experience.

Schein suggests that socialization and training activities are most prevalent for the younger manager—that is, one who has not yet been fully acclimated to the organization. Innovation occurs most often later in a manager's career, when he or she has acquired more status and experience.

Career Pathing at Sears

Sears, Roebuck and Company has developed an approach to career pathing that uses a potent but very common training and development technique: the job. Sears has a long history of using job assignments for management development.[13] For example, for years college recruits started on the back dock and rotated through six or eight other job assignments during the first twelve to eighteen months. At the end of this period, the individual was assigned to his or her first supervisory position as a department manager. During ensuing years, if the individual was still considered promotable, he or she was assigned to a variety of store staff positions—perhaps as many as seven—ending with the assistant store manager and store manager positions.

Career Pathing Fundamentals.   Career pathing at Sears is based on the following principles:

1. The most important influences on career development occur on the job. Everyday job challenges and demands are important socializing and skill-building mechanisms. The job itself probably has more influence on development than formal classroom training programs (see chapter 10).
2. Different jobs demand the development of different skills. A first-line manager's job, for example, stimulates the development of improved hu-

EXHIBIT 20-11
Career Pathing Example in a Retail Organization

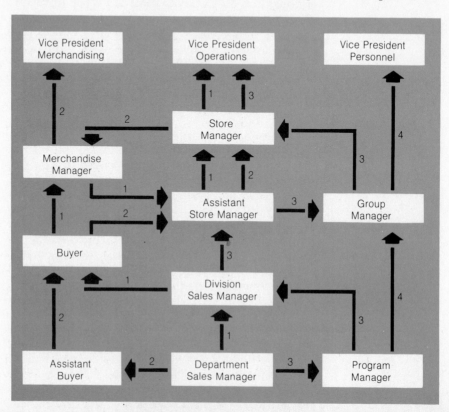

man relations skills, while a position in finance may add to the individual's technical skills.

3. Each new job requires the development of new skills. Very little is learned if a person is put into a different job that demands skills the person has already mastered. A job in a career path should stretch the person to learn new skills or improve existing ones.

4. With a systematic career pathing program, the time required to develop the necessary skills for a chosen target job can be reduced. Without a systematic career pathing program, job assignments often overlap. Some promotions within the same functional area, for example, do not encourage skills development. A systematic approach, on the other hand, minimizes overlap in job demands, and thus enhances the development of skills.

Implementing the Approach.   The Sears approach begins with an evaluation of each job along three basic dimensions: know-how, problem-solving requirements, and accountability. Each of these dimensions itself has subdimensions. For example, know-how is broken down into job knowledge associated with technical, managerial, and human skills. Scores, or points, for each subdimension are assigned to each job, and a total value for each job is then computed.

With the use of this evaluation system, effective developmental career paths can be constructed. Each manager's career path is structured around three experience elements: (1) an increase in at least one skill area (e.g., know-how) on each new assignment; (2) an increase of at least 10 percent in total points on each new assignment; and (3) job moves, which can be upward, downward, or cross-functional.

To illustrate these career path experiences, consider the example in exhibit 20-11. The exhibits shows possible career paths for four managers. Manager 1 begins as a department sales manager with a career path that leads to the position of vice president of operations; manager 2 also begins as a department sales manager, but is career pathed to the vice president of merchandising position; manager 3's career path begins and ends the same as manager 1, but the path is different; finally, manager 4 stays within the personnel function, eventually achieving the vice president's job.

The exhibit also shows many of the possible career experiences that are available to managers in this system. For example, the move by manager 3 from group manager of personnel to store manager entails an increase in at least one skill area. Manager 2's promotion from merchandise manager to vice president of merchandising would involve more than a 10 percent increase in total points. Concerning job moves, each manager at one or more times experiences an upward move. All managers, with the exception of manager 4, also experienced at least one lateral, or cross-functional move. A downward move is shown for manager 1 in the transfer from merchandise manager to assistant store manager.

Before this type of career pathing approach can work effectively, a number of issues need to be confronted. First, managers at all levels must be committed to the new system. As pointed out in the last chapter, moving from a strict vertical ladder approach to one with multiple moves can be met with considerable resistance. Second, managers must not view lateral, cross-functional or downward moves as being blots on their records. It must be clear that these moves are necessary for skills improve-

DOONESBURY   by Garry Trudeau

ment. Downward moves in some organizations, in fact, are made with an agreement similar to academic tenure—that is, the manager accepting a downward move will not be terminated within the near future. Finally, one must be concerned with the accuracy of the job evaluation system. An inaccurate system will identify improper moves and prohibit acceptable moves.

INDIVIDUAL CAREER PLANNING

Individual career planning consists of a number of important elements. The most crucial are a personal resource analysis, a career preference analysis, and career goals.[14]

Personal Resource Analysis

One of the first things a young manager should do in planning his or her career is a personal resource analysis, sometimes referred to as self-assessment.

We may take a lesson from our analysis of organizations, their goals, and their strategies when we develop a personal resource profile. First, the individual should identify various facets that make up his or her important characteristics. Included are needs, skills, experiences, abilities, aptitudes, and so on. Second, evaluate each of these characteristics as being a strength or weakness. For example, an individual can identify "I like to work on challenging tasks" and "I have a number of years as a manager in a high technology industry experience" as certain strengths. On the other hand, this same person can state that "I get bored very quickly if faced with routine job duties" and "I need a graduate degree to progress further in this organization and industry" are weaknesses. If available, a university testing center may be a good start in developing a resource analysis.

Several points should be made about this type of analysis. First, it is helpful to ask other people what they think your strengths and weaknesses are, especially for such hard-to-self-evaluate factors as interpersonal relations and communication ability. Second, it is important to consider your perspective when the analysis is developed. For example, if the brief evaluation above were conducted with the idea that further promotions were sought, then the evaluation would be accurate. Conversely, if the person was looking for long-term tenure in the present job, then some of the strengths and weaknesses could be revised or even switched. Last, this analysis is only as good as the degree of honesty that goes into it. Throwing too many flowers on one's accomplishments or being too critical won't do anything but confuse the issue.

A personal resource analysis is not an end in itself. It is a good start and provides a foundation for further planning.

Career Preference Analysis

The personal resource analysis responds to the issue of "who am I?" The next step is to answer the question, "What do I want from a job and career?" Because this subject deals with preferences, there are no specific guidelines that fit everyone. What may be of assistance are a series of questions that each young manager should answer carefully. The first series of questions concerns *general issues*. For example:

1. *Do I have a geographic preference where I would like to work? Do I want to be near home? near recreation areas? in warmer climates? ski areas? How mobile am I willing to be? How important is the area to my chosen lifestyle?* We all have certain preferences as to where we would like to live, but we must also recognize that the more detailed and demanding our performance, the more limited will be the job opportunities.

2. *What type of organization do I want to work in (profit, not-for-profit, public sector)? What types of industries within these sectors appeal to me (manufacturing, insurance, health care, and so on)? Do I have a preference concerning the size of the organization (large, medium, or small)?* The choices available to the young manager are innumerable. There are opportunities in just about all types of organizations. In recent years there has been a significant movement of managers *across* industries; e.g., engineers working in hospitals, or personnel specialists in social service agencies moving to manufacturing firms. This trend offers increased opportunities for the manager.

3. *Do I want to work for a "go-go" growth organization or one that stresses stability? Would I like to work for a young organization or one that is an established concern?* These are some of the most difficult questions for the young manager. Many people initially want the challenge of working for a young and growing organization, yet few understand that such organizations are more risky to a career. On the other hand, though the established, stable firm may offer less risk (excluding such organizations as Chrysler), one can expect slower career growth than in the younger organization.

Beyond these general issues, the young manager should consider the following specific *job-related* questions:

1. *What kind of job do I want? Do I want a fast track or one where I begin at the bottom and learn all facets of the business? Am I willing to accept a lower initial starting salary because the job is interesting or promises fast career movement after a few years?* The fast track may get the individual to a higher level quicker, but slower movements may provide him or her with a better understanding of the various functions of the organization. A lower starting salary is used by some organizations, especially in retailing, as a screening mechanism for young recruits. If the person is willing to pay his or her "dues" for a few years, the upper managerial ranks offer substantial increases in salary.

2. *Do I prefer to work alone? in small groups? or in large groups? Do I like many committee and task-force assignments?* Understand your preferences and then investigate the policies of the organization. Remember

that as one advances up the organizational management ladder and as the external environment grows more complex, group related activities will probably increase.

3. *What type of supervisor do I work best with? Do I want one who directs my work closely or one who leaves me alone? Do I prefer one who gives me frequent feedback or one who communicates my good and bad points at infrequent intervals?* No two supervisors are the same. Like you, they have their own preferences and needs, so spend time understanding what motivates them. Whatever type of supervisors you work with during your career, remember a key point: learn from them, no matter if it is how to do something correct or how not to do something. Constantly observe, investigate, study, and ask—learn what it takes to be effective in various situations.

Setting Career Goals

Setting career goals is a natural result of the personal resource analysis and career preference analysis steps. In general, career goals consist of two components: time frame and criteria.

Time frame is important because too many young managers set career goals in terms of the highest level in the organization they wish to achieve, without consideration of how they are going to get there. To counter this, many career planning specialists suggest that at least three time frames should be considered. The first is the *immediate* period after graduation from college through the first year of employment. Second, career goals should be set for a period *three-to-five years* after the immediate period. These are probably the most realistic goals to be set because they concern a time where some degree of forecast accuracy can be achieved. Finally, career goals for a period of *ten years* from the present time should be established. Normally, these ten-year goals are quite ambiguous because much can happen in ten years that cannot be forecast. Nevertheless, such goals serve a purpose if for no other reason than that they force the manager to think carefully about what he or she wants to accomplish.

Career *goal criteria* consist of the particular work-related factors that the manager wishes to achieve. The key factors include:

COMMENTS ON THE PRACTICE OF MANAGEMENT
(See p. 698)

The Matsushita selection at the beginning of this chapter presents a number of issues on managerial careers that should be considered by all managers, no matter what their national affiliation. First, the dominant philosophy of a founder such as Matsushita extends throughout the organization and beyond. Management development and its relationship to society in general are strong themes.

Second, the reader must recognize that cultural differences play an important role in career planning in Japan. Essentially, most jobs are taken for life, which means that adaptation to the policies and values of the organization are mandatory. Lastly, the type of educational training in Matsushita's new management school may be a preview of things to come. That is, education and career growth may be considered and discussed in a format that is quite different than that which is currently operating. Normal college training may prepare the individual with technical skills—the higher-level skills may need to be acquired by a separate educational mechanism.

1. Specific job titles
2. Target salary
3. Number of different jobs held during a period
4. Number of people you would like to supervise
5. Level of educational achievement (e.g., M.B.A., C.P.A., and so on)
6. Type of lifestyle you wish to live
7. Level of responsibility
8. Type, size, and growth of employing organization

It may also be helpful for the young manager to select priorities among criteria within each time frame.

Career goals should be frequently analyzed and revised. Far too often, job-related and/or family-related situations can totally revamp one's career planning. Career goals should be examined at least once a year to insure their accuracy with respect to current events.

CURRENT ISSUES IN MANAGERIAL CAREERS

Managerial careers are exciting, challenging, but increasingly complex. We have chosen two important current issues for discussion—dual-career couples and the mid-career plateau.

Dual-Career Couples

An ever-increasing problem faced by individuals and organizations is the managing of dual careers. *Dual careers* describes the husband and wife who both have full-time careers, whether in similar or different fields, in the same or different organizations. There has been a rapid increase in the number of married women who have joined the work force on a full-time basis. More than one-half of all mothers with children under the age of three are in the work force. In addition, nearly 58 percent of all working women are married and living with employed spouses. This means that more than 46 million men and women—out of 98 million people in the American work force—are two-career couples.

At least two factors are possible causes for the growth in dual-career families.[15] First, pure economic reasons may be behind the number of married women seeking full-time employment. High inflation has put a crunch on many family budgets, forcing major adjustments. Also, particularly for young couples, two incomes provide for establishing the "good life" much earlier than their parents could. They have the opportunity to buy large homes, take extended weekend or annual vacations, and purchase luxury items usually *before* children are added to the family. Their parents usually tried to attain this type of lifestyle only *after* the children left the nest. The second reason is need by women for professional growth, development, and recognition. The number of women graduating from colleges has been steadily increasing in both undergraduate and graduate programs. As these women enter the work force, they have the same desires to learn, grow, and advance as their male counterparts do.

Whether the dual-career couple is motivated by economic need or professional development, it presents unique opportunities *and* adjustment problems for both the organization and the couple.[16] For example, if one is offered a significant promotion in another city that has limited job opportunities for the spouse, how should the couple react? What if the husband and wife work for two different organizations that present a potential conflict of interests for the couple? Also, a household still must be maintained, and in some cases there are children who must be raised. Some dual-career couples may believe that some of these problems are insurmountable; others look at it as an opportunity for a new start and a chance to give careers an added commitment. For the organization, there are a number of issues that must be faced: e.g., how to manage recruitment if both are desirable employees for the firm; how to handle problems of travel, transfers, or promotions; whether the organization should get involved in dual-career planning.

When dual-career couples first appeared in organizations, neither the couple nor the organization knew how to handle the conflicts that invariably developed. Over time, however, a number of keys to success have been noted. For the couple, a successful dual career usually results from an emphasis on four factors. First, there must be a *mutual commitment* by the couple to *both* careers. This means that one member does not take precedence over the other on all career matters. Second, there should be *flexibility*—personal *and* job related—by both members. There must be a willingness to change plans, shift gears, and try new ways of doing things. Third, successful dual-career couples have developed *coping mechanisms* to resolve job and family-related conflicts. Finally, similar to the first two points, an emphasis should be placed on *keeping up to date* in one's career. To be flexible and adaptable, each member of the dual-career family should spend considerable time and effort on self-assessment and continuing education.

Organizations, too, must be able to adapt to dual-career couples. Initially, this can involve providing flexible career tracks, possibly involving cross-functional moves, instead of a rigid career path. Second, some internal policies may need to be revised; e.g., less rigid transfer policies (so that turning down a transfer does not exclude future promotions) and special recruiting techniques. Third, creation of dual-career support services could prove useful. Examples could be helping an unemployed spouse find a new job, locating daycare centers or childcare arrangements, assisting in buying and selling homes, revised fringe-benefit policies, and providing couple career counseling.[17]

In summary, it is important for managers and organizations to recognize that the dual-career phenomenon is not a temporary situation. It is a reflection of changing societal and cultural norms on one hand, and on the other hand a recognition that a career is shaped more by the individual than by the organization. Because the individual's career may be redirected from time to time to meet the needs of the person, it is crucial for organizations to develop programs to utilize these talents more effectively.

Mid-Career Plateau

Once a manager has become established in his or her career (stage III or the "rock" in our earlier discussion), he or she enters what has been called the mid-career plateau. In contrast to the fierce strivings and achievement of the earlier stages, most activities are oriented to holding your own and maintaining what has already been achieved. In other words, it is generally not a time for breaking new ground. Yet this is not a tranquil period, one of reaping the fruits of earlier labors and achievements. It can be a time for decline or for embarking on a new career. Research suggests that there are physiological, attitudinal, occupational, and family-related changes that occur at this stage.[18] For example:

An awareness of advancing age, mentally and physically.

A recognition of what career goals have been accomplished and those that cannot be achieved.

A growing search for a change in lifestyle.

Observable changes in work-related relationships.

A growing sense of obsolescence.

The person feels less mobile and attractive in the job market and, therefore, more concerned about job security.

More than anything, the mid-career plateau is an identity crisis with concerns about goals and questions like "Where am I headed?" and "What can I do next?"

The preceding points may sound gloomy for the forty-year-old manager. Our knowledge about this situation, however, has increased to the point where methods and approaches are available to effectively cope with mid-career stress. First, the person should *learn more about the processes of mid-career change* to understand what is going on inside him or her. He or she should be encouraged to face up to feelings of restlessness and insecurity, to reexamine his or her values and life goals, and to set new ones or recommit to old ones. Life planning and career planning exercises have been devised that are extremely helpful in mid-career.

Second, the mid-career manager can be used effectively to *help develop younger employees*. In this mentor role, the manager can grow along with the younger person. By working with younger employees, he or she keeps up-to-date, fresh, and energetic. One of the most important psychological needs of mid-career managers is to build something lasting, something that will be a permanent contribution to one's organization or profession. The development of a future generation of managers and executives could be a lasting and satisfying contribution.

A third approch is to *deal directly with the issue of obsolescence*. This can be done by sending managers back to school for seminars, workshops, courses, and degree programs. The manager not only gains new knowledge, but a great deal of learning and self-assessment can occur by interacting with managers like him or her in other organizations. A better approach is to prevent obsolescence from occurring in the first place. This can be accomplished by giving managers assignments throughout their careers that force them to develop new skills and learn about new developments in their fields. As we have suggested throughout this book, the job itself probably has more impact on the manager's development than most off-the-job activities. With job rotation, the manager is assigned to a job where he or she is working with recent graduates where mutual learning and a trading of experiences can occur. The new job may require the learning of new skills such as computer operations, employee affirmative action laws, manufacturing techniques, and so on. If transfers were expected to continue throughout the career, more use could be made of learning potential in new jobs and new people, and obsolescence could be reduced.

Whatever the approach, the mid-career plateau occurs in all types of organizations. Organizations are recognizing this factor and are building preventive measures into their career planning programs.

KEYS TO SUCCESS IN MANAGERIAL CAREERS

Choosing a managerial career can be one of the most exciting, challenging, and satisfying decisions in a person's life. Successful managerial careers—and nonmanagerial careers as well—are the result of careful preparation, hard work, and continual planning.

As throughout this book, the experiences of practicing managers and the research of management scholars have provided at least a partial list of keys to success that the young manager should consider. We have divided these keys into three categories—those dealing with job-related, interpersonal, and personal issues.[19]

Job-Related Keys to Success

1. **Work hard—do excellent work.**

   On a continuing basis, this is probably the most important success key. Hard work that is well done will pay off in both short-term and long-term results. Isolated setbacks will no doubt occur, but in the long run it is the high performer that reaps the most benefits. Consistent high performance will identify you as a dependable person, one that can be counted on when the chips are down.

2. **Try to stay visible.**

   Sometimes your work performance is sufficient to provide you with visibility in the organization. Other times you may have to "beat your own drum." This can be done by circulating memos and reports to interested parties, keeping supervisors informed of your progress on a project, and so on. The key is to do this without becoming a braggart, which will alienate other people. Remember, you are your best "press agent"—if you don't do it, no one else will.

3. **Learn how to control organizational resources.**

   Controlling resources brings power and the ability to influence others. One of the most important resources is information—knowledge is power. When you are the sole possessor of valued information, others must come to you for assistance. This increases your visibility and your centrality to the purposes of the organization.

4. **Change organizations when it improves your career movement.**

   While loyalty is a quality that most organizations seek, it is not a permanent factor. Too many factors can change that significantly alter your position: a new superior, changes in organizational policies, environmental factors, and so on. When these factors present a barrier to your growth, carefully consider moving to another firm. Frequent job hopping will not be appealing on your resume; however, carefully thought-out moves can greatly enhance your future advancement opportunities.

Interpersonal Keys to Success

1. **Learn how to get along with a variety of people.**

   Current and future managers will increasingly be asked to be generalists. This means that they must become skilled in interacting with a variety of technical specialists, peers, subordinates, superiors, and people outside the organization. These skills involve not only understanding what motivates others, but concern for your own ability to effectively communicate and cooperate in a number of situations, be they committee meetings or one-on-one interactions.

2. **Help superiors to succeed in their work.**

   Your superiors are the key people who will make decisions on your career movement. Try not only to develop good relations with them, but become a valued subordinate by keeping them informed and assisting them when it is clear that you can help. This, however, can create a problem. By being a key subordinate to an upwardly mobile superior, you may be considered as part of an advancement team—that is, when your superior moves, he or she will take you. On the other hand, being an indispensable subordinate to a "deadwood" superior may hinder your career movement—you make the superior look so good, he or she is reluctant to let you go.

3. Find a supportive mentor.

As we have suggested throughout this book, mentoring is one of the most important processes in developing managers. Even if the organization does not have a formal mentor-protege program, become associated with people whom you can learn from, involving possibly more than one mentor. When mentoring is not sanctioned by the organization, choose and maintain your mentor relationships carefully. Remember, you need mentors more than they need you, and losing a mentor can be quite harmful to you. When your mentor is not your direct superior, be careful not to alienate your superior by appearing disloyal or snubbing his or her advice.

4. Handle conflictful situations with care.

If you are part of a conflict, attempt to resolve it as quick as possible, preferably using confrontation and problem-solving methods. Unresolved conflict will usually become worse with time. If you observe a conflict between other employees, but are not part of it, remain unattached. Not only is it not your business, but becoming part of it may force you to take sides, which can be detrimental to you in the future.

Personal Keys to Success

1. Stay mobile.

Managers with records of high achievement and experience in a number of vital organizational functions have great mobility both within and across organizations. Sometimes it is desirable to be valued by other organizations because it will increase your stature with your present firm. High mobility, particularly geographic mobility, has its drawbacks in disruptions to social and family relationships. Achieving a top management position rarely occurs without sacrifices—for example, you may find yourself in a desirable job with a good company, but in a less-than-acceptable location. Remember, managerial career movement requires taking the good with the bad.

2. Can you exhibit the image the organization wants?

Organizations are different in the way they want their managers to look—that is, clothing, demeanor, and general appearance. Find out what the organization wants, but question whether you can adapt to it. This is an issue of norms. If you feel comfortable with these organizational norms, adopt them—if you resist them, be prepared to be labeled as a nonconformist and be aware of the associated actions to force you to conform. Identifying organizational norms is something you should do in the selection process or quite early in your career. The longer you wait, the more difficulties you may run across.

3. Don't be lulled into inactivity by current successes.

Career planning is an ongoing process that requires constant attention and action. Success now will not guarantee future success. Continually revise your career goals and plans.

4. **Develop your own self-improvement program.**

Career planning is as much your responsibility as the organization's. Don't wait on the organization to suggest career improvement methods—show initiative. This can include nominating yourself for new jobs, projects, or positions and indicating interest in education and training programs. One of the most important things for self-improvement is to read current literature. Know what is going on around you in other organizations, what the important trends are, and what you need to be up-to-date. *The Wall Street Journal, Business Week, Fortune, Forbes, Harvard Business Review,* and *Management Review* are just some of the many sources that you should become acquainted with. We have tried to use these sources in this book in hope that your interest will be kindled.

SUMMARY FOR THE MANAGER

1. Managerial career opportunities vary by profession and type of industry. The health care, computer systems, engineering, accounting, and personnel fields offer significant opportunities for managers. Similarly, the service sector, government, and manufacturing are industries where growth in employment is expected.

2. The career profiles of existing executives present some interesting points. For example, educational levels are increasing, most had fathers who were professionals or businessmen, the Midwest has been a breeding ground for many, and most have worked for fewer than three organizations during their careers.

3. The dominant career success factors include concern for results and people, a desire of responsibility, and a desire to achieve.

4. One of the most important lessons from the first job is understanding one's expectations and the expectations of the organization. Unrealistic expectations create problems that must eventually be confronted by the young manager.

5. Other lessons to be learned concern the impact of the first supervisor, the realities of performance evaluation, and the inherent lack of job challenge on initial assignments.

6. Organizational politics are a way of life in many firms and institutions. Managers must learn that political alliances exist and are based on power and influence. Such political activities, however, can be one of the sources of initial anxiety and stress. Future success comes, in part, from learning how to cope with this ever-present stress.

7. Career planning consists of organizational career planning and individual career planning. The two must be integrated for effective career planning.

8. One of the key components of organizational career planning is career pathing. It consists of a series of positions—vertical, lateral, and downward—from the manager's current job. Movement through these jobs in a systematic manner provides the manager with the necessary experience and skills for future performance.

9. Individual career planning involves at least three elements: personal resource analysis, personal preference analysis, and a statement of career goals. Career goals should be formulated not only with respect to time, but also criteria, preferably prioritized. These goals should be continually analyzed and revised.

10. Among the most important current issues in managerial careers are dual careers and the mid-career plateau. Many families now have two wage earners. This creates promises and problems for the family members and the organization. The mid-career plateau occurs for many managers during middle age. Job rotation, training, and mentorship are some of the many methods organizations have adopted to counter this problem.

QUESTIONS FOR REVIEW AND DISCUSSION

1. Why is the service sector identified as a promising managerial career area?
2. Managers are more highly educated today than their past counterparts. Why is this?
3. What role does college play in creating unrealistic expectations?

4. Why are many young managers not prepared for the realities of organizational politics?

5. In what ways does the young recruit's first supervisor affect his or her career?

6. What is the difference between organizational career planning and individual career planning?

7. Some career pathing programs involve downward moves for managers. What must the organization do before this procedure is successful?

8. What is a personal resource analysis?

9. Why is time an important factor in developing career goals?

10. What new problems have been created for organizations and individuals with the emergence of dual-career couples?

NOTES

1. C. G. Burck, "A Group Profile of the Fortune 500 Chief Executive," *Fortune* (May 1976): 172–77.

2. J. A. Sussman, "A Career Profile of the Senior Executive," *Management Review* (July 1979): 14–21.

3. M. C. Johnson, "Mentors—The Key to Development and Growth," *Training and Development Journal* (July 1980): 55–57.

4. See D. T. Hall, "Potential for Career Growth," *Personnel Administration* (1971): 18–30; and E. H. Schein, "The First Job Dilemma," *Psychology Today* (March 1968): 22–37.

5. D. T. Hall, *Career in Organizations* (Santa Monica, California: Goodyear, 1976), p. 66.

6. T. M. Rohan, "Lessons from that First Job," *Industry Week* (August 20, 1979): 94.

7. J. S. Manuso, "Executive Stress Management," *The Personnel Administrator* (November 1979): 23–26.

8. "Executive Stress May Not Be All Bad," *Business Week* (April 30, 1980): 96.

9. T. P. Ference, J. A. F. Stoner, and E. K. Warren, "Managing the Career Plateau," *Academy of Management Review* (October 1977).

10. E. H. Burack, "Why All the Confusion About Career Planning?" *Human Resource Management* (Summer 1977): 21–23.

11. M. Jelinek, ed., *Career Management* (Chicago: St. Clair, 1979), pp. 354–56.

12. E. H. Schein, "The Individual, the Organization, and the Career," *Journal of Applied Behavioral Science* (1971) 404–17.

13. H. L. Wellbank, D. T. Hall, M. A. Morgan, and W. C. Hamner, "Planning Job Progression for Effective Career Development and Human Resources Management," *Personnel* (March–April 1978): 54–64.

14. S. Gould, "Career Planning in the Organization," *Human Resource Management* (Spring 1978): 8–11.

15. Hall, *Careers in Organizations,* p. 187.

16. D. T. Hall and F. Hall, "What's New in Career Management," *Organizational Dynamics* (Summer 1976): 17–33.

17. F. Hall and D. T. Hall, "Dual Careers—How Do Couples and Companies Cope with the Problems?" *Organizational Dynamics* (Spring 1978): 57–77.

18. See Hall, *Careers in Organizations,* p. 85; and D. J. Levinson, *The Seasons of a Man's Life* (New York: Knopf, 1978), pp. 191–200.

19. See M. A. Morgan, ed., *Managing Career Development* (New York: Van Nostrand, 1980); E. Jennings, "Success Chess," *Management of Personnel Quarterly* (Fall 1980): 2–8; and A. N. Schoonmaker, *Executive Career Strategy* (New York: American Management Associations, 1971).

ADDITIONAL REFERENCES

Aplin, J. C. and Gerster, D. K. "Career Development: An Integration of Individual and Organizational Needs." *Personnel,* March–April 1978, pp. 23–29.

Burack, E. H. and Mathys, N. "Career Ladders, Pathing and Planning: Some Neglected Basics." *Human Resource Management,* Summer 1979, pp. 2–8.

Greiff, B. S. and Munter, P. K. *Tradeoffs: Executive, Family, and Organizational Life.* New York: New American Library, 1980.

Montana, P. J. and Higginson, M. V. *Career Life Planning for Americans.* New York: American Management Associations, 1978.

Montana, P. J. "Implementing a Career Life Planning Program." *Personnel,* September–October 1979, pp. 66–71.

Moore, L. L. "From Manpower Planning to Human Resources Planning Through Career Development." *Personnel,* May–June 1979, pp. 9–16.

Morgan, M. A.; Hall, D. T.; and Martier, A. "Career Development Strategies in Industry—Where Are We and Where Should We Be?" *Personnel,* March–April 1979, pp. 13–30.

Ranftl, R. M. "Guidelines to Productive Management," *Management Review,* November 1979, pp. 49–54.

Sheridan, J. H. "Would You Want Your Child to be a Manager?" *Industry Week,* October 2, 1978, pp. 52–58.

Walker, J. W. "Does Career Planning Rock the Boat?" *Human Resource Management,* Spring 1978, pp. 2–7.

A CASE FOR ANALYSIS

Fast Track at Bethlehem Steel Corporation

Attempting to convince bright, young college graduates to take jobs in the U. S. steel industry has not been an easy task during the past few years. Steel companies have a reputation for stodgy management, dirty pants, small profits, and big problems. The trend, however, seems to be shifting as more and more college graduates are investigating careers in the steel industry, particularly Bethlehem Steel. The reason apparently is the desire to participate in Loop, an unusual recruiting and training program that puts new graduates on the management track the day they join the company. Surprisingly, Bethlehem's program has existed since 1922.

Other big industrial companies woo college graduates with promises of challenging jobs and good salaries. But Bethlehem adds what its recruiters call "the third piece of the pie"—a guaranteed shot at management before the newly minted graduate even learns the first real job. This may sound risky, since most employees move into management at most companies only after they demonstrate they can handle subordinate jobs. But Bethlehem contends that the qualities that mark people as management material—leadership and personal integrity, for example—are evident by the time they are college seniors. Offering these students places in the Loop program often allows the company to overcome both the poor image of the steel industry and the higher salary offers made by other companies.

Bethlehem's three-phase program "loops" trainees through all of the company's operations, from steelmaking to accounting to public relations. The first phase is a two-week orientation session at headquarters that gives participants an overall look at the company and thorough exposure to the steelmaking process. Extensive movement through the recruit's assigned plant or office follows. Then there is on-the-job training for two years, with quarterly evaluations. The aim is to have participants rise at least as high as the department-head level during their careers.

Of Bethlehem's 270 top managers and executives, 56 percent were participants. At the middle-management levels and in some functions, the percentage is higher. For example, in steel operations, 78 percent of the managers went through the program while 61 percent of the firm's accounting managers took part. Loyalty also appears to be an outcome of the program. The company says that industrial firms typically lose an average of 50 percent of their new recruits during the first five years of employment. Since the program's inception, Bethlehem has retained 70 percent of its participants through the first five years. Bethlehem executives indicate that employees do not have to go through the program to get ahead. The current chairman, in fact, was hired in 1975 from a large accounting firm. Other outside hirings of top executives have caused some concern among program participants.

Most current Loop classes nevertheless consider themselves to be among the chosen few, a feeling of being somebody special. That feeling breeds a mixture of comraderie and competition among the class, numbering usually over 150 people. For example, during study sessions, engineers explain to accountants the technology of making steel, while accounting trainees show engineering trainees why it is better to use a faster depreciation method to offset inflation. On the other hand, during daily classes with top executives, the participants almost always vie for the attention with their work and even their appearance.

Questions for Review and Discussion

1. What principles of career planning are used by Bethlehem?
2. Identify some of the positive features of the program. What are some possible negative features?
3. Why has the program been a success?
4. Would you want to be part of this type of program?

   Adapted from Douglas Sease, "Grads Trained for Fast Track at Bethlehem," Wall Street Journal *(July 29, 1980), p. 31.*

EXPERIENTIAL EXERCISE

Investigating Job and Career Opportunities

Purpose

1. To investigate job and career opportunities in organizations.
2. To develop an investigative framework that will enable the young recruit to minimize the effects of unrealistic job expectations.

Required Understanding

A basic understanding of the elements of career planning.

How to Set Up the Exercise

The instructor may assign this exercise to individual students or a team of students as an external project. The results can be handed in as a formal report, or discussed within the team or group.

Instructions for the Exercise

Students should contact an organization in the area—either in person or by telephone. A manager within the organization should be identified who can provide answers regarding job and career opportunities within the firm. Examples include an acquaintance employed by the organization, or possibly someone within the personnel function. After the manager has been identified, the following questions should be asked. Responses should be recorded for later presentation.

1. Nature of the work.
   a. What kind of job or career is being discussed?
   b. Is it an entry-level job or above?
   c. Briefly describe the kinds of things an employee is expected to do.
2. Conditions of work.
   a. What kinds of hours are you expected to work? (Watch for overtime, night work, regular hours, irregular hours, weekends, etc.) Are you paid for overtime?
   b. Does the job offer security? Is it seasonal or irregular? When people leave this job for another organization, what are the usual or prevalent reasons?
   c. What is the work environment like? Are there any hazards?
   d. Are there elements of the job that might be unpleasant to the employee, such as noise, heat, and so on?
   e. Can the job be challenging enough to hold your attention and motivate you?

3. Pay, training, and promotion.
   a. What are the maximum, average, and minimum wages for this job?
   b. What are the normal promotional steps for this job? How long do the steps take on the average? Does a formal career planning program exist? How does pay change with each promotional step? Does the organization support a mentorship program, formal or informal?
4. Worker relationships.
   a. Do you work primarily alone or with other people in this job?
   b. Is there a lot of competition between fellow workers in this job, such as commissions or promotions?
   c. Are the relationships between employees on the job formal or informal?
   d. Given the nature of the work, are there opportunities to develop close personal relationships?
5. Worker qualifications.
   a. Is previous experience or training required? What is the source, nature, and length for such experience and training?
   b. Is there evidence of any preference given on the basis of age, sex, or race?
6. Physical qualifications.
   a. Are there any visual, height, strength, stamina, speech, or appearance requirements?
7. Educational requirements.
   a. Does entry into this job require a high school diploma, associate degree, bachelor's degree, master's degree, doctorate, or post-graduate work?
   b. Does advancement on the job require formal education, advanced degrees, special classes, or special training?
8. Psychological qualifications.
   a. What aptitudes, abilities, personality characteristics, and so on are needed to be successful at getting and mastering the job?
   b. Are there types of screening exams or psychological tests given? What is the nature of such exams?
9. Work experience.
   a. What experience, if any, is required for entry-level and higher-level jobs?
   b. What special skills must one possess to qualify for this job?
   c. Are there any skill tests given for this job?
10. Performance evaluation.
   a. When are employees evaluated on this job? Does it vary with length of service?
   b. Who is expected to conduct these evaluations? Are superiors trained in formal performance appraisal methods? Does a formal evaluation system exist? When and in what form can the employee expect to receive feedback on his or her performance?
   c. Are career planning and performance appraisals separate or simultaneous?
11. Equipment requirements.
   a. What items, such as tools or clothing, must be supplied by the employee?
   b. Is an automobile required?
12. Employment opportunities.
   a. To what extent are workers in demand today in this type of job?
   b. Where is the greatest demand, geographically or industry-wise?
   c. Is employment likely to increase, decrease, or stay the same in the next three-to-five years?

Adapted from Edmond Billingsley, Career Planning and Job Hunting for Today's Student *(Santa Monica, Calif.: Goodyear, 1978), pp. 33–34.*

List of Key Terms

Abilities   Potentials for carrying out specific acts or behaviors, which are necessary but not sufficient conditions for behavior.

Accountability   A person's obligation to carry out responsibilities and be answerable for decisions and activities.

Achievement   A motive that causes people to prefer tasks that involve only a moderate amount of risk and involve rather immediate and clear feedback on results.

Activity   The work necessary to complete a particular event in a PERT network. An activity consumes time, which is an important variable in a PERT system.

Activity ratios   Ratios used during ratio analysis that indicate how well an organization is selling its products in relation to its available resources.

Ad hoc committee   A temporary committee formed to serve a short-term, specific purpose.

Affirmative action programs   Programs whose basic purpose is to eliminate barriers and increase opportunities for underutilized and/or disadvantaged individuals.

Assessment center   A multidimensional approach to the measurement of performance and potential.

Assistant-to   A staff assistant to a line manager; though normally lacking line authority, often has considerable responsibility and influence.

Audit   An investigation of activities. An *internal audit* is conducted by an organization's own personnel; an *external audit* is conducted by an outside firm.

Authority   The power to issue commands, make decisions, take action, and enforce obedience.

Avoidance   The administration of a reinforcement that prevents the occurrence of an undesired behavior.

Avoidance conflict resolution   A strategy that generally disregards causes of a conflict by enabling the conflict to continue only under controlled conditions.

Balance-sheet budget   A composite of all financial plans that reflect anticipated assets, liabilities, and owners' equity at a future time.

Behavior   The tangible acts or decisions of individuals, groups, or organizations.

Behavior modeling   A training or skills development technique that emphasizes role playing and videotape review to afford learning through experience.

Behavioral decision theory   Decision models that examine the influence of individual, group, and organization factors in decision making.

Behavior modification   An approach to motivation that uses operant conditioning. Operant behavior is learned through consequences. If a behavior causes a desired outcome, it is reinforced. Because of its consequences it is likely to be repeated. Thus, behavior is conditioned by adjusting its consequences.

Behavioral leadership theories   Approaches to leadership that seek to identify leadership styles that are the most effective in various situations.

Behaviorally anchored rating scales   (BARS): Performance ratings that focus on specific behaviors or acts as indicators of effective and ineffective performance, rather than on broadly stated adjectives such as "average, above average, or below average."

Brainstorming   A technique for generating a solution to a problem that involves the following steps: a group of people is assembled; each person suggests a solution, with no criticism allowed from other members of the group; the ideas are evaluated.

Break-even analysis   A method for determining the relationship between cost and revenue at various sales levels in order to show the point at which it is profitable to produce and sell a product.

Break-even point   The point at which income equals cost.

Budget   A control tool that outlines how funds in a given period will be spent, as well as how they will be obtained.

Bureaucracy   An organizational system that relies on specialization of labor, a specific authority hierarchy, a formal set of rules and procedures, and rigid promotion and selection criteria.

Capital expenditure budget   A projection of the amount of money that will be needed during a given period for the purchase of capital items, such as buildings.

Career   An individual's sequence of jobs and behaviors associated with work-related experiences and activities over the span of his or her life.

Career path   The sequence of jobs planned for or by a person, which leads to a career objective.

Career planning   The process of systematically matching an individual's career aspirations with opportunities for achieving them.

Career stages   Distinct, but interrelated, steps or phases of a career.

Carrying costs   The cost incurred by carrying an inventory. These include taxes and insurance on the goods in inventory, interest on the money invested in inventory and storage space, and losses because of inventory obsolescence.

Cash budget   A projection of cash receipts and cash disbursements for a given period.

Centralization   That situation in which a minimal number of job activities and a minimal amount of authority are delegated to subordinates.

Central tendency   An error often associated with traditional rating scales. It consists of a rater incorrectly assigning similar ratings to a group of employees and not accurately representing the true distribution of performance. All ratings tend to cluster at the middle of the scale.

Chain of command   The route by which authority is transmitted from the top to the bottom of an organization.

Chief executive officer (CEO): The highest-ranking person of authority in a company.

Classical conditioning   The learning or acquisition of a habit (stimulus-response connection) through associating an unconditioned stimulus (UCS) with a conditioned stimulus (CS).

Classical decision theory   A normative approach to decision making that emphasizes achieving known objectives by choosing the alternative that maximizes expected returns.

Classical design theory   The theoretical approach based on scientific management procedures and bureaucratic principles.

Coercive power   An influence over others based on fear.

Cohesiveness   Closeness and common attitudes, behaviors, and performance of group members.

Committee   A task group charged with performing a specific activity.

Communication   The process by which information is transmitted and exchanged.

Communication barriers   Factors that interfere with the process of communication. They include the distortion of messages due to attributes of the receiver, selective perception, semantic problems, timing, and information overload.

Compensatory decision process   A rule whereby a decision maker allows a high value on one decision criterion to offset a low value on some other criterion.

Competence   The ability to perform well.

Conceptual skill   The ability to coordinate and integrate ideas, concepts, and practices. Such skill is most important to top-level managers.

Conformity   Compliance with existing rules or customs.

Confrontation conflict resolution   A strategy that focuses on the sources of conflict and attempts to resolve them through such procedures as mutual personnel exchange, use of superordinate goals, or problem solving.

Conjunctive decision rule   A rule whereby the decision maker establishes minimally acceptable levels on each of several decision criteria. To decide in favor of an alternative, that alternative must achieve minimally acceptable levels of every criterion.

Consideration   Behavior of the leader that emphasizes openness, friendliness, and concern for the welfare of subordinates.

Content motivation theories   Theories that focus on the factors within the person that start, arouse, energize, or stop behavior.

Contingency design approach   An attempt to understand the interrelationships within and among organizational subsystems as well as between the organizational system as an entity and its environments. It emphasizes the multivariate nature of organizations and attempts to interpret how they operate under varying conditions and in specific situations.

Contingency plan   A plan that outlines how to handle a possible but not probable future event.

Controlling function   All managerial activity undertaken to assure that actual operations go according to plan.

Coordination   The orderly arrangement of group effort to provide unity of action in the pursuit of a common purpose.

Critical incident method   A job analysis technique that attempts to study the job in terms of specific, identifiable behaviors or actions that are critical to success in carrying out a job.

Critical path   That sequence of events and activities within a PERT network that requires the longest period of time to complete.

Current ratio   A liquidity ratio that indicates the organization's ability to meet its financial obligations in the short run.

Decentralization   The pushing downward in a hierarchy of decision-making authority.

Decision making   A choice among several mutually exclusive and exhaustive alternatives. The choice is made after a consideration of all possible outcomes, the probabilities of such outcomes, and the conditions associated with each alternative and its outcome.

Decision tree   A planning tool that graphically shows the future effects of given courses of action.

Decoding   The mental procedure that the receiver uses to decipher a message.

Defusion conflict resolution   A strategy that attempts to buy time to resolve intergroup conflict later, when it is less emotional or crucial.

Delegation   The process of assigning job activities

and related authority to specific individuals within the organization.

Delphi technique A group decision technique closely associated with the normal group technique, except that members are physically separated from each other.

Departmentalization The combining of jobs into a specific unit or department.

Diagnostic activities Fact-finding or data-collection that attempts to find what is occurring within a unit or organization.

Differentiation Segmentation of the organization's subsystems, each of which contains members who form special attitudes and behavior and tend to become specialized experts.

Division of labor The assignment of various portions of a particular task among a number of organization members.

Downward communication Communication that flows from any point on an organization chart downward to another point on the chart.

Dual careers Describes the husband and wife who both have full-time careers.

Effort The motivated aspect of behavior. When effort is combined with ability, behavior will result. Effort is the amount of energy expended by the individual in a given act. Level of effort is influenced by the strength of the individual's motives or needs.

Emergent leader An individual who has emerged from a group to assume a leading role as the informal leader.

Encoding Converting of a communication into an understandable message.

Environmental uncertainty The state of the external environment of an organization as defined by the degree of complexity and the degree of change.

EOQ model The economic order quantity model, used to resolve problems regarding the size of orders. A manager concerned with minimizing inventory costs could utilize this model to study the relationships between carrying costs, ordering costs, and usage.

Equal Employment Opportunity Commission (EEOC) Agency established to enforce the laws regulating recruiting and other managerial practices.

Esteem needs Maslow's fourth set of human needs; include human desire for self-respect and respect from others.

Event An accomplishment at a particular point in time on a PERT network. Consumes no time.

Expectancy The perceived probability that a particular act will be followed by a particular outcome.

Expectancy theory States that an individual will select an outcome based on how this choice is related to second-order outcomes (rewards). The choice of behavior acts is based upon the strength or value of the outcome and the perceived probability between first- and second-level outcomes.

Expert power The capacity to influence based upon some skill, expertise, or knowledge.

Extinction The decrease in undesirable behavior because of nonreinforcement.

Expenditure forecast An estimate of the amount of money that an organization will spend during a given time period.

External communication Communication that goes beyond an organization.

Extrinsic rewards Rewards that a person receives from sources other than the job itself. They include compensation, supervision, promotions, vacations, and friendships.

Favorableness The leadership situation, based upon group atmosphere, task structure, and the leader's position power, that contributes to the leader's ability to influence subordinates.

Feedback Knowledge about job performance obtained from the job itself or from other employees.

Feedback control Control that takes place after some unit of work has been performed.

First-line management The lowest level of the hierarchy. A manager at this level coordinates the work of nonmanagers but reports to a manager.

Fixed cost An expenditure that is not affected by a short-run change in revenue.

Flat organization chart An organization chart characterized by few levels and relatively large spans of control.

Flextime A job design that staggers working hours so that employees decide when to begin and end their days.

Forecast A prediction based on study and analysis of pertinent data.

Formal group A subgroup created by management within an organization; formal groups, such as divisions and departments, make up the organization as a whole.

Friendship group A group that evolves because of some common characteristic, such as age, political sentiment, or background.

Fringe benefits Rewards given to an employee over and above wage or salary. They include vacation benefits, pension plan contributions, employee discounts, and other nonsalary rewards.

Functional group A group that is created and specified by the structure of the organization.

Game theory The simulation of real situations to test the effects of certain possible decisions.

Gantt chart A graph on which projected and completed phases of production are plotted in relation to specific times.

Geographic departmentalization The grouping of an organization's activities by area or territory.

Goal orientation The particular goals (techno-economic, market, or science) with which individuals or groups are primarily concerned.

Goal setting A critical activity identified as having an impact on the effectiveness of an incentive plan. To motivate performance through incentives, employees must accept the goals established for a task and/or set them themselves.

Goal succession The change in goals as a result of conscious effort by management to shift the course of the organization's activities.

Goals At the organizational level, desired states that the system is attempting to achieve by planning, organizing, and controlling. Goals are created by individuals or groups within the organization.

Grid training A leadership development method proposed by Blake and Mouton that emphasizes the necessary balance between production orientation and person orientation.

Graicunas's formula A mathematical formula that shows geometrically how the addition of subordinates increases the complexity of managing.

Grapevine A slang term referring to informal communication networks that parallel formal networks within organizations.

Group Two or more individuals who are interdependent and interact for the purpose of performing to achieve a common goal or objective.

Group composition The relative homogeneity or heterogeneity of the group based on the individual characteristics of the members.

Group decision A decision reached jointly by members of a group. Interactions among people affect the group decision process. In addition, group decision making allows for the possibility of conflict among goals to be considered.

Group development A series of stages that most groups go through over time (orientation, internal problem solving, growth and productivity, and evaluation and control).

Group norms Standards of behavior established by the group that describe the acceptable behavior of members.

Groupthink A group defense reaction that impairs the quality of group decisions.

Halo effects The forming of impressions (positive or negative) about a person based on performance in one area.

Hawthorne effect The tendency of people who are being observed to react differently than they would otherwise.

Hawthorne studies Management studies conducted at the Western Electric Hawthorne plant in a suburb of Chicago by a group of Harvard University researchers. The most famous studies ever conducted in the field of management.

Hierarchy-of-needs theory A theory of motivation, proposed by Maslow, based on the idea that human needs form a hierarchy and that as one need is satisfied the need at the next higher level emerges as a motivator.

Horizontal communication Communication when the communicator and the receiver are at the same level in the organization.

Human resource accounting An attempt to compute the worth of personnel by assigning monetary values to their contributions or to their costs in terms of recruitment and training.

Human resource planning Estimating the size and makeup of the future work force.

Human skill The ability to work with, motivate, and counsel people. Most important to middle-level managers.

Hygiene (maintenance) factors Items that influence job dissatisfaction.

Incentive A type of motive that focuses on an event or outcome attractive to an individual; outcomes towards which behavior is directed.

Incentive plan A reward scheme that attempts to tie pay directly to job performance; e.g., a piece rate and sales commission.

Initiating structure The behavior of the leader that emphasizes structuring the task, assigning work, and providing feedback.

Influencing The process of guiding the activities of organization members in appropriate directions.

Informal group A subgroup created by the members themselves within an organization; e.g., people who regularly bowl together or meet to share ideas.

Information overload A condition in which too much information flows through communication channels — leads to ignoring potentially critical pieces of information.

Instrumental conditioning (See *Operant conditioning*.)

Instrumentality The relationship between first- and second-level outcomes.

Integration The quality of collaboration among departments that are required to achieve unity of effort by the demands of the environment.

Interaction requirements The variety of individuals, frequency, and quality necessary in intergroup activities.

Interdependence The degree to which two or more groups are dependent on one another for inputs or outputs.

Interest group Informal groups created because of

common characteristics or interests. Generally, when the interest declines, the group disbands.

Intergroup conflict Conflict between two or more groups.

Interval reinforcement A schedule of rewards that ties reinforcements to time. Such a schedule can be *fixed* or *variable*.

Intrinsic rewards Rewards associated with the job itself, such as the opportunity to perform meaningful work, complete cycles of work, see finished products, experience variety, carry out highly visible cycles of activity, and receive feedback on work results.

Inventory models A type of production control model that answers two questions relating to inventory management: "How much?" and "When?" An inventory model tells the manager when goods should be reordered and what quantity should be purchased.

Job A homogeneous cluster of work tasks, the completion of which serves some enduring purpose for the organization.

Job analysis The systematic study of jobs that attempts to discover the major task dimensions of a job and what the job calls for in terms of employee behaviors and qualifications.

Job content Factors that define the specific work activities or tasks.

Job dynamics Situational factors surrounding the tasks on a job that must be considered to adequately define the job.

Job enlargement A job design strategy that expands the job range of the individual's job horizontally, giving him or her more things to do.

Job enrichment A job design strategy, based on the motivator-hygiene theory, that seeks to improve performance and satisfaction by providing more challenge, responsibility, authority, and recognition to jobs.

Job evaluation A method that attempts to determine the relative worth of each job or position to the organization in order to establish a basis for relative wage rates within the organization. It is a major method for establishing reward policy.

Job functions The general requirements of and methods involved in performing a job.

Job rotation A job design strategy that involves moving the worker from task to task over a period of time to reduce boredom.

Job satisfaction An attitude held by a person that reflects an evaluation of a particular component in the work place.

Job specialization Dividing the work or tasks of a job into specialized, standardized, and simple tasks.

Job stress An individual's internal frustration and anxiety over certain job or organization-related situations.

Key result area An aspect of a company's operations that has direct bearing on profitability.

Leadership The ability to inspire people to perform duties competently and willingly.

Leadership style A behavioral pattern a leader establishes while guiding organization members in appropriate directions.

Learning A relatively permanent change in behavior that occurs as a result of experience. Learning is to be distinguished from other factors influencing changes in behavior, including fatigue and maturation.

Legitimate power A leader's capacity to influence based upon his or her position in the organization.

Leniency An error often associated with traditional rating methods. It consists of a rater incorrectly assigning similar ratings to a group of employees without accurately representing the true distribution of performance, so that all ratings tend to cluster towards the high end of the scale.

Leverage ratios Ratios used during ratio analysis that indicate the relationship between organizational funds supplied by the owners of an organization and organizational funds supplied by creditors.

Liabilities What an enterprise owes.

Line-and-staff organization An organization that has, because of its size or the complexity of its functions or goals, an advisory support staff in addition to the line staff.

Linear programming A method for determining the optimum combination of resources to use in attaining a goal. Used when a change in one variable results in a proportionate change in another.

Line authority The responsibility for carrying out an enterprise's main functions.

Line manager A person involved in carrying out the primary activities of an organization.

Liquidity ratios Ratios used during ratio analysis that indicate an organization's ability to meet upcoming financial obligations.

Management The process by which people, technology, job tasks, and other resources are combined and coordinated to achieve organizational goals.

Management audit An evaluation of the overall operation of an enterprise.

Management by objectives A process in which a superior and a subordinate or a group of subordinates jointly identify and establish common goals.

Management development The process of educating and developing selected employees so that they have the knowledge, skills, attitudes, and understanding needed to manage in future positions.

Management functions The activities which a manager must perform as a result of position in the organization. This text identifies planning, organizing, leading, and controlling as the management functions.

Management information systems A structured complex of individuals, machines, and procedures to provide management with pertinent information from both external and internal sources. Management information systems support the planning, control, and operations functions of an organization by providing uniform information that serves as the basis for decision making.

Management-science approach A method of studying management that emphasizes the development of mathematical models to test management hypotheses.

Managerial roles The organized sets of behavior that belong to the manager's job. The three main types of managerial roles discovered by such researchers as Mintzberg are interpersonal, informational, and decisional roles.

Managerial grid activities A total organizational program that is implemented in six phases to upgrade individual managers' skills and leadership abilities, teamwork, goal setting, and monitoring of events within an organization.

Manpower planning Input planning that involves obtaining the human resources necessary for the organization to achieve its objectives.

Material budget A forecast of how much material will be necessary to achieve a result.

Matrix design A design that includes the control features of functional organizational design and the adaptive aspects of product design, usually found in organizations that include a number of projects, programs, or task forces. In this arrangement, the special program managers have authority to supervise and divert subordinates from line managers.

Mechanistic organizations Organizations with highly specialized job tasks, rigid authority systems, top-down flow of communications, and conflict resolution by the superior.

Message The information a message sender communicates.

Message feedback The response of a message receiver to a message.

Message sender Anyone who communicates something to someone else.

Midcareer plateau The stage of a career at which the individual has no opportunity for further advancement.

Middle management The middle level of an administrative hierarchy. Managers at this level coordinate the work of managers and report to a manager.

Motion study The process of analyzing work in order to determine the most efficient motions for performing tasks. Motion study, a major contribution of scientific management, was developed principally through the efforts of Frederick Taylor and Frank and Lillian Gilbreth.

Motivation The inner strivings that initiate a person's actions.

Motivator-hygiene theory The theory that identifies two basic kinds of factors: hygiene factors and motivators. Hygiene factors (e.g., challenging job, personal growth, recognition and so on) increase satisfaction and, hence, affect motivation.

Network analysis A technique whereby the whole of a project is broken down into specific parts so that each part can be evaluated in relation to the other parts and to time.

Noise Interference with the flow of a message from a sender to a receiver.

Nominal group technique A group decision method in which individual member judgements are pooled in a systematic fashion in making decisions. (See *Delphi technique*.)

Nonprogrammed decisions Decisions for novel and unstructured problems or for complex or extremely important problems. Nonprogrammed decisions deserve special attention by management.

Nonverbal communication The sharing of ideas without the use of words.

Operant conditioning A motivation approach that focuses on the relationship between stimulus, response, and reward.

Operating management Manages the implementation of programs and projects in each area of performance, measures and evaluates results, and compares results with objectives.

Operations manager A manager who converts strategic management's input into routine output for an organization.

Operations research (OR) A scientific approach to forecasting that uses mathematical models to predict which course of action from among the available alternatives will produce the best result.

Ordering cost An element in inventory control models that comprises clerical, administrative, and labor costs; a major cost component that is considered in inventory control decisions. Each time a firm orders items for inventory, some clerical and administrative work is usually required to place the order and some labor is required to put the items in inventory.

Organic system An organizational design with a behavioral orientation, participation from all employees, and communication flowing in all directions.

Organization A system that coordinates people, jobs, financial resources, and managerial practices to achieve performance goals.

Organization structure The formally defined framework of task and authority relationships. The organization structure is analogous to the biological function of the skeleton.

Organizational change The intentional attempt by management to improve the overall performance of individuals, groups, and the organization by altering the organization's structure, behavior, and technology.

Organizing function All managerial activity that results in the design of a formal structure of tasks and authority.

Orientation The process of introducing new employees to an organization and to their specific jobs. *Formal orientation* is under the direct control of management; *informal orientation* is given by peers.

Path-goal leadership theory A leadership theory that emphasizes the influence of the leadership on subordinate goals and the paths to these goals.

Pay secrecy A management policy of maintaining silence or secrecy about individual employee salaries.

People change approaches Modifying attitudes, motivation, and behavioral skills through such techniques as training programs, selection techniques, and performance appraisal techniques.

Perception A process by which individuals (1) attend to incoming stimuli; and (2) translate such stimuli into a message indicating the appropriate response.

Performance The key dependent or predicted measure in our framework. It serves as the vehicle for judging the effectiveness of individuals, groups, and organizations.

Performance dimensions The basis for making appraisal judgments, consisting of the specific aspects, tasks, and outcomes upon which the performance of individuals and groups are judged.

Performance evaluation The process by which an organization obtains feedback about the effectiveness of individual employees and groups. It serves an auditing and control function in organizations.

PERT (Program Evaluation Review Technique) A form of network analysis used to determine time requirements for untried projects. Estimates are made of the best possible time, the most likely time, and the worst time in which the project will be completed.

Physiological (basic) needs Needs of the human body, such as food, water, and sex.

Planning function All managerial activities that lead to the definition of goals and to the determination of appropriate means to achieve those goals.

Policies Guidelines for managerial action that must be adhered to at all times. Policy making is an important management tool for assuring that action is oriented toward objectives. The purpose of policies is to achieve consistency and direction and to protect the reputation of the organization.

Position power A factor in the Fiedler contingency model of leadership that refers to the power inherent in the leadership position.

Positive reinforcement The administration of positive rewards, contingent on good performance, that strengthens desired behavior in the future.

Power The ability to influence another person's behavior.

Private sector organizations Profit-making organizations in the U. S. economy.

Process motivation theories Theories that describe how behavior is energized, aroused, or stopped.

Profit sharing A plan by which a predetermined share of profits is paid to qualified personnel. Under *cash profit sharing*, a person's share of profits is distributed at regular intervals; under *deferred profit sharing*, a person's share of profits is invested in a fund and held until he or she reaches a certain age or leaves the company.

Profitability measures Include the ratio of net profit to capital, to total assets, and to sales.

Program budgeting An extension and refinement of cost-effectiveness analysis whose purpose is to evaluate each organizational activity according to what it accomplishes for a given expenditure; that is, to relate objectives to resource allocation. Used by both private and public organizations.

Programmed decisions Responses to repetitive and routine problems, handled by a standard procedure that has been developed by management.

Project organizational design A design in which a project manager temporarily directs a group of employees who have been brought together from various functional units until a specific job is completed.

Promotion from within A policy whereby management positions are filled by people who are already employees of the organization.

Public sector organizations Federal, state, and local governmental bodies.

Punishment The administration of negative rewards, contingent on poor performance, that acts to eliminate undesired behavior in the future.

Quality of working life A series of organizational interventions designed to improve the workplace for employees.

Queuing Scheduling people or items to minimize the cost of providing a service and the amount of time users of the service must wait.

Ranking An alternative method of performance appraisal in which a judge is asked to order a group of employees in terms of their performance from highest to lowest.

Rating A traditional method of performance appraisal that asks a judge to evaluate performance in terms of a value or index that is used in some standard way. Traditionally involves global rating scales.

Ratio analysis A performance-measuring device that uses ratios (percentages) to compare operating results of similar companies.

Ratio reinforcement A schedule of rewards that ties reinforcements directly to acts or behaviors. Can be *fixed* or *variable*.

Realistic job previews (RJP) The practice of providing realistic information to new employees, to avoid creating expectations that cannot be realized.

Recency of events error The tendency to make biased ratings because of the excessive influence of recent events.

Recruitment The initial screening of the total supply of prospective human resources available to fill a position.

Referent power The capacity to influence based on identification with another powerful individual.

Reinforcement schedule The timing or scheduling of rewards.

Reinforcement theory A motivation approach that examines factors that energize, direct, and sustain behavior.

Reinforcer or reward A stimulus that follows an act and (1) reduces the need motivating the act; and (2) strengthens the habit that led to the act in the first place.

Responsibility The requirement imposed on an individual to take charge of and to answer to superiors for the performance of specific obligations.

Return on investment (ROI) The ratio of net income (earnings) to invested capital (stockholders' equity).

Revenue and expense (operating) budget A monetary plan that details anticipated revenues and predicted expenditures for a given period.

Revenue (sales) forecast An estimate of the amount of money that will be brought into an organization over a given period of time.

Reward bases The various methods for distributing rewards in organizations. Equity, equality, power, and need have served as bases for distributing rewards. A problem arises for management when bases conflict in reward policy.

Reward policy An organizational policy concerning the type, amount, and way in which rewards are distributed in organizations.

Reward power The capacity to influence based on the leader's ability to reward good performance.

Rewards Outcomes or events in the organization that satisfy work-related needs.

Risk The element of uncertainty in making decisions.

Risk propensity A personality characteristic involving a person's like or dislike for taking chances.

Role The expected-perceived-enacted behavior patterns attributed to a particular job or position.

Role ambiguity Lack of clarity regarding job duties, authority, and responsibilities resulting in uncertainty and dissatisfaction.

Role analysis team building Designed to clarify role expectations and responsibilities of team members. This clarification can be brought about by group meeting and discussion.

Role conflict A state of tension created by multiple demands and conflicting directions from two or more individuals in performance of one's role, resulting in anxiety.

Rule A statement that details what is and what is not to be done in a specific situation.

Scaler (chain-of-command) principle Authority should flow directly and clearly from the top executive to each subordinate at successively descending levels.

Scientific management A body of literature that emerged during 1890-1930 that reports the ideas and theories of engineers concerned with such aspects as job design, incentive systems, selection, and training.

Security needs Maslow's second set of human needs, these reflect the desire to keep free from physical harm.

Selection Choosing an individual to hire from all those who have been recruited.

Self-actualization The need to fully realize one's potential.

Single-use plans Plans used only once or several times because they focus on organizational situations that do not occur repeatedly.

Situational leadership theories Approaches to study of leadership that stress the importance of situational factors (leader and subordinate characteristics, the task, and organizational factors) on leader effectiveness.

Social density A physical measure of the number of group members working within a certain walking distance of each other.

Societal environment Forces external to an organization that influence what happens internally. Among these forces are political, regulatory, resource, economic, and technological factors.

Social responsibility The responsibility to promote the overall welfare of society by refraining from harmful practices or by making a positive effort to help society.

Social responsiveness approach An approach to meeting social obligations that considers business to have societal and economic goals as well as the obligation to anticipate upcoming social problems and work actively to prevent their appearance.

Span of control The number of subordinates who report directly to a supervisor.

Staffing The management function of selecting, training, compensating, and evaluating people so that the work in an organization is performed according to established standards.

Staff manager A person who serves as an adviser and is auxiliary to the organization in terms of helping it achieve goals.

Standard A model level of performance to be attained.

Standing committee A permanent committee that deals with specific, ongoing matters.

Status A social ranking within a group assigned on the basis of position in the group or individual characteristics.

Status consequence The agreement of group members about the relative status of members of the group.

Stereotyping A perceptual error in which a person forms a judgement about another person based on ideas or impressions formed about that individual's group. Individual differences within the group are ignored.

Stimulus-response The basic unit of learning (habit) in both the classical and instrumental conditioning models.

Strategic management Develops the mission, objectives, and strategies of the entire organization; the top-level decision-makers in the organization.

Strategic planning The activities that lead to the definition of objectives for the entire organization and to the determination of appropriate strategies for achieving those objectives.

Strategy A comprehensive and integrated framework that determines the nature, choices, and direction of an organization's activities toward goal achievement.

Strictness An error often associated with traditional rating methods. It consists of a rater incorrectly assigning similar ratings to a group of employees without accurately representing the true distribution of performance, so that all ratings tend to cluster towards the low end of the scale.

Structural change approaches Changes brought about through new formal guidelines, procedures, policies, and organizational rearrangements.

Survey-feedback activities Activities that focus on collecting survey data and designing a plan of action based on the interpretation of the data.

Task force A temporary group formed to study a unique problem and offer a solution.

Tall organization chart An organization chart characterized by many levels and relatively small spans of management.

Task types A classification strategy that categorizes group tasks on the basis of one of three objectives: production, discussion, or problem solving.

Task uncertainty The extent to which internal or external events create a state of uncertainty with respect to job predictability.

Technical skill The skill of working with the resources and knowledge in a specific area. Such skill is most important to first-level managers.

Technical change approaches Changes that focus on rearrangements in work flow, new physical layouts, job descriptions, and work standards.

Technology People-machine activities carried out in the organizational system that utilize such technological inputs as capital goods, production techniques, and managerial and nonmanagerial knowledge.

Testing Examining human resources for qualities relevant to performing available jobs.

Theory X and theory Y McGregor's theory that behind every management decision are assumptions that a manager makes about human behavior. The theory X manager assumes that people are lazy, dislike work, want no responsibility, and prefer to be closely directed. The theory Y manager assumes that people seek responsibility, like to work, and are committed to doing good work if rewards are received for achievement.

Time orientation The degree to which individuals or groups are oriented toward short-term or long-term results.

Time series analysis method A method of predicting future sales levels by analyzing the historical relationship within an organization between sales and time.

Top management The top level of an administrative hierarchy. Managers at this level coordinate the work of other managers but do not report to a manager.

Training The process of developing qualities in human resources that ultimately will enable them to be more productive and, thus, contribute more to organizational goal attainment.

Trait leadership theories Approaches to the study of leadership that seek to identify a finite set of characteristics or traits that can distinguish effective from noneffective leaders.

Type A behavior A behavior pattern in which the person has a sense of time urgency, attempts to achieve more in less time, has a high need for achievement, is insecure, and is generally hostile.

Type B behavior A behavior pattern in which the person is easygoing, confident, and generally pleasant and unaggressive.

Unity of command A management principle that states that each subordinate should report to only one superior.

Upward communication Communication from individuals at lower levels of an organization structure to those at higher levels; e.g., suggestion boxes, group meetings, and appeal or grievance procedures.

Valence The strength or value placed by an individual on a particular reward.

Validity A measurement quality of any performance evaluation technique that demands that information regarding performance effectiveness be gathered in a way that insures the relevance of the information to the purpose of the performance review.

Variable (flexible) budget A prediction intended to reflect changes in expenditures that will result from changes in revenue.

Variable cost An expenditure that is affected by a change in revenue.

Vertical integration The performance of a business at different levels in the same industry.

Verbal communication The sharing of ideas through words.

Zero-base budgeting An accounting and planning tool that requires managers of organizational units to justify all planned expenditures and rank them in order of priority. Expenditures that recurred in prior budgets have to be rejustified. Zero-base budgeting originated in government but has also been utilized in the private sector.

Name Index

Subject Index